ROCK BOTTOM

by Jorge Malave-DeJesus

ISBN 978 0 692 18049 5

ACKNOWLEDGMENTS

WOW!! Where do I begin? This journey has been so amazing. No matter how hard I try to put all the words together so that it can seem just as I feel it. It's almost impossible to do.

For starters, I want to thank ELENA DEJESUS(MY QUEEN). Many would never understand the struggles this woman has endoured with us and I wouldn't expect anyone to understand. We all are given our fair share of battles that we must overcome but this work of art has set the bar so high that im still trying to reach it. She is the true definition of a WOMAN but most importantly she is the most important female in my world. She is my mother and I want to thank you mom for being so hard on me and raising us alone. I want to say sorry for all the tears I may have caused you to spill due to my careless actions over the years. I want you to know that everything I did may have not been so great, but I did it with you in mind. I wanted to show you that I would make you proud by any means one day. I love you girl and I hope your proud because Im not done yet!!!

My brother JOHNNY MALAVE-DEJESUS. I am sorry for not being the best role model nor the big brother you may have wanted. What I will say is, that I thank you for never giving up on me when times hit the worst for me. You was there when I needed you and I will always be here for you, forever! You are a great father and always remember that. Keep striving for greatness because thats who we are bro!!! I love you.

My sister NEIDALIZ RIVERA-DEJESUS!!! You are something special girl. The connection we have, has always been magical and it continues to be as its always been. You have grown up to be strong and independent just like our queen. I am so proud of you. You are a great mother and Im sorry for all the pain you may have endoured in your journey but it too has molded you into a work of art that will all be passed down to your children. Thank you sis for always beliving in me when many didn't. I love you.

Major shout out to my boys!! This is for all 3 of you. ELIJAH, J.R AND BENTLEY my 3 kings. Ima set this bar high and my only wish is for the 3 of you to do your best in life. Don't ever let anyone tell you that you can't achieve what your heart really feels and desires. Because of you, is why Im so destined to reach my greatest heights. I love you boys!!

My pride and joy CORAZON DEJESUS my princess!! The day you entered my life I knew I had to get on my shit times 1000. You are my air, my life, my heart and soul if i still have one its yours. There is so much I have to teach you about life, Im so eager I cant wait. This world is yours and I want you to fully believe this. You will be great and I will pave the way. Don't be gullable nor naive when it comes to people, think and think again. I love you and watch how daddy moves.

I want to thank THE DEJESUS FAMILY grandma and grandpa if it wasn't for you two there wouldn't be no us!!! Thank you for this. You all know who yall are and yall know who I really rock with! Tio Joe was more like a father instead of an uncle to me, and I love you for that because I needed you in my life more than you would ever know. Your a real father figure and I commend you for that. Thanks for all that you taught me and are still teaching me. If your questioning if I rock with you? Than it's evident I don't. The ones that know will never question my loyalty. I love you all.

My brothers from different mothers. You all know who you are. If I ever called you my bro and you still rocking with me through all this, than guess what? you are my brother till the end. For those who parted ways, thanks and I wish you all the best!!!(CHIN CHIN, ADRIAN, KUKO, WADU,HOLLY-WOOD,JAYGO) yes. these all my real brothers who thugged it out with me on every level. I Love yall on some real shit!!!

Mr. Jack Pitts have to give a special thanks to you you gave me the opportunity to see life at a different perspective. You are a great instructor and a positive influence. Keep doing what you are doing you cant help us all but you helped me.

Aaron major hope to get the chance to read this I kept my word and I stuck to my guns this was for you.

I want to give a major shout out to all my big brothers thats locked up behind those big walls. I did this for yall because you all believed in my when i was gona give up on myself. If we crossed paths you know who you are. Thank you so much for every push yall gave me and for the helping hand in putting me on game with the real game. If you reading this than I want you to know to keep your head up and keep fighting for your freedom. We did it guys. Thank you!!!

I can go on forever here but i won't gota save some for the next one. It doesn't stop here so lets get it!!!

"Any thing in this book that may feel as though
it took place or has occured in actual life is mere coincidental.
This is a ficticous novel and was put together for
entertainment purposes.

I hope you enjoy the read!!!"

Chapter 1
"Of age"

Sirens blaring! Through the beautiful nightly lit sky in Camden New Jersey. It's about 2am. The night is a bit briskly, but not to briskly for the dope boyz. They were posted out on the strip hitting sales all through the night, handling there shift at ease. The moon was full, the beautiful sky was illuminated by the powerful rays from the moon. The potent aroma of the marijuana being burned became a natural scent in this rural area. Growing up in the southern part of New Jersey has its pros and cons just every other urban city.

With the addicts on the hunt for their next fix, not giving a fuck who or what becomes there next target. Their main focus was on their next blast. It was either rocked up cocaine known as crack, butter, hard or crills. This shit had the power to drive the sanest individual crazy with a capital "C". Talk about paranoid this was the drug to get the job done. If this was what you're looking for paranoia to the extreme. Yea, soft is sold but unlike the rock its effect wasn't as intense, unless pure as fuck. Oh wait now if you chose to inject the powdery raw substance with a used or new syringe than, I might add that you'll be bouncing of the walls, like a shiny pinball inside of a pinball machine.

The clientele for the soft was based more of your lawyers, D.As, Doctors and those with a bigger bank account etc. There the ones who usually took the shit straight to their nostrils while at work to stay up or just to make it through a hectic day in the office. I never could understand how being mentally impaired at work with someone's life in your hands one could functon. How could someone manage to maintain the balanced. A tolerance is created and maintained as you ingest more of anything. You'll be surprised on how the people we put our lives in their hands are functioning addicts on the low. Reputations go untarnished due to the fact that here in Camden NJ no one cared. Who or what you were into it was your business. As long as your money was correct, when dealing with the hustlers, pimps and any other organized crime that you may have been directly or in-directly involved with. It will go well. If not then you deal with the consequence however they may come. There is a saying that many have heard which is said "one hand washes the other, while both wash the face" there couldn't be a better quote than this one, when referring to the street.

So I briefly touched on two of the three main drugs that are pumped heavily throughout the small city better known as C.M.D. aka Crime, Money, Drugs. What was once a beautiful city known for its Campbell's soup and the beautiful homes and downtown stores? Today as much as it saddens me to say. This city has managed to evolve into the country's most deadliest city to live in. It has managed to have the highest murder rate, raped and drugs etc. If your brain has thought of a crime, than most likely this poverty city has already perfected it.

It's broken down into three main subsections, east, north and south Camden. Each of the three sections strived to maintain their own ruthless reputation. With all three combined you have a well-orchestrated cash flow. The city was known to be the most successful in obtaining the purest of drugs throughout the East coast. Especially the "heroin" along with the crack has managed to gross in billions over the years, sucking the life right out of the city. Not stopping there, the life being sucked right out of the veins from those who find themselves with the needle imbedded in them. If this is the cup of tea and is your preference than by all means. How many you need is all you'll be asked? To try it once is to say that you'll keep on chasing it until you have reached that first high again. Which was practically impossible. That high will most likely never resurface agian. That chase alone would eventually leave you where you stand, sit or lay breathless cold. Until your body was found or even smelled due to the decomposing of your organs and flesh eating your own flesh. Maggots would always be searching for an exit, and believe me it was always found. A lot of people who fall victim to these unpleasant experiences are many who find themselves alone struggling with personal issues, physically or mental impairments. The fact that being in and out of county jail/state correctional facilities just add to the already burden on their shoulders. Not seeking any help, better yet not wanting any help better said. Death to these individuals is welcomed with open arms. So once your mindset is locked on reaching the inevitable "guess what"? … It's going to claim what is his.

My name is Manuel Ricardo I'm a Hispanic Puerto Rican I'm very fortunate to be 6'3 which is pretty tall I weigh about 225 lbs. I have a pretty nice build. My hair is dark my eyes are hazel thanks to the woman who brought me into this life. In sure she had to be an amazing woman in her own way. I'm assuming my height and muscular build came from my father. I can't complain about that one. Unfortunately, I didn't have the opportunity to grow up with my biological parents. My mother had two options on the day that I was about to be conceived in the operating room once her water broke. Who would have known that giving birth could ultimately put a woman in a predicament that could cause her to lose her own life on the day that is supposed to be the most important day of woman's life?

"Ms. Juanita" the doctor spoke trying to stay calm as he delivered the horrible news.

"You'll have a 35% chance of surviving this delivery it's completely your decision to either save yourself or save the baby. We are preparing for the worst case scenario" he spoke firm but in a nurturing voice as if he could feel the pain of his news.

What a position to be put in. I've learned to respect woman for more than just being a woman, they are creators and are so strong in so many ways one can't even imagine.

As tears filled her almond hazel shaped eyes, her long curly hair rested on the bed. Her completion was very Indian like cinnamon to be exact. She was beautiful despite the fact that she was hooked on drugs. The doctor was very aware of all of this. A decision to let live was one that couldn't be easy for one to make. This child could have possibly helped her change her whole outlook on life if the procedure was successful. Or would her life be better off nonexistent? No one knows for sure if her life would have actually straightened out with this child by her side. Could this child be saved without the mother being lost?

Juanita's eyes said a lot. She didn't look not one bit happy, more or so frightened. I'm sure many would say that even if she did give a healthy birth, it would just be another repeat of a doped up mother looking for her fix. It's a possibility that this innocent child could be malnourished on a daily basis. Juanita's eyes begged for one more fix. She was in so much pain at the moment. She did what any mother would do in a similar situation.

"I'll take my chances Dr. let's continue with the labor" Juanita requested.

That child that the woman gave up her life for is I. In that moment I knew that I had to live up to her expectations whatever they would have been.

With the doctor and his aids all prepped for the delivery he asked

"I need you to sign here Ms. Juanita" the doctor stated

It amazes me how your John Hancock is needed for everything in this country, whether it is to shop, live and die. I'm surprised they didn't ask for a co-signer too.

"Sign here and here please" The doctor ordered politely. "and good luck Ms. Juanita you are very brave."..... "Doctor make sure he's healthy and put in good hands please" she said with a broken heart she spoke it into existence not even knowing.

Her emotions got the best of her, her hands trembled. For some odd reason she knew deep down inside that she was not going to be given the opportunity to hold and admire her newborn. The operating room lights where shining brightly overhead. Juanita could hear every single sound as if it was magnified. The wheels spinning from the cart containing all of the essential instruments needed for the procedure the light chatter from the aids could be heard clearly. They held back there tears feeling sorry for the woman lying on the bed. All while staying focused in providing the doctor with all that he needed. To save the mother and child was the ultimate goal. The room's temperature was colder than the usual Juanita thought to herself, was she going to make it?

Once the face mask was placed over her face the doctor began to count backwards almost immediately "10.....9......8..........7.......6" By the time he reached one he already knew that she was out cold way before that but just making sure of it.

As he began to do what he was licensed to do.He was working precisely as he did for over a quarter century. The problem was that Juanita was so malnourished. Her body wouldn't be able to endure any more beatings like this one. Drugs will take a toll on anyone no matter who the person was. The doctor could have her looking like and octopus with all those tubes in her body and even with that. It wouldn't be sufficient enough. The odds were completely stacked against her. Conceiving a child is known to be emotionally and physically draining. So if you're not helping the situation, matters could only get worst or even disastrous. The biggest concern was that, the baby was the only reason why Juanita was alive. The doctor seen it this way. Once the baby would be delivered the inevitable was going to occur. Many would say that it was a miracle baby but to be honest. I don't feel losing my mother is anything near a miracle. I would have loved to meet Juanita very much.

"Beep.... Beep.......beep...... " the C-section was in progress Juanita's vitals were dropping slowly, "Williams please bring the paddles" the doctor ordered as a precaution. Within seconds the paddles were with in arms reach as he instructed. After a few minutes the baby was being dug out the whaling of the new born voice was full of life.

Passing the new born over to his assistant "Make sure you clean him up quickly and check his vitals before anything" the doctor was moving quickly. The baby was almost pinkish and very slimy just before the nurses cleaned him up quickly.

"I'll finish up with the mother she seems to be hanging on." The doctor was a little amazed at what he was witnessing. Her vitals moving up and down steadily. He did what he was trained to do. He dosed Juanita up with much needed care as his team watched awaiting further instruction praying all went well.

"Staples" the doctor ordered getting ready to begin closing the wound he just opened. "Staples" replied the nurse handing him what he just asked for.

As the doctor put in the staples Ms. Juanita vitals where stable, it appeared that all would end well even after all that was going on. Everyone's eyes being locked on all monitors not wanting anything terrible to occur but ready in the event it would. The big sighs of breath exhaling indicating a big relief on everyone's end.

"Doctor the baby is doing very well on this end, he is very light and extremely underdeveloped" the nurse informed the doctor. "Keep those hoses in him and keep a close eye on him." The doctor stated. He glanced over his shoulder sneaking a peak at the child with a smile on his face.

The I.V was supplementing the baby with vast amounts of vitamins and nutrient. There was a great chance that he would do just fine.

24 staples later....

"I think she's going to recover just fine", the doctor smiled commenting happily with his work "she is very strong transfer the baby up to the nursery shell be up soon" the doctor ordered

Juanita was in a deep bliss she wore a big smile on her face as if she was listening to everything that was being said about her beautiful child. He was healthy, she couldn't wait to awake to see and hold her child. With this baby being her first there was some hope that maybe she would turn her life around, If not for herself but for him. To be the mother that all females are destined to be. Right?

With needles and tubes running in and out of her body the nurses chatted lightly about how she would have the opportunity to raise her boy or would she?

Juanita was eventually placed up on the pediatrics floor where her baby was. He too was moved into an empty room just for the two of them. The two were being carefully monitored as the doctor ordered. The medication that Juanita was under was beginning to ware off a bit.

The feeling of the needles could be felt as if they were just placed into her once again. The pain that we normally hate to consider, it was more of a sensation to Juanita. They reminded her of the monkey she would learn to shake off eventually. This is what everyone at least hoped for. A fix was on her mind not the baby anymore, not her health. A needle with the purest heroin was entering her mind once again. Its location of the lethal drug was already awaiting her in the apartment she resided in right in her kitchen cabinet. Just the thought of it cause her glands on her forehead to perspire a bit. She twitched.... A few seconds later she twitched again the nurse sitting by her bedside didn't think much of it so she just continued to pick at her thumbnail. Moments later the twitch began to intensify a bit more. The nurse got up to take a closer look at Juanita's monitor her heart rate was dropping ever so slightly. Still not thinking anything was wrong with her she went to sit back down while turning her back on Juanita. That's when she began to shake uncontrollably. She began pressing the panic button, this was the nurse's initial reaction now. You would think that button should have been pressed upon noticing the first awkward twitch but then again I'm not a doctor just going by common sense. In just a matter of seconds the Dr. and his back up had arrive with all there artillery.

"Get the baby out of here please!" he ordered not even wanting the baby to hear any of what was going on....."Load the paddles" the Dr. ordered, he immediately injected Juanita with a sedative which was supposed to get her to stop, but that didn't seize the convulsing not even a tiny bit. With the child gone, He ripped her gown right open exposing Juanita chest. The nurses were already by the doctor with the paddle live ready for use. Juanita flopped like a fish searching for water. Her vitals were all out of whack, the foam spewing out of her mouth was being cleaned up as the doctor worked hard to stabilize her vitals by his staff.

The electrical charge lifted her body up off the bed no pulse, no more foam no more anything, could this be it? The frustration in the doctor's tone could be heard let alone felt.

"Turn up the cc's." he snapped "clear!" the assistant snapped back..... The slamming from Juanita's body sent fear in everyone that was inside of the room... "clear"! He yelled... Mouth to mouth recitation was commenced but to no avail.

"Beeeeppppp......." The pulse was lost, the doctor wasn't finished. "High!" he yelled not wanting this to end this way "clear!" the nurse retorted.

The perspiration from the doctor's forehead began to drip onto the lifeless Juanita's body.

"We lost her!"…. "How could this have happens?" The doctor questioned loudly, the nurse that was watching Juanita in the room lowered her head as if she was to blame for all of this, was she?

They say that if it is meant to be it will be, now if it isn't its almost impossible to make it be. Everything and everyone is believed to have his or her purpose in life. Of course if we figure this out early, than great. Now, if your one that love to go against your own better judgment than guess what...? Deal with the outcome as it may come whether positive of negative.

Juanita knew exactly what she was doing not to forget she was grown and was far from a child, could she of had some support? Of course she could have but then again why and how did she end up on the path that she was in? I don't mean to sound heartless she was my mother but imagine what we may have had to go thru if she had lived but didn't change? We all have the capacity to build bridges in our life, don't we? Now we all have the intelligence to keep building them and the power to also burn them down just as quick as we built them knowing we worked so hard to build them, that is solely up to our very own discretion. In no way am I saying that she got what she deserved but I'm a firm believer that we control our own destiny. So why not try and make it more reliable for ourselves? So our future can be a lot more promising. If not for ourselves but for the ones we are gifted in bringing into the life we live in.

I'm not going to sit here and lie I spend a great majority of my thoughts contemplating on how and why I ended up alone? It can be an emotional ride and I'm very aware that in due time I am to let go of all those thoughts that seem to haunt me. How does one let go of things as such? We can't! Or can we? To be honest I don't think we actually let them go but rather learn how to live with them.

I just turned 18 which just so happens to be the age that I had to be in order to be allowed to read and better yet understand the doctor reports of what had transpired the night of my mother's death. These wounds are painful and fresh with my heart just as tender. It's safe to say that for those who never experience anything as close to mine be grateful. I'm sure I'm not alone in this department though. For the most part you'll get your family and friends who will always say that "it's ok" or that" everything will be just fine"

This is for those individuals. Who the fuck do you honestly think you are? To assume that all is going to be ok? "Fuck you!" And "Fuck what you think!! Or is that what you think that I want or need to hear!" You don't know shit nor do you know what or how this news is going to affect my life Bitch"!

I've heard so many stories of my father and mother it's sad to say but they were all lies and rumors. No one and I mean no one will be able to tell me who these people where. So to be frank I'd appreciate it if you would keep your hypothesis and yourself made conclusion of who or what my parents were or what they should have been to yourself. This is my journey that I have to take, let alone the shoes I'm wearing are the ones I Manuel Ricardo have to walk in. So whether I get over it or not I have to live with this shit, neither you nor the individual next to you needs to opinionate shit. Thank you!

Once I had the copies of the hospital reports and wiped my eyes which was useless because I could feel the swelling on of my tear ducts which would give away that I was going through something tragic shit. I pulled myself together and took it all in for the time being, as much as my heart ached. I held my head up high and finally made my way out of the hospital.

As I headed out the sliding doors my voyage was intercepted by this red-bone who was thick in all the right places. She was leaning on the wall smoking a cigarette she hadn't noticed me yet but in a matter a seconds she was turned around staring at me.

"Hey handsome" she had no shame in her game, speaking what was on her mind I wanted to keep walking but my male whore inside me pulled me to a halt. I didn't want her or anyone to see me or even carry a conversation with me at a time like this. Her sweet scent had me on the line as if I was a catfish being fished out the fucking water at ease. I walked casually towards her. Those sexy powerful green eyes that demanded so much attention had me by the balls... tightly at that.

"Are you ok?" She asked not letting me respond to her first acknowledgement. I knew she noticed that my eyes still were a bit glossy. She had on some turquois scrubs that complemented her eyes to the tee. Her hair was reddish but not your typical box die, more or less you're natural red head. It was curly and appeared to be wet if not all gelled up to keep those sexy ass curls in place. I noticed she had to be about 5'1 in height, just by that you can only imagine how much I towered over her small self. She was sexy, short and thick just how I didn't mind them. She may have been a little too light for me but hey it was just small convo right?

"Sup ma". I finally responded to her. The stare in her eyes was way to seductive and inviting who knows maybe this light conversation would evolve into something a bit more exciting maybe later if I played my cards right.

"I'm good baby girl thanks for asking" I said my natural instant caused my head to drop starring at the ground not even really noticing that I did it. "Bad news Hun?" She asked not letting up. "You can say that ma" I replied trying hard to hold my composure. "Do you want to talk about it"? She asked. Now this woman had to be crazy I didn't know her from a can a paint and I was supposed to just get all personal with her with news that I couldn't even register properly yet myself, the nerve people had. I got to admit though her sweet soft voice had me all fucked up inside not to forget my emotions where already outa wack.

"Maybe another time ma" I replied to her question "I have a few things I need to take care of" I lied knowing damn well I didn't have a mother fucking thing to do. "Are you sure I have a few minutes to spare before I head back to work" she tried again to get me to open up. "Yes I'm sure" only a few minutes before she went back to work was all that kept replaying inside my head. I had to go for the kill. "If you have some time later on tonight or whenever we can maybe talk about it or even kick it for a bit, well that's only if it's cool with you ma?" My mind was racing a thousand miles wanting to know what she was thinking. With my gaze locked on hers I could see through her eyes, she was in deep thought.

There are a mass majority of females that work at the cooper hospital and I've seen plenty, but this one actually wanted to give me the time of day. This woman had no clue as to how old I was or did she not even give a shit? As I kicked a few thoughts inside my head, it was as though she was inside of my head playing tennis with my thoughts because out of nowhere the question came from left field.

"How old are you handsome?" She asked still locking eyes with me. My smile couldn't have been held back even if I tried. I wanted to lie but for what? She had to be at least in her early 20's. I thought against it and blurted out "I'm 18 ma." I answered with much confidence. "What!?" She was shocked I take it by how she reacted. I looked around just to see if anyone was around just in case she would decide to make a small show but good thing she didn't. "18" she repeated not wanting to believe the truth. "Yes I am, is that a problem?" I asked ready to walk away on her fine ass. She gasped for air "no not at all but you do look so much older ... I'm 25 is that a problem with you" she asked "fuck yea!" It was my turn to make a show she got red in the face feeling embarrassed is how I took it. "Nah I'm kidding, it's just right ma." I tried to make her feel better by informing her.

"I'm Felicia call me tonight if you want" she said writing her number on my palm the feeling of the ballpoint sliding on my skin caused me to smile. She glanced at her watch which meant one thing. "It's time to get back to work huh?" I beat her to the punch being observant. "I'm Manuel or Rock and I'll hit you up orita ma ok?" I said to her the look on her face was puzzled "orita"? She repeated not knowing what it meant. "Later ma, it means later" I translated with a half-smile. She smiled back "I knew that" she began stepping closer to the entrance door. I couldn't help but to stare at her round ass as it sashayed away. It was bouncing all over the place she knew I was looking and made sure that I enjoyed the view.

"That's right young'n" an old head was speaking to me I looked over at him and winked and walked away.

As I made my way over toward the terminal my mind drifted back onto how for some odd reason when women know that there being watch and they can find a hint of attraction in the person who is watching them they'll walk with a bit more authority in there step. If that doesn't grab a man's full attention than I'm not sure what will. If that's what you're into. The urine smell didn't helped not one bit. Starring out the window all the smudges on the window looked very fresh. They could have been anything at this time of day, sweaty palm, mucus or even spit it was disgusting. As the New Jersey transit made its way towards the terminal, I have to add that trying not to vomit took a lot of effort. The report in my hand brought back goose bumps again.

Finally getting dropped off at the crowded terminal the sight was one that no one could ever forget due to how a human being could be forced to live the way they did down in this part of town. The down town area was a place people could come to shop and just enjoy the store at their leisure. This wasn't the problem though the sight of homeless sleeping in packs in broad daylight was the issue, after so long it has become the norm in most cities I guess. Some didn't just sleep some probed the tourist others would just shoot up and get high with needles in their arms. Every bench that was put downtown had been claimed way before it was even stuck in the ground by the next homeless. That was there's and no one would say a thing. Panhandling was a way of living and guess what? This is what one choose to do with his or her life. So live it because feeling sorry for you was not my responsibility.

Waiting patiently on the next bus to take me over to federal S.t I stood outside waiting on Broadway, I noticed a help wanted sign starring directly at me in my face. My initial thought was to dismiss it but my gut pushed me over crossing the street heading straight to the sign or rather the store that displayed the sign. I kept my eyes in motion because I never trusted many people moving around me. A stick up or even a random shoot out could occur in seconds. So being a point in an urban city was a must which I'm sure you are all aware of this. "Beeeepppppp!" The sound of a BMWs horn blared almost running into a woman crossing I shook my head and entered the sub shop.

The clock on the wall was the first thing I noticed, I stared at it but time was motionless it didn't work. I already knew that I had roughly about 15 minutes to spare to get back over to the terminal. So just grab the application and drop it off manana/tomorrow/. Well that's what I thought.

"Can I help you"? Yelled the greasy ass apron wearing African American man who was putting together a meal for what could have been a customer or probably for himself. "Actually you can I wanted to know if I could get an application?" I spoke up as I was always taught. "Application?" he shot back I scrunched up my eyebrows as if I wasn't feeling where this was going but I just listened. "Who told you we was hiring"? The big man asked. He couldn't be serious… but the problem was that he most defiantly was. I turned over slightly looking at the sign and he followed my stare. "Oh shit! I forgot all about that shit it's been there for years and no one has ever came in to ask about it.

I've been meaning to take it down actually." He tried to clean up his previous statement and did ok I might add. As he spoke I looked around, this place was a dump. The walls where off colored, the floor couldn't be seen through the film of dirt and greased piled up on it. It was a sub shop that I would never and I mean never come in to eat once I walked in.

I will tell you this though this place has its reputation which isn't the best but it's known to have the beefiest subs in the city so with just that being said I could see how they still manage to survive in the game. I didn't have the opportunity to try there food but I'm sure I would one day but this was my first time actually coming up in here. Going by the image of this place I wouldn't be surprise if you would even purchase a free napkin from this place, but the food spoke for itself I guess. The man had left to the back and after a few seconds he reappeared with another male. The man he was with was tall and had to be at least close to 300 lbs. give or take a few a pounds. He also wore a greasy apron that could mean two things this man was the other worker or he was in charge of eating all the profit. He face was a scruffy which meant he needed a good shaving. The ketchup on his cheek told me he was back there demolishing something serious back there. I could most defiantly see how working here could get a man that fucking big. I smiled just by my own thoughts. "Sup kid"? The man wobbled over towards me. "I hear you looking for a job"? He asked staring at me. His voice was loud and raspy. The sound of the industrial fan over in the corner humming away pushing all the dust all over the place which was also very loud. This could be why this man was already accustomed to yelling. "Yes, I am sir." I replied honestly and sincere. I extended my hand gesturing a sign of respect as any respectful individual might opt in doing, he grabbed my hand returning it with a nice tight grip but I wasn't out of shape a firm shake is one worth extending.

"My name is Manuel and I noticed the sign you have displayed on the lower corner of the window". I informed him. "The what?" He yelled astonished as I pointed to it "the sign sir." I repeated "WOW!" He turned around and looked at his employee "I thought I told you to take that shit down years ago" he joked "man I've been so busy I forgot." the cook joked back. "Busy my ass" the big white man put his attention back on me. "You want to take his place?" The scruffy face man asked joking. I had about five minutes before I had to get back over to the terminal. I interrupted "if I may can I have an application I fill it out and bring it back to you in the morning my bus is on its way" I asked. He jumped on the task "yea sure, Jamal get him an application." He instructed his cook. "When you bring in the application be sure to bring in some working clothes as well, we'll see how you handle yourself tomorrow". I stared at him wondering was this a good move? He snapped me out of my daze. "We open up at 8:00 am." My mind was traveling a million miles an hour I grabbed his hand and shook it vigorously. There is no way that this man couldn't sense my excitement. After retrieving the application from Jamal I moved towards the door. "See you in the a.m." I said exiting the door, I sprinted across the street. Right on Q the bus had just pulled up with everyone loading it ready to get going on his daily route.

I had to attend school in the a.m. and it would be Friday, so I figured that I would miss the day. School was a joke to me. I don't say that in a sense that I didn't like it, I meant it in a sense that the school board and the faculty didn't take our education seriously. I was fortunate to attend Woodrow Wilson which was up the street from where I lived. I stay at a foster home with my foster parent on 27th and federal. The high was only a few blocks away. There is another high school in East Camden area known as Camden high these two high schools where rivals something that has been going on forever. No matter what was going on these two school could not find a drop of truce in between them. In my eyes it could be said that the two school strived to see who could hold the worst reputation for the longest amount of time. You know when there is a problem in a school when they go as far as implementing metal detector in almost every entrance to the building but it doesn't stop there the gated and bars on every window most defiantly can't go un-noticed. Any one walking by just by the image of the school can make their own opinion about the place just on looks and nine times out of ten they will hit the bull's eye based on what they see.

Any individual with the lowest IQ can managed to slip through the cracks, the majority of the woman would end up getting knocked up whether in study hall or even in the bathrooms if there was an opportunity it was going to be taken. I'm sure this all takes place in many other cities but for now I am going to speak of where I found myself. Drop outs outnumbered the graduates from what I observed. I'm hanging on myself. I work and strive to learn something on a daily basis but when your instructor doesn't have the passion let alone show any initiative to teach, how is one to learn? So for me to decide to miss tomorrow it was not a difficult decision to make on my behalf. Woodrow Wilson would not miss me for one day of even a week. My mind was already set as to what my day would consist of the following morning.

Riding the bus lost in my own thoughts, the bus made a few stops picking up a few bodies on the way some would sit up front others made their way over to the back end which I made sure to keep my peripherals sharp. The smell of poop lingered throughout the chunk of metal we all rode. After I almost fell over on every passenger making my way to the rear the driver finally pulled off ensuring everyone's safety. Not!

PCP is also a powerful drug that made its way into the inner streets of Camden. Many say that its birth was from over the bridge, which is Philadelphia. It's a form of embalmed fluid that is used for the deceased. I'm not a 100% sure how and what is used to chop that shit up to make it consumable, but it's ready for the streets, and for the crowd that enjoys that type of high. It comes in a few forms, in mint leaves, a liquid engorged in a cigarette known as a "sherm stick" or even as dust, if I'm not mistaken. Once anyone ingests that mess, there is no telling what that person will end up doing. If you think of it, guess what? You're going to do it whether its positive or negative, saying fuck the outcome.

On many occasions, I've been encountered with many of these drugs especially in the school bathrooms. This is where a lot of peer pressure takes a hold on many young lost kids who all need some attention. This is where a lot of youth get turned out, following the other just to fit in.

In the 18 years that I've been up and ticking, I can honestly say that I've only smoked marijuana twice and drank alcohol once. That was at a small house party, which ended up with two taken lives over by Steven Street. Over some, "she say" "he say shit" that someone probably thought it would be funny to start. One female and two males lives where taken that night, and I saw it evolve right in front of my eyes. "Bing!" The sound of the bell rang as I pulled the cord to instruct the driver to bring the bus to a halt at the next stop which was my stop at 27th and Federal.

Here in this small city it is wise for one to learn how to protect oneself, even though that will be embedding in you as you go through the schools and just living in the area. When one had a disagreement. The two of you would duke it out, with knuckle to knuckle action. Today this has now become modern warfare with your opponent. Blood spilling is what this world has come to, the use of weapons of all types that can be easily purchase with no i.d ,no type of criteria is needed in these streets. You can get your hands on anything. "Money talk bullshit walks" I'm sure everyone has heard of that quote. Then again in the art of war rules could be considered to be out the window. It's your life or mine how bad do you want to live.

My first encounter was in the 4th grade, I was on my way to the bodega with 50 cents in my hand. I had bought a bag of Doritos and a huggie which was a blue one. As I made my way out the store all happy go lucky I was encountered by these two block bullies. Now I'm only a half a block away from my foster mom's house with no brothers, no family and no one to have my back when things would get ugly. Let's just say that the taste of that bag of chips never made it to my mouth nor did that cold juicy. I have gotten beat up by those two boys who were around my age and I had no chance to even strike a blow back. I did what my mind thought was the right thing to do which was run. I ran home as fast as I could scared out my mind. What took place was something I never expected.

"Manuel what in the world happened to you!" Ms. Cathy yelled with a look of anger on her face. The sight of my banged up face took her by surprise. All I could say was "I got beat up" with my face starring at the floor in a pathetic tone. "You got beat up?" Ms. Cathy asked "by who?" There was another question. She asked. I knew exactly who beat me up. They live right down the street, they were known on the block for their little terroristic acts. There was no way I could muster up the courage to tell so I didn't. I think just the fact that if I did I would probably get beat up again just for telling on them.

Ms. Cathy was my foster parent who had custody of me since the age of 10 along with a girl who was around my age as well. The girls name was Jalinda she was my sister not by blood but by relation, being raised in the same house hold with no biological parents we sort of created a family amongst one another. Ms. Cathy took us both in and tried her best to teach us and mold us into well respectful individuals. Ms. Cathy was in her late 30s damn near 40 she was Caucasian woman who smoked like a damn chimney. She wasn't skinny but was far from big she had to be at least 180lbs. she wasn't the shortest but was about 5'5. She always made sure that Jalinda and I didn't need or want for anything. Everything that we asked for was in our hands of course within reason.

"Why did these boys beat you up"? She was still bombarded me with questions. She looked past me "and where is your soda and chips?" She threw another question at me. Her hand was placed on her thick hips. I still searched the floor for all my unanswered question's answers. I let out "I don't know and they took them from me." I said practically in tears. "You let them take your snacks!?" She cut me off. "There were two of them". I tried to justify knowing I should have kept my mouth shut. "Listen to me Manuel. You going to have to learn how to protect and fend for yourself no matter what." Ms. Cathy spoke to me. I listened attentively. "Even if there is more than one, you grab whatever is around you whether it be a stick, rock or anything you see to help you protect yourself from harm and use it only if you are outnumbered." She went on to explain to me. "You always fight head on meaning that if it's just you and one other person you fight them one on one. She starred at me wondering if it was sinking in, which in my mind it most defiantly was. "Ok!?" She asked "yes Ms. Cathy." I replied starring back at her with my swollen eyes. "Now come on so I can get you cleaned up." Her words never left my head until this very day there was no getting rid of those strong and truthful words. It just so happened that two days later I was once again given some change as the usual. Not even thinking about what has happened two day ago I went on my happy go lucky merry way to the bodega again. If I would of know that it would have been round two I may have opted to stay my ass in the house but I did not, not knowing what was about to take place but what I did know was that this was not going to go down the way it did the last time.

The day was sunny and beautiful and the block was jumping as any other day and it just so happen the two bullies were out as well waiting and plotting. The dope dealers busting traps all day on the block was something that everyone had learned to get accustomed to they were actually the ones who made sure our block was somewhat safe from those who didn't belong in this area but of course drama was always in the area and hard to avoid. But when disputes occurred they were far from the one to break shit up, if anything they would scout the brawls for potential workers, look outs and pack runners, they would also sit back and enjoy the show just like every other person on the block. The more ruthless one would display the better your odds were to become a dope dealer yourself. With them knowing that a majority of the kids on the block not having a pot to piss in nor a window to throw it out of they would use that to their advantage. So with a little guidance and a few dollars put in their pocket the young bucks would be running the block in no time. A never ending cycle.

As I made my way out of the bodega guess who was waiting for me? Yup you got it right Bam and mother fucking Curtis. Knowing this was an easy come up on their behalf, my heart began to beat uncontrollably fast due to being scared and just flat out nervousness. All I knew was that it was about to go down. I wanted to run. A bodega is a small corner store with all your essentials that may be needed on a day to day basis. In Spanish it called "bodega".

"Sup man let me get the bag!" Bam ordered in his tough man voice. I kept on walking as if I didn't hear them my main focus was to get to Ms. Cathy's house and try so hard to avoid all that was about to take place. As I walked I noticed a nice size stick up ahead and kept my eye on it as I sense these two on my heels. The stick gleamed as if it was a sign for me not to walk past it so I slowed my pace down a bit. It was Curtis turn to put his tough man voice on "yo he said to give him the bag!" He now repeated what his partner had ordered the first time. Just as he said that, bam snatched the bag right from my hand ripping the plastic bag. My instinct was to pick up the stick and guess what? That is exactly what I did. You would have mistaken me as Babe Ruth the way I swung that stick trying to hit a home run. I got bam right behind the ear and he fell instantly "ahhhhh!" He screamed I'm not going to lie I was scared out my mind as I struck him "give me my bag!" I yelled back in fury not wanted to strike him again but knew I would due to the rush I felt not knowing exactly what that feeling was. "Yo!" yelled Curtis shocked at what he just witnessed, he tried to pounce on me but I was too quick with the stick catching him dead in his mouth. I'm pretty sure he had to have swallowed one of his teeth because the amount of blood that he was spewing couldn't be from a busted lip. He too bellowed out a loud cry. At this point my anger and the image of them bullying all the kids from the block replayed over and over in my head. As I recounted every past episode I struck each one over and over again not letting up one bit. I couldn't and I wasn't. "Please stop, please stop hurting us!" cried bam with a petrified look on his face. He didn't even let out his last syllable and I had his face plastered onto the stick again. Whatever I was feeling had me in a trance I enjoyed what I was feeling. Was I wrong?

"Only if you leave me the heck alone, I don't bother anyone!" I yelled still taking turns on them. The stick had broken on both of them I notice a tooth on the ground which I knew belonged to Curtis. "Manuel!" a very familiar voice yells at the top of their lungs. It was Ms. Cathy. She ripped the stick right out of my hand and bopped me right upside the head with it. My eyes watered as I now felt a small percentage of what I was doing to bam and Curtis. "Pick up your bag!" Ms. Cathy insisted. That was exactly what I did bending over and picking up my already opened bag of chips and juice. Bam and Curtis took the opportunity and bolted home crying hysterically.

The dope boys kept busting traps all while enjoying the scene from the very beginning. This was my very first altercation and I could feel it would be far from my last encounter physically. No cops even bothered to show up which was the norm around here.

Finally inside of the house I could still feel the beating of my heart still pounding hard, my breathing was slowing down. Ms. Cathy still had the stick in her hand I watch it attentively wondering why she still had it in her hand. "Are those the two who have been picking on you?" she questioned. "Yes." Was all I could say at the moment? I sipped on my juice still replaying what had just happened. "I'm sure those two will never pick on you ever again." she informed me of her prediction. I could only hope that she was right. If she wasn't I would either catch it worst the next time or vice versa?

—

"Hello Manuel where have you been" Ms. Cathy asked, upon me entering the house. "I got a job" was all I could say while taking off my low top Nikes off at the door. I knew that once I would tell her about the job I hope she would approve even though the part of me missing school would be something she wouldn't approve of. "You got a what?!" She asked shocked and in disbelief. I repeated to her. It was just a matter of seconds before all the bombarding of questions would come flying my way as she always did. "Where?" She asked me and stopping what she was doing in the kitchen. You see the house we lived in was a two-story with a small basement and a porch out front and in the back. In the front of the house we had metal bars going around the porch and up over the gutters due to the fact that the breakings were heavy in the area and we no longer wanted to be victims to the BNE's so Ms. Cathy had them installed on all doors and windows. Whoever wanted to break in our home had to bring the welding equipment to get through all that steel. The bars were all painted black and all the sidings were all painted white so the house had his own unique identity on the block. Our house was a few houses away from the Chinese takeout spot that seems to attract getting shot up every time there's beef in our area. Well once you enter Ms. Cathy's home you have the living room which is small but has its own color which is a baby blue and white the white has shiny glitter mixed in so he gives the living room its own flavor. The couches are black so they stand out something seriously the entertainment center also is black with a few knick knacks and a few picture frames of Ms. Cathy's foster children who are my sister and I. She also has a photo of her mother who passed away a few years ago. The TV was a big box Sony that we hardly watch because the living room was for "company only". As you pass through the living room there were a set of stairs heading upstairs which led to our bedrooms and bathroom. The dining room had a simple glass table with nice wooden chairs enough to seat four which was more than enough because there was only three living in the house. Ms. Cathy was in the chair wearing her small apron tied around her waist. She and I were speaking our words as she was in the middle of preparing dinner. The aroma in the air was intoxicating with the smell of the seasoning of the adobo and some sofrito and whatever else she would throw in the pots to create a wonderful meal. My words came slow, but had to be spoken truthfully. There was no sense in lying because it already came out my mouth the moment I walked in. "At a sub shop" I answered truthfully but not giving her the exact coordinates. "Oh yea?" She replies she was thinking as she walked towards me. "So how was school?" She asked staring at me directly in my eyes. I looked into her deep blue eyes and answered "I didn't go school today". I couldn't lie to her it would only make her lose trust in me and I wasn't going to lose this bonded friendship that we had Built over the years. "So you got a job at the sub shop?" when you was supposed to be in school?" She spoke firm but not with an attitude she wasn't the type to scold us as if we were animal she spoke and treated us like adults and this is why I couldn't lie to her. My sister Jalinda was the same way. Of course she wanted the best for us but at the end of the day we were going to do as we please eventually. Speaking of Jalinda she was said to be coming home soon by the way. "Manuel was going on why didn't you go to school today?" Ms. Cathy asked. She stared deeply into my eyes searching for lies while lighting a cigarette. "I was at the hospital." I replied looking down at my socks. "Are you not feeling well?" She asked "I'm fine Ms. Cathy". "I went to the hospital to follow up with the reports that you informed me a few years ago that I would be able to received once I turned of age" once I expressed them words she immediately rose up from her seat at the table and gave me the biggest hug and apologize, not for missing school but from what I just learned today about my biological mother. My emotions came pouring back as if I just learned the information for the very first time again I held her and just cried. It just so happened that my sister happen to be turning the doorknob walking right into an emotional situation I'm sure I had no choice but to cue her in the whole day that I had just endured. My sister Jalinda was a year older than me she wasn't biological but like I said from our past experiences you can say that we were because we were so close and if she wasn't my foster sister I would have made a move on her years ago just saying. Jalinda was 4'11" she was African-American she had milk chocolate complexion with dark brown eyes that could keep you locked in her gaze once they met with yours. She had hair up to her shoulders that was always braided neatly in all types of designs, but will always baffled me was how she braided it all by herself she had a few friends that all seem to want to taste her Hispanic brother trust and believe I have my fair share of the ones that Jalinda gave the approval to dick down. I'll get into that later. Jalinda had a sweet laugh once she showed it her high cheekbones couldn't be held down from being exposed. She had very full lips with the straightest teeth to complement them. She had to beauty marks one on the right side of her bottom lip the size of bb pellet which was very cute the other one was on her left cheek bone about an inch above her deep dish dimples... Yeah I said dimples I'm a sucker for dimples but like I said this girl is my pride and joy. She rocked three piercings two on her left ear and one on her right. Her body was also a work of art she had a B cup with a very slim waist with her cute little apple bottom I could see that she was sporting her open toe ballerina shoes with her yellow capris with a snug fit spaghetti string shirt with matching everything when it came to looking good Ms. Cathy always kept us looking presentable and we both were grateful for this. "Manny what is wrong!?" She asked dropping her bag on the couch and heading straight towards Ms. Cathy and I. I held back a few extra tears and just handed her the paper in my back pocket of my Academic jeans. As she read the paperwork for herself, her hands begun to shake uncontrollably as she continued to read these emotions came and went all day, and for some reason I knew this wouldn't be the end of our emotional roller coaster. We all have our history it's all on how we find out about them, then we can honestly learn how to encounter a deal with those past situations which can help us and mold us into what and who we are today. Tears poured down her face onto her black and yellow tank top missing her beautiful smooth skin. She clamped on to me feeling a fraction of my pain. Jalinda and I had our pass just like others which needed to be handled with care. Jalinda is a virgin but technically she's not because unfortunately like most girls who grow up with stepfathers not saying that all stepfathers may have twisted intentions but in this case she received the ugly end of the stick. She was raped for over two years straight by her mother's boyfriends. I guess her mother didn't have the pussy he was looking for so he would sneak up into Jalinda room after getting drunk with her mother and once everyone was passed out he would take advantage of Jalinda in every way possible. As sick as it made me when she told me all of this for the very first time I wanted to find the piece of shit and blow his fucking dick off to pieces. I swore to protect her for as long as we were around one another she could never work up the courage to open her legs up to just any random nigga. I respected her so much for that I see her flee off so many dudes with money, cars, houses even businesses she was just not interested in anything materialistic. If I didn't know any better I would've thought she was a lesbian, but she informed me that she wasn't into that after my curiosity got the best of me.

"I'll find my true love one day no worries or no rush." She told me...

"I'm so sorry Manny" Jalinda spoke sobbing she was the only person I allowed to call me Manny everyone else was either Manuel or Rock. I hugged her and after what felt like an hour we all talked about how we all ended up together and how our lives could be worse and we are happy how our situation became uncovered. Now it was time to move forward 1 foot in front of the other. The smell of the food brought all three was back to reality.

"Are you too hungry?" Ms. Cathy asked us still red and swollen from all of our crying. I'm starving" Jalinda said "oh yeah?" Ms. Cathy replied well soon as you take off your shoes at the door will begin to eat". We both smiled "oh I…." Jalinda tied to explain "no need to explain Linda I already know." Ms. Cathy cut her off we called her "Linda" which meant "pretty" in Spanish. I gave her the nickname and it never left her it stuck to her like gum to the bottom of your shoes. As Linda made her way to the door and removed her little tiny ballerina shoes and walked back with her hips swaying left and right I couldn't help but look. Hey! I'm a man it's in my blood. I'm sure she notices me looking but is just looking I don't drool all over myself as hard as it may be not to. The plates are served and we are ready-to-eat as Ms. Cathy made her way to the dining room. We all said grace. Once grace is over I go to the kitchen and grabbed three sodas two cokes for the women and a Mountain Dew for me. That's my favorite.

"The rice might be a bit smoky due to my lack of focus earlier I apologize". Ms. Cathy apologized. "Its fine Cat" Linda expressed with a mouthful of it, I laughed. "Girl you know better than to speak with all that food in your mouth" Ms. Cathy tells her as we all ate this well-prepared dish that's always prepared for us on a daily basis. Today it was yellow rice with corn in it and pork chops seasoned perfectly with whatever Ms. Cathy puts in it. It's meshed perfectly together just right. Once we all clear our plates like a ritual the cigarette is immediately lit and Linda and I go to go do the dishes.

"I'm tired I'm going to lie down if you need me I'll be in my room just tap on the door before entering." Ms. Cathy says taking her cigarettes and heading up to stairs. Linda and I always take turns with the pots and dishes. Ms. Cathy taught us the ins and outs on taking good care of ourselves and the household because bad habits are hard to break. Which I learned was very true. She hated to smoke but couldn't live without a cigarette in her mouth a pack would last her about a day which was bad in my eyes. She tried the gum, patches and any and every other form of quitting nicotine that is offered in this poisonous world but quitting was something we would consider damn near impossible for her. It just didn't work or maybe she just didn't want it to work. Due to all the chaos of emotions I really didn't get a chance to fully explain my working situation which I thought was a free pass and figured not to mention it till I felt the time was right. I considered telling Linda. In the meantime I scraped the rice pots clean and put the leftover rice and pork chops in a plastic bowl with lid in the fridge. Linda was already banging out the dishes she was fast at washing.

"Manny?" Linda called out to me "what's up sis" I replied "so you didn't go to school today?" No I was so anxious to find out the truth I skipped today and just jumped on the bus and went straight to Cooper Hospital". I informed her "so you going tomorrow?" She asked I knew this was coming "I can't" I replied "you what?" She shot back she stop washing dishes and look dead into my eyes. "I can't" I responded "why?" She barked "because I got to go to work tomorrow morning" she laughed "work? Ha! You don't work Manny" she said laughing at me "I will manana" I assured her "oh my God for real where"? She asked excitedly "at the sub shop on Broadway right across from the terminal" I explained briefly "STOP! Where they sell the beefy juicy subs at?" She asked knowing the spot "you already know sis" I replied smiling. I could smell some smoke but couldn't really detect where was coming from I turned off the stove but I decided to check the back where the single half bathroom was and where the washer and dryer were located in the back in the house "where are you going?" Linda asked "you don't smell that?" I question her question. "Smell what?" She challenged. As I checked the bathroom and the machines it wasn't coming from the back room I decided to finish up helping Linda my mind was probably playing tricks on me… "Happy birthday to you, happy birthday to you, happy birthday to Manny, happy birthday to you!!" It was candles I smelled a big number one and an eight burning slowly. Cathy didn't go to sleep and Linda knew the whole set up. Her smile said it all I looked at the cake and the dancing flames just took me back to every other birthday that was spent here with these two females. The cake was designed .It was something different every year. Today it was a basketball court and ball with the New Jersey Nets team logo which was my favorite team for the past four years Jason Kidd was my boy. I love these two no matter how and why we ended up together.

"Make a wish!" Ms. Cathy yelled "for what I already have you two" Ms. Cathy's eyes watered but no tears fell she held them back bravely. I blew out the candles and of course Linda got me with a fistful of cake right in my face and bolted out the kitchen. "Ima get you Linda!" I yelled wiping my face tasting the frosting form my birthday cake. The ice cream was perfect for the three of us "I know it's been a rough day for you, but just know that Linda and I are here for you" Cathy spoke to me while handing me a small wrapped up box. I immediately tore it open as this point I didn't want to talk about the horrible news anymore. I have plenty of time to deal with that. Linda came back into the kitchen with a smile on her face, one that she knew that I would get her for that stunt but not yet. She too had a small rectangular box in her hand she handed it to me. "Here you go big bro" she was older but being overprotective with her she felt I was the older one. "Thank you sis" I replied still opening Ms. Cathy's gift. It was a gold watch with black onyx and bezels on every link. The reflection from the ceiling lights made it radiate so much, that my eyes were in complete shock. I wasn't into jewelry but this was something that I would love to rock with pride and style. Jalinda's gift was a little different it was a butterfly knife the look in Ms. Cathy's eyes was not a look of happiness but rather and an uncomfortable and uneasy stare. She took the butterfly knife back in her hands and began to show me how to open it and how to close it in swift motions. It looked just like the movies it looked a bit difficult and a bit dangerous at the same time but Jalinda made it look easy I knew that with practice I would open and close it just as good as she did.

"Manuel!" Ms. Cathy spoke out. "Yes?" I replied. "I don't want you to take that to school you can get in a lot of trouble for bringing in a weapon to the schools." She had her eyes locked into minds with a cigarette burning in her hand. "Do you hear me?" She asked "yes I do Ms. Cathy." Even if I wanted to bring it to school I couldn't due to the metal detectors so that was a no-no. "I'm going to bed kids" Ms. Cathy always headed to bed early. Be careful with that knife" she said as she walked away from us heading back upstairs. The kitchen was clean and Jalinda and I had things to do. I thanked her for the gift and she gave me a hug "you're welcome if you need to talk you know where I'll be at Manny happy birthday." She said. She was in college she always had homework to do I wasn't too sure if I was going to college because it felt as if she had no time for herself. Little did I know this was time for herself? I put my knife in a box and would practice every night until I got it. Felicia popped into my head and I decided to give her a buzz after I showered up and got comfy in my bedroom it was already getting dark. I didn't have any plans so I opted to just staying home and gathering my thoughts. Once in my bedroom all washed up and relax I grab the receiver all my nightstand and pondered if I would call her, but then again who I was kidding my mind was already made up. I'm a huge basketball fan so my room is decked out with posters and frames I have a king-size bed which fitted my height just perfect if I'm not mistaken around my freshman year I had to ditch my full-size bed because I knew I would outgrow it due to my rapid growth spurt. I have a nice size closet with two rows of kicks most were forces of different flavors and two pairs of Tim's my Butters and of course suede Blacks. Basketball jerseys hung up fresh and always authentic. A few polos' and a bunch of fitted button ups for a nice night out whenever the opportunity presented itself. Hats were my thing but you can best believe that I had a fitted for every jersey it wouldn't feel right if I didn't. My 36 inch box TV was on another dresser in the far right corner of my room. I'm not gona lie it was a bit messy since I got up this morning with rattled nerves. I turned into Sports Center and lay back on my bed. "609631721….. 1" I dialed taking a deep breath and waited for an answer. Normally I would've waited but I just couldn't help but think about this red bone.

"Yeah you reached Felicia please leave your name and number and I'll get back to you by" her voice on the answer machine. I didn't do the voicemail thing so I just hung up and watch the top 10 highlights, just when I got to the 6th one the phone began to ring. I didn't worry if anyone answered because most of the time everyone in a house knew it was for me. I looked at the caller ID and my heart began to beat faster than the normal. I press talk and just as I did Felicia's sweet voice called out "Manuel" I couldn't help but laugh "now what if it wasn't me?" I challenged to see what her response would be. "I know it was you handsome." "All yea?" I asked challenging some more. "Yes!" You want to know how I know." She asked. "How?" I questioned "Every number is programmed in my phone and you was the only person I gave my number to today." she sounded too confident and I liked it. Key word "today" did you get that? "So who did you give your number out to yesterday?" I joked I had to I wanted to see what I could get out of her. "What?!" She barked sounding a bit agitated or annoyed at that remark. "No one! You happen to be the only one who caught my eye today as matter fact if you want to really know I haven't given my number out to anyone over the past two months tired of all these dudes out here and their games for real!" She was letting loose I couldn't help but to smile on the other end. "Two months get out of here." I couldn't help myself so I challenged a bit more. "Yes I'm for real handsome." I heard a sound of a girl on the other end of the phone. She sounded young so I did what every nigga would do. "Listen ma if you want I'll call you later or manana since you sound a bit busy. "No Manuel you good I'm just here spending some time with my baby girl but I'm about to put her to sleep soon, you okay" she added… baby girl? That played over and over in my head I had to ask her though "you have kids?" It was rude but I wanted to know the deal with his red bone. "Yes I do I have 3 boys and three girls she admitted I was about to hang up on her there was no way I was dealing with a chick with six kids. I'm still a kid myself "wow!" Was all I could say? She began to cough and laugh so hard I was confused "I'm just playing with you handsome I have one daughter and she's my pride and joy" she informed me. I immediately began to laugh my ass off. A couple more seconds and I was going to bang on her and her six kids I thought to myself. "So you have one kid." I asked. "Yes I do her name is Eliza and I'm a single parent, her dad don't want nothing to do with her so I gave him the choice to sign her over or be a part of her life, guess what he chose to do?" She asked "he said no". I answered "yea right I wish he would've said that instead he said where and when do I sign?" She confessed. In my mind I didn't know how any parent could sign over his or her rights over to any child. Why? Would any parent do such a thing to bring a child into this world and then abandoned him or her due to one's selfish needs. For one to raise a child one has to learn that it is no longer about you it's about the well-being of that creation that has been brought into this world. I could feel her sincerity in her voice as we spoke I actually gained some type of respect for her. "So where do you live if I may ask?" Changing the subject. "I live in Collingswood now I use to live in North Camden, but once I had my baby I decided that I wanted better for her." She explained. "So you live alone?" I asked. "Yes and no" it's a three bedroom apartment I have a roommate who has been helping me and vice versa." She answered. "Oh okay so you have your own place in other words?" I asked "you can say that she replied. What are you doing now?" She asked me "I'm in my room talking to you watching ESPN well at least I was you seem to have all my undivided attention now." I answered. I didn't mind that she had all of my attention in fact if felt pretty good to actually have a decent conversation with someone different I have a fair share of female friends but their old news. I can't say that I'm a womanizer but a good girl can't seem to hold my attention for too long. I would eventually move on to the next in a matter of days or even weeks. "I'm sorry do you want me to give you your personal time?" she asked so innocently. Is she crazy I shut off the TV? "No you are my personal time for the moment. I'm all tuned into you ma." I informed her "oh my God you're so sweet or do you talk to all your females the same way?" She asked. "Oh boy?" I knew this was coming. I'm a be honest I have female friends but is just that Felicia I don't have a steady girl or wife I'm too young and I haven't found one to keep my attention for more than 20 minutes." I bit my lip cuz I may have went too far with that remark. It was quiet on the other end she finally spoke. "I'm sorry I heard you handsome I was leaving my daughter's room she fell out." She informed why she was so quiet on the other end for a few seconds. "That's cool ma you got to do what you got to do right?" "No worries" I informed to her. "Hey listen Manuel is only 8:00 PM and I haven't eaten yet I'm starving you want to grab a quick bite nothing more nothing less?" She had to throw that in there I was still stuffed from all the food and cake I just ate there was no way I would be able to eat anything else unless it was her. "I love to but I just ate so much good food and cake and ice cream." I admitted wondering if she thought that I was trying to flee her off. "Cake and ice cream?" She asked "damn!" Must've been a hell of a party?" She was probing and I definitely knew it. "Party?" I laughed no ma not at all it was just a small birthday celebration with my sister and Ms. Cathy here at the house." I spoke into the receiver. I wanted to see her but I really didn't want to eat anything. "So it was your sibling's birthday?" She asked me. "It was my birthday actually." I replied. "Oh really?" She sounded very excited to hear the news. "So you just turned...?" She asked not finishing. "Yes I turned 18 today". I interjected with confidence. "We'll happy birthday handsome now I really want to see you before the night is over." She insisted now "how was the cake?" She asked it was great and delicious It had pieces of strawberry in it and it was marble with thick sweet icing" I explained to her "yummy I bet it was delicious." She replied so where do you live?" She asked me "in the city" I replied I know silly but where in the city?" She questioned on federal" I replied okay on federal and what?" She wasn't going to stop until I gave her my exact location. "27th and Federal Street" I couldn't help but tell her. "Give me a few I'll be there shortly okay?" She wouldn't take no for an answer and I was already waste deep. "What about the baby" I asked. "She's fine my roomie is here and has no plans so I got that covered." She assured me. "Aright then ma.", and ended the call. My stomach was flip-flopping now because this woman was on her way to see me. Well she didn't know exactly where I lived but she was close as hell now. Collingswood is almost about 10 minutes away from where I was. So I had to be ready by the time she arrived. I knew she would take a while because she was going to freshen up you know how women are. I was already fresh all I had to do was get dressed. She told me she was starving and I wasn't so I decided after I got dressed to cut her two slices of cake one for her and one for her daughter better make it 3 one for her roommate since someone was looking after her daughter. A small pimp move I decided to go dark so I pulled out my light blue jeans with black stitching with the black R on the rear pocket for Rock-a-ware and threw on my suede black tims with my black Tim Duncan Spurs jersey with the matching fitted. By the time I handled all that needed to be done my receiver was ringing in my back pocket. It was her "hello, hello" I heard two different hellos on the line it was Ms. Cathy and Felicia. "I got it is for me I waited for a second to make sure it was just us on the line, Felicia?" I spoke "yes handsome it's me I'm a block away" she informed me okay ma turn on 27th and drive to you see the school I'm wearing a jersey. I gotcha she replied I know I had to be out the door quick so she could see me in front of her instead of in her rearview. With the plastic plates in my hands I shot out the door but not before setting the alarm and securing the house. 6,7,3,2 alarm set just in case I didn't come back at a reasonable hour. I was about 50 feet from the school and there was no car in sight I walked down the block and the dope boys were all out as they always are the aroma of marijuana and PCP was thick in the air. The streetlights would flicker and make the block look more malicious than it already was. Fein's were up and down the block copping their drug of choice. I kept walking with my eyes open for anything unusual to come my way. "What's going on Rock?" A raspy deep voice spoke out it was Banga he was accompanied by three other dudes to which I didn't recognize but the one Jigs was with him. "I'm good" I replied. "You good?" I asked but not slowing down "yea we straight?" They replied high out there mines "chilling got to handle something" I replied. "Be easy, we here if anything Rock early." they assured me "say no mas" I replied I was halfway to the school there was a car approaching the high beans flickered twice I figured it was Felicia and just as I figure she pulled up beside me. "Hey handsome you need a ride?" She joked she was driving a Lexus a sexy one at that it wasn't brand-new but it was damn sure clean. I walked around the passenger seat and jumped in. The car was champagne color with original stock rims had peanut butter interior and it smelled good inside the aroma she gave the car was intoxicating. "What's up ma?" I spoke as I got comfy in her whip. I hit the small button on the side of the leather seat to recline and slid the seat all the way back. My legs were long and whoever sat in his chair before I did was really short.

"Damn! Handsome you are tall". She stated as we pulled off she smiled at me and with a big happy birthday. "You're getting old" she joked "yeah I know" I replied laughing, her smile was dazzling she had on lip gloss so the night lights reflected off her lips they were juicy and I wanted to bite them. I know she knew I was looking at her lips and I didn't care one bit. She had on a pink and black Nike tight T-shirt with some matching hoop earrings, her hair was in a messy ponytail with her ears exposed. They were very tiny I thought to myself. She had a few tendrils hanging down the side of her face which added texture to her style. She had a small forehead which was cute; her eyebrows were neat and arched perfectly. They weren't thin but not to think either but went very good complimenting her facial features. Her shirt hugged her breasts which had to be C-cup or a small D-cup she wore tight blue jeans that were probably going to give her yeast infection due to how tight they looked on her from sitting down. I smiled at my own thoughts. I couldn't see her feet but knew she had to be wearing something nice to match her outfit.

"Why? Are you smiling" she asked in her sweet innocent voice "just thought of something no worries ma" I told her "you look very pretty" she blushed immediately "thank you" I didn't have a chance to get ready but I'll take the complement. "She spoke she is full of shit I thought but decided I let go it was her story I'll let her tell it. "You looking fresh is that your birthday outfit?" She asked driving and looking me up and down without missing the road. "No I didn't get an outfit this year". This is something I threw on since I knew you were on your way nothing to flashy". I joked "you smell good to what you got on?" She asked "Joop" I replied back "okay Mr. Joop man" she giggled and joked. "I got something for yall" I said placing the plate on the backseat "was that?" She asked not sure of what was being put her backseat "and who's yall?" She asked confused like a mother fucker. "For you and your daughter and your roommate" I informed her "what is it?" She stopped at the red light I wanted to know where the hell we were going. I just jumped in this car with this chick I just met earlier today not too bright on my behalf. I knew I'll be fine but I still had a slight paranoia. "It's three slices of birthday cake that I wanted to share with you". I told her as the light turned green. "u can eat it later or tomorrow we have a lot left over so might as well you know? " I examined the look on her face it was a complete awe. "You didn't have to do that handsome I can't believe it you're so sweet." She replied "stop that please" I shot back at her "stop what?" She asked confused as shit "with the mushy shit" I said and smiled. She follow suit. "I'm hungry and you going to keep me company while we eat or should I say I eat because you said you're not hungry" she did the quotation hand gesture as she said not hungry she had a cute personality and I was digging it. "So where are we going?" I asked not sure but I want some wings I'm thinking Pizza Hut over in Oaklyn "what you think?" She asked. "Hey if that's what you want than we in there." I replied "Oaklyn" is been a long time since I've been around that part of town is right next to Collingswood. Collingswood was on the outskirts of the city it was known for the area for the higher class white people. So was Oakland, Audubon etc. etc. I had no business over those parts of the area. I was with her so I didn't care and plus it was a change of scenery. We took the nearest main road all the way towards the circle which pointed to Collingswood and Woodlynne. We drove in silence listening to R.Kelly's greatest hits. If I knew any better this woman wanted to get it in, but then again I just went with the flow. Every now and then I would catch myself staring at her thick thighs and her face while she would be focused on the road. I'm sure she saw through her peripherals that I was on her and that I was feeling her. Her hands were manicured and she sported three rings on her right hand and one on her left they were gold I couldn't see exactly what they were but I would know by the night was over. As we pulled up into the Pizza Hut the parking lot was occupied with many cars so of course the joint was packed with patrons. She swiveled her way into a parking spot and threw the shifter in park. We sat in the car for a few minutes she turned around in her seat to retrieve the plate that was inside a grocery bag in her backseat. "I want to taste this because the way you spoke about it on the phone earlier made my mouth water" as she reached for the bag her whole body was shifted in the chair she had curves like a chick in the Nelly video my mouth watered but I kept my cool. She unwrapped the aluminum foil carefully as to not get any icing anywhere on her seats, shirt, and carpet I just observed her. I mean I knew she was some type thick from when I see her earlier but her scrubs kind of camouflaged it a bit. But with these jeans on her now body was on point. Turning on the overhead light which lit up her flawless face. The inside of the car was fully lit and every walking bystander could see straight into the car. I had to remember that I was in Oaklyn and not in the hood. I was good no need to be so discreet about everything. Living in the city raises awareness to about 1,000 no joke. You try to be quick and inconspicuous with the things you do because not everyone has the best intentions for you. You know? She took a piece a cake out with her two fingers her pointer finger and her thumb she looked at the bite and smiled "I'm a sweet junky" she said putting the small bite into her mouth and That sexy smile as she closed her eyes and savored every last crumb. "Oh my God this cake is amazing" she stated with a bit of volume in her voice she was about to go in for another bite but I stopped her before she stuck her hand back into the cake "wait ma you should eat first before you spoil your appetite." If you eat all the cake there you won't eat what you set out to eat in the first place." I tried to explain. I could've cared less to be honest but I wanted to go inside the restaurant and spent time with little mama's. If not she would fill up on the cake and our night will be cut off short and that was not the plan. "One more bite please!" She pled "just one more than" couldn't deny her what was hers. I 'ma eat all of this before the night is over watch." she confessed. "You can eat two pieces but you won't eat your daughter's piece right?" "But" she was like a two-year-old. We step out of the car after she took in her last bite of cake, but not after flipping down the rearview mirror and checking her face and mouth for anything that could cause some type of embarrassment upon entering the restaurant. "You look good ma, don't worry if you had icing on your face I would've licked it off by now" "oh yeah?" She smiled while applying some more lip gloss on her sexy lips. As we walked towards the entrance I could get a full view of her entire body. Shorty had a hell of a body. I kept my cool and opened the door for her as a gentleman should. She wore matching up town she has small feet and that was a plus. "Thank you" she stated while entering the restaurant. The smell of the pizza sauce and the garlic and cheese cause my stomach to turn a bit. It was all in my mind I knew I was already full from mom's dinner, but the fact of knowing you are entering a place that is for eating place tricks on your mind. The lights inside were all dim and the carpet on the floor was burgundy with wooden tables and chairs and of course plenty of booths surrounding the perimeter of the restaurant a salad bar in the middle with all types of salad entrées. There was a wooden sign that read "please wait here" stood about 3 feet tall just as I assume the place was crowded. Not to the max but enough to hear plenty of chatter. I didn't feel awkward but I felt a bit out of place. As I stood next to Felicia and observe everyone enjoying their meals talking to their significant others or family I noticed that there was a mass majority of Caucasian people and just a few Blacks and Hispanics. Felicia could see my eyes scanning the place "are you okay?" She asked "yes I'm fine" I replied "yes you are" she shot back and shared a smile with me. There was a small line forming in the back of us Felicia got closer to me which caught me off guard but I didn't mind it one bit. She wasn't my girl, woman or my wife, but I was with her so I stepped up on her so whoever was looking or checking her out would see that she wasn't alone. About three minutes passed and the waiter came to us "how many" she asked "two" I spoke up. "Booth or table" the waitress asked Felicia. "Booth if is cool with the lady". I replied "yeah that's perfect." Felicia said. As we made our way to the booth the waiter was a taller woman she had dark black hair and wasn't pretty but far from ugly her ass made up for her looks. Her red polo shirt with the Pizza Hut logo on it had grease stains all over it. Guess she must be towards the end of her shift I thought to myself. She had black khakis that hugged her legs which I thought could have been a bit tight but hey who was I to judge her work attire? The booth was pointing towards the street as the waiter showed us our selected booth. The stained glass chandelier above our booth had dim lighting as well the place was nice. I enjoyed the scenery here it wasn't like the city but it was a slight change. It wasn't overly loud with cursing and swearing over any and everything that was going on. It was more relaxed yes you could hear the other people talking but it wasn't as if they were trying to be heard.

"Can I get you drinks?" The waitress asked I saw her name tag and it read Neida. I guess she saw my eyes hit the mark above her left titty and quickly introduce her. My name is Neida and I'll be your waitress". I asked for a Mountain Dew and Felicia asked for an ice tea raspberry. "Coming right up." Neida said going off to retrieve our drinks. I looked at Felicia and she looked back into my eyes. "Mountain Dew?" She asked with a sly smile I knew she was trying to start up smalltalk so I went with it "yeah I love my Mountain Dew." I admitted "I like it too but my favorite is raspberry tea, so are you really not going to eat with me?" Felicia asked pouting. "You can share a personal pan pizza with me." I gave in to her being persistent. "Honestly yes I'm still a bit full but don't worry if my appetite changes ill jump in." I informed her by the time the food would be ordered and prepared I estimated about a good 20 to 30 minutes because it was still people waiting to be fed that were here before us. I looked over to the salad bar which was over to the right of the room. There was also a line of people digging in. Felicia follows my eyes to see what my attention was on. "So how was your birthday?" She asked trying to get my attention back on her. "It was okay I guess." I replied. "You guess?" she asked. "I mean it was okay my day was just an up-and-down day you know?" I said. The waitress was heading our way with drinks and a basket. "Mountain Dew for you and an iced tea for her" she put a red basket with long garlic sticks in it with two small cups of pizza sauce. "Can I take your order" she stared right to my eyes or should I give you a few more minutes?" she asked still looking at me I had to move my eyes because this chick was drawing how you just going to stay locked on my eyes knowing that I'm here was someone else. Or am I bugging? Yeah I know she aint my girl or wife but still the broad doesn't know that for sure. Felicia grabs her attention "yes I'm ready" she snapped not with her normal attitude but with a bit of authority. As to let little Ms. Neida know that she is sitting right at the table too that I wasn't sitting alone. "Okay and what would you like ma'am?" The waitress asked. "12 piece hot wings with blue cheese and a personal pan pizza." Felicia knew exactly what she wanted and what kind of topping on your pizza?" The waitress asked "pepperoni." Felicia replied "and for you?" She looked back at me biting her bottom ever so slightly. "I'm good thank you" I said. As she picked up our menus and spun off to get our food but not before letting us know that it would be about 15 minutes. I looked at her but make sure it wasn't too noticeable. "So it was an up-and-down day for you huh?" Felicia asked going back to our conversation I stared at her pretty face I noticed a tiny scar above her left eye it was tiny but said she was only a foot away and had no other marks on her face I noticed a tiny scar quickly. So before we got wrapped up in my up-and-down day I change the subject quickly.

"Ay ma what happened to your eye I see a scar above your eye?" I asked. She put her hand over as. To feel it once again "is so small how can you even notice it?" She asked. "I was analyzing your pretty face and saw it. It is tiny but is visible up close." I explained. "It doesn't look ugly or anything I think it's kind of cute." I tried to make her feel better about it. "Cute?" She asked raising one of her eyebrows. "Yes cute every scar has a story to it. It's nothing to be ashamed of." I informed her. "It's a learning experience on how to prevent any future scars." I said. "Yeah I see you got a few of them yourself." She joked but spoke to truth. I have my share of scars on my face above my right eyebrow I have one, small one above my little mustache, even a few throughout my body. The ones on my face were from school fights and the rest were for running around and falling when I was a lot younger. "Yes I do and I don't try to hide any of them. They are a part of me." I said looking at her pretty face. "So how did you get the one above your eye?" I asked going back to my previous question. "My daughter" she replied with a smirk. "Your daughter?" Let me find out you baby girl is getting the best of you?" I joked with her. She laughed "no she's not abusing or getting the best of me silly." She replied smiling. "It was an accident it happen when she was three years old. I was cleaning up my eyebrows because that's a feature on my face and I like to keep fresh." She went on to explain. "Yes I like a woman with clean eyebrows myself." I interjected. "I was sitting at my vanity focused in the mirror with a set of new tweezers that I have bought at Sally's beauty supplies when my baby girl came running full speed towards me but I was so focused and what I was doing I didn't realize she was coming towards me that fast I felt her run into the side of my arm which just so happens to be the hand I was using to do the plucking of the follicles." My mouth wasn't completely open as I envision how all this could've happened. My sister is always up in the mirror completely lost and oblivious to what was going on around her when she's doing her makeup and or her little feminine deeds detailing her face. When it came to my sister doing her eyebrows whenever I would come around she would stop and wait till I left to continue with the tweezers. I never knew why but now I see why. "So with the push she gave my arm the sharp tweezers penetrated to my skin but thanks to my eyebrow bone it didn't go any deeper or didn't get a chance to go any lower because if it would of it could have taken my eyesight from me completely. I was sitting there with the tweezers embedded in my skin looking in the mirror until I built up enough courage to pull them out." She relived the whole episode right before me and to think I assumed it was something not so tragic but then again that's the problem with my own one track mind. You can assume how or why anyone could get his or her scar the only way to truly find out is to actually ask and wait to hear the truth of the story on how it got there but in most cases some people do not like to relive tragic episodes pertaining to their scars. "My daughter thought it was the funniest thing in the world she was so small and innocent there was no way I could be mad at her for something she didn't do intentionally." If anything it was my fault for not being a bit more aware of her whereabouts and what she was up to." You know?" She asked "yes I can understand why you couldn't be mad at her I replied the scare was about an eighth of an inch. Like I said it wasn't very noticeable but I noticed it. "So after pulling it out and covering it up, Eliza saw the red blood that somehow knew that something had occurred she wasn't laughing anymore. I cleared up the blood quickly and picked her up and hugged her with her tiny arms wrapped around me squeezing me with all her might. I knew she felt some type of way but I had her laughing moments after just to show her that mommy wasn't mad or hurt that bad. It amazes me how children are so smart they can feel when something isn't right. Yeah she was laughing at first but once she saw the blood her whole demeanor did a 180." She was going in with how and what happened. My mind began to wonder if her I was real or was it one of those glass eyes. I laugh not purposely but just because of my thought. "Is not funny" she says slapping my forearm for smiling. "I know but I wasn't laughing at you I was laughing at what I was just thinking." I replied "so you weren't even listening to me" she countered. "No I definitely was listening" I assured her. "So what were you thinking about that was so funny?" She questioned "well if you really want to know I was thinking, that could it possibly be that the tweezers did poke your eye and now you have a glass eye instead of a normal eye?" I laughed again as a matter of fact she had one hand over her mouth and was laughing hysterically just as hard as I was her eyes began to water because of how hard she was laughing. "How could you be thinking that? I'm telling you what happened?" She asked in between laughs "it was just a random thought." I was still laughing with her. "Well for your info both of my eyes are real." She laughed again "I can't believe you." she joked taking her finger and poking her eye showing me that it was a real eye. She joked I took advantage of the conversation to actually find out for myself I held up my hand and cover one of her eyes and looked at the exposed one and held up two fingers. "How many?" I asked "two" she answered "correct" I replied I did the same with the other eye and held up two fingers again and asked her again "how many?" She said "three" I jump back now she was laughing harder than before "I got you too silly" she said. The joke was on me I guess I should've seen that one coming but I didn't to be honest. Just then the waitress was on her way with a big flat dish with what seemed to be two dishes on it with plates. "Your order is up." She said placing all the food on the table. "If there's anything else I can get you just let me know." She started walking away this time I stood looking at Felicia she was different she was pretty and had a beautiful personality but then again I knew most woman could be very sinister when they needed to be in their own little devilish ways. The breadsticks that were on the table haven't even been touched I picked one up and broke it in half and dipped it in and bit into it. My appetite was coming back the personal pie had four slices cut into it and the wings smelled hot. Felicia noticed that I was in fact a bit hungry now being that it was almost 10 o'clock. She put two slices of pizza on her plate and put two more slices on the other plate and slid the plate over to me. "Thank you for not making me eats alone." She said in a cute tone. "Only because you asked" I replied. "The wings are all mine if you want I'll order another order of them for you" she stated not playing "no problem ma this is good enough." I replied "I'm joking handsome" she said as we ate and had light conversation in between bites and laugh some more she told me a little about her past and I just listen attentively as she spoke like most of us she too had a rough childhood. She had been abused by her mother for years. "Now she and I are on good terms maybe is because I'm not young anymore and I have a child of my own but up until I was 17 it was physical and verbal abuse for every little thing I did whether it was right or wrong. I love her but I couldn't do it anymore after I graduated from Camden high I left the house and lived with a friend until I found a job at a furniture store on Broadway. I worked and attended vo-tech for nursing and just dedicated myself to do right and prove her wrong and that's why I am who I am today." She said proudly. "Wow" she was opening up to me I could feel her pain to a certain degree. "So you're a certified nurse?" I asked "yes I am I've been working at the Cooper Hospital for about five years now they pay good and I like helping people." She confessed. The waitress made her way to the table with the check "did you two enjoy?" She asked politely looking at both of us. "Yes I did" Felicia winked her glass eye at me. I laughed again to myself. I had to stop with the glass eye jokes even if they were in my head alone "I did to" I stated "whenever you are ready u can pay at the register or pay now" she instructed. "So you kicking us out already?" I joked. "no not at all you can stay for as long as you want." the waitress embarrassed face turned red while she tried to sound a bit more convincing with sarcasm in her voice as to not kicking us out. Felicia laughed and gave me a look as if to leave her alone. She walked away. "You're crazy Manuel." She said I went to grab the check before

Lisa's hands were much quicker "what are you doing?" She asked "I was going to pay." I informed her. "Thank you but I invited you remember?" "Plus you're the birthday boy" Felicia said. I nodded my head in approval. I looked over to the clock on the wall and it was almost midnight I couldn't believe how fast time went by. Felicia noticed me looking at the time she looked at herself as well. "Wow" is almost midnight how did I lose track of time like this." She asked. I agreed but didn't mind "my birthday is officially over and I ended it with a bang" I said. She smiled "I had a great time maybe we can do this again?" She asked. "Of course I would love to ma" as we stood up and made our way to the cashier Neida was nowhere in sight. Felicia pays with a credit card "would you care to tip your waiter to your credit card?" The man wearing a white polo shirt with the Pizza Hut logo on it asked his name tag read Carl. "Yes you can deduct a tip." Felicia gave him permission to deduct extra funds off her card. After signing we were on our way out the door.

There were only a handful of cars in the parking lot now. I'm sure these people couldn't wait for the rest of us to wrap up our evenings so they could clean up and go home already. I walked over to the driver side door and waited for Felicia to hit the alarm to unlock the doors, then did what any well-mannered gentleman would have done. I had the door open for her waiting for her to be seated. She smelled amazing as she passed by me. Once inside I made my way around to the passenger side and jumped in. Turning the engine we recapped our time in the restaurant and how good of the time we had. We acknowledge to one another that we liked each other's company which was great, but I wasn't into rushing anything as Felicia wasn't either. As she weaved through the lanes and jumped on the nearest highway she took a detour and pulled over by the Cooper River Park. We would usually stop here to see the fireworks and any other important festivities that were held here. This park was enormous. It had a track around it so the running and bikers could get their exercise in. The center was filled with water known as the River it was a beautiful scenery to take in, also there was a few diamonds for baseball and softball games, a park for the little ones with slides and swings. She parked up and told me to "get out". I did I was told but not before stating

"This is where you're going to kill me?" I joked it was dark only the moonlight was what illuminated the area and a few streetlights at a distance. The moonlight reflected beautifully off the water. I took it that she wasn't in any rush to go home and guess what? I wasn't either. Of course I had to get up and had to work for my first day at the sub shop, but she didn't know that. We got so wrapped up in many different topics that there was no need to bring it up unless she asked which to my knowledge she wasn't. "I bring my baby girl here every now and then this is her park." "That's what she says "mommy can we go to my Park?" In her cute little voice. "I love her so much she is my world" she admitted to me. "I know you do every time you speak of her your whole face shows it" I told her. "She's all I have yeah mom is there now but she is all mine literally without me she doesn't have anyone." She stated "what's up with your parents" she asked I clenched my jaw by the look she gave me she could sell that this wasn't a subject that I didn't want to talk about so we switch lanes on that convo. As we made our way to a nearby bench she sat down as I followed suit. "To be honest I never did any of this with any of my female friends." I admitted usually when I meet a female it wasn't anything but a fuck and on our way we would go. "What do you mean?" Felicia asked. "I mean as far as going out with and hanging out like we did for the past 4 hours" I explained "well for the record is been a while since I had a good time". She said "oh so you having a good time?" I asked "yes I am thanks to you I'm glad I caught your attention today at the hospital." She admitted. "I thought you wouldn't be interested because you look like you was going through a lot at the moment, but I guess I was wrong." She looked for validation in her comments I will most definitely give it to her. "I guess you were" I'm glad you did speak. And you're right I was going through something and one day we can talk about it." I said "that sounds great." She admitted. "Oh wait!" She shot right up and sprinted to her car. I thought she was going to leave me stranded out here because she was out. I just watched and complete observation mode. This woman was a bit loony if she jumped in her car and leaves me out here but once again I was wrong. She came back with a plate and the cake I had given to her earlier.

"You still hungry?" I asked "there's always room for dessert right?" She asked "a big body like yours you have to eat" she joked. "You're right ma but in order to stay in shape I can't lose control and lose my physique." I joked back. "Boy you'll be fine handsome." She told me taken a piece of cake in between her fingers and feeding me a piece I was hesitant at first but knew she would insist. She chomped down on the cake but left the other two slices as I asked her to for her daughter and her roommate. She didn't lie to me when she said she's a sweet junky. "This is good." I'm refraining from eating the other two slices. I took the plate and rewrapped it "nope that's not for you" I joked if she wanted it hey eat on but I knew she would respect that. "Look at me she asked she leaned into me and sucked on my bottom lip almost immediately not given me a chance to even catch my breath. I had a wave of blood running through my entire body and heading straight to my penis area. I kissed her back gently and slowly. "You had some icing on your lip" she use my line on me this girl was smooth and sneaky. I loved it. "Oh yeah?" I think you just couldn't help but to kiss me all night." I joked back. "Maybe you're right or maybe it was just icing." She shot back with a grin I wanted to grab her and just eat her all up right then and there but held myself from falling into my temptation. "Happy birthday" she said I hope you had just as much fun as I did because I had a wonderful time". It was pushing 1 o'clock. "Yes thank you for tonight." I said grabbing her and kissing her again. Once I felt that she was melting in my arms I pulled away. "It's getting late ma and you having to get home to your daughter." I said. "Yes you're absolutely right let's get out of here." We headed to the car as we drove in silence marinating in our own personal thoughts. Pulling up on my block I told her to drop me off at the corner of 28th and federal. "You don't live on the corner do you?" She asked me wanted to know if I was going to hang out on the corner all night. "No I don't ma but it is easier for you to go straight home once I'm out of the car." I showed her I didn't want her on the block. Crazy shit was always happen at the most unexpected time. "Okay handsome you got my number call me whatever you want." She said stopping a few feet from the corner of the block. I gave her a kiss on the cheek and got out of the car she drove off.

I noticed that the block was still doing what it was supposed to do, which was to make money. I made my way towards my house when a raspy voice called out to me. "Rock!" Had to be the one and only "Banga" I went towards the voice he was black as shit but once he spoke again his Pearl whites gave position away. Of course Jigs wasn't too far from him. Wherever there was one other wasn't too far gone. I swear these guys did everything together there was three females with them chilling on a neighbor stoop. They were your typical hood rats with about a dozen kids at home still up probably with the oldest watching them all. I'm not going to lie they look good but the reputation was already set in stone. "What you up to Rock the last time I seen you it was five hours ago?" Banga asked me. I know I didn't need to explain anything to these niggas but they grew on to me and they played a part of the block and whoever lived on the block knew them or they knew of them. "I told them taking care of business you know?" "No I don't" Banga replied "you selling drugs Rock?" I mean if you are its cool but let me know so I can look out for you on the block, if you on the low doing some shady shit you know?" Banga stated he was all fucked up on that wet his eyes opened wide and he spoke with so much sincerity but his voice slurred. He was looking scary as Fuck at the same time. "Yeah Rock we fuck with you a lot and wouldn't want anything to happen to you." That was Jigs speaking he looked and talked just as fucked up as Banga was. He had two chicks in his arm it was Kiki and Cici they were fucked up to probably rolling on ecstasy and wet. Kiki was short as hell probably about 5 feet she had long curly hair, chocolate complexion, juicy lips with B-cups and a cute apple bottom she was a bit on the skinny side but her body was thick all the right places she had a blunt to her mouth. "What's up Rock aint it past your bedtime?" She joked Brie Brie laughed she was over with bang blowing on a cigarette that gave off this horrible strong odor. I knew it was a sherm stick. "Yeah it is I am not going to front that's why I'm on my way home" I followed her flow knowing damn well she needed to be home herself watching over her kids. It wasn't my business and they was too fucked up to take a joke. So I blew it off, now Brie Brie had a caramel complexion it was light but not too light you could say that it was just right she was the baddest of the three she sported a bob haircut with her bangs to the side and not a mark or blemish on her cute face. Lips were all point not to big but enough to suck while you kissed her. Just looking at her the way she pulled on that Sherm stick turned a Nigga on. Her body, oh boy small feet, ass was far from average with jeans that screamed to be on to tight but they were stretched out so bad, her breasts had to be a small D-cup because those breasts were big and round. She was well put together and if the opportunity presented itself I would dig in that but I knew that was Banga's jump off and we all know how Niggas tend to handcuffed there jump offs sad to say. Cici was a bit more tamed, she was bigger than the other two now by a whole lot but enough to feel insecure more than the other two. We're all insecure but some more than others. She was juicy all over but not sloppy she always had her hair done today it was braided with crazy braids all over it. She had a beautiful smile which was plastered on her face insinuating she was also high as fuck. They were all fresh to death Banga and Jigs were all blacked out just in case something broke out they could camouflage in the shadows. The girls wore their own little outfits which wasn't anything to spectacular just fitted jeans with a design tee. I chilled with them for a bit so I wouldn't seem rude but all they were doing was grinding on each other and I wasn't getting it in so I getting out there way. I noticed a couple of shadows all the way down the block. "Ayo somebody coming up the block it look like three of them. Jigs was in his own little world and quiet but got up as soon as I said what I said "where?" His mellow ass followed my gaze we were all on the stoop looking down the block we couldn't be seen due to the bushes "who the fuck?" Jigs mumbled pulling out his 45 Glock, Banga already knew he didn't even bother to look "click clack" he cocked his chrome out 357 Magnum it was big as fuck "go home Rock" Jigs instructed. They are all the way down the block and it was on the opposite side to my house I stepped up and did as I was told no need to be here and I did just as he asked me. The girls also disappeared and were all out of sight. Jigs and Banga relocated as to either creep up on the niggas or wait to actually be able to identify them probably just some customers or something but why all the dark clothing?

I entered the door and deactivated the alarm the house was pitch black I took off my sneaks and left the ones I was going to wear at the door and brought the ones I wasn't going to wear back up to my room. I was tired but made my way straight towards my room got comfy and was surprised by a "tap" at my door. By my sister she whispered "by the way next time let me know when you're going to leave please." Linda stated "I'm sorry I know you were busy and I didn't want to bother you." I admitted "it would've only taken a few seconds." She protested she was right I knew better. "So who is she?" She asked with a smile. I smile back "no one." I lied. "Goodnight I'll see you tomorrow bro." I thought about calling but thought against it, it was late I had to get up early and so did everyone else. As I jumped into bed shut my eyes the sounds that never go unheard of echoed through the night sky. I didn't care and it wasn't for me and I eventually fell asleep.

Chapter 2
"Sweatshop"

The loud "beeping" woke me right out my deep sleep. I had the alarm set for 6 o'clock which was an hour earlier since today was an important day for me. I wanted to be at the shop as soon as it was ready to be open. You know what they say your first impression is your last impression. There was no way that I could display bad impression on first day at the job. I felt heavier than usual probably because I went to bed a little later than usual. I forced my body to get up. I slipped into my sandals and made my way towards the bathroom. Of course, Jalinda was up and ready to tackle her day as always. She always had so much energy in the morning. I never could fully understand how this woman always got up extra early. Was it really that much that needed to be done? I guess so.

"Good morning Manny" she spoke soft as if not to awaken Ms. Cathy. I on the other hand tended to wake up a little grouchy "morning". With a look of not really wanting to talk I replied. She was in the bathroom with her PJs still on but by the way she smelled she had already washed up and was tackling her hair which was all over the place half braided in the rest left unbraided. "Why you up so early?" She asked me. "Work" was all I said pushing her out the bathroom. "Excuse me would help." she said going towards her room knowing that I just took over the bathroom. I shut the door and took care of my morning deeds. Piss, shit and shower I couldn't start my day unless all of the above have been handled accordingly. Once out of the shower mouth fresh I was fully up now. I exited the bathroom and shot straight to Jalinda's room, her door was always ajar. I walked right in, she had on her bra and some tight ass jeans. "Hey grumpy" she joked "it's too early for all that shit" I stated. For me to be standing in her room with just her bra wasn't out of the ordinary we were comfortable around one another. I'm not saying that we watch each other butterball naked, but it wasn't the first time I've seen her in a bra. Even though her flat stomach was worth a sneak peek every now and then, but it never went any further than that. "So you're not going to school today?".... "Again?" Linda asked with one arm on her hip. "I can't is my first day and I don't want to jeopardize this." I countered. "So you rather jeopardize graduating in the last six months of your senior year?" She protested. "I'm not going to jeopardize any of it Linda when I go in this morning I'll explain my school schedule and if there is any way to work around it then I will." I explained. I know she was right working wasn't worth throwing away 12 years of schooling so my plan was to do this as I completed my first day on the job. "What did Ms. Cathy say?" She asked me in a low tone as to not tell on me unintentionally because Ms. Cathy's room wasn't too far. "I didn't tell her about it" I admitted "I mean she knows about the job but I didn't get a chance to get into detail about when I would start." I confessed. The look on her face said it all. I knew it wasn't a good move but it was only for today that I would miss another day. I was already passing all my classes. I knew personally that I would be fine, but of course my sister and Ms. Cathy always wanted the best for me so they would blow things out of proportion at times. "Well you better make sure you talk to your boss immediately." Linda stated. "I will" I replied. "So who was the girl you were with all night?" She turned her lip as she said these words. "Her name is Felicia and I met her at the hospital." I informed her. "Oh so she was getting her shit checked out huh?" …"What she got burned by some dirty dick nigga?" She joked. Linda was so jealous over me when it came to meeting new females she didn't know. "No." I couldn't stop laughing. "She's a nurse at the hospital for your info." I said. Her whole demeanor changed instantly. "I'll tell you more about her later. I got to get ready before I'm late Linda" I said and headed to my room to get ready. Ms. Cathy was still asleep and I wanted to be out the door before she got up. She too was an early bird but not till the next hour. My plan was to be out the door by then. I threw on some crappy clothes which to some might be considered half decent but to me they were going to be used for work. As far as owning a pair of fucked up sneakers or boots that wasn't going to be found in my closet. I debated for about five minutes which pair I would demolish because after today I wouldn't wear them ever again only to work so I decided to go with the black suede timberlands. I went with them because I could wipe them down and if Grease landed on them it wouldn't be too noticeable, then again I was going to work. I thought about calling Felicia just to hear her voice before I walked out the door but my better judgment prevented my intentions. I took $20 with me for the bus ride and for a meal just in case I got hungry. It was almost 7:15 which was more than enough time to get to Broadway on time. I checked myself in the mirror, with much approval I was up and out the door. Clean and clear.

What took me by shock was the crime scene with yellow tape down by the school. There were patrol cars blocking off the road on both ends. The incident that occurred last night wasn't where the tape was, but rather it was six houses down. I had to walk by the crime scene. Not because I was nosey or curious. I had to board the bus on the next block. I was not going around it was not an option, I took a deep breath and began to walk towards the other end of the block. It amazed me how loud the shots rang out last night. Instead of hearing the sirens afterwards, the shots went unnoticed as they always did. No one got into anyone else's business, it's just how it went down in Camden and pretty much in every other ghetto city in America. If anyone did call the cops upon hearing those shots your reputation in the hood was already be set in stone once word got out you like to dial those digits.

The police wouldn't get out there cars and most of the time the calls always went ignored it takes local law enforcement hours to arrive on scean. Around here the residents help out the criminals or better yet don't believe in the police handling justice due to all of the brutal beatings the officers tend to bring upon the Blacks and Hispanics (minorities). You know Rodney King escapades still go on in the streets whether we want to believe it or not. I noticed two blankets on the floor about 8 feet apart. The small yellow cones were spread out on the floor as well. Forensics were taking pictures and doing what they did best which was to examine the whole scene. Digging for clues I wonder who the corps under the sheets were, but then again I diverted my attention on what I was set out to do after almost losing focus. As I continued my journey towards the bus stop.

"Excuse me a young man." a voice called out I kept walking as if I didn't hear a word. "hey you with the black tee" I was in fact wearing a black tea so I still kept walking but turned my head towards the voice. It was what appeared to be a detective the block was dead at the moment but in a matter of 20 minutes or so the kids and parents would begin to drop off the kids at the designated lines in the schoolyard. "Can I have a word with you?" The detective asked. He paced swiftly towards me. What the fuck does this mother fucker want with me I thought to myself as I slow down myself? "Make it quick I'm on my way to work and just like you I don't like to be late." I stated with a serious tone of my voice "did you hear anything or see anything last night?" He asked me "excuse me?" I replied annoyed at the question. "How about we start this again with your name first." I stated "Oh yes I'm sorry I'm detective Shalecki I'm in charge of the homicide division." He spoke proudly extending his hand for a friendly handshake. If you're from any hood you know better and to shake any offices hand I don't care who or what division he runs. I just looked at it and he got the point. "There was a homicide here last night and I wanted to know if you saw or heard anything last night?" He asked again searching for lies within my eyes. "I got up at 6 AM whatever happened last night I didn't hear or see anything sorry." I stated waiting for his response. Detective Shalecki just observe my body language I kept my cool I knew better than that. He handed me his card and just walked away but not before telling me "let me know if you hear anything." "No problem." I replied and went about my business I know who the detective was, the dope boys were always talking about him and how much of an asshole he was. He couldn't get a break in any of his cases he had plenty of homicides on the Eastside alone with about 1000 suspects and no hard evidence to convict not a near one of them. Detective Shalecki was about 5'9, he was stocky with blonde hair with a military cut to be exact he wore jeans with a black polo with his badge and gun on his hip. His deep blue eyes always looked stressed and tired of his own occupation. I guess I would be too if I had to be on the hunt for cold-blooded killers, but could never actually find them. The air was a bit humid and it was sunny. I made it to the bus stop right on time. The bus to Broadway pulled out two minutes after I showed up. There were three Mexicans waiting and an older black lady. I allowed whoever wanted to board the bus first. One of the Mexican stood at the stop. He must be waiting for another bus I thought to myself. The elder lady got on board first. I counted out a dollar in change and was admitted to take my seat. The bus was crowded with a vast majority of hard labor workers heading to work. The bus driver was an old white man who didn't give you a chance to find a seat before pulling off. I stumble side to side heading towards the next available seat towards the back, he slamed on the brakes all of a sudden I almost lose my balance completely. "Ass hole." I mumbled a few passages heard me and laughed. Heading towards Broadway I recapped all the possible scenarios that transpired after I left last night. Everyone was high as hell and guns were pulled. It didn't take a rocket scientist to know that Banga and Jigs were involved in whatever happened last night and or they could possibly be the ones under the white sheets, then again that's all just a theory. To be honest no one really knows, but the people under the sheets and the ones who put them ones under the sheets. In the meantime my mind drifted back to Felicia.

Once at the terminal the smell of all the homeless and the sight of all the trash all over the streets made me wonder. How and why this city come to this. It has become so UN pleasant to see and lets not to forget to mention how abandoned it is by their own governments. Is so sad. Over here on Broadway there is no place to sit, no benches, no empty areas to sit and talk or even hang out. It's all being occupied by homeless stretched out on the floor either sleeping nodding off on drugs, drunk with bags and clothes all over the place. It has gotten so bad that even before you reach the Ben Franklin Bridge the homeless have their own little homeless city. It consist of small tents dozens of shopping carts crates and more trash. It's were all the homeless from that part of town congregate, it's a sad sight.

I was right on time. The shop wasn't open yet so I waited out front. My intentions was to clean this place up once I was shown the layout. If this was a sub shop and is known for his beefy subs imagine how many more people would come if the shop was kept a clean reputation, instead it looked like a germ shop. As I watched all the other shops and stores begin to open. The terminal was occupied by hundreds of people. It was downtown so you had all types of workers getting on and off the bus whether they work at the City Hall, or even at the small boutique shops. It was already 8:15 and the sign on the window at the sub shop read, we open at eight not bad for being 15 minutes late. Just as I looked over I saw Pete in the back of the shop turning on lights and what not, he opened the front door with a big "wow! You're early" you haven't even been hired yet and you're on time "wait till I tell Jamal about this he supposed to be here at eight." His scruffy raspy voice spoke. I handed him my completed application which he threw on the desk in the back and instructed me to flip all the switches I could find except for the red ones. I went on a hunt flipping every switch I came across fans, registers fridges, fountain drinks and ovens "wait not those!" you said all of them accept the red ones. I know but I didn't think you would notice them." He smirked. Little did Pete know? I was on a mission to prove to him I was willing to work, and besides if this would go sour I wasn't going to give up I would look for another gig. I grew up watching all the dope boys with their cars, clothes, and woman, but to be honest is wasn't the path I wanted. For every clear bright day, there's always a dark cold night. If you know what I mean. Being in the game was all fun and dandy but what came with all of that wasn't what anyone really wanted in life. For some once you went in, there was no turning back and I'm speaking for myself for the most part.

Yes, you could be the baddest mother fucka in the bricks and guess what? There was always another big headed mother fucker who wanted you to know that he could be just as bad as, or even better than what you portrayed yourself to be. He was capable of sparking the biggest fire that not even the district fire company could put out. I figured I would give the Joe Schmo life a try.

"Have you ever cooked on a grill before?" Asked big bellied Pete. "On a small grill but nothing this big." I confessed referring to the pretty hefty sized grill. "Well you know how to prepare a sandwich whenever you get hungry at home don't you?" Pete asked "yes I do." I replied "well it's almost the same thing. The only differences instead of sliced bread we use rolls and instead of adding all the condiments you so dearly enjoy you add what the customer likes and ask for." He said with a funny sense of humor. It made perfect sense and it wasn't rocket science. "Did you eat?" Pete asked "no sir I did not." I replied "well good you are going to prepare our breakfast sandwich. Our customers don't start to come in till a little after nine so you can take this as a practice sub." He joked once you turn on the grill remember this, they get hot quick and get hotter as the stay on longer so learn how to play with the knobs. Once you think or see the food that's on the grill looking ready." Pete's words sunk in like a sinker going for a par. "I'll watch you while you put together the sandwich, the dairy products are on the left bottom fridge, and the meats are on the right bottom. Salt-and-pepper and all other seasonings you can feel free to use are right above the bread rolls and buns are behind you." Pete informed me "this was where I had to prove myself I was a bit nervous and hungry so I calm my nerves a so I didn't burn the shop down. "I have to prep some produce I'll be watching go head Manuel." he instructed I flicked the grill on and decided to go with an egg omelet, with grilled onions and cheese would be added at the end. I located the utensils I needed as the sweat began to gather all my forehead I grabbed a nearby towel to wipe my forehead dry. "Hot!" Yelled Pete "is it!?" You already know" I replied. He moved the fans towards me, which were more like dust blowers. The fans are big but due to all the dust on them the air wasn't as cool nor did it circulate as it should have. I will handle all of those minor details after I filled my belly. By the time I did my thing today this place would feel a lot more welcoming to its faithful customers. Instead of quick ins and outs due to the negative reports on how this place lacked cleanliness. The ultimate question was how this place even pass codes. That will not be an issue by the time I got done with this place. The food like I said was always known to be one of the best and I'm sure Jamal takes all the credit for that one. Tossed the beaten eggs on the grill and cut up some bell peppers and onions. I tossed them on the side of the eggs so they would sauté for a while. I grabbed some seasoning which didn't consist of much. Salt pepper oregano and onion pepper was all they used. I threw a bit of all of them but wasn't satisfied with the condiments this place lacked. For now I worked with what they had. I would bring up my request later on no need to begin to ask for anything at the moment I wasn't even sure if I would get the job yet. Bacon strips were cut in pieces and so was the sausage links. "You must be really hungry that's coming out your pay" Pete Barked jokingly. I laughed "Ight". I wasn't going to argue once he tried this little concoction that I put together he would be hooked I was sure of it. I let everything simmer for a bit. "Smells good" Pete yelled once again I didn't say a word. It was so hot in here I though. I wondered how they could swelter in this environment, but I wasn't bitching yet. I cut open a 12 inch role and splash some mayo on it after toasting it I grabbed white American cheese three slices to be exact and put it on the omelet that hadn't been flipped over yet. The meat, peppers and onions cooked just right. I tossed them all leveled on the eggs then folded the omelet in half closing it up once it was ready. With the spatula I pressed down on it ever so lightly so it would cook thoroughly. I grabbed a tiny cup water. I could see Pete looking at me from his Peripherals this was for show now. I had his attention, I looked for an aluminum lid before it was too late and I splashed the water around the omelet lightly to create steam till I heard the sizzling from the grill. The steam rose and I threw the lid over the omelet so I could trap the steam inside this was so the cheese could melt completely inside in a matter of seconds it would be over. The omelet was cut in half and tucked away neatly in the 12 inch role. I headed over towards Pete after shutting off the grill. "Thank you it was getting super-hot in here." Pete joked. He bit into the breakfast sandwich his eyes grew as he chewed. "This is a hell of a sandwich kid" he spoke in between bites. Once I heard that I knew I was already locked in. "You like it huh?" I asked "like it? this is going on our breakfast menu." Would you mind if I went to the grocery store down the street for second Pete I'll be back in two minutes?" I asked "for what?" Pete asked. "You'll see?" I replied. "Hurry up" he said it wasn't 9 o'clock yet but damn near close. I didn't even eat my sandwich before the door was already close in behind me.

I rushed down to the value-plus I was on a mission to get what I needed to get back to work. That I didn't even notice who was on the register. I shot back to the section were all the kitchen and condiments were in search for Sazon and adobo. This would add a twist to what was already being made at the shop. I just hope Pete didn't disapprove. I grabbed two bottles which were two for five dollars and two big boxes of Sazon, on which were two for six dollars. I could feel someone staring at me. I looked over towards my left there was a small petite light skinned girl wearing a red value-plus shirt that smiled at me and asked "you in a rush?" She asked in her soft sexy voice "kind of" was all I said and headed to the register. I made a mental note of her. I would grab her some other time because she was a cutie with a nice little booty. At the register I got rang up by this nigga who looked as if he so desperately wanted to be a woman. His eyebrows were clean and arched so fucking high that it looked as if he saw a ghost and was frightened permanently. I wasn't sure if he had make up on, it but his face did look a bit caked up with all types of shit. I may have been a bit judgmental and probably was wrong but once he spoke I noticed what type time he was on "how Jew doing?" The cashier named Terry spoke with a thick accent. Once his words escaped his lips and spoke I knew he wasn't on the same boat as most niggas were on, but then again now in these days that's an understatement. Which was fine by me as long as he stood in his lane "I'm all right" I replied not wanting to sound rude. I look back at where the little shorty was at. I saw she was defiantly still interested in the kid because she was still staring at me. She moved her stare once she noticed my eyes looking back at her. $11.76 Terry said twice snapping me out of my daze. I handed him $12 and told him to put my change in my bag. "Ju like what you see?" Terry asked "what!?" I snapped not believing what just came out his mouth, but he was talking about the girl. I was hawking in the aisle in the back of the store. "She's cute" I said before storming out the door.

As I made my way back to the sub shop I saw that there were two customers waiting for their food. Jamal was in and was doing what he did best. I made my way to the back were Pete was "I bought a few items that would give the food a bit more flavor and wanted you to try it, if is okay with you before I put it in our customers food." I explained to Pete. He looked at me like I was crazy "was wrong with how we already season our food in here now?" Pete wasn't too amused at the proposition I was trying to show him. He wouldn't understand until he tried it. "I can show you better than I can tell your boss man." I went on to explained if you don't like it, I will worked today for free if you consider to hire me." I know any boss didn't want to pay his workers if he didn't have to. His attention was all mine now. Jamal was wrapping up some orders and joined our little meeting. I could feel he wasn't too thrilled with us not inviting him in but he was busy on the grill. "Was sup young'n?" Jamal extended his hand to greet me. I followed suit. I looked around for my sandwich my stomach was turning and I didn't see it. "Pete? Where is my half a sub I'm hungry?" I asked him. He looked at Jamal "I ate it" Jamal said "it was good as shit" Jamal expressed. I eyed him and Pete. He could feel my tension building, relax man I wanted him to try out your cooking abilities." He tried to sound convincing. "Fuck it!" I said "how was it?" I asked him. "How was it?" He repeated my question. "That shit was on point!" Jamal stated "I told Peter you can have my cooking job and I'll take care of the shop." But he wasn't having it" we both laughed.

Two guys walk in and it was a little past 10 now. Time was going by faster than I expected. "Manual your up." Pete yelled. "Jamal take the order." Let me see what you talking about." Pete challenged. I threw on an apron and waited for the order. This wasn't a breakfast sandwich these guys wanted a cheese steak and fries. It was too early for all that greasy shit for me but hey everyone has their own cup of tea right?

"Two small cheesesteaks with onions and peppers yellow cheese and small French fries." Jamal recited the order to me. "One or two fries?" I asked him. "One" Jamal replied. He grabbed the fries and dunked them in the oil lending me a hand. I did my thing on the grill trying not to screw up the order. I watched Jamal as he worked the deep fryer. I never worked a deep fryer so I watched to take a mental note as I grilled. I opened up the box of Sazon and as soon as I did Pete was over my shoulder watching. "Stealing my secrets?" I asked jokingly. I sprinkled a bit of it on the meat and a dash of it on the onions and peppers letting it simmer for a little. The aroma instantly hit the air. Threw a splash of Mayo and in a matter of minutes both sandwiches were almost done. I gave the customers Ketchup packets. Once they'd take one bite of this they might not want to ruin it with ketchup. I stuffed the role with all the beefy meat as Pete showed me. My wrapping skills wasn't all that great but once I had it together. I wrapped it to what I thought was okay. I passed it over to Jamal. Thank you and have a nice day was all I said. "You too and thanks". The customers replied simultaneously as if they had one voice. Two gentlemen looked as if they work nearby the City Hall, or at least somewhere near it in one of those important buildings downtown. Some steak left over on the grill that I had prepared the gentleman's order. I just added some extras stake because I wanted the guys to try the seasoning. It was only enough for a half a roll but it would do and be sufficient to get there taste buds going. I cut the role in three small pieces. "Yo, young'n it smells good what did you put in that?" Jamal asked?" I pointed to the bright orange packet and yellow bottle with the red cap. If you're not open to try new things you'll never know how or what it is, or know how it would work". Pete and Jamal where basically stuck on the normal. Salt and pepper. Seriously? No matter what restaurant you go to what's on the table? Salt-and-pepper duh. Sometimes we got to switch it up. Pete and Jamal ate their piece and fell in love with how it taste. I knew it was good because he went straight to his pocket and pulled out a $20 bill and repaid me for the seasoning I bought earlier. "That shit stays here." Pete said. I laughed my ass off. "Show Jamal the quantity he needs to use because this is our new touch." We all high-fived then went on with our day. The shop close at 8 PM and I made sure I stayed till it was time to close. So I could talk to him and explain my school schedule. I met all types of people at the shop. You had your hard laborers who come in and order a bunch of subs for the whole construction crew. You had to people who all worked on the block with the neighboring businesses. They all spent some cash with one another it was only right reciprocation is key in the success in a successful business. The white collar workers also stop by to eat on a regular. The majority of our customers ordered takeout. It was rare to see anyone actually eat at one of our four tables. I already knew why they didn't want to sit down and eat. Who would? The dining room area look like shit. I know for a fact that was my first impression when I walked in. It wasn't the best one. So you can only imagine how many others thought the same way. So who could blame the customers? From what I observed Pete was content having the customer's order their food and take it away. As for me I couldn't work here with the place looking like this. I cleaned it up thoroughly and a lot had to be done. I gave thanks to Ms. Cathy for instilling those small traits in Linda and myself. "A clean presentation is an appealing invitation" She once spoke and it turned out to be very true no matter what or who the situation was. I took heed or at least tried my best to obtain and store all the knowledge that was passed on to me by whoever was willing to offer it. I didn't care if you were five years old or

100 years old I could always learn something from anyone. One just had to close your mouth for second and listen and watch. The next customer who walked in around 6:30 PM caught my attention it was the value-plus girl. "Jamal let me get this one" I stated "it's all you playa" for my first day at the shop Jamal and I built a good rapport. He wasn't out to be the boss or even boss me around nor did he act as if I was in the way whenever I made small mistakes. Yes, I screwed up a few orders throughout the day, nothing major just mixing them up. I took it that he and Pete have been working together for almost 10 years. Pete wasn't into meeting or introducing new people to his personal business relationship, it was just work and pay. So for me to be given an opportunity to enter this business relationship with Pete and Jamal I was a bit honored. No real bond as far as going out after work, or even to watch a game of basketball. It was just straight business. Who doesn't like sports? I was much younger than Jamal but I could relate a bit more. "Can I help you?" I asked the value plus girl. She was petite like I said with a small little bubble but that looked as if she swallowed a basketball and it went straight to her lower back side. Her waist was so small I wondered if I could touch my fingertips just by grabbing her by the waistline. I knew I couldn't but you get the picture. She had straight black hair her eyes are dark and mysterious. Her complexion was tan her eyebrows thick but clean, her teeth were also pearly white. I noticed she had to bottom fronts. They were silver it was a bit tacky but she pulled it off. Shorty was cute she had on a pair of black tights with some air maxes. Her shirt was a T-shirt a baby blue one to match her air maxes. Her lips were thin but had form and looked as if I could enjoy every bit of them. I could be jumping the gun but the mind is a terrible thing to waste so enjoy your imagination while you have it. She smiled "hey you... didn't you come to the store earlier today?" She asked. "No I'm sorry I think you have me confused with somebody else." I joked. "Boy please" she replied with her feminine sexy soft voice. "I know I saw you I don't forget my customers." She countered back. "So why did you ask?" I challenge. The store was slow she was the only one waiting to be waited on. There were two other customers who were already waited on and waiting for their food that they ordered. So I figured I had a few minutes to chat with little miss mysterious. "So why did you ask if you don't forget your customers." I repeated. "Because I wanted to see if you would be honest or just lie like you did." Oh damn I know she didn't just go there was all I thought to myself. My mouth open a bit this was going to be interesting. "Orders up!" Jamal yelled so the customers could

picked up their food and make their way out the door. "uuuuuhhhmmmm" yeah typical man" she said "anyway can I get a…" She pondered while biting her bottom lip she was very attractive I can honestly admit. "A small cheesesteak with some mozzarella sticks please." she emphasized please with slight attitude. She sounded a bit undecided. She was hungry and had to get back to work. "Anything else?" I asked her licking my lips. "No that's all she replied "how do you like your cheesesteak ma?" I asked. She gave me this crazy look "I am not your ma" she said I took advantage of this and asked her for her name. "So what they call you?"… "Jacqueline" she replied "plain just meat and cheese." She stated knowing damn well how she liked her food. "right up" just as I turned to give the receipt to Jamal he was already handed me the sub with the mozzarella sticks finishing up the order that I just gave him "she's a regular" he laughed as he handed her the food. How can I be so stupid of course she was she worked on the block duh. I smiled and she smiled back "maybe next time." She said while walking out. "Damn" what the hell did that mean? "She look good right?" Jamal asked. "Hell yea Shorty could get it "I answered back. "why didn't you tell me she was a regular?" I asked Jamal. "Because you didn't give me a chance to." Jamal laughed as he spoke. Remember all the customers you see today are mostly our regulars every now and then you get a walk-in from the people who come to visit the city." He explained to me. Pete was in the back counting money. I guess it pays to be the boss. So he wasn't anywhere near our conversation. I enjoyed today's work. I knew eventually it would get boring but for now it was sufficient for me. The interaction with so many different people all sharing the same feeling which was what? Hunger right? We had 1hr ½ till closing and I told Jamal my plan for the next day at work. Which was to "deep clean this mother fucking place." He gave me dap and went on to explain how come they didn't really get all into the appearance with the shop. "Pete had went through a terrible passing of his kids due to drugs." He explained in a soft whisper. The shop was to be left to them whenever the day came that Pete wanted to retire." He continued I understood now why? The shop was so unkept. "Plus I'm always doing everything in the shop so I don't have a lot of extra time to actually get into the cleaning." he admitted "I got you" I assured him. "Even if I'm only here for more than a while, I'd help out as much as I can to earn my money." I spoke from the heart. I was serious "for a while?" Jamal asked in disbelief "you already have a set date to quit once you get hired. "Hired?" I shot back who said anything about getting hired yet?" I asked. You lasted all day and brought something new to the table plus Pete told me he liked you." Jamal spilled the beans. I wouldn't overreact but my grin said it all. We began to tidy up the place but took our time just in case a customer came walking in. To no avail two individuals walked in but they didn't come alone. They had a tremendous horrible odor with them I wasn't sure what to do I was sweeping but sidestepped them upon there entrance. Just on Q Pete emerged from the back it was Phil and Lex they both were homeless and wore every piece of clothing they owned. They had all types of miscellaneous items on them as well, like wires, scarfs, rubber bands on their clothing. Outfits looked as if it was decorating and deteriorating at the same time. Their shoes were Mitch match it was a very unpleasant site to see I never did enjoy seeing people live a life as such. Their face has scars and horrible acne as if they wouldn't pop their pimples but more or less rip them right off their pores, it was disgusting.

"What do y'all want!?" Yelled Pete "nothing we just came to say hi." They spoke as if they were one. I see so many types of homeless who live a lifestyle of conning and making thousands, but these two men were the real deal. There was no way one would rip their skin open while getting fuked up. "Well hi and bye." Pete barked. As they walked away to leave he addressed to Jamal.

"We had made an order that was canceled." I watched as Jamal retreated the food from where they were kept warm. "Wait!" Yelled Pete. Just as he spoke the two did in a bout face as if they had military experience in their background. Knowing those type of men don't ever let go of their training. They both looked around in their mid-60s. Jamal handed them the large sub which they knew they had to share. Their smiles lit up as if they were two children on Christmas, happy as can be. Together they had about five teeth in total.

"Oh thank you Mr. Pete!" They both sounded as if they didn't eat in weeks. Pete was a kind hearted mother fucker. "Don't thanked me just get your shit together I'm not here to cater to anymore grown man!" He yelled. They both bowed their heads ashamed walking out the door. Pete was a given man but like all men, no man wanted to take care of another man's needs. Your children and father might be acceptable but even with that after a while is time to let them spread their wings and fly when you feel as though the time is right. If we carry them too long they become too codependent on one and that's the worst thing any parent can do to their child.

It was about time to close up the shop when Pete called me into the office. He disappeared into the back of the building where his office was located at. Jamal gave me a sly grin with an "ooooo your trouble." He joked as I left. Jamal stood on the main floor cleaning up everything else that needed to be cleaned up. I walked into Pete's office. It was a complete mess. His desk didn't even look like a desk. It look more like a pile of all types of things that could possibly come in handy sometime in the near future. It varied from papers, Styrofoam plates, duct tape, and a ruler. So many objects that looked out of place, his chair looked as if it had been there from the very first day that he decided to open this place. I noticed it had duct tape on the back of it and on the armrest. That would explain the reason for the duct tape on the desk. He had two big cabinets with missing slots where one would normally keep the files stored in them. The fan up ahead was hanging up there by a thread because it was Harlem shaking as it spun. The floor was also a stain attraction. On the other side of the desk he had a plastic chair, to be honest was the cleanest and neatest thing in the room probably because no one ever sat in it.

"Have a seat Manuel" he instructed me. I did as I was told. He was positioning himself on the other side of the desk. He began to move things off his desk and toss them in to a milk crate he had in the corner. That was overflowing with all types of shit. I understand that not everyone likes to have their things tidy and neat but for some reason how was anyone to run a business and be in such a wreck? Anyway I dismissed all my thoughts at the moment.

"So did you enjoy your day working at the shop?" He asked with a look of desperation in his deep blue eyes. "Yes you can say I did it was different but for the most part it was okay." I answered. I still wasn't 100% sure how much I would get paid nor did I even asked Jamal how much he was getting paid. These are questions you didn't ask you coworker because I knew I wasn't getting paid the same thing that Jamal was getting paid. For all I know he could be making minimum wage for the past 10 years which is flat out fucked up. I'm sure we would iron out all the wrinkles once we both decided if the shirt size was the one I wanted to wear. You know?

"So do you think you'll be interested in coming back tomorrow because to be honest you handle yourself pretty well today. I could use a new face and helping hand in the shop as well." he spoke in all honesty. I already knew that I would be back but it had to be on my terms due to my schooling. I wanted to hear what else he had to say anyway. So I just sat back and listened.

"OH!".... Pete's outburst right there startled the shit out of me. "The new flavor you introduced me to? I've always been told that a little more flavor would drastically improve the food here but I never paid any mine." He was rambling now being honest. I just let him go. "I mean it's a flavor I tasted before at one of my exes house but I never even bothered to ask her what it was that she used. I was too busy stuffing my face every time I went over there." He was grinning like a devilish animal who had his eyes locked on its prey. "You were brought into the shop for reason and I couldn't let it go." I was very amused by this statement. I couldn't hold it in anymore and I let out a small smile. It felt good to be appreciated, this man doesn't know me from a can of paint yet, he's in a given the opportunity to work here with him and Jamal and I was more than grateful. Anything would be better than hugging the block at least that's what I thought. I know the money slinging that shit, would never be anywhere near what I'll be making at the sub shop. At least, in the shop I wouldn't fall into a trap or set up out there that could cause me to lose my life on a daily basis having to watch my back. Was I wrong for choosing this route? Pete was still going on but I left the office a while ago mentally. My body was right in front of him but my mind is home telling Ms. Cathy of my good news. It even made a quick pit stop to Felicia as I wondered about what she could be up to at this very moment. She probably blowing up the house phone looking for me. I didn't own a cell phone yet I thought it was a little too much. To me it was a tracking device and to be honest I didn't want anyone tracking me down no one needed to know my whereabouts 24 seven. If an emergency ever presented itself I could always get to a phone if needed.

"Manuel!"... "Manuel!" Pete snapped me out of my trance. "Are you listening to me?" Pete asked. "I wasn't but I was" I replied with a smile to my face. He shook his head putting his hand on his four head. I knew better than to let myself slip but hey I had a few things on my mind can't knock me for using it. "Are you going to work for me?" Pete asked a bit annoyed. "Yes Pete I would love to work under one condition." I was ready to compromise. I had to if I didn't bring this up he would be mad if I brought it up later out of the blue. "And what could possibly be these conditions that you're talking about?"

He challenged. "Well I know your aware but this is my senior year in high school and I have a little over six months left until graduation and I don't want to jeopardize any of that." I spoke looking him in the eyes speaking loud and clear for him to understand my every proud word that escaped my mouth. You see once you get to your senior year in high school you don't have to stay the entire day due to co-op opportunities, which are for seniors with jobs. They are allowed to leave school early to go to work. So once you sign in and stay until 10, 11 or 12, you may begin to work as long as you show proof of employment. Your days are cut much shorter than the seniors who don't have a job. I would need a letter from my employer stating that I'm his employee and such and such. So far I stood until 3 o'clock because I had no job and plus I love being surrounded by so many woman it was ridiculous.

"So what are you telling me?" He questioned. This man was a bit slow? I asked myself. Just giving him a blank stare with the "are you serious look?" So you had class today but you decided to come and work?" Pete asked "yes that is correct." I replied "why didn't you tell me this?" Pete asked. You never asked plus I wanted to show you that I was really interested in working so I came into work as we have agreed on the previous day. I kept my word." I said. "Yeah I know but I would have worked out a schedule with you Manuel or I would have just asked you to come in a little later." Pete said exactly what I wanted to hear. "Well it was only one day Pete and we can still work out that schedule if you're still interested in me working here with you and Jamal." I stated "Yes, I still want you. What time can I have from your free time?" Pete asked grabbing a pen and paper off the load on his desk. "Well first and foremost I need a letter from you stating that I'll be working for you from 11 o'clock till whatever, with your number and address on it." "Second, I'm available every day after 12 o'clock. I will be starting ASAP." I stated all my small but very important terms. "Well once you come in tomorrow I'll have all that ready for you so you can hand it to whomever by Monday morning. How does that sound Manuel?" Pete replied agreeing on it. "This sounds great"… "Oh and another thing Pete" I said. "Oh man now you're just pushing your luck, you asking for way too much." he joked "nah just kidding, what now?" "Can you call me Rock" I didn't want every customer who walked in knowing my name it was irrelevant. If I wanted you to know my name I would be the one to tell you, plus is not like we wore nametags. "Rock!" Pete sounded a bit surprised "why Rock?" He asked. "A long story but it's what I prefer to be called". "No problem" Pete replied. "Now go out and help Jamal with the rest of the cleaning that needs to be done Rock." He emphasized Rock jokingly but was serious at the same time. "Cleaning this place needs a power washing" I joked back. "Thanks for volunteering" Pete shot back. I walked out of the office happier than I've ever been in the past year. I felt good about myself. "You two men were back there for a while. I finished everything up front already." Jamal informed me. "He was just breaking me down with the breakdown." I replied. "Ayo Pete!" I sat right in the chair I was sitting on right before I left the office "what's up?" Pete answered with the shocked look on his face. I must've startled him a bit "how much am I getting paid?" I asked "Ha!" You was supposed to as that why you were placing your terms and conditions on the table buddy" Pete was right I got caught up in all that I needed to be done for me. I lost sight of what was really important to me. "You'll get minimum wage every six months it'll go up a quarter." Pete spoke "check or cash?" I asked. A check with all your hours recorded and documented. Overtime is included after 40 hours a week $7.25 is your pay rate" he informed me I nodded my head in approval because I did in fact approve. It was 10 till 8 o'clock we were about to close. I shook his hand and decided to call Felicia. "Can I make a call?" I asked Pete. I knew I could call her when I get home but instead I opted to see what she was doing now. He pointed to the phone and told me to "press nine before u dial out." he walked out away he must've knew I may have wanted a bit of privacy. I reached in my back pocket and pulled out my wallet in search for her number I picked up the receiver and dialed the number... after a few rings she finally picked up.

"Hello." her soft voice sounded as if she didn't know the person who was on the other line. "Hello, hey you" was all I said she knew who it was just by them three words. "OMG I thought you was never gona call me." She sounded a bit sadden. "Where are you?" I asked her "I'm at the dollar store buying a few things with my princess." she spoke excitedly. "Oh yeah?" I replied "where are you?" She asked me "I'm just getting off of work about to head to the terminal." "Work!?" I didn't know you worked." She stated sounding surprised "you never asked." I joked "wanna ride?" She asked I was all greasy smelling like straight food I didn't want her to see me like this let alone smell me like this. "Na I'm okay ma Ima catch the bus." I spoke into the receiver. "Boy if you don't stop let me pay and I'll meet you at the terminal, if the bus arrived before I do then just hop on it, but if I'm there before it arrives you riding with us." She had me and I didn't even care. That ended the call. The bus would be there by 8:15p.m and it was already eight she wouldn't make it, I was sure of it. I went up front with the guys they were sitting in the front talking amongst themselves. "Yall ready to roll up out of here?!" Jamal spoke wanting to leave. Pete must've told him what I wanted to be addressed as. "Ready if y'all are" I countered. "I'll see you tomorrow Pete we headed to the back door the alarms were set and the front door was secure. We exited the back door which led to an alley Pete had his Mitsubishi Montero parked on the side of the alley it was a SUV I couldn't picture him in a small two door he was a bit large to be squeezing in and out of a smaller vehicle. Once he turned his engine over all we saw where his tail lights disappeared into the night streets. "You want a ride?" Asked Jamal "nah I'm good, im jumping on this bus it's on its way" I replied. "So congrats on the job it's not that bad is only us three now. with all the women who coming in, they all going to be all over you now. I'm fucked!" Jamal joked laughing. We shared a laugh the terminal could be seen from where we always standing it was a 30 sec. walk if that. I knew I could burn a minute or two. The loud yelling caught Jamal and myself by surprise. There was noise coming from the side of the terminal. It sounded like people were arguing, we walked a bit closer to see if what we heard would confirmed what we were thinking. To our surprise, our ears didn't deceive us. The homeless were scuffling over who knows what.

"That's every day" Jamal said "yea?" I countered "yeah they be arguing and fighting over drugs, food or over any other petty lil thing. Last week they took two of them for fighting, one went to jail, the other went to the hospital down the street. The one they took to the hospital didn't make it. He got beat so bad with the tire iron that they had no choice but to charge the other homeless man with murder. So he'll be somewhere getting his life together by force because it wouldn't have been by choice." Jamal stated. I knew what he meant. Anyone would rather be free and keep living their comfortable life as they desired, instead of living a life behind bars. The scuffling stopped but just as I look back, the Lexus caught my attention. "Oh shit." "Gotta go Jamal see you manana ight?" I dapped him up "you good?" He asked "yea that's my ride." I replied "all right Rock be easy" he said before I left. "No doubt" I began to walk towards the car that was moving slowly. I could see her looking through the people and cars trying to find me in the mist of everything. I tap on the glass on the driver side she screamed and looked my way scared out her mind. She bawled her fist up and says something behind her gritted teeth. I noticed the baby in the car seat. She rolled her window down after catching her breath "you scared me." she whined. "I'm sorry I didn't mean to." I smiled. "I told you I would catch the bus." I stated "oh no you not, get in." I wasn't going to contest to that this wasn't the place for that. "What happened over there?" She asked pointing to the spot where all the homeless were gathered. "Just a little scuffle between them." I answered. "I turned over to say hi to the little princess. "Hi Elisa" her eyes popped out of her face mom how does he know my name?" She asked her mother in a sweet innocent voice. "Oh baby I don't know ask him" Felicia joked with her. "How do ju know me?" Eliza asked in a babbling tone but enough for me to make out her words. "How I know you?" A pretty girl like you the whole world knows who you are" I had her smiling "no dey don't" she shot back. Felicia was right her daughter was adorable she looked just like her mother. "You look so much like your mom you know that?" I asked her. "Yea I know mommy looks like meh" she corrected me. We all laughed and rolled out into the night sky.

"How was your day?" I asked Felicia I looked at her she had on purple and white this girl looked edible like a mother fucker. Her little princess had on matching purple and white just like her mother did. "Well I had off today so I spent the whole day with my princess. Went shopping, we got our nails done and we went out to eat. I had a few bills to pay so I handled them too." I called your house so you could hang out with us but I took it as you were out doing you.I can't lie I called about 45 times. Some lady answered, she was nice but I know she was probably tired of me calling so I stopped." She explained to me. "No she wasn't annoyed at you, if anything she was worried about my where-abouts just as you was." I informed her. "What you mean? You didn't tell her that you would be at work?" Felicia asked "not really but she knew I got a job." I tried to sound convincing. "Awww she was probably worried sick you can't do that handsome." She scolded me. She was right, but I know she would be okay. Well at least I hoped. "Well if you want, I'll drop you off, or we can hang out tonight?" Felicia sounded as if she really wanted to spend time with me, but I really had to handle my situation at home first and foremost. How about you drop me off first and after I get all cleaned up, because I stink.Than, I'll hit you up and if you still want to hang out will take it from there." I propose to her. "Sounds good" she smiled at me. I look back and the princess she had dozed off and I couldn't deprive her from going home and enjoying peace in her very own bed. The whole ride we spoke about our day. I really did all the talking about my first day at the shop. She didn't judge me, if anything she liked the fact that I was willing to work and attend school at the same time. She said that's what she had to do when it was time for her to fend for herself." She informed me that she would feel uncomfortable and tiresome at times but it was a responsibility one had to learn to accept in this life. I listen to every word she had to say about the matter. I know she's been through a lot and I could sense her motherly intuition speaking just out of care. We finally pulled up on a corner, where she dropped me off last night. I gave her a thank you and a kiss on the cheek. "Call me handsome if you wanna link up." She said before I hopped out of the whip "I got you ma"

I stepped on the block and everyone who lived on it was out enjoying themselves. Yeah, just music blaring reggaeton bumping and your hip-hop down the block. This was every week but the weekends were even worse. Your typical individual would think there was a block party going on. I walked down the block towards my house and the smell the weed was tickling my nostrals. That shit was potent like a mother fucker. I stop by a few neighbors and gave them my greetings but kept it moving. I walked up the steps to the house and inserted my key into the keyhole. My heart almost dropped at the sight of Ms. Cathy sitting on the couch. She wore a look of disappointment written all over her face. I kicked my shoes off.

"Hey Ms. Cathy" I tried to break the ice. I should've known that by me not informing her about my whereabouts she will be worried or even mad. "Have seat Manuel." She spoke to me in her normal tone. I took a seat across from her. By the smell of my clothing she could see that I was at work, but I'm sure the issue was a lot bigger than what I had imagined. "Did you go to school today and boy don't lie to me?" Ms. Cathy asked. "no I did not." I answer not even contemplating to lie. My luck even if I did say that I did go to school she would've countered it with, she had made a phone call to the school I had to keep a straight and truthful. "Did you go to your job that you said you found yesturday?" She asked putting together the pieces looking at me dead into my eyes. This was her second cigarette that she lit as I walked in this door this woman could smoke. She had on her cozy nightgown with her cozy slippers on. The ashtray was overflowing with cigarette butts. I didn't understand how someone could fill their lungs it was so much smoke throughout the day. This was what she did but sometimes I worried about her health, even though she would always say that she was in good health. "So you are telling me that you drop out of school to begin this job of yours?" She asked shaking her leg while it was crossed over the other puffing away. "I didn't drop out Ms. Cathy." I replied truthfully. I wanted to see where she was going this. "So you rather work than attend your schooling? ... I understand you want to have some extra money in your pocket, but Manuel is not worth throwing these last months away for a couple of pennies." She explained. She was absolutely right and I was fully aware of this and to be honest it had crossed my mind to dropout, but after hearing what Linda and Felicia had told me I thought about it a lot. At the end of the day it was just thoughts. Yea, I was sick and tired of the school I was in, but I knew that in this "Great American Country." and I use that term very loosely. You need a high school diploma to even work at fast food joint. "No Ms. Cathy, I'm going to finish my senior year.I know how important it is. You have always taught me to complete everything that I begin no matter what the case may be." I replied "So why was it hard for you to tell me that you were not going to attend school today? for whatever the reason may have been?" Cathy asked "no"... But" I tried to answer but she interjected "but nothing Manuel I know you're becoming a man but I need you to remember I worry about you and your sister so much when you are out in them streets. For me to wake up and not see you in the early morning as I always do, that can be a bit odd. Now after looking down the street and seeing a crime scene with two dead bodies lying in the middle of the street what am I to think Manuel?" Ms. Cathy was once again absolutely right, now I fully understood why she was so worried about the way things had transpired throughout the day. I had forgotten about that one. This can easily turn into a mind game if some pieces are out of place. "I didn't have any idea who wherer those bodies that laid beneath the sheets but if you are nowhere in sight and your sister is already gone. Whatever my mind may think even though it isn't true, to me it is the truth until I see you with my very own eyes. Until I finally see the actual truth I will not be satisfied. So please Manuel I'm not yelling at you nor am I mad, but please let's keep each other aware of the other please. My dear God I swore it was you that laid under that blanket." Ms. Cathy informed

"I'm sorry Ms. Cathy my intentions were never to make you feel the way you felt today. It will never happen again." I felt bad because I knew better. The smell in the air had my stomach craving everything that was on the stove. "You know what made things even worse Manuel?" She asked before I was ready to get up "what's that?" I replied. "why my mind thought the worst, this girl kept calling asking for you and if you. It wasn't one that i was use to calling, this one seemed a bit more intelligent over the phone and polite. I mean she must've called about six times." "Who is this child?" Ms. Cathy asked giving me then look as if she was just another typical fast ass. "Her name is Felicia and I met her yesterday Ms. Cathy." I replied. The look on my face she could sense that this one may be a bit different from all the others. "Oh really?" Ms. Cathy smiled "maybe one day I'll meet this Felicia." She stated heading for the kitchen. "Yes maybe one day" I'm a wash up I'm filthy." I stated. "You going eat?" She asked "yes I am, wouldn't miss it for the world." I answered Bolting up the steps. As I got out the greasy ass clothes, my mind drifted back to be Felicia. I pondered on what Ms. Cathy said. About wanting to meet her, not yet was all I thought. As I made my way over to the bathroom I could hear someone enter the house must've been Linda.

—

"How was your day baby?" Ms. Cathy asked to Linda. "I'm tired I have to prepare for my mid-term. I know is going to be a lot of work but I'm ready to deal with it all." Linda stated to Ms. Cathy. She did look a bit tired. "I'm sorry to hear that honey. Remember, great things come to those who work for them." "No one said life would be easy but going through it all will make us better and stronger people as we evolve into what we want to be in life." Ms. Cathy stated in a warm loving tone. "Ms. Cathy you always know what to say and how to say it. I love you so much." She hugged Ms. Cathy. "Where's Manny?" Jalinda asked "he's upstairs taking a shower he had a long day at work. He came in here with his close smelling like cheese steak and fries." Ms. Cathy informed Linda smiling. "I'm glad he's working now" Linda stated to Ms. Cathy. They both stood in the kitchen. "I am to baby, but my main concern for both of you is to finish everything that you guys start. I want you to finish your college courses and I want your brother to finish high school. If he chooses not to go to college then so be it, but earning the reputation of starting something and leaving it incomplete or half done is not what I'm raising. If that's the case don't do it at all." Ms. Cathy spoke her loving and caring words. Yes, I know how you feel about that but have you spoken about this with him?" Jalinda asked. "We did have a long discussion about this and we both came to reasonable understanding with all this. He had already explained this to his employer." "Im hoping." Ms. Cathy answered while heating up the food that she just put together. "Good"… "Oh and how about this new friend that has them all happy and excited whenever you mention her name." Ms. Cathy whispered. "I know she must be something special" Jalinda stated with a little slight discomfort. Jalinda hates the fact that woman are always after her brother. The fact that she doesn't know this one makes her a bit weary of her brother possibly being hurt. When he came in the house and how cheery he was lastnight. Linda was going to make it her business to make sure this girl wouldn't hurt her brother. She would make sure she would handle her if she did. Let me make this clear, how noone really knows how overprotective these two are over one another. About six years ago, one of Jalinda friends were around the house one day playing tag. Her friend Amy tried to sneak up on Manuel in a friendly way with no harmful intention. Someway somehow Manuel fell and hurt his knee pretty bad. Jalinda gripped up her friend and shook her up so bad that she never came around ever since. No one knows what she actually said or did to her but few heard stories of what was done. Linda may look sweet and wouldn't think that she was an evil person and im not saying she is, but then again with all these women I done ran into. I done seen some crazy shit.

—

"Many how was work?" Linda asked Manuel once everyone was settled at the table. "It was very interesting and funny how many people love to order takeout." Manuel replied "so what did you do at the shop today?" Linda asked. "I took orders and pass it along to the cook and whenever he got tired of cooking we would switch." Manny answered. Just the thought of the job, lead back to thinking about Jacqueline. Hhe was determined to make her like him. "How many people work with you?" Ms. Cathy was asking now. "Well it's only me and my boss and Jamal." I answered. "Is not a really big shop you know the one on the corner on Broadway, right across from the terminal? There is only 3 of us now." Rock stated answering all the questions that they wanted to ask. I could sense they were excited for me and like how I was becoming a man. "So no more school?" Linda asked giving me a sly look while taking a sip of her juice. " I have more school to do or should I say finish." "Why wouldn't I finish what I started?" She almost spit out her juice after that remark. I had to throw it out there just to show her that I know what's expected from us. I'm going to do my best to finish these last few months of the year. I saw Ms. Cathy smile out the corner of my eyes. She was happy and I wouldn't want to make her feel any other type of way. We enjoyed our meals just as the phone rang. Jalinda was the closest to the receiver so she answered it.

"Hello?" Answered Linda. She look good her lips all perked out with her little attitude. "Let me see if he is here." She said putting the phone on mute. "It's Erica Manny." Linda gave me an evil look that could kill anyone. "Tell her I'm not here, I don't feel like talking to her." "Uuuumhmmm" Ms. Cathy said lighting a cigarette. "He don't want to talk to you right now." Linda had balls at times and I couldn't deny it. "Bye!" She hung up. I shook my head. "Wow." I said. Ms. Cathy was laughing while a cloud of smoke came out her mouth. "ooooo you in trouble now" Ms. Cathy said "trouble yeah right if anything, at peace." I corrected laughing. "You got to a slow down with these women Manny." Ms. Cathy said. "You know they go crazy over your beautiful hair and your complexion." Ms. Cathy spoke "please" Jalinda interjected "don't pipe his head up Cat." We all shared a laugh together. It just so happen the phone rang again, it was already clenched in Linda's hands from the previous call. The look on her face got more sinister as she looked at the caller ID. I could tell she already know who the number belong to. The look in her eyes would have made anyone a believer, that all that sweetness was out the window without her even speaking. I spoke. "transfer the call I'll take it upstairs Linda." I said getting up from the table, leaving my dishes on the table with the food still on the plates. I sprinting up the steps. The phone was already ringing due to the transferred call by the time I hit my room door. I took a deep breath so I wouldn't sound out of breath. I was trying my best to sound calm...

"Hello" I spoke to the receiver waiting for a response. "Hey handsome" it was Felicia. "Hey Ma, my bad I was going to hit you up. I got a little caught up with the family and shit." I spoke into the receiver. "I thought you forgot all about me, if you busy you can call me later if you want handsome." She said knowing damn well she didn't want a nigga to hang up on her. I should have hung up on her just to see what she would say. There I go overthinking again. "Na ma you good, what you up to?" I asked her. "Well the baby is out and I'm kind of bored I wanted to see your fine ass, but it sounds like you are ready made up your mind as to not coming back out." She was thinking for me. I really didn't appreciate that. I never said that but thanks for thinking for me."

"Pop, pop, pop!" the shots Echoing nearby sounded a bit closer than usual. Shots were ringing out again. "What was that!?" Felicia asked. "Girl you lived in a city you already know what that was." I said. "You see that's why I had to get out of that hell hole." Felicia was dead serious. "Is not that bad." I tried to defend my city. Yea, it was a hell hole but cities like this make people better than most people think. It's totally up to you if you choose to become a statistic or a product of your environment. It was your destiny and you choose it. "Yeah okay I know you seen the news right? Where I picked you up last night two male bodies were found lying in the middle of the street. The crazy part is that no one knows who killed who?!" Felicia really had a distasteful taste for the city ever since she moved. "Yea, but what if the niggaz who got killed had it coming? People just don't go around killing people for shits giggles." I defended. It was a true statement. Yes, I must admit that every once in a while some innocent bystander gets the ugly end of the stick, and we call those casualties. It's no one's fault though. Wrong place, wrong time. Sometime a bullet would ricochet off the wall and harm an innocent bystander buts it's not likely to happen everytinme. So as far as getting riddled with bullets is something that the individual brought upon himself, whether it may be a male or female. You either owe a chunk of change or you running on someone's turf. To be honest, you could just be blatantly disrespecting someone to the extent it's just him or you. If your into armed robberies or even gang related issues, you earned all that was brought on to you. You or no one justify how or why that should've not happened to you because at the end of the day we choose to gamble with our own lives every day coming out of the house. You just don't get killed in the city by violence, anyone can and will die eventually. Rither by choice or by force. The cards are dealt and it's your hand to play it and to be honest no religion or priest or government agency etc. etc. is going to save your ass. When it's your time, it's time go. "Yeah I know but it's not like they don't hesitate to not kill anyone. The crime rate in Camden New Jersey is through the roof, every year is either the number one poorest city or number one in the highest murder rate with the most criminal activities you can think of. Pretty soon we are going to receive a noble violent tragedy prize award, instead of a Nobel Peace Prize. I can guarantee you will win every year" Felicia had jokes. I really wasn't in the mood to go back and forth over this because I would defend my city to the end. "Okay switching lanes it is what it is I don't care who kills who to be honest ma." I tried to change the subject. It was pointless, she moved out of the city so now that she was gone she would be against everything that occurred in the city she grew up in. "You're right handsome, aint no point in getting all worked up over this nonsense." So what did you eat?" She asked "well today Ms. Cathy made lasagna with a side of white rice." I answered "white rice?"

Felicia asked. "Yup, not too many people understood why the white rice with the lasagna, but you can't knock it till you try it. The rice complements the lasagna. It's a perfect match, maybe one day you'll be invited to try it out." I had no intentions on inviting her for dinner or to meet Ms. Cathy, especially my sisters Linda. "Oh really" Felicia sounded very excited. "I say maybe ma I can't make any promises. I stated so she did not get her hopes up too high. "Who was that girl who answered the phone,? It didn't sound like the other girl who answered the first time I called." She asked. "that was my sister." I replied. "She sounds so sweet and nice." Felicia had no idea what she was saying. "If you only knew ma." I left it at that, no need for any details. "So you feel like coming out tonight?" She finally dropped the bomb I personally didn't feel like it but it was Saturday and some type of fun was due. "What did you have in mind?" I wanted to see where her head was at. "We could hit the movies or even Dave and busters in Philly." She was on the right track but Dave and busters was a bit pricey for my budget and I didn't feel like dipping into the stash and dropping to much dough tonight. "That sounds good but I'm not too sure. The movies? it's like staying home and Dave and busters is... well you know Dave and busters." I waited for her respond. "What you had in mind?" I thought for a second. "Can you skate?" I threw in the air.

The sight of flashing red and blue lights bounced off the walls outside, the cops were patrolling looking for a shooter or another body since there was a homicide last night. They were on duty around the clock on this part of town due to that murder. "Skating?" She replied not sure if she understood me the first time. "Yes skating like on wheels on your shoes you know?" I explained. "Wow!" You know how long is been since I've skated?" How long?" I asked wanting to know how rusty this woman was on skates. I choose skating because I could take this time to hold her if she would fall. This was a guarantee, especially where I had in mind to go. "When I was 16 years old." She admitted "damn, you are due for some serious exercise than." I shot back "damn, you think I need some exercise because I'm fat huh?" She asked joking. She was far from fat nor did I noticed that she needed to do any exercise even though working out was good for everyone. No matter if you were fat or skinny, fit or out of shape. It's good to move and get on your feet. "I never said that your thinking for me again, so what do you think?" I asked challenging her decision "where do you want to skate at?" I could sense it in her voice she was a bit nervous. I knew that she would be okay. She wasn't alone and would be with me. "The millennium" I stated "The millennium?" She asked. That the new skating ring over by federal down by the 7eleven?" She was on the money. "So I take it you been there before?" I asked interested if she had been there recently or at all. "No but I heard about it." She sounded as if she didn't want to go but to be honest she was going, if she wanted to go out with me tonight. I hadn't been there in a minute but I was waiting for the opportunity to go and this was it. "So you're coming with me right?" I asked already making up her mind for her. "You sound like you made up your mind for both of us." Felicia was right I already did make it up. I looked at my clock on my nightstand and it was 9 o'clock already. The place closed at 2 AM so it was still very early. "Yea, we can go but listen to me." She barked a little "as soon as it starts to get crazy in there we are leaving out of that place okay?" Felicia was a bit worried. I wasnt into the drama at all especially in here presence. "Let me get ready. I'll call you once I'm out the door." Felicia said. "Better yet call me when you're a block away." I cut her off. "See you soon." She hung up. I had to get her to get comfortable in the city again she grew up here, the city was in her blood. I couldn't deal with a chick who thought she was above all of this, knowing damn well she had the hood in her veins. Is just dormant at the moment. You know? I rummaged through my wardrobes as I heard a "tap, tap" on a door.

"It's open." I responded. "Hey Linda." "I'll be down to help you with the kitchen in a bit." I thought that's what she wanted. "It's all done Manny, no worries." I took care of it thank you anyway." Are you going out tonight?" Linda was probing. "Yeah if you want to call it that" I replied "where to?" She asked "Ima ahead to the millennium." I replied "oh yea?" With the girl who just call?" Linda asked. I had my back to her while picking out one of my money green button ups and polo. I tossed them both on the bed. "Yes I am." was all I said "you want to come Linda?" I asked turning to her, I searched her eyes for the answer but her mouth was much faster than I could search "no I'm good." She answered "just be careful and wrap it up." She spun and left. I smiled. She cared a lot about her brother and I had so much respect for her because of that. So I had chosen to go with the deep money green short sleeve with my dark denim jeans with of course my butters, no fitted just my new watch. Once I was all fresh and ready for a good night out, I made my way to the bathroom. The smell from my Ed Hardy cologne was all over the second floor. Ms. Cathy called out to me.

"Manuel!"... "Yes." was my only reply. One of the many things I've learned growing up with Ms. Cathy, was politeness and I got clowned a lot for it but it never would go away. I made my way over to Ms. Cathy's room where she was smoking and watching her television. "Oh you looking good." She spoke with a smile on her face "you're going out I see." "Yes, I am. Nowhere special I though. I had $53 to my name which was more than enough. "Is it with that girl you just met?" I had no choice but to smile. "Yes it is." I answered "you like this one." I can see it in your eyes." Ms. Cathy knew me like the palm of her hand. "A little" I replied "a little my ass boy. Go in my jewelry box and take what's in it and I don't mean to jewelry." I went straight to her wooden jewelry box once I open it up there was some money I closed it just as quick as I opened it. "I'm okay I got some money." I tried to sound convincing but she didn't want to hear that. She got up and open the box and called out to Jalinda. She had six $20 bills in her hand gave me three of them and as soon as Linda came in she handed the other three $20 bills to her. We both took the money. We always had a few dollars in our pockets, but Ms. Cathy was always like that. It wasn't hundreds upon hundreds, but if we would add up all the money she gave us it was a pretty chunk of change. We never asked how she got all the money, but knew it had to be the government helping her out, plus her lawsuit money she collected a while back ago. It wasn't our business and one day I would pay her back whether it be money or just as she would always say, be successful that's how you'll pay me back. "Thank you." We both thanked Ms. Cathy. Have fun and be careful Manuel." "Take your sister with you" Ms. Cathy said. "Already tried to invite her and she didn't want to go." I replied. "Okay then." I walked back over to my room and sat on the bed thinking. Not long enough, the phone was already ringing in my ear. The number was already a number that was beginning to become more familiar as the days passed by in this house. It was Redbone. I let it ring for a bit before I decided to answer it. "Hey gorgeous." Her laughter brought a smile right on my face immediately. I couldn't really tell you if I would actually fall for this one or would it just be a good fuck, then on to the next. I had all the emotional attachments for this woman but to be true it was probably because she was a fresh piece of ass that I hadn't got the chance to dick down yet. If u think I'm a bit fucked up for being like this. I'm going to keep it 100 with you. The women aren't too different from the men. I live with two of them and I know there are plenty of men out there who have lived with women so the apple doesn't fall too far from the tree. I was willing to give it a shot though. Who knows if this one had the experience to keep a nigga eyes wide open and on point. "Where you at ma?" I asked. You told me to call you when I was a block away right?" She answers so calm and giggly. I must admit baby girl listens to a nigga for real and i felt dumb ass fuck. I definitely like that. I noticed that even though my age was a lot younger than her she still gave a nigga his position he deserved. "All right I'll see you then." Hanging up the phone I shot down the steps, but had to shoot right back up. I forgot something. I went straight to my nightstand opening up my drawer and there it was waiting for me, it was such a beauty. I threw it in my left pocket and was out the door any hop and a skip. I was fresh, felt fresh and was smelling good and ready to enjoy myself.

As I walked at a nice pace to the corner I could see the hyper white lights that belong to the Lex. The block was alive as always, but not as many people as usual since the weekend was here. Many decided to go out and party or maybe they were all on the next block chilling. I was two steps away from the car when I could hear some fast steps approaching at a rapid pace. I looked over to my left it was two patrol officers chasing someone, that had them both gasping for air as if the culprit was moving too swiftly for either of them fat doughnut eaten pigs to even catch up.

I laughed and jumped in the whip. "Did you see that?" Falicia was all hyped at seeing the live chase going on. "I sure did they not catching homeboy." I reply with a grin. "How you know that?" She asked before we pulled off. "because they already turned around knowing better than to step into one of them dark ass alleys you never know what's on the other side." I stated she glanced at her rearview mirror and saw the two officers walking back. "that's crazy." she said in her sweet innocent voice that drove me crazy damn! I can't wait to taste that pussy. "You know where we going?" I asked. "Yup" she answered. She looked nice, she was wearing dark colors. It was a navy blue top with a black denim sports jacket that hugged her tightly. Her hair was up in a messy bun with a few tendrils dangling by the side of her face. She wore gold earrings. Her lip gloss was definitely popping, but I wanted to see her standing in them jeans. Two rings on her fingers complimented her well-manicured hands that look smooth and soft. I imagine the wrapped around my little big man's if you following me.

As for the millennium, it was a new skating ring and a club where everyone who loved music and enjoy to skate would all pile up in this place. It didn't matter where the hell you were from East, North or South Camden, we all had one intention which was to have a great time. It was only about three minutes away from my house so we were there in no time. I had advised Felicia to park a bit further then the place was located, just in case a situation broke out which nine times out of 10 it would. Not that I was going to start some shit, but I learned to be over prepared which is way better than to be under prepared and plus I didn't want mother fuckas judging a nigga because he pulled up in a mother fucking Lex. You and I both know I aint built like that. Felicia parked up. She smelled so good. I just watched her. When she threw the car in park I jumped out and made my way over to her side of the door and did what a gentleman does. I grabbed her hand and we stood by the car for a second. In this place they had metal detectors and security wanding everyone, except for the woman so you could just imagine how many niggas used there ladies to bring in their weapons of choice. Today, I would definitely have Felicia bring in mine.

The cold ness made her jump "what's that?" She asked. Not to happy, relax I'll get it from you in a bit okay. She gave me a sly look. She knew the deal and if not she was about to find out. We walked at a slow pace staying on the opposite side of the road, until we were about to cross headingto the millennium. The sound of the base was echoing and got louder as we took every step closer towards it. Trash filled the streets and sidewalks, the smell of wet and marijuana polluted our every breath, but I didn't care. Houses that had been abandoned or burned down years ago have been converted into crack spots. I could only imagine what else was being held in them houses. Felicia gripped my hand tightly which made me feel that she fell a bit uneasy. I knew that no matter what I wouldn't allow anything to happen to her tonight. That was my main priority over everything. Crossing the street we waited for all the whips to drive by, so that we can find an opening to cross. Because getting hit by car wasn't out of the norm, especially getting hit by random stole.

Chapter 3

"Hold my hand"

Once in line in the long line, I scanned all the different types of people from all over the city looking to have a great time. You had your group of guys looking for victims or just looking for some unsolved beef amongst the crews. The guys were on the hunt to find some smuts to smut out. At the same time looking for a potential come up, if you were the flamboyant type guess what? You could be a possible contender. You had your couples hugging one another tightly. No matter what would happen, once one left the other the vultures' were out on both ends soaring. It was the woman chasing the married men or the men chasing the married women. If you was in a relationship was where the loyalty got tested. We had our white girls looking for a nigga to put it on them rough and nasty. They would all congregate together in their own little clicks, with their pretty blue green eyes prowling. They would all come from Cherry Hill, Collingswood, and White horse Pike etc... I could only imagine what they told their parents, as to where they were going out to. Yea, Felicia was my redbone, and she was right on my hip tight the way she was suppose to be. I like that, you had your disrespectful dudes who wanted a sneak peek at what you had by your side, but to be honest I never minded that one bit. The sound of the base was booming. Everyone waited anxiously to get in. To be grooving inside is what everyone wanted. I know for myself I wanted to head inside. My body rhythm was following the melody of "Mr. Cheeks" hit song "lights, camera, and action!" I could tell Felicia was ready to let go herself. One by one the line continued to shorten, but at the same time it was lengthening towards the end.

"This place is packed tonight" Felicia spoke in my ear "I know, I can't wait to get in already" I answered back.She smiled. I love this girl's smile. She was bad. I knew it would take a while, but I was on a mission to drop them drawls down tonight. There was a couple in front of us, who were getting wanded by a big black dude and his partner who was a short stocky Spanish man security guard. The screaming of the wand went berserk right at the guy's waistline.

"I't's my belt" was his immediate response. The security man gave him a sly look. To say, nigga who you kidding. "Go put it away in the car or you and your lady are shit out a luck tonight." He spoke deeply being dead serious. The man knew better than to protest. He and his lady spun and left. It was time for us to be searched, well at least it was my turn. I knew she wouldn't get searched. It must've been old boy first time in here. Everyone who's been here before knows that, all males got searched point blank. "What up Playboy?" the bouncer said patting me down. "chilling, ready to let loose in here." I replied then came the wand. "You and your lady enjoy your night and be safe." once inside I grabbed Felicia's waistline and grabbed my butterfly knife inconspicuously slide it into my pant pockets. She looked at me as if she felt she was being used. I gave her a peck on the lips, she smiled immediately.

"What size are you?" I asked. She looked down at her feet. She had some small ass feet. "Four" she replied. Now, The Millennium was pretty big and had a huge ring. It was where we did all our skating, they also had a small bar in the right-hand corner. A few pool tables and a couple of arcade games. Tables and seats were around the whole place either occupied or just use as a coat racks. The strobe lights illuminated the place with all types of colors. Some were even in sync with the base of the music. "I'm going to the bathroom" Felicia stated. I barely heard her right before she spun and walked towards the restroom. I nodded and we separated for a while. I made my way to the counter to retrieve our skates. The girl at the counter wasn't the one I saw before. She might have be positioned somewhere else in the building.

"Sizes?" She asked loudly wearing her millennium black T-shirt, with the words Millennium in yellow. She was Hispanic. I noticed this off the rip, she had a small mouth and my imagination took me way beyond the present. How big could it get I thought and giggled to myself. She had to be about 5'1 her hair was colored with highlights aiming towards a copper with black. Her hair look very attractive. I know making a move on this Shorty wouldn't be in my best interest, but as she went to retrieve the skates. Her hips just sashayed left to right with authority. She didn't walk too far towards the back, but she had to sense my eyes all over her body,shorty was thick and fine. I noticed her Vasquez boots she wore. They look cute as ever on her tiny feet. She came back with two pairs of skates in her hands she smiled. She rang me up for the skate rentals which came up to 15 dollars even. I handed her a 20 dollars.

"So who are you here with?" She asked me licking her lips which were pink and juicy. I had no choice but to do the same right back at her. "A Friend." I kept my answers short and to the point nothing more nothing less... Just in case you never know who this girl knew. "I bet she is cute." She responded. Handing me my change. I went to grab the skates but she grabbed my hand, "hold on big boy." She spoke. Reaching under the counter "I'm a hook you up." she replaced the insoles of the skates with brand-new insoles. "We supposed to do this at the end of each night but I want to make sure you good." She stated "yeah don't need any unwanted fungus skating my way." We laughed. "How about my friend skates?" I asked. She threw her hands on her hips. "Forget your friend she can get all the fungus that comes with them skates." She was tight, I had no choice but to smile. Woman are too much. I was about to walk away but she grabbed my hand again. "Just kidding." She smiled hooking up Felicia's rentals as well. "I can't have you with no friend with fungus feet." she joked with me. I always admired a female that look good and had a splashing personality. I felt a cold hand on my arm. I grabbed it on a reflex not knowing my own strength.

"Ouch Rock you're hurting me." a female voice spoke. I recognize the voice immediately. Her hands were always cold. I learned a wild back ago that a woman who is up to no good will possess hands of ice, but a woman with hands that were always warm ment she was caring and loving individual. I'm not 100% sure of how true this may be but to be honest it has to have some truth by it or it could straight bullshit. The hands that caught me off guard belong to no other than Erica. The girl who handed me the skates gave me a look, that ment that she was done with me for the moment. "Why" you didn't pick up the phone earlier when I called your house." Erica was annoyed and causing a scene for no reason. Erica was dark chocolate with straight black hair. Today she had it in a side ponytail. She was a bit taller than the rest of my picks. She was bad with beautiful white teeth and had a body of a goddess. I had sex with her on numerous occasions but it was just that sex. There wasn't anything more or less with her. I know woman always seem to get a little attached as times passes by and I explained this to her on numerous occasions. She was well-informed, but it really didn't matter to her though. I knew better or at least I thought I did. "I was busy what makes you think that I had to drop whatever I'm doing to cater to your needs?" I spoke cordially but at the same time I felt my blood begin to boil. I knew that she wasn't going to let this go so easily. I don't care what you were doing all I know is that when I call you, don't tell your sister to tell me that you don't want to talk to me!" She was swinging one arm and the other on was on her thick ass hips. She wore baby blue top making her skin complexion just pop. Not to mention all that white gold she wore was all together just right. Her baby blue and white chucks complemented her small feet. I pictured her naked, even though it wasn't that hard to accomplish. I snapped out of my daze and realized that I was here with someone who was probably watching me or even searching for me. "Listen Erica, Ima holla at you another time but to be honest I might not." I had to be blunt I didn't have time for the extra bull shit. I'm very aware it is all my bull shit, but it was time to cut it off .She was disrupting the flow things and she wasn't going to let up on her own. "What!?" She shot back but her words went dead in the music. Usher's "yeah" featuring Lil John and Luda came on. The strobes were doing their thing and all the skaters taking care of business. I look for a table that was semi-occupied and headed right to it. It was away from the pool tables but close enough to the bar. I scanned the entire room looking for my redbone diva. I didn't see her or may have possibly overlooked her. I came here with the intention of just skating and dancing. Alcohol was sold to just about everyone as long as you paid for it. No one cared that most of us were under age. Unlike most joints you would be carded and a wristband would be issued but not around these neck of the woods... The cops wouldn't even think about running up in his spot. We have a hard time getting them to aid the wounded when it's really a time in need. So for them to even think of coming up in here just to be on some disturbing the peace type shit, it wasn't gona happen. We are all in here to enjoy ourselves, whether it is illegal drinking, underage drinking, drugs and weapons we were gonna do as we wished . Aint no one crying out for help yet so let us be. The smell of the wiggles and bud was already lingering all around this place. I'm sure it was coming from the bathrooms. You could tell it was some exotic. It was either Kush or even some Dro. I could be wrong too. I began to strap up my skates. My head was down and I was focusing on what I was doing. It wasn't until I felt someone's hands reach up under my shirt from behind. The hands were warm, it could be only one other person . I just tested the waters and waited, how far she would keep feeling and roaming on my body. Noticing that I enjoyed the hands over my back she stopped. "Boy you a freak aint you?" Felicia spoke in my ear. I just smiled and pointed to her skates. She plopped down right beside me and took off her sneakers and slid right into the skates. "How they feel?" I asked her.

"I'll tell you in a minute." I watched her attentively as she tied them up. Her breast hung down exposing all of her cleavage. I was enjoying every bit of it. She glanced up and caught me staring. I wasn't looking I was literally staring at her breasts. "You like what you see handsome?" Felicia asked me. My smile gave away the answer right even before I could even get a vowel out. "I know you do" she answered for me. I grabbed her sneakers and I grab my boots and headed towards the lockers over by the bathroom.

"Pick a number ma." I asked of her. The whole wall had blue lockers with keys. The key would be released, when the money was put into the coin slot. I dug in my pocket and handed Felicia a handful of change. She already was on it, she went straight to the number 77 which was on the front right near the bottom. I watched as she bent over. This girl was teasing this shit out of me and I liked it a lot. Once we secured the things in the locker. She decided to hold onto her keys. "Why don't you give me your car keys, this wasn't the time or place to misplace your keys." I asked "I got them." she replied. I pulled out one of my boots and asked her "you can just put them inside my boot." "ill no, not in those smelly things." She whined joking. She didn't protest. instead she stuffed them all the way into the front of my boot. "You see them not going anywhere, you can keep the locker key around your wrist." I assured her. That way they would be safer in the locker than in your hand. I know, it's that I'm used to holding all my own things down." She winked at me. Once the locker was shut and secure we rolled away from the lockers. "I'm not the best skater so don't laugh if I fall." Felicia was worried about falling. Little did she know I knew I was bound to fall at least twice because of how crowded the floor was? You could be the best skater in the world, but once someone bumped you off balance it would take a miracle for you to not fall on that ass.

"E.I!" The whole club went into a frenzy that Nelly's hit came on... Felicia pulled me up towards the ring, she was ready to let go and I wouldn't stop her nor would I slow her down in any way . We hit the ring which was already tight so there was no stopping once you entered. The flow was moving counter-clockwise, she smiled and sped away from me. I let her go away. The moment we lost eyesight of each other I decided to show her my skills. I began to skate backwards against the crown. It would only take a few seconds before I would run into her. I swiveled in and out trying my hardest to avoid hitting any-one who was flying straight at me. I heard the voice over the speaker yell ou,t "someone is on a suicide mission!" That was the DJ who today happens to be DJ Show. He was referring to me. That's just informed everyone that someone was out there posing as a major threat, to keep there eyes open. I was a hazardous threat he was talking about. I noticed Felicia in the turn still looking back wondering how come I wasn't gaining on her from behind, little did she know I was already gaining on her through the front. The moment she turned around, she screamed and jumped once she saw my face. Perfect!, Got her. I was laughing uncontrollably,

"Oh my God why would you do that!? you scared the shit out of me!" she yelled, where did you go?" And how did you pass me I didn't even see you?" She asked so many questions excitedly and surprise on how well I maneuvered on the skating ring. " While you were looking for me from behind I was coming the other way". I had to gloat a little. "You are so crazy! How? You can't skate the opposite way?" She asked. "I didn't even answer the question. Instead, I tagged her and spun around "you're it" we enjoyed every second of the game we played. I would slip up and run into her own purpose, just to feel her body. We watched the skate crews do their routines, they got better every year they came around to show off their skills. "How come you don't join a skating crew?" Felicia asked me. We made our way to the side. She wanted to get to know a bit more about me. "I'm not as nice as those guys." I replied. I see how you move and you have skills." Felicia replied "Ima be honest I'm not all that social when it comes to being clicked up with homies or any type of groups. I'm not sure why I am like that but is just how I rather be." I spoke honestly which was more than the truth. These guys were all in a crew. They were all from some part of the hood and some were even from some gangs. So we all know what presents itself with all that and to keep it real that was never my twist. "I like to come and enjoy myself with a friend or my sister. For me to show up squad deep, it's always doomed to end up in some type of unnecessary drama ." She stared in my eyes as I spoke nodding her head. She was agreeing to all that I was saying. It is best not to surround yourself with extra bull shit sometimes. I wish I would've learned that when I was a bit younger. Instead of putting myself through all the extra shit i did in school, hanging around all the wrong people. Felicia must've went through a lot of situations that I would sooner or later find out,only if she would allow me to venture into her past. So for now I would not probe. This wasn't the place nor time.

"You wanna take a shot with me?" Felicia asked. "No not really I didn't come out to drink ma." I replied "well you going to take a shot with me and I'll leave you alone for the night." Felicia tried to sound convincing. I wanted to contest but thought against it, when I should have stood with my initial judgment. We made our way to the bar which was even more crowded than the ring itself. I went to dig in my pocket but Felicia pull my hand out. She moved her pointer finger from side to side signaling to me that she had it. "No I got it." she said. She made her way closer as the bartender, he noticed her tiny body creeping closer, acknowledging her with a nod. "Let me get two double Jaeger bombs." She yelled. he spun retrieving the drinks. I drank but I didn't drink too often so whatever she ordered was something that was clueless to me. "What is a bomb?" I asked her. It sounded scary. I didn't want to ingest any type of bomb was my initial thought. "You'll see handsome." Felicia humored me while the drinks were being concocted by the bartender. He did his little fancy tricks with the bottles in the air. He spun them and threw them behind his back and whatnot, he poured from 2 feet above the glasses. He was very talented I must admit. Felicia had her arm wrapped around my waist and I had my arm wrapped around her back. She was so much smaller than I was but it was exactly how I like my woman. The drinks were ready and it was four shot glasses, with four other glasses that stood side-by-side one another. I looked at her like she was from another world or maybe in some serious need of a few AA meetings. She slid the bartender a 20 right out from her bra. It was very amusing to know that woman could keep a lot of things inside their bras. I smiled cuz you already know my mind was running wild.

"You ready?" Felicia asked. "O hell no, why order so many drinks?" I asked in disbelief. Yea I was bitching. "It's only two a piece." She joked "I see eight" I countered. "I know but four of them are only red bulls she explained I just stared at her. I wasn't used to drinking a mixture like this. Give me a beer and a few shots and I'm good to go. "You take the shot glass and you drop it in to the red bull and chug it down in one gulp." She went on explaining and now the whole bar was staring at us. I couldn't back down now and trust and believe I wasn't planning to. "You ready?" She asked. "Let's go" I barked on three we both drop the shots into the red bull and downed it and went straight to the other one. The taste wasn't bad at all, the mixture of the two drinks went hand-in-hand together complementing one another. "Wait till that hits you." Felicia said. in my ear pulling me towards the ring.

About 20 minutes later I was pop locking, skating, and flirting with every woman in sight. That Jaeger bomb had exploded inside of me and had me feeling so fucking wired. I took notice of how my whole demeanor had changed. Felicia was buzzing but I'm sure she wasn't as Buzz as I was because I was all over the ring.

"Are you okay baby?" Felicia asked "what! Am I okay? You see me, I'm having a blast, let's go take some more water bombs?" I joked "No, you don't need no more of them." She laughed. She was right I didn't but I wanted another one. She has some napkins in her hand. She wipe some of my sweat off my forehead. I was hot and my shirt was gone. I was skating in a beater. So muscle city was being broadcasted. Felicia was right on me wherever I went. I was feeling it and I wanted to fuck Felicia right here, right now. My tongue done slid down her throat already and she did not resist it at all. If anything she played tug-of-war with it. "Let's go to the arcades." I was in the mood to play some Mortal Combat and whip Felicia's ass. We slipped out of our skates but didn't return them just in case we wanted to hit the ring once more before we left. The tournament was on and it would be on until the next hour. I was getting a bit tired watching all the crews do their thing, not hating on them because them boys and girls has some serious skills when it came to the tournaments and competitions. It was tricks, dance moves and great crew routines. Making our way to the coin dispenser, I took out some bills and just fed it into the machine. "which one you wanna play ma?" I asked Felicia "it don't matter you going to lose in all the games we play anyway." she joked with her arm around me. My mouth was dry. I gave her all the coins but stood with about $13 worth. Ima get a quick drink, go ahead play I will be right back." I spun off and headed towards the concession stand. I ordered a raspberry tea because that's what I remember what she liked. I felt some hands on my ass, but it wasn't Felicia's. I was looking and she had her back towards me playing Pac-Man. It was Miss Erika....Again.

"Girl what the fuck you doing?" I snapped. "Touching what's mine." She spat. "Yours?!" Ha! Your bugging." I replied. I know I see you with your little high and mighty Redbone bitch, I guess you tired of the black bitches huh." Erica was also buzzing I could smell it. "You need to chill, I'm going to handle my date and you're going to get back to what and who you were doing. I'll talk to you later." I shot back with a twisted grill. "I'm going to fuck you one way or another you see." I didn't even reply. Shorty was a case waiting to happen. Ms. Cathy was right I had to get away because she really thought that in her mind. I still wanted her. I crept up on Felicia who was engaged in a convo with some nigga, who must be trying to press up on her. Being that she was all alone. That was the game, fucking vultures. I said to myself. I know everyone in this mother fucker done seen us all in the open grinding all over each other skating all night, but hey it's all fair game. I knew better than to have baby girl alone. I moved swiftly now, the skates have been off so my feet so I felt superlight I was up on Felicia in no time.

"Sup ma you ight?" I asked her. "Yeah handsome I'm good I'm trying to let homeboy know I'm good but he must be super thirsty." Felicia spoke not taken her eyes off the game. "Ayo my man you thirsty?" I gestured to the big gulp drink I had in my hand being sarcastic "like a mother fucker". The grill he gave me subsided immediately "Damn nah Rock, I'm good I thought she was alone and you know how it is." This nigga didn't know me. How the fuck he knew my name? I asked myself. There was plenty of dudes from school up in here but even so, this particular nigga didn't know me nor did I know him. I meant to interrogate this situation but Felicia took my attention off him and he spun off with no other words. "What he say to you?" I asked baby girl. "He was asking about you?" She replied "and what you say?" I asked "what you think?" She asked being smart ass fuck. "You told him my name?" I asked trying to eliminate her from how this mother fucker knew my name. Shit like that erked me. I don't socialize with every dick and harry for everyone to know me. You must not know how hard it is to stay underground. It's not easy to do in your hood. Trying your hardest to keep the bare minimum of people to know who you are, but for some reason it always got around. It's very difficult and had to be one of these girls up in here. Anyway, I dismissed the thought and got back to my date.

"Thirsty?" I asked Redbone. "Am I, I hope it's my favorite?" She asked "damn its soda." I reply she gave me the only mug, she took a sip her eyes lit up. "No is not is raspberry tea" she cheered up. "You already know ma" "come on let me whip that ass on Speedway" it was unoccupied and we both jumped into each of the seats. We played and used up all the coins until we had enough of the game. The crowd was going in everyone was in their own world either dancing or drinking doing whatever they wanted to do up in here.

“Thank you handsome.” Felicia hollered over to me. “Thanks for what?” There was no need to thank me I didn’t do anything. “For bringing me here. I am enjoying myself and it’s been a long time, it’s hard to find free time when you’re a single parent. I’m glad I made time for us tonight.” Felicia was enjoying herself and I could tell because she couldn’t stop smiling from ear to ear. I was more than okay with that. “I knew you would like this and plus you deserve it.” I started taken my eyes off the screen to look at her. She leaned over and planted a kiss right on my lips. The blood began to pump I was getting aroused. “Every now and then you have to enjoy yourself, you can’t put too much stress on your shoulders. You can always help everyone else every now and then but we have to step back and remember you have needs that need to be satisfied and I’m not talking sexually.” I had her attention now. We kicked it in the arcade until our quarters were beginning to run low. We saved enough for the pool table and the Mortal Combat. The juice was all gone and I had to release some bottled up piss that I’ve been holding in for hours. It was almost midnight and the party was nowhere near ending.

“Ima go get us some more juice.” Felicia stated “Ima hit the restroom then I’ll meet you in your arcade room.” I stated walking off. My journey to the bathroom was stopped by the girl who was working the counter. “Ayo funky feet.” She yelled out. I automatically stopped and gave into her humor. “You still hiding back there” I joked back. “I’m back here for the rest of the night pa.” she spoke I found it to be so sexy when woman who were of Latin dissent would actually use their native language in a conversation, you know like Spanglish “oh man that’s too bad maybe another time then.” I kept it light. I knew I shouldn’t be over here kicking it to this sexy female. It was hard to resist. “Maybe another time when I don’t see you with that ugly ass Redbone. I should have let her get fungus on her feet.” She spat rolling her eyes. She was talking shit while smiling. My mouth dropped. “wow!” I couldn’t help but to let out a laugh. No matter how bad the woman was, the next woman will always critique her and bash her. It could be because she was prettier than her or she felt that she couldn’t compete with her. It was rare to find another woman to complement the female you are with, especially if she has some type of connection with you sexually or even attracted to you. I took advantage of the moment and asked her for her name.” It don’t matter you got a girl.” She replied “you’re right” I was about to walk off, not before screaming her name to me “Vanessa!” She blurted out. I kept on walking, I heard her but I wasn’t just going to stand there and let this broad disrespect me and my date. Yeah, I may have been wrong but she wasn't gona enjoy this. I'll catch her on the rebound and let her think about that one for a minute. As far as Felicia being ugly she knew she was dead wrong. I don't fuck with ugly broads. As I excused myself from all the crowd and made my way over to the bathroom, the smell of the PCP was stupid thick in the air. I could catch a contact just by walking through the thick clouds of the strong stench. I smelled a lot of horrible smells but this fluid had a very unique sent to it that could be distinguished from any type of essence in any environment. I noticed two of the individuals on the far corner with a flock of bitches around them so I made my way straight to them. The circle that was around him immediately backed up and just allow me to roll all up on them.

"Ayo Rock what's up!" Jigs slurred with a stick in one hand and a mixed drink in the other. "Shit chilling, enjoying my night, Whats sup with you two? I haven't seen you in a minute." "You already know Rock, we laying low. We will be around in a bit." "How the block feeling?" Banga asked. I knew exactly what he meant but I still didn't know what occurred that night nor did I really want to know. "It's a bit caliente and I got hassled by the DT the other day, other than that is the same as it always been." "Oh yeah, that fucking pig Shalecki fucking with you?" Jigs asked puffing on his boogie. "We going to handle that pig one day." He was a bit upset of the news. "Na he just asked me if I saw or heard anything but after not getting anywhere with me he dropped the issue.", "No worries than you already know." We dapped up and I made my way over to take a piss. I had a date to get back to. "I'll see y'all, be easy." I said. before leaving "Early" they both replied. As I made my way towards the bathroom I could feel eyes on me. I wasn't to sure who they belong to, but my intuition was letting me know. I stood on point. I was glad I ran into those two crazy mother fucker's. Now, I knew it wasn't either one of them two under the blanket that morning. Yeah, I must admit I thought it was one and one but I guess they got the best of whoever tried to do whatever that night.

Is like no matter where in this establishment you would run into a different cloud after cloud, talk about aroma therapy. The bathroom was straight up marijuana. The odor was amazing I enjoyed that smell. They were all congregated in the front I made my way straight to the back. It was crazy how a men's bathroom could be mistaken as a coed bathroom due to the group of men and women drinking and smoking in it. With all the laughter that was going on, my mind drifted back to Felicia who probably already ordered the drink and who knows what else she ordered. I wondered who else could be pressing up on her right now, knowing that I left her alone. I flushed the toilet and was ready to zip up and get up out of the bathroom when I heard a

"Tap tap "on the stall door. "Someone in here" I let be known. I saw small feet under the door and immediately knew who they belong to. The door opened and I was immediately taking back on how strong this girl was. She pushed me back. She drop down in a squat, whipping my dick back out and did what she knew how to do best. By then my little fight was far overdue. I just went with the flow my eyes just rolled around in pure ecstasy. I could hear the commotion in the front but didn't pay no mind Shorty came in here with one intention which was to make me come hard. I looked down at her with her helpless eyes looking up at me enjoying how she saw me enjoying her work. I was buckling at the knees she made it disappear and reappear over and over again I grabbed her hair and pounded her mouth so hard all you her was her gagging as the saliva ran down my balls and not to brag but my Dick was a bit longer than your average Joe Schmoe, and lets not forget, It was pretty fucking thick. I guess she could sense how I was about to blow. She stopped but kept stroking it vigorously with her right hand. With her left she un did her pants and in a matter of seconds. I watched how my dick slid in and out of that wet juicy fat pussy. Her hands were posted on the walls, her legs were sprawled around the toilet as I went to work. The drink I had in me was wearing off but I could still feel the buzz. I was hitting her hard, slapping her ass even harder. She tossed that shit back harder and it was to the point of no turning bank. I fucked up, I know. I gripped her shoulders and finished her pounding like at mad man. All her moaning and yelling echoed even through the music. The guest in the bathroom either got really quiet or they decided to leave us at our own privacy. After a couple minutes of stroking, my sperm went straight into the toilet right below us. I held her up because she was trembling as if she was going to collapse any second now. I didn't waste no time, zipping up and getting up out of their but not before Erica blurted out

"That's my dick?" She was bugging "you wish." I shot back, exiting the bathroom. I hope I didn't smell like sex. That would be detected in a heartbeat but Erica never had a bad odor to her. I went to the bar and ordered two shots of Henny which came out to just under $10. I grabbed the shot glasses spilling a bit of it on my hand. I walked towards where I was supposed to meet Felicia about 10 minutes ago. I noticed her on the Pac-Man machine again. I thought of how much this girl love to play that game. I felt weak. Could it have been because of my little quick escapade? I can't believe I let myself fall into Erica's trap, but then again that was gona happen one way or another. I kissed the side of her neck trying to figure out her move.

"Damn! Handsome where you been?" She asked turning around. "Two shots?" she answered her own question. "all that's where you was, at the bar." She grabbed a glass and made a toast "to us." she didn't even give me a chance to say anything. All I could do was follow Suit and drink the shot right up with no protest. I took the glasses and I looked at my watch and it was getting later. I had to get up for work in the a.m. I'm sure Felicia had to get up too. Maybe not, either way she had to attend to her princess. It was about to be the end of the night for us. The Henny brought back some of the buzz from our last drinks.

"You okay handsome?" Felicia asked "yea I'm good, A bit tired but I'm good what about you?" I countered. I'm great thanks to you and our wonderful night we are having with each other." She smiled leaning in for a quick peck. "I gave it to her without any hesitation dispite what i just did. I told myself that we weren't intimately involved,. So it technically didn't count. Who was I kidding though? There was some ruckus coming from the back part of the ring. I glanced over but couldn't really make out what was going on. It settled down a bit, I didn't feel no imminent threat.

"I'm hungry" Felicia brought my attention back on her. "Are you?" I asked. I must admit I was feeling a wave of hunger myself. "Do you want to eat something here or you rather go catch a late night bite at a diner or something?" Felicia asked. I wasn't in no mood to drive around and look for a spot to eat. "No we can order a meal in here." "Is that cool which you?" I asked her "sounds good to me" she replied. Now mind you, this place wasn't showing no type of quieting down nor was anyone ready to call it a night besides us. The place was still jam-packed with everyone trying not to bump into anyone else deliberately. It was something you couldn't avoid. Moving through the flock of people, I notice the girl who handed me the skates. I took this opportunity to return the skates with Felicia so Vanessa couldn't get all psycho on a nigga. "Come on let's get rid of these heavy as skates" Felicia said. "You read my mind." We made our way straight to the rental spot. There was a few people in front of us returning there skates as well. "Here you go Ma." I said handing her our skates. "did yall enjoy yourselves." Vanessa asked starring at Felicia. "We sure did thank you." Felicia replied. She wrapped her arm around my waist and pulled me closer.

We ordered two burgers, some nachos with one big drink. We already had the cup so we only pay $.50 for a refill. I carried a light conversation with Felicia, but I felt a bit strange. I could feel someone was watching me. I looked around but I didn't see anything out of the norm. My burger had disappeared into my belly almost immediately. It was a husky one at that.

"So what you got planned out for manana?" Felicia asked. I laughed. The way she said tomorrow sounded way off because "n" was pronounced differently. I corrected her smiling. "That's what I said handsome." She returned the smile back at me stating. "Well I have to go to work, after that I'm not sure what is on my schedule. "I informed her. I'm sure she was going to try to lock something in with us for tomorrow. I wasn't agreeing with any of it just yet. In order to make this girl want me I had to make her miss me. You know? "OMG!" "Look at that!" Her eyes were almost out of her socket I look back but didn't see anything. "No look over more, that way". She instructed pointing. What we were watching was a man being pinned up against the far back wall, He had a barrel in his mouth. I couldn't make out who these guys were because of the herd of bodies surrounding him. Very few noticed but the ones that did notice didn't seem to give a shit. That's how went down no one ever got into anything that didn't have anything to do with you. "He's going to kill him" Felicia said. She was getting all rattled up by now. "No he's not. Don't worry about it, It's none of our business if he does. I tried calming her down "you see this is why I had to get out of the city." She protested. "Just a few minutes ago you was telling me how much of a good time you were having, now you talking shit." I informed her of herself. It's to truth you can't be a two-faced individual. "Fuck them for all I care let them kill each other. Come to think about it, it was all happening where Banga and Jigz were at. Let me find out these niggas found some more shit to get into. Oh well, I got back to eating my nachos. Felicia lost her appetite. So I tried to finish off her nachos too. I love nachos and cheese, or was it that I was hungry? I looked over to my left, guess who was approaching the concession stand? It was Erica with her face all twisted up. She rolled her eyes at me and just ordered her preferred food of choice. She was with one of her friends that I couldn't remember her name but I knew she looked familiar. She looked a bit ratchet. I still focused on Felicia as she spoke about how she wanted to do something tomorrow with me. I was paying close attention but at the same time watching Erica through my peripherals. I couldn't trust this girl nor would I let her run up on Felicia or some slimy shit. The bathroom situation replayed in my head over and over again. I fucked up! I fucked up! I knew this. It was going to get ugly up in this side of the building. The guys over there were still arguing over who knows what. East Camden was being shouted and North Camden was shouting back. The DJ didn't make the situation any better due to his slick remarks and the "ooooss" in the "no he didn't" shout outs.

Erica and her girlfriend were talking shit now too. I know this because they was pointing and laughing. I kept my composure and tried to keep our conversation inviting and worry free. The meal was gone. Felicia ate about half of her cheeseburger than decided to empty the tray. I cut my eyes over to Erica as Felicia made her way over to the trash can. She blew a kiss over at me. I shook my head ready to get up out from this joint shit was about to get ugly, but Erica couldn't hold her tongue any longer. She threw a verbal shot Felicia "look at that red bone bitch thinks she the shit!" Felicia looked at her dead in her eyes she kept her mouth shut and walked by on my side.

"I know you hear me bitch! Let me know how my pussy taste?" She barked at Felicia. By now we were passing the pool table Felicia was inside and I was of course on the outside I noticed Felicia grab the ball off the table being very UN noticeable to anyone else. I don't think she knew that I saw that but Erica was already a few steps on our heels gaining fast. She was about to make a move on Felicia.

"Don't ignore me you trifling as bitch!" Erica knew exactly what she was up to, and her little girlfriend was following suit with all types of comments being shot at Felicia "Yeah bitch you know you hear us!" Erica was gaining on her. Felicia spun around so quick catching Erica dead in her tracks,. Erica was moving so fast that she couldn't stop her body's momentum completely before Felicia had splashed her in the face with the pool ball. I noticed it was the blue one. The impact hit her mouth so hard that it caught everyone off guard, especially Erica. Erica was a fighter everyone in East Camden new tha,t but her mouth was put to a halt today. She got up quickly bleeding profusely all over her chin and shirt. She charged at Felicia, scratching the side of her face. Felicia used all of Erica's momentum to throw her off of her. She still had the ball in her right hand. Erica showed no sign of quitting Felicia decided to put her down. She gave her a left hook,

"Red bone bitch huh!?" she barked. Giving her another shot while shouting back every word that was yelled in her direction by Erica and her friend. At the same on time the other end ,it erupted in frenzy with chairs and punches being thrown left and right I was just making sure Felicia didn't get jump. I took my eyes off to watch my back and Erica's friend was already on Felicia's heels. What caught me by surprise was a braided female gripping up Felicia's friend and beginning to trash her face immediately. My jaw dropped at how both Erica and her friend were getting their asses handed to them by Jalinda and Felicia. "Yeah" who would have known Jalinda was all up in here playing incognito and shit. I knew I felt eyes on me. I pull Felicia off Erica

"That's enough ma she aint going to fight back no more, she's done!" "Give me the ball." Felicia was quiet and had this look on her face that made me worry a bit if an ever got her mad. She was mad as hell her eyes were red and infuriated with anger. I took the ball from her hand requiring a bit of force due to her blood and adrenaline pumping through her veins. I slid the ball in my pocket. I made my way over to my sister who was having a field day with Miss. little ratchetness. "Linda let's go!" I barked. I reached down to grab her hand which I didn't have to say it twice, her hand was locked on my right. "Hold my hand!." Just as I said those words to shots rang out. I clutched both Felicia and Jalinda's hands hard and tight, and as everyone ducked not wanting to get struck by a bullet. I made my way straight towards the door I didn't stop until we reached our destination which was out of the fucking club.

"Go to the car I'll meet you there!" I took off to key off Felicia's wrists and ran back against all the bodies running out like a stampede. I couldn't make any stops I had one thing on my mind and that was the locker number 77, it was emptied. I had to get up out of their and that's what I did. I didn't go out the front. I search for the nearest backdoor exit.

Back at the car Felicia was still infuriated by the whole situation.

“I know I shouldn’t have come to this spot.” Her hands were shaking. “Its okay girl that bitch deserves that she anyway.” Jalinda assured her. “She did, but who are you anyway?” Felicia asked clueless “Girl I am Linda, Manny sister. I was all up in there watching over my brother, these bitches get crazy over that pretty ass nigga.” Jalinda joked. Being serious at the same time. “You his sister?” Felicia couldn’t believe it. “So why was you whopping the other girls ass?” Felicia asked. Because the other bitch was about 2 feet away from jumping on your ass while you was handling your business with the other bitch.” Linda went on to explain.

“You can fight girl I saw how you handled yourself.” Thanks, I saw you too beating on old girl too, she had no chance with you. Your brother had to rip me off of that bitch.” “I’m Jalinda” she extended her hand. “I’m Felicia your brothers date.” “I saw.” Jalinda replied. They both just sat back and waited as the police ambulance sped by to help anyone who may have been in need of some medical assistance. “We good girl” Linda tried to calm Felicia. Linda already knew how to handle most of these situations, do what you got to do get out quick. Get away from the scene as fast as possible after you do that everything should be okay.

“Where is your brother girl we should go back for him?” Felicia stated to Linda. She liked how this girl was determined to make sure Manny was good. “No give him a few minutes, if he don’t make it by then, then we headed back for him.” The car unlocked and the lights pulsed at the same time. Manuel was coming from behind them. Felicia and Jalinda jumped in the car and waited. The red and blues were all over the block now, but as usual there a penny short and a dime too late. Everything played out perfectly. Manuel was walking up to the vehicle. Felicia held her hand as if it was hurt. I wouldn’t be surprise after that episode. Finally inside the car Manuel was in the backseat, he handed over the keys up front to Felicia.

“What took you so long?” She asked starting the car. “let’s get out of here fuck all that. They probably looking for yall crazy asses.” Everyone laughed. “I bet.” Linda replied. It wasn’t something to be proud ot, this wasn’t a laughing matter, but at the end of the day everything that transpired was provoked by no other than the ones who got dealt with today. I may have something to do with that too, but they took it the extra mile. As far as the gunshots I have no idea who or what started all of that commotion nor and i wasn’t interested in knowing who did what. I noticed as Felicia drove she used her opposite hand to maneuver the steering wheel. She winced at every turn she made. She either broke a knuckle or it was sprained. We all sat in silence as Felicia navigated to our destination. All three of us were recapping what just happened. I like how this little Ms. Redbone carried herself tonight. To be honest I didn't think she was going to let Erica get inside of her head like that. The way she moved, not saying a word planning her next move way ahead showed me she was on point. Despite not showing any signs of anger, she held her composure and kept herself in check until she couldn't take it no more. The sudden stop brought me back to reality. We were on the corner on my block. Linda looked wondering why she stopping on this corner. I gave her the head gester indicating her to get out. We both got out. I felt bad for not letting this girl know where Ms. Cathy's house was but it was my way of being a bit cautious.

"I'll meet you at the house" I told Linda. "all right." Our house was closer than you think. I came over to the passenger side. "Are you okay ma?" I asked Felicia "yes I'm okay" I don't understand why bitches always tend to think shit is sweet when it comes to a light-skinned bitch." Felicia was mad all over again. "She had all that coming to her." I try to let it slide Manuel. I'm sorry for getting out of hand tonight." Felicia was going in. "No it's not your fault you did what you had to do." I'm impressed but at the same time I feel bad because I invited you to this spot." I tried to put it on me. "Is that girl really is sister?" Felicia was talking about to Linda. "Why you asked me that?" Did she tell you that she was?" I asked "yes she said. She was but I don't believe her." Felicia confessed. "Well why don't you believe her?" I asked already knowing the answer. "Because she don't resemble nothing like you Manuel." And to make matters worse she came out of nowhere." Felicia was a bit skeptical. "Well ma she is my sister not blood but like I said before she's my foster sister and to keep it 100 she's my sister for real. I treasure her with all my heart." That's why we look nothing alike and I know what you mean when you say she came out of nowhere, I invited her to come out with us but she refused, I'll get on her about that when I get inside. The way she looks after me I do the same but if I'm not aware that she was in that spot, how could I be able to know she's was okay. She was playing sneaky games and i wasnt feeling them. She was supposed to be in the house not spying on me." I was tight I aint gona lie. The episode could have went down 1,001 other ways, But I'm glad it went down the way it did tonight, because both of these two women are safe and secure. I had a bone to pick with Linda though.

“Let me see your hand.” I grabbed her right hand. It was swollen. “Close your fist tightly” I instructed her to do so, her hand was closed tightly she hissed like a snake. “open and close it again.” she did as I asked “does it hurt?” I asked “a little” it’s a bit swollen but it don’t look broke and I did the same with the other hand. “Put some ice on it when you get home.” “Yes doctor.” She joked. I’m glad she found some humor in all of this. “Are you mad at me handsome?” Felicia whopped this girl’s ass, and she was worried if I was mad at her. How could she be worried if I was mad at her over something that I may have started intentionally but unintentionally at the same time if that makes any sense? “Why would I be mad?” Better yet we’ll talk about this tomorrow okay? When we are both rested up and clearheaded. How’s that sound?” I didn’t want to get all wrapped up in this at the moment. On the other hand I should settle this now. If I let her marinate on all that was said, she’s gona start to ask all the right questions. Oh well. I leaned over and kissed her passionately to the point that she let out a slight moan. I could have her tonight I thought as she melted in my arms, but I decided not to. I wanted to make her want me a little more. I laughed at my mental thought. “What?” Felicia asked smiling with uncertainty. “Nada ma, call me when you get home okay.” I told her. “All right” she replied.

I left the car and went straight inside all the lights were off. Alarm was set. I shot right upstairs. Linda was in her room sitting on her bed. Her room was always Nice and neat. TV was off. She had on her cozy clothes and got comfy on her bed. So I was going to make this brief.

“Mija, how come when I asked you if you wanted to come with me you answered that you didn’t want to come?” I asked in a low tone but a serious one. “Because I didn’t want to go out with you and your little friend.” She answered back. I looked at her knuckles and they were bleeding a bit. She was tough and she had box game too. “How long were you at the millennium?” I was all over that place and I didn’t notice you up in the air.” I asked. “I got there when you and miss thing were on the raceway game.” She answered. “And you just took it upon yourself to not inform me that you was up in their?” I countered. “No need I saw you, and that was good enough.” She replied “ugh... not really.” “What if something would’ve broken off with you and I had no clue you was involved, than come to find out it was you on the floor getting your face pounded out?” I waited for a response. I didn’t have to wait too long. “Boy please” she thought she was Holyfield I tell you. “I’m serious

Linda I can't protect you if I don't know where you are. Especially if we are in the same building and I don't even know it. My voice was getting a little louder. I was getting a little worked up. I toned it down a bit. I knew she could handle her shit but I knew I was right and she knew it too. "I don't know why you are tripping Manny, you see me I'm good right?" She threw in the air "yes we are good because I pulled both of you off them dumb bitches." "If I wouldn't have done anything the two would probably be still pounding their faces into the ground to this very second." "Then what? Wait for the police arrive and have them pull you off the girls, then see you booked for aggravated assault?" You didn't even notice how bad y'all beat those girls up did you?" I asked. "No! I was just protecting you Manny I saw her charging your way so I blacked out." She admitted. I can't be too mad because she did pop up in the best of time. I didn't want my sister getting into a jam she couldn't get out of you know? I know she going to hold her shit down. She has to and learn when enough is enough though too. "I hope you told your little girlfriend the same little speech you given me." She demanded as if it would be unfair if I didn't. "No I didn't at the end of the day Linda you are my pride and joy." I admitted. Her face lit up. She got up and gave me a hug. A tight one I could feel her nipples all over my chest. She smelled good to. "Go put some ice on that hand, Holyfield." I joked. She danced putting her fist up. "You already know" Linda bounced back and forth swinging "girl ill worked that ass" I jumped at her. She fled away. Her ass jumping up and down. She was my heart and I hope she understood all that I said. I headed to my room I stripped down and was ready to call it a night. I didn't feel like stretching this night out any longer than it had to be. I stashed my butterfly knife. I was glad that I didn't have to use on anyone tonight which was a good thing. The day I would use it or even pull it out, would be a day that would turn into tragedy for someone.

"Ring ring" it was way too late for the phone to be echoing through the house. "Hello" I answered "hey handsome" I'm just calling to let you know that I'm home and I'm fine." She informed me. "Fine you are ma" I joked. "Listen, Ima call it a night I gotta get up early to go to work so I need my beauty rest" I joked back. "Yes you do with your sexy ass." She replied. "good night baby girl" I was trying to end the convo. "Let me know if you want me to pick you up, it don't matter when you get up. If I'm not busy I got you." She informed me. "This girl was on it I thought to myself. "I got you goodnight." The call ended. "Damn Dick whipped all ready." Linda poked her head in the doorway. I laughed I didn't even touch this girl yet." Imagine when I do...

Chapter 4

"Empty pockets"

The alarms of the metal detector were just as annoying as any other beeping noise you could think of. No one in their right mind would ever enjoy that shit, Who would of thought, entering a school establishment you would have to go through an airport customs, literally. The scanning and searching of all the materials on our possession wasn't like the clubs, where most of the ladies didn't have to be put through such security precautions. It was the complete opposite they got searched just as thoroughly as the males entering the building did. Woodrow Wilson had a capacity over 1000 students, all of which came to learn or just pump drugs straight out of the classrooms and bathrooms with no exceptions. Straight to the money. The building had three floors consisting of freshmans, sophomores, juniors and seniors scattered all throughout school. No real structure, just get in where you fit in and learn as much as you could. Sooner or later the majority of the students would either drop out, flunk and some did in fact pass just for showing up. It was a win-win for an easy diploma if you asked me. The crowds that stood outside the building waiting to enter the building either waited across the street, at this enormous park or right out front of the school building speaking to friends and smoking their cigarettes and marijuana joints. It was rare that you smelled wet in the air but then again every now and then you had your individuals that were so codependent on the drug that the smell of the mint leaves would tingle your nostrils every now and then. I couldn't understand that one but hey each is your own. The females all looked as if they were about to go out to the club, heels or some fresh kicks on with there matching outfits looking sexy as ever.The aroma of the different type's perfumes on the ladies seem to be so intoxicating they would flare up everyone's nostrils. Sad to say they were amongst the crowds with the joints being deep throated for a morning rush. My mind drifted back thinking and imagining how many of these women in here have gotten their juice boxes banged out in the bathroom or it even in the empty classroom. These types of things happened on a regular skipping class just to get a quick nut off. I've been privileged enough to experience that and every chance i got i was all over it. You would always hear the gossip around the school. Ladies would always gloat if it was worth it.

"He got some good dick." Then you would hear the fellas "man I had her bent all over in the bathroom toilet seat, shorty a freak for real." I must admit I enjoyed my few episodes of the quickies in the bathroom. Why wouldn't I?

A good portion of the females graduated but the ones who didn't ended up dropping out due to pregnancy. The sad part was no one knew exactly who the baby daddy was. I wouldn't be surprised if I had a couple of little juniors running around, then again I highly doubted it. Let me not think about that right now, Lets get back to trying to enter the building. It was my turn to head through the metal detectors. My Jansport was all black, it was a semi empty book bag that was snatched up by a hated truancy officer. He went by the name of "Davis" this big light-skinned ass guy was a problem in the school. His crew was just as problematic as he was. They were called the true gang. There was about 30 of them. All on the same fucking mission to be on a niggas ass. They didn't care if you was black, latino or white, Asian persuasion or from a turtles ass. They had a few lawsuits against them, which to no avail. They all ended up being dismissed because as we all know there excuse was that it was self-defense and that she/he was being combative and resistant. Fucking ass holes!

"Mr. Ricardo, how is the slinging of the coke in the dope business going for you?" Mr. Davis asked. I didn't utter a fucking word. He and I had our little differences back in my sophomore year. I hit him so hard for coming out his neck about my sister, he never talked that shit again. Yea, he still makes his slick remarks every now and then but that's what he wanted. To provoke you into saying or knocking him the fuck out so he can get some more paid time off. After being Frist and passing the detector, getting wanded was next. I was in the clear to move about the building without being harassed for the moment. Yes, it was hectic every morning up in here. No one said that gaining your high school diploma was going to be a walk through the park you know? I shot down to the cafeteria which was always overly crowded with the masses of people. We had two dining halls and even with them two it wasn't enough to hold up the capacity of all of us in the two designated areas. You would see a great majority of people standing while eating. A warm donut and milk was always my choice. The staff always tried to put pressure on the students to get out the halls with their food but who were they kidding? They tried so hard to cram everyone into a confined area. Yeah okay, that was a mission all in itself for them so eventually they gave up. No one listened, not because we didn't want to, because what they wanted was a confrontation. Once something of that magnatude would be provoked, it wouldn't be a pretty situation. It would escalate into something bigger ion a matter of minutes.

I had the information and paperwork already filled out by Mr. Pete. I wasn't even going to homeroom. As soon as the bell rang, I was going straight to the front office to get this approved immediately. "What's up Rock." a voice called out, It was Chino. He's in my homeroom class. Chino was about 5'5 short with a muscular build. He had green eyes that were a bit slanted as if he had a parent that would be of Asian descent. I slid over to where he was over by the vending machine with two other dudes who were from his part of the hood North Camden. Sandra and Jazmine were posted with them both with iced teas in her hands. I dapped up Chino and kept on moving swiftly. I spoke to those who I knew and only to those who knew me. I made it my business to not befriend all of the niggas around me. They didn't have my best interest but many I kept close. The school had it's gangs or sets just like many schools. My answered to every last one that was looking for prospects, I told them all with respect that I was good. They respected that I kept to myself but at the same time I was far from pussy. I stood my ground no matter who or what the situation was. You'll be surprised at how much respect you can gain by being your own man. A lot of dudes seems not to have the strength from within so many would seek that route, hey whatever floats your boat right? As I was making my way over to the front office. I noticed Julissa she was a senior. She wanted to get real serious a few months ago. I had to tell her that it was not gona happen. She knew what it is was from the very beginning. She accepted the terms on our mutual agreement. I thought she got the impression that I would fall for her because she was one of the baddest in the school. Yea, her sex game was on point but that wasn't gonna work on me. I noticed her from a mile away. Today, she wore white tights with her little green and gold ballerina shoes, with a matching top. Her hair was color box blond and was pinned up in a messy bun. It exposed her pierced small ears. The gold hoops dangled as she talked to the girl in front of her. She didn't notice me yet but her apple bottom protruded from her backside perfectly, her 36 c-cups were flawless. Damn! How my mind drifted back to our countless escapades all over Camden. She hasn't noticed me yet. The conversation was deeper than just clothes, probably a sexual encounter I thought to myself or she was just ignoring me. I kept it moving, it didn't bother me not. I strolled on by with my swag on a 100. Whatever she was talking about went right out the window completely. I say this because she left old girl and grabbed my arm almost imnidiatly, I guess she wasn't ignoring me.

"Damn boy you aint even going to speak?" She was all smiles "oh shit my bad." I lied like a mother fucker. "I didn't see you" I said she stop dead in her tracks and put her left hand on her hips "Seriously Rock!?" You didn't see me?" She questioned "Na I'm sorry too much on my mind. "I lied again "I'm going to see you orita because I gotta go straight to the front office." I said. "Well what a coincidence, I have to go there /tambien/."/too/ she replied. She put her arm around mine. I already knew she was still on the kids top but I wouldn't allow myself to get involved no matter how many times she would plead. She already let me know how she felt, if i continued to give her the good pipe game she would only get wrapped up even more all over again harder each time. Nope not me. She smelled wonderful I though she has such a feminine scent. I never even asked her what was it that she wore, but it was aromatherapy to my nostrils.

"So how was your weekend ma?" I started light conversation trying to buy some time since the bell was due to ring in about five more minutes. "Boring Pa, it was lonely and lonely and lonely some more." Julissa explained to me knowing damn well she was out somewhere doing her thing. I never knew why? She thought she had to lie to me or maybe she was actually a goody-goody girl. Yeah okay, was my initial thought? "How about yours?" she asked. Repeating what she asked. "How was my weekend?" My mind replayed all the events starting from Friday like a quick preview in a snapshot movie. "Well... my weekend was a little bit dull as well." I replied. Not really feeling the need to go deep into explanation of all the crazy events that transpired. "Maybe next weekend, you'll hit me up so our weekend can be a bit better than dull what you think?" Julissa asked licking her juicy lips. She had a pretty face her jawline was visible but not overly. Her eyebrow had a tiny hoop ring on the left one which made her face look a lot sexier. Her skin was flawless, she had one beauty mark on her right cheek. She was all smiles after her last comment. I wasn't feeding in, I changed the subject I already knew that when I wanted that ass it was up for grabs but for now I was good.

"So you figure out what you going to do once you graduate?" I asked her "I'm going to Temple if all goes as planned then, take it one semester at a time." She spoke as if she was determined. That was a great way of thinking was. I on the other hand was going to take a break, even though the odds were against me times 1000. The majority of people/students who decided to take time off before going back to school, usually didn't make it back or just flat out never finish anything they start due to all the extra obstacles they put into their own paths. That's why it's said that one should get it while it's still fresh and the ball is already rolling. "what are you going to do?" Julissa asked me. "Not too sure yet ma." I replied "so why you gotta go to the front office for?" She asked "I'm trying to get up out of here by 10 o'clock." I said "10 o'clock you better have a job or a real good excuse in order to get out of here and you know that boy." She spoke as if I didn't know that already "ring, ring, ring ,ring" the sound of the bell was echoing all throughout the halls. You would think that everyone would be in a rush to get to class not in Woodrow Wilson the crowd began to disperse slowly but I mean slowly. "Ring ring ring ring." The sound of the second bell rang moments later. This was the late bell and the crowds were still roaming.

I had already entered the front office. I wasn't the only one waiting to be seen. Julissa was standing right next to me it was 8:15 and the staff members were all occupied typing away answering all the phone calls back to back. I looked over and saw two seats open and opted to get comfy. No need to stand all morning waiting for the staff to acknowledge me. Julissa looked at me. "you lazy." She joked. I just stared at her body while she swayed ever so slightly, shifting her weight left and right. Her ass was round and fat. I know she knew exactly what she was doing and I didn't give a fuck. I pictured bending her right over the counter and just going all up inside of that, you think she would let me? .....Hell no! I laughed at my perverted thoughts. She caught me staring and said "what? /tengo algo en los pantalones/?" She asked so innocently wiping her right and left butt cheeks. /asking if she had something on her pants/ "No you good." I replied. "So why you laughing?" She asked answering her own question. "/te gusta I know/" /you like/ she stated cocky and confident? "ya tu sabe ma." I replied /you already know/.

"Manuel!" yelled a voice from the rear "how can I hope you young man?" The voice belong to no other than the Vice Principal Mr. Johnson. A bald older man with a chinstrap, big belly but not fat. I stood up and spoke up "I need to get this job form approved I gotta be at work in the next couple hours." I explained Julissa looked at me "ooooo a working man!" the staff also threw in their two cents. "That's right Manuel get that money the right way." I walked back over to the vice principal office. "Have a seat" he said. He had one of these loud voices that could easily be used to intimidate the younger freshmen. As time went by you learned that's how his voice was when he naturally spoke. "So where is this so-called job at?" Mr. Johnson asked. Sensing I could be lying. "Sub shop on Broadway." I replied. "on Broadway?" He asked "yes sir" I replied. "So you're telling me that you wanna work at a sub shop for the rest of your life?" He asked staring me dead in my eyes "No Mr. Johnson but it's a job for the summer so I can help out at home and provide for myself, instead depending on Ms. Cathy all the time." I explained. I didn't want to make this a career but at the end of the day, this was a small time gig. He hawked my face as if not wanting to believe my intentions. Mr. Johnson and I had our visits with one another due to my behavior and my slick mouth towards authority. Who had no respect for their students but as far as posing as a problematic individual everyday, was not the reputation I had. Just because this is what I thought didn't mean that, this is what everyone in his building thought about me. "Well, give me a moment to verify all of this information." Mr. Johnson stated. I went to walk out but was stopped dead in my tracks. "Where you going?" He asked. "I'm giving you some time to verify?" I replied. "No need for you to leave, it's not like I'm going to drive over to this so-called "sub shop", he threw his left and right fingers up as if they were quotation marks. I smirked. He picked up the receiver and began to dial out, looking at me after a couple of seconds hanging up the phone. "no one answered" Mr. Johnson said. "Okay so called again. It's a sub shop they probably on the other line are busy." I countered. He dialed again. "Hello my name is Mr. Johnson and I'm the vice principal here at Woodrow Wilson high school, are you expecting an employee today to work for you from my school." He eyed me, this man was something else. I could not be mad though. I could only imagine how many times this man has been hoodwinked. "Okay thank you sir he'll be there." He hung up and handed me a pink slip. "Take this to your home a teacher and you'll be able to leave at 10 o'clock. In my mind I was jumping up and down. I didn't start till 12 o'clock. I had time to burn. "Listen to me Manuel, I'm proud you found a job. My congrats goes out to you but don't lose focus. Look at the bigger picturem you're a smart young man. The world is in your palm, don't just settle for scraps when you could settle for millions." Mr. Johnson was right. I also understood what he meant but for now I wanted to get up out of here. "Thank you Mr. Johnson and I'll keep that in mind." I replied. He knew this was going to be the last time he would see me until graduation. I'm sure that in his line of profession he had seen all of the successful ones and all the ones that took life as one big joke. Maybe he grew an attachment to a chosen few, as for me I didn't get too good of a vibe off him. It didn't really matter either. I slid right out of his office. Julissa was still being seen by the staff for whatever purpose she was there for.

My homeroom was on the third floor. I found the nearest stair well and bolted up. The stairs was a hotspot, when I say this I don't mean it as a good spot. I mean that in these areas is where there weren't any superiors to look out for the victim or victims. This is where a lot of the tragedies would occur. Once you were caught off guard no one was near you to help you. The staircase worked against you. This year alone there's been at least 15 assaults and I don't mean a punch or slap in the face. I'm talking serious bodily fluid being spilled out of someone's body. Some were gang-related, others over some "he say" "she say shit". The rest were over women but most of all over money. I wasn't worried about the spots not because I'm a bad ass. If you stayed in shit, guess what you'll end up in deeper shit. Plus my box game was on point. You know what cracked me up the most?

"Excuse me" I asked politely to the couple practically having sex in the middle of the stairway. They kept on giving each other mouth-to-mouth as if one was losing air begging for resuscitation. They continued as if I wasn't even there or passing through. It's crazy how they do all this security checking all over the place, but there was no preventing someone from getting injured by school supplies? How hard was it to make a quick weapon? In science class the chemicals alone could obliterate someones face, Just think of all the other materials that could be used to assault someone. If they didn't allow guns and knives in their eyes everyone was safe right? How can one be so blind and dumb to the criminal's mind?

"Hey Ms. Robinson" I spoke to my homeroom teacher as I entered my homeroom room. The class room consisted off a bunch of females and a few males. Who all looked asleep in their own worlds mentally. "Good morning Mr. Ricardo how nice of you to join us." She replied, Everyone noticed the rectangular piece of bright pink paper in my hands. "Oh shit Rock got a gig!" Yelled

Benny from the back I ignore him, He had a slick mouth piece at times. In homeroom we all joked a bit when we were in the mood. Today i sensed that he was in the mood. It was seconds before the next comment was exiting his ashy ass lips "so where is it McDonald's or Taco Bell?" Benny had no pics, but guess what neither did I. "Na it's taking care of your mommy and daddy." oooooooo" the class erupted. "Damn Rock, why you always got to take it there?" Benny love to dish it but could never take it when it came from me. Benny was like most of us growing up in foster homes. I continued to dished it all over him fast. Shut your mouth if you wasn't ready for the comeback. You should of kept your mouth closed before you started spiting all that shit, plus you should brush your teeth cuz all that shit stink." I shot back before i diverted my attention. "Ms. Robinson, I was told to give this to you." I handed over the pink paper. "Ok good Mr. Ricardo" She scanned the paper and put it in a file "you can go at 10 o'clock." She informed me. It was that easy. Why just we made it way worse than it was, I was I sat down right next to Melissa. She was a white girl who had light green eyes. She was a full blown slut. Her reputation was shot and I knew better than to stick my little man's up in that.

—

10 o'clock came and went, I was out the building by 9:55 AM, it was a big relief. I don't know what felt better, me about to go to work or the fact that all this schooling after 12 years was coming to an end. It was one thing to strive for what you wanted to accomplish, but schooling tended to get a bit tedious day after day after day. These last final months have been given me a feeling that I couldn't seem to explain. It felt way beyond joyous. I walked to the federal strip taking in the scenery, the one I never had time to look at. My morning walks were quick and swift. I was always a few minutes behind schedule. Today, I didn't have to rush anywhere. I couldn't wait to get back home. Not because I missed it because I could.

I passed the nail salon and watched these two older ladies hop out a Mercedes that was parked along the curve. I gave them the right away "excuse us." The taller one spoke in her sexy seductive voice.They both looked way older than 30 but then again I could be wrong. We all know it isn't wise to assume. Either way I couldn't get my eyes off of them until they disappeared into the nail salon on 29th St. The shorter one turned around and took another glance at me or was just making sure I wasn't gona steal her car. I smiled and kept on walking. This was a different atmosphere, everyone was in school and all the grown folks were going about their normal commute into work or just running errands. You had your dropouts on the corners getting that fast money. Looking all fresh, with clothes and shining jewels. Finally home, the gate on the porch was locked when I arrived at the house. The door was wide open which was fine because the security gate wasn't going to get broken open. It was too much work to get by that gate. I unlocked it and made my way in. Ms. Cathy was in the kitchen cleaning with her music playing her slow jam throwbacks. "Mrs. Jones" was playing. She didn't notice me. I imagined this is what she did every day when she didn't have any errands to run. A cigarette in her hand, and a rag in the other. Making sure everything was exactly the way she liked it clean. I stood there watching her I wonder if my mother would have been the same way as Ms. Cathy? Or would this house be flipped upside down. No matter what I thought I love my mom but most of all I love Ms. Cathy's cigarette totting self. She raised me well enough to see how one must conduct themselves. She was singing the song. I learned a few years ago, he was singing about his addiction to heroin. I always thought it was a female that he was obsessed about. Ms. Cathy spun around with a jump and a shout

"Boy why you creeping up on me!?" She held her heart I laughed but it didn't look too funny by the way she clench her chest. She tried to play it off as well with a big smile. "I'm sorry, I didn't want to interrupt your little jazzy jam with Mrs. Jones." I joked. "Want to dance." I asked wanting to learn a few moves. "Boy you can't dance." "All you young people know how to do is pop lock and make babies." She joked back "Please." I replied I grabbed her hand and had a dance with Ms. Cathy till the song was over. She didn't protest. I bet it's been years since she danced with anyone. I made a mental note to take her to a jazz show or even a grown folk's jam in Philly one day. Once the song was over she sat down and lit another cigarette but I took it out her fingertips.

"Slow down Ms. Cathy please." I spoke with much sincerity. This lady smoked like a freight train. It was ridiculous how many cigarettes just one little old lady could inhale. I put my life that her lungs were the color of charcoal. She didn't argue but she did asked me why I wasn't in school, she must forgot about our conversation the other day. about me going to work. I pulled out a copy of the paper that they asked me to give to my homeroom teacher. She looked at it and smiled brightly.

"You're grown up so fast Manny I'm so proud of you I would've thought you had plenty of years left till you began to work. My boy is becoming a man." A tear fell from her face, "Stop don't cry, It's all because of you I'm becoming a man." I showed the respect she earned deserved. "Y'all be moving out soon and have a bunch of little Manny's running all around and forgetting about little old me." That last command took me by shock. How could she say such a thing? "Why would I ever forget about you Ms. Cathy?" There is no way I could do such a thing you have provided so much wisdom and care for Jalinda and myself. I'm only going to work I'm not going anywhere till you decide to kick me out." I explained. Then it finally hit me Ms. Cathy raise a few foster kids back in her day. They probably never came by to show love in fact all the years that we've been together I've not once witnessed anybody come by only her sister's friends and that was rare. Ms. .Cathy was a mother to me and I know I may not express myself in the matter that I should but what she said has opened my eyes once again.

"Ms. Cathy you have been more than a mother to me and you have no idea how much love I've learned to have for you. No other person has taken time to show me and discipline me the way you have done for Linda and myself. I am sure now she feels the same way. I wouldn't trade you for anyone in this world. I am your son and you are my mother and I say that proudly if it's okay with you." I explained. She raised her head with tears running down her face and gave me a biggest tightest hug that felt like eternity.

"Yes my son I will be your mother to I rest in my deathbed only if you allow me to." This morning was not supposed to transpire this way but I'm glad it did. You could never predict how ones day would turn out I don't care how carefully planned out it. You could aim it in a direction and get there but no one could predict of all the detailed event that were to transpire along the way there. These words felt so good to be express to the woman, the caregiver who deserved it the most. Ever since that day Ms. Cathy wasn't known as Ms. Cathy anymore she was my mom and I was her son.

"Now go clean that room that looks as if a tornado ripped through it." Mom spoke she was right I didn't fix it up this morning I was too excited. "Are you hungry?" Mom asked "actually no I'm good I ate breakfast at school." I replied. A donut is not a breakfast child." I laughed I'm fine mom and bolted up the steps. Ms. Cathy never not once ever force us to call her mom which was why I never did it but I saw that she didn't have to because as I got older I learned what a mom was and Ms. Cathy was the perfect example. So sooner or later one acknowledged this and today was that day. I had a few hours to burn which was a little over two hours that I didn't know what to do with. Once I was done with my room I could smell Ms. Cathy was putting something together on the stove. I wasn't all that hungry just by the smell it caused my stomach to turn. I threw on some raggedy clothes that I didn't mind ruining...again.

"Manuel!" Ms. Cathy called up the stairs. I peeked my head out "yeah?" I shouted back down "Come and eat." She said. "I'll be down in a minute." I replied,

A bagel with eggs, bacon, sausage and cheese that thing was husky I joked with Ms. Cathy "did you leave any food or did you just put it all in this?" I pointed to the bagel. She laughed. "You can't work on empty stomach right?" Mom asked. She was absolutely right. I looked at it trying to see how it was put together because I knew it was going to be slamming so I analyzed it before I decided to demolish it. The cheese complemented the sausage, the bacon was perfect and crispy just how I loved it.

"Why you keep staring at the sandwich?" She asked with a lit cigarette in her hand while blowing smoke out her mouth. "No mom, it's great I'm getting an idea." she stopped short "ideas?" Don't be taking my secrets and spreading them all over the city." She joked. I know she was serious though "I'm not." I replied. How are you and that girl Felicia doing?" I stopped chewing "look at you can't even eat at the sound of her name." Damn child" she was grinding me up. I laughed "we are okay mom but we are just friends." I tried to explain in between bites "I know that's what your mouth say, but who are you fooling?" Mom was on the money. "Well if we did make this an official relationship you will be the first to know. You know how I am with these girls I can't stay focused on one for too long." If I didn't like you there was a good probability that you wouldn't be around for too long. Ms. Cathy knew it was the truth and I knew better than to bring them around to her. I had all types of woman calling this house. "Boy you don't got to tell me I know you a little player." Ms. Cathy didn't like that, this is how I was. She always told me that it would bite me in the ass if I didn't cut it out. Being a hardheaded mother fucker I didn't listen too often. I always thought if it happened, it would and I couldn't stop it no matter what.

"Be careful with this one manual if you don't watch yourself. You could easily become a victim in her world." Mom warned me about Felicia. "Why do you say that?" I asked. "I see how you are with all the woman and I would never wish bad on you, but whenever this girl is brought up in a conversation your body language tells it all son. This girl has a hold on you that's all I'm saying." Mom's words were pounding me hard because she was right. It's one thing to think something about yourself but we can't really observe our own body language at times. It's true is was a dead giveaway. I made sure to put all those thoughts in the frontal lobes of my mind and not to get all wrapped up with Felicia. It wasn't a good time to get involved. I'm glad I didn't have sex with her yet. The other part of me already had her undressed, moist and wet in my mind bent over taking me all in her. Yea, I know the mind was a terrible thing to waist and im a freak.

"I'm glad you're taking my advice or at least I hope you are." Mom snap me out of my daze. "It doesn't feel too good to be hurt by someone you care about." "That's all I'm saying, clean your dish I'm taking a nap." Mom walked out of the kitchen leaving me to marinate on all that what was thrown at me. I locked up the house and set the alarm.

—

The day was as bright as fuck, the sun was gleaming. You could hear the laughter and the yells from all the elementary school kids down the street. There innocence roared through the air as they played. I passed by them all. I could see all kids enjoying their time during early recess, getting some exercise and blood circulating through their bodies. Some play kickball, I loved that game when I was a lot smaller. Others play hopscotch, jump rope, playing catch or the infamous game of "tag" while others just stood and talk to their friends. I wondered what they spoke about, probably cartoons or toys who knew. I took the long way to any bus stop, I had options and time to waste. I ended up taking Steven St, just to stretch my legs some. "weed out, weed out" a young boy shouted informing everyone that he had that ganja. "I'm good." I replied and kept it moving. About half a block down you could hear "5-0, 5-0" by the lookouts. To no surprise, they were right. The jump outs were surrounding a house. It look like a rade or just a regular jump out. The jump outs never needed a warrant. They did what they wanted or at least that's what they thought. Most cases got thrown out due to the search and seizure warrant not being used. For the most part all they wanted was the guns and money. They were protecting and serving right?.... Wrong! Not here, they would be searching and seizing the opportunity to take what they wanted from you. Especially, if you was part of an illegal organization or even just someone who didn't know how to be under the radar. Leaving you with the drugs so you could keep on pumping. Don't worry they would come back and flip your pockets again. Then you would wonder why cops were being attacked or even killed left and right. You would think that with all that bogus shit to serve and protect, they would actually do what was needed from them when needed right? Wrong again! That badge and automatic handgune went straight to their head and caused them to act like the criminals. Instead of behaving and following what their job description and oath was intended to stand for. It's gotten so bad that the jump outs would extort so many who sold on the strips. I mean money making strips. I'm not going to get into detail where the strips are located but if you know how to read just grab the Courier Post one day and enjoy it. I ended up at the bus stop where Popeye's used to be. Right across Cousin supermarket by the time the Broadway bus made it's way towards me. I still had about 40 minutes left to burn. I just waited patiently. I watched the junkies dig into the trash cans and in the process just looking for a quick buck and suck. This was my city and I was proud to have grown up in the city no matter how bad or rough many would say it has gotten. Like they say, only the strong survive. Yeah I know so cliché but it's the fuckin truth.

Once on board the bus I made a quick look towards the back before I paid for a one way trip. No matter what bus you got on boardm, they all smelled like straight fucking piss. It wasn't the best thing to ride but it was cheap and gas efficient since I didn't have a car at the moment. As I made my way to my seat I saw a very familiar face. I didn't notice but her stare gave her away. I wanted to be rude and just act like I didn't see or notice her but I thought against it. This was my opportunity to talk to her and she was alone in her tiny uniform shirt. It just so happened that she was on the same bus, she had to be heading my way as well. Duh... She look fly, her long black hair was pinned up on the right side. She was wearing some head phones, listening to music bopping to the tunes in her ear. I wondered what she was listening too. There was a seat across from her and one right next to her. I went for the one right beside her. There was no way I was letting this opportunity slip my fingers, nope not today. By then she had her eyes locked with mine. I was waiting for her to say something smart and I wish she did.

"All them open seats and you have to sit next to me." She was feisty and I loved it. She spoke with a sly smile. I went to get up and sit somewhere else. I knew she was writing the check she didn't want to see get cash. I began to move. She grabbed my arm. "I'm playing." Jacqueline joked. "you aint got to tell me twice if I'm not wanted I'll go sit elsewhere." I countered. "I see that." She replied. "No stay here." She pled. "Off to work I see." I asked pointing to her logo on her shirt. "Yeah all week." How about you?" She asked "I'm headed to work myself." I replied. "You smell a little too good to be headed to work." She spoke as the bus made another stop picking up and dropping off people to their destinations. Jacqueline and I enjoyed our light conversation. "Well I just signed out of school. I went home to change clothes and left." Is not like I put on cologne to work even though it might be a good idea because I see you notice." I stated with a smile. She returned the smile. Jacqueline was very attractive small and cute. Her voice was soft but the way she carried herself I sensed that she had or may have had a complicated lifestyle. I could be wrong though.

"You're a senior?" Jacqueline asked. "Yes I am." I have six months left to graduate and I can't wait." I informed her. "That's nice." She replied "how about you ma?" You finished school already or what?" I asked. "Or what?" She replied with smile she had a sense of humor. "I dropped out my junior year I wanted to finish but it got real hard for me." She put her head down as if she was disappointed in her past decisions. "Is not the end of the world ma." I put my left hand under her chin getting her to raise her head. "Keep that head up, there's no need to look down." She forced a smile. "I know you're right but with my son growing up so fast he is so small and needs so much. I don't have any time to worry about what I got to do for myself. I just let the thought of going back to school go." She let go, and just spilled her guts out. I never understood why? Women always ended up opening up to me so freely and quickly. "So you gave up on yourself?" I asked her.

"You can say that, it's not about me anymore." Do you have any children?" Jacqueline asked me. "No I do not" I replied. "So you have no idea what it is to feel like you have to give your all too another person and wished this person will turned out to be a great person as your only intention is." She spoke with an abundance of joy about her son. I knew what she was saying. "You are right I may not know how hard it may be but what I do know is that if you truly want to better your situation, it could be done whether you have six or 12 kids. It's all on the individual if he or she really wants to make a difference in the child's life and his or her life." I pause for a second "I'm not saying that it's a walk to the park but nothing is meant to be easy especially if it's for one's benefit you know?" I stated starring at her deeply in her eyes expressing to her the truth and that no matter your living situation the sky is the limit. She payed close attention to my every word. Her lips look soft and moist. I wanted to grab her and give her a kiss but I knew damn well that I wouldn't dare to move in for a kiss. This girl had too much on her mind to be dealing with more bull shit on her plate. I decided to play my position and lend an ear and listen, and a shoulder to lean on. I could tell that my few words had hit her like a ton of bricks. I may be only 18 years old but I've been through my share of problems and obstacles that I failed miserably on many occasions. I've learned how to get up and dust myself off and try again. It felt good to have that extra push from someone or anyone who was willing to pass on some knowledge when you needed it the most. Today, I was the one passing it on to her because somewhere down the line it was shared to me Now she had to hear it. After two more bus stops the bus was stationing in the terminal.

"So what time you have to be in to work?" I asked her. "Now I'm a couple minutes late." She replied "wow I'll walk you to your job if it's okay with you?" I asked but stating actually "that's cool, what's your name again?" Jacqueline asked "Manuel but a lot of people call me Rock" I informed her "Rock?!" She asked. "Yes Rock" I'll explain that another day." I replied as we exited the terminal walking side-by-side. I towered her by almost a foot and a half she would look up at me to talk to me it was just how I liked it. We strolled towards her job, passing right by the sub shop. Broadway was always busy, everyone was always looking to spend money and looking for the best bargains. Jacqueline had a nice round butt she caught me looking at her she smiled while talking shit.

"You need to keep your eyes up front." She joked. "You right." I replied only a few feet away from her job. I gave her a quick hug and a kiss on the cheek. "Remember what I told you think about it when you can." I stated "I will. I'll see you on my break." She replied entering her job.

I spun heading to the sub shop I heard a loud plop, plop, plop. I wasn't sure what it was until I seen the older Buick with two flats plopping down the street. Whoever owned that car had to be pist having two flat tires. I could only imagine being pist with one but having two. It was already 12 PM. The shop had a few customers and the guys were handling everything smoothly as they been doing for years. Yesterday, I hit the floors hard and cleaned the fans. The floor actually look like a floor and the air inside was circulating in the room freshly.

"Rock!" Yelled Pete did your V.P give you a hard time?" He yelled as all the customers kept their eyes on me as I made my way over towards the back of the counter. "No he didn't he had no choice but to approve it Pete. It was legit you know?" I put on my apron and washed my hands and put on my gloves. "Go take the next order." Pete ordered as he fell back and disappeared to his office. "What up Jamal." I greeted my coworker while attending the next customer. "you already know play'a, taking care business early." It's been a pretty busy morning and is about to get even busier this afternoon." He spoke while chopping up the stakes and doing what he did the best. "Let's get it, I got you." I informed him. Customers came in and out. We actually had a few who stayed in and ate. Jamal crept up on me and told me it's been years since I see someone sit down and eat their food in the dining area." "That your work Rock." He informed me "my work?" I laughed and gestured "it's the food Jamal I aint got anything to do with that." I replied seriously. "nah it's the cleanliness that you brought up in here and yea the food has a lot to do with it, but that plays a major part as well, plus we been using the seasoning you put on." He joked.

—

As the rush slowed down I decided to take advantage and hit up these walls and windows that needed a Jenny Craig makeover, yes it was that bad.

"Ay Rock!" Yelled Pete "why you always got to yell Pete?" I asked. "that's how I talk , it's nothimg personal." We need some more of that orange shit you brought the other day." He was referring to the Sazon he handed me two $20 bills. "Spend it on that." Pete said the seasoning was on all the food by now a little here and there. "It's called /Sazon/" I tried to break it down for him. "Yeah whatever, yeah that shit." I took off my apron and headed over to where little Ms. Jacqueline worked. By the time I got there I noticed her across the street with some dude leaning on a Lincoln town car, it was blue and it has some nice 22's on it. It had no tires , They looked like rubber bands around the rim instead of tires. Homeboy was fresh looking like your typical drug dealer with his husky chain on. His gear was on point. The car could've been a dead giveaway. Yea, I am stereotyping like a motha but at the end of the day it is what it is. It don't take a dummy to put two and two together. I kept on as if I didn't notice anything and bought what I needed like I had planned to. I was not really in a rush to get back so I was gona try to catch a few sentences were her. After I paid for all the boxes and bought one big bottle of adobo. I ended up only spending $24.75 than I remembered Pete said to use it all. I made my way to head out the door and bumped into my teeny meanie.

"Hey you.... When you get here I didn't even notice you." She asked. "Had to get a few things I saw you though." Let her know I saw her with her man or whoever that was. "Did you?" She asked. "yes I did." I replied. "That was my baby dad." She confessed automatically as if I was pressing her. "You don't have to explain who you was with ma, that your business not mine. I gotta go. I'll see you around though." I spun and headed to the shop. I figured she was involved with someone but I didn't want to see it for myself. I wanted to slide up in shorty, but we'll see how this one would pan out.

"You got some change man?" A homeless man asked as I headed back to where I was suppose to be. I gave him the change I had in my pocket and kept it moving. Keeping up with all the masses of the people heading in every direction cause to get whiplash. Broadway alone had more than 100 different shops. I counted out six to the value plus from the sub shop were little teeny mini was working at.

Finally back in the shop I handed the changeover to Pete he quickly tossed it back into the register not even counting it.

"You aint going to count it?" I asked "why, Should I?" He asked "do you. Count if you want it's all there nobody stealing from you." I shot back. I looked over at Jamal "What's good Jamal?" I sparked light conversation with him as I put away the seasoning. "My baby mama and I are going through some crazy shit right now." Jamal spoke loud enough for everyone to hear what he was saying not intentionally. He was getting all worked up as he spoke. Woman had a tendency to do that, no matter the age or nationality. "So what did you do that your baby mama tripping bro?" I asked so he could vent. What ever I could do to help him out I would . Without hesitation. "Damn it sound like you on her side already." Jamal joked. "Nah a couple months ago I slid off and had some fun with this shorty I had met" The look on my face spoke for itself 'Are you serious'? Look, before you go in on me let me explain real quickly. My baby moms and I had a big argument over some cash she wanted to go and get her nails and feet done. Mind you I had to pay the car note too. I told her she had to wait till next week." "Jamal went on to explain!" Pete yelled interrupting his story. "Two cheesesteaks and a dozen wings." I immediately went for the wings assisting Jamal. He went on to explain to me but not before letting Pete know "coming right up!" We worked, well together I thought. "She wasn't trying to hear that because I have her and my son spoiled like two rich brats." He joked. "So this little bitch got the nerve to accuse me of cheating and that I must have another chick on the side. She didn't stop at that, she went on to say that she must be using up all my money." Mine you I haven't cheated on my wifey in over 10 years. She know all I do is work damn every day all day. Where would I find time to mingle with these chicken heads out here? Rock those days are done for me." Jamal plead his caseb all while wrapping up the sandwich once it was done. I had already drained out the wings. "any sauces?" I asked the customer. "yes please, blue cheese." Replied the light skin man out front with a light blue polo. "Order up!" I handed him his order and Jamal went right back to his little dilemma. "You two got this up here I see." Pete stated walking right by. The store was empty now. "So she think you to creeping huh?" I asked grabbing a rag to hit the walls and windows, Jamal followed suit. He went in. "That night I was so pissed I went to a bar up the street from our crib. One I normally go with her every now and then to shoot pool. I went alone that day. It was late as hell and this fly little mami came all up in their dolow, no friends or no man. I was already tipsy off my henny and coke. It was about to be my ninth one so yeah I was a bit blasted. Mind you now I'm spending my money from the car note. This is how pissed off I was. So no car note paid or any nails done for my baby mama." Mami had me wide open, he let out a laughed "I know it's crazy but it gets better." He informed me. This Nigga was digging the hole deeper and deeper as he drank. "So little Shorty turned out she was from Philly right across the bridge. She was looking for a good time, by that time all I wanted to do was forget about everything. I could care less about anyone or anything in that moment. You don't know how that shit feels to be the bread winner for my family and I get treated like shit, hell no!" Jamal really was feeling some type of way. "So Shorty and I jumped in my car. I took her to the Campbell Soup parking lot and pounded her brains out so bad that she bled all over my seats in my car." I couldn't believe what I was hearing. As we were cleaning up the dingy ass walls he kept on telling me how he had this chick screaming and crying his name in the car. "You would of though I was raping or killing this woman." He said. I was bugging. "So you drove Shorty home?" I asked "Yup all the way to the Badlands. She invited me inside and we went at it again. I didn't leave her spot till the middle of the night. "He confessed. I shook my head in disbelief he was in a serious relationship with his BMs and one big argument led to all of this. "So what she got to do with all this?" I asked him, he gave me this dumbfounded looked "Are you serious Rock?" Jamal asked me laughing. "This bitch got my number and called me and spoke to my BMs and told her everything!" My mouth hit the floor. I was speechless, that was some slimy shit. "Wooowww!!!" Was all I mustered to say. "Yea wow is correct." So my BMs don't want to give me no pussy and she swear up and down I'm cheating on her every day now my nigga." Jamal caught his breath I took the opportunity to ask a few questions but was interrupted by these two couples that came inside the shop to order some food cutting him off for second.

"How are you doing can I take your order?" I asked. It was two black males around 20 to 25 with a white girl and a Spanish girl. The girls looked like trash and I wasn't even into trashy chicks. "Yea give us some time." The caucasian girl spoke letting me know, "Just let me know when you're ready." The nigga with the scruffy hair on his face was hawking me as if I owed him some money. I didn't pay him no mind but Jamal noticed it. "A Rock you know homeboy?" Nah, I don't I know he sizing me up. I aint sweating him though." He looked high as hell anyway." We burst out laughing. "You already know." Jamal stated "I'll tell you the rest in a bit." I made my way back to the counter I looked at all four of them. They had on neat clothing with dingy ass kicks.

"Ayo what the fuck you looking at!?" Barked the scruffy face ass nigga. "You see something you like?!" He asked me more like yelling. This shit caught me off guard a bit. I kept my cool I was at work. The last thing I need to do is to fuck somebody up because they can't control they mouth. "Nah not at all I'm just waiting for your order." I spoke in a cordial tone. "That's what I thought!" Scruffy barked back. His little girlfriend was trying to get him to calm down. "baby chill he aint even saying anything to you, you bugging." Little Miss Thing was right. She tried but Mr. Scruffy was writing a check that was about to get bounced back by me. I always learn how to avoid a confrontation, but sometimes confrontation had to be handled the way it was supposed to be handled. Which ment to get physical, and this was always the way I tried not to engage in any altercation. Even though I was due for a nice ass whopping and I was ready. I learned a long time ago win, lose or draw was my motto. Mr. Scruffy was still eyeballing me. To make this a bit more interesting his buddy with the receding hairline decided it was a good idea to throw some more gasoline on a fire that was already simmering.

"I'm... I'm saying if you got a problem than pop off!" Mr. Stutters stated stuttering. I laughed I couldn't help it this illiterate mother fucka had a speech impairment. "Listen you going to order or what?!" That was Jamal making his way up to the counter. He already was in a bad mood. He wasn't going to let this episode go on once he noticed that they weren't going to calm down.

"Man who the fuck you think you talking to just make my food and fall the fuck back!" Barked scruffy. The two females didn't know what to do or say anything. They just stood by the soda machine watching shaking their heads. "I would if you would stop running your fucking mouth and place your order first you stupid mother fucker, matta fact! Get the fuck out, y'all aint getting shit now!" Jamal barked mad now. I was too but I wasn't going to bicker back and forth with these two bitch ass niggas. "You... You... Gon... gona make our food because we hungry as shit." Mr. Stutter tried to chime in. By then Pete was already heading out to where all the commotion was coming from... I was just glad that it was just us in the store.

"Hey! What is going on here?" Pete was loud but his raspy loud ass voice got even louder. It was as if he had a megaphone. "It's your workers!" Yelled scruffy McGruff. "What about my workers?" Pete asked. "They not tryna to take our order." He informed Pete. The look Pete gave us wasn't one that gave us the impression that he believed what the customers were stating. He was the owner and he knew what he had to do. "I'm a take your order?" What can I get you?" Pete grabbed the note pad and began to jot down what they wanted to eat. It took them about 10 minutes, talk about being intoxicated. Once the order was fianlly taken Jamal and I prepared it. I made a mental note of Mr. Scruffy and Mr. Stutters just in case we were ever to cross paths again.

"Hey go outside and smoke that!" Pete Barked smelling the cigarette the Spanish girl lit up. I could feel Scruffy hawking my every move but if he wanted it he knew where I was at. I dismissed all that bitchassness. We fixed there order im not gonna lie i wanted to piss on that shit but knew better .They paid and were handed the bag of food and dismissed. Pete was the first one to start up the grind up session. "Now why? Would you two engage into a verbal dispute with two individuals who are highly intoxicated?" Which one of you can answer that for me please?" He asked. "Pete I tried to talk to that mother fucker with some humbleness but it wasn't happening he was arguing with himself in his own mind." I tried to defend our case "my point is how you can defuse the situation before it gets out of hand?" Pete asked. I got where he was going with this he wanted to teach how to turn a confrontation into a transaction gone bad and make it go good. I decided to learn instead of trying to defend our case. "I was about to whip his ass Pete you already know me." Jamal spoke truthfully. "I know this but we can't beat on all our customers that get disrespectful. I wanted to bash in a couple of faces in to but I can't unless it gets to that point. When you are running a successful business you can't be known for beating up your customers Jamal." He joked with us but spoke with all seriousness at the same time. We laughed ."You always give the customer the power not because he's right but because once he orders his food and pays he's gone." Pete was absolutely right, once the orders were taken and pay for they would leave within seconds or even minutes. "I knew that you two didn't start altercation not because I heard it, just because this is how a business goes. It's our job to show them disrespectful mother fuckers they will not provoke us or pull us down to their level. Jamal and I listened and nodded our heads attentively. "You want to fight do it on your own time or just come to the back and you can duke it out with me for a while." He joked "you can't handle this." Jamal joked back "Your Holyfield days are over." I threw in the air. "Oh yea don't sleep on the old man." He joked back heading to the back. Jamal looked at me

"You wanted to hit him I saw it, don't lie?" He smiled while he said those words. "I was a bit mad but nah I didn't want to hit him." I had a wide grin when I replied to his question. "Man you can lie to yourself but I wish I had a camera so you could have seen your whole facial expression." Jamal was enjoying this and I notice it immediately. "So let me ask you this Jamal?" "Sup?" He replied. Have you had to actually physically fight a customer before?" I asked already putting it together what Pete had let out earlier.

"Twice" Jamal answered holding up his two fingers. "So you just go right on and do beat up all the customers huh?" I stated, now it was my turn to throw some sauce. "Man Rock you just have no idea these mother fuckers be here all intoxicated getting real disrespectful towards a nigga, and we both from the city so that shit don't fly no matter where we at right?" He spoke with all honesty "I hear you." I replied. "Well Pete knows of the 1 knock out right out front. I wouldn't disrespect the shop by stretching someone out in the dining area nah that aint me, but don't get it twisted Rock if it goes down then hey it happens. The other altercation that happened, old boy who was talking out the side of his neck was asked to meet me in the back alley. Pete was fixing something on the grill but I slid out back and we got it in for a few minutes. He tagged me a couple times but no more after that I put him out too." Jamal was in his fighting stance going in with the details of his fair share of fights at work due to dealing with the average tough guy complex when they get a little alcohol in they system. I listened. "Yea it can get crazy so I already know what to expect." I said. "You already tried like Pete said. You tried to defuse the bomb before it detonated like you did earlier with them to nut ass smokers. You did the right thing. I was observing but once I seen your face go from humbug to this nigga don't know, That's when I had to interject because if it's me. Pete won't throw me out because he already knows that I try to keep the peace first. When push comes to shove its yard out. He knows this from my past encounters. Hold up don't think for one second that our boss is a saint. I had to hold him back from pounding out some guys, who came up in here on some give me some money type shit. Pete is a fair man but once you pass that disrespectful shit he can go from 0 to 60 in a heartbeat, like I was watching you about to go." He joked the door swung open and stopped us both in our conversation, we both locked eyes on the two customers who just walked in.

"Damn! What are yall looking at?" Jacqueline sweet sexy self-spoke in her soft voice. Jamal gave me the nod as to handle that." My bad ladies but when two gorgeous women walk up and here it can be a bit of a good distraction." I eased up to the counter spitting that shit. The girlfriend she was with also had on a value plus shirt on. She was a couple shades darker than Jacqueline but she was much thicker, not fat but had more weight on her. She was a bit taller not by much. Her friend put her head down and smiled. I took it she was a bit shy. She had full lips and a nose ring. Her hair was in micro braids. I also liked that look on my females. I peeked down at her feet and saw that she wore crisp up towns, white at that. I could see Jacqueline watched me watch her friend. So I redirected my attention back to her sexy self.

"What's up how can I help you?" I ask lightening up the mood. "I'll take the regular Jamal." She looked at Jamal. I wrote down a regular on the memo pad. "What about for your pretty friend? The one you didn't even introduce her to us?" Jamal said. "That's rude." he finished off. I laughed. "Her name is "Kia" and I'm not sure what she want. That's Jamal he is my pain in my butt." she informed Kia while pointing over to Jamal and you already know who that is" she said referred to me. Jamal came over and extended his hand taking off his glove to shake her hand.

"Hi how are you doing it's a pleasure to meet such a fine woman as yourself." Jamal flirted a bit. "Nice to meet you too and thank you, you're not bad looking yourself." Kia gave him some play I observe how they both handled themselves. Kia had to be about 27 because she looked a bit older than Jacqueline. While they got acquainted I slid over to little mamas.

"So how's your day at work going?" I asked her "its okay I mean my feet hurt but I'm alright." She spoke. I was lost in another thought on how she told her friend that she already knew who I was when we clearly never even met. I knew that she must have told her about me prior to coming into the shop, I found it a bit awkward how woman made their own reservations. when it came to a thing / people they didn't want the next person to become attracted to or want. It was all good with me but damn did she forget I saw her earlier with her baby dads? I didn't have time for drama and trust and believe I was not fallen into no one's trap.

"Are you listening to me?" She snapped. "I am so tell me?" She asked. I had no clue what she wanted me to tell her so I took it in another direction. "Tell you what? How beautiful you are or do you want to know what I want to do to you?" I spoke to her almost in a whisper. She put her hand up to her mouth "Oh My God you're so crazy Rock" Jacqueline was shocked at my answer. It never fails. I went on to help Jamal with their order and try to find out as much as I could about her friend, not for myself. Just to check if Jamal was waist deep or just on some flirtation mode. "What you need?" I asked. "nothing I got it already but you can cut open the 6 inch roll." Jamal had it all on lock.

"So was up with Kia?" I asked being nosy as hell. "Well she is 32 and she has two kids and is a single mom." I looked at him and smiled "damn nigga you don't waste no time do you?" I joked. "why would I? I might not see her again unless she wants to." He was cheesing from ear to ear. I could have sworn that we just had the ultimate conversation about how bad things were at his house but hey I guess he didn't care. That shit gets boring I bet. "Can you hook it up with some extra packets of ketchup in the bag please?" Jacqueline asked.

"So what's up you going to get her number or what?" I asked "I'm not sure Rock you already know I'm on thin ice at home." Jamal was thinking with his head and not the small one. "You right my nigga." I applauded him for his loyalty towards his wife. Me on the other hand I jotted down my house number, folded it up so I could hand it to little Miss teeny meanie. She and her girl-friend spoke to each other and I could tell she wasn't even paying attention.

Two more customers walked in. A much older couple I took their orders and told them that their orders will be up shortly to take a seat. I handed them there fountain cups.

"Oh thank you darling. The older lady with the gray said with her husband of many years. He held her hand. I noticed Jacqueline and Kia admiring the older couple. He helped her with everything his wife needed. "He is such a gentleman ma'am." Kia spoke to the couple "Oh dear they get like this after they're done with all their headaches and games." The older lady smiled as she spoke the truth. "Either way I wouldn't change him for the world." She spoke very appreciative about her long lover. "I would change her in a heartbeat." The elder man Joked back. Jamal slapped my shoulder "Old head is a fucking G." Jamal stated. I must admit I too admire their loving nature of how they express themselves so freely towards one another joking. The girls were in love with their relationship and I'm sure they wish they could find their soul mate to grow old and die in each other's arms. The ladies left the couple alone and got back to us walking back up to the counter

"Oh my God they're so cute you see them?" Jacqueline asked "Yeah I see, now that some true love and loyalty. Just imagine how many arguments they done had in their lifetime." I stated. "Yeah but it was all well worth it because they are together and still madly in love with one another." She spoke I handed her the food with my number. "See yall around" Jamal stated "maybe sooner." Kia winked at him. After a while the food for the elders was ready so I decided to bring it to them. "Oh thank you darling, you didn't have to that's what he's for." She smiled referring to her husband. The older man handed me two quarters and held my hand "that's for you son" he spoke and in a flash they were gone. That was my first tip and it was a priceless one. I could only imagine how much knowledge these two had in their memory bank. "He tipped you?" Jamal asked "yup". I replied "you want half." I asked Jamal. "nah that's all you My G." Jamal replied. He laughed as we exchanged words. I took it as he already knew the old man and have once given him a tip before.I will hold onto those two quarters for as long as I could. I have my reasons. The day was finally coming to an end and it's been a good day. Wrapping up the night who would've thought it had come to this. Just when you think all is done and settled in complete it never really is.

I decided to give Felicia a ring."Hello?" She answered. "was sup?" I spoke into the receiver. The shop was all cleaned up and it had made a great improvement since I started. I was not taken any credit but the atmosphere felt a lot more welcoming. "Damn handsome I thought you forgot all about me." Felicia said over the phone. "Nah just been a bit busy that's all how are you?" I asked. "I'm okay thank you for asking." She replied. "and your princess how is she?" I asked. "She is great sleeping at the moment." "You at work?" Felicia asked. "Im just getting off about the jump on the bus." I answered her. "No you're not, I'll be there in 10 to 15 minutes." She hung up just as quickly as she finished her last word so I couldn't protest. Jamal and Pete were up front looking out the window and talking about who knows what. "Pete is there anything you need me to do before I wrap this up?" I asked "Yes check the back door, I think it's locked." He directed. I shot straight to the back and the old man was right it wasn't open but the deadbolt wasn't secure, I secured it. I made my way back to where the rest of the guys were sitting. "Well gentlemen it was a great day and remember what I said to the two of you today." Pete stated exited by the side door. I had a bag with a 12 foot sub and some wings that was ordered and never picked up. Jamal had a 2Liter of Pepsi in his arm. "We got you boss, vow down to customers while we work." Jamal joked "that's right at work!" We all shook hands and watched Pete disappear in the dark.

"You need a ride" Jamal asked me "nah Shorty coming to scoop me." I replied "okay, okay, playa, playa." Jamal joked. "Not even close." I defended myself from the assassination of character remark. "I am going to wait until she gets here." Jamal was a goodhearted man I notice he put the soda down and began to talk about how he and his girlfriend were going through it again, but the conversation changed courses as soon as he remembered Kia.

"Ayo Rock whenever you talk to Jacqueline ask her about her friend so we can do the double date thing." I listened as he spoke with a smile, it was dark and we were in the alley so it was hard to see him. His pearly white teeth gave away his big smile. "Don't look at me like that. I aint trying to fuck it's just a night out with them nothing more or less." He tried to sound very convincing , knowing damn well I knew if the opportunity presented itself he would be all up in them guts because she look fine. We joked for a bit, but the sound of glass cracking under footsteps brought us back to our awareness. We were a bit vulnerable at the moment. I had to set the bag down freeing my hands just in case. I left my right one in my pocket. Jamal noticed my move and put his back to the wall. Their was a shadow coming closer and closer, my heart beat began to rise a bit faster than normal my hands were lose.

"You... You... Th... Thought we wasn't going to come back? "We already knew exactly who that was. His man didn't have to utter a word because I knew he had to be with himj too. The attention was focused on me I'm guessing they didn't notice Jamal paved on the wall with his black ass. It was good because he actually had all their focus on the light-skinned mother fucker who happened to be me once again. The only thing running through my mind was they holding or not. I guess I was about to find out. Mr. Stutter was on my right and Scruffy was on his left. They still were a good 10 feet away. The hairs on my neck rose and my heart rate began to accelerate as they got closer. I tried to envision my attack quickly because the gap between us got closer and closer. I could only see two out of the four. My focus was all on myself now.

"You look scared you bitch ass nigga." Scruffy Barked still 4 feet away and gaining. I didn't say shit I waited till he was up close, so I could show him how scared I really was according to him. 2 feet.... 1 feet.... My right hook exploded landing perfectly on his glass chin but my left went straight to his boy. Jamal was all over scruffy as we exchange punches with stutters. He managed to split my lip open, I could taste the blood in my mouth. It was a taste I knew to well. He pulled out a knife noticing his punches were not slowing me down at all. I pulled out my butterfly and all eyes were on it as a floating open. Stutter's eyes were wide open. "It was wrong if yall thought shit was going to be sweet?" I Barked. He was backing away as I stepped forward quickly. Scruffy managed to get Jamal on the ground, Jamal was a bit older and a lot bigger so he tended to get a little fatigue as he fought back. Stutters looked back. "get him man fuck that puss...!" The back of my butterfly caught him right above his eyebrow splitting it open immediately, not the sharp end but the back end. The blood gushed out blinding his eye sight. He fucked up and dropped the knife and I picked it up in a quick lunging motion. A stomach blow sent him scurrying away. I diverted all my attention to Scruffy. My heart rate was thundering as I jumped on him, it gave Jamal some time to catch his breath and regroup himself. Two jabs to his mouth had him pissed. I put the butterfly away because I didn't feel I needed it with this clown ass nigga. He swung and caught me in the back of my ear. I must admit that blow threw me off a little bit. That sharp blow infuriated me even more. His next shot was countered by my left and I gave him a nice combination to his stomach and face. I punched the wind right out of him. The smell of liquor and PCP smacked me in the face hard. "Let me finish him Jamal Pled. I step back given Jamal the opportunity to claim his win. I looked down the alley to see if I could see his boy Stutters, lurking in the midst of the darkness trying to sneak up on us again . That piece of shit was nowhere in sight. Jamal took out all his anger and aggression on this man. I noticed the Lexus drive by you would think all of this was taking forever but in all actuality it had to been only a few minutes that wisp by.

"Fuck this nigga!" Yelled Jamal still beating the shit out and Scruffy face. His face had blood all over it. Come to think of it all of us were smothered in blood. I grabbed Jamal and pulled him away from scruffy which wasn't an easy task? "Don't let me see you come back into the shop or yall both dead!" Barked

Jamal. I figured we should've killed them if he was going to threaten them but fuck it, it was time to go.

"Your soda" I reminded Jamal. Scruffy was out cold on the floor. Jamal ran to his car and I ran over to the Lexus. I'd see him tomorrow. We both were okay and alive that's all that mattered to me in that moment. I jumped in the car.

"Let's go get out of here." I spoke out of breath. "Oh my God! What happened to you? are you ok?!" Felicia asked worried. "Just drive please I tell you in a bit." I barked not really meaning to, we sat in silence for a while. My mind was all over the place.

"I'm sorry for yelling at you." I wasn't in the right state of mind at the moment I apologize." I tried to diffuse the situation, she had no part of. "It's okay are you okay?" Do you want to go to the hospital?" She asked again. "No I'm good why would I need to go to the hospital when I got you?" She blushed with that remark. "Ima take you to my house and fix you up right quick, then I'll drop you off at your house, how's that?" She asked "sounds good since I don't want to go home right away anyway." I said. Too many questions to answer once she seen my swollen lip. Questions that I didn't want to answer, were soon to come crashing down but I guess I'd rather they be asked by Felicia at the moment than anyone else. I'll deal with Linda and mom later. We drove until we hit the outskirts of the city.

We reached Felicia's small apartment that was on the second floor. It was nice actually it was clean and it was quiet. I noticed a silhouette in the living room..

"That's my roommate she pointed over to the person on the couch. In a quick blink of an eye the silhouette got up and left. "Sit down." She instructed. I sat on the chair in the dining room. The table was glass with a glass fruit bowl in the middle of it. White table mats laid on the table for each chair. She came back with alcohol , peroxide and gauzes. This girl was prepared. "What you going to do surgery?" I joked asking her "Oh god no I'm not a doctor." She replied. She patched me up for a few minutes,than planted a big wet kiss on my lips. Her moist lips took my mind off of the pain for a few moments. She straddled me on the chair with a kiss on my neck. My hands on her ass were gripping on for dear life, it was soft and round. I managed to slip into the waistline of her pants to get a more accurate feel of how soft it really was. She didn't stop me she continued to nibble on my neck and ears which was a no no. That was my spot, my erection got bigger, she could feel the blood flowing. She began to grind on it while kissing me. She felt it and kept grinding on it,she moaned ever so lightly. My hands made their way to her breasts, which are round and soft as well. I expoosed one and plopped one into my mouth biting the aerial softly, she purred like a kitten. I couldn't take it anymore I stood up picking her up.

"Whoa!" She wrapped her arms around my neck tightly. I walked over to the sofa and sat back down as we were on the chair. This time she slid in between my legs tugging all my belt and jeans until she found what she was looking for. She pulled out my little man's which was far from little but I loved to refer to it as my little man's. She put it in her mouth. I kick my boots off because I was not going to pass this up tonight. She jerked and sucked softly but with a firm grip on my penis, my eyes rolled back so I just grabbed her hair and let her do what she wanted. She licked my balls while stroking my manhood... I was in ecstasy and I didn't want it to end. I grabbed her breasts and she moan at every touch. She was wet as hell I was 100% sure of it and couldn't wait to feel it all. I wanted to taste that pussy in my mouth already. She tried to deep throat me but it led to a gag. It was too long but I gave it to her she tried it was good enough in my book. 10 and a half inches wasn't an easy task. I unloaded inside of her mouth hard. She looked at me as every drop went straight down her pipe. It was my turn I stripped her off her clothing and wrapped her legs around my head. I let my tongue take her to ecstasy. Her pussy was swollen and well kept up with, is smelled like a mixture of fruit and I was determined to identify every last one. I gently licked her click as she grabbed the back of my head moaning. By now I knew she didn't care that her roommate heard her. I licked and sucked nibbling on her from time to time. Her thighs trembled tremendously as she climaxed. I swallowed all of that juicy nectar that came from her insides. Her back arched from the sofa as I commence to perform my tongue dance and routine on her. She couldn't take it anymore so she pulled me up so I could enter her. I met her face to face and I teased her by putting in my head of my lil man's just so it touched her lips of her vagina. She tried to scoot down but I kept my charade up.

"Stop I want you to give it to me!" She barked. I had her exactly where I wanted her begging for it. I reached down to my jeans and pulled out a condom.

She snatched it out of my hand "you playing." she opened it up horny ass fuck and slid it on in the matter of seconds. She wasn't joking when she said she wanted it. She gripped up my dick and made sure it was headed into her cave. I slid it in slowly, her cries didn't go unnoticed as I went in inch by inch. Her deep breath was something she couldn't hold back. I'll say about six was already vanished inside of her. Her hands grabbed my waistline as if she couldn't let me go in anymore. I respected that because I was into hurting woman my mission was to satisfy and please her. I kept it at six and some and stroked slowly at a nice rhythm, she came again. I watched my dick go in and out on every stroke. Her breasts were nice. I search for stretch marks but didn't detect any. Her nipples were light brown and were erected fully. I sucked and bit on them as if I could get a couple milk out of them. Nothing. "I want to ride it." Was all she said jumping on top as we turn positions and she tried to ride it and I knew she wasn't going to take it all in? I hardly knew anyone that coul. Unless, Shorty was wide open and hollow inside. she would be a trooper for real. I finished her off with doggy style and busted all up in that condom. She dropped down naked and satisfied as I did the same. I was impressed with her performance I love the woman who could take charge and show some dominance it was a major turn on.

—

After getting dressed we headed back over to my place where we parted ways. I told her the whole situation of all the events that occurred tonight with us and that fight. We agreed on a friendship unless we both agreed on taken things a bit further.

The block was jumping with sales and a couple of bodies around doing their own thing. You could hear some arguing and could only imagine over what?

I entered the house locked it up and set the alarm.

I headed straight to the kitchen it was almost midnight. The piece of paper on the microwave read: The plate inside is yours. I press start and tore the food up like I was a starving hostage. My lip was still sore and my only thought was on how bad the other two faces had to be on the two who tried to get out on us earlier. There face must feel a lot worst. I showered up and passed out along with everyone else who was in the house.

Chapter 5
"Take a hit"

After hearing everything that was said by Linda and mom that following morning I was frustrated. Yes, I knew they both meant well. They needed to know that, I am a man and situations occur that we didn't expect. We had to deal with the situation as it came. If one would slip we had no choice but to get back up. Maybe they were right, I should've ran, who was i kidding. Running wasn't an option. We learned to stand up for ourselves. It was sad to say my life could have been taken away that easily. There was no telling when we would leave this planet. In my eyes I wasn't going to run from anyone not sure why but I wouldn't. Maybe it was my pride or just the thought of actually dying was the end result regardless of the matter. I wanted to test those waters and I did. I probably am talking a bit ridiculous but then again it's my life let me manage it at least.

—

After what seemed to be a couple of months working and getting all my classes in order. I was handling and making it all work. I managed to handle it all without any major concern.

Jamal and I decided to take up the girls out to a date to Dave and Busters. In the meantime, we had a sub shop to run . After that altercation that took place that night Jamal and myself have formed a tight bond. I know he had my back for real, just as I knew I had his. The days came and went fast. It was Wednesday in the middle of May and it was hot as hell. Mr. Pete had decided to close up the shop early on this particular day.

"I have a meeting with my lawyers and some friends this morning." Was all he said to us not really wanting to explain anything. We didn't blame him he didn't have to, he was our boss. "Don't worry you two will still get paid a full day's work." He added seeing the look of disappointment in our faces. I needed every dollar because I was saving for a car. I had already $3,000 in the stash in my room. I would give mom $100 whenever I could but has become a hassle. I would have to hide in her jewelry box because it was like pulling teeth with her.

"It's your money you worked hard for it spend it on yourself. I don't want it nor do I need it!" She would bark. I wondered if she thought it was drug money. I felt bad that she didn't want my money. Linda didn't care where it came from she was snatch it right out of my hand fingernails and all would disappear.

Speaking of Linda she had managed to find herself a boyfriend. His name was Joel and she was all over him. What took me back was on how similar this nigga resembled myself. He was tall, light skin even down to his eyes resembles mine. I've always been told that sisters always look for boyfriends that simulate their brothers or even their fathers but I always thought that was bullshit. I guess not now. I been pulled him aside and gave him "the talk" I'm sure we all know and heard "the talk" before. In case you're not sure I'll tell you. It's this dead serious conversation you have with either your sister's boyfriend or even your mother's new boyfriend.

"Let me holla at you" I singled him out the day she brought him over to the house. My sister and mom already knew what I was up too. They both enjoyed this as much as I did. As I walked up towards federal with my twin I asked him a series of questions.

"So what's up with you and my sister?" I looked him dead in his eyes and they twinkle a bit, he may look like me but I was cut from a way different fabric. If you were a hood nigga you could look past any façade a nigga trying to put up. "We just friends" Joel answered. "Wrong answer Playboy." I shot at him while making the sound from jeopardy when you got the answer wrong. "I mean we dating and taking things slow just to see how things go." This nigga couldn't lock his eyes with mine and I didn't really like that not one bit. "Which is it you friends are dating you aint doing both." I was always taught to look a man in eyes as you spoke to him. Not his feet, not the floor he walking on, not the sky, not his shoulders but dead in his eyes. Weakness is exactly what I sensed.

"I'm up here." I spoke stopping at the bodega on corner of 27th and Federal. "Listen, how can I give you my permission to continue to date my pride and joy if you aint man enough to look at me in the eyes and hold a simple conversation?" He was locked on my eyes now. "My sister aint no broad you going to fuck and kicked to the curb like a piece of meat. If you plan on doing this to her you might as well keep on moving now." I waited to see his reaction. This dude was older by a few years but he wasn't in my league. "I don't plan on leaving her Rock." Joel spoke "You don't want to leave her yet because you aint get that pussy yet, but when you do it'll be a whole another story right?" I challenged. My sister was going to do what she wanted at the end of the day. Until than i still would interrogate every mother fucker the same for as long as I lived in her life. That was my job and I enjoyed it. "Even if she do give me some I'm not going to leave her. Those are not my intentions." Joel was talking now. "So how many girlfriends you have?" I asked. "None" he replied "you're wrong again." I challenged. "Well one if you count your sister." He tried to fix. "I don't know man I feel you lying to me." I challenged some more. "No I'm not Rock, to be honest..... please don't tell your sister this." He leaned in a little closer. I didn't know where he was going with this shit now. "Wassup." I said. "I'm a virgin, but please don't tell your sister this. I don't want her to judge me." Joel just broke and I had him by the balls. This nigga aint ever dip and no pussy. I couldn't believe what the fuck I just heard. Linda hit the jackpot! To make matters even better my sister didn't even know. I didn't even think men like this even exist, but guess he was going to tell her because i wasn't. Nope not me. "You what?" I couldn't help but to this concept a little more. "Come on let's get something from the store.

We entered the bodega and all I could think of was what Joel had just expressed to me. Was he telling the truth? I'm not 100% sure, but then again why would anyone make this up? Unless he knew that my sister was a virgin herself, and the only way anyone could crack that box open you had to be a virgin yourself . Yes, like I said before she was broken in before, but that was by force. Linda was untouched and I wanted to make sure her first wouldn't be someone she would regret. If there was a way, to help weed out the fraudualent one with my assistence so be it. I know niggas, trust and believe we will lie about anything to get in them panties.

"Grab what you want it's on me." I told Joel. I made my way over to get a chocolate milk and grab two packs of powdered donuts. He grabbed some hard candy and a strawberry kiwi mystic. I already knew that was for Linda. "Is that everything papa?" The man behind the counter asked. "You got some playboys back there? My friend here aint never seen no pussy and I want him to see some good good, before he end of scared of it once he sees it for the first time." Joel didn't know where to hide his face. His face got so red it was hilarious. "What!? He no get no pussy?" The clerk asked in his broken accent. "Awww man you don't know what you missing papa!" He continued. I paid and we exited the store. "I should have never told you Rock. That's some fucked up shit." Joel was a lil upset. He'll be ight I thought to myself.

Mutha fucking Banga and Jigz, pulled up on the corner literally as we walked out. They were in a burgundy Crown Victoria was some big ass deep dish rims. The rims almost reached up to my waist. This niggaz had money to blow. The music was blaring it was 50cent's "gangsta shit" all the windows were down and the backseat was loaded with three women. I didn't recognize any of them but they looked at me and my soft as twin. I watched as Banga and Jigz jumped out leaving the girls in the back going deaf by the music.

"Rock! What the fuck is up G?" we dapped up and they both hawked Joel as if he owed them some money. "Who the fuck this nigga?" Jigz sized up Joel "Chill this my sister boyfriend or another player trying to get in her pants." I winked at Banga. He got the clue and walked over to him "If you do her dirty I'll cut you dick off than mail it to your house." Banga went a bit overboard but fuck it he got the message. Joel nearly swallowing his own Adam's apple. "I won't" he spoke back with his chin up. Okay I see he has some balls on him I thought to my self. "Let me get these Dutches give me a minute Rock." Jigz and Banga said right before they shot right into the store. " Joel, I'll meet you back at the house." I stated. I didn't get to finish and all I saw was the bottom of his air maxes moving towards the house. I couldn't help but smile as I watched his feet hit the pavement. Linda what are you doing? I asked myself. I ate my donuts with my milk before my milk got warm. The girls in a car looked at me and licked their lips. I wasn't sure if it was because they were hungry or because they liked what they saw. It could be because their lips were so dry due to all the marijuana smoking in the car. I smiled at my own thoughts. Banga and Jigz came out of the store with bags as if they bought everything in the store. Banga had all the bags and Jigz was eating a snickers. "Munchies." I said. "Man you already know." Banga said "Ayo has that detective fucked with you again?" Banga asked in between bites. "hell no, I haven't seen or heard from his ass since that day." I answerd. "Oh no? well let me know if he harasses you again." Banga spoke handing the bags to the girls in the backseat. Jigz was smiling but I wasn't sure why? He lit up the el taken some hard puffs. It was definatley some loud. That shit stunk. "I will. Yall good." I asked after answering the question. "Yea we straight, just wanted to know if that asshole was still fucking with you." I'm not sure if you notice but we got some workers on the block now too and we wanted you to look after them. Just make sure they do what they was supposed to do Rock?" Jigz stated not even asking me anymore. He said passing the el to Banga. The look I gave him said it all. There was really no need to say anything. Im not gonna lie it was tempting as fuck though.

"Come on Rock it's easy money. You don't have to do anything but make sure they're on their shit on their shift." Banga tried his persuasiveness. The look once again answered for me. "All right my bad we forgot you not into that shit. We got to try though." Jigz laughed. "Thanks man but no I'm good." I replied. I looked over to the girls and they was eating away. I decided to change the vibe. "Why you got them fine ass shorties starving like that? They fucking that food up look at them?" I joked "Man they not starving. They eating right? Mutha fuckers in third world countries starving, those bitches eating?" Joked Jigz taking the el back. "Them bitches are just high as fuck." Banga said laughing. "Don't eat all my food!" He barked at them, they couldn't even hear him. They probably couldn't even hear each other inside the car, with how loud the music was.

"We know you about to graduate soon Rock. What you want to do?" Jigz asked. "How the fuck you know this?" I asked "We know everything." Banga chimed in. "Yeah okay." I replied. "Nah my cousin is in one of your classes and he told me. He also said that you don't fuck with nobody but females, Mr. Play'a, play'a." He finished. I couldn't hold back my grin it wasn't a lie but it wasn't the truth. "Not sure yet, why what's up?" We going to throw a block party for you and my cousin than, Whoever you want to bring let em know." "How's that?" Jigz asked. "Not bad but you aint got to go out your way." I spoke "I know but it's for the block and you two knuckleheads." He stated. "Aight whatever." I replied. Here take a hit, it's just some loud... I should've known better. I took two pulls what the hell right? It was only bud. My eyes got watery. I thought my throat wanted to climb out my mouth. I coughed hysterically that shit was potent as fuck. I was so fucking high it was ridiculous how fast that shit took a hold of me.

—

"So you want to ride?" Jamal asked while closing up the shop with Pete it was only 1:30 and I didn't have any plans. "Yeah sure why not." I accepted his offer as we made our way towards his car. The day was too nice to waste. "So what you about to do?" I asked him. Man I don't know, aint nobody at my spot and my son is at my mom's. "What are trying to do?" He asked. "I don't care what we do man. I don't want to go home and all the shorties are still at work where we should be." I joked. "I know." Jamal said reaching into his ashtray and pulling out a clip and lit it up. He turned on the CD player. "Oh Boy" Cameron's voice echoed through the speakers. I hopped right in and in no time we sped off. The bridge lights were right aroud the corner and on the Ben Franklin Bridge we headed towards Philadelphia. I didn't give a shit at the moment. I needed a breath of fresh air. He passed me the joint. I pulled it a couple times and passed it right back. This bud taste a lil different from Banga's. All I know is this shit had my mouth dryer than a mother fucker after a few pulls. After entering Philly which only took about 10 minutes Jamal drove around until he reached his destination. I'm not from Philly but I saw so many women with phat asses and pretty faces. I wanted to be from philly now. Sike! My city had some heavy show stopper too. I can't front. I was breaking my neck though trying to keep up with all the woman I was noticing. He circled the block in search for a parking spot. He noticed a car getting out so he sped up and parked up.

"Ready to have a good time." He asked. "Hell yea." I replied. I didn't know much but I know we were in downtown Philadelphia. We finally hopped out, Jamal through some money in the meter. I noticed the masses of men and woman walking back and forth. The diversity was amazing. "Beautiful women! Damn I love this!" Spoke out loud. Jamal heard me. "You aint see shit yet he said while smiling. Nothing yet we walked for about 3 to 4 blocks sightseeing. Growing up in East Camden all my years and living so close to Philly. I never actually took the time to cross that bridge. I was gonna make it my business to enjoy my neighboring city. I now saw why called baby New York. The crowds of people were all over, plus the stores were all-cashing in all at once with people who were willing to spend all their change in their wallets and purses. The sign up ahead read the bananas and the spot was open.

"Here we go." Jamal stated mind you, we just got off work so we weren't even dressed to impress but since our day was cut short we hardly looked as if we was working in the sub shop, we smelled like it though. As we entered the door security popped up in Jamal's face they growled at one another for a minute. I didn't know what was going to happen, but I was on point just in case. I felt bad for the big slack wearing security guard in case something jumped off. I know he had backup but by the time his backup would arrive his ass woWhat the fuck you mean I can't come in?" Jamal barked back. "Because I said so!" They both looked as if there were about to engage in a physical altercation the tension was broken with a big hug with laughs and shouts. They knew each other. I let out a breath relaxing a bit, this mother fucka Jamal "listen my man doesn't have no ID but he of age." Jamal referred to me "Man you already know bro, get the fuck inside." The big bouncer informed. He patted us down and in moments we were inside the club. It was bright day light outside but in here it was night time and the place was jumping with all types of bodies. The song by state property was booming through the speakers. We made our way over to the table that was unoccupied in the far corner. We had a great view of the place and the dance floor was heavily occupied. The loud bass sent chills through my body. I already knew I was going to hit the dance floor. We took our seats, this sexy female with light skin vanilla, bright green eyes, blonde hair came over immediatly.

"Hello." My name is Ashley and I'll be your hostess for today." She yelled to us over the thumping of the music. Her breasts almost popped right out her shirt as she leaned forward. I didn't mind because worst case scenario I could catch one with my mouth if it did pop out. Jamal tapped me "order what you want it's on me." He also spoke loudly. "Get me what you getting." I yell back. "I'll take two Long Islands." Jamal ordered. "Two Long Island anything else?" The hostess asked. "Nah that's it for now." He replied to Ashley. "She sexy aint she?" Jamal asked. "Hell yeah, they're all around us." I said looking around us. "When was the last time you been to a club during the day?" Jamal asked already knowing the answer. "Never" I replied. "who was that man at the door?" I asked being a nosy Latino. "That's my brother." I looked at him. "Nah seriously, he's my biological brother." Jamal informed me. "He's been bouncing for years. He bounces and he hits all the clubs in downtown. It's a great job, he's well known and respected." Jamal gloated about his brother. "So why don't you get into that? You are as big as him too." I asked. Jamal laughed. "Man I tried but my girl wasn't trying to hear that, she said that's an excuse to party all night long on a regular." Jamal admitted. "It's a job that look like a lot of fun?" I replied. "That's exactly what she say. I'll have too much fun at work so I just didn't push the issue but believe me if I were to be single again I'm all for it. Look at all these women." The place was live and just like that the music switched over to "Green Day" This place did cater to everyone. It was diverse when it came to music but for a moment it caught me off guard. "What you think?" Jamal asked. "I like this. I never been to a club in Philly before Jamal it's all new to me but I'm definatly feeling it." I replied. I wonder how many of these mother fuckers were blasted on drugs so early in the morning. At first I was a little confused, how the hell was this jumping at these hours. My better judgment informed me that a lot of people had to work the graveyard shift, so how could one enjoy a night out if they were stuck in the manufacturing companie third shift? So the owner was one step ahead of the game let's make it nighttime all day. He did and from what I was looking at it was a smart move.

Little Ms. Ashley came swinging her hips over our way, boy did this vanilla wafer look eatible as fuck. I held my composure. "All right guys here goes your drinks the long islands were pretty husky. I noticed Jamal handed her a $10 bill. "If you need anything I'll be around just look for me." She said walking away. "Is she crazy to go look for her?... In this big ass place." Jamal held his glass in the air "this is for the shop" we both laughed I followed suit. "Clank!" was the sound of the glass hitting the other. I took a sip of it and this shit had a kick to it. "What the hell is in that?" I asked Jamal. He was still slurping, his dancing eyes did all the speaking. This had to be one of his favorite drinks.

"It has several different types of liquor like vodka, gin, white rum, white tequila and triple with a splash of cola for taste or even lemon. Why you don't like it?" Jamal asked. "It's strong as hell." I replied "It's supposed to be Rock it's a drink." He informed me after a few sips of the long island. I could feel it, I wasn't drunk but a tad bit buzzed. I knew I wasn't sober because I was grinding all up on two bad ass shorties. They had my tall ass sandwiched. Young Guns was blaring. "Everybody in the club get in tipsy!" Jamal wasn't too far away he was all up on this dark skinned black beauty. She was moving that ass all over him, she looked good. He gave me the thumbs up. I was grinding hard on the blonde in front of me, I would alternate with the Burnett. I didn't know either one of these two, but that's not why I came here anyway. I knew I wouldn't see these two again and I was more than cool with that. Their hands were all over me. I mean all over me. I was getting molested byl these two right on the dance floor. I wouldn't be surprised if my wallet was gone. Just that thought alone forced me to instantly check my rear pocket. I also followed their little game, my hands explored all of them as well. It was a bit harder for me to feel up on the Burnett. Her jeans were glued on her super tight.,with the flick of my finger the top button of her jeans gave me a little wiggle room. The strobe lights were danced around thew room. I reached down her pants and she pushed my hands even deeper. She was wet and I was stupid horny. I wanted this girl. After the song, I made my way over to the table, Jamal was on my heels. Both cups were empty. I was tipsy as the song had just been playing not to mention still high off that bud. I felt great! I notice four shot glasses on the table were we sat at. At first I thought we were at the wrong table but realize it was definitely our table. Ashley was making her way right over to the table. I guessed to collect money or take our order for more drinks.

"Those drinks are from a man who claims to be your brother." Ashley spoke looking at us. "Okay that's good tell him we said thank you." It was his brother Jamil. "You ready?" Jamal asked me looking at the shot glasses. "I'm not going to drink them both right now." I replied sounded like a little bitch. "You are not going to drink the shots my brother sent us?" Jamal was using his guilt trip tactics. "I didn't say that nigga, let's go fuck it!" I grabbed the shot glasses one in each hand, just as we were about to throw back the shots. The two girls that I was dancing with, rushed over with a bottle in their hands. These two were intoxicated. "Wait for us!" They both yelled. These girls were already trashed. Lets not forget to mention they had a fresh bottle of gray goose in her hands with shot glasses. Jamal leaned into my ear. "You know they just paid $150 for a bottle right?" The look I gave him. I couldn't bekieve that shit. They had to be two spoiled girls or had to be tricking. They prolly had some great paying job, who was I to bash them like that I had to admit. I didn't care I will find out in a bit. We all held up our shot glasses and they called out the toast. "Party hard!" Just like that the shot glasses were emptied. These two girls had to have some Boricua or African-American in their blood because there asses was just right, Nice breasts a bit ditzy but hey who cared. Linkin Park came on they both grabbed our hands leaving the bottle on our table. They dragged us to the dance floor it was on . We had to fuck these two either in the bathroom or in the car. I didn't care I was starting to feel it now. We danced and partied until we were all sweaty and tired. I dance with a few other woman, no need to be all over just one or two when there were many up in here. Jamal was gone, it was just me with the two snow bunnies. They informed me they are from Center City about a quarter mile from the Ben Franklin Bridge and we where invited over if we wanted. I told them I would talk to Jamal. Little Miss Burnett came over and sat on my lap and started grinding on me till she felt my dick perfectly. She grinded on it perfectly every time. I wanted some of her. I already knew she was all for a quick fuck. So was I. After about 20 minutes Jamal popped up with a big smile. What the fuck was he up too?

"Pour me a drink baby girl." The blonde did as she was asked. "Here you go cutie. He downed the drink and was still smiling from ear to ear. I wondered why the hell he was so happy. He had to be in the back with his brother busting it up. The girls sidestepped for a few. "We are going to go to the bathroom." They informed us.

"Ayo where the fuck you go?" I slurred a bit. I noticed. "I was in the bathroom with that shorty I was dancing with." My mouth dropped hearing this. Jamal was falling in love. Not with the any woman but with the feeling of cheating. There was no preventing it or evening stopping it, even if he wanted to. "Yeah right!" I challenge. "For real Rock!" I went to take a piss and she was right behind me." He looked dead into my eyes as he spoke. It reminded me of the night at the millennium with Felicia and Erika. How she crept up in the bathroom too. "So how was it?" I asked. "Boy that girl a freak!" Was all he said. "What's up with those two broad's?" He asked not having enough. "Niggahh you just had your fun." I joked. "Nah I can go another round." Yes, I could be a friend and try to talk him out of cheating again but let's look at the bigger picture. He had already blown black beauties back out in the bathroom, while I thought he was busting it up with his brother. Two he is feeling it and he's having a great time and three what are the odds of seeing any of these chicken heads ever again? FUCK IT!

"Well they live a few minutes from here and they want to chill with us for a bit, back at their spot. I'm not telling you to do this, but then again I'm not telling you not to." I knew I was already intoxicated but as for Jamal he was a lot bigger. All the stories he told me this was a walk in the park for him. "Fuck it we out, shit I told you we was going to have a good time and we are. I'm already waste deep in this and to back out now I don't think so." Jamal already had his mind made up a while ago, when Pete told us we could leave early and still get paid. Money wasn't an issue because I had some bread and so did Jamal. By the way this evening was going. We only spent $10 on the two long island that Jamal had bought three hours ago. His brother sent over four shots. The two brats came over with a bottle, and we were already wasted.

Blondie and Burnett came walking back over to our table. I could only imagine what they were doing in the bathroom, coke, speed? Who knew. They were walking off balance. Their eyes were glossy but I didn't care to keep it hundred. Burnett sat on my lap and Blondie sat on Jamal's lap.

"What's up? Y'all coming back to our spot for a few or are we leaving alone?" Blondie asked. "We don't even know your names?" I asked. Not really given a shit but buying some time. "Well my name is Samantha and I'm 23, the one on my lap confessed. I am Britney and I'm also 23. Anything else you want to know before we leave?" Britney joked. "Nah let's go." Jamal stood up carrying Britney right off her feet. "Whoa you're strong." She said turning towards him. It was too late the damage was done. "I can bring that bottle or leave it we got more alcohol at the apartment." Samantha said. "Shit." I grabbed the bottle and put the cork back on. Exiting the club we dapped up Jamil. The bright sunlight still pierced the sky, forcing all of us to hold our hands up over our eyes. The brats had on their sunglasses already on their faces.

"We parked over there so wait up for me so you can follow." Britney stated walking away. "Don't drive away!" Samantha said. They wanted to fuck and I was going to hit that if everything went according to plan. Jamal and I walked towards the car. "yooo I tore Shorty up in that bathroom Rock. I wish you could've been there, you could've gotten all in that too my "G". Jamal joked. I laugh my ass off. "We gona run through these two in a few fuck that." I stated we slap hands twice ."You already know." Jamal replied. In his car he rolled some loud. I never thought he smoked, he'd always came to work clear eyed. He was not the one to come in all high and disconnected. He inhaled the thick cloud of smoke and held it in for what seemed like forever. Cars ripped by us of all sorts. I kept my eye on my side view mirror waiting to see the brats pull up or pass us by. The sound of a horn blared twice. It was yellow but more like a canary yellow Mercedes. The chrome emblem on the front stood out perfectly. It pulled out right next to us it was the girls. Blondie blew us kisses and yelled through the window. "Follow us." Jamal smiled. "Ima get her." Jamal stated putting the car in drive as he pulled out of the parking. We followed the bens as it moved in and out of traffic. Britney was a speed freak, I could tell. She was driving like a lunatic. Jamal wasn't too far off. She cut off every car that held her up, which only forced Jamal to cut off the cars as well. I took notice that this is how everyone drove down here in Philly. You had to play the game or be played. Jamal handed me the spliff and I took one big drag inhaled and held it. My heart slowed down as I exhaled, my lungs let out the cloud of smoke. Instantly, everything hit me even harder. The alcohol felt as if I had ingested 10 more shots. I was really feeling fucked up.

"Wow!" I spoke "you are alright Rock?" Jamal asked looking at me with some concern. "Am I." I replied with a big grin. "I'm feeling it yo." I said with a slur. "Yeah I know my

G I can tell. "You ight though, just enjoy yourself I got you. I'm ight but I'm not fucked up. Jamal reassured me. After a good 10 minutes that felt like eternity we pulled up in a small parking lot. The gate needed to be lifted in order to pass through. The code was punched in and we followed them right in. This building look like a factory from the outside or was my vision that impaired? "You ready?" Jamal asked me. "Hell yea." I replied. We going to smash these two grab, bite to eat then were going home. Try not to drink anymore." Jamal instructed me. "If anything just smoke." He stated. We exited the car, immediately the girl were in out faces.

"Hey baby come on." Samantha grabbed my hand. "Where are we?" I asked. "We are at my apartment silly." Samantha replied. "why it look like a warehouse?" I asked "it's just how it looks on the outside, the inside looks way different." She tried to explained. Once inside we passed a small lobby with a wooden bench and a picture on the wall. To the average person no one would think that this was an apartment building. Right in front of us was a large garage door. Britney pushed the button and this big door slid right up. We all stepped onto the open platform. It was a huge elevator, a very old one at that. My stomach was turning. "I'm hungry." I let out almost in a whisper "I'm hungry too." Samantha agreed "Well we got a lot of food upstairs. You can eat what you want or I'll make you something." Samantha informed me. "Word." Jamal spoke. I guess he was hungry too. Who wasn't we needed to balance this cloud we were on. "You smell like some good loud." Britney stated leaning on Jamal. "We were smoking in the car." Jamal informed them. "We want some." Samantha whined. "Oh yea? Well I got some. We will discuss business when we get to the room." Jamal joked looking up. "This slow as elevator has my stomach all fucked up." I said. A hard and loud thud, the elevator came to a halt. The door slid open and voilà we were several hundred feet in the air.

Samantha and Britney walked ahead of us. Their asses jiggled and bounced as they led the way. Jamal tapped my shoulder pointing to all that ass in front of us. I laughed. "I'm a put it on her." I spoke. I didn't whisper it just came out. Samantha turned and smiled. "You can't handle this." She joked. She didn't know what she was getting herself into but I was about to show her. Three more doors down to the left, there key was inserted in the keyhole and inside we all stood. Just out of habit my shoes got kicked off by the door. I wanted to explore this nice ass apartment. It was spacious. The sofas were white leather, the carpet was black and fluffy as fuck. A big screen was placed over by the wall.

"You don't have to take your boots off but thank you anyway." Britney thanked. Jamal and I were halfway in the room. We did an about face and followed them. "No need to thank me it's a habit." I plopped down on the sofa it was so soft my body was just so relaxed. The AC was on and it felt nowhere near how I thought it would feel. The atmosphere was calm and cool. Britney jumped on my lap and straddled me. "You like?" She asked nibbling on my neck which always got me aroused forgetting about the food and all. I palmed her ass with my big ass hands but she jumped right off. "Not yet." "You say you was hungry, what you want to eat?" Sam asked. "Matter fact, come with me." Samantha grabbed my hand.

"Ayo Rock Ima roll up." Jamal spoke sitting down on the loveseat. Britney sat right next to him.

"So what you got?" Britney asked. Britney was nice she looked like a small Barbie. Her spaghetti strap shirt exposed a great portion of her chest. Her long brown hair hung down by the side of her face, her tiny shorts made her bottom look so big. They were so tiny.

"I got whatever you need baby." Jamal stated pulling out a half of ounce of some loud. "Well I want a quarter." She stated "I don't have a scale so that might not be possible." Britney disappeared Jamal watched her pretty feet hit the carpet floor as she walked away. Seconds later she reappeared with a digital scale. How ironic this girl did drugs for real. Jamal threw some of that sticky icky onto the scale until it read 7g. She reached in her back pocket and pulled out some bills.

"What you gona charge me for that?" She asked staring at the bud already being put away in a bag. "Give me $150" Jamal pushed it. "$150" she countered. "That's fine." Jamal was caught off guard with that one. With no protests she dished out $150 at ease. Jamal continue to roll up the joint he was about to light up. Britney followed suit. In the meantime, my ass was in the kitchen with his big ass refrigerator that looked as if it was made of steel. On some futuristic shit, with the matching microwave. I was opening every cabinet that I noticed. They were all cherry wood I was all up in them. They had all types of junk, Pringles, Oreos, and cookies, pop tarts etc. These girls never had to go to the bodega unless they needed some blunts I thought. I ate until I felt a bit sober which wasn't going to happen because Jamal and Britney barged into the kitchen too. I could smell the aroma that was all too familiar to me tingling my nostrils.

"Damn! You wasn't lying when you say you was hungry. I looked over to my right and on the refrigerator I saw a delivery pizza advertisement. I looked around and look for the telephone receiver. I found it posted on the wall. I picked it up and dialed out the number. "Oh my God what is he doing?" Britney asked lighting her blunt. "He doing what he does." Jamal said. "and what's that Sam asked. "What I want." Rock interjected.

"I would like to place an order...... umm let me get some wings with the special." I spoke into the receiver while puffing on the spliff. She was mesmerized by Rock. "alright I'll take that special." "What you want?" Rock asked. "It's on me." He assured them. "What did you get already?" Britney asked "24 wings and a cheesesteak." Rock explained to them. "I want pizza" Sam spoke up, "me too." They both agreed on a pie. "What do you want my G?" "A sub and you already know how I want mine." Jamal stated. Just like that the order was placed. I handed the phone over to Sam so she could give the address. "It came up to $36.76." Sam stated. I went back to the Oreos. "You have milk?" Jamal and Britney disappeared with the Pringles. I grab Sam from behind, she was melting in my arms. She reached down my pants while I was chomping down on the Nabisco's. She grabbed my manhood but pulled her hand out so fast, as if she had got bitten by a snake is something. She put her hand up to her mouth.

"Oh my God that is big." Sam said exaggerating referring to my little man. I spit out the milk as soon as her words left her mouth. "Don't worry about that." I joked drinking the milk which left a milk stash above my lips. She kissed it away. Temptation and curiosity got the best of her. Samantha reached back down my pants with one hand and unbuttoned them with the other. Samantha had to weigh at least 150 pounds she was around 5'6 she had hair up to her shoulders with hazel eyes. She wasn't bad to look at. She was cute. Her body was plump and I couldn't wait to enjoy it. I got more erect as she began to stroke my little man. I got week in the back of my kneeswhen she put him in her mouth . I never knew why this would always happen but it wasn't a feeling that I didn't mind at all. It drove me insane. I held onto the counter as she gave me a welcoming to her home. There was no way she could take all of that down her throat. Her eyes looked up at me and she tried to do the impossible. I'm not gona lie she managed to almost get it all in. The gagging was too much she had to come up for air. I watched her closely. Every now and then I would tilt my head back because the enjoyment was hard to resist. I grabbed her head but I didn't pound her face in. I was good and satisfied on how she was managing the situation. I tended to only face fuck woman if i noticed they didnt have skills in that department. She slurped, I wondered if they could hear all the sucking and slurping in the living room. Not that it mattered, I didn't care not one bit if they did. Jamal probably had little Ms. Thing bent over doing him. That was our mission. Samantha's mouth was a cave and a very spacious one at that. I looked over to my right and saw the bottle of Grey goose. I grabbed it and cracked it open taking a quick swig to get my mind off busting a load all down her esophagus. She moaned as she went to work. She had saliva all over my shaft and I love the way she used both hands twisted and pulling.

"Oh my God." The feminine voice took me by surprise. "Get that girl!" Britney stated talking about my little man's as well. Samantha didn't stop she didn't Miss a beat "Give me the bottle, she snatched it out of my hands, don't choke on that thing." I handed her the bottle and she licked her lips as she left. I'd bet any amount of chips she was just as wet as her friend. I felt a bit embarrassed. I felt my lil man lose its pump a bit but Sam made sure it stood hard and ready. I let her suck me wet then until I was dry. I busted all in her mouth. I couldn't hold back anymore. Her head game was serious. She had a nigga feeling to good. She swallowed every drop, she moaned as if she came as I did. Her hands look so small holding onto me.

"Oh my God I can't wait to get up on that mother fucker!" She said excited. "Why wait?" I asked "yeah you're right!" She was horny as shit right now. I pulled on my pants and grabbed some more Oreos. I reached in my back pocket and pulled out my wallet grabbing two $20 bills. Give this to them since they were in the living room. I waited in the kitchen my little man's was already semi-hard and I wanted to bust this bitch ass. She came back with her jaw hanging.

"What's wrong?" I asked. "Your man is fucking the shit out of Britney. Her face looked as if she was in pain but her little moans said different." Sam said. "That's good she supposed to. Your going to get yours in a minute." I assured her. "Boy please." She said passing me the bottle. I took another swig. She grabbed my hands "We going to see if you can back that mouth of yours." We made our way to the back room. We headed to the baby blue door. She led the way and opened it up, the big old bed took my vision and I jump right in. It was big and bouncy. She had a small library which told me that she liked to read. Another big ass TV that was to the far left of the room. To the very right there was a small desk with a closed laptop this girl wasn't no dummy she had her shit together. The carpet on the floor matched the door. Her sheets were white as snow. She pulled her shorts down and what was under that, was straight skin no panties or nothing. The tattoo of her name was on her left pelvic bone with some stars and design lines. Once her top came flying off, her breasts were hidden behind a sports bra that kept them in place. She wiggled out of that as well. She like to be naked. She stripped down like nothing. She had one thing on her mind which was me.

"You like my room?" She asked getting closer and closer to me. "I like what I'm looking at now, fuck the room." My pants were unbuttoned. She tore off my jeans until my boxers were all she could see. My little man was peeking out of the bottom, in a flash my boxers came flying off too. My shirt wasn't off yet because she didn't get there. She was on a mission and i was too.

"You have a condom?" I asked. This girl was moving way too fast and she looked too cute but not cute enough to not put one on, fuck that. "Yes I do baby." She went into her little jewelry box and presto. Three condoms appeared they weren't my preferred usual but anything was better than nothing. She ripped it open and put it in her mouth while stroking me, My erection became engorged with blood using her mouth she put it on. She was a pro at this shit. The condom only reached a little pass half which was fine I guess I didn't think she was going to actually jump on this wild stallion and go crazy anyway. "Want me to glue two of them together?" She joked. That was funny I never heard that on before. I had to laugh. I looked at her breast they were nice and firm. Tan nipples were erect and ready to be nibbled on. She tried to give me a kiss but I gave her my neck instead. She got the point I'm not getting into all that kissy shit sorry. One, I just met you in the city that I never really been into. Two, her dick sucking game was superb, like they say practice makes perfect. So nah I'm good. I gnawed on her neck bone which made her shake. That was my little secret she moaned with satisfaction. I too let out a slight moaned. She hit my soft spot and I loved the shit for real... I felt her pussy with my left hand and it was very moist begging for penetration. She had me straddled. I position myself for a direct hit. My palms gripped on her soft ass holding her position. My mouth was filled with her breasts. I waited until she lowered herself a bit so I could thrust up in her juice box slowly. She eased her waist lower and lower. Her moans became louder and softer. She tried to contain herself. I loved it how a woman moaned it was sexy as fuck. She pulled back. Taking me in with small strokes, she did this for a while until she was ready. I could feel her juices flowing down my manhood down to my balls. My hand gripped her ass tightly. I would thrust my hips up and she would let out a moan. She lifted herself up so I couldn't hit it too hard.

"What's wrong?" I asked. "You know whats wrong, that shit is too big for the pussy." She laughed while enjoying. "Okay I could've sworn you was talking a lot of shit earlier." "I'm not baby." She replied. I had her under my control now. I turned her over missionary and let her enjoy it her way. I done heard so many stories of men with big egos that tried to go straight for the kill on a woman with their gift. Not all men possess such a tool so if your gifted don't abuse learn how to use you shit niggaz. I fucked her nice and slow but hitting it just right. The moaning and the scratching on my back felt so good I had no choice but to follow her rhythm. "a little bit harder baby." She asked in a sexy soft moan. I went in deeper stroking while sucking on her neck. Her hands had my ass cheeks palmed tightly. I was a freak I didn't care how it was done just no homo shit and we was good to go full effect.

"Right there! Baby right there!" Her eyes teared up. She let her body go limp, and began to shake uncontrollably. I kept up my temple. By now my dick was sliding in and out with ease so I turned her over doggy style. The look she gave me led me to believe she wasn't ready for this one. "Don't worry baby, I got you." I assured her pure pleasure nothing less. I let her back up into it. She was in charge I let her set the tone as she moaned. Her waist moved in circular motions taking me inside stopping halfway. She pulled away hitting the same spot again. I took it as this was how far I could go and went in on her not over exaggerating it. She threw it back in on me I made sure to catch her. Her cries were exploding and I was about to come and I was gonna come hard. "You want more baby?" I asked while thrusting. "Yes give it to me! Give me more!" she yelled back "give me your mouth she turned around quickly the condom I notice was busted but it was all good because I didn't come yet.Instead I bust straight inside her mouth, It was just as big as the first load. She gulped it all up all tear eyed. "Don't cry ma I'm not leaving." I joked. She smiled swallowing "Oh my God that felt magnificent." You know what you doing with that thing." She applauded me I fell on the bed right on cue, Jamal came in I covered up.

"Playboy the food just got here." You got nice breasts." He says spinning around. In my mind we all saw each other naked,. My sinister thoughts began to roam the possibilities.

My sub was on point with just the right amount of cheese. Everyone was chomping down on pizza and wings. It was quiet for a minute or two. Jamal broke the silence. "Here you go bro." He handed me a $20 bill. "Was that for?" You gave me $40." Jamal stated "Right I told you it was on me." I replied not taken the money. "I know but I'm not gona make you pay for all the food how that look." He spoke I was not going to argue so I took the $20 bill and stuffed it in my pocket. The order came with two sodas and I wasn't a big soda drinker but I managed. I looked at the clock on the wall and it was almost 7 PM. Jamal noticed my eyes and took a glance back. We both knew it was time to wrap this up but not yet. I wanted to see how much more fun we can have. After we all had full bellies and another spliff was in rotation by Miss. Brittany. I looked over to Jamal and gave him a wink. He looked lost, but I had to quarterback this one.

"So let me get this straight we all saw each other naked tonight or should I say today right?" I asked with a huge grin. Britney put her head down as if she was embarrassed. She walked in on Sam and I when she was giving me a hell of a blow job. Sam looked at me puzzled. "Yup I sure did see everyone in here in this room naked or at least half naked." Britney spoke up. Seconds later Sam let it be known. "I also saw everyone naked today." She started laughing, we all had smiles on our faces. The Loud was doing and working its magic. I had the spliff, I took two deep pulls and passed it to Jamal. "So how about before we part ways and probably never see each other again in this lifetime. We all just have one small orgy?" I stated with all seriousness.

"Oh my God!" Are you always this straight forward?" Britney asked shocked that I even impose such a suggestion. Jamal burst out laughing "damn bro that's why I fuck with you" So I winked at him again, now he caught on. I didn't care I wanted to feel Britney's pussy too, call me s dog if you want. "Ruff, Ruff mother fucker". Samantha grabbed Britney's hand and disappeared to the next room. "You are something else Rock." Jamal joked. "Fuck that I want to break shorty in too." Referring to Brittany. "I want to smash Samantha." Jamal admitted "I'm with it." Jamal put his two cents in. "The worst thing that can happen is that they say no, but my gut tells me that they will be down with the proposition." I explained. This will be my first orgy and I couldn't wait. We was all still buzzing off all of the drugs and alcohol but it wasn't as bad as earlier. I spoke for myself. Jamal was already rolling up another L this nigga couldn't get enough of the bud I noticed, or was he nervous. I'm not gona lie I wanted to know what they were contemplating on the next room.

"Yo Rock don't be looking at me, when we do this." I burst out laughing. Jamal just spoke it into existence "Man now why the fuck am I going to be eyeing you when we going to be busting these two Shorty's asses?" He joked, but I was serious that was weird shti for him to say even if he was joking. I looked around for the bottle it was tipped over by the sofa empty. I felt the floor to see if the rug was tipsy yet, but it was dry. It didn't spill over.

"Aye yall got no more liquor?" I shouted loud enough for them to hear. "In the kitchen bottom drawer next to the dishwasher." Britney yelled back. "I know yall not starting without us?" I yelled back "boy shut up!" Samantha joked. Jamal had already found the bottle it was a Henny bottle. My eyes popped out of my face. "It's either this or Jack Daniels." Jamal said uncorking the Hennessey.I was down but damn! Light and dark wasn't the best mixture when it came to liquor. He took a swig and passed the L and the fifth. I just stared at the bottle.

"That shit aint gona get you nice by staring at it." Jamal joked. "Ha, Ha funny guy." I replied joking back. Jamal cleaned up a bit putting the extra food away..So if it did go down the mess wouldn't be all over the place. The sofas were white so you could just imagine the pizza sauce all over the whiteness. That shit would probably be a bitch to get clean. By the time the two brats were done doing what they were doing the L was all gone. What came through the hallway made both our jaws drop they were actually going out there way to freshening up. They were down. I mean they were down! Britney came out and some lace lingerie red and black. She went as far as putting a red bow around her hair she looked very pretty and sexy. She was vanilla all around not a stretch mark in sight. A rush of blood came straight to my little man's. Britney had on white and baby blue it wasn't lace but more of a silk material but she too look so sexy. These girls were going to perform all the nasty deeds today. The smell they brought into the room was intoxicating and very seducing. Jamal looked over at me and smiled shaking his head. I wasn't sure if he was disappointed or couldn't believe what was about to go down. Samantha walked over to the radio and press play. It was low enough for us to talk and hear one another perfectly. It was a Destiny's Child hits, Samantha walked over to Jamal dropping her tiny robe exposing all of her curves to him so he could get a full view of her. He licked his lips. She straddled him while kissing his neck and performing all that she did to me earlier. Britney walked over to me swaying those thick hips and touching her body while dancing a bit trying to build up my desire for her. It was working because my man's was hard as hell all over again, if she only knew. Getting on her knee she stood right in between my knees touching me through my clothing. She had all my attention, she kissed my belly button teasing me following the rhythm of the music. I was so excited that I wanted to grab her but she was faster than me she got away. "Hey baby girl can I have a kiss." Samantha asked Brittany. They both walked into the center of the living room and began to kiss one another passionately and very intimately. I watch their hands caress one another's bodies. Jamal was just as excited as I was. He was on the edge of his seat ready to pounce on them. Samantha unclipped Britney's bra and in seconds it came flying my way. Britney imitated all that Samantha was doing. I wondered how many times Samantha done did this and with how many dicks. I watched very attentively as they made their way over to the carpet. "Where are the condoms?" I asked before I would completely forget about them. "On the dresser. I bolted to the room and spotted two condoms these would have to do. Back into the room they were still going at it no bras or panties. Sam was kissing Britney all over until she hit her mark. Her clitoris was fully erect inside of Sam's mouth. I tossed Jamaal a condom but told him not to put it on yet. I wanted to get head from both these brats and I already know Samantha has skills in that department. The moaning got louder and softer Britney was in ecstasy. I crawled over to Britney's face and nibbled on her neck and breast Jamal wasn't too far behind. He caressed Samantha's ass since she was on all four eating Britney's pussy. He finger popped her pussy while she enjoyed sucking on Britt's pussy. Britney was reaching for my dick so I came up out of my jeans and my boxers, putting my lil man's in front of Britney's face. She didn't hesitate for not even a second. She grabbed it with her right hand, plopping it right into her warm wet mouth. I caressed her beautiful breasts while she went to work. Sam was moaning. Jamal had her going crazy over there, he had both hands finger fucking her vagina and her ass. The look on his face was priceless he wanted to kill this girl with his thrusting of his hands. After making Britney cum, Sam turned over to Jamal ripping his pants off and getting to work on his manhood, slurping and sucking was all you heard over the track that played "I need a soldier with little Wayne." Britney got comfortable and really tried to deep throw my little man's, mind you she had deep throated him further than Samantha my toes curled up. I could see Sam's pussy from behind, this was a fucking dream. I didn't want to wake up. Britney noticed me enjoying Sam's pussy so she guided me towards it. She sucked on my balls as I penetrated her from behind Jamal and I slapped hands. I went to work on her. She had to stop on occasion to grab some air I was digging in. I slipped out and turned my focus on Britney. She straddled me and tried to ride and that she did. She was screaming and biting but she wouldn't stop I was all the way inside of her, Britney's face was buried in the pillow as I went to town on that pussy. I could feel her juices sliding down my dick. Sam was still sucking the skin of Jamal's dick until he couldn't take it anymore. Jamal eventually turned her over and started to dig up all inside of her too. "Cum with me baby"! Sam was pleading. "You want me to cum with you"? "CLAP!,CLAP!,CLAP!" Jamal shouted back sweating. The sound of the ass clapping was louder as he was getting ready to reach his climax with her just like she asked. The fuck session wasn't going to stop till everyone's juices had been spilled in pure ecstasy. Both girls in the center of the room getting it in doggy style now.

They were touching and kissing one another as we blew their backs out. Britney pulled Sam's hair and vice versa. "OH my God OH.... OH my gooddd!" Yelled Britney. I pulled out and put it in her ass "OH my God no, OH my God no!" She screamed but guided me in slowly at the same time. I was inside FUCK MY ASS! FUCK MY ASS!" She screamed ""with that big dick! YES! YES! She play with her pussy as I stroked her ass, I was loving this. "Jamal FUCK MY ASS TOOO!!" "FUCK ME HARD!" Jamal did as she demanded inserting that ass. I pulled out walked over with Britney, now they were side-by-side. I slid back inside, they kissed and grabbed one another talking nasty to each other "OH yes, you're a slut!" Sam yelled "yes I am, yes I am" Britney yelled back. "Fuck me till you come all over these sluts." Sam yelled. I slapped Sam's ass while fucking Brits ass. Jamal did it to. "Let's switch." Jamal stated just like that we switched from ass to pussy from whichever girl we wanted at the moment. We were smutting these two out for real and they wanted us to keep going. I felt I was about to explode so I held back and gave myself a second to regain my composure. There were juices all over me and they weren't mine. "I want two Cocks inside of me." Britney pleaded. Jamal looked at me with a "hell yeah." After putting both of them hammers inside of her she cried and begged for us to stop. "No you take that dick bitch, take that dick! Thats what you asked for it." Sam talked her into staying strong. I had to laugh at these two girls. I only had about 3 inches in Jamal had another three in her "ahhhhh" she was screaming "ahhhhh yes two big dicks I love thissss! DONT STOP!" she didn't know what she wanted, this girl was a freak Sam kissed her breasts and kissed our bodies all over the place. She was next, she took it a bit better then Britt she beg for us to take it easy. Her pussy was wide open her ass was pink from all of the pounding and her pussy was spread wide open. Britney had her pussy in her face so she could occupy herself instead of yelling. I grabbed breast from every angle but it was time. Jamal began to stroke faster and faster I followed suit pulled out ripping off our condoms, we jerked off until we have both of their faces in front of us. In seconds their faces were splattered from both hoses. All in their eyes hair face mouth nose they enjoyed it all over them. "God damn! It was fucking amazing." I barked busting at the same time. "yea it was." Jamal agreed with me. "Yes it was." Sam said. "Damn it was." Britney stated getting up and heading to the bathroom hand in hand with Sam. Jamal and myself got dressed litting up another L "Damn my G, today was a hell of a day." He said "I know man." I replied looking at the time. It was passed 9 PM. "Oh shit! We got to go Rock." My girl going to kill me." Jamal was all wide eyed. The damage was already done now "you wanna go let's go then." I assured him it was his call. He rubbed his head in deep thought.

It's amazing how the mind works while you committed the crime or committing the sinful acts, you are not worried about it when it going down. Once, the deed is complete and it's too late to take back up now, your conscious wants to get involved. "Yeah let's roll." Jamal spoke without even thinking twice after I said what I said. We took the bottle of Henny and left the food. It was an even trade or not. We left the house without looking back. It was a bit rude but hey who was gona stop us? I could only imagine the brats coming out of the bathroom in complete shock to see that the two men that had just given them the time of their life had just gotten up and disappeared. "Ayo my wife is going to kill me!" Jamal stated again once inside the car. We realized that we couldn't get out because there was a code that needed to open the gate. "Now what?" I asked "This is ridiculous for all we know there are looking out the window and laughing at us." Jamal joked. I had no choice but to laugh along with him. Right on cue there was a vehicle at the gate this was our chance and just like that we were gone and on our way back to New Jersey.

" Hand me the phone in my glove box." Jamal asked keeping his eyes on the road. I did as he asked. "Hit the power button on the phone." I waited for it to turn on completely and immediately it began to vibrate for at least three minutes straight. "It was vibrating something serious." I said while making sure I got it to his hands he looked down "damn." He said "was wrong" I asked "I got 17 voice messages and I bet I know they're all from my girl." Jamal was in a panic and bitching. I'm glad I'm single. I took a swig of the Henny. A loud crackle of the dark blue sky followed with lightning only meant one thing was about to happen. "Just what we need." I stated. Jamal grabbed the bottle and drank while maneuvering through the Ben Franklin Bridge "listen I was with you the whole time Rock, if anything we was at your spot. Is that cool we were not over at your spot, but that's the story." Jamal stated. "If it helps bro then hey you was at my spot with me drinking and smoking." I assured him. He punched the numbers into his cell. The water was pouring he swerved a bit. I grabbed the bottle "man drive you going to kill us before we can tell her where we was at." I joked. "Nah Rock I got this."

"Hello" he spoke into the receiver I could hear her voice screaming all the way in the passenger seat. Jamal held the cell away from his face and his face was scrunched up. I held in my laughter. I know it's not funny but damn a female has a lot of power over a man who is in love with her and she put it down on him. "Are you done" Jamal spoke in a calm voice over into the receiver. Obviously she wasn't but Jamal hung up on her. "You just banged on her?" I asked confused as hell. "Yup you'll see." Jamal stated in less than three seconds the cell was vibrating again. "Hello?" Jamal answered in a cordial tone. I can't talk to you baby if you hollering and screaming like a mad woman." He challenged, it was quiet Jamal looked at me and winked he had been with this woman for years and he knew how to operate the situation. Well at least I hoped. "Yes, I know my cell was in the car and I got caught up with my coworker at his place drinking and smoking, you know the young boy I told you about." He spoke to her "Rock roll that up." He tossed me some bud. "the Dutches are in the glove box." I search but there wasn't any Dutches. "Damn! We ran through all of them" Jamal stated once I gave him the thumbs down. The look on my face made him laugh all the smoking we done did. He got some nerve. Once we hit Camden we stopped at the mobile to grab a few. while I did he stood talking to his girl. I jumped back into the car and he was done with his pleading for forgiveness. His grin only could mean one thing. "Everything is all good." He informed me. "Not everything Jamal what you think she not gona smell all that sex on your underware?" His eyes popped wide open as if he thought of everything but that. "You are on point I forgot all about that part." Jamal admitted. The rain was still coming down. Jamal rolled up and grabbed the Henny from the backseat what he did was something I would've never thought of. Everyone should know how strong the smell of Henny is. He went on and spilled some all over his jeans and shirt. "You are tripping." I stated laughing at him. "Desperate times require desperate measures." He admitted "good luck." I replied and we smoked and joked all the way back to the spot. "I'm a catch you tomorrow at the shop." Jamal stated "here this is for you he handed me the rest of the bud in the bag it wasn't much but two els could be rolled easily. Ima taken the Henny is that all right?" He negotiated. "Yea because you going to need it more than I will. I joked after dapping him up and watching him speed away. I dipped into the house. It was almost 10 o'clock when I walked up inside. My sister Linda was in the dining room eating. "You just now eating Linda?" I asked her. "Yeah I just got home I was out with Joel." Linda didn't look too happy while she spoke. "Was wrong Linda?" Did he try something with you?" I asked getting closer to her. She sniffled. Changing the subject. "You smell like weed Manny you better change first then we can talk mom isn't asleep yet .She's in the basement." Linda warned me. "I'm slipping" was all I said bolting up the steps, stripped off my clothing and jumped in the shower. I couldn't plainly disrespect mom. It's funny how Linda started to call Ms. Cathy mom as well after she heard me go with it. It was only right.

—

"Is your brother home?" Mom asked with a basket in her arms. "Yes he's washing up" Linda stated not given up too much information. "Did he eat?" Mom asked. "not sure" Linda replied taking small bites of her food. "Well I'll see you tomorrow baby good night." Mom said planning a kiss on Linda's four head. "What's ever bothering you can't be that bad so let it go honey." Mom said as she walked up the stairs. Speaking to Linda. Ms. Cathy always could sense when something was in our way, or even in our mind a little too long bothering us. We never had to say a word since she practically raised us. She knows us better than we actually thought she did. I could hear the footsteps in the hallway. "Knock, Knock" Was the sound on the bathroom door "yeah!" I answered. Your food is in the microwave if you're hungry." Mom spoke to the door. "Okay mom thank you." I replied "you're welcome. I'll see you tomorrow good night." Mom spoke "goodnight mom." I replied by now I did have the munchies again so I did make my way back downstairs and to my surprise Linda was still there playing with her food. "You still down here?" I asked grabbing her plate and heading to the kitchen. I threw both of them in the microwave and hit start she came in behind me. "looked at me." Linda spoke she looked at me deep in my eyes. "You are high." Was all she said? "No I'm not" I tried to lie..... The look and her hand on her hip broke me. "Okay yes, I am but it'll go away soon." I sounded stupid. "Did you just hear what you said?" Linda asked. I laughed. "I know very dumb." I admitted. The ringing of the microwave brought my attention back to my munchies. "When and why the hell did you start to get high?" Linda asked in much disapproval. "A couple weeks ago I'm going to stop it's not an everyday thing. I did do it a few times today." I couldn't and wouldn't lie to Linda right now. "You better stop that shit. It isn't in you and no need to start something that can spiral out of control and take you right under." Linda was right we headed to the table. I had carry both plates over. Her face wasn't a pretty one. I told her what I did "I'm sorry I'll stop." I tried to make the situation lighter and smaller than what it really was. "You promise?" She asked batting her eyes "I promise." I figured it couldn't be too hard to quit. "Eat" I spoke to her. "What's on your mind? Why the long face?" I asked her "It's Joel" Linda stated "what about him?" I ask. "He wants to lose his virginity to me but I'm not ready to give mine up yet, I mean I want to but I don't want him to treat me any different once I give it up." Linda admitted. "Well look", I spoke with my mouth full "If you're not ready he has no choice but to accept that or if you really want to check him, tell him you're waiting to get married. If that don't work. I'll talk to him and tell him my way to make him understand." I chewed with my eyes low and with a sinister grin. I will bash Mr. Joel's face in for putting my baby girl in a situation like this, you can't rush this shit was all I kept thinking. Linda wasn't eating with me any longer she was playing with her food. She took a sip of her juice and I forgot mine so I took some of hers. "You are silly." Linda stated "It's the bud." I held up my two fingers imitating a joint. She shook her head and laughed. I was stuff. "Oh Manny, your girlfriend called asking for you earlier." Linda informed me. "One she is not my girlfriend you are and two she don't want me like that and three I'm not sure if I even want her like that." Linda blushed and pushed me as I got up to grab our plates. I'm going to wash them. Go call her she sounded as if she been dying to talk to you. "Linda stated. "She's a good girl give her a chance." I almost spit out the juice I was drinking. "What did you just say" I asked not sure I heard the right thing. "Go call her" Linda repeated. "Alrighty then." I went to my room leaving Linda in the kitchen. It was an exhausting day who would've known that all of the fucking and sucking I was doing could drain you so much. I turned on the TV not even really interested in anything that was on or evening what had to be said about anything. Mentally, I was spent and physically I was spent as well. I wanted to fall out right on my bed but my sister's words got the best of me. I had to call her just so it would make her feel wanted at least. The phone rang about four times before someone spoke into the receiver. "Hello" I could hear the baby shouting in the background. I had to take a double glance at my clock on my nightstand it was getting pretty late and Eliza was causing havoc over in their I noticed. "Mommy can I have some more please. "Eliza's voice clearly being understood over on her and that a phone. "Please." I imitated over the phone. "Oh my God you too." Felicia joked. "What's up ma /como tu esta/?" I asked her/how are you doing/ "I'm doing well, I'm here waiting for this one to drop. Felicia sounded a bit exhausted herself. "Maybe if you give her what she is asking for she might fall out." I spoke thinking as if I knew what was going on over on that end. "Ha you must be kidding, there is no way that little missy Lisa is getting any more candy." Felicia was speaking to both of us as she emphasized her words. I couldn't help but laugh. "You think this is funny?" She joked. "A ma but I think its cute" I defended my behavior. "I'll deal with you when I see you but for now I'm a deal with this one first." Felicia was referring to Little Miss hyper sugariness over there. "So why did you give her candy if you knew that she would be up bouncing off the walls if she had it?" I questioned. "Well when I came in from work there was candy wrappers all over the place and my roommate and little Miss Eliza were running all over the house like two lunatics." She informed me. "Ooooo so your roommate is to blame?" I asked "The worst part is that she not even here she went out and thought it would be funny to get my baby all hyped up and split as soon as I walked in the door. "Once again I had to laugh. "Is not funny handsome, it's late in this little girl is wide-awake." Felicia emphasized once again. "My bad but look let her run around in her room and eventually she'll fall out." I didn't know much about children but it only makes sense "eventually too much of anything will make you mentally exhausted then the body will follow." I tried to give her some advice. "What, give it a shot and I'll call you later." Felicia stated. "How about tomorrow because I am so tired myself." It was a short conversation but at least it was an acknowledgment on my part. "All right, see you tomorrow." Felicia didn't ask it was more of a for sure thing. "Whatever you say." I replied. "Don't be like that. She whined. I laughed at her. "Okay we'll link up manana tabien." I assured her "good night." she said before hanging up. I looked at my wall following a roach that was behind my TV until Linda came walking in. "So you just gona stare at it." I laughed my ass off. She actually looked at what I was looking at in the deep daze. "Kill it Manny." Linda whined all these women whining around me. When does it ever end. I thought. "Leave him alone he bothering me." I joked with her she sat on my bed next to me. I scooted over. So now you're protecting every roach in this house, and to make it crazier you're giving them sexes." Linda was hilarious when she wanted to be. "Yup that one is

Joel and he's waiting for you to splatter his guts all over the wall if he don't tighten up." I joked now she was laughing so hard she squeezed my shoulders. "Damn!" I said. "Manny so what's up with you and Felicia?" Damn! Linda I'm so tired I don't even want to talk about any of these women at the moment." I admitted not trying to be rude. "long day at work?" She countered. "At work? Not at all we had a half a day today and everything else that I got into today is what has me drained today literally." I dropped a clue. "You are such a pig Manny are you ever going to change." Linda asked slapping me on my chess playing. "What you talking about Linda? I'm not doing anything that I've not been doing already." I confessed it "The weed?" She got me okay you're right about that one and Ima stop doing that dumb shit." I admitted. "Well you need to before you end up like the rest of these cracked out fiens out here." Linda scolded me. "I know you are absolutely right." I agreed with her. Shots rang out like a wave of thunder as we spoke to one another. She held me tightly, she hated the sound of gunshots. You would think that by all the years that we've have heard of so many either close by or even from a distance she could get use to the sounds echoing through the air. She seemed to never get used to it. I told her. "You okay? Don't worry we are all the way up here." I tried to ease her worries. "All you hear is shots after shots, why do these crazy ass niggaz always want to kill each other." Linda was mad. "You know when I'm asleep I wake up in the middle of the night because of the shots it's an everyday thing." Linda went on "I know but you gotta remember this shit isn't just here in Camden, it's in most of all major cities so is not like you can run from it." I tried to console her as I could. "I'm not scared is just what is the point of shooting and killing one another over every petty thing. If you want to shoot and kill, go be all you can be in the God damn Army." Linda stated still holding me. The shots were still going back and forth but it wasn't close by I estimate maybe three or four blocks away. "I know you are right but one day we will be stable enough to get up out of the city." I stated. The shots ceased after about 20 or 30 went exchanging between whoever. I could only imagine who got hit and why? Taking the thought right from my head Linda spoke. "We'll see who it was in the news in the morning like always. The shooter always gets away so much for the police force." Linda was mad. I'll let her vent she had a lot of stress with school and finals...etc. etc. Linda got up to leave my room she was done and I could feel her pain and disappointment with the city. I love you and get your beauty sleep." She said. "Make sure you get yours too, my door will be open if anything." I assured her moments later I was out.

Chapter 6

"Smoke another"

Looking back is hard to believe that this day is here already. The graduating class of 1993 is a year that is going to stand out for the rest of my life. Putting up with all the extra bull shit that came along with learning in public schools. This wasn't something that I was going to miss at all. Dispite it all, I'm glad every event transpired the way it did. Today, I am accepting life for what it is today. My eyes are open more than your average bear. I am not 100% sure what to dedicate my life to after this, but I'm sure I'll think of something. No need to rush anything. Ima let life take it's course one day at a time. I'm a firm believer in self salvation. Many may not understand my logic behind this. Could it be that many may be too brainwashed to see it any other way? Being brought up a certain way in any household would leave a major impact on ones beliefs.Right? Lets not forget to mention the America Society's brainwashing system working at its best with full force. What I mean by that, is that I control my own destiny. I don't look for something that may or may not exist. Religion is not a way of life for me. I live in the here and the now. I could give a shit what happens once we hit the dirt. Even though it was a path that was introduced to me as the years strolled by, but I could never see the logic in it and accept it. Many religions had to many contradiction, amongst so many other flaws. No disrespect to anyone who practices religion but it just wasn't for me. That was my opinion, until further noticed. The sound of Mr. Pete's loud ass voice snapped me out of my deep thoughts." Rock!" Pete barked. I looked over. "yes?" I replied shocked. "The phone." Pete said "the phone?" I repeated. I rarely had any personal phone calls at the job. It wasn't a behavior that I wanted to project while working. Every now and then I would call out but I would always make sure whoever I called, wouldn't call back or just block the number from the shop. I made my way over to Mr. Pete's office. As we passed one another he gave me an odd look, my stomach began to knot up as soon as he gave me that look. Something wasn't right "hello?" I spoke into the receiver. "Manny!" It was Linda. "Linda what's up? You know I'm at work my heart began to speed up." I cut her off thinking she was bored or something, but then again my intuition steered me towards another thought. "It's mom Manny." Her voice cracked a little. "What's the matter with mom?" I asked emphasizing every word. "She is in a hospital. She was home and she just collapsed onto the ground right in front of me. Manny I'm so scared I don't know what was going on but I called 911. They took forever but when they finally came they put her on a stretcher and on an oxygen machine and rushed her to the Lady of Lourdes Hospital." Linda was talking fast and frantically in between shallow breath. "So where are you right now?" I asked. "At the Lady of Lourdes Hospital." Linda answered "I'm on my way, don't go anywhere." I stated. My eyes began to water up and my chest began to hurt. "I'm in the emergency room Manny." Linda spoke. "I'm on my way I said." "Everything is going to be okay Linda." I couldn't help but to leave immediately. I didn't know what was going to happen. I needed to know the cause of mom's collapse. I told myself that she would be okay. That is all I kept repeating in my head. I couldn't hold back my tears, they just fell. I never actually cried for anyone but this was my mother not my foster mom or just some old lady. She was my mother. I snatched off the apron and headed straight to the front door. "Mr. Pete I got to go." I stated not even caring what he had to say. "I know Rock just be careful and be strong." Linda had already told Mr. Pete what was going on. As I went to push the door Jamal yelled over to me "Rock!" tossing me some keys. "take my whip." He demanded. "I got no license." I replied "neither do I. You know how to drive right?" He asked "yea". I replied. "Ight go handle that." He stated. The customers looked at us wondering what was going on. "Good looking." I was out the door heading towards Jamal's car. My only task was getting to my destination in one piece. Everything is going to be all right is all I kept saying over and over. After dashing by Camden high, I was about 2 maybe 3 minutes away. Everything is going to be all right. I was all fucked up mentally. Why out of all the innocent people in this fucking world did it have to be Ms. Cathy? What the fuck did she do to anyone besides, continuously help the ones who needed it the most. I tarnish my mind with negative thoughts. I had to come to a conclusion that thinking negative would only bring upon the inevitable which was? Negative results and that was not an option. Not today not ever, I forced my mind to flushed all the negativity out of my head. I was parked in the parking lot in deep thought. I turned off the ignition and took one big deep breath. Spoke out loud. "She is going to be all right." and

I exhaled. As I made my way into the emergency room it was jam-packed. I hated hospitals, nothing ever came good out of anyone's visit here. Well maybe if you were given labor, but even that had its ups and downs. You had people wearing mask, while others had on bloodied T-shirts. The crying and whimpering was all you could hear. It wasn't a pretty sight. Linda spotted me in a heartbeat coming up the hall. She ran and clung on to me for dear life sobbing. "Manny I hope she doesn't leave us! Manny please do something!" She sobbed begging. "Linda looked at me." I grabbed her beautiful face and made her watery swollen eyes meet mine. "Everything is going to be all right." I spoke to her. My words hit her hard, she could feel deep down that I was gona be right. She hugged me tightly. "I love you Manny, please don't you ever leave me." Linda said crying into my chest. "I will never leave you, you don't have to worry about that." We made our way over to where she had her belongings. We passed a lot of people who had some serious injuries. The emergency room was always jam-packed. You would think they would come up with a better system to take faster care of everyone who needed it the most. That was just my opinion.

"Did you eat?" I asked Linda trying to get her mind off the worst. "No." She spoke softly holding my hand tightly. Let's go to the vending machine so you can eat and tell me what happened." I stated. We walked over to the vending machine where two tiny kids were pushing and playing with the buttons desperately trying to get something out of the vending machine. I looked at the screen and it said. "please insert money." I put in a dollar and told them to push the button, they could barely reach the buttons but managed to push what they wanted by standing on their tippy toes. A bag of Doritos came tumbling down. I pushed open the trap door at the bottom "/ cojelo/" I spoke to the little girl ./grab it/ She grabbed the bag. Her and her brother or friend quickly sped away. "Gracias" the boy said while leaving. "That was nice." Linda applauded my efforts. "habla me" what happened"? I put in five dollars in the machine and started punching in buttons. I wanted my donuts and Snickers, Linda pointed at chips and tasty cakes. She began to explain to me what happened earlier in the house. "

Well I decided to come home from school early because I felt something wasn't right." She explained. I grabbed all the snacks switching over to the beverage machine. I put in two dollars. I grabbed a chocolate milk and Linda grabbed an ice tea peach. We headed to our seats. "So, I made it home mom was in the kitchen as always preparing something to eat. I could smell it, it smelled amazing like always. I took off my shoes, she noticed me as I came in. "Are you hungry baby?" She yelled over to me with a spatula in her hand and a cigarette in the other. I smile because this woman was always smoking no matter what she was doing with her time. "Yes I am. What are you making?" I asked moving towards her. "I'm making cheeseburgers she smiled but as she said her last word. That's when she dropped the cigarette and grabbed her chest. The look in her eyes screamed for help. I was so scared." "Mom!" Are you okay!?" I asked horrified. "She shook her head dropping the spatula. I grabbed the phone and ran to her help her sit down. She was already on one knee so picking her up would be almost impossible. I leaned her up against the wall. Breathe mom, breathe please! Her shallow breath seem so limited. I held on to her, I reached over and turned off the stove. I let go for three seconds, just to open the windows and doors so some fresh air could circulate throughout the room. She looked into my eyes, her blue eyes look like ice. Manny I was so scared." Linda recounted the whole scenario. She was beginning to cry again. "Okay, okay ma don't cry baby girl it's all right." I wiped her tears off her face. In my mind, I knew it was the fucking cigarettes that she was always sucking on as if it was candy or something. "So the paramedics came right into the house with the stretcher. With a little help they took her immediately, asking me what happen and a bunch of other questions. I told them exactly what I'm telling you. They hooked her up on to the oxygen mask with a small cylinder tank. I closed the windows quickly and locked up the house. I was right with them in the back of the ambulance. I left everything even my keys, how stupid was that?" Linda stated in between breaths. "It wasn't stupid, you weren't thinking of yourself. You was thinking about mom. I got my keys so we are good." I corrected her for being so hard on herself. " As soon as we entered the hospital I asked to use their phone. I called the operator and asked for the sub shop on Broadway and got connected a.s.a.p to you. Your boss picked up and I told him what just happened, he assured me you'll be right there. He didn't lie because look, you are here with us." She went on to explain as she ate her tasty cake cream filled cupcake. I ate my donuts, taking in all that was just revealed to me. "How did you get here so fast Manny?" Linda asked. "I drove." I replied. "You mean someone drove you or did I just hear that you said you drove?" Linda asked perplexed. "I drove." I reiterated. "Who's car?" Linda asked. "My coworkers." I answered. "You don't have a license Manny." Linda laughed. "Didn't need it at the moment." I stated it was a dumb and unconscious decision at the moment. I could of easily have gotten pulled over and lost the car. On top of that my license could of gotten suspended way before I even got it. I made a mental note to go to the motor vehicles on my next day off and handle that, stop being so careless. "So when are you supposed to return the car back?" Linda asked. "Whenever I'm done I guess, he didn't give me no time schedule but I'm sure he wants his car back before he gets off of work." I informed Linda. "Ms. Jalinda." A tall thin white man in a white overcoat called out. He must be the doctor, who's looking after mom I thought to myself. Linda grabbed my hand and headed towards him. He noticed us heading his way and met us halfway. His skin was pale as if he was always stuck in a hospital, he was cleanly shaved. He was just my height, he met me at eye level. He wore some running shoes that looked as if he had them delivered this morning, crispy. Green scrubs under his overcoat, with a stethoscope around his neck. His name was shown on his overcoat read M.D Harrison. "Linda?" Mr. Harrison spoke directly to her. "Hey Dr. this is my brother." Linda looked up at me. I looked over at him we shook hands firmly. "Nice to meet you." "Is it good news or bad news?" I asked straight up. "Well..." As he began to speak Linda clenched my arm cutting off all the blood circulation immediately. "We have Catherine hooked up to a breathing machine, which to be honest I think she'll be using for a long time if not forever. I'm going to run some more tests, and run her through an MRI scan than we will take it from there." The doctor looked into my eyes with a very serious stare, his green bright eyes seemed cold and numb. I could only imagine how much those eyes have endured in his lifetime, working in this field. They say your eyes are the windows to your soul.

"Can we see her doctor?" I asked wanting to see mom. "Not just yet we have her under close observation, give me about an hour or two. I'll let you know if you can go and see her for a while." The doctor spun around after he asked us if we had any questions. We had no other questions. I grabbed Linda and headed back to our seats. Linda had her head down while holding her chips not even eating anymore, she was worried. I will admit so was I? I heard the most important piece of information which was. "for the rest of her life" which meant she would live a while longer if not plenty more years. Yes, I also understood that the oxygen machine and tank probably would have to stay with her at all times. Mom was okay for the most part. "What you think is wrong with her?" Asked Linda. "I can't answer that Linda I don't want to say something that will make us more worried than we already were." I answered in my most honest opinion. "I bet you it's those cancer sticks she stay sucking on. Why can't she just smoked one or two? No she has to smoke every carton that the store sells." Linda was mad but she was mad over something she had no control over. "Mom is what you call a chain smoker Linda, that's how she smokes. She's not going to quit because in her mind the cigarettes are not doing this to her." I explained. "I bet if I wrap that chain around her neck she won't be a chain smoker anymore." Linda joked trying to ease her mind. "Damn you want to kill her before she even dies Ma?" I joked back. "No Manny." She whined. "It's that she is so stubborn." Linda stated. "I know, but we are going to help her no matter what the doctor says. It might be something unrelated or related to smoking, but whatever it is we will make sure she is going to take better care of herself." I informed Linda as we sat in the lobby. Linda eventually dozed off on my shoulder. My arm was starting to fall asleep right along with her. Her big head was heavy. I tried to move it ever slightly so I wouldn't wake her. Her smell was always so fresh and sweet. Her hair smelled like fresh flowers. I looked around the lobby area and it was getting a bit lighter with the injured people being moved to their rooms, that didn't mean they didn't stop coming in. The hospital was a moneymaker for real. It was just a shame on how the money had to be made. What took me by surprise was how this lady and a small child came in, screaming and crying. "Where's my baby!? Where's my baby!? Is he okay?" She yelled at the top of her lungs. The nurses came running to her aid immediately trying to calm her down. "Please don't let him die, please don't!" She yelled uncontrollably. The child beside her also cried frantically. I didn't want to know what happened or why? But I knew it had to be very bad. By the way she was screaming about her baby. I looked over at the clock on the wall and I noticed three hours had passed us by. It was getting late. I woke Linda up shaking her back and forth, trying to get her up. She whined but got up. She became conscious again. "Did they say we can come see her?" She asked. "No but I'm going to find out." I replied getting up while stretching my body and headed up to the front desk. Linda was on my heels not skipping a beat. "Excuse me I was told by Dr. Harrison that in about two hours I would be able to see Catherine. I wanted to find out her status because it's been three hours." I cordially asked. "Give me a minute sir." She replied. "Sir?" I felt so old when people would direct me as Sir. I held Linda while we waited. She was cold and the AC in the facilities were below zero, okay I'm exaggerating a bit. It was really cold in this place and that's how it felt. "Excuse me sir?" The lady behind the counter looked in my direction getting my attention. "You can go and see her if you want at this time." The nurse stated from behind the counter. "Ms. Catherine is in room 314. "She informed us handing Linda a visitors pass as well as myself. Once we were let by the big gray doors we searched for the elevators. Linda pushed the button immediately once they came in sight. The lights of top counted down from 13. The floors were spotless but the air was stale. Doctors and nurses walked back and forth getting torn in between patients. A small line formed around us waiting to get an elevator as well. I looked at Linda who seem so anxious. "Are you okay?" I asked her. "Yeah I'm fine just want to see her that's all." Linda admitted. "We are, just try to stay strong not for me or you but for mom." I said. "I'm trying Manny you know how I feel about you two." She replied. "I know" I said. Wrapping my arm around her shoulder. Once we entered room 314 it was dead silence. The beeping of the heart monitor and the breathing machine was all that could be heard. The TV was off and the room was dim. We tiptoed till we reached mom's bedside. My eyes watered at the site of mom. She had tubes in her mouth and in her nose. It was a site no child would like to see their mother in. My mind wandered as to how someone could breathe with all of them clear tubes in and out of their mouths and nose. Linda was crying there was no holding her tears back. It wasn't a pretty sight. I grabbed her hand it was warm. She wasn't conscious at the moment.

"Mom please don't leave us, we are here. We've been here all along and we are not going anywhere.... Please mom wake up if you can hear me." Linda spoke softly with alot emotion. I was also tearing up, I squeeze mom's hand tightly. I knew she could feel the presence of someone holding onto her. I felt a light faint squeeze back but I wasn't a hundred percent sure. I thought it could be my mind playing tricks on me, but I felt it again. It wasn't my mind, it was mom squeezing me back. "She's awake." As whispered to Linda. "How do you know?" She asked "She squeeze my hand." I said. Linda went to the other side and held her other hand. "Mom is Linda and Manny can you hear us?" Mom asked. "Are you okay?" How do you feel? Linda wanted to ask her 1,000 questions without even get an answer to the first question. "Manny she squeeze my hand!" Linda smiled excitedly. This was the first time she smiled. "L..ind...a" mom tried to speak out which was a mumble that no one could really understand. "Mom get your rest, we are right here. No need to stress your voice." I spoke. "Ma..n..uel." She also mumbled. "Yes it's us, your two kids. We are here and we are not going anywhere." I stated hoping she heard every word. She squeezed Linda's hand tightly now with much more strength than the first time. "Mom you going to break my hand." Linda joked as she always did with her. A sly smile was shown on her face, she could hear us. I was happy that she was conscious of us being in the room with her. "I love... you.. s..o muc..h" she mumbled with no energy. "We love you more." Linda and I spoke both of was wiping our eyes. This was a very emotional moment for us especially for me. I couldn't deal with losing both of my mother's . It would be far too much for me to endure more pain. I'm not sure how I would react upon receiving some more tragic news like that again. "Cigarette." Mom mumbled "I know she didn't just as for cigarette." Linda barked. I shook my head confirming our conversation Linda and myself had down in the lobby. "Mom are you serious, you're lying in his bed and no one knows what was wrong with you. Manny and I are so scared worried in here. The only thing you can muster up to say is you want to cigarette!?" Linda was mad at what mom uttered out her mouth. "I'll.... ..be f...ine." Mom mumbled. "Yes I know you will but you don't need no cigarette. Were you going to put it? In one of them plastic tubes?" Linda replied being sarcastic as fuck. Mom didn't reply. "Linda is right mom, a cigarette is a last you need at this time." I agree with my sister. I had to because if the cigarettes was the problem Linda and I would have to work together to get her off those cancer sticks immediately. It would be hell but it would be our main focus and keeping her healthy and alive. If it had nothing to do with a cigarette than maybe we would let her smoke again, who the fuck are we kidding. We won't be able to be around this woman 24/7 to ensure that she doesn't pick up another cigarette. In our presence we could try and do our part. Just so she knows that at least Linda and I care about her and want what is best for her well being. We love this old woman. She is all that we have besides one another and we wanted to keep her by our side for as long as we can.

"The doctor is going to run some tests to find out what really happened to you and the MRI will tell him what caused you to collapse earlier." Linda explained to mom. "I'm okay." Mom mumbled. "Yes you are okay because all of these hoses coming in and out of your body. This is what is keeping you alive." Linda challenged. Mom spoke with her eyes closed she was drained. Our hands were still clasped with one another. We were so busy entertaining mom that we didn't even notice the nurse creep up on us. "I'm sorry for the interruption but we are going to be taken Ms. Catherine for some more studies." The pretty tall tan skinned nurse spoke politely. She was tall and even with those scrubs on you couldn't help but notice how curvaceous her body was. She had high cheekbones, she wore micro braids that I would have loved the pull. "Ima stay here with her." Linda suggested. "You can stay but you can't come with us. She's going to the MRI unit where no one else can enter." The nurse explained to Linda shooting down her volunteered company. "Excuse me, what's your name?" I asked in my soft latino voice. I felt mom's hand tighten on mine. "I'm sorry my name is Breanna and I'll be looking after Ms. Catherine on my shift." Brianna replied. "So how long do you think she'll be going through all these tests?" I asked getting to the bottom of how much time we would have to go home eat shower and come back. "Anywhere between 4 to 6 hours. "Brianna replied swiftly. "Wow" Linda chimed in. "Yeah I know these tests aren't short. We want to do a full body check up and get to the root of what happened to Ms. Catherine." Brianna looked at me in my eyes as she spoke. "So if you want, you can come back tomorrow morning because visits are over at 7 PM and is almost 6 PM already." Brianna was right as much as I hated that she was. Mom could hear all of our exchange words but she stood quiet, her grip went limp as the news of us not being able to stay echoed in her ears. "Can you can give us a few minutes please?" Linda asked. "Absolutely." The nurse replied. We brought all of the attention back to mom. Well at least Linda did. I searched for a phone. I had to call some reinforcements to move about the city at ease. "Who you calling?" Linda asked. "Back up" I replied "hello?" Felicia spoke into the receiver. "Ay ma wassup?" I asked lightly. "I'm alright, here with Elisa at the house." She replied. "Why are you calling me from the hospital line?" Felicia asked. How the hell does she know I was in the hospital? This woman had a GPS wired on me I thought. "What?" How the hell you know?" I asked confused like a mother "I work at a hospital, so we call the lady of Lords a lot. The area code." Felicia replied. "Well my mother.... I'll explain later. I need you if your not too busy." I stated. "For you, I'll always make time." She replied. "Well I need you to meet me at the terminal in 15 to 20 minutes." I stated short and to the point. Informing her what I needed to be done. "You are at the hospital why would I meet you over there?" Felicia asked. "I'm a drop off the car to my coworker, then I'm ride with you back to my spot." I explained woman always wanted to know details. "I'm bringing my baby is that cool?" She asked. "Of course it is why it wouldn't be." I assured her. "Well I'll see you in 20 then." Felicia confirmed. We said our goodbyes to mom, gave her our kisses and told her will be back in the morning. She let go of our hands. "be c...arefu..l" she mumbled.

—

Pulling up at the sub shop we went around the rear of the place. I parked up where there was a spot available. "This is where you work at?" Linda asked. Yes it is, don't be popping up down here just wishing to get some free food." I joked. "All man you are fucked now. I will be all up in here getting me some free food." Linda Joked back. We made our way towards the front entrance. Jamal and Pete were cleaning up. I walked in getting ready to help them out. "What are you doing?" Pete asked. "closing up." I replied. "We got it Rock, how's your mom?" The look I displayed said it all. "She going to get an MRI done and a bunch of other test must be done so they can identify the problem." I explained. The shop was dead. Linda sat at one of the tables. "That's my baby sister Jalinda. I introduced her to Pete and Jamal and vice versa. "So when you going back?" Jamal asked. "In the morning before I come into work." I reply handing him his keys. "Good looking." I show my gratitude. "Man, that's what we hear for Rock I got you." Jamal replied. ""Look Rock if you need time to handle things at home you got it." Pete informed me. Linda listened attentively. "Thanks Pete but I need the job just as bad as I need to be by mom side." I admitted. "I'll be here, my sister will be by my mom for the most part and will alternate if needed." I explained. "Did yall eat?" Jamal asked. "No actually we didn't. We snacked on some chips but that was hours ago." Pete came over to us what they bag in his hands. Grab a soda and take that there for you and your sister." Pete said. "Thank you." Linda was hungry. I knew she couldn't wait to dig in that bag it looked heavy too. "Damn how many orders did yall fuck up today?" I joked. That was Mr. Pete's work, he screwed up bad today." Jamal joked. "Bullshit they ordered a fucked up order." Pete defended his screw up.

We all shared some much needed laughs. I noticed the white Lexus drive by the shop and right on cue I got up and looked to make sure. "That's my ride guys, I'll see you tomorrow. Thanks again and be safe." I stated to my boss and coworker. Linda was up on my heels as I stood up. "Nice meeting you." Linda spoke. "Likewise Rock stay strong and remember we hear." Pete assured me.

Out the door we headed towards the parallel parked Lexus. I opened the back door for Linda, her hands were full and Eliza was locked in her booster seat on the right. I made my way up front. I leaned in and gave Felicia a kiss on the cheek.

"Thank you is been a long day." I started some small convo. "Are you okay?" Felicia asked. "Yeah I turned over to greet the Princess, "Hi Eliza." I said in a caring tone. ""Halloo" Eliza replied extending her greeting. "You see that girl next to you?" I asked her. "Yes." She replied. "That's my sister Jalinda, is it okay if she sits next to you?" I tried I wasn't the best with kids. She had a doll in her hand and passed it to Linda accepting her position. "Who's this?" Linda asked. "It's my friend Barbie." They joked around for a bit. "Hey Jalinda" Felicia said. "Hey girl." How's everything?" Felicia asked. "Not too good but making the best of it you know." Jalinda exchanged a few words back and forth. I got lost in deep thinking of how would things have been if Linda would've never showed that when she did. I didn't even speak the whole ride until we reached Federal Street. "You can pull up on the block and park anywhere you see a free parking." I immediately went to the right side but let Linda out first. I grabbed Eliza by the hand. "You want to see my mom's house?" I asked her. "Yes" She replied taking my hand. I opened the security gate making sure everyone was in a safe. That was my only interest at the moment. "Alarm off" the box informed me upon entering the house and disarming the alarm. My shoes were off Linda did as we always did too. Felicia took notice and did the same. She had on Tweety Bird socks, you don't have to take off Eliza shoes. "But I want to too." Eliza corrected me. She too came off her tiny shoes. How foolish of me thinking the child wouldn't want to follow suit. "Making youself at home, Ima warmed up some food so we all could eat." I said. "Manuel we ate you and your sister eat we are good." Felicia informed me. I handed her the remote to the TV, as they got comfy on the sofa and turned on the cartoon network. I could here Eliza with all laughs as she watched her cartoons. In the kitchen Linda and I put the food in the oven.

"You can shower up if you want Manny, I'll handle this." Linda stated. "No I'll shower once everyone is gone." I replied. The phone rang twice and I made my way to the receiver it was for Linda. "Who is it?" She asked it was Joel she disappeared for a few minutes. I put the subs in the oven with the wings. The fries and a pierogies went to the microwave. I laughed at myself because I know now why Jamal and Pete were joking around about how bad the order was screwed up. It was a big one. I let it sit up under the heat for about 15 minutes. In the meantime I went and kept the company entertained. Eliza was enjoying the television. She was caught up with her mother, they both shared a good laugh. I sat across from them so I could stare at them. Mostly at Felicia. I replayed our sexual encounter at her house, who would've known that a small scuffle could get a nigga some pussy. I might need to get into a bunch of scuffles. I noticed her looking at me through her Peripherals. She had on her glasses and her hair was loose which made her face look so cute. "Manny." Linda called over to me from the kitchen. "Yeah?" I stood up and headed towards her. "Wassup?" I'm starving let's eat." she stated. "I know, give it a few more minutes." I laughed with her. "Eliza." I called out from the kitchen. "do you wanna eat some french fries." I asked. "Yes, please "she answered back almost immediately. She was so polite. I should of asked her mother is what I should've done, but hey what the hell. "Only if mommy eat some with me." Eliza chimed. "She is so cute." Linda spoke. I could only imagine what she was thinking. She was already plotting on having a baby. By the sound of what she said. "she is so cute I want one." As if it was a life size baby doll or a baby chimp. I just looked at her. "Yes of course mommy can have some." Linda interjected my reply. "There is not enough for her." I joked. There was more than enough. "Stop it Manny." Linda was all smiles. I was glad that I could put a smile on her face due to our tragic day. She was beautiful. Linda opened the oven and I watched her. The wave of the heat hit her face and forced her to look back at me catching me, catching a glimpse of her round ass. She smiled and returned her attention back on the food. "Is sizzling Manny." She stated "all right so let's break it down and eat it." I joked.

"Hey ladies, if you can please join us at the table to share this cheap meal with me and my beautiful sister." I joked about the situation. Elisa came running over to one of the chairs. "Can I sit here Manuel?" I loved how she said my name barely audible. "Yes you can baby girl." I replied.

"Come on mom I looked over at Felicia. She was taking her sweet old time walking over to join us. She looked tired and sexy all in one nutshell. I went back to the kitchen "Linda split a sub down the middle. There not that hungry, we can eat the sub" I informed her. "How the hell you know?" Linda asked. "Because Felicia told me that they had just eaten before she met us at the shop." I replied sticking my tongue out at her like a child. She smiled. "You think you know everything don't you?" Felicia challenge. "No I know a little bit about a lot or is it a lot about new bit?" I asked jokingly. Once the plates were set, we all shared a meal. Linda and I ate the most but there was plenty left over. I'm glad Pete had given us this meal because I would've paid a pretty buck for all of this. "Mommy are we staying here tonight?" Elisa asked her mother so innocently, without evening noticing the severity of her questioning. "I like it here." She stated. "No baby we have our own house, don't you like our house?" Felicia asked. "Yes I do mommy." Eliza and her mother had a small conversation. It was fascinating how a child's innocent mind thinks and just talks with no filter no nothing. It just thinks and talks right off the gun bust. No wonder everyone would say that children are so innocent and don't lie. Felicia changed the subject and directed her attention to Linda and I.

"If I may ask, when are they going to let your mom out of the hospital?" She asked. "We don't know yet but I'm hoping soon because I'm missing her already." Linda stated. "They're going to run some tests on her to find out what caused her to collapse the way she did earlier today." I informed Felicia already getting tired of repeating the same information. "My mommy can fix your mom, she takes care of me when I'm not feeling well." Eliza was bright. "Awww my god she is so sweet." Linda complemented Felicia's daughter. "No baby I can't, they need a doctor to help their mom. I'm only a nurse." Felicia corrected her daughter. "Oh" Eliza was playing with her fries, she wasn't hungry not one bit. I notice and decided to clean up the table out of force a habit. I began to think of mom and wonder if the doctors had given her any solid food yet. I doubted it though usually when test were involved, one would usually be fed by an IV. I'm sure she was feining for a cigarette and some real food right about now. Linda sat back and just entertained the company. Jalinda's focus was on Eliza, she was bedazzled by this young intelligent little girl. They played patty cake, Linda was screwing up every time. Felicia took it upon herself to help me. I saw that coming a mile away. "I'll take these Rock." She grabbed all the plates and cups on her side. I wrapped up the extra food that went untouched by anyone and threw it in the fridge. That would be eaten by the end of the night I was sure of it. "Felicia what you doing?" I asked. "I didn't invite you to my house to do dishes." I stated. "I know you didn't but a helping hand is needed every now and then, wouldn't you agree?" Felicia suggested flipping it so smoothly. "Yes you're right but not today and not by you at least."…. "And I say this with all the respect in the world." I booty bumped her. If mom only knew some stranger was in her kitchen playing with dishes. She'll probably have a conniption I thought to myself. I took over the dishes handing her a towel so she could dry off the dishes instead of washing them. She noticed my hands very attentively. "A man that can handle his own in the kitchen?" "Very attractive." Felicia said with a smile on her face. She dried them up and placed them on the counter upside down. I looked at her and she looked back up at me and perked her lips for a kiss. I leaned over and planted one on her sucking on her bottom lip. "Oh no." She whispered. "You started it." I whispered back. I wanted to take her upstairs and get rid of all my stress that I had pinned inside. I couldn't be so disrespectful in mom's house today. I mean not like it never happened but out of all the days not today? She wasn't here so this wouldn't count or would it? Linda came in with tiny Eliza right on her heels. "Why don't y'all go to the living room or wherever and let Eliza and I finish up in the kitchen." My sister know my horny ass wanted to beat this girl pussy up. "Yeah mommy, I'll help her." Eliza shouted. "Okay but then we have to go home because it is getting late baby okay?" Felicia informed her daughter. I looked at Linda and she gave me a wink. Already knew what that meant, I moved out the kitchen with Felicia. I should have taken her upstairs but to be honest I didn't feel right. Instead we kicked it in the living room for a bit getting to know one another on a deeper level but as friends. "So are you ready for graduation Rock?" She asked me padding me with her Tweety bird socks. "Yes I am and I'm excited that it's finally over for now. I'm not too sure on what's next on my agenda as far as school goes you know?" I admitted. "Yes but don't rush your yourself and remember don't prolong it for too long either. Don't you lose sight of your future. You don't want to end up with the why's and how you should've never stopped or lost focus. "Felicia was right and I honestly didn't want to lose sight of my future. For now, I was going to enjoy the little bit of time I had off. "I feel you." I admitted. I watched as she shook her thigh out of nervousness or just anxiousness. "Why you so shaky?" I asked. "You really want to know?" She challenged. "No I just ask questions so that they go unanswered." I joked. "I'm keeping from jumping on you and tearing you up." She joked smiling. Her pearly whites was a site worth watching. "Oh boy, I could've sworn we already been through this before, if I'm not mistaken you tapped out on me the last encounter we had." I joked. "Shit anyone would tap out with that thing." She looked down at my waist. I laughed. "You still didn't let me fully handle my business." She whispered. Just as I was about to take her upstairs, little Eliza came sprinting to her. "Mommy." The kitchen is all clean." Eliza yelled excitedly. "Good girl, what did she do?" Felicia asked. "I dried while she washed." Who is she?" Her mother cut her off "Linda." Eliza replied almost immediately. "Okay and what else? I help sweep and mop." Eliza recounted the events that occurred while Felicia and I were indulged in our conversation. "Wow that's a lot, you did all that? Then what did Linda do?" I joked. "Sounds like slavery to me." I had everyone laughing. Linda slapped me on my shoulder. "Shut up Manny"

"Well we gotta go." Felicia stated. "All man why mommy?" Eliza whined. "Because you little missy have to go to bed, its past your bedtime and you are not going to be keeping me up every night." Felicia put her mommy foot down. I thought it was sexy and powerful. Eliza's head dropped and she almost cried. She like being with Linda, I guess she felt at home with a friend. "Look what you did." I stated to Linda. Linda got down on one knee, eye level with Eliza. "Don't be sad, we will play again another day okay?" Linda lighting up the mood. "Really?" Eliza stated. "Yes, not sure when but we will." Linda was good with her. I actually admired the fact on how she was handling the situation with little Eliza. Eliza was all smiles again "come on mommy let's go so I can sleep until it was time for me to play with Linda again." Her words cut through Felicia. Her face displayed a hint of sadness as Eliza spoke such words about a girl who she had never seen and was looking forward to seeing her again. Felicia forced a smile. "Okay baby let's go." I stepped out first to make sure all was well. I walked them to the car and gave Felicia a kiss on the cheek.

"By Princess." I said to Eliza waving through the glass window. "Bye Manny." She called me by what Linda calls me. This girl was smart, maybe too smart for her own good. "Call me when you get home so I know you're good." I said. I look back at the house and Linda was watching over me. She was always watching over me. "I will." And just like that I waited till the taillights of her car made it to the end of the block and made a right at the end. I looked over to the Chinese store and heading in that direction. The store was small so it was set up so that all you could do was order and get the hell out, the candy was displayed through a thick 3 inch bulletproof glass that has some deep marks from being shot at on numerous occasions. The pictures of all the plates available were also on display right above the glass. The rest was covered with anything to disrupt a view to the other side. To the right was a steel door that was heavily secured. Just locks on top of more locks to secure more locks. Talk about security. I waited as the two niggaz barked there order into the hole in a glass. "10 minute." The lady replied. "let me get a vanilla Dutch." I asked. The look on her face showed shock and disappointment. I had the bud Jamal gave me and I was going to smoke that shit. Mom was in the hospital and I was a bit stressed the fuck out. "Sup G you got something to put in that Dutch?" Asked one of the guys who ordered their food and was waiting. He stumbled a little and slurred his words. "Yeah I'm good." Short and to the point. I headed back to the house with my dutches and to no surprise, Linda was still posted on the door waiting for me to reappear. "I know you didn't order no more for which you greedy ass?" Linda joked. I thought about concealing the Dutch but what she was going to bitch regardless, unless.... "What you going to do with that?" Linda Barked with one hand on her hip. "With what?" I replied as if I didn't know what she was referring to. "Don't be acting stupid boy." Linda shot back. I pass right by her with a smile I bolted upstairs with shoes and all on. "You better take them dirty ass shoes off."... "I'm telling mom." I laughed while heading upstairs. She was joking she wasn't telling nobody anything. I know damn well she wasn't saying shit. I came back down with the bag Jamaal had given me still untouched. "Manny what are you doing?" Linda whined following me to the kitchen. I split the Dutch like I saw Jamal do countless times, Only difference was my line wasn't as straight as his was. "You really about the smoke that shit!?" Linda asked with her hands on her hip again. "Relax it's only a little bud." I spoke seriously. I was right it was only bud not crack, I kept telling myself this over and over again repeating this in my mind so it wouldn't feel so bad. "That's a gateway drug Manny." Linda stated with all seriousness. She waited for me to reply to what she just. What could I say she was right. Instead, I focused on my task at hand. I was getting frustrated because the leaf on the Dutch Floating off. I slobbered all over the leaves and place them as they went. I had to literally use the counter as my platform. "Jamal made this shit look to fucking easy". I almost yelled. "Well you're not Jamal." Linda still kept on fucking with me. She opened up the bag and in seconds the strong aroma slapped both of our faces. "That smells good." I looked at her with a shocked stare. "I can't believe you just said that?" I was expecting all man this shit stinks." I tried to mimic her tone breaking up the bud. She started to break it up with me. "Why is this so sticky?" She asked. "Because it's that sticky icky." I joked by the time I had the L rolled up. It looked like a boomerang I laugh because it wasn't a work of art but it had to do. "Where u smoking that?" Linda asked. "In your room let's go." I stated. "Oh hell no, not in my room." Linda barked. I was cracking up if she would've been def. I know she would've spoken after saying what I said to her in instant. With that I turned right back around I checked the drawer where mom always kept her lighters and extra boxes of cigarettes. "Bingo!" Now I was all ready to float up in the sky. "Come on I'm going out back." I invited her. "I'm not conspiring in your little adventure." Linda replied I headed to the back. I sat down on the top steps of the back porch the sky was a deep dark blue with a bunch of white bright stars. I looked over across the yard and no one was outback or in any of the other yards that I noticed. That could be because everyone was out front. I lit the L took a big puffin held it in... Exhaling I heard the door from behind me open it was Linda. "Why you leave me alone in their?" Linda asked with a sweatshirt on. "I told you to come out with me didn't I?" I am not feeling anything yet. "Yeah but I didn't think you was actually going to go through with this." She said pointing at the L. She also had her sleeve covering her nose and mouth as to avoid getting a contact. I turned back to look straight ahead, I took another puff and that's when I felt my eyes getting heavier than the usual. My speech slurred and got a lot smoother. "Are you smoking because you are worried about mom?" Linda asked me the inevitable question. "Yes." Was all I said in my reply? "Well let me get some too." She asked. "Yeah right don't start Linda." I replied. "For real, I'm so worried and stressed out myself." She admitted. "You was just getting on my ass about this and now all of the sudden you want some?" I stated. "Yeah" she replied. "Fuck it."

I stated taking another pull before passing it over to my foster sister. I looked around a bit paranoid as if someone was about to creep up on us or even the police. I looked at Linda and she still didn't take a hit. "Just suck on it like a straw and take a deep breath." I instructed. She put the L to her lips and did as I told her. I would know if she was fraud if she didn't burst out coughing out a lung or two. She did as I explained but held the smoke in her mouth. "Now take a deep breath, like when the doctor tells you to take a deep breath." Right on cue she almost coughed up spitting up a tonsils, Lungs, esophagus all her insides were trying to climb out of her mouth. I laughed uncontrollably. She gave it back still coughing. "Are you okay?" I asked her with one arm around her. "Yeah" she had watery eyes but she was fine. From where we sat in my yard we had a view of the side of the school building. I noticed a group of guys walking slowly, they couldn't see us because the backyards were stupid dart. I noticed them by the street-lights. I passed the L back to Linda to see if she wanted anymore. To my surprise again, she took it but this time took a slow drag instead of a big puff like she took in the first place. "I feel it Manny." She informed me. Her eyes were low but I couldn't tell if they were red. "What are you feeling?" I asked. "I feel so relax its indescribable Manny, this doesn't feel so bad." Her words hit me harder than I expected. "I repeated what she said in my head I didn't want her to get a liking to this but to be honest I think it was too late for that. "How do you feel Manny?" She asked. "I feel like for the next however long this feeling is going to last, that I'm not here. My thoughts aren't as hard, my body feels as if it's warm, my nerves and my anxiousness are nonexistent at the moment. I feel good ma. I'm glad you are here with me and I'm sure mom will be fine." I went on to explain to her. "Whoa... I feel the same way." Linda moved in closer by now the L was practically gone. Once I passed it back over to Linda I went inside and retrieve the trash bag. I couldn't let mom see the evidence if she did come back home. I guess I was being paranoid. She'll kill us if she found out we were smoking weed in her house. I was eyeing the ally, I was paranoid as shit. This had to be the only part I didn't like too much. "Manny what are you doing?" Linda asked. "Nothing, come inside if you're done." I was headfirst in the refrigerator. I went for the freezer to get me some Ben & Jerry's chocolate chip cookie ice cream. "Ooooo, I want some of that." I laughed at Linda I bet you do want some." We stuffed our faces with all kinds of food the phone rang, Linda ran like hell to answer it. "Hello Felicia." Linda was geeky with his this big ass cheesy smile while eating. "Manny?" He's taken a shower I'll tell him to call you later." Linda was bugging and she hung up on her. "Why you hang up on her?" I disapproved of her move but she was right I couldn't talk to her like this. "We chilling and this is our time. You can call her later or my manana." Linda was high as a kite her eyes were bloodshot red. The kitchen was a mess with especially the counter, chips, cookies and juice we had to clean this shit again before we went to bed it was all I was thinking. I looked at Linda she was in the living room fiddling with the radio. She turned it up to power 103.9Fm and DMX was playing "what these bitches want from a nigga." She bolted back to where I was in the kitchen. I was scooping the ice cream with a Dorito, her body looked alot better than it usually did. It must've been the weed, she was dancing. Linda love to dance I enjoyed the way she moved to the beat. The music was blaring we was so high. I put the food down and followed her rhythm with my hands, her body was soft and to be honest I was getting horny as fuck. My hands caressed her curves. She wasn't my blood sister and we wasn't fucking all we was doing was enjoying a good dance. Nelly "If you want to take a ride with me." We switched it up with, we both had moves. The way she was throwing it back there was no way she couldn't feel all of me all over her ass. She was hitting it hard every time. So I was for sure that she felt my little man's. She turned over and literally began grinding on me harder I had no choice but to show her I was the dance king in this house I dropped low so she could feel all of the little man's. I should've known this was gona open up a whole other can of worms. I grabbed her ass to break her down but she seen me dance on numerous occasions and counter my every move. Her arm was around my neck only made it harder for me to do what I do. Her face looked as if she was enjoying every moment of this a little too much. I was enjoying her body myself, things were escalated rapidly we went from dancing innocently to a little bump and grind while sweating. My hands held her tightly and she held on to me. Inhaling one another's breath with both our hearts pounding out our chest. Her nipples I noticed were erected, she moved my left hand onto her breasts. They were so soft and more than a handful while still dancing, obviously the one thing on our minds was a sexual encounter no matter how much I know I couldn't cross that line. Linda was all in, kissing and nibbling on my neck. My little man's was rock solid by now, she managed to get me to kiss her soft juicy lips. Her tongue was wet and warm, my taste buds explored her tongue. My hands caressed to the point I slipped my hand to the backside of her pants,her skin was smooth and so pure. My little head already had it's mind made up. I was going to take my time with her slowly and gently enjoying all of her juicy nectar. Linda was a great kisser she may have not done any fucking but I know she's done some kissing. She definitely knew how to move those lips and tongue. Her hand massaged my head and ears. She was touching me the way she always desired to but never knew that I would accept such pleasurable actions. "I want you Manny." She whispered while kissing all of me. My shirt was off in minutes feeling my abs one at a time. My chess, nipples and everything else she made sure she touched. Her lips moving downward with me pinned on the refrigerator. "You want me Manny?" Her voice was so seductive and sexually arousing. I did want her I was determined to tear that wet juicy pussy right up. I was horny and this was my opportunity to eat her all up and claim this untouched pussy. "Yes, Linda I want all of you." I replied "take me Manny." "Take it all for yourself." Linda was talking and saying things I knew she really didn't want to happen or did she actually want me just as bad? I done went through so many shows with this girl, about this guy and that guy that there was no way she wanted me Manuel Ricardo to take her virginity. I had to be one of the biggest dogs in East Camden. Could I be so selfish and just think about myself and what I wanted? I wanted to stick my thick long dick all up inside that pussy? It was screaming for some flesh to penetrate inside of them walls. My mind was made up when her hand went down to my little man's. Both of her tiny hands grabbed a hold on it she dropped to her knees and flicked her tongue off my head, stroking my shaft back and forth. "This is what you want Manny?" She spoke in between licks. "Oh yeah, Linda suck me baby suck me good." I replied looking down at her. I couldn't believe this was happening in Ms. Cathy's house, in her god damn kitchen at that. Linda sucked on the head as it was a blow pop her only focus was my head. An exciting feeling came over me she was sucking me so good my knees buckled every time. My shaft had her saliva all over it, slippery and stroking it firmly and with some speed. I wonder how many pornos had Linda been watching to acquire such skills and techniques or was she fucking on the low? She didn't even attempt to put it all inside of her tiny mouth. My balls were being sucked on at the moment. She stroked my Dick as the balls were being teabag. This was a dream come true, there was no turning back from this now I let her do her thing until I was ready to explode. I stopped her. "no I want to taste all of you, come Manny give it to me Baby." She ordered I held it back for a few more minutes. I grabbed her and picked her up in one quick motion dropping her right on the counter. "Oh papa you are too strong, I ripped off her shirt her nipples were small but were hard as raisins. I sucked and bit on them gently she moaned in ecstasy. "this is what you want mami?" I asked biting and kissing her. "Yes! Only by you baby, only if it's you Manny. I always wanted you." She held my head speaking her heart out. Her breasts were fully exposed no marks. The only marks were from my teeth, no stretch marks. She was flawless under her clothing. I couldn't wait but I wanted her to experience, the experience she desired role play. "Come on Manny fuck my tight pussy." Fuck me papi." I know you want it because I want it." I slid her pants right from under her. Her body was fully exposed. She was sitting on the countertop, I scooted her to the edge so that her pussy was hanging nearly off the edge. I put her legs up on my shoulder and got low and moved my tongue down her navel passing her waist. I wouldn't stop until I reached the destination I was looking for. Her lips were tucked away neatly as if never being moved or touched by a soul, her small clit was hidden underneath the sensitive layer of skin that concealed it. It smelled clean and was shaven down to every follicle. Her thighs matched her whole skin tone as if she tanned naked but then again she was African-American so her skin was flawless. I was in heaven enjoying all of this. She let out a slight moan but not out of pain but out of pure ecstasy and enjoyment. Never being touched in these areas may feel abnormal but once it is done you become hooked immediately. I flicked my tongue on her click she threw her head back "oh my God!" She hit her head against the cabinet behind her. I laugh but continued to go at it. I slid my tongue down her small slit right down the middle. "Manny what are you doing to me baby!!" She was yelling, she was loving this shit. I was going to make this feeling last a lifetime. "Yes baby eat your pussy.... Eat your pussy!" she demanded. "how does it taste?" She asked. I didn't say anything I was too involved but I moaned in agreeing with all her words. I nibbled a little as she began to shake, her thighs slap my ears almost causing me to go death. I dug my fingers in her thick thighs and hit my spot. My tongue slipped in and out slowly feeling her every crease and tender flesh, she began to cum uncontrollably "Manny, Manny, Manny oh my God yes... Yes... Yes...yyyeeesssss!!!!" Her thighs felt as if they were a vice grips holding my head in place. As she came all in my mouth, It felt like she was putting me in a chokehold. I didn't stop until I felt her about to come again, this time she came more than the first time it was time for me. I couldn't wait to let my little man feel how wet and warm Linda was. She grabbed him with her hand and looked at into my eyes. "Slow baby please." She spoke serious as all hell. "Okay baby." I slid my shaft up and down her lips so I could get all wet by her natural sweet juices so I could ease up inside of her.

"Pop!! Pop!!pop!!..." The sound of shots rang out waking me up out of my sleep. I jumped up and Linda was right in my arms laying on the back porch. "Oh shit Linda!" I shook her up. "what?" She answered grouchy as fuck. "." We passed out in the backyard and my dick was fully erected. "Oh my God Manny put that thing away." Linda's arm was resting on my little man. "I wonder what you was dreaming about boy." She smiled standing up. "No you don't." I shot back trying to gather myself, embarrassed. The moon was bright as ever it was late, we shot inside. The clock on the oven red 3:16 AM "wow" it's late. We fell out." That's what weeds does to you? It puts you to sleep?" Linda stated in a question heading to the fridge "It did tonight. I must of been beat." I spoke. "That is a waste of money and time remind me to never do that shit again." Linda said drinking her orange juice. She began to clean up and I helped with everything. "Manny please quit smoking please." She emphasized please. "I will." I replied. "You will or you'll try?" She asked. "I'll try." We called it a night. I didn't even get the chance to call Felicia. I'm sure she must've called again but it was late. I looked at the caller ID and yup just as I expected, four missed calls one from an unknown number and two from Felicia and another from a foreign number that I didn't recognize. It was probably for Linda. I stashed the rest of the bud and eventually stared at my eyelids.

—

The sound of the alarm buzzing two hours later after I fell asleep blared in my room but especially in my ears. My intention was to slam it against the floor but I knew I had to get up to go visit mom. I went straight to Linda's room not even shutting off the alarm pushed her door open. She was sprawled out on the bed sound asleep. I jumped on her to wake her up. I kept saying her name until she would eventually hear my voice. She sounded groggy and she protested “nooooo.” I’m so tired Manny.” Linda spoke with her face buried in her pillow. Turn off that damn alarm of yours.” Why would you leave it on?” She was irritated since my room was next-door. My alarm was loud as hell. Get your ass up we gotta go see mom.” The words left my mouth and hit her head hard, she shot right up as if she was a groundhog peeking out of his hole. “All right.” Ima get ready.” I was so happy and how genuine her love is for mom. I got up and got dressed as soon as I jumped out of the shower, Linda was in the kitchen preparing some breakfast. It was almost 7:30am, we had to get moving I thought. I call Felicia but I decided to just ride the bus with Linda. She had to go to school anyway. I wasn’t going I had way more important things to handle today. It took Linda almost an hour to get ready. I wondered why the hell this was a must for females. “Let’s go mija! I gotta work today too by the way.” I yelled up to her from the bottom of the steps. I had the sandwich she made me in one hand and the plate of sausage and bacon in the other. “I’m almost done Manny damn.” She replied. How the fuck wasn’t she ready yet? Stomach was full and I was all ready to hear what the doctor had to say about mom or wasn’t I? I could hear Linda walking down the steps my mind drifted back to the dream of us. I rubbed my head while opening the front door. The blazing sun blinded me temporary. I stood on my porch and watched as the parents hustled back and forth with their children to get them to school on time. Linda popped up behind me “let’s go” I turned to look at her and she was always looking crazy sexy. Her choice of clothing made that so. She had on jungle green capris and some black forces with a black tank top that hugged her body tightly. Her hair went from all over the place to it being twisted all over. “No wonder you took so long.” I said. “Why?” She challenge. “That nappy head you had to attend too.” I joked she punch me really hard and smiled “shut up I forgot my bag” the lip gloss was slapped on her lips heavy as always. I was wearing work clothes I wasn’t in the position to get fresh, I’ll save that for later. “Today you going to shine for both of us.” I stated complimenting to her. “I said as she walked back inside to get her book bag. I looked up and we was out the door in a hop and skip. As we walked to the nearest bus stop I had to talk to Linda about the possible outcomes that could possibly happen to mom. My gut told me she was okay for now but it wasn’t too promising for her in the future. I learned to follow my intuition even though sometimes I’ll go against in which I should know better than to do. “Linda?” I called over to my sister. "Sup Manny?" She replied I know I'm supposed to be the strong one here but I want you to know that, I try my best to keep my head up in every situation that comes our way." I began to speak, she was walking almost as if we were glued together. I didn't mind she was mine and was secure by my side. She listened attentively. "Excuse me." I politely walked through a crowd on the corner. I want you to know that when you and I walk through that depressing hospital it can go two ways." She looked at me. "what do you mean two ways Manny?" She asked still listening closely. Arriving At the bus stop on 26 St and Federal, we waited along with two other people when who we didn't recognize. "I mean that there only two things that the Dr. is going to tell us and that's either good news or bad news." I informed her "so you're trying to tell me is to expect either or?" She was right on the money Linda is far from dumb, she was catching on quick. "Exactly we have no choice but to be strong for mom even though by now I'm sure she already knows whats the issue. The doctors probably told her last night if not this morning." I explained. I had to prepare for the worst because going in there hoping and wishing for nothing but good news was the mentality one should always have. One had to be realistic about life as well. It was always to be optimistic but to have balance was even better just in case the worst came. "Why you talking like that Manny." Linda whined. "You know something that I don't know Manny?" She asked me worried. "No I don't Linda, but I went in the hospital thinking all crazy when I found out about my biological mother and when the news came that brought me down mentally because I set up my own mind up for failure." She looked up into my eyes. "I'm sorry." She showed some sympathy the bus showed up but it wasn't the one we was waiting for. The other two people who were waiting jumped on board, and left Linda and I alone. "You don't have to apologize we already dealt with my situation. I'm telling you this just in case okay?" I asked her, getting her to understand what I'm trying to say. "I understand what you mean Manny to be strong right?" I kissed her for head. It was nice out and I noticed our bus approaching it read "Lady of lords." I'll pay for myself. Yeah I was cheap like that, just kidding. Linda was a student so she had a pass. She didn't pay how privileged was that? Linda was on my heels we rode in silence side-by-side taking in the view of the filthy streets of East Camden. It was home. Despite all the terrible things you hear about this poor city is still has a lot of potential to rise from this poverty. What good is a governor who gives two shits on how we live. That's why it is the way it is. You have Mount Laurel, Cherry Hill, even Pennsauken all on the perimeter of Camden doing great their streets are clean with barely any potholes no trash etc. etc. Why can't we get some funding to help clean up our small city? We passed the bypass crossing over towards Camden high, to our left was the park which was already flooded with basketball players and your local dogs and children. This park was known to have the fountains that shoot water in the air about 10 feet in a circle formation. It's where all the children spend their hot summer days with their families. Shoes must be worn due to the broken glass that is all over the place though. Even with all that, they still managed to have a great time. I remember running through the water when I was smaller. Grown ups would get wet as well, I looked over to Linda and she was looking at all of the teenagers headed towards Camden high. I mean they look like ants. Woodrow Wilson's rivals as I stated before. To me this high school looked a bit bigger but I was riding with Woodrow Wilson high. It was only right, no big difference it was the same clicks and crews all broken up doing their thing getting high before they heard the bells. Only difference was the people themselves. Both schools were tough on the security just as all the other schools in the hood. There had to be a lease 1400 heads up in this school. It was a scene to look at. Cops patrolled and truancy patrolled. More than a few fights that did not break out on a daily basis was not a normal day. Good thing we were just driving on by because I didn't have time for any extra bullshit. I spoke too soon.... The bus driver stopped two blocks away from the hospital to pick up someone. My eyes were in complete shock when I noticed who just boarded the mother fucking bus. By her waist and dark complexion I had an idea who it was but once she paid and turned to find a seat my eyes confirmed my initial thoughts. I already knew where this was going to go. Linda stood calm as fuck as she always did. She felt no threat at the moment nor did she had to because I was right by her side. "All look who it is." Erica locked her gaze on to me. She still look good, her face was back to normal she healed quickly. I smirked. "So you still thinks it is funny!" She barked sitting diagonally from Linda and myself, I pay her no mind. Linda had her fist balled up now. I held her hand, To ease her thoughts through my touch, This Bitch was still popping off at the jaws. "So you wanna ignore me!" She barked. Mind you now she had the whole bus attention. Everyone was looking at her to see who she was directing those disrespectful harsh words to. Still a block away "you know my cousins are going to fuck your light-skinned ass the fuck up!" It all fell on deaf ears. I had one thing on my mind and that was mom. "Oh and your little girlfriend going to get it too. She thinks she's slick huh?" Erica was trying hard to get under my skin, but it wasn't working. She had gotten trashed because of her mouth and evidently she still didn't learn from the last ass whopping. I had to take a better look at her as she spoke. She was missing a tooth and that made me really laugh. The bus driver pulled up at the hospital and slowed down after I rang the bell Linda stood up and allow me to go first. I made my way towards the back door and kept it open with one hand on it. Erica came out her mouth one more time but didn't finish her statement Linda was all in her mouth.

"Bitch your cousin going to do what!?" Linda barked. Hit in her with two pieces back to back. "His girlfriend is going to get what!?" "Nothing bitch if anything happens to my brother or his girl, Ima kill you myself!" I didn't move because the bus driver was yelling for me to let go the door so he could barricade us inside. "Let go of the door young man!" Linda split her shit, all this bitch had to do was ride the bus and shut the fuck up. She ran her mouth and now your face paid for it." Let's go Linda just like a trained killer, she's stopped and got her short self-off the bus. We speed walked into the hospital and disappeared into the crowd. The bus driver call for the police but it was too late. Stupid mother fucker. I looked at Linda she was breathing heavily. "You okay?" I asked her. I grabbed her hand which was shaking uncontrollably due to her adrenaline pumping heart. "Yeah I'm good." She said in between breath she was cut and was leaking blood on the elevator floor. We was in the hospital so it would be easy to patch this up once inside mom's room. There should be more than enough Gauzes and alcohol pads and Band-Aids for this little wound on her knuckle. Linda had a fight game but she never flaunted it. She always tried to stay humble about all of our encounters. "Linda why you beat that bitch face in like that?" I had a smirk on my face. "Two reasons the first one, was because you're a man and I know you wasn't going to do shit but make her even more pist. Two, she wouldn't shut the fuck up about the threats and all that extra shit. So now she can pick up her face off the seat next to her because I got that dirty bitch good." Linda spoke with attitude. She was right I wasn't going to touch her at all. I was going to get her madder at the fact that I wasn't feeding into her bull shit. Her cousins? I knew them and they knew me if they wanted to try me they knew where I was. I wasn't running or hiding from anyone. The door opened I grabbed Linda's hand as if she was my girl like I always did. As we made our way towards the end of the hall I scanned the room looking for a white shirt. I wanted to know what they told mom because if I let it up to mom to explain to me she'll just sugarcoat it and have us believing that everything is all right. Just so we wouldn't be all worried and panic. This is how she would describe the tragic news to us, very nonchalantly which I thought was wrong. I had to understand her point of view in not wanting us to be hurt as bad. I noticed two men in white overcoats in room 304. I waited until I noticed they weren't in the middle the conversation to get their attention. Let me emphasize this, there was two of them in one room. Why there was a need for so much knowledge in one room.... "Excuse me?" I called into the room they both turned and looked back. They had this disgusted look on their faces as if I interrupted a surgery or something. I know I was a bit in the wrong but I wanted to know. Dr. Harrison changed his expression on his face. As he put my face in his memory bank and remembered me from last night. He excused himself from the other doctor and other patients "Manuel?" He extended his well-manicured hand "have you seen your mother yet?" He was reading my mind by asking these questions. "How is she?" Linda blurted out. "Well let's go somewhere so we can talk privately. Linda grabbed and squeezed the shit outta my left hand. We made our way to an empty room. "We can use his room for a few it won't be filled till the next half an hour" Dr. Harrison stated Linda and myself were stanThere was absolutely no feeling in my fingers. I looked over at Linda and her eyes were already to the brink of dropping tears but she inhaled a deep breath and let it out slowly. "Let us hear the good news first doctor." I said trying to hold my composure. "Well Ms. Catherine is a strong woman. She'll be fine as long as she cuts back on smoking, or just gives it up completely. It'll be a whole lot better but I'm sure all three of us know that this isn't going to happen." Dr. Harrison stated. "Why you say she won't quit?" Linda asked. "Well Ms. Catherine and I had a long discussion about this topic and we went in circles for almost an hour. She stubborn and to be honest she has no intention of quitting or slowing down which will only speed up the bad news that I have for you." Dr. Harrison paused. We could let it all sink in. I'm nodding my head to let him know to drop the bad news on us. "Ms.

Catherine has a sign of cancer in her left lung which is relatively small but in case you're not informed on the whole cancer epidemic it has the ability to spread rapidly. What makes cancer so deadly is that it attacks when it wants too. To slow down the process Ms. Catherine would have to slow down on the cigarettes." Linda couldn't hold it in anymore she broke down. I knew this was going to happen there was no stopping it or preventing it. I held her tightly. "She's going to be fine but you have to help her quit. I'm not sure how you will accomplish this but it has to be done so she could live many more years." Dr. Harrison notice Linda's hands and grabbed it. "How did this happen?" He asked. The look I gave him and a shake of my head said enough. "I'll get my nurse to address that out for you it looks infected." Thank you Dr. Harrison. "You're welcome now go see your mother. "Do you mind if we have a moment." I asked him to try and settle Jalinda down. "Sure" just like that he disappeared. I held her and dropped my tears because this was going to be a challenge to get mom to stop let alone quit. This is why Linda cried uncontrollably. "She not going to stop Manny. I don't want to lose her Manny, I can live with that. You two are the only people I have." Linda cried on my chest. "That's our job and will have to do our part." "I know but it's not gona work Manny you and I both know how she is." Linda stated. I grabbed her face and wiped her tears with my thumbs. Listen to me, everything is going to work out and if it doesn't at least you and I know that we tried our best. Now let's go and see mom." I told her, she didn't respond. We left to go to the room 314 were mom was wide-awake and noticed us immediately. "There you are I've been calling home since last night. I'm ready to go home." Mom stated with a smile on her face happy to see us, but little did she know a long talk was due once we got released.

Chapter 7

"Class of 2000"

"Manuel Ricardo!" I may not be the most popular individual in this big ass school, but the up roar of all who knew me or even heard of me let it be known. It was a very beautiful sunny clear day, anyone would say that this was the perfect weather for a senior graduation. I was so excited. It had to be about 800 seniors graduating today. The men wore black caps and gowns and the female wore burgundy. The graduation was held right out front of the high schoo,l it was about 2 o'clock on this lovely afternoon. The families and friends surrounded all of us. Many stood on their 2 feet not by choice just because of the lack of chairs that was to blame. That wasn't going to stop the celebration from proceeding. I was in the far back row since my last name started with an "R" I didn't care, all that mattered to me was that I finally was able to actually say. "I have a high school diploma not a GED but an actual diploma." It took me a lot of tiresome days and nights studying to prepare for the exams, pop quizzes and every other difficult test one had to pass to get to where I am today. Mom and Linda were amongst the crowd hollering and cheering. I remember when Linda graduated she was also so excited. Her smile illuminated the whole Eastern part of the world. I wondered how she was feeling that day. Now in this very moment I know exactly how she felt. Butterflies had built a nest in my stomach and had their own celebration inside of me floating in my belly. I scanned the area. I stood tall with my chin up. I made sure I sat and walked with the perfect posture. My height stood out over everyone.

Rock! You did it!" Someone yelled. I displayed the biggest smile. I knew Banga and

Jigz would be somewhere up in here since his cousin was graduating as well. Till this day I still didn't know who he was. Jamal had told me that he would be present but it was like a needle in a haystack looking for him. I made my way up closer to the podium. She was waiting for me, with my diploma in her hand. The vice principals and all the higher ups had seats behind her. I looked over to my side. I noticed a few faces who were in one of my study halls. I never really associated with them but by their attire, I knew that they were one of many who may not get the opportunity to graduate. No Wait! They did get the opportunity they chose not to put in the work to graduate, allow me to correct myself. So their choice was to try again, the embarrassment was too much to handle. When the juniors are now seniors and are in the same classes as you. That alone can tend to break your pride in half and cause you to act out in many ways that can hurt you in the wrong way. "Congratulations Manuel." Mrs. Espinosa stated loudly so that I could hear her voice clearly. "Thank you very much." I replied shaking her well-manicured hands and grabbing my diploma. I held her hand and looked over to the crowed so that whoever wanted to take the picture of us.

This felt so surreal. I held my diploma up as high as I could. I wanted the world to see I was overwhelmed with joy. "I did it! Yes!" I yelled. I made my way back over to my seat as I heard the next name being called. My time to shine was over for now. The next graduate proceeded to enjoy his moment of fame, which was only fair. He too put in all the time and work to accomplish what needed to be done. I could hear Linda yelling. "Manny you did it we love you!" I look back at them and mom and Linda had their hands locked in one another's held up high in the sky. "I love you too." I yelled as loud as I could. The two most important woman in my world were here with me. It felt great having her see with her own eyes, what she drilled in Linda and myself had finally been accomplish. Year after year starting from third grade even after I screwed up. She begged me and lectured me on the significance of obtaining a diploma. "Once you have it can't nobody ever take it from you?" Those were her words. She was right, it wasn't in my hands but in the Garden State of New Jersey. I was certified and it was legit. Even if I lost this one my records were all accounted for. The graduation ceremony lasted about 2 1/2 hours of countless speeches and the music was very boring but it was part of the ordeal.

I met up with Linda and Mom once everyone was given their diplomas and all of the superiors concluded their speeches. The ceremony ended with everyone throwing up their caps at the sound of the "GRADUATING CLASS OF 2000." Cheering and screaming amongst all the graduates was the finalization of the ceremony. I never seen so many people smile it was a site worth taking in. Mom clung on to me. Linda wasn't too far back. "So how do you feel Manny?" Linda asked excitedly. "It's amazing it was actually worth it." I replied. "You bet your ass it was worth it you think all that shit I repeated year after year was all a smokescreens?" Mom asked. "No and I'm very grateful you took the time out to instill it in us that quitters will never succeed in this gruesome world we live in." I recited one of mom's lines. "You can bet your last dollar on that too." Mom stood by her quoted words. "Come on were going to go out to eat. Felicia is on her way." Linda stated. She had to work, it was an emergency that was why she wasn't with mom and Linda in the crowd cheering. I know that if she didn't have to work she would've been right there cheering right beside my beautiful Angels. "Let's get away from all these people I need another cigarette." Mom stated reaching in her purse. She knew better than to light up next to me. I didn't care how much money she spent on those damn cancer sticks. I would snatch it right away from her mouth and disintegrate those bad boys. I couldn't just let her smoke and kill herself right in front of me. I looked at her and she walked very swiftly away to take a few puffs. I didn't chase her. Linda had my hand held tightly so I couldn't really let go. "Where you want to go?" I kept my eyes on mom. "Manny am talking to you, you know she's going to do what she wants so get on her ass later." Mom only took a few puffs and toss the rest looking back at me. My visage was one not to be fucked with as she knew this.

"I'm sorry baby but my body craves it so bad." Mom was apologizing sensing I wasn't to pleased. "I don't want to ruin your day." I didn't say a word. I wanted to kill whoever sold those fucking cancer sticks. All three bodegas that are in our area were instructed by me to not sell her any type of nicotine products, even the Chinese store was warned. I told them what the deal was, From us living in an area for years they knew it us all too well. I went as far as threatening to burn the store down if I found out there was selling cigarettes to her. The other stores were off-limits because they didn't know me from a hole in the wall. All the owners felt my pain and agreed to not sell mom no more nicotine. I knew it was working because one day she came into the house bitching and complaining.

"I don't know why you would tell the stores not to sell me any cigarettes! I'm going to get them one way or another." Mom complained lighting a cigarette. She finally has gotten the drift. I was dead serious. She's smokes in her room or in the bathroom. When Linda and I are around she knows better because she'll just lose a cigarette. So why waste more money when we are around. The doctor ordered her a few oxygen tanks and mask, Just in case she does tend to lose her breath. She would be fine until she can go to the emergency room. Even with those tanks. It specifically states on the label. "Warning highly explosive, no smoking." Now do you honestly think she cares? I caught her with the mask on and smoking and at the same time. She found it exhilarating. I think mom might have a death wish to be honest. I would do my best to prevent it from happening alone with my sister Linda.

"Ayo bro!" A familiar voice called out from behind us. I turned around it was Jamal "you showed up." I thought you was around but I couldn't spot your big ass." I joked. "Yea I'm here with my cousin he gestured to Malik who was in my homeroom. He was a chill back guy he and I spoke a few times but nothing more. I walked over to salute Jamal and his cousin they were deep because a few ore heads popped up. "Congrats Rock." Malik dapped me up "likewise it's finally over for now. I congradulated him as well. "For now" he stated. "You're right for now. "Rock this is my wife, son and thats my aunt with her uncle and my other little cousin." I shook hands with all of them introducing myself. It was my turn.

"This is my wonderful small family. This is Ms. Cathy and you already met Linda, these two women are my world." I spoke very highly of them making them feel very important because they were very important to me. "Where you going?" Jamal asked. "Were about to go out to eat." Linda answered. "All yea were too?" Jamal asked, but no sooner did he get the words out. The blaring of a horn came closer and louder, who could be the maniac.

"All there go girly." Jamal looked over my shoulder stating. The Lexus appeared. I looked, it was Felicia just like Linda said she was on her way. She jumped out screaming. "Congratulations baby I'm so proud to you!" "I guess I'll catch you at work or tonight hit me up Rock." Jamal stating getting back to his cousins celebration. They disappeared as we walked over to the Lexus she had white shoe polish painted all over her windows with sayings like "class of 00, you did it baby"! All types of quotes. She jumped into my arms planning a big kiss. I look to see if I saw Eliza but no sign of her. The little booger was growing on me. Everyone has been introduced and off we went. We headed out of the city. It seems as though the ladies had already planned out what was going on today. Which was fine with me. We had a casual conversation while we drove to the so called restaurant. About 20 minutes into the drive we pulled into a parking lot of the "Italian bistro" around the Cherry Hill area. The logo was big and robust all in one. I had never eaten out in this place but we were all excited. "We are here." Felicia put the car in park. "I'm sorry I missed the ceremony but I'm here now and we are going to celebrate till we get kicked out." Felicia was hyped in her scrubs. They had Looney Tunes all over them. "Kicked out? Girl what you plan on doing?" Mom asked jokingly. "Nothing Ms. Cathy I'm just happy to see him. I'm going little overboard." Felicia corrected her behavior. Linda was laughing. "What's so funny Linda?" I asked. "Nada let's eat I'm starving." Linda stated. "I opened the door for mom helping her get out of the Lexus. We made it inside the place. It was a bit up scale and flashy. It wasn't a five-star restaurant well probably a three or four. The place had chandeliers and everything seemed to sparkle so radiantly. The bar was in the center with a balcony for whoever wanted to enjoy a meal outside. This place was a very nice spot. I thought to myself.

"Oh my." Mom said upon entering. I always drove by this place and always wonder what it looked like inside." Mom was excited to. "Felicia and I wanted to go somewhere different. so today wouldn't be an unforgettable day for Manny." Linda said with Felicia right by her side. "We sure did, we looked at all types a restaurant but this one stood out so we went with this one. Felicia stared into my eyes as she spoke. We made our way to the please wait sign. "Manuel Ricardo?" The short Caucasian green eyed female called out with a clipboard in her hand. Her dirty blonde hair was done up neatly. She wore all black with the restaurant logo on her left breast and her name tag on the right which read Angelina. The earpiece didn't go unnoticed. "Yes thats me." I reply having a big cheesy smile platered on my face. "Okay great, your table is ready we have reservations for you and your party of 4."Angelina spoke to us but into the earpiece at the same time. I looked at Felicia and she winked at me. The Reservation gave us the green light to jump in front of all the other people who have been waiting for who knows how long. ""Follow me." Angelina stated. She had a cute body but but she wasn't my type. I wasn't sure what it was but something told me that she wasn't. We all followed Little Miss Angelina all the way to the table that was towards the left of the room. I couldn't help but to look at all the plates on the tables, there were all empty. The smell of the pasta and garlic was filtered all over the air. I was hungry now more than I thought I was earlier. Our table was neatly set up with all types of dishes. The only problem was that there were all empty like I said. "I think this is the wrong table." I stated while everyone was taken their seats. "Why you say that?" Angelina asked. "Because all the plates are empty." I joked. "You have to order silly." Angelina smiled that's when I noticed her grill was all bent out of shape. A Light bulb went off. She handed us our menus and we all got lost with all the fancy Italian words. There was some type of language being used I was in 100% sure but it looked like Italian with English. We all tried to focus in on the menu, I had to break the silence. "So whose going to translate this menu in English for us. I failed French and every other language course in the high." I joked everyone laugh uncontrollably. "I'm right with you on that one son. This is confusing the only words I understand are the drinks." Mom said "Linda you look like you already know what you want." I stated. "Yes I sure do all I did was pick one and it's a hit or miss if I don't like it I'll change it." Linda joked. Felicia was all laughs. "Ima order the Parmesan with the Alfredo and cheese." Felicia said. You could tell she had been here before. "That sounds good." Mom said I'll take the same. "Can I get you your drinks?" Angelina came over with a pad and pen in her hand. She started with Felicia which was right across from me. Linda was next to her and mom was in front of Linda but next to me. "Brisk iced tea." Felicia said. "Do you have juices?" Linda asked. "Yes, we have orange juice, kiwi strawberry, mango and lemonade." Angelina recited as if she answered that question 1000 times. "I'll take the kiwi strawberry please." Linda asked politely. "I'll take a Jolly rancher." I looked at mom not knowing what the fuck she was talking about. Felicia giggled. The hostess jotted it down with no problems. "How about you sir." What can I get you to drink?" "I'll take a Mountain Dew with extra ice please." I ordered. "You still need time for your order ?" Angelina asked "yes were not ready but do you have a menu with pictures on it." I joke but was dead serious at the same time. You are too much no I don't but everything is good." She went on. "what do you recommend?" I asked. "I like the spaghetti with the homemade meatballs with the Parmesan on the side." Angelina knew what was good because I'm sure she ate and tried everything on the menu. "Linda jumped in I'll take that." "I'll have the same." I stated, Felicia ordered her Alfredo twice one for her and one for mom, all that was said and done. "I'll be back with your drinks in a minute." Angelina walked away. Her ass bounced in her tight fitted slacks "I can't believe you asked for a menu with pictures on it Manny." Linda was tripping. "I know, You are something else Manuel." Mom was also laughing her ass off. "So you like the place?" Felicia asked I looked around yes is very nice. The prices on the menu are a bit steep but hey I guess you gotta pay to have a good time in a place like this." If I can recall the lowest price for a decent meal I noticed on the menu was about $15 from there they went up rapidly. "I came here almost 7 years ago." Felicia informed me. "I was with my mom and one of her boyfriend's. We ended up getting kicked out because they got so drunk and started to argue. It was so embarrassing. "This place is such a peaceful place to eat you don't hear screaming and hollering like Pizza Hut right?" Felicia was right this place was so quiet .You could hear what the cooks were saying from the back. "This is nowhere near Pizza Hut. Pizza Hut. That place was super loud." I admitted "I like Pizza Hut." Mom said. "Yes I do too." I agreed with mom. "Where not that far from the mall?" Linda interjected changing the subject. "No were about a mile away from it." Felicia informed Linda. "If you want we can shoot over there when were done here." Lisa suggested. "Sounds like a good idea." Mom replied. Just as the sentence was finished our drinks were being placed in front of us. Also, the empty plates were being removed from our table. Angelina move swiftly and in seconds they were all gone. She left a basket full of breadsticks and marinara sauce in the center of the table. I was dying to know what the fuck was a Jolly rancher. I slid mom's cup over to me taste it. My face balled up immediately. I was expecting a sweetish drink instead I was hit with a sweet bitter alcoholic beverage. Everyone was laughing at me. I guess that's what I get. "Mom you serious?" I asked her. "That's what you get for being nosy." Mom stated laughing taking her cup back. "What did you think it was Manuel?" Felicia asked dying with laughter. "I don't know a juicy drink like what Linda ordered." I replied feeling stupid. That was the talk of the night I already knew how that was going to go. "It's a mixed drink. I know you noticed a big bar in the center of the room." Felicia stated the obvious "yeah I saw it but I didn't think they had a drink on the menu named Jolly Rancher. I tried to defend my case but it wasn't happing. Mom was in her own little world sipping on her drink with a smile on her face. After a few minutes that seemed like forever, our food was smoking hot and on it's way over to the table. The dishes were flooded with food. I now understood why the food was pricey. They were servings for at least three people each plate. The breadsticks were a bonus and let's not forget to mention the salad that came with the meal on another small plate. The main course was a hefty plate. My eyes pop out my face literally at the sight of the serving rations. So much food for one person to consume at one time. I was ready to put a hurting on this dish. I stared at each plate as it was placed on the table. My mouth watered something serious. Mom's and Felicia's plate was well put together. The pasta had white sauce all over, so did the meat. I just wondered what it tastes like. Linda's dish was spaghetti with big ass meatballs that were the size of softballs. It smelled delightful.

An hour and a half later everyone sat back with their bellies full with no room for anything. Linda and mom excuse themselves from the table. "So how was your meal babe?" Felicia asked. "It was delicious." Was all I could say? I literally couldn't breathe I was stuffed. "I'm glad you enjoyed it maybe you can enjoy me for dessert tonight?" Felicia was hooked on little man but fuck it I enjoyed fucking the shit out of her." We can work something out." I joked. "Where is the baby?" I asked. "Home. She should be getting ready for bed." I looked at my watch and it was already almost 7 PM. The night was young but aging quickly. Angelina came over with her letter pad. "Is that all for tonight?" She asked in her sexy voice, to bad her grill was shot. "Yes to my knowledge that is all." I answered looking at Felicia. "Yes, I'm good let's wait and see if your mom Linada are done." Felicia spoken Angelina listened then chimed in. "Yeah I just met with them on my way towards the bathroom. They are wrapping things up with their end." She handed me the pad and left. I went to open it Felicia's snatched it out of my hand. That's not for you to see." Felicia stated. "Why can't I see it? Ima pay for it." I replied knowing damn well I wasn't paying for shit. "Because I'm treating you. If I wanted you to pay I would ask you to pay or even split it." Felicia replied. Yes, but the next one was supposed to be on me?" I challenge. "Yeah you're right our next date just you and me." She corrected. "Okay you got it then." Linda and mom were on their way holding each other arm in arm. "Let's go to the mall." Linda whined. "I'm all for that?" I joked. "What you mean to spend some money." Linda shot back mom was feeling nice she was all smiles. "I'll be right back." Mom stated. So now it was just three of us at the table. "I'm full. " Linda informed everyone. "Mom is crazy, she was hitting on the older man at the bar." Linda spoke and pointed at the older man on the corner of the bar. He was bald with glasses he wore a button down shirt and looked as if he was important. "Oh yeah and what happened?" I asked. "Nothing mom shot him down after she got him all wound up. Telling him "I'm sorry I'm married and from the looks of it you are too." Linda mimicked moms voice. I looked around for her but didn't see her. "Your mom is married?" Felicia asked. "No but she uses that when she wants to get out of a conversation that is started by someone else who is interested." Linda laughed as she let Felicia know of mom's mischievous acts. I couldn't help but laugh myself. "What's that?" Linda asked pointing to the letter pad. "The bill." Felicia replied holding it tightly. "Let me see." Linda stated reaching in her small purse. "Nope." Felicia replied Linda pulled out a $50 bill. "Here this is for the bill." Felicia gave her a look of disgust. "I got it Linda. I just had this conversation which your brother, it's my treat." Felicia stated. "It's our treat this as our gift to him were gona help out." Linda stated. Looking back at Felicia. I think Felicia knew better than to engage in an argument would Linda so she took the $50 and put it away. "Here comes mom." Linda noticed. She was right she had about nine employees from the restaurant with her with a big old cake with two lit candles on it. Once they were close to the table they all yelled "congratulation Manuel for graduating class of 2000!" The whole restaurant clapped and cheered. This woman was crazy, after blowing out the candles the cake was cut up into four pieces and shared with ice cream. "Come on mom I'm full." I whined. I couldn't believe these woman had all types of tricks up there sleaves. "There's always room for dessert baby." I could smell the nicotine roll over tongue. I wanted to trip but I decided that I wouldn't at least not here. After paying the $120 tab the host boxed up our cake and off to the mall we went. It was right down the street so it wasn't a long drive it was short and the mall was crowded as always.

The Cherry Hill Mall was always flooded, it was our mall for all your ballers. This one was for those who didn't feel like driving to Gallery, Franklin Mills or even the King of Prussia. It had two levels and it was the spot. Macy's was on point with there clothing. We all looked our part as we strolled throughout the mall. Mom, Linda and Felicia had to buy everything that they saw. I made my way to the footlocker and grab me some new black Tims. I did ruin the ones I used for work.

It was getting late but who would've known that I would run into little ol Jacqueline. I didn't know where mom and the girls were but she rolled up on me hard. "Hey you?" Her sweet soft voice spoke. "Sup ma what you doing up in here by yourself?" I asked. She had a few bags in her hand and I noticed one was a Victoria's Secret's. "You know treating myself to a little something." Jacqueline was bad and I couldn't wait to beat that shit up if I ever got the chance. "Lingerie?" Must be a romantic night for you?" I joked. "You can say that if you want to but it's for my eyes only." She replied. "I know you going to wear that for your man no need to front. I respected a woman who can keep it 100 with me, just like I keep it 100 with whoever at all times." I wanted to see if she was willing to spill the beans. "Boy I don't have to front I aint got no man worth me getting all sexy for, one that can appreciate this for what it's worth. I got a BD's and that negative ass nigga wish he could get this back. Nope he done fucked up one too many times." Jacqueline was on the money. "Maybe I'll be able to enjoy that one day if you're not too busy?" I challenged. I looked over her shoulder and I noticed Linda from a distance we was in front of the fountain and I knew Felicia wasn't too far back. Linda did a 180 as soon as she saw me and snatched up Felicia into a store. "Maybe, we'll see...she smiled. What you up to?" Well just needed some boots. I'm here with my family and friends." I replied. "So you came here for some boots at this time?" She asked. "Yeah but I just came from the Italian bistro from dinner after my graduation it was my gift for my family." I informed her. "Oh shit all done with school huh? I might in fact wear this for you?" Jacqueline was all in my face now. She had to look up. She smells so good. "I'm a call you later on tonight." She informed me. "So you finally going to call huh?" "If you say so." I replied. "I wanted to call you the same night I got the number, but I wasn't trying to appear too desperate." She admitted. "How you gona look desperate? The whole point of me giving you my number was for you to call so we could link up." I stated in disbelief. I understood exactly what she was saying. "I know and my friend Nikki stay bugging me to call you, because she want to link go with your boy." Jacqueline admitted. So you don't want to chill? That's what's wrong with this picture." I replied. "Not at all have I wanted to, but with you I would already know I'm not gona control myself because you are a sexy mother fucka." She said. "Come on ma I'm your average nigga nothing to brag about." I stared at her eyes. "You look like you controlling yourself well to me." I informed her. I noticed she was crossing her legs so her juice box must've been moist. I thought to myself. She smiled. "We'll look Ima wait for your call and we will take it from there." I said. "You work tomorrow?" She asked. "You already know."

If anything I'll stop by and we can kick it, let your friend Nikki know." I said. "All right pa." I gave her a kiss on her cheek and went on the hunt for the others. I passed by Modell's and decided to step in there and check out what they had. I looked around for a bit checking out the jerseys and hats. I didn't see anything there. "Can I help you sir?" The Modell's worker asked "No, I'm good just looking around." I replied. "We'll let me know if you need anything." I spun around and ended up leaving. I had changed my mind. I wasn't really in the mood for a new jersey so I left. "Manny!" Yelled Linda with Felicia right on her heels. "/Que Paso?/" I asked./what happen?/ "come look at this." Linda grabbed me and spun dragging me into the wet seal store. It was a female store. I noticed many females so I didn't protest not one bit. I noticed Mom checking out some sunglasses. "We need a male's point of view." Felicia stated. "I see you found what you was looking for." Linda look down at my bag. "They are either all Blacks or the original butters." Linda already knew what I like and what I didn't wear. My smile gave her the answer. "Men are so predictable." Linda said holding up an outfit. "I like this but I'm not sure which one I want she picked up another one. The one in her left hand was a button up blouse with some slacks, the other one was something similar to a suit. "Which one Manny?" She asked. I told her "the blouse with the slacks is nice and very conservative." "You gotta try them on first, you know that." I said. I called over to. "Would you doing over there?" looking for some new shades." She had one in each hand and a pair on her face. "I like the ones in your left hand." I opinionated. "Oh yeah, how about the ones I have on?" She asked. "Yeah they're nice too." It seems as if all eyes were on us. "They are buy one get one free Manuel." Mom said. "Take all three I got you." I informed her the smile on her face was priceless. I wouldn't change that smile for anything. All I ask for is for my girls to stay happy. I followed Felicia and Linda to the dressing room. This was where all the mami's' were, getting naked and trying on all types of outfits. Falicia stood by me. "So girl you see anything you like?" I asked Felicia given her my undivided attention for a bit. "As a matter fact I do." She replied looking at me while licking her lips. "What may that be?" I asked. "You." She replied. 'Oh yeah?" I joked. "Oh yeah." She joked back.

"Manny! Linda called out from behind the fitting room door. "/Estoy aqui mija./" /I'm right here/ I informed her. "Excuse me." The small blonde girl came walking over. "Can I ask you for your opinion?" She asked Felicia and myself. "Do you think this looks too tight on me?" I looked at her. She had on the jeans that look way too tight. So tight that you could follow her fart traveling if she'd let one go." "Can you breathe?" Felicia joked. "Yeah but I can't barely walk." The Blondie joked back. "Then there you go, you have your answer." Felicia joked back. "Yeah, but you'll loosen up after a while little mama. They look good to me. I think they look good on you. Just don't make any sudden movements." I joked. Linda's door swung open and she stepped out with an all black jacket with the black slacks with a white blouse. "Wow." I said as soon as I saw her. "I like that a lot." Oh yes Linda that is very nice." Mom popped up out of nowhere. "It's cute baby." Felicia stated. She looked in the mirror and looked at her backside front and side. She liked it I could tell her smile was lit up. "Is not crazy tight but it shows off your curves very nicely." I informed her. The blonde over heard when I said overly tight and scrunched up her face. I guess she felt a bit insulted even though I wasn't talking about her. "You don't think is too much?" Linda question "I think it's different and very sexy to see a woman in a suit. You look very professional." I said. "I agree." mom stated. "I like it too Linda. I didn't think it would have looked like that once it was on the rack, but you rocking that girl." Felicia changed her mind on the previous outfit. "I'm a take it." Linda made up her mind. I put on one of mom shades that she had in her hand. "How I look?" "Very confused." mom said laughing her ass off. I joked around for a bit "stop Manuel." "Linda look at your brother." Felicia instructed. Linda poked her head out. "Oh my God you better stop." She laughed at my childish behavior. I gathered myself and waited patiently for the girls who were all done shopping. Women being woman took about a good hour and some change. I couldn't believe how expensive mom's glasses turned out to be. She spoke "boy if I would've known that they were $100 a piece I would've left them right where they were." "Don't worry about it mom." I informed her. Linda's outfit was $110 which was a bit pricey but she didn't care. I made it a mental note to buy her one for her birthday, which was around the corner. "You ready to leave?" I asked all three. Felicia didn't say word I guess she was down for whatever as long as I was calling the shots and she was with me. "Yeah let's go. We taking up all of Felicia's time." Mom stated. "No, Ms. Cathy you are fine. I'm happy that I can spend time and get to know y'all better since I never really have my own family to actually enjoy." Felicia stated. We decided to head out to the mall since it was almost 10 PM and that's the time they started to close up and kick everybody out little by little. Mom and Linda walked ahead. Felicia grabbed my arm and I looked around as to make sure I wouldn't blow my own cover with any other spectators. "So what do you want to do tonight Rock?" Felicia asked. I like how she called me Manuel when she was around my family and switched it up when we were alone. "You if that's what you want to do?" I asked. already knowing that this is what she actually wanted. "I'm tired baby how about tomorrow?" Felicia asked. This came to a complete shock to me. I'm here thinking that I was going to punish this girl tonight and here it is, I got shot down. How could I end this night with no pussy? I wasn't going to show her I was caught off guard. I knew this game already and boy this girl was dead wrong for trying to play me with the oldest trick in the book. "Say no more, I'm tired myself." I replied. Showing no emotional discomfort. "You not mad at me?" Felicia asked. Now she was feeling guilty all of the sudden. "Mad." Oh no." I'm good." I kept it light. "You will call one of your other bitches to fuck you, I already know." Felicia said with her added two cents. I didn't pay her no mind this girl was acting up and already. I knew this was going to happen either today, tomorrow or the next week it was no stopping it. I walked straight to the car with everyone else. She unlocked the door and off in the dark sky we drove until we reached 28th and federal.

"Thank you sweetie." Mom shared her gratitude towards Felicia. Linda just got up and left, I was about to open my door slide out when she held my hand. "Hold on." I waited but kept my eyes on my sister and mom. I made sure they were safe as they headed into the house. "You love them a lot don't you?" She asked referring to my mom and Linda. "More than life itself, if it wouldn't because of them. My life wouldn't be as complete as it is today." I admitted. "I can see that Rock. I see how your eyes glow when you're with them. Your smile and even when you speak about them." She informed me. The car horn in back of us caused her to drive since we was in the middle of the street. She drove around and found a parking spot.

She turned off the car and leaned over to me and what she did, did in fact take me by surprise. She unzipped my pants. "I looked at her a bit shocked. "What you think, I aint leaving you hanging on your birthday?" She whipped out my little man's and lick the tip, mind you we were about 25 feet from a church on Federal. My blood flowed right to where her tongue was licking as if it wanted to shoot right into her mouth. Once it was fully erect, the chatter and laughter from outside the car could be heard. I peaked and what I saw just made me more excited. I couldn't believe how we went from talking about how much I loved my family to getting some birthday head. The voices came from a small crowd that was about two houses down from the Lexus. The laughter was directed straight to us. I saw the street lights above the cars that weren't any help. The site of Felicia's head bopping up and down could be seen clear as day and i didn't give a shit. I took it all in and just ignored it all. My mind was searching for ecstasy and I was going to find it. I reached over and slid my hand down the back of her jeans until my palms had her juicy ass squeezing it tightly. She sucked the skin off my dick. My feet were pushed up on the floor boards on the car. "That's right girl, get him!" I heard from the outside spectators throwing in there comments our way. I couldn't help but to smirk. Woman and men were so nosey why couldn't they just looked the other way? No they had to witness everything for themselves. The slurping caused the erection to go up even harder. They wanted to see the whole show and not miss any parts of it. I bit my lip slipping my finger in her wet pussy. She let out a moan, I played with her pussy till I felt my fingers all wet. The warmth from her love box had my dick throbbing. Felicia noticed and began stroking harder and sucking more. I couldn't help it nor hold it anymore. She couldn't swallow me whole but my right hand was pushing me deeper inside of her soft wet juicy mouth. I shot my heavy load all down her throat and left my finger inside her pussy. She moaned as I jammed my finger deep down inside of her. Toes curled, she kept slurping every soldier that came out of my shaft. The crowd cheered and clapped as the show came to an abrupt stop. I licked my fingers because I'm nasty like that. Felicia was embarrassed as her adrenaline slowed down. She tried to conceal her face.

"Oh my God they were watching the whole time and you didn't say anything." She pouted. I laughed. "Who cares baby would you have stopped if I would have said something?" I asked "no." She replied "alright then let's get up out of here then."

We shared laughter all the way to the house which was only around the corner. The sound of the base dumping was heard almost immediately, let alone felt in the air. I always love the car with a bang. The car given off all this ruckus was parallel parked in the middle of the street. Felicia stopped at the half street. She was no dummy and I'm very precautions. I decided to jump out so she could hang the right and go about her business. "Call me when you get home baby girl." I said shutting the door not waiting for response. The car was unfamiliar but it was nice. It had shiny wheels but resembled a truck more than a car to be exact. In fact it was a money green expedition. I noticed it was tinted out all around with limo tint. It was pointless trying to see who occupied the truck. I made my way towards the house but a familiar voice called out my name.

"Ayo Rock!" The truck turned off his four ways and parked on the corner with the whole front and hanging off the corner. It was Jigz "What's up G." I notice him as he hopped out of the truck a bit hesitant. "You good? It's me." Jigz stated leaving his truck and the dumping behind him. His jewels were shining brightly. His necklace dangled side-by-side. The diamonds were playing double Dutch with the streetlights. I felt tired and weak due to my explosion in the Lexus. I had to wrap this up. "So how does it feel to be a high school graduate? "Jigz asked with a wide grin. He had a blunt in the back of his ear I noticed but I didn't say shit. These niggaz was getting it, this nigga smelt like money for real. Fresh to death from head to toe. Switching back and forth from one whip to a different whip. His eyes were a big glossy. He was feeling it. "It feels good Jigz but I'm not up there like you yet." I joked. "We gave you the proposition and is still there if you wanted my G. It is in your hands to take it and sit back and watch the bread stack up." Jigz spoke "you already know Jigz." "That's not me right now." I said with all honesty. "And this is why I personally want you to handle this strip because you don't play and you voice your opinion and stand your ground." Jigz was sounding convincing, look let you peoples know that I'm trying to get rid of that." He pointed over to the truck. "Get rid of what?" I asked puzzled. "My baby girl right there." I was still lost. "The truck Rock, the damn truck. "Jigz said. "Oh yeah what's wrong with it?" I asked. The look he gave me was a vicious one as if I just played him. "What the fuck you mean? What's wrong with it? Rock you know I'm about my money and there is no way I do backward business. "Jigz stated firmly to my insult. "So was wrong with it?" I repeated. "You gotta be crazy." Jigz joked "I'm saying Jigz... I wanted it unless? ... "Unless what?" Jigz interjected "nothing is wrong with it?" he finished.

"Look I'm trying to cop me something new and I'm tired of her." Jigz was dead ass. I laughed at how these mother fuckas put names and went as far as adding genders to their precious cars. "I never seen you with this, so how the hell you tired of her.?" I asked with my finger symbolizing quotation marks. It was not meant for everybody to see all the bitches I have accumulated. They only come out every once in a blue Rock. Too many eyes and definitely too many stickup kids but I got something for they asses." He pulled up his button up and show me the chrome. "So what you want for her and where the fuck is Banga?" I asked. Those two mother fuckas were inseparable. "He should be on his way we going to go to La Tierra Columbiana in Philly." Jigz informed me. "Oh all right going to splurge I see." I joked. "you know it papa." I'm asking for $5000 Rock, as it is. They can have it with the 24's and the TVs, and the system everything is included." I rubbed the back of my neck as I heard the numbers. If I wasn't mistaken I had $4000 in the stash but I was still short a stack. "What's the lowest you will take so I can make some money on it Jigz?" I was trying to see how far I could take this. The truck was fresh and I wanted something big even though I didn't have my license yet. I could get that as soon as possible. I'm too tall to be jumping in and out of a go-cart. I need something suitable for me. I held my composure as always. "Man looked Rock give me 45 and you keep the extra nickel. "Jigz was sparking the L that was in the back of his ear. He was on Hustler mode now for real. I looked at my watch and it was damn near 11 o'clock. "So $4500 right?" I asked "yup early, only for you." Jigz caught himself given me a deal. Some more thunder came from behind us. "That's gotta be Banga." Jigz stated. The car crept up slow and Jigs pulled his 45 Glock out and loaded one in the head in one quick motion. I stepped aside just in case. He held it at his side as the limo tint on the Buick was so dark that no visible trace of anyone was noticeable. "Nah that's not him." Jigz kept his look on the whip and stood focused on point. In case anything were to pop off, who is in your truck?" I asked. "2 bad bitches they in their getting twisted. "Jigz admitted "damn 2 of them." I said "yeah and they all mine Banga gotta find his own flock of bitches." He joked. "That's why we need two whips." He stated. "They sipping on Henny and probably rolling up as we speak." He exhaled a cloud of smoke as he bragged about his girls getting trashed in the truck. "You want to come? "Jigz asked. "Nah I'm good I had a long day maybe another time." I had let the words out before I noticed what the fuck I just said. It was too late. "Ima hold you to that. "Jigz said. "But no for real, /el carro lo quiero vender/ let people know jefe."/the car I want to sell it let people know/Jigz said. "You gotta get an alignment because the rims are fresh and I never made time to get them aligned." He admitted. "I guess the weed don't lie huh?" I joked. "might be. "Jigz replied. "There that nigga go right there." He noticed Banga candy apple Vic pull up. The music wasn't thumping loudly, but the thumping that came from the Vic sounded as if someone was in the trunk trying to signal for help being trapped inside. The thumps where vicious. Four ways on and the two main bosses of the block were right here chillen with me. There much wanted new recruit. "Yo my nigga I only got two bitches because the other ones weren't ready so I left them. "Banga joked also shining. I could only imagine how much money these two had on them. We all dapped up and joked around for a little bit. "How many you got in the trunk? "Banga asked. "Only got 2 for me and none for you..." Jigz admitted joking "Oh man I thought you was going to have at least four. "Banga was high as hell too. Grabbing the L Jigz just handed him. "What the fuck y'all up to?" Let me find out Rock finally want some of this block money?" Banga wished for confirmation. "I'm waiting for him to give me the okay." Jigz lied. "I didn't say shit." Nah we was talking about selling the truck." Jigz informed Banga "who the hell he know that want to drop five stacks on the truck Jigs. "Banga was jumping to his own conclusions. "These niggas out here broke Jigz." Banga was talking shit but stating the obvious in his eyes. I didn't like the assassination at my character like that. "Man I told him I'll give him $4000 right now take it or leave it." I stated trying to call his bluff and let these mother fuckas know, just because I don't sling that work don't mean a nigga broke. Jigz almost broke his neck looking at me. All eyes were on him and Banga being the hype man, helped me out more than he knew it. "Damn! Nigga I know you didn't turned down 4G's don't tell me he'd lying." Banga was coming at his face as they always did. "Man hell know if somebody gave me 4G's right now. I'll give them the keys right now shit!" Jigz was cornered and now my hand was exposed. If this Nigga sold me the truck for $4000 I was taken this shit with no license and all. I didn't say anything I just waited to see who or what would jump next and just I expected Jigz let out. "What's up G?" it's easy to talk when your pockets are empty. "Jigz let out. "Shake on it that I get the keys right now and we'll handle the paperwork another time." Banga looked at me, then at Jigz. I had my hand out and there was no turning back now. He gripped my hand but I have a grip myself. "Early! Is all settled than where my money at?" Banga joked. With the L in his mouth. "I'll be back." I stated. I bolted to my room, Linda was sitting on the couch on the phone and I didn't even take my shoes off. In my closet in seconds with my heart racing. I pulled out my air force ones box. I pulled out all my money that I had been saving for the past few months it was $4000 give or take 20 or $10 off I was sure of it. I looked in the mirror and took a deep breath and picture me in the truck. My mind was made up and the deal was already sealed. I bolted back downstairs that sounded like a roaring stampede of Buffalo. "Damn! Manny what the hell. You okay?" Linda said. By the time she was done I was already going down the front porch steps with a nod of cash wrapped in a rubber band. "Get the fuck out of here." Jigz was salty like a bitch catching her man creeping "this little nigga got the bread." Jigs was sick. "Yes he does and now you gotta walk with your ugly ass bitches all the way across the Ben Franklin Bridge and hope and pray you make it to the club before closes." Banga was talking mad shit while passing the L to Jigz. "I handed him the money and he fluttered through it checking to see if it looked official. "It's all there count it." I hit him with the final blow. "He reached in his pocket and pulled out another knot that was much thicker than the one I just handed him. ""Nah for some reason I trust you and if not is my fault for trusting you." He said. I knew he was going to count that shit as soon as he had the chance. "Yo it's getting late let's get moving my G, that's it. It's gone let the young boy enjoy his truck, it pays off to have a check you can cash you know. That's how Rock is raised he don't talk just cause he got lips. This nigga is smart." Banga applauded my moves and winked at me. We walked over to the truck. Listen, we will do the paperwork this weekend get your license as soon as possible." Jigz stated. I knew I shouldn't of bought this car but what the hell. It was fully loaded, he opened the door and the roaring of the Vico C reggaeton echoed all through the block. The cloud escaped smelling like straight up loud. Jigz jumped in and turned down the system. I could hear the female voices chatting and laughing. Banga open the back door and I saw both of them in thigh-high miniskirts with cleavage all in the open. It was two Spanish woman and they were all done up looking light showstoppers for real. "Diablo" I stressed.

"You see but no you don't want to roll with us. "Jigz joked. "What papa we not good enough for you." The box blonde haired one asked in her sexy accent. "Not at all mami /estoy muy cansado/ that's all." I stated /I was really tired/. I should jump in and roll with them but no I had to work in the morning. "Come on ladies we are taking my car." Banga stated as Jigz shut off the engine on the truck "Why I like this one is bigger." The black hair Spanish girl spoke while hitting the L. "I bet you do like the big ones but i like money better." Jigs joked. "Not like that Jigz." She confessed. "Yea I know" Banga stated. "Here my G is all yours be easy and keep the alarm activated." Jigz joke but was dead ass and I knew it. "You already know y'all have fun and don't hurt nobody tonight." I joked back. "That's always the objective but always an alternative." Jigz joked. The bottle of Henny was in his hand. The bitches left by his side and they made their way to the Vic. "Let me know when you got your els" Jigz yelled back at me. "Tabien." I replied. I looked at this truck it was husky. I couldn't leave this mother fucker sitting there like this. "Manny what you doing!?" "Ben aqui" I instructed to the question /come here/ shutting the door she was at the corner in seconds. "Damn! This is clean." Linda said referring to the truck. "Isn't it?" Why you just staring at it?" Linda spoke. "We going to get fucking shot just for staring at whoever car this is, it looks like we plotting." Linda spoke the truth. "I'm not shooting myself and I'm not going to shoot you." I let it all marinate to see if it sunk in her small head. "What you talking about Manny. I know you not gona shoot us, but the owner will if he sees us just staring at his car." I'm leaving." Linda began to walk back to the house. The people came in and out of the Chinese store and just looked at the truck. It was clean and fresh. "/Mira!/" I said. I held the keys up and she couldn't believe what she was seeing. "You don't even have a license and don't tell me that it's yours because you aint got no money for a car like that." She had her hand on her hip and talked with an attitude. "You're wrong and right." I don't have a license but Im getting it and second I did have the money to buy this but now I'm broke because I just spent it all on this." I push the buttons and the beep warned. She was inching closer and closer. "You bought it for real?" Linda was super hyped. "It's ours and yes I bought it with all the pennies I saved from working at the sub shop." I informed her. "Stop playing how much Manny?" Linda asked. "It doesn't matter it's paid for and this weekend I'll get my license and the title transfer when I get paid." I stated. I pushed the button again. "Get in girl." I said "let me lock the door to the house." She raced to lock the door.

Inside the car is smelled like straight loud and female perfume. "It smells all feminine in here Manny." Linda stated the obvious. "You bought it from a woman?" She asked. "It doesn't matter is all mine and pay for I said again. I'll wash it up tomorrow and get the smell out of it." I turned the ignition and it turned over at ease, the music was low. "That radio is nice Manny." The radio lit up the inside of the truck but it was pointless because you couldn't see inside even if you try. I turned the knob.The bass hit even harder than Linda began to dance in her seat. "Look at all that room in the back." She yelled over the music. I looked and it was spacious, she was not lying on that note. I put the car in gear to drive off. I knew I had to take the big road because to be honest I never drove a truck like this. I pulled off slowly and got acquainted with my new vehicle. I took through Pennsauken and jumped on 78 and just drove until I had enough. I wanted to drive to Felicia's but change my mind. I felt good to be honest I felt like a boss. I pulled up to the other whips and I had no choice but to look down on them, not because I thought I was better but because that's how high up I was in the truck. It felt great to own something that you were taught to save penny after penny for. I made it all the way to South Camden then back over to east. Linda turned on the radio. "Tell me how much you pay for this?" She asked rubbing the shiny dashboard. I stared at her. "$4000 don't tell anyone please this is between us." I spoke seriously "what? That's it?" She asked very doubtful. "It stolen?" She asked "no why would I buy stolen car?" I replied "because no one will sell a truck with rims and a system fully loaded for just four grand and to make it more unbelievable it's a almost a new truck." I laughed you gotta know people sometimes. "Were you get it from?" She was bugging with all these questions but then again she knew everything that I did. That's what I get for developing this relationship with her. She wasn't going to stop until I told her and answered all her questions. "Jigz" "No wonder, it's probably wanted in a murder or a robbery Manny." Linda was right or at least could be right. I doubted that he would set me up like that. I'll kill that nigga for real. I never killed anyone but I think I would do just that. "It's all good trust me." I stated hoping I was right. A lot of different scenarios came along with buying a car off someone off the street. One could never know like Linda stated. It could dam will be stolen as a matter fact I never even seen a title. It could be even worse. My mind was going crazy now how stupid could I be? It could possibly have been used in a crime, and knowing these two crazy ass niggaz I wouldn't put it past either one of them. A murder, robbery or even just being under investigation point blank. Anything was possible. I dismissed all of those thoughts out of my head and looked over at Linda. I guess the look on my face was one that showed worry. "It's all good Manny." She said putting up the music again, now she wanted to think positive after she put all these fucked up thoughts in my head. We have known each other for years and I never did shit to either one of them. For all I know we was all good, so good that they wanted me to hold down the block for them on a business level.Then again how many niggaz in the hood have hidden agendas on the next man? Too many I answered myself. A strong smell of Loud smacked me right out of my trance that I didn't even notice what Linda was doing.

"What the fuck Linda where the hell did you get that from?" I barked at her very upset. "It was in the ashtray Manny damn you don't have to yell at me." She replied exhaling the smoke out of her mouth I pulled over right on 22nd St. and snatched that shit out of her hand. The looked I gave her wasn't a good one "what?" She asked. As if she didn't do anything wrong. "What are you smoking?" I barked again. "What you mean what am I smoking?" She asked not knowing the answer to my question "yes exactly what are you smoking?" I barked. "I think is weed." She said with no type of assurance or confidence. "And how do you know?" I asked again. "I don't know but it smells like It." she answered. I smelled the el but didn't taste it yet until I was sure exactly what was in the L. Even with my lack of knowledge on drugs I couldn't it be 100% sure of what it was myself. "Why you so mad Manny?" Linda asked. "Because you was quick to pick up this already rolled up L, and smoke the shit without actually knowing what the fuck is in it. I didn't hand this to you did I?" I asked still a bit furious. "No." She answered with her head down. "Exactly you found in this dumb ass car and was so quick to lite it as if you knew exactly what was in it." Preached to her but I was dead serious because I was. I finally came to the conclusion that it was only weed that it wasn't mixed with anything else besides that. I didn't smell anything out of the ordinary that gave me the impression that it was laced with PCP or any other hard drug and am so thankful that it wasn't.

"Linda let me tell you something if you don't see was being rolled up, not that you should be smoking shit anyway, know that if you didn't see it get rolled then you should not smoking it. Now you know Jigs and Banga right? I asked "Right." She replied. Well you know them two are crazy ass niggaz smoke wet and lace there blunts every now and then. Well maybe you don't know this but I do so for you to pick up an el that they left in this truck should've been a red flag. The same way you came to think of all the thoughts about the truck and why the hell did I buy from them. You should've used that same thought process about lighting up the el. You can't trust no one when it comes to drugs or anything that's going to be ingested into your body ma. Yes, I'm a bit mad cuz I thought you would be smarter than that. I'm glad that you're not tripping and I see that you are just high." I said. "Yes, I am definitely high and I'm sorry and I see what you're saying Manny. I should've known better than to put that shit in my mouth." Linda understood and apologized. I sparked it. "Well let's finish it and get home." I stated pulling off in the truck. I wouldn't know what I would've done if that L was laced. How would I explain this to mom? Let alone to the people at the hospital if the L had been laced with some harder drugs ,instead of just plain Jane marijuana. The hairs all my arm immediately turned into Goosebumps at the thought of Linda getting drugged up unintentionally due to my carelessness. This little cruise wouldn't have ended well. My fear of all of this and the prosibility of her becoming dependent would of torn me apart. I inhaled and pulled on our block and scanned for a parking spot. I looked over at Linda and her mind was lost in the sights of our rough but lovely small city. "/Toma./" I said and passed her the L she reached over and grabbed it. Never no parking on this dumbass block but only one and it look way to small. I wondered how the hell I was going to get this big bad bitch into this parking spot. I never parked a beast this big, actually I haven't parked any car to be straight up. I put on my four ways and got ready to attempt this move. The view was too high up in the right and the four ways were throwing me off my focal vision on the corners. Pulled her up closer to the car on the side of my truck so that I could get an easier but it wasn't happening. Linda was literally kneeling on the back seat looking out the back windshield to try to help me out but she was high and just made noise effects.

"I can't see, get out and get me in." I asked her. I pulled down the window and just listen to her as she yelled. "more,.... more,.... and more" it took about a good five minutes to get this big bitch in but it was all said and done. Windows up in alarm set Linda pass me the L. I took two more pulls and disintegrated it on the bottom of my sneakers. "I'm high as hell." I admitted to her. "Me too and I'm thirsty." She informed me I looked to the Chinese store but the bright yellow sign off. We had to settle for soda which was probably the only thing we had in the house which was fine. I looked up at mom's window and the TV was on her lights were off. I damn sure didn't want her to catch me like this high out my mind and to make it worse my sister was blasted right along with me. Even though she was the older one out of the two, but at the end of the day I would have to bite that charge. The block wasn't popping. It looked like a ghost town everyone is broke or everybody went to bed getting some rest before work something. Once inside we smashed some cake that was left over from the Italian bistro and let me tell you I searched every cabinet door for a glass of milk. There was not a single drop of milk in this house. I swore if a woman would've been lactating, I would've filled up the glass and enjoyed the shit out of this cake with it. My thoughts caused me to crack the fuck up. Linda was popping soda cans open because she already knew the deal, soda in cake. "What you laughing at?" She questioned smiling at me I want some milk and the only store open right now is the 7eleven and I'm not walking down there." I informed her "walk?" Manny you have a car." She stated the obvious. "I know but I'm not going through the hassle to park that big as truck in that tight ass spot again. And even if we did leave the parking spot would be taken unless you stand there till I get back." I joked. She spit up the soda and I was holding my stomach all the laughing I was doing. "You crazy ass fuck. Manny you know how long I'll be waiting there for you to give back?" She joked back. "You're in your fresh new car, there is no way you will be right back. I'll be there standing there looking stupid as hell." She said she was right my main focus would be to get the milk but being high I wouldn't stay on track for sure. The cake and soda wasn't as bad. The muchies made almost anything acceptable. I cut out two more slices for Ms. Cathy just in case she wanted some. The rest would be demolished before we went up to our rooms and went to bed. I was tired and I knew I had to call Felicia back because I'm sure she called over here and no one picked up.

—

The horrible sound of the alarm clock blaring into my ears, I was late for school was my first reaction, but my tassel sitting on my nightstand reminded me I didn't have to wake up for school. The smell in the air forced me to wake up. It felt way too good to stay in bed. The coffee was strong and the bacon and eggs smell too fresh to pass. I brushed my teeth and shot straight downstairs. I became instantly enraged at the site of mom sitting in the dining room with her mask. Yes, the mask that is supposed to pump and fresh air into her lungs. What made me get super physco was the site of her smoking a cigarette while hooked up to the tank. That was image that put me on tilt.

Are you fucking serious!?" I barked I walked up to her smacked the burning cancer stick out of her hand and the pack that was on the table right by her elbow. I grabbed it and shredded every last stick. "Manuel."

She spoke removing the mass. "What is it with you mom do you want to die and leave us here in this world alone without you, you don't love us?" I yelled while turning off the burners on the stove. "No! I do want to die Manuel, I was going to put it out but..." "But nothing" I cut her off for someone that doesn't want to die and has been diagnosed with first stage cancer by a professional doctor. Who is still in her dining room smoking cigarettes back to back as if its her last day alive." I snatched ashtray and emptied it. "But to make matters worse she's on her oxygen machine which clearly states very flammable and no smoking signs all over the fucking tanks!" I was way beyond mad. "You don't understand." Mom protested. "No I do very clearly you don't want to live! What my eyes are portraying is a clear indication that you Catherine do not want to be on this planet or any other planet as a matter fact! Someone who wants to live to see their grandbabies grow up whenever that may be conceived is speeding up her death to arrivealot faster than it has to.... Now if I'm wrong then you please tell me that I am and please make me understand what I don't understand mom!" I was about 2 feet from her I lost it. I was letting it all out because she needed to hear this not later not tomorrow but now. "Why are you down here hollering and ranting about now Manny." Linda had this scared on her face. The look I gave her didn't require an explanation. She saw it and believe me something had to be wrong for me to be hollering a mom. "He's overreacted Linda, don't worry about it baby." Mom said under the mass. She sounded like a scuba diver. "Overreacting and I wonder why he's overreacting mom." Linda stressed the issue you could tell that she rolled right out of bed and came straight down because of the loudness in my voice woke her straight up. I darted to the kitchen and put me a plate together. I was calming myself down. I decided to put a plate together for Linda too. "Tell her mom." I stated. Her voice was hard to understand with the mask on but I'm sure Linda understood every last word since she was a few feet away. "Now you know better than that." Linda scolded her. I came back with two plates. Mom had a half a plate in front of her so she was good. I sat on the opposite end of the table with my face looking at my food. Linda took her seat. "So you say he's overreacting huh?" Linda asked. "I don't think that's overreacting mom. I think that if he would have never came down you would still be down here smoking and inhaling the oxygen together as if you can't live without either one." I just ate and listen as the two tried to debate cordially, but it wasn't going to happen because mom was just as stubborn as we all are. How well did you think this was going to end? It's not so bad. "Look last time I checked I'm grown." Mom was fed up she got my attention now "I know I need to slow down on the cigarettes but I'm grown and I don't want to quit smoking. The doctor said I could continue but it was a good idea to quit. I won't die but I'm not helping the situation not one bit." I didn't say shit, neither did Linda. "I've been smoking for my whole entire life and to think quitting overnight isn't easy as it sounds, well let me tell you to something.Instead of yelling at me telling me what I need to do, why don't y'all help me." Mom voice was cracking she was getting emotional on this. "I need help and I wish I could just quit just like that but obviously neither of you know what it feels like to be empowered by something so meaningless. I'm so fortunate, that I'm the one with the addiction instead of one or both of you." She was all teared up now I felt bad on how I acted out on her. I know she spoke for truth because in my whole life that we have been together which has been many years and every moment it was spent with her smoking. No matter the time or place she had a cigarette incinerating on a daily basis. Linda and I just listen as she spoke her feelings out to us. "You think I want to wake up every morning with this mask on my face? You actually think I want to put you and your sister through all of this embarrassment? My lungs crave this nicotine and it might just be mental but our minds are very powerful and it can be known to kill ourselves willingly." These words stabbed me dead center in my heart. Embarrassment? It echoed through my eardrum. Why would she think we would consider herself in embarrassment? These were my thoughts. I'm not sure what Linda was feeling but all I know is that mom was going through her own demons and I had to try and help her. "Mom I'm sorry for yelling." I said with all sincerity in my heart. I didn't know it was that bad and you are right I don't know what it feels like to be in your shoes.... I should have talked to you about it instead of lashing out." "Manuel you didn't mean no harm and believe me son I know this. You don't need to apologize because it's what your heart was speaking in the heat of the moment. If you don't care for me or my health you and your sister could just keep living your life day after day and pay my life no mine. Once you see that you words didn't seem to help you went on to do other tactics like throwing out my packs, hiding my lighters you even went as far as threaten the nice people who own the bodegas around here. Telling them not to sell me cigarettes." We all shared a small laugh. "Now that showing me that I mean something to the two of you and this is why I'm opening up to you now. I'm not as strong as I may appear to be. I am human and I have my weaknesses just as we all do." Mom was spilling the beans. "Mom we love you so much and trust and believe, that losing you would be the worst thing to happen to us. What can we do to help you and what are you willing to do to put this into effect and what is it going to take?" Linda asked a triple combo questions wiping her eyes. I nodded as she spoke and chose her words correctly. "Knock knock!!!" and the buzzing of the doorbell caught everyone's attention. I got up immediately because no one knocks on our door ever. I checked the people and it was Jigz. "Who is that?" Mom asked in her voice no one. A friend. I replied. I looked at Linda she went back and talk to mom. I slid out the door. "Yo what's up?" I answered "My bad Rock but I left something in the truck and I needed ASAP Jigz was talking a little faster normal. I noticed Banga's car down the block on the corner. By the looks of Jigz clothing and his face they still hadn't been to bed yet. "Yo Jigz I smoked that el you left in your ashtray." I actually thought that's the reason for the visit. "Phssst" he blew through his lips as if he didn't even care about that. "I don't have the keys holdup." I shot back inside and grab the keys from the nightstand. Mom and Linda stared at me as I move swiftly. "What is he doing Linda?" Mom asked her. I don't know but I'll ask him when he get back." Linda played it cool. Mom was going to know about the truck but not like this. I was outside and Jigz was out front. He walked over to the truck I pushed the button to unlock the truck" hit it again." Jigz instructed the back door unlocked I was about a foot away he reached up under the floorboards and pulled out what looked to be a fully automatic. My eyes popped out of my head. "Watch my back for the boys." Jigz instructed me there was two cars coming down "holdup." I said. I wasn't sure if it was the boys even though there weren't regular patrol cars but once again the DTs tended to use unmarked vehicles. "What the fuck Jigz, how you forget about that in the whip? On top of that I went for a drive last night with my sister with that in the back." I spoke aggressively. "I know my G but I totally forgot you know the bud and the alcohol didn't help at all. I'm glad you didn't get pulled over because if you I would've been sick." The car is legit but no license is enough to search I think but you know how these pigs get down in the hood"... Jigz explained. "You good." I replied. Damn I'm just happy Linda and myself didn't keep driving longer last night was all I kept thinking.

Chapter 8

"Roll up"

"Beep... Beep!" The horn from my truck ripped through the cloudy morning probably waking everyone who was still in a deep sleep. I wasn't exactly sure which house it was but being only five houses from the mechanic shop it had to be one of them. I looked over to my left and notice the big Canon in the park. Two bodies were slumped on the floor right beside it. A couple homeless sleeping was all that came to mind. The air guns from the shop loosening lug nuts and whatnot screamed every so often. I didn't see the body I was looking for. There were people up and about either going or coming from stores. The dope dealers at the end of the blocks were up early getting that cash. I was about to honk again until I noticed a small body exit the corner house. It was her Jacqueline, she was small but was all women. I pulled up and rolled the window down.

"You need a ride?" My smile was inviting. She walked over and opened the door and hopped in almost needing a ladder to get in. I smiled at her. "Whaaaatt?" She asked smiling with her sexy voice. "Nada just mesmerized by your beauty that's all." I worked it on her. She blushed. "Boy don't start." She replied. "I bet you're hungry." I asked. "I am where we going." Well I want a good breakfast and I only have you for an hour before I got to go in to work, and if I'm not mistaken you on the same boat?" I stated but it ended with sort of a question. "Yes you are right." She replied. "Well McDonald's is up the street from our jobs so we can hit that up and eat inside or just eat in the truck is up to you. It's not the best breakfast but we on borrowed time." Me knowing how ghetto that McDonalds is I really would've preferred to eat in the truck so we could enjoy one another's company. "We eat in the truck and chill if that's all right." Jacqueline wasn't the type you had to hassle with every little thing and I like that. Quick and to the point. "So I didn't know you drove." She stated but asking at the same time. "I know the last time you saw me was on the bus." I spoke. The bass in the truck was on volume one and is still thumped a bit. She would move her hair out her face. She was beautiful. Her body was following the reggaeton beat. "So this is you pa?" She as referring to the truck. "Yeah I just copped it yesterday why?" I asked. "Because is big and is clean and I don't want to get it all dirty when I eat." She joked. "You good unless you eat like a three year old." I joked back. So how was your sexual encounter last night with that sexy lingerie?" I had to ask. A punch to my arm is what I got for that remark. "I told you that was just for me to feel sexy for myself. A woman does that sometimes you know?" She stated trying to justify the reason she was buying lingerie. I acted as if my arm was badly hurt "damn my arm is sprained and you just made it even worse." I held my arm holding in my smile. I was playing it off good anyone in there right mind would've gave me a Grammy for that one. "I'm sorry." She pled. I got her now I laugh to myself. She grabbed my arm and massaged it. The front seat was so huge that there was room for more bodies up front. I enjoyed the contact, she was soft and gentle with her touch. My eyes were glued on her. I wasn't going to put a dent on this mother fucker the today. I extended my arm so she could do the whole arm. My hand was on her thigh I gripped it up as I suspected it to be soft I was right. I looked over quickly she follow my hand with her eyes. I stopped and focused on the road. It took me about seven minutes to hit South Camden into the parking lot of McDonald's. She was still rubbing my arm "does it still hurt pa?" Jacqueline asked softly and seductively. "A little." I lied. I didn't want her to stop. I flexed my arm a bit, she squeezed it "damn you fit too, there is no way my soft as punch hurt you boy." She joked but she still didn't let go. "It didn't hurt physically it hurt emotionally." I laughed and so did she. "You are too much boy." She said. I pulled up to the intercom in the drive through." What are you in the mood for?" I asked. I knew what I was in the mood for but I didn't even take it there, not yet I thought. She looked at the breakfast menu. "I'll take the breakfast bagel with an OJ." She said certain. "Welcome to McDonald's can I take your order please!?" The voice on the other end of the intercom yelled loudly. "God damn this shit is loud." Jacqueline said with her face all twisted up. "I know who you telling." I agreed. "Yes, can I get the number 2 with the orange juice with an extra orange juice on the side please that'll be all thank you." I spoke into the intercom "anything else?" The female voice yelled again. "No that's everything." I replied "$5.60 pulled around." I pulled off before she could even finish saying what she was saying. What? Why? You're not going to eat with me? That was the whole point of our so-called breakfast date." She used her fingers as quotes and joked. "I ate already. I wanted to take u out before work because I wanted to see you." I said paying at the window. I handed her a $20 bill and waited for my change. "$14.40 thank you. You might want to turn the speaker down because that is really loud back there." I informed the worker. "I'm sorry I will." She replied handed me a small bag, then the drinks. "Napkins are in the bag sir, have a good day and enjoy your meal." The lady at the window said. "Thank you ma." I replied. "She loves her job or she is feeling you." Jacqueline said taken the bag out of my hand. "She was cute." I said jokingly. She looked at me in disgust as I pulled over to a park. I made sure I was far from every other car in the lot. I laughed. "What, big girls need love too and I heard they can take care of their man." I threw it in park and got comfy. "You gotta be joking Manuel." She asked "It's Rock please." She was sexy as fuck, her lips were pink and glossy. I wanted to chew on them but I kept my composure. "/Come ma/, /eat/." I instructed. "Toma/here/." She handed me her hash brown. "You got a long day ahead of you eat up you need your energy." I turned up the music a tiny bit but it boomed as if I wanted the City Hall to hear what we was listening to. Gargolas by Archangel was playing. By the way Jacqueline moved I noticed she could dance. She ate in small bites like a mouse. We talked about our day and what was on our to-do list for the night. I drank the OJ and played with the radio trying to adjust the bass. It was way too strong. I didn't mind but I wanted it low for now. "What you trying to do?" She asked because I was messing up her vibe. "trying to adjust the bass." I replied. "why?" She asked. "It's too much." I replied. "I'm not familiar with the radio I just got it so yeah." She laughed at my silliness. "So Rock how many girlfriends do you have?" She asked being dead serious asking personal questions now. I smiled. "For real though.... why do I gotta have girlfriends and not just one?" I defended myself. "Yeah okay." She sipped on her OJ. "You are a pretty boy and you are young. So yeah." She use my line against me. "Well to keep it 100 with you. I expect you to do the same with me." I'm messing with one chick but is not serious and I like you so she might get booted." I told her. She was blushing but covered her mouth with one hand as she chewed on her food. "And you?" I asked her she swallowed and began. "I have a few male friends that are just friends. One of them is gay and the others know that it aint gona happen. My baby dads is all on my ass. The last time I had sex was four months ago with him." She admitted. "Four months ago?" I challenge with a look of disbelief on my face. "I'm serious Rock. I'm not trying to fuck him anymore. He is a dog and he shows me this right in front of my face. I cut him off completely." She defended her cause. "So why you still fucking him?" I asked looking at her and licking my lips. "Don't do that pa." She said "what?" I said doing it again. "That!" She barked. Not looking at my lips. "I fucked him because I get horny too. I rather have sex with him then a random nigga in the street." She let it out. My mouth dropped how real she was. I definitely like that and she earned extra points for that especially. "So how about you leave that nigga alone and just let him be the father to your son and when you feel lonely you can call me." It was a risk that I took but I went for the kill. "What if you're with that girl that you messing with?" She challenged. Then I might drop her just to be by your side." I said biting my bottom lip. She stared at me and chewed slowly trying to read what I was really thinking. I smiled and so did she. I switched the subject, I planted the seed and now it was all on her. "So what is up with Nikki?" I asked her. "Man that girl won't quit asking about your boy." She replied. "So why don't yall let niggaz know when yall want to link up so I can tell my boy Jamal." I stated. I noticed a homeless guy going window to window asking for change. I knew it was just a matter of time before he got to the truck. "Because I don't like to be like her all pressed over no man." She act like she hasn't had sex in years." Jacqueline joked. I laughed with her. She had a personality and that was needed in any girl I fucked with. "So I'm not worth being pressed over." I joked. "/Yo no dije eso/"/I didn't say that/. She defended. You be to busy and I'm always busy, so I'm not trying to be in anyone's way. The kid don't really be busy at all so he stay free." I let be known. I definitely like you pa." She said inhaling deeply trying to alleviate my doubt of her not liking me. "So when you feel as though you have any spare time let me know and I'll let Jamal know. We were supposed to set up a double date which still didn't go as planned." Remember?" I asked. "Yeah that was my fault, no babysitter. I'll prepare better for the next one." She admitted. "Even if you don't want to hang out with Nikki, we can do whatever." I spoke looking at her. She pointed at the window on my side, the homeless man. I scrolled the window down it was hot and this man had on everything he owned as usual. His face was full of perspiration. I dug into the cup holder that Jigz left full of change and grabbed a handful. "Can you spare some change young brother?" The man's breath was bad and his teeth were almost close to none. I stuck my hand out and empty my hand in his. "You better be using this to grab something to eat. Don't let me see you slumped over because you high with my money." I stated in a firm tone. I know it wasn't for no food it was either drugs or alcohol and that was all on him. "I will, I promise the older man replied. "/Toma/, / here/." I looked out and it always felt good to help out someone who was deep in the gutter at times. You can't help them all but giving to one will make you feel a whole lot better. "You're too nice pa." Jacqueline liked that one. I looked at the watch on the dashboard and it was time for us to roll. "You ready mama?" I asked her. She glanced at the watch and turned her bottom lip. "Not really." She said. "You too cute." And just like that I was in search of another parking spot around the sub shop. I wanted to park somewhere where I could keep eye on the truck but then I remembered Jamal and Pete always park in the back. After I dropped Jacqueline off at her job. I notice her baby dads on the other end of the street again. She noticed me noticing him. "This nigga be all on my heels, he's a stalker for real." She informed me with an attitude. "Listen, don't let him spoil your beautiful day and remember what I told you. If you're lonely call me, fuck him." I reminded her. "I will pa." She leaned over for a peck on the cheek but my smoothness got the best of me. I lip locked on her. The slight moan she let out only confirmed she enjoyed me. She didn't pull away, instead she enjoyed a real soft genuine kiss that was passionately delivered for real. The rush went straight downward. "Wow." She felt her lips "I gotta go I will see you orita/later/." She said exiting the vehicle. "Tabien/ok/." I replied she hopped out the truck and I blasted the music so it could be heard throughout Broadway. Her baby dad didn't notice her jumping out the truck. I bounced and parked up right next to Jamal's whip. I noticed Pete dumping some trash out in the dumpster. He was slipping, he didn't notice my footsteps approaching him from behind. "Empty those pockets old head." I said in a joking manner. I wasn't sure what time Pete was on but to be honest I couldn't sleep on him. "You better be ready to shoot cause you aint getting shit." Pete must've knew it was my voice because he was talking crazy. He probably didn't even have any money on him but his pride got the best of him in that moment. "Just kidding old head." I said. He turned around in a fighting stance. I laughed. "You just don't walk up on people and joke around like that." Pete stated in his raspy voice, he too had a cigarette in his mouth. "You hear me." Pete asked "yeah, I had a few things to do so I decided to drop in as soon as I was done." I informed Pete "How's your mom doing?" Pete asked about Ms. Cathy I inhaled and just shook my head in disappointment. "Is not easy to quit these things." Pete held up the cigarette in his left hand. "Yeah she told Linda and myself about that this morning. I'm going to get her some patches later and whatever else I can find that will get her mind off the cancer sticks." I said. Pete and I talked for a bit outback on the side of the shop, he gave me some great advice to try and help her instead of screaming at her. That'll just make it even worse. "Worst case scenario if she really wants to quit, you might want to consider rehab maybe that can be of some help. Even though I'm not sure if it possible, but it is always a possibility." Pete informed me. Pete was a good guy and I appreciate all that he had to say to try and help me in my little situation that I found myself in. "I'll keep that in mind Pete so how has the morning flow been?" I asked changing the subject. "Is been okay, I can't complain we have been picking up ever since I hired you, you must be a good luck charm kid." Pete joked. "Yeah why can't I bring some luck my own way?" I joked. It'll come naturally you can't force it Rock." That was our last word before we decided to enter back into the shop. I smelled some food on the grill. There must be some customers out front. I clocked in and wash my hands and through on an apron with some gloves. I was already dug in and accustomed to how we all worked. We had a small but efficient team. Food was on the grill but Jamal was in the middle of taking an order. "What's up bro, you want me to take that?" I said from behind him. "Definitely." Jamal said. "He moved back to the grill, that was our thing when someone was on the grill you didn't intervene with that person's order because you were most likely you was going to ruin it, not purposely but the chances were higher. I took the orders of two breakfast sandwiches and a 6 inch sub with everything on it. After orders were finally complete I grabbed a broom and talked to Jamal about Jacqueline. "So you fucking Shorty?" I looked at him almost breaking my neck. "Nigggaaaa I having even chilled with her yet to even set things up. Now I saw her at the mall last night. When I was with Felicia, Linda and mom. Shorty caught me leaving the Footaction and let me tell you she look guuuuud damn bro." I emphasized. "I know right. I've been seeing her come in and out of the shop for the past few years and I already know. I'm too old for her but if she would give me the time a day I will plant a seed in that garden." Jamal joked giving me a high five. "I bet yo ass would." I joked back. "But nah Rock was so wassup with her girlfriend?" Jamal ask. Pete walked up to the counter. "You need to share some of them bitches and stop holding out." We all laughed. "You can't handle these broad's Pete?" Jamal stated. "Who can't handle what?" Pete countered. "Mother fucker old but I'm far from senile." Pete joked. We were busting it up crazy. Customers were in and Pete was already taking there orders. "Jamal I'll take the orders." Pete instructed. We waited for the memo sheet for the order. I continued to tell Jamal about what took place this morning. "I took Jacqueline to breakfast this morning right?" When? What you mean you took her to breakfast? You mean the New Jersey transit to yall to breakfast." Jamal always had jokes. "Yeah whatever and all she kept telling me was that Nikki wanted to see you and we wanted to link up with them, yada yada yada." I joked. "So i tried to put it together. Ima tryna to put it on lil mama." Jamal was all out with it now. He grabbed a few sheets from Pete and read it off "grab two orders of fries and 3 foot long rows and some mozzarella sticks." Jamal said turning on the deep-fryer. I went to go retrieve all that was asked for. He threw the steaks on the grill and handled the rest. "So when are we going to get it in with them?" Jamal had a grin on his face "I'm not sure." I replied slicing the rolls down the middle. The fries were simmering in the deep-fryer. "I told Jacqueline, that as soon as she and her friend weren't too busy, to let me know so I can let you know. That way you can get up out of your situation ahead of time because that last-minute shit might not work." I said. The chiming of the spatula was thundering as Jamal chopped up the stakes doing his thing on the grill. What all go on these?" I asked him. "I got it what else you tell them?" Jamal asked. "That's about it." I said. "So if they decided to call you last minute fuck it call me and let me know we are in." Jamal informed me. He really wanted to blow shorty back out. "Nah bro I can't have you in some shit all over this broad." I tried not feeding into his infatuation with Nikki. "Man Rock you better call my crib and tell me what's up. I do as I please shit." I looked at him like yeah right. "I know" being sarcastic. I pulled the fries and mozzarella sticks and packed them up in separate containers and marked them. "Two more customers came in and Pete was out front talking to some lady. I took the orders and the rest of our day went with a nice flow of customers. Taking orders and putting them together and getting them out of here hot and fresh. We moved all day in sync. I decided not to tell Jamal about my personal gift that I purchased for myself. Instead, I wanted him to see me tower over him in my truck after work. It was close to 7:30pm and it was slow. "Ayo Pete do you mind if I run to the plus to grab a few things that we discussed earlier?" I asked Pete. I didn't want to leave the shop like he did on a regular basis but asked instead. "Take Jamal with you, yall could use some fresh air." The last statement caught me off guard. "come on Jamal." I instructed "where?" He asked. To the plus Pete said make it quick." I informed him, aprons off and gloves in the trash. There was a pharmacy shop close by and I would hit that up first just in case they didn't have the patches for mom.

"What you grabbing from in here?" Jamal asked. Some patches for my mom." I informed him "how she holding up?" He asked. "You see what I'm buying right?" Not too good I take it." Jamal answered his own question. "Could be better but we'll see." After buying two boxes that were almost $15 a box. I hope that it'll help a little bit. I really wanted mom to slow down with her habit especially after what Pete said. We headed over to the plus and all eyes were on the two ghetto mother fucker's from the sub shop entering the store. I noticed Nakia almost immediately I scanned for Jacqueline but I didn't see her. We walked over to the seasoning isle but we didn't need any of it today. Nakia scooted her way towards us. "Can I help y'all with anything?" Her sweet thick self asked with all eyes on Jamal. Nakia noticed me looking around. "She in the back Rock, she'll be out soon." Nakia said, Ima let yall two talk for a bit before we slide out.

I saw my baby girl with her value plus sure on and those tight as jeans were her black forces showing off her ankles. Her smile lit up as soon as she saw me. "What do you want?" She joked. "I want what I can't have." I joked back. The store was empty but the homo was on the register... "And what might that be?" She asked smiling. She was all up next to me, she smelled so good. For all I know she could've been in the bathroom taking a mean as shit and here I was saying she smelled good as hell.

"Yo ma ya tu sabe/you already know/." She smiled "oh yeah?" She asked. "So was you good this morning?" I asked. I remember how her baby dads was up on the block. "Oh man, you don't even want to know?" She said. "Yeah I do, what happened....?" I was nosey as fuck. "That nigga was tripping so hard. Who the fuck was that in the truck and where did you meet him? He was bitching." I laughed. It's crazy because I swore he didn't see her hop out my shit. "Is not funny." Jacqueline said laughing along with me. "And what did you tell him?" I probed "I told him to worry about his son, not who I'm talking to or who I'm seeing." I knew that would sent him over the edge and it sure did." She smiled. "That's good, I'm glad you spoke the truth instead of lying and trying to make up 101 excuses." I said. I look back at Jamal and he was all in a deep conversation with Nakia. I had an idea... I would take Jacqueline home and Jamal would take Nakia to her spot I wasn't sure how that would go but it was worth a shot.

"Jamal let me holler at you right quick." Nakia left. "Yo you want to chill with girly tonight for a little bit?" I asked. I just wanted to know what their status was. "I actually told her that if she wanted we all could link up near closing time at the shop and I would take everyone home." Jamal was on his shit. "No you worry about Nakia and I'll worry about Jacqueline cool?" I stated not on some smart shit but on some do you type shit and he knew what I meant. "Al-right bet." Jamal said. I shot back towards Jacqueline. "Ima see you later okay." I informed her. "Nikki, see you soon." Jamal stated to Nakia. "You taking me home tonight?" Jacqueline asked. "maybe" I joked knowing damn we would.

Jamal was on my heels as I headed to the door. "See you papi" the flamer said. "Nigga you better chill it aint that type of party over here. "I was just joking." I didn't even reply. Jamal didn't like that one bit "homeboy need to chill with that funny shit" Jamal stated. "Man fuck that flamer, So what's up with old girl?" I asked him taking his mind off the dumb shit. "We going to chill tonight right after work, so you already know." Jamal said "Ayo let's cut through here I gotta put this up." I said heading towards the alley "put what up? And where?" Jamal asked. I didn't answer. We just kept walking. I don't know she says something about her spot or whatever. I wasn't really paying attention because I was all in her ass and thighs and those juicy as lips." I laughed. "You are crazy man." I let be known. "What about wifey I asked him. "Oh boy don't even mention her. Ima have to deal with her mouth as soon as I walk up in that house. She going to trip and believe me she going to trip but as long as I'm home in our bed she'll be all right." Jamal said. "Where the fuck is you taking me Rock we gotta head back to the shop." Jamal stating the obvious. I pushed the button on the keypad for the truck and the horn beeped and the lights flickered "damn that truck is nice." Jamal said. "Is it?" I asked playing stupid. I wonder who the hell that shit belong to." We were about 10 feet away. He still had no clue. I pushed it again this time with it out my pocket. He looked over "Oh hell no!" Jamal was shocked. I smiled. I had nothing to say but I was happy every time I looked at the truck and knew that I owned the keys, it was an amazing feeling. "Yo bro this shit is clean, when the fuck did you cop this?" Jamal asked "a couple days ago." I said not revealing too much information Jamal circled the truck. "you gotta let me hold this one day bro." He stated in awe. "I got you, you know I got you." I was serious I would let him hold it down after what he did for me that day with mom. It was only right there was no way I could deny him that. The look on his face said it all upon opening the door. "You don't even smoke and you got this car smelling like straight exotic." Jamal spoke. "Man that's the bud you gave me that day." I lied again. "Hell no it aint." Jamal looked at me. This shit smell like some Dro, that shit I gave you was sour and this smell aint no sour." Jamal stated knowing his bud. "You ready." I asked ready to finish our day at work. Just as I said that I felt a drop hit my ear. It was getting dark but the sun was already set somewhere. I felt another I looked at Jamal.

"It's going to come down tonight." Jamal said. I threw the bags I had in my hand on the floor of the truck and slid inside the shop. "Bossman!" Jamal yell for Pete. I looked up front and it was clear. I looked at Jamal. "Watch this?"

He said. "I'm a fuck with Pete." "What?" All that hollering?" Pete came out of the bathroom. "Can a man piss in peace? "He joked. "I need a damn raise." Jamal blurted out with his arms folded and a dead ass look on his face. "What?" Pete asked "you heard me old man I need a raise today." Jamal Barked. Pete looked over his shoulders to see if there was any customers, our reaction was to look back as well. "mother fucker I just gave you a raise how much more money you want?" You make just as much as I do. I think you make more." Pete joked "hell no I don't, but yes you did give me a raise but I need more because apparently you paying Rock more." I started to look at him. He winked. "Why would I pay Rock more when he just started not too long ago?" Pete was confused for a bit. "I don't think so you saw what he is driving?" I didn't know Jamal wasn't going to take it that far, he damn sure did "what? Who's driving what?" Pete go look for yourself it's next to my car." Jamal was bugging. I know he didn't mean no harm by it but damn. Pete disappeared and I stared at Jamal. "You tripping man." I said "I'm bidding I want to see what he says. "Whoa whoa!" That's yours Rock?" Pete came back in with his loud as voice. I nodded I didn't have much to say. "How many bricks did that run you?" Pete said. At first I didn't catch it. Than it hit me.

"No bricks just save every penny you paid me since I started at the shop." I said with my head up high and with a truthful serious face. Pete looked at Jamal. "You see that's what you need to be doing saving more money instead of spending every dime on weed and alcohol." Pete joked with some truth behind it all. "Man I got kids and a girl who spends damn near every penny before I even get to see it." Jamal joked back. "I got the same problem over here only difference is I'm not married. At least I don't feel like it." Pete joked. The water was coming down slowly hitting the glass window out front. Just before closing we had a few more orders, but no sooner did the two value plus girls come in with bags over their heads. I laughed as I saw them both. Jamal laughed too.

"What you don't want to ruin your hair." He joked. "Shut up." Nikki said it with her cute little self. Jacqueline had water all over her face. It wasn't a long walk but it was about a block if that. "Oh shit." I said "What's up Rock?" Jamal looked at me. I handed napkins to the girls and shot to the back. Jamal followed me "what's up with you?" "Damn I was supposed to meet Felicia." I say completely forgetting about what I had told her. How could I be so dumb? "I'm slacking." I was disappointed in myself "Well you can see her later since a playa fuckin up."

Jamal tried to make light of the situation by joking. "Nah nigga I was supposed to see her this afternoon." I said. "Oh shit! How the fuck you forget to do that and now you want to remember?" Jamal wasn't helping the situation. "You are slipping on your pimping." Jamal joked. "I am." I replied "call her "Jamal suggested. "Hell no, I'll see her when I can." I replied" Come on lets go holla at the girls." Jamal said as we was on our way to the front "Rock!" Pete yelled out. "Yoyo." I slid right into his office. "have a seat real quick." I was adding or subtracting back here and sorry to be in your business but you have a $23,000 truck out there with rims and all and if you've been saving all the money that you've been making from the shop that only brings you up to at least $8000 you are still almost $15,000 short at that from the truck Rock. I need you to be honest with me. If you are dealing let me know so I know what to expect." Pete was serious and I couldn't believe this was happening. "Look Pete I know that looks crazy Pete. Ima be honest with you I'm not no drug dealer, that life is not my twist. I prefer to work for my shit no matter if his scrubbing floors or even washing dishes and yes that is an expensive car but when you know people who know people you come across very good deals, as if you will go to the auction you know? I'm not going to tell you how much I pay for but it wasn't all that expensive. I saved a lot since working and know that I wouldn't bring no drama like that into your place of business Pete." I was sincere and straightforward. I'm sure that even if I was he wouldn't have cared anyway just as long as I didn't bring all that noise up in here. "All right then Rock. I apologize for the lack of trust but I don't know what you up to while you're not here, plus I like you and don't want to see you get lost in the cold streets." Pete was honest and thorough. "Thank you and I'll let you know whenever I decide to test that road out. In the meantime I'm here with you and Jamal." Pete smiled as I spoke. "All right now get out of here and clean up my shop." Pete said to me. I laughed "already done" I joked I made my way up to the front "you good?" Jamal asked. "Yeah I'm good, what yall up to?" I asked. Waiting on you pa, why you got me up here all by myself?" Jacqueline stated .I scooted up on her side the rain was tapping on the window it was coming down harder now. The lightning would light up the sky for a split second but the cracking of the thunder would let loose ripping through the air. The shop was clean, it was about that time to close up. We chilled and just waited till Pete finished his paperwork I wondered if Linda was okay. Jacqueline grab my face and looked in my eyes. "Are you okay pa?" Jacqueline asked a bit worried. "Yes I'm good." I smiled. "You sure you seem distant. I thought you would be happy to see me." She said. Jamal and Nikki were both in a deep conversation. "I am I just want to get up out here and chill with you." I said. "How was your day?" She asked. "It was a bit busy but it's always a little busy when it came to people wanted some good food, especially when that boy over there is the chef." I spoke so Jamal could hear me. "You already know gotta keep them happy and coming back." Pete showed his face. "Oh what the hell is this?" He spoke loudly. "Something wrong with this picture." Pete said. I looked around to examine everything "what?" I said everything is taken care of." Jamal said. "Oh yea?" Why isn't the door locked and how come I see two beautiful women in here and there isn't one for me waiting on the side for this old man." Pete was shot out and he was crazy too. "Don't worry Ima fine you a sexy mama to keep that ass occupied?" Nikki ghetto ass had to feed into his bull shit. "You see that's what I like to hear. I like her." Pete like any new face he saw. "Let's get up out of here guys." He said. The rain soaked my shirt, hat, boots and everything else I had on. Jamal took advantage and tried to conceal little Nikki from the rain. I did the same but it was pointless. "My hair!" Yelled Jacqueline. I ripped off the bag she had over her head and slowed her walk down. "What are you doing?" She whined. "We are both already soaked, so how about we just enjoyed it. Jamal and Nikki were already in their car. I had Jacqueline posted up on the side of my truck, the sound of the raindrops bouncing off the hood sound light pellets hitting the hood. "You are so crazy." Why do you want to stand here and get wet?" she asked under my arms. "Because I may not get this chance ever again in this lifetime." I grabbed her chin in my hand and went straight for the kill. My lips touched hers in a very sensual passionate way. Jamal's horn beeped and I could hear his tires moving away from us. I didn't care "mmmmm." She let out a slight moan of satisfaction at that moment. Her hand slipped right under my shirt and I was getting aroused again. The water slipped into our mouths which wasn't a problem but it was a bit annoying. I grabbed her by the waist and walked her to the passenger side. I opened the door and I helped her in. I looked around and saw a set of headlights but I didn't pay them any mind. Once inside I turned the engine and we sat for a moment.

"I'm so wet is not even funny." Jacqueline said "I bet you are." I joked. "Not like that!" She contested. I laughed. The water was coming down hard so I had to pay close attention to the rode. "You can't even see can you?" Jacqueline tried to wipe down the big ass windshield. It was fogging up on me real bad. "I can see a little." I laughed because her small hands only got about a quarter of the glass, check if there is some napkins or a shirt in this motha fucka." I knew there wasn't but I wanted to see if she'd check. Then again who knew what she would find back there. There was an assault rifle in this bitch that I didn't know about. I played with the buttons on the dash to get this window to clear up it wasn't easy I tell you. Jacqueline was in the back. I saw her rummaging through nothing because there wasn't anything in the truck. I saw her through the rearview.

"/Pa no ay nada/,/there isn't anything/ her latin voice was so sexy, Oh man I wanted this girl, the words just glided off her tongue so naturally it was something that could be replicated but it was nothing compared to the real deal. Our native language was something that needed to be embraced. I hit the AC and the air began to clear the windshield miraculously. "You got it!" She affirmed. Happy that we wasn't going to die in a collision. She hopped back up front with me. It's empty back there I didn't see anything." She defended why she come up empty handed. "I know I cleaned it out this morning." I joke. Once again a jab came straight to me. I swerved a little bit because I wasn't expecting it. "Damn now you want to kill us huh?" I joked. She cover her mouth "No pa I'll stop with the punching." I didn't know I hit that hard." She said in all seriousness. I laughed "you do hit pretty hard and you better stop before I bite that ass." I said joking. This little midget was not affecting me with those little punches, but I let her feel powerful at moment. "So I'm taking you home?" I asked her. "If that's where you want to take me then yes." She stated more like a question." I rather not but you are soaking wet and I don't have a towel I'm guessing you want to get all dried up." I replied. "Yeah that sounds fine plus I got to go and attend Josiah. My sister probably has plans and I can't be an asshole because she's the only one I trust with my baby boy." Jacqueline spoke highly about her baby and sister. "That's very considerate." I said. "I wanted to chill with her but I had to see what Felicia was up to first. I did her wrong today it wasn't my intentions but it happened. I was about a block away from her spot and I noticed the Lincoln and at the top of the corner. So did Jacqueline.

"Damn the stocker, he need to find a girl and leave me the fuck alone." She was annoyed at the site of his car. "You can drop me off at the corner." My heart wasn't with all that I wanted to drop her off at her doorstep like I should do but I had to understand where she was coming from. She didn't want no problems between her baby dad and myself. There was no stopping it, it was going to happen no matter what. I thought about pressing the issue than realized it wasn't that deep. All I knew was that his BMs was tired and wasn't feeling this nigga anymore. I had to clear up something before she left. "Look ma before you leave

I need to know if you fucking him still?" I don't care if you are, I mean I do if you going to be with me but if not is whatever. I just need to so I know what to expect from him." I laid the cards out all on the table. "Rock I told you that it's been four months and I'm not into him anymore and Ima be real if I was talking to him I would be in his car not yours so keep that in my. Let me handle him and you just stay in your lane and be there for me if and when I need you. I'm a call you tonight right now give me a kiss." I listened and did as she asked I left an imprint on those lips with my teeth. She moaned and I'm almost sure she got wet at the same time. "Damn pa you so rough." Her eyes watered. "Sorry come here." I sucked on her bottom lips softly. She jumped out and I watched her ass as she walked. Her body was all I really wanted at the moment but deep down inside I knew she wanted something a bit more intimate as far as a relationship. I waited till she was in her house before I drove by with my bass thumping. I drove my truck's tint was limo as well.

—

I spun the block looking for the Lexus but I didn't spot it, I thought I missed it so I circled the complex again. I saw it parked up by older Volkswagen or at least I thought I did. The foggy windows impaired my vision again. I backed up as to see well because I thought my mind was playing tricks on me but they weren't. It was her car and she was in it. She had no clue as to who I was or why I was parking up directly in front of her car. I sat in the truck looking and watching. For about three minutes I was lost in my thoughts. The sound of her car door slamming snap me out of my days. I beeped and rolled down the window she turned around and kept moving.

"Felicia!" I yell so she could hear me. "Who is that?" She asked. "Rock." She did a 180 and came flying over to the truck. Her friend or whoever that was kept walking into the apartments. I unlocked the door and she jumped in already knowing what was about to transpire. "Comfy?" I asked all wet. "Why was you just sitting here watching us?" You had us scared to death you know that." Felicia was dead ass. She was right with all the weirdos out here chasing and stalking women I should of know better. Listen, I came to see you since I stood you up earlier today I felt bad." I said. Well you should because I was out there hungry waiting for you, that's what I get for listening to you." Felicia had all right to be mad. I couldn't even be mad at her for being mad at me. I had to make the situation better than it was "so how was your day besides being stood up?" I asked trying to make things lighter she stared at me with a venomous stare. I held in my laughter as I stared back. I couldn't hold it. "What? You want to hit me go ahead ma, will that make you feel better?" I move my face closer to hers but instead of hitting me she slapped a bunch of kisses all over my face. I enjoyed the smooches, "My day was very complicated. You'll be amazed at how badly hurt people tend to get when they are out working or even out just chilling. I saw so much blood today and that's not even my job description but the ER was so jam-packed that they pulled me from the back to help." Felicia had a very hard job. I knew it wasn't the most comfortable. I reached over and held her. She laid on my chest. "You want to come up?" She asked. "For a bit I gotta get these patches to mom?" I stated. "Patches?" She questioned. "Yeah nicotine patches, she wants to lean off the cigarettes. It kind of got a little hectic this morning." I said. "Well at least she willing to try." Felicia said. I parked up and we ran to the entrance,in moments we were inside her apartment.

"Mommy!" The little princess yelled she was all cheers when she heard the door open and the jingle of her keys. She jumped right into her mother's arms. "Hey baby can I ask you something?" Felicia asked her daughter "yes mommy anything." Eliza's cute little voice answered. "Why aren't you in bed baby?" Felicia set her up for that one. "That's easy I wanted to see you before I went to bed mommy." Now either that was rehearsed or this little girl was just too smart. Felicia looked at me with an unbelievable visage. "Hey Rock where have ju been?" Eliza asked. "Working." Was all I could say? "Tell your sister I said hi." And just like that Felicia was gone with her daughter in tow. I sat down at the dining room table and waited. I couldn't imagine how good of a memory Eliza had. Was my child going to be that smart when I had a child? I asked myself. I noticed a phone by my hand and dialed out. I called home. "Hello?" Ms. Cathy answered. "Mom I'll be there shortly I had to stop by Felicia's for a quick minute." I said. "All right I'll see you when you get here, did you get them patches for me?" She asked. "Yes I did two boxes of them." I replied. I could hear her wheezing a bit over the handset. "Good your sister just got here so we'll see you soon." That was all and that was the end of conversation. "Who was that?" Felicia asked. Mom I just telling her I'm be there shortly." I informed her. She bit my ear. "So who's car you driving now?" She asked kissing my neck. "Mine I replied." "Oh yea?" I didn't know you had a car?" She said touching me. "No one did I just bought it." She went to talk about it some more but I slid my tongue down her throat to shut her up. It was a rap from there. A bit of sucking and licking and the clothes were off just like that. She rode me right on that chair and I finish with blowing her back, that had her yelping and screaming for me to take it easy but I was in my bag. Her face was buried in the pillow, even with that she couldn't hold it back even if she wanted to. I gave it to her good. My erection subsided slowly as our lungs search for air. She didn't even bother to put her clothes back on she was still enjoying the aftershock. Her legs were still a bit shaky. "You okay?" I asked. "Am I?" She questioned sarcastically "I'm good baby I hope you are good too." Felicia was open I had to go and I was ready for my departure and get back on the road. So am I gona see you tomorrow?" Felicia asked this was what I didn't want but then again there was no one to blame but myself. "We'll see, you saw what happened today, I don't want to say something then not pull through it is busy at the job at times." "But I will let you know." I informed her. Trying to let the issue just drive right by us. "I'm a get you a phone." Felicia said. "A what?" I shot back "a phone." She reiterated. "For?" I questioned. "So I can call you?" She said. "Nah you good." I don't do phones." I replied. "Don't you think if I wanted a tracking device I would've bought one already?" I said. Not meaning to sound mean but in a way it was too late to sound as I did. "A tracking device huh?" She barked back. "So that's what you call it Rock?" She asked a bit annoyed. "Well that's what it is, if you want to get technical." Anyway, we will discuss this another time I have to go." I ended it with that. Felicia was on my mind and so was Jacqueline. This was bound to get worse or better the thought was crazy to even think of it. For some reason I knew nothing good was going to come out of this. There were too many emotions getting involved and they were moving too fast. By the time I made it back to mom's house it was late and I knew I had to place one of these patches on her no matter what.

Finally parked up, it was a miracle there was room for this big bitch on the block. I managed to get her in a spot. I left my boots on the porch because I wasn't gona wet the carpet nope not me I wasn't biting that charge. The phone was buzzing as soon as I walked in. I picked up and it was Felicia. "hello" she answered "wassup ma?" I said pressing the numbers on the microwave. "What was that about?" I question as if I was oblivious as to what her ranting was about. "You know what I'm talking about?" She sounded annoyed. "Look Felicia I'm tired and I'm about to eat. So unless you don't switch this shit up Ima hang this phone up and disconnected this tracking device too." Low blow.

"Are you serious? Why are you so mean?" She asked trying to humble herself. "Mean because you dragging out something that don't mean anything. I don't want a phone. So if you buy it I'm not gona take it nor will I buy one myself." I stated. I heard the stairs cracking but I didn't notice anyone coming down. "Beep, beep, beep." The microwave called me. The smell was to die for as it always was. "It's only a phone and was the big deal if I do get you one?" She asked. "Is not the phone I'm worried about, it's how many calls I'm going to get throughout the day and if I don't answer. I gota hear all the extra shit that comes with it. Fuck that I'm not beat?" I spoke the honest truth. Dick was a motha fucka when it came to these chicks. "Why you so offensive though that's what I want to know?" She asked. "We already made this clear we was going to take this shit slow and not rush into anything crazy serious as far as relationship wise remember?" I asked. "Yes, I remember but this pussy all over that Dick of yours..." "Click." I hung up, she wasn't going to ruin my meal. I had the inter-com button on the handset Linda picked up "wassup Manny?" Felicia going to call back check her real quick please Im eating." I said. "I got you did you grab them patches?" Yeah come down." I replied. I blew the spoonful of rice and beans because it was smoking something serious. Linda came right on down in my boxers, her ass was all over the place, no bra only a wife beater. She noticed me looking she knew what she was up to. Crazy ass girl I didn't mind though.

"What is up with you and girly?" Linda asked. My look told her everything. "You can't be putting it on them like that Manny. You already know how they trip." Linda wasn't lying. "She talking about she want me to get a phone but she will buy it for me." I ate as I spoke in between bites. "Oh boy, are you in trouble." Linda joked the phone rang. "It's her." Linda said noticing the number "handle that." I instructed. "He is eating he going to call you when he done." Click" Linda had no pics she didn't give three fucks about Felicia, She knew that maybe one day she would have to trash her. "Why won't you just get an ankle monitor?" Linda joked. I almost spit of my food that I was chewing, she had the patches in her hand and opened the box up read the instructions and said. "I'll be right back she bolted upstairs. I was right behind her leaving the food and all we crept up in mom's room. She was out like a light. TV was still on and she was breathing just fine with her oxygen machine. Linda was planting one of the patches on her while she was sleep. I just watched. Mom's room was always neat and clean just as she always practice what she preached. Mom's arm wasn't exposed but Linda managed get it exposed just enough to place the patch on. Mom moved and moved a bit more I just looked wondering why she didn't just wake her up I thought. I heard the phone ring again but for some reason the one in mom's room didn't make a sound. It was lighting up but no noise was coming from it. That's how bad these girls be blowing up the phone but hey Linda's boyfriend be right along with the calls too. At one point it was all me. I felt bad because she had to silence the phone to get some rest, maybe I should get a cell phone. Linda managed to put the patch on her and kiss her good night, I followed suit.

Back to my food I kept the box down here and put it in a cabinet. This will be the backup stash. "So back to Felicia" Linda said. I acted as if I didn't hear her. "She is pretty Manny." Linda said trying to get me to talk. "I know she is pretty. Felicia and I talked about this already, there is no need to rush into something that neither of us are ready for." I repeated. "You mean you not ready for but she is more than ready." Linda wasn't helping and the phone was ringing again. "I'm a curse this girl out." Linda said looking at the caller ID." Oh wait it isn't her... Hello? "Jacqueline?" Linda said looking in my eyes if looks could kill. I would be dead a long time ago, but it's a shame you gotta do that shit manually. I grabbed the receiver and she shook her head in disgust. "Wassup ma?" I answered the call. The huffing and the cracking in her voice brought my defense of all the way. "/Que te pasa mija?/, / what's wrong/" I asked her "My...b... baby dad he was over here tripping.... He was scaring the baby and my sister." Jacqueline was distraught for real. "He hit you?" I asked. "No he left but he is bugging." Jacqueline was all tears over the receiver. My heart was racing and I knew all of this was my fault. "I'm sorry mami." I apologize for me playing a major role in this. "Sorry for what pa?" Is not your fault I'm a grown, he and I had our chance to make this work a couple of times, and it just didn't work out. Ima move on he needs to do the same." Jacqueline said in a worried tone. I felt for her but what more could I do to make her feel better? That was between her and her baby dads knowing me though I had to get involved just because I wanted to know what this lame ass nigga was talking. I know he mentioned me. "So what he say?" I approached to try to see what I could get out of all this drama. "Oh man where do I start?" She said. "Take a deep breath." I instructed her to do. I heard her inhale and exhale slowly now where is the baby?" He is in his bed sleep." Jacqueline admitted. "Okay so after I dropped you off at your house what happened?" I began. Not really ready to hear what was about to be said. "Well I walked in and he was with his son playing near the window. My sister was on the kitchen which was only a few feet away." She was recounting what had transpired at the house detail by detail just like I wanted to hear it. I walked in and my son went crazy like he always does.... She was getting emotional again, calm down ma. Once she did, she continued “okay so my son is trying to get to me but he won’t let him go. He begins to cry because he wants me to hug him right?” She stated but asking. “Right?” I agreed. I walked over and grabbed him but as I grabbed him he sees your truck drive by at the same time and that’s when he decided to get all crazy. I grab my son off his hand but by now my son is screaming. My sister is watching just in case he gets to crazy.” she went on to explain “Who the fuck is that nigga in that truck bitch?!” He barked at me. “Watch your mouth around the baby.” I said. “Fuck that! Who the fuck is that!?” He asked again. “None of your damn business!” I said trying to get the baby to quiet down at the same time. She explained.

“Well know this, if I see you with him whoever he is I’m a beat the shit out of you and take my son away from you. You can play with me if you want.” He was mad. She said as she reiterated all that was said. “Did he hit you?” I asked. I knew that would be my drawing point. I already knew he was a coward just by the way he had threatened to beat her ass and to solidify my assumption. He was indeed a coward. I was correct due to the simple fact that he was willing to take the baby from his own mother. Only because she was moving on without him. “No he didn’t but he acted as if he was, my sister was freaking out I’m not gona lie I was scared too. I knew if he touched either of us I would stab him than call the cops on his ass if he even so much spit on me.” Jacqueline was enraged and I felt bad and at fault. I said what I honestly felt in my heart.

“Look baby girl I like you and am feeling you but like I said today we not trying to get into anything serious because we both have things in our lives that need to be addressed. So if you want me to back off so all this unnecessary drama can go away then I will. It’ll hurt me but at the end of the day I’m not worth you losing your baby over.” I sat back in the dining room chair and waited for a response. I could hear Linda in the kitchen doing who knows what... prolly being nosy. “Rock if I decide to have something with you that’s my decision. I like you and don’t think for one second that my corny as baby dad going to take my baby just like that. I’m the one who does everything for that boy not him. Plus if I give him that satisfaction, that will only mean that I can’t do as I please or see anyone because he’ll think he got me like that. Hell fucking no.” Jacqueline wasn’t going to let it go just like that. “I feel you but listen to me I’m here for you but if that nigga try and come at my neck don’t even try and hold him or me back. I may look humble but my bite locks." She was silent.... "It's not going to get that far pa." She tried to make me feel better. "I know a lot of niggaz like him and it can get worse if you you do stick to your guns." I spoke with all honesty, this nigga probably had a flock a woman but this one was special. One she had his baby, two because she was bad and her sex game had to be on point to drive this nigga insane. I'm not even bout that crazy life but if a motha fucker came at me, guess we would find out "are you okay though?" I asked changing the subject little by little. "Yeah I'm good thanks to you." She said. "Why me?" I asked a bit confused. Your in my corner and I can't handle this alone but I feel safer with you by my side." She stated. "I got you let's just be smart about all of this alright?" I said to her. If I was going to keep this beautiful jewel by my side I had to be on point every day. I already slipped up by letting this nigga see my whip but fuck it, if he wanted me he would have to come and get me.

"What are you doing?" She asked a bit more calm "nada about to wash up and relax gotta get up in the a.m." I replied. "Need some help?" Jacqueline asked knowing damn well I would love for her to help me wash up. I knew she was feeling emotional and to be honest I knew that if I really wanted to I could slide up and that and claim that pussy or I could be led right into a straight set up where her baby dads. As of right now after this episode. It was very likely because he threaten her with her son.

If you're a mother you would do anything to keep your child out of harm's way without thinking twice about anything let alone anyone. It could be that she could be a grimy ass chick. We could never put any pass anyone. Being put in a predicament like that could turn into a desperate measures situation and a motha fucka wouldn't be allowed to size me up, fuck that. In her baby dads eyes all he saw was a target that was sitting on some bread. If you are from the hood and are about that life than you can most definitely relate. "Maybe another time." Was all I could to say "I'm a hold you up to that." She replied. "You work tomorrow right?" I asked her. "Yes but I'm thinking of finding a spot to move away from this house, it's time to start fresh." Jacqueline was thinking now. "So did you just decide on this now because it's useless if you move and bring all your troubles along with you?" I said not trying to offend her but stating the obvious. "Yes, you're right that's why if I do move it will just be me and my sister and my son, I can't start over in the past. Is not going to work even if I wanted to. As much as I thought I could actually change everything before it all gets worse. I really don't want my son to see all this. He doesn't deserve all this drama, he sees it all and feels it most now." Jacqueline was focusing on their future which was great. I didn't frame her into coming out with any of this but it was a heart spoken gesture. I feel it, all she wanted the best for her son. Like any mother would want for their child. If I could help I would. "I see you thinking a lot now, it's good to start fresh and look past what took place today. Most of all focus on tomorrow I commend you on that. If you ever need me for anything I'm right here." I informed her. I was tired and I didn't feel like staying up for hours. Linda had just went up to her room so I was left downstairs to lock up and make sure all was secure. I could hear the argument outside. It sounded as if it was close by, a females voice high-pitched could be heard taunting a male. I peeked out the window. It was drizzling and I could see the three silhouettes two houses away. I wrapped up the conversation with Jacqueline and told her that I would speak to her tomorrow. She blew me a kiss and wished me a good night. Her way of speaking just drove me insane. Spanglish was how she would put it all together so perfectly.

—

With all the needed to be done, as far as the title transfer and everything else things were going along safe and smoothly. I tried to stay out of the way but at the same time handling all my affairs and I use that term loosely. Jacqueline and Felicia were my main girls and to be straight through and through I thought about introducing them to one another, just so I can have them both around me in the open without hiding one from another. Who was I kidding this wouldn't be a smart move at all. My game wasn't that tight. My mind tends get carried away at times but imagine if I did pull that off. I could only ponder and utilize my imagination where I would see it fit.

—

With it being almost winter time you could say this because the temperatures were dropping and my Scully stayed on my head. Felicia calm down and decided not to smother me as much but on the other hand she probably had another man on her left side. Jacqueline finally moved out out her spot like she said she wanted to do. She was still close enough to the hood but was more on 35th leading up to Westfield not too far from me. It was all the same to me because she was still close by. Her baby dad was still bugging but he didn't know where she rest her head at which was a good thing but you and I know it was only a matter of time until he got wind where her beehive was located at. Till this day I'm a little salty because helping her in the transition to move to her new spot I scratched the sideboard in the back of the truck. I felt as if I personally got scarred physically forever. Yes I know pathetic, She apologized 1,000,001 times. It bugs me out to see how thoughtful she is still to this day she always does it. It's my fault for using my truck to move most of your shit, so as far as me getting bent at a shape it didn't last too long. You would think that with all this time passing me by I would've had Jacqueline wrapped around my finger due to my little man's talents and moves, but it hasn't even occurred and to be honest this could be why this girl respect me so much more. Yes, I'm sure she knows that our chemistry is very noticeable but for me it's the fact that what could happen once the deal was sealed is what I'm thinking thats holding us back from one another. Why are we stopping one another from given each other what the other yearns for. Every now and then her baby dads shows up on the block on Broadway to talk to her about, how he is sorry and yada yada yada. Jacqueline stuck to her guns and I also gained a tremendous amount of respect for her. I commend her but I thought she was taking things a little too far. She wasn't allowing him take his son. I understand not letting him know where you are and where the baby rest at that was a risk that took some serious willpower. If my baby moms pulled a stunt like that? I wouldn't rest until I found out all that I needed to know and on top of that I would raise hell even to a much greater degree. I'm aware he wants to take his son and bond with him but by what she said "he has to show me that it's not about me or this pussy. It has to be all about our son." Those were her exact words. She didn't care how many roses he sent or how many rings or bracelets he spent his money on she was dead ass and I was seeing this with my own eyes.

Mom was still holding are strong to them nicotine patches but every now and then she'll smoke a cancer stick or two. I know it's defeating the purpose but to see her downgrade from 100's to shorts and going from two boxes a day to a box every two days only lets me know that she is trying her best and in all actuality that is all we have ever wanted. Now instead of a freight train blowing smoke in 24/7 she's more like a chimney blazing wood on a chilly night and to me that isn't totally acceptable but it is progress. As far as Linda she and Joel? They have been serious and to be sincere it sucks but what else can I expect? She's not my girl and she wants to be happy even if this tall as light-skinned as mother fucker looks like me to the T. She is almost done with a great portion of her associate's degree and has told me that she actually wants to pursue her bachelor's degree which to me is wonderful.

—

"So what you plan on doing Manny?" Linda asked me one morning. "What you mean?" I replied not really understanding the literal meaning of her question. As far as school Manny you been out for a while, don't you think it's time to open up some doors and see what's on the other side and see what options are available to you? Being that you are still fresh out of school and you are the individuals that the community colleges and trade schools prefer because your brain isn't fried yet." She spoke seriously but in a joking manner at the same time. I nodded my head agreeing to what she was saying.... "Damn you haven't even considered anything have you?" She asked already knowing the answer to her question. "I mean I have but I haven't at the same time." I lied through my pearly whites. The blank look she gave me made me confess. "Okay you're right and I haven't even considered it, not even a second." I admitted. "I know you didn't you don't have to tell me this. You have these two broad's on your hip and you got this laid-back job and it's fucked the rest of the world." She said speaking the truth. She may have taking it a little too far but I couldn't even defend my case because she was on a roll as far as everything else. "It's easy to get side tracked from everything that's really important and Ima be honest if it aint for you or mom. I wouldn't even be working in the shop I would be Holden down 28th with Jigz and Banga because that offer till this day is on the table with high pay and security and my own hours." I said sounding dumb as ever. "You forgot one Manny?" Linda said "was that?" I asked "no benefits and no retirement or pension." Her low blows came sharp and thrown like real champ. The silence in the car was all that could be heard as I approached Joel's crib. She left me with all that to ponder and that is what I did until I ended up getting sidetracked again.

—

Jamal was in later than usual on this Thursday. His face showed a bit of frustration. I decided to let him get situated before I started to ask if he was all right. I fucked up someones order somehow confuse it with American cheese instead of provolone cheese was my task at the moment. Today couldn't be like this all day, at least I hope it wouldn't. Customers came in with their bear coats and Pea coats of all flavors. It was getting colder as the season was already shifting. I thought about Christmas and wonder who was getting what.

"Two subs with provolone." I yelled up to the customers. "would you like a free drink sir? I apologize for the wait." I did this whenever I screwed up which was rare but hey I'm not perfect. "Sure let me get a Pepsi." The middle age man said. I pulled a can of Pepsi from the fridge and off he was happier than ever. Taken another order and Jamal was where he usually was at the grill. I still didn't break the silence, but I did pass him two memo slips. I charged the man and headed to help Jamal. Linda was right I didn't want to do this for the rest of my life. I would prefer to run the place but working like this wasn't bad but it wasn't what my life would consist of on a daily basis. "You not gona believe what the fuck I got myself into Rock." His face had this overly worried look. I knew this look because this one had more emotion in it. "It's so bad it probably can't even get fixed back to how things ought to be." With those words coming out of his mouth I immediately assume that someway, somehow this Nigga managed to slip up and get caught up with his wife again. I met his girl twice and she was respectively pretty and they look happy together, then again I can only speak on what I saw with my own eyes at that moment. "This gotta be bad." For you to say that the way you just day." I stated watching him work the grill. "It is broke and I don't know how to fix it. I thought of everything and nothing seems to come to mind. It hasn't erupted fully but I know that this is going to be used against me in every opportunity that presents itself." Now I really wanted to know what this was all about because it might be salvageable but then again there's a good chance is not gona work out ever the way he was putting it. I checked the front and it was clear. One customer in and in a few seconds he would be out the door. "I'm not sure I even wanted to know what you done got yourself into Jamal." I spoke in all honesty. Negative energy can be transferred over to you very quickly, if you never take the time to realize it. "Oh you are gona hear this I couldn't wait to get here just so I could tell you." Jamal admitted. "I'm not sure if that's a good thing or a bad thing." I joked lightly trying to ease the levels of his frustration. "No listen to it Rock." Jamal spoke slowly so I could grasp his every syllable noun verb etc. etc. He leaned up on the fridge and went into explaining his dilemma. "As you already know that Nikki and myself have been sucking and fucking for a while now right?" He asked. Pete was rolling up on us. I looked over and made eye contact with him. He sensed the seriousness of the conversation and decided to stay and listen in on what was the meeting we were having. "Oh boy this can't be good." Pete said folding his arms on his chest positioning himself to hear what was about to be said. Jamal and Pete locked eyes for a quick second. Jamal lowered his head in disappointment. "We'll look Ima need you to help me brainstorm this one for real..." Anyway he got back to his story. "Nikki and I have been seeing one another on a daily basis for the past few months okay and not every time we see each other are we fucking and sucking, but we are hugging and kissing and a good portion of our encounters with some sexual favors are exchanged." He took a deep breath.. exhaling, our attention was all on Jamal at this very moment. "We knew that due to all of our time spending with the girl, feelings and emotions are growing that apparently neither one of us can stop or even slow down even if we wanted them to stop. Especially if we were so far gone that it wouldn't work it would be too late. I'm not gona sit here and lie to you, we are all men and Pete you've known me for some time now. I love my wife even though we may have a relationship that your average Joe Schmoe wouldn't take if it was free. No one would understand it no matter who looked at me and my wife. The ones who know us say that we are just crazy for still being with one another... At the end of the day I do love her right?" I nodded my head agreeing with his way of analyzing his relationship and his whole outlook on how truly he really loved his woman. It could be that he is so adamant about actually losing her this time for good or he just wants to sound good. Either way he was my boy and I had to give him my support. "My wife he asked me to go to a family reunion out and Pennsauken right?" Pete and I stayed silent, I usually skip all of these family functions whenever they are brought up, because her family and I always have our little differences that aren't so bad for them but because it's "Jamal" they tend to blow it out of proportion on my end." I go back and forth with her about not wanting to go but sooner or later she convinces me to go with her. I still to this day can't wrap my fingers around how she did it. It makes me wonder if she knew or if she has some type of suspicion or just might not know anything to be honest." Jamal was talking fast and thinking very hard at the same time. "Customers stopped him in the middle of his soap opera wanting to place an order. I wanted to hear the rest, but it had to wait. "Commercial gentlemen." Pete joked and I had no choice but to bust out laughing. Jamal tried to hold his but had to admit this was a commercial in the real. Pete took the order and we got to work. A few more customers came rushing in as well.

I felt bass coming from the front but it wasn't directly out front. I was occupied into what I was doing. Two males and a girl that had to be at least in their 20s came walking and she looked very pretty. One of the guys look familiar but I couldn't pinpoint where I saw him. It wasn't a good feeling but it wasn't a terrible feeling either. I ignored my emotions. I took the order and by eavesdropping on their conversation I gained knowledge that one of the two male's names was "Streets" it was a coincidence that Jacqueline's baby dad was called "Streets" as well. I now knew where I saw his face from... He didn't know who I was but then again he could know and was just playing it off.

"Hi can I help y'all?" I asked staring at the nigga named street dead in his eyes. He returned the stare, but it wasn't one that indicated any real threat. I examine his posture so I can get a better understanding how he moved. You'll be surprised on how many niggaz could be read without realizing it. When you fight or box so much it becomes almost as if you're always in training mode or even fight mode. Your posture and stance is something that couldn't be erased. He was shorter than me but he was bulkier than I was. He had on jewels all over, rocks in his ears that weighed down his earlobes. A necklace with a number one charm on it had white gold or platinum not too sure. It could just be sterling silver for all I know. I noticed a scar above his left eyebrow and another on his four head not a very noticeable one but with the florescent light in the shop it wasn't tough to miss. "/Dame un momento/, /give me a moment/." Street said. The other customers order was wrapped up and ready to go. "Order up." I said loud enough for him to hear me. The girl that was with Streets stared at my movements. She had on some grey tights with some sneakers. She was fresh in her little fitted vest. She walked over to the window. I examine her plump ass on the low. I wasn't going to be blatantly be disrespectful it was nice and round though. I know she could see my reflection off the glass because I use that to my advantage plenty of times myself. "/Mira loka que tu quiere?/" Streets asked her /what she wanted/. "Cheesesteak with some mozzarella sticks I wrote as she spoke. Her voice was soft and sweet voice. Her dark black curly hair fell to her shoulders. I waited for her to turn around. "What do you want on your steak?" I asked look over her way.... She turned around with an attitude. "Just put cheese and onions and katsup on it." She said not looking at me but talking to Streets. Not so sweet I thought correcting myself "And what about for yall?" I asked "/dame/,/give me/.. The same with fries instead." Street said. "what you want "Kay"?" Streets asked. Girly headed back to the window. "I'll have a burger with onion rings with everything on it." Kay said "anything else?" I asked "no let me get two Mountain Dew." Streets said. That girl she was sexy but looked dangerous. "Look Streets he leaving right there." Girly he said pointing to the parking spot. Streets jetted out to move his car. He was back in no time. His attitude wasn't crazy hood but it has some swag to it. His boy Kay look like all he did was get high and shoot shit up. All blacked out hoodie and hand on his hip all the time. He too had on some husky studs in his ears that. The Lincoln parked in view and confirmed my intuition. This is the nigga who threaten his BM's and said he would take the baby from her if she continued to see me or any other nigga. He wasn't Puerto Rican. I noticed his accent which wasn't thick but I knew it had to be Dominican or even Cuban not 100% sure but I would find out now. I actually had him up and close, my blood began to boil. He and his crew decided to sit at the booth and talk amongst themselves, but it wasn't amongst themselves. I could hear them perfectly now of course I wasn't going to be noticeable and just stand and listen. As Jamal went to work. I decided to clean the windows, yes to hear what I could. It wasn't right but hey I needed direct info and why not get it from the source. I thought about how I could spark up a conversation without triggering them that I was probing. Then he came to me. "Ayo G." I yelled over to Jamal he looked and I winked at him. This was my angle.

"I tell you man, chick's aint loyal when it comes to boyfriend and girlfriend type shit." I tossed in the air wiping down the windows. Jamal and I have developed this little scheme a while ago and it tends to bring out feelings with the customers at random. Not sure why but maybe because everyone knows very little but are very quick to give an opinion. I once heard this somewhere and it works if triggered correctly. "Who you telling homie?" Streets chimed in immediately. Got em! Was all I thought I winked at Jamal again? "I know you can't trust them as far as you can throw them." Jamal said. "I wanted to get shorty so bad, I just don't know how." Street was talking to his homeboy. "Don't worry man we will handle that she can't hide forever." Kay spoke in a cold manner. Now minding my business I continued to do what I was doing. "I forgot to ask you is this for here to go?" I looked at girly so she could make a decision. "To go" Kay said. "No to stay I don't want to eat in no car and get all dirty with all of them potholes and shit." Girly said with a nasty attitude that was kind of cute. "For here man." Streets gave the final decision. "Jamal that's for here." I said. "This nigga she fucking with got her head all fucking sprung, that she won't even let me touch her." Streets was pissed. "That dick game papa." Star said teasing." I now could see why the stars were behind her left ear, they represented her nickname. "Homeboy dick game gotta be on point." She entice. "I bet if I cut his balls off she won't be on his dick anymore." Kay said. I had to laugh. I wanted to spark it right then and there in the shop and put an end to all this bull shit. Exposing my hand to them and let them dictate my emotions, I knew better and I knew that I had to study my enemy in order to win the war. "How don't you know who this nigga is?" Star asked." He never around and his truck no one knows where it be parked up or don't want to tell me." Streets said in a disappointing tone. "Order up." Jamal said. All three sat there and ate their meals talking very freely and believe me they gave up their hand without even knowing who or what dealt the cards. He was much older but stupidity came in all ages and sizes. It's been said that one mind is a terrible thing to waste so I had to put mind to use.... After it was all said and done Jamal got back to his story. Nikki is somehow related to his wife by third or second cousin, and she didn't say a word at the reunion. It all came so quick and unexpected. "I don't know if she is going to tell or if she going to keep it on the low but she gotta tell me something." Jamal was worried sick. "When is the next time you gona see her?" I asked. "She worked down the block Jamal." You should handle that before she does." I didn't mean to tell her off, but to minimize this or cut her off it had to be done is my opinion." Man I don't want to see her right now Rock let's talk about something else." Jamal was stressing bad "What was that about with them three who came in?" Jamal asked once the trio left. "That was Jacqueline's baby dads and he was talking greasy about whoever fucking Jacqueline going to get it." I said. Jamal's eyes were wide open like a deer caught in the headlights. "He don't know?" He asked. "No but he might find out sooner than he think......

Chapter 9
"Get out of here"

After finally getting the chance to have sex with Jacqueline things between us also began to heat up, unlike Felicia she knew it was all about being around for one another and just a little bump and grind in between everything. From what I saw she contained her emotions in check very well.

It was late but not too late. I had already taken off all my clothes and I was not really in the mindset to go anywhere. Jalinda on the other hand came into the room all ghetto fly. She had on her fatigue capris with her all black k-Swiss with a black fitted shirt. She looked like a tomboy for real. "Where the hell are you going?" I asked. "The Army not taken anyone at this time." I joked. "The Army wish they had a soldier like me on their side." Linda joked back looking at herself in my full body mirror. I could hear mom coming, "Mom look at this." I hollered over so she could come in. I looked at Linda. She did look cute I'm not gona lie she knew how to put it together. "Where you off to dressed like that?" Mom asked in a humorous tone. "I want to go to Pennsauken Mart." Linda said looking my way. I change my stared to the TV. "And what do you need from there?" Mom asked already noticing that I was not in the mood to go anywhere. "I don't need anything but I do want to go." I got a little bit of money and I really wanted to see if they had anything new over there." Linda stated still admiring her body in the mirror, I kept my eyes glued on the TV. "Well you better talk to your brother about that one." Mom threw me under the bus. "Me? She better call the Army reserve to take her ass over there." I joked. Mom laughed. Linda turned around and jumped right on me. "You got jokes huh?" She was tagging me with light body shots, she had me straddled. "You two are a mess, and lock the house up once yall decide to go out." Mom said. "You want to come?" Linda asked mom without even knowing if I was going to take her. "No baby I'm tired." Mom replied to her question, knowing damn well I was taking Linda to the Mart. "Come on Linda get off me before I hurt your tiny ass." I warned. "Hurting who?" You the young'n or you must forgot." She was right I was younger her but she knew better. In one swift motion I had her pinned down? "It's easy to talk shit when no one isn't fighting back huh?" She struggled. It was useless I was way too strong for her. I noticed she had something in her pocket, so I decided to be nosy. "What is this?" I pinned both her wrists with one of my big ass hands and searched her pockets. "Run that." I pulled out some bills. "What else you got for me?" I asked joking. "It was her butterfly knife "Oh yea what is this little pretty pink." After I took all that she had, I got up and put it in my pockets. "My shit." I joked. She got up fixing her own outfit and looking back into the mirror. "You play too much Manny that don't count you cheated." She whined like a two year old. "What? You started with me chump... I mean champ." I joked. "You can't handle me, I'm too strong for you." I antagonized her. She jumped on me again and tried to choke me out. It was pointless I flung her over my head and tossed her right on my bed. She bounced right off and landed on the side of the bed. "No you did it." This girl did not want to quit. "/Ya Tate quieta./" /stay still/ I told her. She listened. "Come on let's go, get ready." Linda stated. "I really don't feel like it ma, I'm tired and I want to relax." I replied "you don't even have to work tomorrow." She interrupted. "I'll buy you a funnel cake." She bargained. Let me tell you this everyone knows about funnel cakes up in Pennsauken Mart. They were infamous for that shit. My mouth watered just by her saying that. All right let's go but give me a minute and you fixing my bed if you want to go, here." I said handing her back her items.

I threw on my fresh black Tim's and my jeans, with an all-black hoodie and fitted cap. If she was going to be hood I wasn't going to let her be on her own. I pulled my Army cap than called out to her "Linda." She came rushing in "wassup? What you want some more?" She joked. This girl was all amped up. "Calm you're ass down, here put this on see if you like it." She took it and disappeared . Something told me to chill tonight, but Linda was ready and she looked like she wanted to hang out with just me today. I went against my better judgment, which was something I never did but today I did just for Linda sake. I had some bud, I grabbed some, the potency of the high grade bud was remarkable. This was going to calm her as down I thought to myself. I put on my watch and in a minutes we were out the door. The block was turnt up and doing what they always did. Partying and causing havoc when they could.

I opened the truck and told Linda. "I'll be right back.".... "Grab me a drink." She jumped in the truck after yelling over in my direction. I grabbed a vanilla dutch and a homemade iced tea. We could share this.

Back in the truck, "that's for us?" Linda asked. "yes, why?" I asked. "I thought you said no more." She informed me. "Yeah but your ass is a little to hyped for me right now." I joked. "So it's for me then." She challenged with a smile. I didn't say anything. I turned the engine over and she fiddled with the radio. DMX was playing. "You mighty gangsta today." I said before she started to turn it up. I pushed in the lighter and put the car in drive. For the record, my rolling game has gotten a lot better. I mean it's gotten quicker but not better. The lighter popped out and in seconds the L was in rotation. Linda went from army strong to chill out in about five minutes. "You good?" I asked her. She was sucking on the straw from the ice tea. "Yeah" she answered in a smooth calm voice. "Save me some." I said hitting the L. I was high as shit I was not even going to front. I drove normally but every now and then I would catch myself at a stop sign for a little longer than I had to. The blaring of the car horn behind me would bring back to reality. I knew this was dumb idea to get high and drive but we only lived once. Linda turned down the music and decided to talk.

"Manny?" She looked over "wassup?" I replied keeping my eyes on the road. "Would you be mad if I got pregnant?" She asked. My mind went blank for a second, I wasn't sure how to answer this. I mean no, but why now? The thought surfaced. "What did you say?" I had to hear it again. "I mean I'm not going to get pregnant now but if I did with-in the next year would you be mad?" She asked rephrasing the question. I could see the bright "M" all the way in the horizon from up ahead indicating we were almost there. "Listen you don't need no babies right now, I'm not gona be mad but you gotta be sure that this is what you want." I said to her. It was the weed that had me being so straight forward with her at the moment. Normally I would have eased into this answer. "Yeah but I see Felicia and Jacqueline with their kids and they seem so happy Manny." The bud had hit his girl on some other shit this time. She went from be all you can be to be the mommy you can be. "Yes, they may appear to be happy and I'm sure that they are but they also are super stressed. They can't do anything without considering who and where they're going to have as a babysitter. They can do this or do that because their baby is around. Is not that simple Linda." Mom will be my babysitter while I finish school." She said. "Mom? Yeah right!" I stated. "So you want mom to raise your baby and smoke all the cigarettes around him or her?" I took it a bit too far but I had to. Maybe she would think before coming up with another random conversation like this. The L was gone and we were both roasted. We stood in silence as I pulled into a parking spot. This place would sell whatever they could, from house hold items up to fancy shoes. It was a flea market and inside is where all the merchandise was fresh and original and a lot of bootleg shit as well. If you couldn't tell which was which. If you couldn't than hey each is your own. That was for the ones who couldn't afford the authentic merchandise. Depending on your budger than you were more than welcome to enjoy the array of affordables. Jewelry was sold from platinum to aluminum bull shit. This was the hang out for all the hustlers to splurge on some hood rat. Most came just to pick up a shorty for the night in the arcade or just even walking around this place. It was a huge rectangle with so many stores. It was so big that there entrances were marked in chronological order with a letter starting from "a". The barbershop was known for the freshest lineups during the day time till the late-night. The sold stereos for your home. car, computers, and rugs etc. etc... Whatever you wanted or needed could be found up in here and I meant that. If you couldn't find? It was because you wasn't looking hard enough for it. I decided to park further away from all the clutter of cars because of accidents and your natural born haters who got there rocks off vandalizing vehicles and whatnot. I looked over at Linda she was all in the the sun visor mirror.She pulled her hat down low so you couldn't see her eyes. "You look like a tomboy." I joked. "Don't start." She spat. "And so what."... I look good and you know it." She said. No comment. I opened the door making sure my keys were on my pocket. The butterfly knife when ever I went out. "Parked up at C3." Linda said. As soon as you open the door the roar from the loud music and all the chatter of people echoed all throughout the hallway. The buzzing from the tattoo gun at the entrance was working at it's best. Anyone that wanted a show could see it through the glass. You could actually see the tattoo being permanently put on to the customer skin always drew a few spectators threw the transparent glass. Linda and I stood there for a moment and watch as the white girl got a scar on her forearm for the rest of her life. The bright red plastered look all over her face didn't go unnoticed. She was going through an agonizing amount of pain. I laughed "look at her face." I told Linda. "That bitch, is bitching." Linda pulled me away. Smoking was permitted in this place, it wasn't a problem. Cigarette butts and trash all on the floor. This place was ghetto for real. I wondered who had to be the one to sweep this place up. I bet it had to be a few of them with how big this place was. It was impossible not to get bumped into due to all the crowds of people. I dipped into a spot where there was some official outfits on display, Linda was on my heels. She moved toward the female section I was just looking .I wasn't going to buy just anything unless I saw something I really like. The guy up front was a big stocky Russian looking guy. "Can I hope Ju?" He spoke in his loud raspy voice. "I'm good just looking." I notice him checking out Linda. For all he knew she was a nigga, but a good look over would state the obvious she wasn't. I would have to say that there had to be at least 200 stores and that's just a low estimation. I couldn't emphasize it enough. The amounts of woman that came up in here were all bad of all flavors. Some were cuffed up and all the others just want to be spoiled by a potential Baller. Others just want to fuck and trust and believe they will let that be known. No strings attached just "here and give me mine." The best way to enjoy was to either stroll at a snails pace because once you got to where you started you would be physically exhausted. You had your hustlers selling a little bit of everything. Why wouldn't they take advantage of the masse of people, to get rid of a pound or two broken down quick and easy cash. I didn't need any of that I was blazed. Linda's almond shaped eyes told me she was just as blasted as I was no questions asked. I scanned for her and noticed she was across the store we just left, she was looking at some scarfs and a few miscellaneous objects that caught her eye. She wrapped a deep navy blue one with gold trim around her neck.

"It's three for five dollars." The Chinese lady stated as clearly as she could. Her husband or whoever he was, was walking around patrolling his miniature store. "Oh yea that brings me up to this point this was the easiest place to steal from, I remember these two guys decided to steal some jewelry. Until this day they haven't caught them. The mass of people in here can be used to your advantage. Let's not forget to mention all the stores in the center of this rectangle had no walls so it was an alleys with no fences or gates etc. etc. If your dip game was sharp enough you would be good. "Manny which one?" She asked. Holden up about five different type of scarfs. She pulled with all of them, "they all look nice I'm sure you going to put them together with any outfit real nice. How many colors do they have altogether styles and all?" I asked her "about 15." She replied counted them all searching for the ones she didn't already have a hand. "Yes about 15"she said again the Chinese man came walking over I looked right at him "how much for all 15 of them?" I asked in my head. The amount came up to $25 if he stuck to his deal already posted. "$23" he said in his broken up lingo. I blew air cut my lips as if I had a flat tire. Linda didn't say a word she already knew what was going on. You had to try to hustle the hustler. I bet he paid a dollar for each scarf and I was not going to take that from him but he had to give me some leeway. I wanted them for at least $20. "Come on we can check out the other store." Linda face wasn't a happy one. "How much?" The lady yelled over to me rubbing her fingers together as if she was indicated money. "$18" I said. I know I was pushing it a bit too far but I had to lowball. Linda was already almost completely out the store.... "$20 no lower." The Asian lady said to me. Linda turn right around as I bought her a variety of all scarfs. You have to remember when you are dealing with anyone who is selling anything, you just don't jump on the first price thrown at you, why would you do that when you could possibly pay that much less? Linda put her arm interwind with mine as we walked. This always kept the dogs away but their eyes always stay glued on her. I couldn't do anything about that. Anyone can look but when you staring and your lips get the talking at the same time that's when it becomes a problem. We looked at the pagers and cell phone spots and to be straight up I like some of the gadgets they had. They weren't the best but it was sure enough to let you know that someone was on that ass.

"Jalinda!" A female voice yelled over the crowd now it could be a coincidence that my Linda wasn't the one being called, but it was my Linda. I followed the voice and it was "Alexa" one of Linda's friends from high school. She ran over dipping through the crowd of people she was tall and skinny but she made up for that from behind she was also Puerto Rican. She carried some serious plumpness from behind. Her hair was blonde with black highlights. she always wore it out with her curls. I loved that shit. I had that pussy and it was good. She didn't have big breasts but they were a mouthful. "What you doing here?" Alexa asked a dumb ass question as if she didn't know already. It was either to spend money or window shop. They embraced than directed her attention over to me. She gave me a kiss on my cheek. Her sweet smell brought back memories when I had her begging for mercy. Sorry I can get a bit cocky when you know you put in work in the bedroom. She had two dimples not on her cheek but one next to her eyebrow and one to the right of her bottom lip. It was something different when she smiled she look so pretty. "Manuel what's up papi?" She rubbed my belly. Linda slapped her hand playfully. "Shopping." I said answering her question. "/Ay chavo?/"/there is money/... She walked with us for a while until Linda decided to ditch her with her favorite line

"I'll give you a call sometime next week Alexa hope you find what your looking for.".... Alexa got the hint. "Make sure you do, I'll blow your house phone up." Alexa stated being dead serious but playing at the same time. "Don't even start that shit again." Linda said in a more serious tone. When I was messing with her after Linda gave her the green light to fuck with me. I trashed her in every position I knew at the moment. This was at her house when her parents left town, she lived over by Pollock and it was me and three other girls besides my sister. They had a nice house I still remember her room. "Manuel." Alexa called over to me. "You want to see me again?" She asked desperately. I was about to answer her. "No he already booked he aint got no time for you or any of them other girls he done Dicknotyzed." Linda was off the chain. You still think I'm playing when I say she very overprotective over me? I laughed. "Damn Linda you hooked us up now you acting up." Alexa challenged. "Yes I did and you didn't know how to act so no it's not gona happen again." I threw up my hands insinuating the decision has been made. I'm not going to go against Linda and ruin our trust. I looked around and made my way towards the pellet gun shop where they had all types of toys for grown-ups. If you were into hunting this was the spot, they had so many gadgets. Alexa eventually left when she saw her relative or even her friend. "Crazy as bitch" Linda said over to me. I laughed. "You see what you do to my friends?" She joked I was all smiles. "I didn't do anything I give them what they asked for." I countered back. "That's the problem Manny if you would just ignore them and act like you aren't interested they wouldn't be tripping." Linda was in her bag now. She let me fuck them but now I'm the bad one right? I looked at all the paintball guns on the wall, they had all types. Single shooters, three round burst and of course my favorite fully. You wanted to shoot 150 paintballs in one shot, this is where you had to come to get your gun custom made. The glass counter carried an array of BB guns that were all manufactured to look like Real guns. They range from 380s to 22's all the way up to 45's and ARs. I love coming in here looking at all the toys. Knives, ninja stars, swords and nun chucks etc. etc. this was a store with a lot of collectible items as well. I whipped out my butterfly knife one swift motion.

"So you are a collector?" The white guy with the white beard asked me. "No this was a gift from." I nodded my head towards Linda who was lost in the guns. "Very nice gift." The older man said. "Yes it is listen I wanted to know if you could engrave something on it for me." I asked him. Linda looked up at the guy. "Oh it's you the girl who bought two of these." He said recognizing Linda. Linda smile. "Is your finger all better?" He asked. Linda held up her hand "good as new." Ballen up her fist. "She is feisty." The old man joked. "Who are you telling?" I said going along with his remark. "Is she always so tough?" He asked me. Not even waiting for a response. "I didn't recognize you with all that camouflage you wearing Jalinda." He did remember her now. I just stared at him until I got his attention again. So how many times did you get cut?" He asked holden up my butterfly knife. "Not too many." I replied. His face didn't believe a word I said. "So what is it that you want on it?" He asked me. "I want you to engrave something on it, you know like you do on the swords." I stated. His facial expression led me to doubt that it could be done. "I don't know let me check." He said. Linda walked up on me. "What you going to get on it?" Linda was being super nosy. "Nunya." I stated "nunya?" She repeated back to me. "Who was that?" She asked. "Nunya ya damn business." I joked. "Ima get Manny and Felicia on it." I lied. She punch me, this girl love to throw her fucking hands. "I bet you wouldn't be able to swing those hands at me anymore when I break them." She took two side steps away for me. "Don't run now?" I joked now. Okay he came back and with my butterfly in his hand. "We can try it but I can't be 100% sure that it'll work." The old man said. He had me in deep thought. "Why?" I asked. "Because the swords are much thicker and wider but we can attempt it if you want." He said. He slid a pencil and a piece of paper my way, "Here write down what you want me to engrave on the knife." Linda picked up a bow and arrow she didn't have the bow fastened and aimed it at me. "Damn ma, don't mark me." I joked. "You want me dead?" I joked. She put it down immediately. "No never that." She said. "I know after a few minutes a couple came in and walked out quickly. I began to walk around myself "What the hell?" Linda yelled startled. I looked over "wassup?" I walked over to her, there was a lady chilling in the cut. I guess she was the security in this mother fucker watching over everything. She was also older but look creepy as fuck. She smiled. Linda sped away,

"Check it out." The older man said. I walked over and I grabbed the knife and opened up as quickly as possible just so I could get a look at the back of the blade. "Manuel, Linda and Cathy forever." I stared at it for a few minutes admiring how each letter was crafted so perfectly. The smile on my face caused Linda to be even nosier. "Let me see." Linda whined. I handed her the blade she whipped her blade out like a pro "do this one to." She demanded. "Yes ma'am I don't want no problems with you." The older man Joked putting his hands up, no problems. Linda examined the blade and didn't let it go until hers was in her hand with the same words in her palm. "Thank you." We both said in unison. The total came up to $14 and we was out. "So how about that funnel cake?" Linda reminded me.

The lady that makes these cakes have been in the spot for over 20 years and everyone love her funnel cakes. The only problem was that it was on the other side on the opposite and that we were walking on. "You want to walk around or cut through then go up?" I asked her. "It's right up here Manny what are you saying?" She corrected my thinking. I was about to argue that I wasn't wrong, but instead I looked and noticed she was definitely right. So we shot right over to the spot. There was a line of about nine people so we waited and waited and waited some more. The hissing of the air brush guns were right diagonally from where the funnel cakes were. If you ever ate a funnel cake fresh then you knew that those things take a minute especially when you have a line out front of you. Nine times out of 10 everyone ordering the same thing. I stood on alert watching everyone who walked by and walked up on us. I didn't trust anyone even though this wasn't the place to draw.

After getting our cakes we sat down and ate watching all the passerby's. Everyone in deep conversation with their partner/friends etc. I laughed to myself. Linda had powdered sugar on her nose and I wanted to leave it there until we got to the car but I couldn't let my rider walk around like that. "/Toma/"/here/ handing her a napkin. "Your nose." Her head dropped out of embarrassment. She stuck her pink powder tongue out at me. "You better had." She replied it was about 11 PM and this looked as if it wasn't going to shut down no time soon. "I'm surprised you didn't invite one of them chicks you fucking to come up in here with us?" Linda spoke were her mouth full being a smartass. "Why would I do that when you invited me, not the other way around?" I answered. "Yes but even if I did don't you think it was only right to invite one of them? Linda said. "Felicia seemed to be the only one who has most of your time lately." Linda stated. "Are you jealous?" I smiled. "Not jealous Manny but I think you should give her a chance." Linda liked Felicia I could tell. "I'm still young Linda I can't be locked down and we already had this conversation." I said. "You won't realize what you got until is gone is all I'm saying." So cliché. I threw a piece of funnel cake at her and hit her on the chin. Her mouth open in shock. I got up and left with the rest of my cake... Knowing her she would go overboard... Too late, I felt something hit me right on my left shoulder. Her laughter didn't go unnoticed and the rest of the shoppers around us started to enjoy our playful bond towards one another.

I felt this uneasy feeling in my stomach coming over me. It felt like a knot forming and it was working its way up to my throat. My mind went into deep thoughts of concern. Linda was all on my back, still joking going about herself. I tried to show that everything was normal, but realizing something was up but I couldn't pinpoint what or who it was. "Mom"? Came into my mind and I said her name a little louder than I intended too. I went to the nearest payphone and decided to dial home. No answer. "What is wrong?" Linda asked. "Nada just checking up on mom ." Happy with my answers. She perused close by staring at the display of items around the mart. My buzz from the bud was either playing with me or my gut was on point. I didn't know which one overpowered the other. All I knew was that both had me in a tug-of-war with one another. "Hello?" A raspy tired voice answered. "Mom!" I practically yelled over the receiver "Yes baby?" Mom answered. With just as much emphasis in her words. "Are you okay Manuel?" Mom asked me. I found that question to be very odd. Why would she asked me this? Why wouldn't I be? My stomach got even tighter "yes I'm okay I'm still here with Linda at the mart I was checking up on you. I know you were asleep but still." I answered her truthfully. "I'm laying here I'm not asleep yet...."The call went silent for a moment. It's almost midnight when are you to plan on coming home?" Mom questioned. "Real soon I know it's late." I replied. "Yes it is and be careful I'll see you two here shortly." I was about to hang up. "I love you Manuel." Mom said. "Love you too mom." I felt a little relieved that mom was fine but I wasn't fully satisfied yet. I whistled to get Linda's attention and managed to grab about 75 other people's attention along with hers at the same time. "/vamonos/"/let's go/I said. I know she didn't hear me due to all the ruckus but she got the idea. Her lips pouted I didn't care we was out. "Why?" She whined. This couldn't be happening right now. "Because it's late and I'm tired mija." Her eyes were still bloodshot. She was still feeling the bud so was I but it wasn't as effective as when I took the first hits. Linda's lungs were still being broken in so she would feel it a little bit longer since her tolerance wasn't that high.

“I saw this shirt that the man was putting together for this couple and it gave me an idea.” Linda said. “What are you saying?” I asked, “Let me get this shirt then we can leave.” “No let’s go.” I said. She didn’t even argue as we began walking away. I force myself to go back and get this so-called shirt Linda wanted. I couldn’t tell her no, Why would I? I was still going against all my natural feelings. Shit, I may in fact be over reacting like many do I thought to myself. Linda and I took a look at the posters on display. There were all types of drawling’s whether cartoon characters with either violence, love or animals etc. etc. It was already 11:40 and we were next to be seen by the artist now this man was too talented. He would airbrush anything from sneakers, clothing, basketballs golf balls etc. etc. Didn’t matter he would get it done for you. I felt eyes on me but then again there was a mass number of people around me so my paranoia was taken a toll on me. I looked around with my hand in my pocket trying to identify any real threat that would cause me to feel this way but I couldn’t locate it. It wasn’t anything of anyone I was bugging.

“Look at this one Manny. I think this one would look nice for us.” Linda had a smile on her face it was priceless. I admired her charm so much I wouldn’t know what I would do if someone ever tried to hurt her. “Nice, for who? You and Joel?” I asked. The portrait cartoon character was of a male and female back to back with weapons in both hands which look like a Bonnie and Clyde type. I thought it was very well articulated there was no question about that. “No!” For me and you.” Linda almost killed me with her look. I threw my hands up again “my bad.” It was just a couple’s thing.” I tried to defend my initial reaction. “I know it is Manny but the other one I saw him drawling was along the lines like this but he did it with a twist.” Linda said “ooh /tabien entonse./”/ok than/. The woman ahead of us with her kids was almost completed with their shirts. She had about three done with two more left. I watched as the two boys and three girls all cheered and talk to about their shirts excitedly. They had barbie and superheros on them. “What mom said?” Linda finally decided to inquire. “She’s good.” I replied brief and to the point. It was finally Linda turn to talk to the artist she spoke to him as if it was a big secret. He asked us to position ourselves over the by the wall where no one was standing.

“To the left a bit.” The artist director our movement so he could get a perfect view of the two of us with those big ass florescent lights up ahead. My position was with my back on her back looking over to the side and he had her face on the opposite side looking over. "Hold it right there." After a few moments. "Let me see you girl." The artist spoke to Linda. I mean mug the shit it out at him. I couldn't see Linda but I'm sure she had her infamous mug on. I held the thought of all the shit that happened to me that caused me to mug so many people in the past. Using what slick shit came out there mouth or even all the back biting that was found out by everyone. I even used the thought of mom smoking and Linda and Joel arguing.I was using to it. I was in deep thought with this shit. I was feeling the emotions with all this shit. "All right u can relax. Whatever you're going to with your hands do it now." The artist informed us. I threw up my fighting stance. I could stand here all day. All I needed was a face to put my hands to use. I thought to myself . I woundered what Linda was doing. After a good 15 minutes "all done." Was all the artist said? He was a tall black guy and I must say the boy has skills for real. He showed us the shirt letting it dry on his canvas. My face was exactly how I looked. Our completion everything else look just as it was. "Look at that." Linda smiled brightly. "That came out official." "Thanks" The artist showed his appreciation for his work. Everyone had their own talent and this man knew this is how he could make a lot of money. Can't knock the hustle and believe me I'm not, the way this place was overcrowded with all types of people he was killing it. "How much?" I asked he looked at us. $40 Linda reached in her back pocket and tossed him a $50 keep the change, and just like that we was up out of there. She didn't stop looking at the shirt, her features were crafted to the tee but what stood out the most was what she told him to write in cursive writing "We gona ride out." And on the back up top in the same letters read "Forever CMD." It was hot and the city skyline was in the background. It was mainly the Ben Franklin Bridge but with a piece of North Camden and South Camden borderlines. It was definitely worth the 40 piece. I snatched the shirt "this is for me right?" I joked knowing damn well it was because it would drown Linda with how big it was. "Yeah right this is all mine." She teased. You can get one next time if you aint in no rush. The place was dwindling down by the minute. The wave of individuals subsided. It was still bumping though with people but not as much as when we first arrived. Our exit was all the way on the other and so we headed towards it. Passing the arcades the aroma of marijuana was strong and in the open. People were turning up. No one could care less of the cops patrolling. What made it worse was that there was a Bible and Scripture spot right across from the arcades. Talk about contradiction I could have sworn that the couple running that spot enjoyed the aroma that was always being emitted from the arcades. You would think that once they would've noticed all those other sinful deeds that came along with the arcades. The owner would've relocated to another area to sell his godly merchandise. Unless they actually enjoyed the smell? Yes, I tend to look into things a little deeper than just the usual . Instead look at it in all possible angles. Might be a bit fucked up to say but is to truth.

"Put that away before you drop it and dirty it before we even make it to the car." I said. I felt like a father at times not too sure if it was because I didn't have one or just because I knew I had to murture faster than I anticipated. I was still young and playful believe me.

"Pennsauken Mart will be closing in about 10 minutes so if you please go to the nearest exit we would appreciate it." The loud P.A system barked at all the stragglers. "Yes that's us mija." I said to Linda. "They can wait us leaving." Linda was back in her bag with the gangsta attitude. "Where was the bud when you needed it?" I joked. "That's how you feel?" Linda protested. I laughed she stepped up to me. "I'm at tell mom you hit me." She threw a combo at my chest and ran before I could say or do anything. The combo had already landed quickly. As we approached our exit, the buzzing of the tattoo gun was still humming. You could imagine of all the profits this place would rake in. We stood there to look again, this time it was a white male with no room on his skin to even fit a beauty mark. That's how covered this guy was with these tattoos. The man doing the tattoo was also covered with all sorts of ink and he still managed to somehow find some room on the other man's body to add more. "That's what I want to do to my body." Linda said sounding very serious "what?" I shot back at her with a disgusted look. "You want all that ink on your body?" I asked her hoping she was kidding. "Hell no Manny." She corrected. "I want what he has in his ears." Linda stated. I had to take another glance over at both of these white mother Fokker's. "They had big ass holes in their ears with what looked like long ass toothpicks but thicker. I mean these holes were huge. You could fit your full finger in them Holes and still has some room left over. I scrunched up my face in total discuss. If that's what you like than hey by all means, it isn't my body you know? Linda pose she pulled out her keys and use the key ring to act as if she had holes. "How do I look?" She asked "like an idiot." I shot at her. "Let's keep it moving." A heavyset security guard from behind us said. "Yes sir." Linda replied sarcastically.

We were out in the dark with the night sky, the air was briskier than usual. The sky was loaded with stars. The parking lot lights were on but didn't do their job correctly. In fact if it wasn't for the full moon from up above this parking lot would be damn near pitch black. There were about a dozen cars out here and let me tell you I'm glad I wore this hoodie because it was a bit nippy. The air was Crisp my truck stood out from the distant as we passed practically nothing. The cars that were out were scattered throughout the lot. I hit my alarm and the lights blinked right on cue. I noticed a car part further behind the truck but didn't pay it no mind.

"It's chilly." Linda said. "I know I'm tired and I can't wait to hit my bed." I reply. "Uuummmhhhmmmm." Linda urged. "This wasn't so bad Manny was it to?" Linda asked I smile. "No it was fun actually we should do this again." I proposed. "Yeah I'd like that." Turning the key to turn the engine over was what I was intended to do but that was interrupted by the Loud "BANG"!!!! That made my neck get whiplash. "What the fuck!" I barked holding my neck. I glanced in the rearview and noticed a box shape vehicle behind me. . Already knowing what this was for immidiatlly.

I looked over to Linda "Whatever happens I want to know that's Jacqueline's baby dad and it's about to go down wait here don't move." Linda was quiet and had this cold stare in her eyes. I hopped out of the truck with my neck all fucked up. He rammed the rear of my truck again "YO BITCH!" I barked pissed. It was on now. Get the fuck out of the car. I was on the side of his car trying to open his door trying to pull him out. His window was up so I couldn't tell if it was actually him in the car, but at this point it didn't matter who was in the car. We were far past talking now. I'm not the talking type anyway. The passenger door open and a body rose out of the passenger side. It was Kay but I had to be sure, "YOU KNOW YOU DONE FUCKED UP!" He walked around the back at a Lincoln. "FUCK YOU PUSSY IF YOU WANT IT COME GET IT!" I shot at him furious. It was in fact Kay his voice confirmed it all the way. "The sub shop boy got some heart now." Kay was antagonizing me by now he was almost within arm's reach but not fully yet I watched his feet and his guard was completely down. As soon as he got close enough he came up quick not what they right or left but an automatic handgun. It put me on Pause for second. My butterfly knife was in my right pocket and there was no chance on me drawling that out without him letting off a round. He had me at a stalemate. The driver of the car decided to come out seeing that I wasn't a threat at the moment. The back door open. It was Streets and Star both wearing gray. They gave me sly ass grin. "ALL YOU HAD TO DO WAS LEAVE HER ALONE." Street barked. "THATS MY BITCH!" he spoke pissed ass fuck. He spit right in my face. "Damn and to think I actually thought you was good looking at the shop." Star stated I held my composure wondering what and how I was going to get out of this mess. Linda was still in the truck I don't know what she was doing but I was glad she was tucked away in the cut. I don't even think that they even knew that I was with her. But then again if they were watching they must've known. "LOOK SUB BOY IMA TELL YOU THIS ONE TIME AND ONE TIME ONLY....." He was within my reach but he threw the first solid blow which connected on my left side of my jaw. I felt the impact, this nigga had a mean hook. Kay was all up on me just in case I decided to jump. "DONT EVEN THINK ABOUT IT!" Kay barked at me. "IF YOU DONT STAY AWAY FROM MY BABYMOMS THERE IS GOING TO BE ALL HELL TO PAY." YOU'RE SISTER AND YOU MOM ARE ALL GOING TO SUFFER FOR YOUR STUPIDITY. My blood was way past boiling and there wasn't no cooling it down right now. This nigga done threating my whole family and not to mention he just cracked me right in my jaw. How the fuck did he know? I thought of letting all this go, if all he was gona do was give a small speech. I would plan my next move later but he brought my loved ones into all this an now my head was dancing with the demonds. I SWEAR TO THAT PATHETIC ASS GOD YALL WORSHIP IF YOU MOVE I WILL LEAVE YOU ASS SLUMPED RIGHT HERE!" Kay was pissed. I could smell the PCP right off of him as he came closer. So I'm hunched over on one knee and little Miss /Estrella/,/Star/ decides she wants to get in on the action by kicking me right on the side of my stomach taking me by total shock. That blow left me breathless. There goes my ribs I thought as I searched for air on the ground. Her all black Tims were being put to good use today. "YOU HEARD WHAT HE SAID!?" She barked. SO THE WHOLE TIME WE WERE IN THE SHOP, IT WAS YOU FUCKING HER BRAINS OUT!?".... He paused mad as hell. YOU EVEN HAD THE AUDACITY TO THROW THIS SHIT RIGHT UP IN MY FACE LIKE I WASNT SHIT!" Another kick but this one landed on the side of my head. I spit out blood. I felt a bit dizzy but I knew I would regain my focus once my equilibrium balance itself out. So I just ran with the beating until I saw my opportunity. It came when Kay finally took his eyes off me and began to talk to streets. "Streets let me kill this nigga, show him what happens to spics that fuck with another man's girl." His hand got closer but his vision followed his voice as he spoke to Street, pushing up off the floor I charged right as Streets. I drove him right into the side of his car door. It was an older lincoln so it was all body metal. A loud thud caused his body to be imprinted in the door. "uggghh!" His air was knocked right out of him. His grip was too tight he held onto my neck and arm, I pulled back and turned with him. I knew I had to get his body on the outside of mine because Kay was ready to shoot. I knew that he wouldn't if he couldn't get a clear shot off. I had to spin him around. He had his left arm loose and was catching me dead in the face, I wasn't a wrestler and I kind of wish at the moment I was. I wasn't completely down and out yet but he was getting the best of me something serious. Star kicked and punched me from behind I felt every last blow especially the one that landed in between my legs. "I SHOULD CUT THEM OFF!" She barked. That one had me seeing stars, I was out of air with that blow. My grip on streets loosen up. "THAT'S RIGHT MAMI HE FELT THAT SHIT! Blow after blow I wasn't doing too well. "YOU ARE GOING TO DIE TONIGHT! YOU FAGGOT ASS PUSSY! SAY YOU LAST PRAYER YOU BITCH ASS NIGGA!" Kay was still pointing that loaded gun at me. He wanted me dead and I couldn't do anything. Streets had me on the ground with his legs straddled on top of me delivering blow after blow. Every time he let one loose I saw the fucking lights go out like shockwaves in my head. Every blow was precise and to make matters worse. The back of my head would bounce off the ground every time. He was strong but I somehow managed to reach in my pocket, I didn't pull anything out yet because Kay was still locked and loaded watching my every move waiting for me to get do something so he could plug one in me. "BEAT HIS ASS STREETS!" Yelled Star. She was cute but at this very second I wanted to kill this bitch, along with every other mother fucker out here. Help would've been appreciated at this time but my only wis was that Linda was long gone by now. This wasn't her mess and I couldn't live with her seeing any of this, it was too much for her to handle. I couldn't I blame her for leaving me, could I? No she was protecting herself this wasn't your ordinary brawl? Her life was more important to me, rather than seeing her be here laying right by my side getting her face bashed in as well. "IM DONE WITH YOU! NOW IMA GO STRAIGHT TO YOUR HOUSE AND FUCK YOU SISTER THAN KILL HER AND YOUR MOM!?" Streets was demolishing my face, a big part of me was given up a fight that I knew I couldn't win. I couldn't understand how he found out so much about me. Half of me was dead or even on the brink of being on unconscious. I heard a choking sound, but my eyes were to swollen shut to see anything. The voice of Star brought me back to what the fuck was actually happening to me. My knife was out in one swift motion this was my chance to save myself. I caught Streets right on the side of his arm. "YOU BITCH!" I pulled out the knife and went for another poke. He was off of me holding his arm. I looked over and the sound of Kay gasping for air was what gave me a wave of hope. This wasn't over. He was on the floor holding his neck with his hands. His hands were red due to all the blood he was so desperatly trying to keep in his body. The sound of him choking and spitting up his own blood gave me the biggest boost of energy. Linda and Star were mixing it up. Streets was holding his arm. I pulled Star by the hair and got her up off Linda, "/COJE TU COSA/,/GET YOUR THING/ AND GET OUT OF HER!" I barked. "NO IM HERE WITH YOU!" She wanted to ride but the sound of the sirens could be her within a distance. ". GO! NOW!" She ran to the truck and ran away just like I told her to. I wasn't sure where she was running to but she ran. I walked back over to Streets He had two guns in his hand. He was pointing them at me once again. "IF YOU GOING TO SHOOT THAN SHOOT BITCH!" I barked already at my limit getting closer to him. Star was on the ground looking up at us. She knew better than to get up. I could see the red and blues common "GET IN THE FUCKING CAR STAR!" Star didn't hesitate not one second. "YOU KILLED MY MANS ROCK REMEMBER THAT I FUCKING GOT YOU." Streets Barked. He was backing into his car to get in I wanted to charge at him but I was scared of being hit and ended up like Kay. They jumped in and peeled off before the cops could come close enough to see him leave the scene. Linda was my initial thought. I saw the taillights disappear in the night sky and looked over at this motionless body to the right of me. It was his right hand man's just lying there dead as fuck. I jumped in my truck I had to leave but the smell of gas only indicated one thing. There was no way my truck was going to start. It leaked all the gas out from the Lincoln bagging up the rear. The red and blues appeared in front of the Lincoln blocking him in that brought me a big sign of relief on my end. The chopper in the sky had me pinpointed so running was out the question. I noticed my watch fragments all over the asphalt. Mom and Linda is all I could think of. I only I hoped we can afford an lawyer. I looked down at Kay shook my head. "Should've been your own man." I said to his soulless body.

"GET ON THE GROUND, GET ON THE FUCKING GROUND!" The Pennsauken police barked. I looked over to streets and he was surrounded just as I was. I had no time to do anything it all happened so fast. "PUT YOU HANDS ON YOUR HEAD NOW!" The white tall husky officer barked again. "IM NOT GOING TO SAY IT AGAIN NOW!" I did as they told me. I took in many deep breaths to enjoy the cool air. I wasn't sure that I would enjoy any tomorrow. Dropping on my knees, the chopper up a head had his spot-light illuminating the whole parking lot. I stalled some more so Linda could have more time to go where ever she was going, hopefully home. "LAY ON YOU STOMACH!" After each order being barked at me two or three times. I wouldn't decide to comply not because I was being a smartass, but because I had a responsibility and that was to keep her safe. Tears filled my eys, my heart was hurting so bad. I felt it wanted to explode. The bird had his spotlight on me so that was good news. The ambulance showed up in the area but didn't come in close until I was fully cuffed and slammed around by the rednecks. "You like killing boy?!" He asked. The one kick me right where Star kicked me, this caused may my whole body ache and pain. I got a beating on top of the beaten that I had already gotten. "So why did you kill him? The initial arrest-ing officer asked "He owed you money? Or was it because he looked at you the wrong way?" He was being very sarcastic as fuck. I didn't say a fucking word, anyone in their right mind better than to engage with the cops at a time like this and if you didn't you better learn that shit now.

The DTs finally decided to show up to the party while I was in the back of the cop car squished. I hated it. I couldn't move. The ambulance still didn't even get a chance to enter the scene because this was a homicide as they may call it. The corners and forensics were called immidiatly and did what their job entitled them to do. They took photos, measurements samples and a bunch of other shit. I was wondering why the hell I didn't stay home tonight as I had planned. No matter how hard I wanted this to not be. It was happen-ing regardless. What I should've done and what happened is very irrelevant at the moment. So now I had to get my story straight. The cold steel around my wrist pierced my skin tightly. I was sitting in this patrol car and my knees practically were on my chess. How the hell could these cars be altered so that you couldn't even move. It was to uncomfortable? I stayed in the backseat of the patrol car for seem like eternity. Everything was going by in slow motion. My head was throbbing and I could taste the blood in my mouth excessively.

Streets most definitely got the upper hand on me tonight. He got me good and I wasn't afraid to admit it. Yes, I was out number but there are no rules in the art of war. We all know and heard of this shit. I noticed a uniform officer approaching the car I was confined in. He had this big smile on his face as he open the door ever so slightly.

"You obviously know why you being arrested don't you?" I kept my lips together. "Was wrong boy you can't talk all of a sudden?" The redneck asshole wouldn't quit. "Homicide" you know what that is?" He was getting annoyed at the fact of me not speaking to him. He slammed the door and disappeared. My stomach had a knot and I was scared as fuck. What was going to happen to me? I wanted to go home. I wanted to wake up from this dream already. I'm not made of steel my nerves was acting up and I wanted to scream so loud but I couldn't find the strength too. Kay was dead and I was there suspect. They didn't care who or what did what all the wanted to do was put all the pieces together rapidly. My mind was running its own marathon. Come to think about it these mother fuckers didn't even read me my rights. For what I know, which is very little. They're supposed to do this when the cuffs are being put on right? I watched as the DTs examine the area that was blocked off. I couldn't see if the Lincoln was still in the distance or did they let them go. I remember puncturing Streets good. He had to go to the hospital soon. If not he was likely to bleed to death. This is what I was really hoping for. The redneck finally jumped in the driver seat of his patrol car.

"Listen boy, I can't help you if you don't talk to me. What happened out here and why did you kill that man?" He waited for a response. I wasn't going to give him shit. "Your hurt. Just tell me what happen and I will take you to the nearest hospital so you can get clean and checked out." Still no answer. This dumbass must think I am mentally challenged aint? He had no choice but to take me to the fucking hospital whether he wanted to or not. He didn't have a damn choice. As bad as I looked he pulled off. A part of me wanted to actually think that he did truly want to help me. We knew that these cops were for self and looking for a promotion. They don't give a shit about me or even the man dead on the floor back on the asphalt. We drove for a while until we reached the nearby hospital, which was no bigger than the Cooper Hospital. My ribs hurt bad, it hurt to breathe. We went through the side entrances that was around the corner from the emergency entrance.

"Come on the officer spoke pulling me by my arm I winced in pain. I really was in so much pain but felt a lot better once I made it to a bed. He spoke to me until I reach the room in the far left corner away from everyone, The lights were bright and irritating my view. I was immediately put on a bed and being cuff to it with both my left arm and my right arm to the corners of the bed. "This is to make sure you don't run anywhere boy." The cop said. This piece of shit was racist as fuck. He enjoyed this a little too much. I couldn't move nor was I going to go anywhere. It took almost an hour for the nurse to finally come in. I was fucked up!

"Hi my name is Mandy." Mandy spooke. She was pretty as hell for a chubby girl. Her eyes were green and her hair was blonde. She had to weigh around 160-170 pounds she wasn't very short but was far from tall. "Can you tell me where it hurts sir?" She asked not knowing what to call me. "Manuel." I said "He's not much of a talker." The redneck hillbilly decided to chime in his two cents.

"My left side of my rib cage and my head hurts really badly." I said telling her everything that hurt the most. "Oh shit now he wants to talk." The cop said. "Fucking prick!" He didn't like that at all he sucked his teeth like a bitch that he is. He mumbled loudly.

"Sir, can I ask you to step outside please." Mandy asked very politely. He didn't like that at all, he sucked his teeth again. "I'm sorry." Mandy said feeling around my stomach and looked under my shirt to see if I had any bodily injuries. "For what ma?" I asked. "For people like him who can't see past themselves." Mandy was sweet. I noticed she had two beauty marks on her left side of her face. One next to her left nostril and the other above her eye socket. "It's okay you don't have to apologize.... But it does hurt a lot." I cut off my own statement. She was pressing down on my side. "You might have a couple broken ribs." she said. "Great" I replied. "Are you in a lot of trouble?" Mandy asked. Checking my heart rate with a stethoscope. I didn't know how to answer the question. So I changed the subject. "How many bad guys do you see coming here on a regular?" I asked her. Her hands were very soft. She wore rings on three of her fingers but none were on her ring finger. "Well... Let me see yesterday there was three guys and the day before that was about four, so I can say pretty much a lot." She smiled showing me her perfectly white teeth.

I smiled back. "You are pretty beat up Mr. Manuel. I hope the other guy is just as bad." She whispered. I didn't say anything "What's your last name?" She asked "Ricardo" I answered. I wonder why she cared but at the moment I enjoyed our conversation despite the circumstances. "How old are you Mandy?" I asked. "I'm 26." Why you want to know?" She asked shaking her head being a smartass. She checked my eyes. "You have a couple pop blood vessels in your eye. They will heal up as time goes by, but try not to rub them." She said. "I don't know maybe when all of this is all over and done with we could hang out one day." I tried to push my luck. She smiled. "That would be nice." Mandy replied. "The doctor will be in shortly, try and relax and I'll come see you before they take you away Manuel." She touched my arm trying and ease my anxiety. I'm sure she noticed I was a wreck. She walked away she was thick from behind, I mean thick. I dozed off for what seemed like forever but it wasn't. The male doctor woke me up he was speaking to me.

"Were going to run some x-rays on you to make sure you are okay to go. What is your pain level Mr. Ricardo?" 10 I answered. I'll have one on my nurses bring you some pain meds to try and help ease the pain." The doctor informed me "thanks..." I said. He disappeared just as quickly as he came in. Two men walked in wearing what appeared to be some expensive suits, there badges displayed on there waistline shining brightly. I prepareed myself mentally this was going to be interesting.

"Well well if it isn't Manuel Ricardo from East Camden." The taller one said as if he knew me from the hood. "My name is Robert Definchi and this is my partner Detective Hasnoff. They both were tall but he looked a bit more passive than his buddy Definchi. I could be completely wrong. He had dark hair and wore a scar on his chin. I could only imagine how he earned that beauty mark. "Alright look Manuel, you happen to be at the scene where a body was found lying dead on the ground. Lifeless. Is there anything you would like to tell me before I let you know what's going to happen with you?" Definchi explained asking at the same time. Mind you these two pricks are never on your side no matter how lovely they paint the picture. They didn't care about you. All they wanted to do was secure their case. Most likely it has everything to do with you, so shut the fuck up and let them try and put everything together themselves. You can use what they know to your advantage. If you just shut up and listen to what they say you could protect yourself and build your own defense. I got comfy in my bed we at least trying wincing in pain with every movement I made.

"Manuel you look like the victim here and I'm sure you are and maybe we can help you with this, but you have to tell us what exactly went wrong out there tonight." Definchi said in his most sincere tone. He definitely could be great actor. I tell you with the show they'd put on right now it was hilarious. At the moment I gathered that they want me to think that I'm the victim in which I really was but in their eyes there using that to get me to talk since I am the victim but once I say what I say is all going to be turned around and used against me as they tend to do. They also want me to tell them exactly what happened so that they are unsure as to what really took place. No one has said anything as far as Streets or Star. Kay is dead obviously so he cant say shit and Linda must have gotten away. I looked at them as if I didn't understand what they were saying.

"So why did this man attack you?" Detective Hasnoff asked. He stared at me deeply in my eyes looking for clues and motives. Was there anybody else with you when it happened?" Hasnoff asked. Another question. So Linda was in the clear from what I'm getting from all this, and Streets and Star weren't saying shit either. Where were they going was all of this. "If you don't say anything you going to be going away for a very long time if not for the rest of your life Mr. Ricardo." Hasnoff seem to be the more laid back one but still they weren't to be trusted ever. "So this belongs to you?" In the clear bag was my butterfly knife with blood all over. This caused me to swallow hard but I didn't show it. When we run this at our lab you know this is going to put you in jail for ever?".... Definchi stated. "Your fingerprints will get process once you begin to feel better than you will be screwed." I tried to wipe it out before they got there but I wasn't hundred percent sure if I did a good job. My nerves were all over the place so it was possible that I could have missed a partial print or two. The engravings I put on them caused me to feel even more like an idiot because I should have known better. So if they didn't have any prints on it they would pin it all me because the names on it. So that might backfire on me know matter how or which way I look at it. I stared at them in deep thought. I couldn't trust these two nor any other person in a uniform. "Can you call me a lawyer please, if you don't mind?" I said putting an end to their bull shit. I was in pain and dealing with this shit could wait.

"He wants his lawyer?" Hasnoff stated to his partner fucking around. "Don't worry you'll get your lawyer and he'll probably be a PD and guess what?" I raise my left cut eyebrow. "He's on our side." Definchi said. He was a fucking asshole with his slick back hair. They finally got the message and left. I looked around for a phone. "What are you looking for?" The redneck cop came back into the room. Ain't nothing for you to get a hold on in this room. This room is specially designed for killers like yourself." I hated this man. I know he was doing his job but this piece of shit didn't know shit. He already in his mind swore that I was a killer/murderer without even knowing the facts. I waited for the hospital to release me which took forever. I ended up with three cracked ribs and a fractured cheekbone with a bunch of scrapes and cuts. The important thing was that I was still breathing and very well much still alive. I ended up given Mandy permission to write me if I did end up in jail which looked very much inevitable. I also gave her my house number to be honest I wasn't sure why the hell I did that. She was pudgy but where I was headed I needed all the friends I could get. So fat, skinny or ugly it didn't matter I was high on the oxides Mandy managed to give me before I left. I wasn't complaining anymore after that one the ride to the county jail took longer than I had anticipated.

—

Meanwhile the streets were cold and the bottom of her heels hurt from all the walking. Her brother was in trouble and she couldn't do anything for him. Was all Linda was thinking? Tears were running down her face as the thoughts over powered all of her emotions. She clutched her butterfly knife that still had Kay's lifeless blood all over. With one foot in front of the other until she reached her final destination. Linda was furious and scared. All she knew was that everyone was in jail. She didn't know she killed Kay but she would soon find out. Why couldn't I help when all this had erupted? Why did I stay in the truck and wait till all of this got out of hand that bad? Linda kept beating her mind up as if she was the one to blame for all that took place. She wasn't at fault. She did what she could do and many would say that she took it overboard. Knowing that the two males who were involved, there intentions weren't just to beat her brother down and let him go. They had plans that were to personal and a life had to be taken. These guys were all fucked up with their actions and were ego driven to the max.

“I will kill them if anything else happens to my brother! I swear to God there brothers, sisters, father and mother, I will kill them all!” Linda spoke out loud with so much fury. She wasn’t focus on anything else but what was ahead. She didn’t even notice the Lincoln pass right by her which was a good thing because Streets didn’t notice her either. Glad they both went unnoticed because all of that could have been another casualty waiting to happen.

—

Back at the spot Streets was still bleeding profusely “aggghhh!” IT HURTS STAR WHAT THE FUCK!” Streets was bitching mad as hell. “You gotta go to the hospital streets!” Star barked at him. “FUCK GOING TO THE HOSPITAL SHUT THE FUCK UP, GET SOME NEEDELE AND THREAD AND SEW THIS SHIT THE FUCK UP. I’LL DIE BEFORE I GO TO THE HOSPITAL!” Street was scared of getting caught up at the hospital which was likely. It was a good way of staying clean and clear off the radar though. Star did as she was told, her eyes were swollen too. Linda put a good beating on her. She stitched Streets up while streets was bitching and complaining. “It hurts right?” Should of taking your ass to the ER.” Star was being a bitch right now. “SMACK!” Streets let his left hand lose and cracked her with a 5 finger on the side of her face. “I told you to stitch me up and shut the fuck up!” Star was all shaken the fuck up. “That’s the problem with your bitches you can keep your legs close and don’t know when to listen to a nigga.” Star was shaken up now. “What now? You don’t have shit to say.” I had to smack you so you could do what I asked you to do from the very beginning. That some backward shit Star.” Streets was drinking a fifth the Henny while Star continued to patched him up good. The blood has settled but now the alcohol was taking a toll on him.

“Come here.” He pulled Star close and unzipped his pants. She already knew what he wanted and she did what he wanted. she wanted to or because she feared him something serious. She sucked on his manhood hard as hell and he didn’t let up until he drowned her with all his cum all down her throat. His cum oozed out of Star’s nostrils and mouth. As Streets came he pushed her head so far down on his shaft that his cum had nowhere to go. He came in ecstasy as she was left to clean up the mess of all his bodily fluids blood from all herself. Streets was a savage and a woman beater. He was heavy into selling crack cocaine and had his crew in the Northgate Apartments had shit on smash.

He must be all fucked up by all the shit his BMs told me. Then again woman tended to lie on a nigga they couldn't stand anymore. They would go to the extreme, like he's a deadbeat,a snitch or he got a small dig etc. etc. I even heard of a woman going as far lying on there baby dads that he had AIDS. That was some crazy shit. If that was the case bitch you have aids too don't you think? Women would say anything to ruin a guy's reputation and vice versa. They will say anything to get you fucked up and killed all in one shot. You break you girl's heart boy, you better watch out because she isn't just going to leave it at that trust and believe.

"Ayo babe you saw how we took ourselves out of that mess?" Streets was glorifying on how they managed to get away from the scene. While I am in cuffs and Kay is laid up in the freezer somewhere. They were drinking and celebrating because they had managed to get away. "Hell yeah! I thought we was fuck for real." Star admitted. They killed my man's and he is going to pay for this shit one way or another." Streets was mad he was sobbing. "Who was that nigga that killed Kay?" Streets asked. "That wasn't a nigga. Star corrected. Streets looked at her in disbelief. "So you mean to tell me you let a bitch roll up on you and on Kay, killing him and whopping your ass at the same time?!" Streets barked at Star. She had to choose her words wisely. I didn't see her till it was too late Streets, don't even put this on me." Star spat leaving the room. Streets fell back on his Lay-z-boy and let his mind recount what just happened. He couldn't fathom the thought that a female killed his mans

"Who was this bitch?" He asked himself. "Probably some chick he fucking "Star said coming back into the room. "We got a lot of homework to do mija and I'm not gona rest till we find out who was this bitch." Streets said before passing out.

—

Linda rushed up the steps at her house and banged and rang the doorbell repeatedly. Forgetting she had her own keys to get inside. She rushed in and sprinted up the flight of stairs screaming "Mom! Mom!" It was too late because mom was already at the top of the stairs staring at her daughter in complete shock at the way she was acting rushing up the stairs. The knot in her stomach traveled all the way up to her throat, to only be cleared out by a burst of cries. "Manuel where is he?" Mom choked up. "He's in trouble mom, he's in trouble and it's all my fault Mom! I'm sorry please help me, help him more I can't do it alone! He's all I have mom?!" Linda let out her cries. Her emotions got the best of her, her strengths and her courage was useless in her mom's arms. "I knew something was wrong, I knew it! Why didn't he just come straight home when I spoke to him!" Mom was crying uncontrollably now. This was horrible both of the woman of my life were feeling as if I had abandoned them and tore them apart. I was helpless, they were helpless in the moment. There wasn't anything I could do for either of them. "Linda what happened?" Mom asked. Her breathing began to slow down and she clutched her chest. "Linda. I... Can't....bre.a.th..." They both rushed to her room and hooked mom up to the breathing machine immediatly. "Mom are you okay?" "Don't you leave me right now too?" Linda warned mom. "Calm down mom Ima tell you everything that happened. Mom grabbed Linda's hand and noticed the dried up blood on them. "Does that hurt?" Mom asked. I'm not sure mom but listen we was on our way out of the mark, when we got attacked by these two guys and a girl. I was in the car watching to see if Manny was going to handle it."

"Calm down baby please." Mom said to Linda coming her down a bit she was talking to fast. "Deep breath." Mom said. "The man pulled out a gun on Manny and Manny had his hands up as if he didn't want any trouble. Then the other man and girl began to beat him mom. They were beating him very bad mom. I was watching as they tried to beat him to death. My eyes couldn't believe what they were seeing my superhero. I just watched as he was getting his body and face beat in by all of them." Linda began to cry again as she recounted the events and how she just sat there doing nothing. "I couldn't watch it anymore. I pulled out my butterfly knife that Manny and I had just gotten engraved in the mark. Took a deep breath and snuck up to the man that had the gun. I rammed my knife deep into his neck. I stabbed him where I thought would do the most damage right in the side of his neck mom." Linda pulled out the knife and re-enacted what she did to Kay. Mom's eyes were big as hell. She saw the weapon that she thought would never be used. She was wrong it was a dark burgundy with the dried up blood all over it you could barly see the pink now. She followed it with her eyes as Linda showed her how she used it.

"The guy fell on the floor, he dropped the gun and then the girl tried to attack me too. I wanted to stab her to but I rather fight her. In one quick motion I put it away and began to box her face in until Manny yelled at me to run. "Run Linda go!" I didn't want to but I knew I had to listen to him because I always do mom." Linda had her head down in a shame for leaving her brother alone to defend himself. "Give me the knife." Mom said reaching for it but Linda's grip on it was tight. She didn't want to let it go. Linda please give me the knife. Mom asked again. They're going to be looking for this we have to get rid of it baby, I'm sorry but we have to." Mom was a wise woman who knew a lot about something. She was right if they did come in search the house and let just say perhaps find it on Linda's possession and match it up to the one that was used on Kay. She was going down Linda was hesitant but knew and saw the logic behind mom's actions. She hugged her daughter and tried to comfort her the best that she could. "I'm scared mom I don't know was going to happen to Manny." Linda spoke into mom's shoulder sobbing uncontrollably. "Don't worry baby we will wait for his call, in the meantime go wash up and put all your close in a bag before you jump in the shower.Come on I'll go with you."

Linda was a murderer and mom knew it so now she had to protect her baby girl. Mom's baby was doing what she never failed to do, which was protecting her brother. After all the cries and sobs they eventually fell asleep in each other's arms. This was going to be a challenge for Linda and mom. No one could tell how any of this was going to pan out. Many have lost loved ones and some could care less. The ones that know what it feels like to have a family member stripped away from you. It feels as though a chunk of your heart has been stolen away right from your chest.

Back in central bookings in the Pennsauken Township Rock laid on a slab of concrete. The holding cell was dingy and the air was stale. The floor looked as if it was pissed on by many. A silver toilet was mounted directly on the sink and barely had any water flowing from it. The water was lukewarm and only a tiny bit squirted out just barely hitting your lips. I tried my hardest not to let my lips touch the water fountain if that's what you wanted to call it. The walls were white but look beige as if they hadn't been cleaned in decades. The roaches ran across right under the gate that was supposed to be a door. My stomach turned at the smell and sight of all of this. I had to take a shit but I had no toilet tissue. Where the fuck was I?

"How the fuck do these mother fucker's want me to use the bathroom with my hands cuffed and chained right in front of my bellybutton?" Rock was talking to himself. "These fucking shackles where needed for what? Where the hell was out going to run to?" He noticed a camera in the corner of the room he looked up at it. "I gotta take a shit!" he yelled at the camera hoping someone would take notice of his pleas. To no avail no one seem to care. Rock was going through the motions of being stripped away from his freedom.

To all of those who never had this privilege in your life make sure you keep doing what you doing and keep living the way you. This is a privilege that you nor your worst enemy would want to experience and wait, I use the term privilege very loosely. Now for the ones who have had this opportunity you and I both know the emotions that I was feeling. I satt in this 6 x 8 room with nothing but my thoughts and horrible odors. I wasn't able to move my body the way it is accustomed to. Plus these fucking chains aint helping shit.

"Linda I hope you made it home, I'm so sorry to put you through this. Please forgive me I never meant to hurt you, all I ever wanted was for you to be happy and safe." Rock was talking to Linda but the sad part was no one was listening but the walls. "Take care of mom for me if you can please." This was the first time away from his mom and Linda. They were his only intermediate family. He was mentally breaking himself down. The sound of the keys brought him so much inspiration that the cop was going to set him free....

"You hungry." The white sheriff asked. "Yes, Rock answered desperately. He tossed him a bag. that landed right on the sweaty dirty floor. "I gotta use the bathroom." Rock said. "There's the can use it." Sheriff said in a rude manner. "I need tissue and I have to take a shit." Rock said truthfully. "Give me a minute." The sheriff said with a smirk. He was an ex Marine or Army brat, his crew-cut gave me that impression. I reached for the bag and opened it up. I saw a milk carton and pulled it out with my hands a half inch apart from one another. It was awkward and extremely uncomfortable. I had food and that was a good thing. The sandwich was bologna and cheese that gave off this foul odor. What made this even better was the milk. It was soil. I spit that shit right the fuck up. This couldn't be how I had to be treated for defended myself.

"Ayo! What the fuck...." Rock was passed. "Ayo! I know I'm in trouble but what the fuck is this shit you feeding me!" Rocks cries and demands fell on deaf ears. No one cared in everyone's eyes in a facility like this. You was an ordinary criminal who reaps what he sows with no, ifs, ands or butts. The sound of the keys came towards his so again. The sheriff was staring at him. "What the fuck you hollering about?" Has smirk was still plastered on his face? "You gave me spoiled milk man." Rock said. There's your tissue and who cares if your milk is bad. This isn't the Holiday Inn boy." The sheriff tossed him his tissue and walked away. "How am I supposed to wipe my ass like this?" Rock barked. "Figure it out smartass." The sheriff never came back. After beating himself up for what seemed like forever he ended up taking a shit and not being able to wipe his ass . Rock was fucked up. He cried and he actually prayed but he knew it was pointless. It amazed my how quick one would look for god when their hands were tied. The journey was coming to one end. The thought about death even crossed his mind. Maybe this wasn't what he really wanted to do but at the moment he wished he was dead in peace with his biological mother. He laid on the slab of concrete that was a foot above the ground. The blowing of the vent cause him to shiver. He couldn't get a good few minutes of sleep with all that was happening. The chains were overpowering his comfort. When he laid on the side it dug right into his side. His back his neck and his lower back was all in so much pain. His hands and toes were numb. The meds that Mandy had given him were wearing off quickly. He didn't know the time and it was very quiet. The only sounds being heard was the buzzing of the flies and the light, high up above him. What seemed to be a couple of hours turn to be into a whole night, that eventually turned into morning?

"Mr. Ricardo the judge will see you shortly." A different white sheriff informed him. "Excuse me" The man turned to look at Manuel "what?" "Can you tell me the time?" Manuel's eyes were burning in his body felt so weak. "Is 6 AM." Just like that the sheriff walked away. "Is 6 AM I've been in here all night and I can't even see no sunlight or hear anything you can't be serious." The more Manuel spoke to himself the more serious he knew the situation was. His mind raced 1,000 miles an hour without stopping for a pit stop. He pissed on his shit, that didn't want to flush. The smell got alot worst. What was he going to do? Was there a way out of this? Where was mom and Linda?

Were they going to come and get him out of this hellhole? Or were they not? All these questions bombarded Manuel. Thoughts and were soon haunting his every thought. The keys came back.

"Let's go Mr. Ricardo the judge is ready for you." The sheriff related. Manuel thoughts were all positive ones. He was going home because he didn't do anything as far as he knows. With no strength to even walk. The sheriff pulled him towards a small room all the way to the back. Where he came across a TV screen with a chair. The camera was visible. Rock noticed the old man wearing a black robe, his white hair was clearly visible. "Don't say anything unless he ask." The sheriff said. "Do you hear me?" Rock was already frightened and to be honest was already fully submissive to the tee. "Yes sir." Rock had already been broken in. He may of not known it at the moment but truth be told this was a psychological war that wasn't an easy one. If you were unaware of the ropes. It was easy to be broken down and molded into a submissive individual in a few hours. Rock was a statistic. He was fresh and new to all of this. "Manuel Ricardo." The judge spoke. "Yes sir" Rock answered as if he was in the Army for years. You live on 28th and Federal in Camden New Jersey?" The judge asked. "Yes sir" Rock answered again. "Are you aware why you are under arrest?" The all-white judge asked "No sir!" Rock said. The judge looked up. "You are being charged with first-degree murder and possession with an instrument used in a crime." The judge stated coldly. "Do you understand this now?" "I didn't kill anyone." Rock barked back. "Well Mr. Ricardo this is why you have the right to take all this to trial but in the meantime you will have to sit and wait." The judge said. Rock was in complete shock this shit was too real. He couldn't believe it. I will set your bail at $ million sign the papers in front of you." There weren't any papers in front of him until the judge said those words. A bunch of papers appear right in front of his person. He signed and dated all of them just as he was coerced. His next hearing will be in three months. The sheriff will let you know when you are done here. Just like that the TV was off.

"These copies are for you." The sheriff informed Rock. My mind was stuck I didn't know what to think nor did I want to think. I couldn't do anything I had to wait and see what the future held for me. You will be shipped up to the jail shortly, shortly never came what was I going to do just sitting here in the holding tank?

Chapter 10
"Feed me"

Linda answered the phone that was glued to her hand, she slept with it since the incident. Her eyes still burned due to all the crying she's been doing for the past few nights. She looked over to mom and she was still sound asleep.

"You have a collect call from" the operator voiced. "Manny." You will be charged for this call, to accept the call please press 1, to block press...." Before the operator's voice could go on Linda didn't give it a chance she press one immediately. Very excitedly she woke up mom. "It's Manny!" She said. "Manny where are you?" Linda asked with so much concern and worry. Without given him a chance to speak. "I'm in the holding station waiting to be transported to the county jail. Rock was depressed you could hear it in his voice he was giving up all hope. "What's going to happen?" Linda asked. "Well first and foremost how are you?" Rock asked. "I'm okay, I really am okay. I want to see you can I come see you?" Linda was breaking up again inside. "Listen I need you to be strong, you can't come see me yet. I'll call you and let you know when you and mom can come see me." Linda cut him off. "What are they charging you with?" "First-degree murder." Linda tossed the phone to mom and began to cry uncontrollably. "Linda what's wrong?" Mom said picking up the receiver off her bed. "Manuel what is happening? Why is your sister over here losing it?" Rock had a knot in his throat that wouldn't move down or up, it was just there stuck there. "You got five minutes." The sheriff barked. Mom heard it and began to do what she knew. "What's your bail Manuel?" Mom waited for the answer Rock was still trying to regain his composure. "$1 million." Rock said in a monotone voice. "Charges?" Mom asked. "First-degree murder and possession of a deadly weapon." Rock read off the paperwork in his hand. "Are you at the county jail yet?" Mom had went through all this with one of her past affairs. "No not yet." Rock replied to mom. He was losing all hope fast. "Tell Linda I'll be fine and to forget all that happened." Rock tried to speak subliminally mom caught on quickly. It was early and this wasn't the wake up no one or no family ever wanted to hear. "Manuel stay focused no matter the outcome of all this and be sure to call me as soon as they move you to the county jail. You are not alone we are here for you." Mom began to whimper ever so slightly but she knew she had to be strong, not for herself but for Linda and Manuel. "Mom... I love you so much please take care of Linda, you two are all I have." Just like that the phone was shut off. Linda left to her room and mom just sat on her bed clutching the receiver in her hand. In a very deep thought. She didn't have nowhere near the money to bail out her son, nor did she know any good lawyers that would be affordable. She was going to do all that she could to keep her word on her end. She made her way over to Linda's room and the sounds of her sobbing could still be heard in the hallway.

"knock,knock"mom walked in. She took a deep breath "It's all my fault I killed that man not Manny, it's not fair for him to pay for what I did mom!" Linda was going hysterical but in a sense she was right, shouldn't no one have to pay for another's actions but then again what if the person involved was your baby sister or even your mother? Would you do it for you loved one? Your whole life you been protecting them. Could you honestly say that you would take the fall for them so they wouldn't suffer? Or would you do what many did and blow the whistle on your own family. So you can go scot-free? It's a different decision when it isn't just a thought. When a situation that's deep presents itself, is when you find out who you are without second guessing the matter. If you are that person you always claimed to be this is when one would be put to the test. "Linda come here." Mom wrapped her arms around her beautiful child. "I need you to calm down for a few minutes so we can put together a plan and help Manny. Sitting here, beating ourselves up isn't going to help anyone. I know it hurts and believe me I want him home just as bad as you do. At the moment these are the cards that been dealt." Mom tried to sound strong. "These aren't the cards Manny was dealt. This is the hand that I was dealt and I should take responsibility for my actions right? That is what you always taught. Why would this be any different?" Linda asked being absolutely right. "I know baby." Mom rubbed her head. "Your brother told me to tell you to stay focused and finish your schooling, and for you to never ever talk about what happened to anyone." Mom informed Linda. "This is serious what took place that night can't be repeated to anyone to Linda." Mom was drilling it in her head. "If you do it, it won't just be Manuel in jail. You'll both be far away from me." Mom spoke letting it all sink in. Mom turned on the TV in Linda's room.

She always watch the news whenever it would come on. To her surprise Manuel's truck popped up again at the mart. KYW News Radio was all over the scene. They went on, on how the police had discovered a lifeless body and had the suspect in custody. Linda and mom's eyes were focused on the images that were shown on the TV screen. "The investigation continues." The news reporter stated. This was all that they needed to seen, well at least all that mom needed to see to put all her doubts to rest.

"What did Manny tell you mom?" Linda asked still laying on her mom's shoulder sobbing. "He said that he loved us very much and to not worry too much because he is okay. Also, that he would let us know when to come up to visit him at the county." Mom didn't really get into all the horrible details but as time would pass. Linda would see for herself that this was real, and that it could have been easily be her if she really wanted to turn herself in. "Do you think he'll be in jail for a long time?" Linda asked not knowing the severity of the crime that she committed out of pure rage protecting her brother. "I don't know baby we have to pray and hope all goes well. If you would of never did what you did your brother could very well be dead right now Linda. Know that if it wouldn't have been for your bravery you nor your brother would be here today." Mom did her best lightining the weight load on Linda's shoulders. "They were going to kill him." Linda said. "I'm sure they were but they didn't thanks to you." Mom kiss Linda on the forehead. "I have to make some phone calls." If you need me I'll be in my room and remember what I said. "No one is to know anything." Mom couldn't stress this enough. Linda laid in her sorrows. The whole day not eating or doing anything, this was taking a major toll on her. She dismissed all of Joel's phone calls even though he had nothing to do with anything. Mom didn't force her to do anything, in due time she would get the strength to get back on course with her life. Mentally she had to find herself again. If not for herself but for her brother sake. He always just asked of her to stay strong and focused and her studies.

Jacqueline notice Manuel's photo in the news and immediately called her baby dads. She wanted to know what the hell happened to him. She remember her baby dads telling her he had to go to Pennsauken Mart and after seeing Rocks car on the news her stomach began to turn up side down.

"What's up girl?" Street answered in his cocky arrogant tone sounding drunk. Star was laying right beside him. "Don't was sup me nigga!" So what happened the other night?" Jacqueline spat with a nasty attitude. "What you talking about?" Street asked nonchalantly. "Don't play stupid with me." She spat again. "What's wrong baby your boyfriend didn't call you this morning?" Street was jabbing her right in her face with his choice of words. "He might not ever call you again baby. He killed Kay the other night." Jacqueline's hands trembled as she heard the words come out of her baby dad's mouth. "You are such an asshole, what you think just because you got him locked up I'm going to go back with your cornball ass!? I'm not! Your useless and pathetic Streets! That's why you won't ever get this pussy again, so stay with your infected hoes! You will never touch me again. His dick game was way better than yours will ever be. You know what boo? Ima ride with him to the wheels fall off something you always wished for." Click! Jacqueline let loose on him. She loved Rock. Not for his dick game but because he treated her as if she was number one. He made sure she had her head on right. He showed her how to comb through things with a fine tooth comb. She fell in love with him by mistake and it felt great. She felt it in her heart that she would truly ride with him at the moment. Time will tell because loyalty is a something that you couldn't buy or rent at the nearest store. It was earned and shown through the ups and downs. Streets was infuriated Jacqueline's choice of words. They hit him stupid hard.

—

After being stripped and fingerprinted they finally decided to throw Rock in the wagon. You would be so surprised on how bad one would want to be transported to the county jail after all those hours restrained. It was your ordinary jail, known for the gangs, violence and rapes. It housed nothing but savages. It was a maximum security jail that was stricter than most, but just like all county jails there was drugs and your fair share of guards who were just as dirty as the prisoners they housed. Once again stripped and thrown in a holding tank with a few others until they were ready to be moved to quarantine. That wouldn't done until the nurse had drawn your blood and did a full body physical to ensure that you were all good. All this took time and moving quickly wasn't a must right now in this place. In Rock's case he wasn't good at all but guess what he had to deal with his medical condition. He had a few fractured ribs and trauma to the head. You would normally think that they would actually make sure you were taking care of thoroughly, but nope not in these walls. If you were in a lot of pain "be sure to send a request to see that Dr." that's what would be what you had to do. Enduring all of your pain was what one would go through raw and uncut. The shower was cold as fuck and beyond filthy. Mildew was all over the walls and floor, but he was very much excited to finally put on his uniform. It fit perfectly sad to say. His Skippy's were snug on his feet as if they were made espeacially for him. Heading back to the holding cell without the cuffs. He felt but wasn't free not even a bit. His wrists and ankles were sore from the jewelry they had on him for the past two days. If this wasn't cruel and unusual for a punishment than I don't know what was. Stripped from all his rights and freedom was all Rock could think of, Many of us are so uneducated that we tend to forget yes, we may have committed a crime. This didn't mean we no longer had our rights. If anything our rights became a bit more defined, only if one would go about handling your rights in the right manner. We could still indeed enforce our rights if you would follow the chain of comand and trust and believe me it works. Remember this! All prisoners have rights as well, do not allow any one to make you think otherwise. After about an hour or two Rock was finally thrown into quarantine. He was escorted by two correctional officers wearing black shirts with their chest all puffed out. Rock stomach was flip-flopping everything was handled so slowly but at the moment things were progressing up so rapidly. When would all this be over.

"You will be going to quarantine for a few days tops, once medical and a psych clears you. You will go straight to population once all that is done." The guard stated. "Mind your business too" The Hispanic CO informed Rock. The walk came to an end at the main gate deep inside. "clank clank!" The gate was open. "Proceed to the next gate until you reached a bubble." The other guard who happened to be black instructed. You could hear all of the noise and banging echoing off the block towards the hallways. This was complete chaos Manny thought to himself. He was nervous and yes he was scared. "I can't believe this shit." he said to himself.

"Fresh meat!" Yelled the prisoner. "I want his ass up in my cell CO." Yelled another. "ADR!" yelled another. It was complete pandemonium. ". "You look lost bitch." This wasn't going to stop. Rock kept his head up high showing no fear as he always did. He managed to contain himself in every situation that presented himself. In the inside he wasn't so contained. Making his way to the bubble the guard smirked and coldly stared at him making him feel worthless. This was all a joke to these mother fuckers. "First time?" The prick asked as if he cared. Rock already broken in answer every question darted his way. "Oh nice we have a newbie." He joked to his fellow companion inside of the bubble. Rock looked around. "Who are you looking for?" The prick asked. Laughing uncontrollably. This wasn't helping the situation not one bit

"Orientation will be called soon and your door will be popped? Listen for it and don't asked me anything and I won't bother you for shit. You have a problem grieve it or handle it. It says here you are here for first-degree murder so you'll fit right in. Any questions? Good" He answered himself not giving me the chance to say anything. Your cell is b-16 top bunk now get out of my face." The beer belly prick barked. The sound of a door popped but there were so many. He had to focus in and really look at the numbers until he spotted the number the guard had instructed. Rock was so lost that he felt dumb. The banging on the glass by the C.O broke his concentration. He pointed to the opposite side where he was looking and walked over to the cell b-16 top bunk he told him self. The kickbox with my clothing and my socks and underwear were weighing my arms down. The door swung open, the prisoner inside sidestepped to allow me in without uttering a word to me. He looked charcoal black. He wore a scar on his face right on his jawline. I put my box on my bed and just felt the mood. I was tense who could blame me. I had my back to the wall and just waited till the cell door slam shut. This was a very awkward moment for me. I couldn't say the same about my cell mate. Who knew how long he's been in here and how many different faces have passed through this cell.

"Where you from?" His voice was deep as fuck. It wasn't loud but low deep, you could feel the vibrations of his voice bouncing off the walls as he spoke. "East." Was all I said until the next question came? "What you in here for?" He asked. I handed him my papers because I didn't feel comfortable telling anyone and everyone I was here for fucking body. He took it gave me a side ways look as if I was hiding something. He examined the paperwork. "Damn! Was all he said? "Where you from?" I asked him. "I'm from Fairview Apartments by the square." He replied. "What you here for?" I asked him. "Drugs and sales." He rummaged through his box in search of his paperwork. I noticed how his whole perception of me changed immediately once he ran my paperwork. I'm not saying he should but I'm assuming that murder one carry some weight to it. "Here they go." He said. He had the same paperwork as mine, only his was more wrinkled from being buried down in his box. I noticed his name was "Malik Johnson." I read the papers until I saw his case number and his charges. Possession and intent to delivery. I counted off five of them. I handed him the paperwork and I introduced myself. "They call me Rock I'm not sure what's going to happen but I'm here. This is my first time in this place. I aint got time for the bullshit. You leave me alone and I'll leave you alone plain and simple." Rock was always straight through and through. "I'm Malik." I am not new, I can show you the ropes a bit. Niggas here look for anything to get into so if you show weakness then you're gona be a great target. Are you in any gangs?" Malik asked "Nah" I answered. Well that's good because that's a big issue here. "You look mixed." Malik questioned. "I'm Puerto Rican 100 percent." Rock answered. There is a bunch of them all over this spot so you might fit right in." Malik said. "The phone is a hassle to get on. They are only four of them on the block and over 200 niggas that want to get on." Malik went on putting Rock on game with how things were ran and what was expected. "Commissary is every week with a $50 limit. Your people gotta send you some money or you just get a job in the kitchen or something. We go out for an hour on the block for day room of yard when they feel like it. This is where you can do whatever you want to do. TV, push-ups, play cards or dominoes etc. etc. Only at this time are u allowed to do any of this. If you look out the window you can see outside. You can talk to your people from all the way up here using hand signs." Rock interrupted sounding confused. " wait, with what?" "Hand signs I'll show you them don't worry about it." Leak was given me my prisoner's orientation from the inside. This was what really mattered this was the real orientation. Not the bullshit one we was about to get. We eat our meals early as shit 6'oclock, 11 o'clock and 5 o'clock that's it. It's the same shit every week so get used to it. If you want McDonald's or pizza you should've stood where you was at, which is home." Malik joked. He had a personality after all. "Showers?" I asked in need of one. A really long and hot one. Once a day either in the afternoon or evening pick it wisely because that's all you get. "This isn't going to be your permanent block anyway. In about a week you'll be getting move. I should be out of here soon myself." Malik informed. I'll see you on the inside. I'm going to a max unit and so are. You can thank that hefty case you holding on too." I kept my cool and just listen to all he had to say. "Visits?" I asked which was really important to me. "Your family can come up once you fill out the proper forms that are in the bottom of your box and hand them in asap. They can come up twice a week three people at a time." Malik had all this down pack. Anyone in their right mind would notice that this wasn't his first time behind these walls. I paid close attention to all that he said, but the most important thing that stood out was.

"Mind your fucking business if it doesn't have to do with you, do not get involved because then all you doing is bringing the heat your way. You don't want or need that shit, unless you like that shit." After hours of talking I registered all the main components of being a celli and how to conduct myself. The last thing I wanted was to not disrespect any person that I was forced to live with. This was the worst, It could end very well at the same time you could set yourself up for an ass whopping. No one would help you get out of this once that gate/door was locked.

"The guards are not here to help you no matter what. If you have to speak to one, make sure you take someone with you. The last thing anyones needs is rumors being surfaced about you ratting or doing favors of any kind for these pigs. Rock they are not your friends and they will throw you in the hole in an instant." Malik said snapping his fingers emphasizing instant. "Are all the cells like this?" I asked him. "What do you mean?" Dingy with all this mildew on the bricks." I asked hoping I didn't offend this mans cell. "No actually the ones on the blocks are better than these, these are like this because so many people come through them. The jail hardly keep up with them." Malik said "My bad for cutting you off." I said. So he could go back to his in-house orientation. "It's all good." "If you are into fags you will be taking care of all day in here. When you get upstate if you make it up there." Malik was making sure I did not miss a beat. "Upstate?" I asked. "Yeah, upstate if you blow trial you will do your time up state where it's more laid-back." Malik informed me. "If you're not into all that gay shit then stay all the way away, dudes will kill for there nigga. I scrunched up my face. "That shit is disgusting" I admited my opinion. "Yeah I know it's disgusting but remember there's a lot of niggas that turn to that life style so just let them be." Many are not going to see the streets again, so man it's literally their best friend." Malik informed me. "I'm good I'll definitely stay away from all that." I assured myself. "If you got beef to handle make sure you handle it ASAP. Don't wait till later or tomorrow you gotta either squash it right then and there or wait to you get call slipping. The guards don't leave the bubble only when they're doing count. Like I said they will let you handle your business, just don't make them do any paperwork." Malik informed me he was basically telling me the wolves can kill each other. "Oh you can fight?" I asked after he ended his statement. "Fight, stab, jump and kill whatever. Rock just do it wisely and don't get too involved with all these no good niggas." Malik said. He knew all this too well. "How many times have you been coming in and out of this place?" I had to ask. "I'm 38 now and my first case was at 16. I'll say almost half of my life." Malik admitted. "This scar on my face was from a nigga who assumed I was rat. Once my paperwork came he was dead wrong." Malik spoke about his past. "That's another thing if you don't have the paperwork on any nigga, don't go spreading rumors because that will get you killed too." "If you don't know leave it at that don't try to stir up the hornets' nest with something that it ain't because everything is documented. Just like your paperwork states all who were involved in your case. You have no Co-d's all you have is a charge and a dead body and that body can't talk. So it's your word all the way, you can use that to your advantage." You'll have to wait for trial and all that long ass process but in the long run you may luck out. I know they took photos of your face in the hospital. The hospital records are going to work in your favor. Self-defense looks promising on your behalf. It might not Rock don't get your hopes up. All this will have to wait until you have your retrial if you blow trial. You have to stick with it. You can't give up no matter what they try to pin on you." Malik was smooth with how he spoke, he was much shorter than I was. The look in his dark cold eyes looked as if he witnessed a lot of tragedies in his time. He wasn't slow but he did have a problem with staying out in society. Authority could be something he stated. I was grateful to have ran into this man, and thankful to have learned so much in the little amount of time. It eventually got late in our conversation began to die down. I decided to take a look outside through the window where I noticed the wave of people out there doing hand signs. I couldn't believe how many people cared and actually showed their support to their love ones behind these walls. The field was at a distance I saw all types of people, beautiful women with their small children learning and teaching them how to do hand signs. The heavy tired breathing from Malik did not go overheard he was out like a light. I switched off the light and just got lost out the window wondering when my opportunity will come to light. I didn't want to stay here for the rest of my life. I had to take heed of what Malik said and that I couldn't give up on myself. I had to fight no matter who or what tried to throw me under the bus. I had to roll from under the bus so that I wouldn't get rolled over and lose my life. My life is precious and I would not just let anyone take it from me. I had to take care of this and get back to my family who needed me back in their lives as soon as possible. My eyes began to burn and a few tears began to form in my eyes. I had no choice but to fall asleep deep in my thoughts.

The sound of the door popped loudly and my name was shouted to the P.a system. It was still dark out and it was very few people left outside. I glanced out the window. I had to be still asleep because I felt like I was dreaming. I stumbled towards the door. It was quiet the block was dim. I didn't know where I had to go. I decided to head towards the bubble. I was in a T-shirt and pants heading out in my sandals, violating rule number one. Never get comfortable in prison. The sound of slight moaning could be heard faintly. I knew I had to be dreaming now. Someone was either taking it or receiving it right now. My stomach cringed. This couldn't be fucking happening. "Mr. Ricardo." A female's voice called out to me before I could get to the bubble. She was dressed in her nurse attire, baby blue scrubs with some white sneakers. Those sneakers appeared to be abuse for some time. She was pretty but was a lot older than I was. I walked over towards her, she had a small red bucket. Her stethoscope was around her neck. The part she puts on your chest was down in between her cleavage. I couldn't help but stare. She followed my eyesn noticing.

"Have a seat please." I did as she instructed. Her eyes were leaning towards a gray but then again. I was still half asleep. She wore braces and I thought it was cute. She tried to hide them whenever she spoke. "How are you feeling?" She asked me. I'm okay I guess." Shaking my leg uncontrollably. She smells so good her hair was dirty blonde and she had it up in a messy bun. I couldn't help but to look and admire her aged beauty. She must've been a hell of a woman in her younger years, even till this day she was still head turning. The moan in the back ground grew a bit louder.

"Oh gosh, sounds like someone is having a good time." She joked. I didn't find it funny. "Hope you're not into that?" She stated, but asking at the same time. "No I'm not into any of that." Let me see your arm." She held my arm with her soft touch. How I wished I was with Felicia or with Jacqueline. Fuck it even Erica I didn't care, I wanted to be with a woman. "You don't look that bad." she tried to make light of how fucked up my face was. "Thank you, you don't look to bad yourself." I replied in a shy manner taking advantage if the convo. It was Russian roulette but I had to test the waters. "Boy I'm an old hag." She said sounding as if she meant every word. She checked my blood pressure. "Do you have a heart problem or condition?" She asked me. "Not that I know of why?" I asked staring deep in her eyes. I lick my lips, she turned her stare. "Your pressure is a little high." She stated. "Is that good or bad?" I asked her. "Well its bad if it doesn't go down but if you don't have any history of heart problems or conditions you should be fine. "Lift your tongue up." She instructed placing a thermometer under my tongue. "Hold that." She said. I couldn't talk, all I could do was stare and admire her and wonder what she wore under them scrubs. She wasn't skinny, she was just right. She has some meat but she didn't have too much meat on her. It was just enough to hold onto and keep me warm at night. The moaning in the back settled finally.

"I'm a take your blood and check you for diseases and infections in your body. Is there anything that you want to get checked out specifically?" The nurse asked. "No but can you check for everything and anything since I'm here. I might as well right?" I asked. "Any concerns?" She asked guiding the needle into my veins. "Well not really but now that you brought it up yes." She smiled trying her best to hide her braces. "You can smile, you have a gorgeous smile." I said. She let her smile show, it was pretty even with the braces. "You have braces because you want your teeth straight. You want show off that perfect smile but now you want to hide it." "I don't understand that?" I said. "I know but it's a habit I developed when I first got these put on two years ago." She admitted. "What's your name?" I asked. "Amanda" She said. Well look Amanda whenever you come and see me if you do ever come back I want you to smile like you are proud to have a gorgeous smile." I worked my cheesy lines on her I had her smiling now from ear to ear. "Doesn't it feel so much better to not hold back your smile?" I asked her. "Yes it does." She drew two small tubes of blood, and broke to ask the ultimate question. "Why are you here? You seem like such a great man." Amanda stated. I took a deep breath. "If you don't want to tell me is okay Manuel." Amanda was nosey as fuck too. "I will tell you but can you keep it between you and me?" I instructed her not really too proud of what I did or should I say what am being accused of. "Of course." she replied to my request. I debated on telling her the truth but I knew better than that. That would only backfire and just make me look like the rest of the guys who claimed that they didn't commit the crimes that there being charged for. "I'm here for murder one." I said with my head down because it wasn't something that I was proud about. I didn't care who asked I wasn't proud to say that I was in this fucking hellhole for a fucking body. "First time?" She asked taken off my armband and putting a band-aid on my arm, where the needled dissected the desired amount of blood from my veins. I nodded my head answering her question. "You didn't do it did you?" Amanda seeked the truth. I smiled. I wondered how and why did she took it upon herself to say that I didn't commit the murder. "We will see ma." I left it at that not wanting to get deeper into this conversation. "I'll be seeing you around, don't worry stay focused on you and your case and things will work out for the best." She told me. I headed back to my cell, I wasn't done though.

"Manuel Ricardo up front." This was getting annoying. This time it was the psych I had to see now. He wasn't on the block like the nurse he was in the back of the block in a small room. I sat down he was an older man who had to be in his late 50s. he was wearing a sports jacket with some jeans, his glasses were pretty thick. I sat down and he began with the questions. "How are you feeling?" The doctor asked. "I'm losing it?" Was all I could say? "Explain?" The doctor asked. "I feel like I'm dreaming all of this and when I sleep I can't sleep. I feel down and depressed." I admitted. "Suicidal?" The doctor asked. "No not that far but my mind will not stop running. How do I shut it off?" "Voices?" He asked. "Yes I lied. "What are they saying?" "I'm coming for you?" I said. "Who's coming?" The doctor asked. "I don't know but they're coming." I kept it going. "I'm going to prescribe you was Seroquel, Ambien, Celexa, Prozac he went on with the drugs. I didn't care I had to get my mind still. "You here for a murder right?" The doctor asked. "Yes." I answered. Do you think the man you killed is haunting you?" The doctor couldn't be serious or was he? Fuck it I thought he was probably right. I counted he had almost four pages of notes about our little meeting. "If you need to see me for anything just put in a request or sick call for the psych doctor okay?" The doctor instructed. "Yes I will thank you." Manuel remember these voices that you hear are the voices of yourself. Don't let them run or dictate your actions. He spoke in all serious ness looking like he was on meds himself. I headed straight back to my cell and hopped right up on my bed. I'm was begining to dose off and my fucking door pops again. You had to be kidding. My name was yelled to the PA system. My face had hell written all over it. I was beyond pissed that this wasn't a dream. The fact that I couldn't even get a dream started was fucking with me to the highest degreee. A tall white man stood a few feet from my door.

"This will just be a second." He said. His shirt was red and had the letters ABC on it. What the fuck this mother fucker wanted? To teach me the alfabet. I thought to myself.

"I'm with the ABC Bail bondsman .I have a few questions for you. Is your name Manuel Ricardo?" "Yes it is" I answered. "You are here for first-degree murder?" He asked. "Yes." I answered. "Your bail is $1 million.... Got damn! That's a lot of cash!" He stated loudly astonished. Well let's see 10% of that is 100,000 if I'm not mistaken. Do you have that kind of money laying around to get up out of here?" This prick couldn't be serious. I just gave him my get the fuck out my face look. I knew he was trying to help but he wasn't because he wanted all the money for himself." I'm just kidding I know you probably don't." He said still waiting for an answer to come out of my mouth. "No I don't!" "How about a house?"... "No." I answered, "A car?" He asked. "A truck." I said but it's long gone." I informed him. "Cops got it?" I said. "Yeah that's definitely gone. So no valuables or assets that you can put up for collateral?" I walked away on this prick. "Sorry just trying to help." He said to my back. I didn't feel like anyone in the city could help me. I was in an ugly situation where anyone who tried could possibly get sucked in my wave of self-destruction. I knew I had to get all my grind and get out of here from the inside out, not from the outside in. I knew what my cards were, no one else except Linda knew. I wasn't going to drag my baby girl into this mess, nope not at all. The last person I had to see was the public pretender. He wasn't even the one that was going to ride with me all the way. He would be the one to pacify me and just make me feel more helpless that I already was feeling sad to say.

Three months to my preliminary and I had no one in my corner. This was going to be a long lonely journey. I had no choice but to prepare myself for. By the time all the extra bull shit was done it was almost chow time. I was hungry and trust me I didn't give a shit if they served shit on a stick I was going to eat that shit. I laughed at my own stupidity and dozed off for a few.

"Ayo! Rock! Rock!" Malik was trying to get me up. I was out like an opponent knocked out by Ali. I jumped up. "Huh?" It's time to eat you gona eat right?" Malik informed me already dressed and ready to stuff his face. I jumped off the bed barely landing. No wonder I never tried out for the Olympics my dismount was horrible. After almost collapsing I went to brush and wash my face. “No playa, we don’t got no time for that. They locking doors already.” Malik tried to tell me. I washed my face Malik had half his body in the cell and the rest out the cell.

“Let’s go Mr. Johnson!” A deep male voice barked. “Slam!” The cell door went. “Ayo! IM STILL HERE!” I barked all groggy and still half asleep. The body that just walked by walked backwards to my cell. “Ayo?” I barked back. “Who the fuck is ayo?” The C.O barked. I don’t know your name and is my first time up in here and I’m starving.” I tried to cop out. My stomach turned instead of trying to get pretty, you should’ve got up and went. Don’t wait till it’s time to go eat to do all that extra shit!” He was rude and a real asshole. “I didn’t know man.” I tried to explain. “You see these stripes?” he pointed to the side of his arm. “These are stripes so I’m not your man nor a C.O I’m a sergeant so you direct me as Sgt. or Mr. Oyster.” This man had a real power trip that could be smelled from 1,000 feet away. “You hungry?” He asked “Starving.” I replied. “Good next time you’ll be ready.” He walked away from the cell. “Are you fucking serious!” I barked. “So you not gona feed me?” I barked at the white piece of shit!”

By now the guys were already coming back to the block from the chow hall. I was still carrying on at my gate to the Sgt. I noticed Malik coming and he noticed me from all the noise I was making calling the Sgt. All types of bitches and pricks. “Rock!?” Malik looked at me to the gate. “He burnt you right?” I was furious. “Yeah that pussy as cracker burnt me.” I spat taken it out on Malik by accident. He sense my fury. He walked away. All the cells were open but mine. The sound of keys were jingling in the distance. I peeked and it was the Sgt. with a colleague. I wasn’t done with this situation.

“You are a piece of shit Serge. That was some bull shit!” I Barked. I was already in hell so why not let the demons out. Malik was by the side of the cell not saying a word. They hadn’t let him in yet. I knew I was dead wrong but I had to show these pigs I was to be respected. I’m was not a disrespectful man. “Listen Mr. Ricardo!” Serge Barked. Either shut the fuck up or Ima beat your ass! You got burnt! Own that shit, next time you’ll be on prepared when it’s time to go to chow! This isn’t the Marriott nor the fucking five-star hotel. When we say eat you eat point blank. If you got a problem with that, bail the fuck out!" Serge was bright red. The whole blocks attention was on cell b-16.

"Fuck you pussy come in and beat my ass!" I knew he was pump faking and I was going to pull his card. "Cuffed him." He ordered his colleague cuffed Malik. Now I was really pist. "This shit ain't got shit to do with him, why the fuck you cuffing him for pussy?!" I was beyond pissed my skippies were on. He handed his colleague his belt, cuffs and walkie-talkie. "Look out." He opened the cell door and walked in. My back was against the wall. He put up his hands. "Let's go punk you got all that mouth." I looked over at Malik and he gave me the nod of approval. This couldn't be happening. The Sgt. swung and hit me dead on my cheek. I stumble back in the wall. The bed held me up.

"All that mouth your a little bitch!" The block was going insane with the. "Whip his ass yo!" And the "Get ems!" and the banging on the doors. I regain my consciousness quickly because this white mother fucka hit me hard. He swung again but I dip this one. He was slow because he was too wide. So I knew I had to be up on him with speed. He swung twice, this time I dipped the first but the second one caught me right on the side I couldn't understand why my fighting wasn't in sync since Streets put it on me. I shook off the thoughts and just went with the flow to quick jabs took the Sgt. by total complete surprise. His hair went back on both hits. I watched his eyes fill up with water. I was sure of it now he was just as pissed as I was. He swung at me with great force I couldn't sidestep or even dip these blows because the cell was super tiny. He connected all three blows one to the face and to the stomach.. I was winded, I couldn't show him that. My broken ribs reminded me how fucked up I was still. I took in a deep breath and two step forward followed with a combo of my own. I wasn't going for his body though. I wanted him to remember my face when he went home today and as he looked in the mirror and saw my presence was still with him. I felt my face swell up. The adrenaline was kicking in for the both of us. It was convict versus police how it should always be. I saw a red spot under his left nostril. "I struck oil bitch!" I said. "Oh yea, he returned the gesture busting my bottom lip that swelled up immediately. We both exchange blows till his colleague heard something on the radio. "Serge." Just like that he walked out. Not with a victory but he proved his point and I prove mine. He was the boss and I had to abide by his house rules but I prove mine.

I like to fight and I'm sure he'll think twice before burning me again. I wasn't playing and this wasn't the image I wanted to portray but guess what it was the image everyone got to see.

"Ayo Rock you gotta be one of the craziest niggas I've met so far this bid, you are alright?" Malik was surprised. I starred in the mirror that look like a slab of aluminum mounted on the wall. You could barely see your reflection. "Here" Malik had some toast wrapped in some tissue with an orange. I took it. "Good-looking Leak." I began to peel the orange. "I had a feeling that he was going to do some slim ball shit like that, so I brought it back for you."." Leak explained. "Let me tell you this. I've seen this guard be a prick but it's been years since I see him get it in with a prisoner." I didn't think you was gona engage in his bull shit Rock. You got him good though." Leak was smiling. "I take it you enjoy the little fight?" I asked eating the toast with the katsup on it, by the way its blood not catch up hope you're following me.

"Hell yeah that was a total shock I didn't think you like to fight like that Rock." Leak was flattered. I shrug it off as if it wasn't shit. I enjoyed to fight but many always assumed that just cause I'm a smooth pretty boy that I can't. I let them think what they want and wait till they are ready to test the waters. I smashed the toast and orange that Leak brought back for me. I laid back down on my bunk and went into deep thought. An hour passed by. I heard something but I didn't pay any attention to it. "Ayo Rock it's for you." Leak said. "What is?" I asked. "I don't know but it has your name on it. Mr. Ricardo." Leak handed me a foam tray with a lid on it. I opened it and it was my breakfast on overload. I smiled and scarfed the shit down. "You want some?" I asked leak with a mouthful. "Nah G" I ate that's all yours eat up you earned it for real." Leak admitted. I was stuffed. I didn't or should I say couldn't finish all that food. That night they move leak up out of the cell. I decided to move to the bottom bunk but to be honest I enjoy being on top not sure why But I felt better on top. I stood up on the top bunk until they decided to move in someone else. It wouldn't be anytime soon I hoped. I was going out of my mind. The drugs they gave me were so strong that I would be so drugged up that I would miss meals accidentally. I felt so good and out of it that food wasn't even my main interest. I would go up to pill line which was on the block and the nurse would hand me a small cup with 7 pills. I didn't know the skittles from the M&Ms to the Reese's pieces. I would swallowed all of them with no problem. My mind was so stress free and nine times out of 10 I didn't know what the fuck was going on in the unit. To be honest I didn't even care. I was high from the sun up till the sun came back up again. Could you imagine? I was becoming a junkie. My lip had went down from the exchange of blows from the Sgt. but my ribs still felt a lot of pain even after the fact. I was dumb as fuck to even engage in a physical combat with that man with a couple fractured ribs. He could've easily put a serious beating on me and call some real serious hemorrhaging inside of me. The more I thought about it, the more I realize I had to be very mindful of all my action. The next man would have not care who or what is wrong with me. It's either you or him in the art of war right? After about 8 1/2 days I was finally cleared to move to general population. Since, I was all clear with the medical department and I was fully drugged up. I got moved over to the max block were all the hard-core criminals were held at. I had the butterflies again because it was yet another drastic change that I had no control over. It was a journey so we had to roll with the punches. I was feeling woozy from my morning pills which were wearing off, my body was asking for more. I haven't heard from anyone nor did I care. All that I care for was my little paper cups. I felt myself becoming more and more codependent on the pills, was I just imagining things?

"Manuel Ricardo." The C.O in the bubble called out to me. You in 46 cell top bunk" he stated. It took me a bit to focus and it felt as if all eyes were on me. Apparently I was so drugged up. As I made my way towards 46 cell I was a bit drowsy. It wasn't as bad like the first couple of times. I was already familiar with the quarantine but the block I was on had the same structure. Only difference was it was not a quarantine block anymore. It was the block where I would rest until who knew when. It was a lot more rowdy here than the previous one. I figured it being that these mother fuckers were going to be here for a hot minute fighting trial or just waiting to be shipped up. I managed to slip in the cell with no problem at least that's what I thought. I wasn't in here for more than five minutes when this mother fucker unknowingly called me a fucking junkie. He noticed the rage in my eyes because out of all the things he said all I her was "you a fucking fiend ass nigga." My reflexes demanded me to go in on this nigga. He was nowhere near a fighter. He was what you call a dog with all bark trying to intimidate all who passes through with his mouth. One thing is to run your mouth when you know for certain that you can back it the fuck up, but it's a whole another story when a nigga runs his mouth not knowing how to back it the fuck up. Niggas like this are the ones that need to be broken in as soon as possible.

"Please... My fault yo... My fault!" The gangster pled. I wanted to continue to beat on him for his lack of concern and being disrespectful towards others but I was always taught that once an enemy is down and you no longer feel no threat. You let him regain his stance just to see if he's talking a bit more rational. If not its yard out on his ass again. The man in my cell was Randy he was a dusty ass nigga from the projects in North Camden. It was a fucked up way to break the ice in situations like this one.

"You can call me Slash." Randy said. "Slash?" I question. I was on my second confrontation already. "I didn't mean to go in on you like that." I tried my best to clean up the thick tension now. "Nah it's my fault for running my mouth thinking something that it wasn't. I just seen you knodding and the first thing that came to mind was this nigga a crack head because that's how they be out there and in here." It made a lot of sense but I was no fiend and I'll be damn if any nigga would come out his face at me on some crack head shit. "How long you been in here?" I asks Slash. I was expecting him to say a week or two because his cell was a mess for real. This was no way I was going to sleep, let alone live like this. "I've been in here for almost 10 months." He answered. "Damn!" I replied. "Yeah he was feeling his lip because I bust it right open. I'm not going to front I didn't like praying on the week but how was I supposed to know that this man couldn't fight. His mouth was crazy. "So what you got left?" He pulled out his box he has some commissary he was set for a bit. "I'm not talking about what you got in here personally I'm talking about how much time you got left in your case." I was shocked that he thought I was trying to run his shit too. I had a feeling this place was going to cause a bunch of problems. I had to find a better way to avoid all of this extra shit. "Oh, well I'm fighting an arm robbery that ended in a homicide but I wasn't in the mix when the homicide happened." I stared at him as if he must've thought I was stupid as hell or just mentally challenged. That statement that just came out his mouth sounded iffy as fuck. I had to hear him out though. I sat on the top part of the desk and he sat on his bed. "I don't get it?" I said. I wanted him tell me what happen that day of his arrest. I was bored and dinner wasn't until the next couple hours and I wanted to make an assessment on this nigga and see what his deal was. "It was three of us. Two of us are booked and my other man is free not sure if he's running or they just don't know where he is. We went over to Mount Ephraim on Friday night to hit the bar up right before they closed. It was Friday and we heard that foot 21 was jumping." Slash was going into his memory bank to withdraw all accounts that went on that day. I looked at him very attentively. Foot 21 has all the hottest sneakers and gear in that area so it was going to be an easy lick. At least that's what we thought. Earlier that day I went in with my man to check out what they had and to case the place. The spot was jam-packed with all types of drug dealers and bitches spending bread to get fresh for the weekend. It was so busy that it took almost an hour for the salesperson to get to us. I should've known better than that but hey I didn't at the moment.We copped our kicks and he bought a shirt to go with his kicks and we dipped. We shot to my man's crib which wasn't all that far from the store but far enough to get low." He was very animated as he talked. I kicked off my Skippy's because this nigga wasn't no threat at least I thought he wasn't. He didn't have his gun so I was good or was I? He went on recounting all that had transpired on why he and his man's got hit for this arm robbery. "Instead of us changing our gear we put on our mask and went in three deep with our guns in hand. We barked at the customers who were still in in the store and the sales workers to get on the ground. They all did and I was happy because I was bent off them E's. I popped triple stacks, four of them so I was feeling it. I didn't want to hurt anybody but if I needed too then you already knew what was going to happen." The way this guy talk was as if he had no type of education with his lip all curled up hands all over the place. "I held down all the customers on the floor which weren't many but enough to keep me busy. My man and his man's were also all fucked up on wet and E. They both headed to the back of the store to find a safe to get the cash. We were only supposed to be in their 2 minutes tops. It might have been two or maybe one but I felt as if we was in there for 10 minutes." I laughed because I could feel how this was going to end. I listened.

"Ayo let's go hurry the fuck up!" I yelled at them I could hear arguing in the back, I wasn't sure if it was them to or if they were arguing with the owner to open the safe's door. I wasn't sure but I was curious to know what was holding these two mother fuckers up, Get it?" He laughed asking. "But nah I went to the back and these two crazy ass niggaz were beating the shit out of this Spanish man who was helpless on the ground begging for them to stop. Open the safe my boy barked at him kicking him in the face over and over again. I was like how the fuck this nigga going to open the safe if this nigga wouldn't stop kicking him long enough for him to get a chance to open the safe." Slash paused for second so his words would settle in, he had me though I still wanted to hear the rest. "So what happened?" I asked being super nosy. The man was unconscious in and out of it. My man pointed his tech in my face and told me to go and watch the front. "I turned around and sped right to the front. I ended up running out the front because these niggaz was on some extra shit. Come to find out they decided to kill the Spanish nigga because he was so out of his mind, he couldn't even think clearly enough to open the safe." Slash explained. "So they got caught?" I asked. "Nah, no one got caught until three months later. They ended up unloading the clip on main man and taking the whole safe out of the store and carrying it to the house. I wasn't nowhere to be found. One I was pissed because this nigga put a barrel in my face as if he was going to kill me and second it was practically my idea that almost turned into killing that nigga or even killing me." The detectives pulled me over one day and pulled me in stating that I fit the description of one of the robbers due to the gear I was wearing. It's bullshit because how many niggas have the same gear as the next man?" He had a point I thought to myself. "So that's my angle, they got my man's the same way because they said we was all in the store hours earlier casing the store. When it was all busy with the flow of customers. I sent word over to my man and told him to keep the story short and to the point. Yes it was us in there but we was there to shop and that was it. As far as his man? He nowhere to be found" Slash stated hoping his story would work. "No one knows of his whereabouts which is good, if we didn't know where he was the cops didn't know either." I go to my hearing next month then trial a few months after." Slash was acting a bit weird but out of all the things he said the last part is what got my wheels turning. He didn't mention him being questioned about the body nor did he say anything about his man being charged for the homicide on top of that, his last statement was all uncomfortable to hear. He said that if he nor his man's knew about the third person whereabouts then that was good because the DTs didn't know either. So are you telling me that if you two knew than the DTs would know? Or did that just come out the wrong way? I know, I heard what I heard but was he in so deep in his lies that he couldn't keep up with them. Something smelled funny and I wasn't going to jump to conclusion but I was going to find out the truth one way or the other. I wasn't going to get into all of that right now. I had to clean up this cell first. I couldn't live like this.

"Damn! So that's exactly what happened?" I tested him. He was much older 27 to be exact but a liar came in all ages. "Hell yea shit got real." Slash said or was the drugs a proven fact of how your brains can get fried? "Yo Ima clean the cell up is that cool?" I asked not wanting him to feel as if I was going to take his cell over. "nah you good." Slash said. Ima pickup all my shit." "Good looking." I replied. "What you in for?" Slash asked. Leak was right these cells are much better but what was the point when you live in like this I thought. "Murder." I left it at that. "Damn!" Slash said. If I was gona live like this for the rest of my life I was going to live it properly. I told myself without knowing what I was truly saying.

—

"It's my fault my brother is put away. I need you by my side, I need you here to tell me that it's not my fault Joel." Linda was at Joel's house in one of her deep depressions. It's been more than a week and a half since she's heard or seen her brother which was killing her from the inside out literally. Joel was a preppy guy who hasn't really been in the streets other than when he is on the rode going and coming to a destination. It isn't your fault baby because if you wouldn't have done what you did, you could very well be dead. Now if you can't see the logic behind your brother's actions I strongly think you should do some serious thinking on the positive sides of all this." Joel spoke truth but it was so easy for anyone to see it in that aspect. How could anyone understand and feel why and how she thought the way she did about all of this. I fucked up was what Linda thought. She wasn't supposed to say anything about anything that went on that night. Out of all the people she told you Joel." No one was in Joel's house, his parents were out of town but just the tone in Linda's voice caught him off-guard. He had never seen Linda so upset, she was all up in his face. "You don't know what we been through honey! You have your perfect old little life with your parents and expect the whole world to live a happy and dandy life. Let me tell you this, life isn't as easy as you see it. Well at least not for the ones who have been through so many hoops and obstacles to get where we are today. That man you think he did the right thing is my heart and I'll do anything for him because our life was a struggle and apparently it still is......" Linda was in tears. Joel still was shell-shocked. He didn't argue back he realize how much of an impact this whole ordeal has been for her so he let her go on. Besides it was true, yea Joel lives in the hood but he lives more on the borderline. His parents are in fact still very much united. It may not be 100% happiness but they were still together. Linda may have went overboard with her mouth but she had to let it out. Plus after Joel hearing that his girl, the woman he lost his virginity to is a murderer he didn't dare to even counter what she had just said.

"I hate you, I hate myself but I love my brother... I... I... Can't do it anymore!" She was still going on but now she was falling deep into a deep depression. Joel hugged her. "It's going to be all right baby. I'm not gona tell you how because I don't know the answer to that because I can't feel your pain. I'm here with you please be strong because I know you are stronger than this." Joel picked his words wisely it's been a week and a half since Linda has been to school and Joel has been worried about her a lot lately. He somehow wish he could lift all of this weight up off her shoulders. He hugged her tightly to show her how much he really loved her. "Please don't leave me too." Linda looked up at Joel deep in his eyes. He was tall but there stare was met and felt so pure and powerful. He bent over and kissed her softly Linda melted in his arms. She did love him to the fullest not because he technically was her first also but just the mere fact that he resembled Rock in almost every feature of his physical level. What was just a soft kiss evolved into a more passionate kiss. Joel grabbed her by her plump ass and put her right on the kitchen counter. She was swept right off her feet literally her arms wrapped around Joel's neck, he bit her neck and she was still in tears. Joel wasn't sure if he should keep going or just let her keep venting for herself sake. The salt from her tears made it down to her neck straight into Joel's mouth. He licked them following all the way up till where they were falling from. He was literally trying to drink away all her sorrows as much as he could. Linda noticed what he was doing and became more aroused. She took off her shirt which was a fitted silky button up, slipping off every button until her black Victoria's Secret bra was exposing her beautiful breast mushed together making them look so desirable. He didn't miss a beat he was all up in them but he was a bit uneasy about something. He stopped. "Why you stopping baby?" Linda was horny and super wet she wanted him to end all her unwanted emotions by giving her the emotional satisfaction, it's been too long and she wanted it bad. "Let's go upstairs." Joel said. Her face was in disappointment she wanted him here and now by the time they would make it upstairs they will have to start all over again. Joel saw her hesitation, he swept her off the counter and threw her right over his shoulder. "Oh my God Joel!" Linda was upside down. "What are you doing? She smiled and pure joy. "You took too long" Joel took the invitation to get the job done right and keep her in the mood, he climbed with her all the way up to the third floor. Now this nigga was super horny and he wanted some pussy bad too. Because this wasn't two or three steps it was two big flights going up without stopping. "You going to drop me." Her voice bounced in between steps. Linda could see the back of Joel's butt and the steps she thought he was really going to drop her eventually. "I got you baby." Joel said in between breaths he almost didn't make it but he did. Tossing her on the bed with little and no energy the image of Linda sexy body bounced off the bed. He tossed her. Locking the door and it was on. Linda's tears were all gone and she was all smiles. "You strong baby." Linda said as Joel crawled on his bed with no shirt straddling her she fell back into her sexual escapade where they left off in the kitchen. Joel's room was rather large his bed was a queen-size bed his room had two windows one facing the street out front and the other overlooking towards the neighbors backyard. The dressers made of oak wood that matched the headboards, both had mirrors on them. Linda bit his nipples he flinched but soon allowed her to do what she wanted. He stripped her off her jeans that were stuck on her thick thighs. Her socks and all came up off of her body, all she wore was a matching brawl and booty shorts. She nibbled on his neck that was bound to leave a hickey ,he didn't care he wanted her and if she wanted to mark her territory it was all good with him because he was all hers and she was all his for the most part. Unclipping her bra to suck on the fluffy juicy breasts was his main goal until he achieved this he wouldn't stop. Linda's moans were soft but very much felt to anyone who could feel and hear her. Her voice was so feminine, he sucked and bit her areolas as she did to him. She hissed in pure satisfaction. She grabbed the back of his head. Her beautiful soft legs wrapped around his waist as if he wasn't going anywhere until she had enough. He kissed and licked her every upper body part of her. Erected nipples he went down south where he knew where she needed and wanted all of his attention. He teased her by kissing the sides of her hips and biting her outer thighs, just below her belly button. She cried and wanted more of his role-play, it was on point. Linda taught him a few things but he was excelling rapidly. He managed to slip off her shorts all the way down to her toes. Linda's hands and feet always match with one another. It was in her nature to keep her feet fresh. Joel took advantage of the prettiness and her flawless feet. He kissed the top of her feet and licked and sucked on her toes as if she was the cleanest and purest girl in the world, well at least in his world she was. Linda laughed but once his warm wet tongue roamed her feet.

Her laughter transformed into soft sexual moans. He did it to both feet not leave in any part of her untouched by his mouth, he ran up her heels passing her ankles his kissed softly and passionately headed up north on both sides. He had Linda going crazy, the thought and how much time he took with her only cause her to become so moist that a small puddle was forming on his sheets sliding down her ass crack . He smiled to himself at the site of what he was doing to his girl. She probably came twice without him even touching her, his tongue managed to find her love button but he grazed her love button with his tongue. He moved towards her inner thighs she was getting impatient, her thighs spoke for her. She tightened around his neck, but he pried her open. "Relax baby I got you." Joel said. She followed his instructions he licked his two fingers and slid them up and down her slit on her vagina without penetrating. Linda was shaking her thighs were having a seizure. Joel rammed both of his fingers inside of her and she came. Her cries were all cries of satisfaction. His two fingers weren't the smallest but at the feeling of them forcefully going inside of her love box cause her to lose control, he slid them in twice and pulled out. The arch in her lower back, she was no longer lying flat on the bed. His tongue and her clitoris were both in a slow but teasing wrestling match. He would lick his tongue up and down enjoying every move and twitch that Linda's body would do caused by his actions. He slid his tongue down her vagina and followed her stream all the way to her ass. "Baby wait".... she lost it. "Oh yes baby I like that she was getting turned out by Joel. Joel ate her ass out for a bit while finger fucking her pussy at the same time not forgetting to lick her click. He found the rhythm and had her back was arched as if she was possessed.... "I want you baby I wanted." Linda asked very sexual in her sexy voice. "Do you baby?" Joel taunted. He slid off his pants and boxers without her even notice and still maintaining his rhythm. He was now three fingers deep into her pussy and one in her ass. Linda didn't nor could she fight back all that he was doing to her. Joel was rock solid and he wanted her so bad but he wanted to make sure his baby was taking care of first and foremost. Bout to get nasty he went up and kissed her. "Who do you want?" Joel teased. "You baby fuck this pussy." Linda was in it for real Joel lined his man up and in one swift motion had all 10 inches deep in her. "Ouch.... Yes!" Linda yelled "fuck me good!" Linda was telling Joel. He stroked her pussy with his man hood. Linda wasn't broken in like, this mother fucker was giving it to her good. I guess all that stress and depression between the two had to end in a good way. Joel was dicking her down he had a grip on her neck with his hand and on the other side with his teeth like an animal she couldn't get away from this one. "Yesssss! Baby like that oh Yesssss!" Linda was all orgasms and rivers flowing down his shaft all the way down to his balls. "I want to ride you baby." Linda said. In a swift motion Joel was on the bottom and Linda was where she asked to be without losing his positioning. She rolled him over, her breast all in his face he tried to catch one with his mouth but she was moving too good so instead of enjoying them slapping his face as she moved forward he was almost in a couch position so he could feel her soft breasts slapping him all up and down his face. His hands were embedded in her soft thick ass guiding her inward with every thrust and push she was putting it on him. The splashing and clapping of her pussy smacking his balls and pelvic area was all wet. Joel was feeling like he couldn't hold it any longer. So he moved her on all fours. "Coming baby." Joel said. "Come baby! Yes come all over me." He had her doggy style and put it on her harder. Linda had to have come at least 6 times already. He stuck his finger in her ass as he fucked her wet juicy pussy. "Put it in my ass baby." Joel froze for second but did as she asked of him, he slid right in her ass. It's been said when you sex a woman in her ass you take her soul literally. Linda was lost and enjoying every naughty sexual thing that was being performed on her. Joel let Linda lead the way eventually Linda was throwing her plump bottom back while he massaged her click from behind. "I'm coming baby." Joel said to Linda moaning "come with me baby" "I'm coming." Joel said again trying to hold it all back she pulled his dig out and began to stroke it where her hands hard and fast. He looked at her, her eyes were tearing up running down her cheeks her lips were wet and her face displayed pure ecstasy. Joel released all over her breast as she kept stroking his manhood until he fell on the bed, he was done. Linda wiped her body off with his shirt then laid up next to him their heart rates were up and still breathing rapidly. They held one another and the smell of sex was in the air. "I love you Jalinda." Joel said. "I love you too baby."…. Oh my God that felt so good baby." Linda gave praise.

—

Back in the county jail the same routine is taking a toll on Rock. He's been going through the motions with his own thoughts. The meals are garbage and the ones that have potential aren't enough to last him five minutes in his stomach. The drugs are whats keeping him going. Block out/dayroom was only for an hour which was bullshit. By the time you got involved in a game of dominoes, a game of pinnacle, even get into a TV show or even a workout it was time to go back to your cell. How could this be life and to be honest I personally didn't see or wanted to see myself doing this for the rest of my life. I'd go insane and I'll kill myself or even kill somebody if this had to be life. Why I was up in here, ended up traveling fast. I wasn't the only one that was in here for a body, but not many had the balls to go toe to toe with the sergeant that's known to treat to be a prick and treats like shit. Every now and then I would get. "You the nigga who black the Sergeant's eye?" He had a deep purple eye, I had my marks too from us going at it with one another but since he was a much paler individual. You know the rest of the story. I never went around boasting and glorifying what happened that day. You'll be surprised on how fast words really did travel around. It wasn't just in these walls, it was everywhere. Everyone love to gossip about anything and anyone in this world. Male or female. I fell victim to this numerous times but it wasn't a habit that I wanted to possess entirely. I had to work on this. Don't get me started with the phone situation. This was a whole another topic. You would think that since there are 200+ men on the block that they would make more than four phones available for everyone. Well of they didn't. Anything to start a chaotic situation. I didn't have any money yet so it didn't bother me. I stayed my ass in my cell until I was allowed to hit the showers and go to chow. Slash and I would play some spades and Rumy for hours until I grew sick and tired of the card games. It was very frustrating for the most part. I wondered what and how everyone back home was. I wondered if they miss me at all, were they trying their best to get me out of this mess that I was in? So many thoughts ran through my mind. It drove me insane that so many went unanswered. I often thought of my truck that had to be somewhere in an impound lot. I knew it wouldn't be cheap to get out with the daily increase would climb through the roof. It would be too expensive to get out and possibly go up for auction. In a matter of days it would be $30-$40 daily, until it reached an outstanding balance that couldn't or wouldn't be worth paying for. "You got some paper?" I asked Slash. "Some writing paper?" He replied "yes I want to write a letter to my family." I admitted. He dug through his things and pulled out a writing pad along with two stamped envelopes. "You can take these, I bought them but nobody hits me back so fucked them." Slash said sounding fucked up. It was already late and I had a few things on my mind that I had to get off my chest. To much shit was was beginning to bottle up. This could be very dangerous on my behalf to have all this pinned up stress and frustration. I didn't need that at all, so I had to put it down on paper before I would let it out another way.That shit could cause me some serious bodily harm. The sound of the tier runner running around for the guards and other prisoners could be heard. I looked out the cell and I noticed three-tier runners running around like chickens without their heads, passing food, notes, contraband etc. etc. I dismissed the scenery and sat at the desk. My celli was humming a song on his bunk. I sat at the desk and began to put what came to mind down on paper.....

Dear my beautiful mother and beautiful sister,

I want to begin this letter by wishing and hoping that the two most beautiful women in my life to find themselves in the best of health but most of all in the highest of spirits. As for me I find myself in ugly but manageable situation. It's a bit out of my comfort zone but its times like this when we are really put to a test. A test to see if we will always stay who we've always been or we will be quick to switch up. I will not become a major part of the problem, that has been placed in my life's journey. I'm sure the two of you know that as for me I handle whatever is thrown at me. Even when it feels that I may be defeated.

Mom you raise me to be a man and always protect the ones that I hold closest to me and that is what I intend to do until my casket carries my body and it. (That'll be no time soon I hope) The reason for my hesitation in writing to you is, I didn't get the opportunity to purchase some writing supplies. I'm sure you can help me with this. If not I'll figure something out. I haven't called because these collect calls are going to be through the roof as far as the Rates and so forth. Therefore i will not be a bill or burden on you. I miss you two so much. I close my eyes and I see both of your smiles.When I open them they are gone almost immediately. I am in emotional turmoil but know that I'm making the best of a bad situation. My court date isn't for the next few months and I hope to see you there. Linda I know you may be beating yourself up over a couple of things but know that this is what my life was intended to be in this very moment. You may not feel as if this is fair, and I know it's going to drive you insane. You can't let this torment your mind. I'm picking my words cautiously for reasons you should already know. It's no one's fault as to why I'm here. Please let yourself breath and remain focused on the objective at hand. Which is finish your schooling and enjoy all of what life has planned out for you. "I am okay!" I love you too so much and I know that you love me just as much.

A note was slipped under the door. I didn't pay any mind because I knew it wasn't for me. I was wrong. The note had my name on it.

"Ayo Rock! Watch you're fucking head because now you're in my territory and you have nowhere to run in these walls!" I read it out loud and I mean mugged the shit outta my celly. "Is this is a joke?" I asked standing up. "I don't know Rock. "Slash spoke quickly. "Why the fuck would I be getting threats in this mother fucker? I don't even socialize with none of these clowns?" I was getting a bit hyped. "The only niggas that I had any altercation with was with you. You probably told your homies and now they trying to get at me huh!?" I was about to send a serious message with this nigga. "Oh hell no! That aint got shit to do with me I put that on everything Rock, that's my word. Yes we had our misunderstanding but what happened, happened and that was it. Yea I know a couple of heads in here but nah, that message isn't from my niggaz that I fuck with." I somehow believed this nigga but had to keep my guard up with him. Not everyone can get punched in the mouth and just accept that. I know I would have a serious problem with it. "I'll handle that later." I said getting back to my letter.

I put my visit form in, I hope when you get the chance to come up to see me you will. I really love to see and hear from you.

The note was distorting all my thinking. I wanted to know of the coward who slid this shit into my cell. This wasn't going to be an easy step and I had to switch out my whole mentality to play ball in this league. This was a league that I wasn't aware of. If It was a fighting game I was all for it....

Sorry I have to cut this letter short, just remember the past is the past let's focus on now and the future from my heart to yours.

Your son and brother,

Manuel Ricardo

Chapter 11

"I'm perked up"

With the snow approaching rapidly, the days were getting a lot windier and much colder. Hustlers on the block in their bomber jackets, Tims, hoodies and Scully etc. etc. You got your hood rats out looking for nigga to snuggle with the night. It seems that nothing ever changes if you are dopeboy. Yea you get in it but all you do is post up on the block and get high and practically freeze unless you all yacked out with some henny or that vodka.

It's Tuesday and it's almost noon, mom is in the kitchen on the phone chatting away with her old friend. She's waiting for her coffee to be almost ready so she can pour herself a nice mug of it.

"Yes girl I miss him so much its hard." Mom spoke into the receiver Linda was in school handling what she needed to be handling. Mom felt alone. She lit a cigarette, with me getting locked away I can only imagine how much stress has built up in the house. I only wish that mom and Linda maintained their lives as normal as possible as if I were close by. As far as mom smoking heavily again. I wouldn't put it past her. I believed Linda would try her best to keep mom on the path to recovery. "Well I'll talk to you later, it's been good to hear from you." Mom spoke ending the conversation. She walked over to the living room and turned on the TV and watch the news briefly. She admired the photo of myself when I was younger. She just stared at it. "I'm so sorry for failing you Manuel.... I tried my best to keep you away from harm's way." Mom was talking to me but to the photo. She inhaled the smoke and held it. Her tear ducts couldn't hold back the fountain of tears any longer. It's been some time now and she was tired of being so strong. It took so much energy out of her. Why not take advantage of the alone time that she had, and release all those deep pinned up emotions that she's been hindering from escaping her soul. "pl...easeee.... forgive me my son..... It's all my fault. If I would've been more of a great parent, you wouldn't be in a situation that you're in." Mom was letting it all out. I had admit, it feels good to let out these pinned up emotions every now and then. Yes, the situation is bad but it could always be worse. To release your mind and set it free, was a joyous feeling even if you had to cry it all out. "Clank!" The sound of the mailbox lid landed as it did every day around noon-ish. The TV watched mom instead of mom watching the TV. The sound removed her from her thoughts.

—

"Hey" Felicia said answering her phone. "No I had off today plus I'm so tired, what's up?" Felicia spoken to the receiver. "What you up to?" Felicia's friend from work asked. "Have you heard anything from Manuel?" Her friend Amber asked her. "No I haven't heard anything. I'm going to call the county jail today. I've been so busy lately, I'm actually going to take advantage of the day to tie up a couple loose ends." Felicia admitted. You would think that I would have heard something from Felicia but like it's been said. Out of mine out of sight. Nothing could be more true than the infamous quote. "I still can't believe you were dating a fucking murderer." Amber had the audacity. "He isn't a murderer." Felicia defended her love. I know he didn't do that shit it's not in his character." Felicia said. "Yeah hope you're right but just be lucky you didn't piss him off enough for him to kill your ass." Amber was a true hater. It didn't matter who or what Felicia was doing, Amber always had to throw some salt on it. "All right I'm going see you at work." Click. Felicia banged on her. How much more stress can a woman endure. You would think that your close friends or associates will be a little compassionate on what you going through, but nope. Misery loves to be accompanied by anyone who will let themselves fall victim to it. In this case Felicia wasn't in no way shape or form named "company". She wasn't going to let someone so selfish and determine, to bring others down.such as Amber. She wouldn't allow herself to be caught on the fishing line. Instead, she did the complete opposite. Her princess was all knocked out and she took advantage of the day. The 411 director managed to get her the phone number to the county jail. It was a recording that you had to jump to hoops and climb mountains just to get to a live person. After almost 30 minutes, she had gotten the confirmation that she wanted. She got Manuel's address and housing unit. She was told his cases and his upcoming hearings, you be surprised on how easy it is to obtain vital information from certain people. The administration could care less if it was a stalker or even a Joe Schmoe trying to cause some serious problems to you. They give it up all willingly with no if and or butts about it. After hanging up the phone she sat there in complete silence just staring at the handwriting.

"Was this man worth my time....?" "Is he really a killer....?" "Would he have killed me if I have push him to the verge..?" or.... Is he innocent...?" Felicia stomach was in a knots, all these questions were going through her mind as she repeated them softly to herself all at once. What was she doing? Was she ready to waste valuable time on Rock? "Do I love him...? Why Haven't he reached out to me...? Does he not know my address...? Or my phone number...? I miss him so much, it's unbelievable how a stranger could have my mind all fucked up. I love him!"... Felicia didn't have someone to speak to who would understand her. So she did what any other woman who wanted answers would do. She wrote down her emotions on a paper and began to vent to herself, to get a better understanding of her emotions and feelings.

—

Door close quickly as mom tried to keep the cold breeze out. The chill ran up her robe it couldn't be stopped. "Is going to be a cold winter." She said to herself. As she flopped back down on the sofa. She grabbed her mug and set the mail down on the table. When she got the chance she began to look through it. Many were Bills.... Bills.....and More bills. She was saying as she surveyed the pile. Linda's.... Bills...... Linda's... "Oh Manuel!" She was instantly brought to a bliss, she put down her mug and began opening it carefully. Her anxiousness got the best of her and she ended up tearing the one side completely off. Her smile was enormous. It made her look plenty of years younger. It took only a matter of seconds before her smile turned into a frown, then into tears again.

"You are a great man and I know that you'll be a great father one day." Mom spoke in between breaths she held the letter close to her heart as she finished off the emotional letter. The letter wasn't meant to cause any real emotional pain, but reading her son's words after all this time would spark an emotion in anyone who had a heart. Mom got on her grind. She called the impound and called the sub shop to pick up any money owed to her son. After the call she agreed to go to the shop and speak with Pete and explain to him what happened to her son. Now that she knew where he was and knew that he had to be there for a while. She could be there and do her best to uplift her son spirits as much as she could. That wouldn't be an easy task but it was what Manual needed and if it helped, then it's what she would do. By the time she handled all that needed to be handled, she ended up walking back into the house. She was surprised to see Linda sitting at the table with the letter in her hand.

"Mom he is okay!" Linda hollered after reading the same letter mom read this morning. "Yes baby he is, your brother will always be okay as long as we do what he ask us to do." Mom said from her heart. Many may have thought they went overboard on how much they looked up to Manuel. He was that type of person that demanded respect and had to be acknowledged. Not by force but by on how he carried himself and how he treated others.

"So why are you here so early?" Mom asked Linda. "Well the instructor said that she had to leave early so we could leave as well." Linda said with a smile on her face. "And how did you get here?" Mom probed. "A friend at school lives over by cousin's supermarket and she decided to drop me off." Linda replied. Linda noticed the ashtray and counted out nine cigarette butts. Mom noticed her eyes. "Stressing?" Was all Linda asked? "Am I? I miss him so much, he would kill me if he saw this ashtray filled up the way it is." Mom admitted. "No he wouldn't kill you, you're doing all that on your own. Linda hit mom hard with her own statement. "I know..."Mom put her head down. "Just because he is absent doesn't mean you or we going to pick up old habits again and not caring anymore." Linda said in a serious firm loving tone. "I'm a keep this letter." Linda said about to head upstairs. "Wait I want to read it again..." Mom said with her hand out and a smile on her face.

"Are you hungry?" Mom asked. "Am I?" Linda answered. "Well I'll put something together while you do what you need to do." Mom said to Linda. "Look at me." Mom asked Linda. Mom was noticing the dark spot on her neck, but decided to say absolutely nothing. "What?" Linda said catching mom's stare. Mom returned the smile with one of her own. They both knew what the deal was without saying a word. It was a female thing. "Better wrap that thing up." Mom said heading towards the kitchen to prepare a meal for her daughter. Linda face was so embarrassed her hickey could be noticed from Pollock. She bolted up the stairs to get some comfy clothes on. Her plans were to go nowhere but spend it with mom. Mom decided to get the truck from the impound and utilize it for her and Linda. She was going to give it to Linda with my approval to be for real. As much as I cared I was all for it, but then again Streets would be all over town looking for the truck. Rock couldn't allow that. If he found out that it was being driven by a female, and that particular female was the one who offed his right-hand man. Nope it wasn't going to happen. I would not get caught slipping twice, especially with my sister's life. The smell of the freshly cooked meal brought Linda right back down to the kitchen in her PJs with socks on her feet.

"Just on time." Mom said. Finishing up the fried chicken tenders with fries. "I want cheese on my fries" Linda said headed to the fridge. "Grab the Cheez whiz." Mom instructed. She put three spoonfuls in a cup with a splash of milk. "You want some?" She asked mom. "No I'll eat mine without it, thank you." Mom answered. In the microwave it went for about 45 seconds.

"Mom do you think he'll be out soon?" Linda asked a question that she wasn't ready to be answered. Mom inhaled serving a dish full of tenders and another of fries separately. They both would eat out of the same big dishes as if they were appetizers at a restaurant. Exhaling she said. "If he is convicted baby which he might, he could be in there for a long time... "Now if his lawyer helps him, he'll due time but it won't be forever." Mom spoke in all honesty not holding back because that's what she always did. No matter what the subject was about. It wasn't right to sugarcoat any of this because this was a touchy subject that had to be laid flat out on the table. I knew I might have to do a life sentence and if so we all had to anticipate the not guilty verdict as well as the guilty one. Mom intentions were not to discourage Linda but to bring awareness to her about what could occur. Mom decided to switch the conversation up. The spotlight was on Miss. Linda.

"So how are things with you and Mr.Joel?" She immediately began to blush. Mom smiled dipping her tenders in some katsup. "Uuuhhmm." Mom joked. "We okay." Linda tried to keep it short hoping mom would let it go. "Okay." Mom asked knowing there was a whole lot more to be spoken about, but she wouldn't force her either. "All right then." Mom ended. "I really like him mom he is the sweet." Linda was open like a 7/11.. "Too sweet?" Mom repeated. "Would you prefer someone who is mean and that abuses you on a day to day basis?" Mom stared at her deeply in her eyes searching for the answer before it was given. "I don't mean it like that mom. I'm not sure if I can even explain what I'm feeling inside." Linda chewed on her cheese fries. She grabbed the crystal salt shaker and splashed the fries until she was satisfied. "Well baby how does he make you feel?" Mom asked waiting for a response. "He is always the one to uplift my day when I'm down and out. He's always telling me how reality is and is blunt with his advice knowing that they could be really painful. I'm not saying it in a bad way though." Linda tried to explain what she meant to mom. "so he treats you good, he makes you smile, and he tells you what's on his mind and you love this." Mom pointed down south to her private area. "Oh my God mom. No! I mean, yeah!" Linda didn't know what to say she was so embarrassed. They both shared a laugh that was so desperately needed at the time like this. "So you think he's the one?" Mom asked. "I'm hoping he is but I don't want to get my hopes up too high." Linda was right. Deep down in her heart she wanted Joel to be the man in her life for as long as she would allow him to be. If she would admit this to him or mom, her cards will be exposed. This was all that she could control. Her love box belonged to him now. The way that man would put his moves on her was something she wasn't going to let go anytime soon. Mom and Linda kicked it for a good minute. "When you plan on getting back in the dating game?" Linda asked. "Girl, don't nobody want this old thing. I can't even breathe how I would get my thing on." They slapped hands laughing loudly amongst the two of them. "Stop mom, you still got a lot of life in you if you want it." Linda got serious. Mom reach for a cigarette but Linda intervened. "We are eating." Mom didn't object. "We going to get you some good loving, what you think?" Now it was mom's turn to blush. "Can you imagine how happy Manny would be to hear that you have a boo." Linda joked. "He'll be happy or jealous one of the two." Mom joked. Linda noticed the money on the table. "That's for him?" Linda asked. "Yes it is, it's not much but it'll help him call us and put some food in his belly. You know that boy loves to eat." Mom smiled. "Doesn't he?" Linda agree with mom. "I have some money too if you want to send him some more." Linda was always one to look out for Manny ever since they were children. "No you keep your money, if you choose to send him something go right ahead. We can't overdo it because we are just making ends meet by ourselves." Mom spoke the truth. She always handled the house. Now she was getting a little bit of help since we started to work. She was right though, we couldn't go overboard with the sending of the money. You had to be a selfish mother fucker to want to be jailhouse rich. I could easily be a burden and that was something I didn't want to be. This was my mess so I had to deal with it. You would be amazed on how many niggaz and bitches in these walls, were just another bill in this bitch to their families on the otherside. I wasn't going to be just another stressful monthly bill in this mother fucka to my family and mom knew exactly how she had to play this.

—

That same week mom and Linda showed up at the sub shop. They wore their jackets and scarfs, looking beautiful as they always did. The shop was open and pretty busy even after Rock left his spirit there. Mom and Linda came in and picked a spot to sit. They waited patiently for Pete to acknowledge them. Now Pete has never seen or met mom neither has Jamal. They both were familiar with sexy ass to Linda though.

"Look who it is." Jamal joked looking at Linda. Linda smiled and just sat there. Pete caught a glimpse of her. "Oh man!" Pete barked out his loudmouth joking. "Trouble's here". Mom watch him. They stared at one another for a second or two trying to figure each other out. "Come into my office." Pete instructed. They both got up and headed pass the counter were Pete lifted up a part of the counter that would allow them to pass. "How is Rock?" Jamal asked as they got closer. Linda forced a sly smile. "He is okay I guess." Linda Brushed right on by him along with mom. "Tell him I send my love." Jamal said. It was surprising to say this but Pete's office was nothing like it was when Rock left it. It had been cleaned up from wall to wall, and floor to ceiling.

"Have a seat ladies. I'm sorry for the mess." Pete was far from serious. The place was neat and tidy for once "I only wish Rock could see this it now." Pete bragged. Its crazy how I had to get locked up in order for this man to clean up his fucking office. "So any good news?" Pete asked loudly, staring at Linda and mom. "We haven't really heard a lot from him but he wrote us the other day and he told us that he is okay. He wants us not to worry too much about him." Linda spoke quietly. Pete just examined her and kept his eyes on mom. If I wasn't mistaken Pete could of found mom attractive but it wasn't a sure thing. Mom noticed but she wasn't there for him, especially on that note. All she wanted to know was what Pete was going to do for her son, as far as payment. "I'm sorry I didn't get your name." Pete extended his hand to greet mom. "Catherine." Mom replied taking his hand. Mom's hands always look nice and were well maintained, just like the rest of her body. "How are you feeling?" Pete asked. "I'm okay." Mom answered perplexed. Her look gave away her thoughts. "I'm sorry it's just because I remember when you were in the hospital that day. Rock was so afraid and hurt that's why I asked. I didn't mean to offend Catherine." Pete said regretting every word of it. If he could slap himself he would've. I think this was one he wanted to really nail himself. "Oh No... No I'm okay thank you for asking. Just trying my best to stay strong you know?" Mom cracked a smile. This was all that Pete needed to see. I told you mom smile was an astonishing, it would light up the whole North and South Camden when she smiled. It is filled with so much life. That was a smile I've always loved to see. Now, putting it on her face whenever I had the opportunity was the greatest. Pete smiled just as much as she did. Pete wasn't a pretty sight to look at but he wasn't the worst. Linda sat back and analyzed what was going on in this room. Could it be? She asked herself. No I'm tripping. Her conscience was saying. Mom and Pete were doing a tiny bit of flirting. This wasn't bad, in fact it was more than okay. Linda thought.

"Well if there's anything that I can do for you and especially my boy Rock don't hesitate to ask me for anything. " Pete informed snapping linda out her daze. "You sure?" Mom asked. "Yes! He's brought me so much luck in the shop I'm sure his spirit is still roaming somewhere in here. There aren't enough words to show my gratitude." Pete said. "He's not dead." Linda said joking. Pete laughed. "Yeah I know but your brother brought me and this place back to life, so I owe him that much." Mom smiled some more. "As a matter fact "you" are the one who showed him how to cook with that orange seasoning and that adobo stuff right?" Pete's smile was waiting for his confirmation form mom. She smile giving it up. "Yes it was me, he is a quick learner." Mom spoke highly of her son. "Well he brought that tradition in here and now all the customers go crazy with that orange shit." Thank you." Pete praised mom. "No thank you, you gave my son the opportunity to work for you and he really enjoyed the shop." Mom said. "No the pleasure was all mine." Give this to him. He didn't really work the whole week but I'm sure he'll need this more than I do at the moment. It's a gift from me to him." Pete peeled off almost $400 and handed it over to mom. I wasn't sure if he was trying to impress her but mom took it before he could change his mind. "Thank you I'll tell him you sent it." Mom was more than grateful. You're welcome. He should know my number, he can call collect or whatever the case may be. He has a job when he gets out too." Pete was generous but he was all truth behind his words. Mom and Linda appreciated that, they admired him for that. Any other person would have made up some bullshit and just spun the shit out of mom throwing Rock to the curve. It was bad enough he was thrown under the bus already. With that being said Linda and mom got there things together and headed out.

"Thank you so much Pete" Linda said in her sweet feminine voice. "The pleasure was mine." He winked at mom. Mom smiled and left showing off her voluptuous curves.

"Linda can I have a minute with you?" Jamal stopped them in there tracks. She already knew what he wanted or at least she thought she did. "Wassup?" Linda gave him a minute, mom just sat back and waited at the table close to the door and listened. "I don't know exactly what happened that night and I'll probably will never get a chance to find out. Shorty that work at the value-plus is the shorty your brother was fucking with. She came in here the other day talking like she knew a lot of shit. I can't really ask a lot of questions, but her baby dad defiantly had something to do with all that bullshit that went down." Jamal whispered everything that he knew over to Linda. News travels at the speed of light, you would be surprised. Linda stood there taking it all in. Her blood was getting hot. The hair's on the back of her neck stood up as she listened to all this. She remembered her brother's first words when the loud bang hit the back of his truck. "If anything happens, that's Jacqueline's baby dad's car behind me." The episode replayed in her mind like it was a movie. It wasn't a movie though. This was the real deal. "Did your brother tell you anything?" Now Jamal was probing. He was trying to find out who was with Rock at the time, but Linda was no dummy. No one was to be trusted. I don't care who the hell it was, not even the fucking pastor they could trust!

"No I don't know what happened, and to be honest I don't want to know but thank you for your help Jamal." Linda played possum. That was her best move if she wanted to succeed and help her brother get out of jail. Linda had to stay focused on what her main objective was. Which was to achieve triumph by any means, without holding back on anything or anyone. Whatever else was on Jalinda's agenda wouldn't really be known, until she would accumulate all of her facts. Leaving with a sub and wings they vanished with the wind.

The breeze on this chilly evening was enough to drive anyone crazy. I never could understand why the average human was never be content with anything. Whether it was the food we ate, the weather and even our so-called soul mates. We were never fucking happy with our circumstances.

"Can we go to the store down the block mom?" Linda asked mom. "Why not, we are already down here." Mom agreed with Linda's request. "What did the black guy wearing the apron want to talk to you about?" Mom asked with a concerned look on her face. "Oh nothing really he just wanted to talk to me about Manny. He wanted to know if I knew anything that went down that night. You know mom the nosy extra shit." Linda said with a smile on her face. "I take it you kept your lips sealed?" Mom wondered knowing better than to ask such a question. Linda gave mom a side eye. "You know it." Linda joked. "Good cause I don't trust him." Mom spoke not giving Jamal the slightest chance.

Entering the store Linda and mom purused the aisles. Take note, that Linda and Jacqueline have never spoken over the phone. They have never gotten the opportunity to meet one another. Now Linda was aware of this, but how was Linda going to use all of this valuable information to her advantage? No one knew but I was dying to find out how she would get interwined with her.

"Can I help you ladies?" Her name tag read Nakia. It was Nikki sexy ass coming up to mom and Linda. "No I'm just looking for now." Linda replied to Nikki without making eye contact. The way she said it was with a little spunk in her attitude. Nikki withdrew from asking anything else. After about 15 minutes of walking around, the one she came in to see had finally decided to show her face.

"What are you looking for baby? Anything in particular that I can help you search for on this side?" Mom asked. "No mom I'm not looking for anything just play along with me. My name is Jasmine okay." Linda whispered as she noticed Jacqueline approaching her. "What you talking about girl?" Mom was super lost. "Just follow my lead." "Hey!" Jacqueline's beautiful face appeared with all smiles. Speaking in an upbeat tone. "Heyyy." Linda gave her the same upbeat vibe. Mom was just focusing on the items that were in the aisle she was in. "I noticed you been looking hard for something. I'll be more than happy to help you find what you're looking for if we have it?" Jacqueline's name tag gave up her identity and it was sufficient enough for Linda to get to work on her next objective that she was formulating as she was going. "Well I'm looking for these nails that just came out." Linda was lying out her teeth. "I told you Jasmine they are not here." Mom came out of left field with her remark, but it was good. "You said nails?" Jacqueline asked. "Yeah, they come with a bunch of small stickers that you dip in water for a bit and they stick right on your nails." Linda kept her game tight. Jacqueline was thinking. "Let's check over here." She suggested. Mom looked at Linda. She winked at her. Mom was super lost but the cards were hidden at the moment. All three were looking for this items that Linda was describing but no one would find it. Maybe that was because for the first 15 minutes Linda was scanning the store for an item that wasn't going to be found. This was her angle. "How about these?" Jacqueline asked with a serious look on her face. She was really trying to help find, what she would never find in this store. Linda studied her. "No that's not it ma." Jacqueline stopped for second. Rock was the one, who called her that. Jacqueline fell deep in her thoughts. Linda knew her brother so she knew how to play her shit when playing the bitches, that Manny would fuck with. She snapped back to reality. "I'm sorry" Jacqueline went back to looking for the item. She pulled out some nail art, that wasn't either. "What's wrong?" Linda asked. Mom was still searching herself for this made up item. She even thought it could possibly be in the store. "Girl nothing just had a flashback about something. Well, I mean someone." Jacqueline was opening up. Tell me about it or him I have that happen to me all the time. "Jasmine what you think about this?" Mom picked up some nail polish. "I don't like the color." Linda said just barely looking at it. "Who's that?" Jacqueline asked in a low tone. "Oh her, she's my aunt." Linda replied. It took all of mom to keep her composure. Whatever Linda was doing and whatever game she was into mom wanted to flip. She walked all the way to the other end of the aisle removing herself from the nonsense. Linda and Rock beared no resemblance at all. The odds of Jacqueline figuring out that Linda and Rock were related were slim to none. "Of who, if you don't mind me asking?" Linda was nice and she was going to prove it. "This guy.".Jacqueline answered not giving up to much information. "I know It had to be a guy silly, but who is he. "Linda laughed getting real close to this girl that she barely even knew. Quick as fuck. "I'm not sure if I even know him to be honest." Jacqueline said putting her head down. "I'm just so confused with these men now in days. It's like the bad ones want to talk to you, lock you down or keep you to themselves. There the ones thats don't want to treat you the way you should be treated. Now, the good guys get taken away from you, when you actually think that it could be him to bring you the happiness you ever dreamed of." Jacqueline was speaking from the heart but hasn't said any names yet.That night there was two males and one chick. So either the one she killed was her man or the other one was. It was a lot she had to conclude and there was no way that she was going to get it all done in this brief conversation. This is where Linda had to get creative. Not knowing how but she was willing to, shoot for the stars. No not that Star. "Girl I'm going through something with my boo and I'm not sure what to do with him either." Linda tossed another lie in the air but it had some slight truth behind it. "Oh yea what's going on in your relationship?" Jacqueline probed flipping the script. "I think he's cheating on me." Jacqueline's eyes opened wide as hell. "Stop, don't say that Jasmine." Linda had her on the hook. Linda nodded with her chin tucked, she ran her hand over the items in the aisle. "Why do you think this?" Jacqueline asked. "He doesn't look at me the same, he is feeling a bit more distant. Before we used to cuddle all day and all night. We would talk about everything under the sun and moon. He has changed so much. Linda paused for a second. I'm not sure if it's me or if it's the sex or I don't know." Linda played as if it was frustrating. Jacqueline felt the pain. "Don't beat yourself up because this is just an assumption girl. Unless you're 100% sure. Right?" Jacqueline said. Trying to make her feel better. "I mean yes, you are most definitely right ma but still you know when a woman gets that feeling from deep down inside its never wrong for the most part right?" They were really engaging in a conversation that had absolutely no substance to it. It was all created by Jalinda. "That's not necessarily true Jasmine because sometimes our mind is so adamant on finding some truth to out thoughts, that our own mind will trick us into actually putting these things together that have nothing to do with the actual facts. Our thinking will attack our heart and soul and trick us so bad, that if we think it hard enough. Our mind will really make us think that something is going on when nothing is going on at all. I'll tell you this from experience. When I was with my baby dad I swore up and down that he was faithful. I didn't care what others told me about him nor did I care what or who saw what. If in my mind, I didn't see or catch him in the intimate act with the next chick. He wasn't cheating but when his side piece brought me a video of them sucking and fucking, all my beliefs about him being a faithful went out the fucking window in a blink of an eye. He was a dog, a woman beater and a deadbeat father. To make matters worst he is the piece of shit who is making my life a living hell. If I chose to stay with him, I wouldn't be able to see anyone nor would I have any friends. He thinks he still controls me without my consent to be controlled. Linda was wise, by the way little Ms. Jacqueline spoke was giving away major clues. She starting speaking in the present but if her man was dead she would be speaking in the past. So the dead one wasn't the one she killed. Little by little Jacqueline was spoon feeding Linda all that she needed to know voluntarily. Linda glanced over to see what mom was doing, their eyes met and Linda winked at her. Mom continue to do what she was doing. Which was absolutly nothing. "I'm so sorry to hear that ma, maybe you should put a PFA on your baby dads." Linda suggested. Knowing that wasn't going to happen. "Girl a PFA aint going to hold that crazy psychopath back from me and his child. That man will go to jail for a while, than come back out on some other shit. I'm better off ducking and dodging him." Jacqueline was paranoid as she spoke looking around. This tall slender man came from the back looking around. It was the value-plus store manager. "I got to get back to work." Jacqueline said feeling as if she wasn't working at all. "Okay I'm sorry. I don't want you to get caught up talking to me. Listen, this weekend you want to hang out for a bit? So you can clear your mind because I want to clear my mind up and I don't know anybody out here like that." Linda was pushing it. "Sure." Jacqueline replied. "When and where?" Jacqueline asked. Meet me here at the terminal on Saturday, next weekend we can go out from the terminal. Linda requested. I mean is that cool with you?" Linda asked. Next Saturday at the terminal? What time?" Jacqueline asked. "6 o'clock" Linda replied quickly. Linda went to walk away. "I'm sorry we didn't carry what you was looking for Ms." Jacqueline had to play it off to make it look good. Mom heard and headed to the door. "It's okay thank you for the help." Linda yelled walking out the door.

Mom was on her crazy ass daughters heels. "I can't wait for you explain what the fuck all that shit was about." Mom snapped not too happy with Linda's behavior. Mom rarely cursed for her to come out of her character like that was a complete shock. "I will mom lets get out of your first."

Back in the cell, my days felt so long. It was killing me slowly literally. I still didn't pinpointed who the fuck sent me that coward ass kite. I was a bit uneasy and part of me felt scared, but who could I, Manuel Ricardo a.k.a. Rock possibly have beef with? For starters I just got in here. I began to kick around a thoughts in my head, like who could possibly want to cause harm to me because for now I was somewhat safe. Unless, Slash was going to pull something. I laid on my bunk with my Skippy's on ready for action. He had already told me that we were cool, plus I went out to eat a few times and didn't see anything to out of the ordinary. Than again I wasn't up to speed to actually see what would be un ordinary. Whoever this was had the upper hand over me. I didn't know anything about this environment. He could maneuver a bit more swiftly than I could. The thoughts bombarded me, could this be over another femalen other than Jacqueline? I know, I done had my share of one night stands but it still wasn't adding up. Did Streets have that much pull that he had his boys already in here ready to put in work, for him on me? For some good odd reason the last solution seen the most plausible, one that I could actually believe. I've done tagged a few niggas back in the day, but they were small petty fights. Nothing worth holding a grudge over, but than again that all depened on the fuck was going to hold that grudge. At least they weren't to me, there was a complete silence in the cell. I couldn't understand how they would cram four criminals inside one sardine can. It got so bad people were sleeping on the floor on the mats. The color green on the doors were driving me insane. My mind was playing tricks on me the door opens once again my name is hollered over the PA system.

"Medical." "Great." Where the fuck's medical." was my remark." "Damn you about to see some bitches." Slash was more excited than I was, probably because I had no idea where I was about to go. "Bitches?" Nigga, nurses." I said. "Nah nigga the females are on the floor were medical is." Now he had my interest. "Oh yeah?" I looked in the mirror and put a bit of water on my much needed freshy. "You about to see them. Their fat ones, skinny ones, ugly ones, fly with all types of bitches up there." Slash was desperate like a mother fucka. I hope I wouldn't get like that, but then again as horny as I was I knew it was inevitable till I got like that. "Look just go up the steps on the side and you'll see the bubble. Give him your past and you're good. They'll handle the rest." Slash instructed "alright." I'm out." I said heading out the door "Oh wait you aint supposed to talk to them but do you, we criminals and we already in jail." Slash informed. He had a point. As I stepped out the cell the rowdiness on the block was at level 10. The shit talking could be heard much clearer out of the cell. I kind of enjoyed the quietness in the cell to be honest. "You aren't hard nigga!" Someone Barked. I kept my head up high walking. I grabbed my pass. "Go straight upstairs to the bubble." The Sgt. instructed. It wasn't the Serge I fault. I didn't have any words for him so I went on my business to go see some females. My celli was right as soon as I hit the bubble and gave them my pass I was told to "Sit over there on the bench next to the wall, they'll call you in a few." Now this Serge look too familiar. It was my rival. I did as he asked. The whistling from the woman was incredible, their block was cleaner than ours. Go figure.

"Hey sexy! One yelled there was no way that I could pinpoint who was yelling what. "I like my man tall and fly." Another one yelled. I tried to keep my composure but the feminine voices had me going insane. It felt so good to be complemented, even though I felt like shit. I couldn't hold back my smile. That's when they really went bananas.

"Oh my God look at that smiled! Boy how old is you?" The words my celli said to me bounced around my head. "Girl he scared, you wasting your time." Another one said to her girlfriend instigating and it worked. "18!" I barked. "18!?" A voice yelled from far ahead. I nodded. "Hell no, 18 you at least 24 she shot back. I shook my head. "You look good as hell!" I'll snatch that cradle anytime the female yelled. They all broke out in laughter. "Come over here so I can suck you dry baby." The woman behind the green door wasn't playing. If she could get her claws on me I would be in trouble. I laughed. "Don't listen to her you don't want that nasty shit." Another threw some hate on the other girl. It was getting loud I couldn't distinguish what was being said. "What's your name?" A voice to my left yelled. "Manuel!" I yell back. Boy stop talking to these horny ass bitches, They trying to get you caught up with the Serge, he an asshole." The other tried to get me to chill. I ain't worried about him. He know who I am." I said with my chess out. "Damn! You are crazy." Miss horny pants said from straight across. "Manuel what?" The same girl asked Manuel Ricardo!" I said proudly. It wasn't a smart move but hey I had a weakness and the woman were it. "Oh Shit! The one on the paper that killed that man at the mart." She said. I put my head down not answering. "Yea that's you isn't it?" They all waited for my reply. Let me get that paper ma." I barked confirming the accusation by asking for the article. "Now how the hell am I going to get this to you boy?" She asked a good question. Could just get up and walk over there and get it? I decided to but that wasn't a wise move at all. "Where you at?" I asked looking around very well lost. I noticed the paper being waived under the door. Damn, I said under my breath. I counted 12 cell from the stairs. What the fuck I thought. I went to stand up. "Sit down." Sgt. yelled through the P.a system. My palms were up, I surrendered. "Look, Ima slide down to the next cell until it get to the end so you can grab it on the way out." The girl shouted. I was impressed how the females move in here. I'm sure the Serge noticed it but he didn't give a fuck about that one. "What they call you out here?" The same woman asked "Rock!" I repeated. "Rock!" I yelled again. I would love to suck that rock hard dick. The woman in front of me wasn't playing she was horny as fuck as well. I had to admit she was bold. "Ayo Rock!" Yelled a soft voice. I didn't pay it no mind because I wanted to catch it again. "Ay Rock!" The voice spoke again. "What's up ma?" Why the hell are you up in here?" The sweet voice yelled over to me. Now my head was spinning even more. "Who is that?" I asked confused as fuck. "Yeah bitch shut the fuck up, he don't know your ass!" These bitches were gang waring with one another. "Mind your business, you stank ass bitch." The sweet voice went rogue in seconds "Rock!" She called out again. Who the hell is that? I couldn't pin-point the voice. "You really don't know who talking to you huh?" The voice asked. "No baby I'm sorry." I admitted. "Boy she nobody." No need to apol-ogize. "My admire was super jealous. "It's Kiki!" Was all that she said. I let it sink in for a second? "Oh shit! What's up ma?" I said a bit excited. It got quiet real quick all of a sudden. So we could talk a bit. "Why are you here?" Kiki asked. I wanted to see her sexy body but I couldn't. It wasn't the time and place. "It's a long story." I said in a stressed out voice. "I know, I read the paper but I didn't think it was you. Last time I talk to you, you was fin-ishing up school remember?" Kiki asked. "Yeah you was with your friends Jigz and Banga." I remember. Yall were all fucked up. "Yeah that night the shootout happen." Kiki was talking too much now. "Yeah but enough about that, when are you getting out?" I asked her. "I don't know yet." I just came in two weeks ago. I'm waiting on Jigz and Banga to get me out." She said. "All right, you'll get to go home soon." I said. "Listen, Ima call home tonight or tomorrow and I'll let them know you up in here so they can look out. You know them crazy ass niggas love your ass. I never knew why but they fuck with you heavy Rock." Her words made me feel good. "You do that just tell them to keep an eye on mom's house that's all I want." I said. Having an extra set of eyes on mom and Linda couldn't hurt. "I will Rock, stay safe and don't trust no one of the slimy ass niggas in here because they not your friends." Kiki was right. "You too baby girl."

"Manuel." The nurse yelled out the glass door over at me. I stood right up and followed her into a small confined room. The woman in front of me were much older than I was, she was wearing pink scrubs with baby blue sneakers. They look like Nikes. "How are you feeling?" She asked without even looking back at me. "I'm feeling okay." I found that question a bit off. Why wouldn't I be feeling okay? I thought to myself. "That's good" at the far end of the room on the right there were some more cells that were just as confined as the others. "Have a seat." The lady instructed to me. She had a chart in her hand, I looked at her butt and she almost caught me looking. She had a cinnamon complexion with just a few grays but the way her skin look, she took good care of herself. She had very few wrinkles. She smelled good too. The smell of tropical blueberry perfume had a hypnotizing effect on me. I thought back at what I said about Slash about the ladies. It was too late. I was already worse off than he was. I mean don't get me wrong. I have standards when it came to women, but it's a whole different ballgame when you can't pick and choose the apples on the apple tree. You are given a selection but out of that selection a majority are a bit shot.

"It looks to me that you may have..." The words took forever to come out her mouth. I remembered that AIDS and HIV test that I had taken. Could this be what all this was about?" Have I contracted a sexually transmitted disease? Now fucking what? I waited for her to finish this shit couldn't get any worst. "Low iron." The nurse said. "Also your blood pressure is a bit high. I need to take your blood pressure again to make sure the results are correct." I let out a deep breath. "Nervous?" The nurse asked. "Was I?" I thought it was something worse than that." I admitted. She finally looked at me in my eyes. "Like what?" She stared. I couldn't keep it locked on. I steered my vision to my feet and hers. "A disease or something bad." I spoke very ignorantly of what I was saying. She opened my file again.

The screaming and yelling could be heard from the cells in the medical unit. "Excuse me?" She ran towards the cell, along with a few other nurses. The had to be the nutjobs on medical unit or the ones who acted like they were crazy. I just sat there patiently. No one was watching over me at the moment. I looked over to my right I saw gauzes and tape, to my left Band-Aids and more gauzes. I decided to take a roll of tape. I put it on my waist band quickly. I remembered in our cell, the only type of sticking tape Slashed uses was the tape of the deodorants and lotions. It was crap it wouldn't stick and it looked trashy. With this, it could possibly hold. I moved it over to my private area just in case this lady wanted to get the touchy feeling. I noticed a female walk by. Amanda I said to myself. I hope she would walk by again and on cue she did. "Pisssttt." I hissed like a poisonous snake. She stopped and glanced. She smiled but kept it moving. I didn't press the issue. I didn't want her getting caught up on some bullshit fucking with me. The other nurse was back. "I'm sorry about that honey, it gets crazy in here with the patients." She admitted "Can I asked you something?" I asked. "Sure." "What is your name?" She smiled. My name is Peggy but everyone in here calls me Ms. Peg not piggy but Peg." She joked. She had a few missing teeth but her smile was sincere. I smile back. "Let me see your arm." I held up my left arm and she did her thing. "Try to relax Manuel." She informed me. The monitor was in my mouth all over again. I sat there letting my mind drift away. I saw Amanda walk by again, She was a thick white girl, I would love to handle that one day. "It looks good to me." Ms. Peg said. A few more tests and you can go on your way. "Take your time I'm in no rush to go back into a small cell." I stated with a smile. She understood my pain. "No privacy?" She stated more like a questioning. "Nope not at all." I replied. "Once you get out here you have to stay out. This isn't a place to spend the rest of your life hun. Ms. Peg had to be a grandma, her words fell so motherly. I took it that she didn't know why I was here and I wasn't going to tell her either. "Yes I hope so too." She checked my pulse with her fingers on my wrist. I was so glad I moved that dumb ass tape. I would've felt so embarrassed if I would've gotten caught with that shit. "The doctor will be in to tell you about your iron and pressure." Ms. Peg left but Amanda came right in. "Hey you." She smiled. "Wassup beautiful." She blushed. "You're so sweet." Amanda said. "Listen I think you screwed up my blood pressure when you took it because they saying that it's crazy high and Ima die." I joked my ass off.

Her jaw dropped. "How you gonna say that. I know how to do my job, You was just so excited to see me, that's why your blood pressure was high, You couldn't handle it." She joked back and I smiled. I gota go. I'll see you around." She winked and she swished her ass all the way out of sight. She was absolutely right even now with her being in my presence I wanted her to check my pulse, but on a much deeper level. The doctor came in wearing a white overcoat, he was tall and of course a white doctor he had blonde hair that spiked up. "Mr. Ricardo." His pearly whites showed. They looked as if he had just got them installed in his mouth. His skin was smooth, he had to be over 30. He was a wealthy mother fucka. At least that's what I assume. I could be wrong but for some reason I highly doubted that. I'm going to put you on iron pills for your low iron, Do you get cold a lot or most of the time?" I nodded my head because he was on the money. I stayed cold. "As far as your blood pressure you should be okay because it's normal at the moment. Any questions?" He asked me.Getting ready to get rid of me. Since I couldn't get my answers from Ms. Peg, I decided to ask him. "Dr..?" ... "Yes?" he anwered. I wanted to know when my STD and AIDS results would be in." I asked. "Your results should be here within the next week or two" anything else." He asked. "No." I replied alrighty then take care. I'll see you if anything." The doctor's final words came and went and he disappeared. Amanda came back in. "Are you okay?" This girl was going to get herself jammed up. Was all I thought? "I'm okay why Wassup?" "How are you?" I asked her. "Tired." She answered. "Want a massage." I was bugging. She shook her head. "You are crazy." and yes. She flirted back. "But you can't because you're in here." "That was a low blow." I said to her. "Go get your pass and be safe."Take this." She put a pill on the counter I snatched it up. "What is it?" I asked in a whisper. "a perk." I was out and the pill was already traveling down my throat as soon as she told me what it was. There were two other niggas on the bench, it was a white man and a black guy. They both looked up at me. I didn't say anything but I did give them a head nod acknowledging them. The girls were hollering at them too. I wasn't sure what was being said, but all I do know is that when they noticed me they went crazy again. "Ayo Rock!" Kiki voice didn't go unnoticed. "Wassup ma?" Sign up for the Christian church I'll see you there okay." She yelled. "Keep your head up." I headed towards the bubble. Rock I want that dick in my mouth?" Yelled the hornball, she was still bugging. I kept it moving. I saw the newspaper but I didn't have to go towards it because the girl on the end cell somehow managed to shoot it to the steps literally. She made good progress. "Must be real popular." The Sargent said. I didn't say shit, got my pass and headed straight down the steps only to see the carrier post about two steps from the top. I kicked it to the bottom and tucked it as soon as I had the chance.

—

"Can you tell me what in God's name were you doing with that girl?" Kicking off their shoes Mom headed towards the kitchen. Linda didn't say a word on the bus the whole way home. She had to dissect every word and replay every conversation until she was happy with what she had come up with. You want some coffee or hot chocolate?" Mom asked Linda. "Hot chocolate." Linda replied in Spanish. Linda didn't know much Spanish but she knew enough to hold a brief conversation with anyone thanks to her brother. Mom took out some expososa crackers and spread some cheese whiz on them to enjoy with her hot cocoa. You're not going to eat any of this?" Linda referred to the food she had gotten from the shop. "That's too heavy for my stomach right now baby." Mom wasn't about to eat that. "We can eat it later if you want." Linda asked not wanting to eat alone. "Yes, later sounds good." Mom replied. Linda switched the convo. "Mom you saw that girl that I was talking to in a deep conversation with at the store?" Linda was going to tell mom what was going on. "Yes you were engaged in a deep conversation with that girl." Mom acknowledged. "What I don't understand is why you had to lie about your name but most of all lie about me." Mom was suspect about Linda's actions but all that would be put to rest once she understood why Linda did what she did. "Mom I didn't mean for you to feel unwanted but I couldn't let this girl know who you truly were." Mom had this confused look on her face. "What, wait but why? This child done lost her mind". Mom said speaking about Linda. Linda laughed. "No mom, "Are you sure baby? I know a good psychologist." Mom joked pouring chocolate into the big mugs. Linda love how mom made her hot chocolate. Manuel was also a big fan of mom's hot cocoa. It brought back memories of when they would drink it on the cold days of winter and on Christmas. Linda and mom both shared some smiles. Mom wanted to get to the end of all this madness that had transpired earlier today. Eating the crackers Linda began slowly let her mind put together her words carefully.

She didn't want to alert mom of why she needed all this valuable information for. Linda was no real threat to society or was she? She went on after swallowing her chocolate with the marshmallows. "Mom that girl is one of Mannys girlfriends." Linda said mom face showed no emotion. "No he was dating that girl Felicia wasn't he?" Mom asked. "Yes he was but we both know our Manny, he's never happy with just one." Linda informed mom. So what does that mean?" Mom asked. Linda was getting frustrated with all this as she thought of the worst. She took a deep breath to calm her frustration down a bit. Before Manny got into his altercation with Jacquelines baby dad he told me, that the car that crashed into the truck. It belonged her baby dad's car that night" Linda let it all sink in. Mom's eyes opened up as soon as the pieces were locked in. "So you mean to tell me that little bitch got you two set up!" Mom didn't play when it came to us. Her face showed fury. "Mom I didn't say that." Linda spoke. "Yeah but it sounds like it." Mom rebutted. Linda sipped her cocoa, She stared at mom waiting for her to calm down a bit. "I wish you would've told me this before we walked into the store. I would've broken that bitch's pretty little face!" Mom wasn't showing no type of calming down now. "That's exactly why I didn't say shit about her. I had to do my homework because if you would of smashed her face in then what?" Linda said "What do you mean then what?" Next time I see her, I'll do it again." Mom was all hyped now. "Exactly this is... My brother, your son.... I have to handle this carefully." Linda answered her own question to mom in a firm tone. So Mom could feel her words. Eventually , mom calm down once she saw the point Linda was trying to prove. "So what did your little conversation with little miss too cute get you?" Mom asked sarcastically. "Nothing important but I got a date with her next week." Linda admitted to mom. She had no clue what Linda was up to but mom's devilish smile was from ear to ear. "What are you going to do to her?" Mom asked wanting to hear something horrific? This scared Linda a bit. "Are you okay?" Linda asked. "Yes, I'm fine but I want someone to pay for what is going on with my son." Mom was dead serious but there was no way mom would actually think Linda was going to hurt anyone. "Remember?" Linda reminded mom. For a moment Mom had to be possessed by something. Mom attitude would change immediately as the words exited Linda's mouth. "Let me handle this mom. I'm not gonna do anything stupid but I want to get this girl to love me as a friend. I need her to confide in me and tell me all her deepest darkest secrets." Linda spoke calmly. No one knew what Linda was visualizing but for the most part befriending this girl wouldn't be an easy task. At least that's what anyone would think. "Whatever you do let me know what I can do to help you." And be careful Linda. "Mom spoke heading to the kitchen to light up a cigarette. Linda just shook her head. Mom help Linda? Do what? She could barely breathe but I'm sure mom had a lot of animosity pinned up inside. What could mom possibly help with. Linda decided to go to her room and gather her thoughts some more. "I'll be upstairs mom." Okay baby I'll see you and a bit...

—

"I'm a criminal!" Rock barked to himself. "I can't believe all these extra lies these people are putting in the paper." "That's not even how it went down!" Rock was beyond pissed and Slash got right out of his way. He didn't bother to say anything until he knew that Rock wasn't fired up. Rock was facing a life sentence if convicted, any person could tell you this. If not he will go home or get a lesser sentence. "Don't let that paper get you all bent out of shape, these mother fuckers just lie about anything and everything they can think of to make that dollar." Slash looked at Rock and saw how fucked up he looked, not about the paper but he was high and he was enjoying it.

"A yo? You all right?" Slash asked. "Man I'm high as hell." Rock said. "Off of what nigga we don't get meds until later?" Slash questioned "My shorty up stairs blessed me with something." Rock said. He wasn't thinking rationally at all talking way too much. He was exposing his hand and he was too high to even notice it. "Damn nigga let me get some because you look like you smoked a pound some sour." Slash boasted. "She only gave one but I'll hook you up when my other meds come. I'm not gonna need all that." Rock was sitting on the toilet he would snap out of it then go back into a daze. He tossed the paper on the desk. "Let me read it." Slash took it and read the article. "How you get this paper?" Slash asked. This nigga had a lot of questions to? Shorty upstairs." Rock answer slowly but relaxed. "Damn you just a fucking celebrity up in here already huh?" Slash joked. Rock smiled trying to stay up and watch Slash. If he really wanted to be grimy, he could very well take advantage of Rock and take his face off but only If he had the balls. That wasn't going to happen at that moment. "Wow you did kill the shit out of that nigga Rock." Slash opinionated looking at the article.

"First shop, then murder"

On Friday at midnight, the Pennsauken police department was called about a fight that was taken place. Pennsauken Mart is known for his convenience to his customers and all their bargain deals. Every now and then you get a call to the local police department if things got out of hand with an unsatisfied customer, but it's rare when the police department is call for a fight that ended in a murder." These were the words of the Pennsauken police commissioner.

Police gave this account: at approximately 10 past midnight a fight had broken out among two individuals in which one was murdered with a fierce stab to his jugular. The suspect was apprehended at the scene within minutes of the crime. The ambulance arrived but it was useless the deceased did not have a pulse upon the arrival of the paramedics. They did treat the suspect that looked as if he was being brutally beat by the deceased. It may look as if the suspect was acting out of self-defense but it's unclear at the moment and is under investigation. A weapon was found at the scene that may also belong to the suspect in custody who is being held at the Camden County jail. Authorities have identified the suspect by the name of Manuel Ricardo, he's a Camden residents whose address is unknown at the moment. An autopsy will be conducted on the deceased within the next couple of days. No identification on the deceased has yet to be confirmed, some marijuana was found on his possession with only two witnesses that say they drove by and called the police for help. They say they have been released without further incident near the exit. This case is still being investigated by the Camden County Police Department and the Pennsauken police department. They are encouraging all and any witnesses who may have seen anything out of the ordinary that night to please come forwardn and do what's right. Please call the local tipline department and notify the Chief of any valuable information you may have concerning this case.

"Ayo." Slash called up to me, I was laying back in my bunk on cloud one hundred. Fuck a cloud nine, It wasn't as high as I was. "Wassup?" I answered. Hey they say they got witnesses in this article." Slash tried to tell me. I wasn't in the right state of mind to talk about the case. So I just "uuuhhummm" and yada yada yada. My meds came to me as they did every day on the floor on the hour, three times a day. I got up and slip them under my tongue as the nurse and CO watch me as I swallowed. They thought I did. Once they were out of sight I headed straight to the cell and spit them on the tissue so the tissue to soak up all the saliva. I broke them all in half. "Take them Slash" I instructed him. He jumped right up. "Which ones?" I slid his portion to the side and stashed the other in a tissue in my sock. "All of that." Slash was surprised he couldn't believe of the amount of pills that I had just gave him to swallow. "You want to feel nice right?" I said a bit irritated. "You said you wanted to feel nice about an hour ago didn't you? "If you don't I would of never broken them down then nigga." I kind of fell as if I was forcing him to take the pills now. "Say no more if I die is on you." Slash joked "It's on you for taking them." I joked back. We stood up till like 2 AM playing chess and talking about a bunch of nothing. I couldn't wait to head up to the seventh floor so I could find out who was running their gums about me. All the shit was bouncing around in my head, this shit wasn't going to stop until I got to the source. I was feeling abandoned and I was ready to let my hands go and see how far they would take me. I know I'm talking nonsense and I know I'm not in the right state of mind but this place was really starting to fuck with me. My mind is distracted and no one is here to help me regain my consciousness of it.

Eventually we both passed out. My Skippies never left my feet, it was a fucked up feeling but I wasn't as comfortable enough as I wanted to be. I was about to change this feeling. I wasn't a hundred percent sure how would I accomplished this but I knew one thing for sure. If I was going to live behind these walls for the rest of my life there is no way possible that me Manuel Ricardo was going to be living in fear, let alone be receiving threats in this hellhole from anyone. Win, lose or draw my name would either amplify or signify something then what is been perceived to be or nothing at all point blank.

Chapter 12

"My turf"

"Chow time! Chow time!" The P.a screamed for early breakfast. The routine was already set like an internal clock. I was up before the P.a system had a chance to bark. The meds could be a lot better, but hey I wasn't complaining? The tension could be felt in the chow hall this morning. No one never knew when something was about to go down. It was my turn to grab a tray, it was oatmeal and toast with milk. My left hand held the tray and my right was balled up ready for anything. If I felt anything close to a threat, it wasnt gona be an easy fight. The thought of all this was going to be my life, knowing there was no easy way out of this. Walking to the nearest available seat would've been great but all hell broke loose.

"PUSSY!, WHAT YOU THINK THIS SHIT IS A GAME?! The white guy was getting out on the Spanish looking guy. "You take something from me and say you gonna pay it back. You pay that shit or I want my shit back or my money bitch!" The white guy was punching this nigga all in his face something serious tellling him about himself. I counted 11 blows. The papi boy had no chance.. He couldn't do shit because he was stuck sitting on the stool at the table. His legs were in a straddled position. I took notice of how fucked he was due to his positioning. I took heed of all of it, it wasn't a great idea to sit the way he was sitting. Just when I thought it was all over, that's when a small plastic sharp object pierced the Spanish boy skin. His left arm tried to protect his face. That didn't work at all, the homemade shank pierce his arm like nothing.

"Ima pay ju I told ju, don't kill me pleaasee!" Papi boy tried to plea for his life in his broken accent. The lender didn't want to hear these word. It was a little too late and his patience had already ran out. What he wanted to hear was that his money was there already. "Fuck you! I gave you plenty of chances you fucking spic!" Tackled by the CO's just before he could let off another poke. They swarmed him, everyone was forced to head back to their cells with empty bellies. Fortunately for me I was stuffing my face as all this shit was taken place. It all happened so fast but my belly was more import- ant, than to watch two niggas kill each other. After my meds was given to me. I was zoning out as usual.

What took place in the dining hall replayed over and over in my mind. I kind of felt bad for the Spanish guy but it wasn't my problem. He should've paid his debt to society I guess. "Ayo Rock, you saw that shank that mother fucker had in his hand? "Slash asked. "Hell yeah, it was small but it worked like a charm. That was a piece of a chair's leg." Slash informed me. "A chair's

leg?" I asked. Not fully understanding what he actually ment. "Yea you see those chairs over there?" He pointed towards the block where the bubble was at. I noticed the plastic chair he was showing me. "You get one of them legs and you sharpen it up." Slash said. I was still not sure how he was to sharpen the leg up but whatever. I let him keep talking. "The floor is cement and this is a toothbrush. Look, like this Ima show you this just in case you ever want to get creative." The toothbrush was a security toothbrush there was no way I could see him make a weapon out of it. He showed me anyway. I watched him attentively, he dropped a bit of water close to the edge of the toilet and began to go up and down rubbing one end of the toothbrush on the corner. When it looked as if the water was all used up he did it again. He entertained himself for a while. I kept my lazy eyes on him just in case he got any ideas. I was high yes, but don't get me in a situation and try to take advantage of me. Maybe he could of gotten away with it the first few days, when they had me in here almost oblivious to my sur- roundings. I was on my meds but by now these meds were nowhere near hitting me as hard as before. I was still far from sober but conscious enough to react if needed. Was I a functioning addict? Plus, this tiny as shank that Slash was put together could definitely do something if used properly. He had to really put in work to do some serious bodily harm. It was only about 2 inches and from what it looked like now, it was down to one. He eventually tossed it up at me. I examined it, it was pretty sharp to pierce someone's skin, but like I said way too small.

"Now imagine if it was longer?" Slash said taking my thought right from me. You can hurt someone right?" Slash asked. "You mother fucking right." I replied. I played with the present and just imagined how it would feel to poke someone in the eye with this tiny shit. I would laugh if someone would pull something like ths if I were to get in a fight. You would get to pull it out and that alone would have me so pissed. I tossed it back to Slash. "You want it?" Slash asked. I laughed. "Nah I'm cool I can't do shit with that.That will probably get in more trouble carrying that and actually using it." I Joked. Slash laugh. "Word." He agreed. I still kept my eyes on him. He flushed the weapon, I watched it twirl till it eventually it was gone.

—

Holding Felicia in one arm and a baby in the other we were sitting at a park "Why are you so evil?" Felicia asked me. I didn't reply I held my daughter in my arms. She was beautiful, she played with my nose. She was barely one but she loved me. Felicia's daughter Eliza ran around playing with the other kids. "Look at me daddy, look at me!" Elisa yelled over to me. I watch her do flips in the grass. I smiled. "Go baby do it again." Felicia watched me watch her. "So tell me Rock, why are you a killer?" I didn't or couldn't find the answer to her question. I wasn't a killer and she knew this I thought she did. I fell a tight grip on my nose that cut off my oxygen from my nostrils, the grip was hella tight. It was my daughter, she clamped on and wouldn't let it go. "Yes daddy you kill people?" She spoke. Her tiny lips mouthed off , the exact words to what her mother was asking. I couldn't get her little hands off my nose. My hands were full and somehow I couldn't move them. "Felicia." I called to her. "Good girl baby." She encouraged our baby to hold on harder. There was no way this baby could cause all this pain. There was some dripping down my nose, it was my own blood and the blood made its way to my mouth. "Baby let go." I begged in pain. "Please." "No Daddy." The baby said." I couldn't believe what I was hearing, let alone feeling. The ripping of my skin felt as if I was being tortured. "Throw it to me." Eliza cheered on her sister. "Ouccchhhh!" Why was this happening to me?

"Rock! Rock!" Slash was shoving me, to wake me up. I jumped up swinging. "Get off of me!" I Barked. "Yo it's me, your bugging it's a dream!" Slash tried to get me to relax. I felt my nose. "Oh shit!" What the fuck yo!" I said catching my breath. "You okay Rock?" Slash asked me. "It's only a dream." He informed me. "A crazy one at that." I replied. I never in my life had any dreams remotely close to anything like this one. "He gonna let us out to go to the gym you coming?" Slash asked me. "Yeah why not?" I replied. "Ight, they going to let us out soon. Get up." I hopped down a little woozy, the meds wore off a little. "What was you dreaming about?" Slash asked. I tried to explain but it was hard to remember. I did remember was my nose being ripped off cold-blooded." I stated. "damn! That shit sounds like a hurt." Slash joked.

—

In the gym on the seventh floor, they had a court amongst a few other things to get into. The mass of men were all around, in their cliques Spanish with Spanish white the white and your Blacks were with their own kind. This shit always seemed to occur wherever you would go or end up.

The people themselves always felt the need to segregate themselves from all others who aren't of the same color or speak the same language. We tended to continue to live the segregated life. Why? There were a couple chess games going on. A basketball game was being picked up. I took notice and scanned the area. It's been a minute since I gambled and I wanted to play. I walked over to the people who were picking up teams. I just stood there waiting to see who did what or who said what. I didn't care who I played with, all I wanted was to free my mind from all of this. I noticed a familiar face, I stared for a hot minute to make sure it was him, it was. It was leak I was about to head over.

"Yo! My man." I looked over then looked behind me to make sure he was talking to me. "Yeah you ." The voice spoke to me "Wassup?" I replied. "You play?" He asked. This nigga had a slick back, with two teardrops on each of his eyes. He was around 5'9 "Yeah I play a little." I replied. "Come on you with us." I looked at the team, it exactly what I expected four short stocky Latinos and I was the fifth. Our opponents were all big black mother fuckers. "You ready?" He asked. I took a deep breath and it was go time. "Game go to 21. The biggest one out of all of them spoke up. "Call your own fouls." He ended slinging the Rock straight at my chest almost sending it through. "Checkup." Everyone ran around trying to get open as I look for a pass. We had two tall men who were myself and the guy who picked me all the other three were no bigger than 5'6". I never could understand why all the Spanish guys were so short. I had to be one lucky mother fucker. I saw the opening but it was intercepted before it even left my hands. I had to adjust, big man "Black" took the shot. "Swish" two points. I was in the paint, I play ball and I knew how to be center. I'm told that's where I normally can do the most. Passed it down low to the light-skinned man on my team with a regular, his waves spinning something serious. The elbow to the chest through me back caving my chest in. This nigga almost made my heart skip two beats. He was super strong. I thought to myself. There was no way I could guard this monster. They ran the same play twice.

"Come on papi guard him!" My teammates were getting agitated on how all their points were on me, down bottom. This mother fucker was big, he had upper body strength that had to be unhuman. Elbow to the jaw that woke me up out of my daze. I was getting fucked up. Now we had spectators with "oohing and ahhhing!" "You a little nigga, my opponent was given them a show. They were up easy. We still has zero. I gain my consciousness and remembered what my coach used to say. Foundation is key. I got real low on him. So he had to use his legs. Same play I read coming in. "Stolen" right up. It didn't go in, he fouled the shit out of me again. "Call it papi, call that shit." I shrugged it off. I was not gonna call shit. We had the ball. I was impressed on how my team handled the ball, banking two 2 pointers and a layup. They weren't too big but the papi's were short and fast as fuck. I tried to hold the bottom down. We were boxing each other out which look like an elbow punching match. I got the ball spun off of him and in it went. "You won't do that should again bitch!" I didn't like that remark at all. I knew it was his way to get at me on a mental note and it did bother me a bit. I was going to show him on the court who was a bitch. I ran around making him chase me, not full speed. I showed no sign of stopping. The score was 10 - 8 they were up. "Come on Rock!" Yelled someone. I paid it no mind. My head was in the game. "Get the steal!" I yelled to the shortest one on my team. He had long hair, it was in a straight braid down his back. He went for the layup with two of us open and the ball went sailing to the other side of the court. "Step your game up! Barked the charcoal mother fucker. He looked as if he had on a ski mask. He didn't have a shirt on, this brother was cut the fuck up though. "Check Rock!" The exchanging of the blows went from both ends. Noone called anything. I thought this shit was ludicrous but hey we were all men. "14-8" they were climbing and not looking back. They easily jump to 18 in seconds. I was out of breath, and from the looks of it so were my teammates.

"/Oye vamos!/"/let's go/yelled a bald Latino with tattoos on his arms. He tried to fuel us up. I noticed Leak on the sideline I focus on the game. I would talk to him after the fact. These Spanish mother fuckas aint fucking with us." Stated the man with the cornrows. I didn't like that comment at all. These niggaz weren't even that nice. I played with some real ballers. I hustled stealing the ball and taking it straight up. "Ooooo!" The spectators were hyping up the game. There was no need, we were down by a few. My team kept playing hard though, we were not given up. It began to heat up on the far left side of the court at the 2 point line "fuck you!" yelled the papi with slick back. "Fuck you pussy!" Yelled the man covering him. A contact sport was always better off played with a bit of contact. Why not utilize all your body muscles. These two were shoving and pushing, balling reckless with one another.

"Chill!" I stepped in. "Play the game!" I spoke up trying to finish the game. "Stick my man I got yours." I informed my teammate thinking he wasn't going to take my advice, he prove me wrong. A game is better settled on the court as it started than off the court. There wasn't no need to ruin the game because you can't control your fucking temper because than we would really lose. "What you going to do?" The man I settled for tried to use the psychological bullshit on me. He used all his force backing into me hard getting closer to the rim. I leaned and he pushed back really hard. The ball was hitting the ground hard. I sidestepped quick after I leaned forward hard as fuck. He must've thought my body would be right on him because he threw his body back hard stumbling over his own brutness. "Ooopppps!" I snatched the ball right up. The crowd went crazy, just what I needed. My team was bawling out laughing we were still down but only by three now. Homeboy got up with vengeance I had to keep my eyes peeled on him. Double team was all over me, I saw my open man. I hit him with the pass, up and it was off. I was literally gasping for air. "Time." I called. I needed air. "Ain't no time." Barked the first man I was sticking. "Fuck outa here, times nigga!" This nigga had me fucked up. "Come on guy's quick huddle." This was the only few seconds that I had to put some faith into my team. "Look/yo no conosco a ninguno Te ustedes pero yo se que yo quiero a ganar." ponle prescion y tu va ver que vamos a ganar./" I spoke to them in the language that we could understand better. /I don't non any of you but I know I want to win.Put pressure on them and watch how we win this/. The look on their faces was shocked. They didn't expect it to come out the way it did. The game intensified and the fouls grew harder with every play. We were getting beat the fuck up down there. The blows came and went both ways. They were a lot bigger but an elbow hurts in the right spot no matter how big or small you are. Every one of us had looked as if a water hose had hit us due to the amount of sweat being let out our bodies.

Finally, up by one with the score 19-18 our way. "That's right let's finish this shit!" I yelled at the top of my lungs grabbing the rebound. Two swift passes finished off with a swift shot, not even hitting the rim. Now we were up

20-19. I hustled with the layup but it didn't sink. I saw my team losing faith again. It was too early to lack confidence in ourselves this game wasn't over. "It's not fucking over let's play!" I yelled. "/Vamo que no se cavao!/" I yelled over to my teammates and his buddies, but it was over. Cornrows blasted a 2 pointer ending the game. He called out his shot. The rainbow along with the trajectory view, anyone that had a vision could have seen that ball heading straight into the hoop. "Fuck it!" Yelled another. "This is our court." They had all the right to talk all the shit they wanted. They won the game. We shook hands not really wanted to. This was how every good game ended. The blows were felt, but the respect wasn't given. "Good game yo.What's your name?" Cornrows asked. "Rock!" I replied proud of my name. "I'm Shakes." He informed stretching his hand. I gave him pound. I walked around and got to know a few more people. For some it was just a fist pound and I kept it moving. It was all good but wasn't kissing no one ass. They seen the effort I put in playing a game so they decided to give me a little respect. "Good game pop." Slick back said coming over with three of his boys. "Yea good game" I agreed. "We gonna play again some other time." Coco said. "/Tabien./ /ok/" I replied. I noticed Leak approaching, I walked mettting him halfway.

"Man! You a baller for real." Leak joked. "Na, not really but I can try." I joked. "No I seen you doing your thing out there." Leak said. "Not at all I'm a little rusty." I replied. "No you're teammates are rusty you know what the fuck you doing even if you may be rusty." I dapped him up for the compliment. "What's good leak, You good over there?" I asked not even knowing where he was living. "Man I'm always good in this mother fucker. How about you?" Leak asked. "Man this is pretty rough, Im not gonna lie." I admitted. "It gets better once you learn how to keep your mind busy and stay occupied. Your body will adjust and adapt to any drastic change in your environment, no matter where you find yourself and I mean that." Leak spoke from experience. "I hope so." I replied. "Who you shacked up with?" Leak interjected. I didn't know what he meant by that. "Shacked up?" I asked him sounding dumb. "Yea, who you living with?" He asked again. "Oh" with some nigga." I didn't sound too convincing. "Just one?" Leak asked. "Yea for now." I said. "Wassup with him? he cool?" Leak wanted to know whats up."I don't even know leak." I spoke with all honesty. I had no one in this place. Leak was the only half decent man I could talk to and be straight up with. Especially with not knowing the ropes or who was who. "Who is he? He out here?"Leak asked. " I scanned the yard until I spotted Slash. He was with his crew rapping and spitting.

"He over there with his crew dropping a demo." I joked. Leak look back at the crew and burst into laughter. "Which one?" He asked holding his stomach still laughing. "The one with his hand on his boys shoulder." Leak stared for a while, trying to get a good look at Slash. "What they call him?" Leak asked. "Slash" I informed leak. Maybe he could dig something up on this nigga because as far me I couldn't do much. I didn't know too many heads up in here. "Slash" leak repeated softly to himself. "Ayo everyone talking about that shit that happened over on your end. No one knows it was you, well in pretty sure now they know. You a wild mother fucker. I'm surprised that piece of shit didn't bag you that day." Leak said. "He got me good but we both got some good blows in. I think if I would have had more room. I would've definitely boxed him out." I tooted my own horn.

I was cut off by the CO.Yard was over. I couldn't stand this shit.We had to part ways. "If you need anything don't be afraid ask "Rock." Leak informed me. "Vice versa leak, if I got you got it." I informed him. "Ima try to get you moved over to my side, if not I'll shoot over there with you because we going to be here for a minute." Leak said. "Make it happen its what eva." It was time to head back it felt good to have a decent conversation with someone. I didn't know leak but then again I didn't know anyone in this place except the nigga that wanted to stop my pulse in here, but I could only hope that when the time came I would be ready. The day went by and my meds were already dissolving in my system. I was back to floating on the moon again. I wondered if Leak could actually make that move happen. Until then I had to be content with my current situation.

"Yo Rock." Slash called up to me. "Wassup?" I replied. I asked my peoples about that kite they sent to the cell, and they told me if you had beef it was my beef too. Since we up in here together." Slash informed me. "Why would you tell your peoples? It was supposed to be my business?" I asked a bit annoyed. "Look Rock I live here too. I may look as if I'm not thinking about it, but this is our cell. If some nigga decide to come up in here on some gangsta shit I'm riding. Before you got here, I was in this cell all by myself. So for anyone to think that they can barge up in here and do what they want, it's not going down like that. I'm riding with you push comes to shove." Slash spoke keeping it real. "I respect that and I'm glad you are willing to ride out but for the future what goes on in our cell is between us. Is that cool with you?" I asked him. "Aright you got my word." Slash said. We left the issue untouched and played a few games of chess. I wasn't the best but I played my best every time. I was getting better every time I played.

Three envelope slid under the door, I just looked at them. Slash jumped up. "Its mail." He advised siphoning through them, than handed them over. "They're all for you." He said a bit sadden I wondered when was the last time he had gotten mail. My heart raced as I looked at the envelopes. I never cared or even looked in the mailbox at home, but this feeling I was feeling felt so good. Maybe I haven't been forgotten. Just the thought that someone took a moment to write a few words to me made me feel wanted. I read my home address twice, the next one was Felicia's. I wonder what they had to say. I decided to go with mom's first. I knocked over my King forfeited this game. Slash got the point.

Hey son,

I never thought I'll be writing to you in prison, but here I go. I miss you so much, just putting these words together is getting me all worked up. I'm sorry! As I write, I'm smoking a cigarette. It seems it's the only thing that quenches my thirst. I stress these day even more with you gone. Please don't hate me for this. I worry have you eaten? How are you feeling? I try to tell myself that you are fine. It isn't enough your words have to bring me at ease. Seems like yesterday you were asking me for some ice cream whenever we went out to the park with your sister. I miss those days Manuel. I want you to know that, what you did were actions of a true man and a protector of life. Life seems unfair and challenging in many angles. Trust me, I have been through my fair share of dilemmas. It's not the challenges that are the problem, but how one handles and maneuvers his or her way through these challenges. This is what truly make a person stronger than ever. The outcome will only be based on how well you handle what's needed to be handled. This is where it all counts. You will feel it's worth at the end. I can't predict your journey nor do I have any say in it. What I do know and what I'm very sure of, is that you turned out to be a man of worth, with true masculinity without my help. (Smile my son) Do not give up on us because we will never give up on you. We love you so much. I'm know your love is the same. Enclosed I sent you a money order so you could get the things you want and need in there. It isn't much but anything for you. I'm proud of you son!

Love always,

You're Mother

PS...Jalinda is doing just fine and in madly in love with Joel. She will be writing to you soon.

Her words caused my tear ducts to release tears as I read. How could I let this happen? There had to be a way out of this, my mind and heart both wanted out. I felt a surge of overwhelming emotions hitting me in my stomach all at once. I failed my mom and my sister. In there eyes I was a hero, but in my eyes I was nothing more than a failure. They couldn't see the logic behind all of my moves, and yes I rather it be me then Linda any day of the year. I read the letter three times each time it hit me harder than the last. Mom was smoking all over again, probably cartons after cartons. It was my fucking fault. The cell was too quiet, all you heard was me trying to keep my nose from running. My sorrows were getting the best of me. I inhaled deeply, exhaling even slower.

"You all right?" Slash asked. Sensing that I was going through it. "I'm good." I lied. I was hurt nothing anyone could say or do could make or change how I felt. "It's going to get better Rock." Slash said. I wanted to snap but that wasn't going to help anything. "Man! I hope so." I replied trying to let my mind go for a second. I was too hard on myself for leaving mom and Linda. I had to man up for them. If they believed and counted on me I had to keep my shit together for them. Imagine if they would see how much of a bitch I was being at the moment. They were probably wouldn't be looking up to me the way they did. I needed some serious self talk to get me on track. It was done there was no taking it back point blank. I didn't even bother to open the other two letters, not right now I didn't want to go on another roller coaster ride...

—

Linda was just getting off the bus she was coming back from school. Same routine she did every other day when she had no ride. She was getting frustrated but money was tight and a vehicle wasn't on her agenda at all.

"All right girl, I'll see you tomorrow." Her friend said her goodbyes. The air was Crisp. She wore tight ass jeans with some fresh ass Jay's with a fitted top matching her red and white Jay's. Her vest was open so she decided to zip that bad boy up. She wore her hair in micro minis with a red scarf bundling up her micro minis on one side. Lip-gloss stayed on her juicy lips. Her eyebrows stood fresh to death as they always did. With her book bag on her backc she began walking up federal with only a few blocks to get to moms house. She hadn't even noticed the car creeping up on her. Her mind was preoccupied with who knows what but her steps were swift. I explained to Linda countless times, always check your rear view it could get real costly in them streets. Turning on the block, the vic pulled up right on her. It was Jigz and Banga.

"Hey cutie." Banga spoke out his window. "Nigga please." Linda shot. "Nah I'm just joking listen. Banga tried again but Linda kept her step upbeat. Seeing he wasn't getting anywhere Banga jumped out and speed walked to her almost jogging to catch up with her. "Holdup girl damn!" Banga said. Smelling like straight ganja. "What!?" Linda turned around with a fire in her attitude. Linda didn't play no games, she wasn't for them unless she knew you. "Damn! Sorry for bugging." Banga stated with his palms up in a no threat. "How is your brother?" Banga asked. Linda put her hands on her hips, her butt was tilted on one side. Linda was right. She caught Banga looking. "I'm up here!" Linda pointed at her face snapping her fingers to get his attention on her face instead of her bottom. "What do you care?" Linda asked. "Your brother and I are all right, we never had any indifferences that were noticeable besides the drug game." Banga was wasting his time with Linda. "He is good, no thanks to you though." Linda kept on with the shots. Banga shook his head and laughed. "So it's like that?" Banga asked. "Yeah like that." Linda spat back. "Well if you talk to him tell him that Kiki called me." Banga was on the defense mode now, he wasn't trying to be nice anymore. He wasn't trying to cause any harm to her from the start. It probably was by how he first tried to initiate the conversation, that got Linda keeping her defenses up. "And she told me that she bumped heads with him in the county. I got him with some funds as soon as I go and see her. Also tell him that my offer still stands whenever he beats the case, but this is really important that you tell hime this. Remind him that his sister is an asshole." Banga through that in the mix. It work because Linda smile. "Oh so you do smile." Banga tried again. "Well I'm out tell him to hold his head up, and don't take shit from anyone up in there. He repping my hood." Banga spun off and jump back in the whip. They peeled off with the music blasting.

Shutting the door, Linda stood at the door gathering what just happened. She couldn't wrap her head around at the fact that her brother had sent a message while locked away or on how easily it was for her to be ran down. Yea nothing occurred but that could have easily been Streets, with his side chick that could have ran down on her. She was lost in her own thoughts. She would have been caught slipping with nothing, not even a weapon to protector herself. Even though her hands was all that she really needed but you never knew now and days. Her heart finally regained its normal pulse.

She headed upstairs to call Joel."Oh I'm sorry mom." Linda spoke into the receiver hanging up the phone mom was on the line.

It was time for the last meal of the day and I was starving. I wondered and thought about all the things I would buy with the money mom sent me. From what I was looking at the meal was "basura"/trash/. I ate it though why wouldn't I? It was all that I had at the moment. The loudness from everyone talking about their plans upon release could all be heard. I watched and observed everything. I noticed a few transactions here and there but continued as I didn't see anything.

"Ayo, you bitch ass nigga." Someone yelled. I heard it loud and clear but I didn't take any offense to the words because it wasn't intended for me I thought. I was a highly mistaken. With about four bites into my meal the words echoed again. "I'm talking to you pussy!" "Manuel!" Now my ears shot up as if I was a dog and heard a cat or his master's voice. I looked around but there was no identity to the voice. "You in my territory now nigga!" I couldn't take it anymore so I stood up. "Sit the fuck down!" Yelled the guard on duty watching over us. I did a quick look over and sat down eventually. "Stand up again and that's your ass!" The cocky prick yelled at me. My intention was to come at this prick but I couldn't he wasn't the one I wanted. The one with the slick mouth was my target.

My heart pounded fast with every thought. Who the fuck could this be? At this time the food became obsolete, I didn't care for it. I watched everyones eyes and focused around me. Why me? Was my thought. It just so happen that my time is just beginning and it's already off to a rough start. Hey who said this was going to be easy right? I noticed a face to the far left peeking over at me. Could my eyes be deceiving me? If I was not mistaken that mother fucker look like Curtis. I switch my view so I wouldn't give up that I knew who the coward was yelling over everyone's food. It couldn't be him. It had to be him and trust me I was gonna find out. My mind couldn't be playing tricks on me.

I discarded my trash and put up my tray heading back to the housing unit. Curtis's face stood in my mind the whole time.

"A yo Rock?" Slash was in the cell. " Wassup?" I gave him the Rocks eyebrow. "Who was that faggot ass nigga yelling, He yelled Manuel was he talking to you?" My reaction was to keep Slash out of this but I could use him. "I heard it but I couldn't pinpoint where the noise was coming from." I tossed in the air. "I saw that bitch ass nigga." Slash Admitted. Got'em was all I thought. "You saw him?" I asked eagerly. "Yeah my nigga." He was sitting right across from me on the next table." Slash sang like a bird. Now I knew why cops got pay so much money to solve murders/homicides. They didn't have to do shit. All they had to do was ask a couple questions and play stupid. I didn't care this was valuable information to me. "Oh yeah." What was he white, black or Spanish?" I questioned. Damn I could've sworn you look right at him." Slash Challenge me. "Nah I got up to look but you heard that fucking pig." I replied. He looked like a papi boy, he got tattoos on his neck and arms and shit." These words put the icing on the cake. It was exactly who I thought it was. It may be easy to forget names but a face and discription was more difficult to forget. "I knew that was him, he look too familiar." I said out loud accidentally. "Oh so you do know him?" Slash asked. A bit relieved knowing that I knew who he was talking about. "I don't know him like that but we had history with each other and it ain't positive." I admitted. I felt like I opened up enough to him now. I wasn't going to show him my whole hand but if he wanted to ride out the way he said he would. I wanted to find out and beefing with my celli wasn't going to get me too far anyway. "Ain't positive?" Slash asked. I just looked in the mirror.

Alot of people just want to be a part of anything, ranging from a church group down to a local bar from around the way. Many join these groups feeling alone. Many find happiness and comfort in others. It didn't matter who or what. They would do anything to become united with some other people just be identifiable. Slash was much older than I was, but he was gravitating towards me more than I would ever gravitate towards him. . I knew Slash had a few experiences that I could learn from and as time passed by maybe he could learn a thing or two from me.

"I fought that nigga a while back ago." I said to Slash. If Curtis was up in these walls, Bam had to be somewhere close by because those two were always together like some ass cheeks. "Damn, you don't look like someone who gets into all this extra street drama?" Slash admitted to me. "I don't you are absolutely right Slash. That's not my MO or my twist. Don't get me wrong if I have to I will jump on a nigga quick but as far as me going out and starting shit Nah." I explained to Slash so he could get a better understanding of my personality, since he already tested the waters physically. "We grew up around the same area on 28th, but with so much was going on in our lives. We never really bumped heads until now." He is still holding onto a grudge over a fight you two recently had?" Slash asked sitting at the desk. I was posted on the doorway. "Recently?" I laughed. "He and his other half got into it with me when I was a young buck." I recounted the story quickly. They would get me when I would be going to the store and kick my ass. The next time they tried to pull this stunt on me again. It was like a dog that was always fucking with the cat every time he sees the cat minding his own business. The dog eventually is going to pin the cat in a corner and that cat isn't going to know what to do. He going to get scared and lose control right? His claws will come out and his hair will stick up. He'll shows his tiny sharp teeth and hiss. The dog still isn't scared so the dog gets closer and as soon as he does the cat slashes the dog face with his incredibly sharp claws. The dog backed the fuck up now right? The dog is done and can't believe that the cat put a serious slashing on him. So he backed off?" I wasn't sure if I was making any sense but by the way Slash was looking at me I knew he was getting the picture. "So you're the cat?" Slash asked. "I'm a lion now but yea I was the cat." I replied. "So now what?" Slash was being nosy now. "Now I wait and let him tell his crew who I am, since he put himself on blast. Once he tells them his fabricated story his boys will put two AA batteries in his back, piping him up to come and see me again." I spoke it as I saw it transpiring already in my mind. "When he decides to come, I'll make sure to put it on him a lot harder. I'm grown now and stepped up my box game all on my own, while he was out there bullying all the weaklings in the neighborhood with his sidekick." I was done talking about that lame. "But what if he gets the best to you?" Slash asked. I smile. "I'm glad you said that. If he does I have no choice but to tip my hat off to him because he is a better fighter. I'm not going to hold a grudge for the rest of my life. That shit will only consume too much unnecessary lost energy. Being in the situation I'm in, it can't be abused. I will need every bit of it you may never know when the next match will be, you know?" "How old are you again?" Slash asked joking. "I'm a young soul." I replied. "Man fuck that you talk as if you are a bit older than 18." Slash implied. "I'll take that as a complement. You tryna run a game?" Slash asked. "In a bit I gota read the rest of my letters I got but yeah most definitely. "You still didn't read all them yet?" Slash asked. "You can't eat all your candy in one sitting right?" "My mom taught me that one." Slash laugh. "Damn right you can't. Well you can but you will be assed out later." I got comfortable on my bed.

Curtis was a grimy ass nigga and I knew he was coming. I didn't need anyone to ride with me but if Slash was on my side like he said he was, then I was one up on him. I knew Curtis needed all his boys. So he wasn't coming alone. If Leak was with me time would definitely tell. I was going to show him, who and what I was made of. One man army is how I perceive myself to be. It didn't mean I couldn't be touched because my jaw still hurt from when the fucking Sgt. connected with it. My thoughts took a toll on me for a good minute.

The scent of Felicia's perfume tickled my nose bringing me back. I smelled Jacqueline and is smelled the same as Felicia's. My nose was playing with me. I couldn't remember which girl wore what. My first instinct shouldn't have been questioned but I did anyway, it was intoxicating. I enjoyed the aroma, it got me higher than I was already. My next dosage of meds would be arriving shortly. I loved the high, it was helping me deal with all this internal stress. Wait, let me rephrase that it was postponing my stress because once the meds were off. It all came back tumbling down like a ton of bricks landing right on my head.

I rubbed my head which was in need of a serious haircut, my nails were long and my skin was getting really dry. I couldn't wait to go to commissary. I was done examining my hands and skin after about 20 minutes. I fianally opened, not waiting anymore to finally read and feel another wave of emotions.

Dear handsome,

I don't know how to start this letter but for the most part I hope you are in the highest of spirits and are letting god guide you in all that you do. I have so many questions, but I don't know if and how I should ask them. Why did you leave me? You have no idea how much you've grown on to me in the little amount of time that we've been a part of one another's lives. I know that you didn't want to rush any of this between the two of us. I took much respect to your wishes Rock. I have fallen for you so hard that I don't know how to explain how much you actually mean to me. You got up and left with my heart in your hands, without even giving me any notice that you are not coming back. My heart is bleeding through these words as I write. Im sorry if I sound like an emotional wreck and this isn't something that you need to be reading at the moment but this is what you have created. The reason I've taken so long to get in contact with you is only because I heard what happened in the news and read it in the paper. At first I was nonchalant , but than time came and went. My calls went unanswered just like my drive-bys at the shop went unnoticed. Your vehicle was never parked in the back anymore. Let's not forget to mention my girlfriends at the job accusing me of dating a cold-blooded killer. My heart tells me it's not true, but everyone around me tells me to wake the fuck up and let your ass go! What am I supposed to do? Are you safe? Talk to me Rock. I want to know all of you in and out. There can be a bundle of secrets hidden under your bed, but eventually they'll come to light so right now in this very moment I want you to be 100% honest with yourself first and foremost but with me also. I'm willing to put all my cards on the table and take my chances, and play with your hand. Only if you are willing to do your part. I'm not forcing you to make up your mind right now because I know you already have your hands completely full at the moment. I want to know everything about you, no matter what the truth is. I will be by you side. Eliza asked for you and your sister and I don't know what to tell her. Is your family mad at me? I've called your house and like I said no answer. Well I don't want to bore you with all my feminine emotions but please tell me what it is that I can do to help you handsome. If I can do it. I will do my best to do it and if I can't I'll still try and make it work out. Write me back soon, I sent some money so you can call me. I hope you still know my number. Just in case you forgot its (609)541-4456. It's only $50 but I got you on the next round baby take care! XO XO XO

Always yours,

Felicia

P.S I miss your little big man's!

This isn't what I needed at all I thought as I looked at the letter in my hands. This girl was caught up in my world with nothing to hold onto. Was this a good thing? Could I use this to my advantage? I began to think of ways to make all of this work but my conscious was saying 1 million things. Having a friend by my side will be just great, but Felicia didn't just want to be my friend. She was playing for keeps there was no way that I could tell her the truth, she was crazy. For all I know she was being watched or even played like a marionette. I couldn't risk any of this until I figured out what would be my destiny within the courts. Would I tell her this? Probably not so how was I to keep her close by? I too had questions but very few answers

"Slash". I called down to him."What's up?" He answer sounding a bit dozed off. "Let me ask you something." I said. "go head" I couldn't help but laugh because Slash was a character in his own way. "All right this chick im fucking with just wrote me and from what she's writing. She told me that I took her heart and that she has fallen for me hard." I took a deep breath. "And?" Slash interjected. "I'm getting there she wants me to keep it 100 with her and tell her everything as far as who I really am etc. etc." I paused. "So?" Slash asked. I'm not sure if I can do this because I'm not sure if this is legit or if it's a set up to find out more dirt about me." I sounded foolish but like mom told me don't trust any woman unless your heart tells you otherwise." I waited. "What are you worried about?" Slash asked. "It's not so much, what I'm worried about. The point is how much and what does this girl already know? Who has she been getting her info from? Who has her under the magnifying glass?" I asked myself being super cautious or just probably really paranoid while speaking to Slash. His eyes were literally out his face. "Damn nigga you might be looking a little into deep into that letter. What if she just wants to know the truth all on her own?" There is probably nothing more or less to it." Slash stated. He could be 100% right, but my mind wouldn't let it just pan out so easily. I might be wrong and in time I would notice. "What else is she saying that has you all fucked up in the head?" Slash asked. I looked at the letter. "She goes on to say that she will fold her cards and playoff mine if I allow her too. She will be by my side and do whatever I asked her to do." I answered back to him. "Damn my nigga. It's not rocket science. She want to ride this bid out with you Rock and you pushing her away off the rip.I've been through this situation a few times and Ima keep it real. I had my fair share of woman. They would ride out with me but the truth of it all. Is that they all fall off eventually. It gets very difficult for them and too stressful with the visits, letters, and the money. It's as if we actually become another bill in their household agendas. I was hurt when they left me for dead because I fell for them just as your girl explains that she fell for you. It sounds as though she isn't going to give up on you Rock so if I was you I would see how far you can keep her by your side. If you do and I said if you do get convicted, it's a blessing to have a shorty by your side. Mom and your love ones aren't going to be able to fulfill your desire, but a woman to be by your side she will." Slash spoke with all seriousness and what appeared to be straight from the heart. The way he spoke and reminisced about his past relationship could be felt through his choice of words. He has shown me another part of him that I could either discard or even apply in my current situation. "I feel you man so I should just tell her the truth and keep her close huh?" I asked still not knowing what I would do and how I was going to do it. "Whooaa! Tiger I didn't say that." Slash joked. I said feel it out. You never tell her everything but you tell her enough to keep her interested in you. You want her to keep wanting to know more about you. If you tell her everything then there's nothing left for her to explore about you." You understand?" Slash asked me. I nodded I saw his point. I would tell her more of me not about my situation, what happened really didn't concern her at all. I tried not to focus on this too much. I am young, no need to stress myself out with this woman. I decided to open Jacqueline's letter. I should've known better none of this would bring any relief to my problems. It felt great getting the envelopes but the words that were written on them carried a lot more weight and one never knows what's inside these envelope.

Taking a deep fucking breath.

I'm so so sorry please don't be mad at me. I never intended for any of this to happen! Please write me back and tell me that you are okay. I'm so scared I don't know what to do. My baby dad threatened to kill me if I even thought about writing to you. I can't believe all of this, it's all my fault I wish I would've never met you maybe you would still be out here working and living your life. I'm so sorry I'm such a horrible person. I knew this nigga was out of his mind but I never thought it would ever get this far. He always comes around bragging and talking all the shit. "Where's your boyfriend now?" And I told you not to see him!" I run your life you are my property." These are the words that come out of his mouth on a regular basis. I hold it all in my anger and play it off as if it doesn't faze me, but as soon as I give him his son. I break down and just cry and cry and cry so much Rock! I'm such a piece of shit, you were nothing but nice to me. No one has ever filled in this void that I have inside of my heart. You are so much different than all these men out here. Rock I don't know what else or how much more damage this man can inflict on me and in my life but if you want me to testify on your behalf I will. I rather him be in jail than someone who I know is supposed to be out of them walls. Anything that you need from me Rock I'm here money, visits, and letters whatever. I'm not leaving you behind because you didn't leave me behind when I needed someone by my side the most. So how could I treat you any different? I hope that you find it in your heart to forgive me for what my baby dads has put you through. If you choose to not write a word back to me then that's fine because dead and alone is what I deserve. I miss your smile so much I shut my eyes and I can see you so easily. You have earned a special place in my heart that no one can ever take away from me. Thank you for all that you have done to make me a stronger independent woman. I hope to hear from you as soon as you can. My new number is (609) 541-3732 you can call me anytime you want. I get paid this weekend so you'll be hearing from me and I hope I hear from you back! Muahz!

Ur ma!

I was speechless. "This girl has gone mad." I spoke out loud. "Do I want to know?" Slash asked sensing the tone in my voice wasn't very inviting. "Na my nigga "this one I have to wait for the outcome of this case to talk about." Some thing weren't for everyone. "I'm here if anything you know?" Slash didn't beg nor did he press the issue. I liked that. "I got myself in a tight situation." I thought out loud again. Slash didn't respond. I didn't expect him too but I couldn't do shit about anything. I reread this letter more than I read Felicia's. This letter has so much clues for me to use. She knows pretty much all that occurred that night. Or at least I assume she did. Then again, her baby dads was that stupid to even say what he did that night to me? Or was Jacqueline going off the newspaper? Could she be writing because he made her right to me to see what I'm going to do. Could he be checking to see if I was going to reach out to her? I took her heart as well. Why me? All these unanswered questions that I didn't know under which rock to look under for the answers. Whatever I needed she'd be there. Why in the world do I always seem to dickmatize these woman unintentionally? From now on I'm only fucking women for five seconds or less because my little man has got me in a pinch that I can't seem to get out of. Is not her fault that I'm in here. Why is she beating herself up over this? Or was it her fault? The way I see this I can keep in contact were her until her baby dads ends up killing her. If he finds out which could benefit me if he does do something incredibly stupid. I could definitely see him doing some dumb shit. I could use Jacqueline in my court case to try and pin this case on him? I honestly didn't think that would work because it's only a thought. I could kick little Miss sexy lips to the fucking curve and ride this out by myself without her because she is just going to end up causing more drama in my families lives and in my life as well. It seemed that the more I tried to make all this work inside my head the bigger the headache was forming in my brain. This is something I clearly needed to think about when my head wasn't clustered with so much other unneeded bullshit. I really enjoyed being with Jacqueline. She was very different from all the others, besides the drama which equaled out to all the rest of the lokas/crazies/ out here. Maybe I should have let her be when she came up in the shop that day. My womanizing wouldn't let any attractive woman slipped by my hands. Even with all the clues I still didn't obey. This is what I get."It be said, you reap what you sow." Something like that. I kind of feel bad for her. She is probably going through it with that lame ass nigga. I can only imagine him beating on her, all high and drunk in front of his child. Fucking pussy! Why couldn't Linda have killed that piece instead! I couldn't believe what my mind was saying, how the fuck could I have allow myself to think of such an action. To put my sister in another murder was straight up unorthodox. I put away the letters and it just so happen it was time to go eat again.

"Chow time!" Slash jumped up get ready. I also jump down and put on my slides. Those words ,no matter how much I wanted to pay them no mind wouldn't leave my mind. It was Linda, mom, Felicia and Jacqueline. The four amazing woman in my life that I couldn't let go so easily. Of course, some more than others but it's like they too have become a part of me internally. "You good?" Slash asked looking back at me, he was two steps ahead of me. "Yeah I'm good my nigga, it's the letter that got me a bit fucked up in my head." I admitted. I looked around as I walked checking my surroundings making sure I was good. "Told you now imagine when the lovey-dubey shit start and you can't touch or lay out with them." Slash joked as he sped up to catch up with his boys. I maintained my steady pace, losing focus. It was ridiculous how a lousy letter could change someone's demeanor in a blink of an eye. These were no lovey-dubey letters but I could only imagine what Slash was referring to if they were I would be in even more depressed individual. To keep things on a better note I love my woman and that will never change for as long as I lived or for as long as this bid was going to be. If I had to masturbate for the rest of my life and look at porno magazines than guess what? I would die with my little man's in my hand before going another direction. Keeping two crazy bitches in my corner may not be the best idea but I tell you this it felt good to know I had a place in someone else's heart, that wasn't intermediate family...

—

The rush of pain hit me right above my elbow. I couldn't move my arm because someone else's arm had me in a hold. "You pussy Rock! This isn't your turf I run this turf!" Another sharp pain in my lower back. I was in complete shock I couldn't find the words. I didn't see my attacker but his voice was clear as a brand-new mix tape. It was Curtis but who was the man holding me? Was it Slash? Or was it Leak? His hold was like a vice grip getting much tighter as the seconds went by. Others watch but kept on moving to their destination towards the chow hall. The look on their faces show no remorse as I helplessly just got poked up as much as Curtis has planned it out for me. The commotion was low enough to be ignored. "I told you I would get you thought I wasn't, it was never over." My eyes adjusted as I finally saw the faces above me now. It was Curtis and his man's. I never seen this big light-skinned mother fucker in my life, but then again neither have I seen the rest of any of these niggas in this jail. It wasn't enough to carve holes in me, the stomping was the icing on the cake. My eyes watered but I didn't let not one tear fall. I couldn't no matter how bad this pain was. I took it all in like a man. I've been hurt so bad that I was beginning to feel numb to pain, my head was lightning I couldn't feel the blood in my fingers. Why isn't no one here to help? I thought to myself. What took a matter of seconds felt like it would never end? I must have lost consciousness because Slash was by my side on his knees trying to get me to say something. I couldn't I was holding in so much pain. The attackers were long gone. "CO! Help!" Slash yelled at the top of his lungs. The medical unit was on the block. My heart was racing causing so much more blood to spill.

"You need to calm your heart rate down, it's pumping too fast!" A familiar voice spoke to me. It was Peg or at least sounded like her. I smiled. "Stay strong boy, you not gonna leave as yet." We got to get him up out of here now!" Ms. Peg shouted. My life was over at the age of 18 I ended up in the worst possible situation a man could end up in. Could it be that I was such a horrible person to deserve all this trauma? Or could I possibly live a more positive life in the next one? Why was it that men held grudges for long periods inside of them, then came to vengeance so brutally? Was this my destiny on this earth? Was my purpose to die on this jailhouse floor?

"No my son your purpose is much greater than you feel." A voice from a distance spoke to me now I knew I was dead. The word "son" had me by the throat and I was out of breath. It couldn't be there was no way I thought to myself. MS. Cathy was here with me. "Is it so hard to believe? I knew one day you and I would be reunited once again." The voice came closer. All I saw was a silhouette. "Aren't you happy to see me?" The soft feminine voice spoke. I was cold, shivering to be exact. Was I dead, alive? "Almost son." The voice answered every thought that came into my mind without me even speaking out loud. "How could you hear me?" I asked. "Baby up here everyone can hear everyone there are no secrets up here." The shadow of this figure became more visible. Her hair was done up very neatly her face was clear and smooth. She had on a white dress that hugged her body snugly. She was beautiful. She possessed a lot of life. Her smile was so radiant. Her hands were so clean and well-manicured. She was gorgeous her features resembled mine it was my biological mother, not MS Cathy! She was everything I had expected. I walked closer to her the energy that she was given off caused me to stop my shivering, instead she gave me a burst of warmth. She felt so powerful. "You are so much more handsome in person than from the view up above son." Her hand touched my left cheek. I hope you understand what I did for you and why I had to do this son." It was my birth mother, my eyes filled with tears and I wasn't holding them back. They were meant to fall and they fell out of happiness not anger nor pain. "Mom I'm so happy to see you." I choked up. "Don't cry baby I'm here now we can talk about it all." The purity and humility was something that could be overlooked, but here it would be impossible to ignore. "Come with me son and all that pain and suffering will be over. I took two steps forward.

"Dr. his heart rate is dropping slowly!" The doctor's assistant spoke loudly. Prepare for CPR they were losing me. The nurses and doctors all got ready for the inevitable. He lost too much blood go and get some more donor packs." The doctor ordered. One of the assistant ran off. Being flown in I didn't quite understand because the hospital was only about five minutes away from the jail. I could feel as they touch me and the noise of the equipment could be heard clear as day. I was dying and I was leaving with my mother. Linda and

Ms. Cathy were going to be alone from this day on out when I left with my biological mother. I hope she would understand. I had so much catching up to do with my mom. I would get to know all her secrets and she could know all of me. "He's dropping Dr.!" I was looking for an easy way out something Ms. Cathy taught me never to do, how could I betray her? What would she think of me? Linda needed me by her side, how could I be so selfish and abandon the ones who are dependent on me? It's rising!" The nurse yelled over to the doctor. "He's fighting the doctor sat back and watched. "I'm fighting." I thought to myself who fighting? Im leaving with mom fuck all this jail shit. "It's dropping again." The nurse said. That's when it hit me the hardest. I had total control of what my destiny would hold for me. It was all up to me to stay or leave. To die or to live. This was amazing. I can either vanish from earth and be free from all my pain and imprisonment, Or go be with my biological mother free and happy. The way I've always dreamed of it or I could just stay my ass right here.

—

My mother tugged on my hand edging me towards the way. "What's wrong son? You don't want to stay with me?" She asked sadly. "I do mom." But" she put her index finger on my lips. "Then walk with me." I took two more steps forward. "What about Ms. Cathy and my sister?" I asked her taking one more step. "They will be just fine with you watching over them son." mom said. "We are losing him!" The nurse yelled at the doctor. "Not yet" the doctor replied "I can't mom, I'm sorry. Please don't be mad at me but I need to be there for them they need me more than ever right now. It's not fair to abandon them so easily when things get harder for us." I tried to sound convincing speaking from my heart. "Son is up to you, I'm not mad just know that I'm always by your side when you feel things are too rough to handle." That's what I needed to hear. "Time is ticking son you have to choose now." Mom kept walking as if I should follow but I didn't I was going towards the other way. "I love you son." "I love you too mom!" My heart felt like it was being ripped from right inside of me, I wanted to run back to mom and stay with her but I couldn't.

—

My leg was twitching as if it was falling asleep and I wanted to shake off the annoying feeling. "There he goes." The doctor spoke happily. He's back with this."

Going back to work on me. I had new blood being pumped in through my veins, they managed to put me back into shape. But the worst part was soon to come yet after countless hours of stitching me and making sure all my vitals and organs were intact. They made sure nothing was severely punctured along with the heavily medication that I was being induced with I eventually fell out for some time.

—

Meanwhile back at home mom gets two disturbing phone call that I have been in a brutal and fatal fight. She was going hysterical all alone. Linda was out with Joel so getting in contact with them was impossible. "What do you mean I can't go see him!?" Mom was barking with a cigarette in her mouth.

"He is my fuck and son and you are supposed to ensure his safety not call me and tell me that he's in a fatal condition. What the fuck are you all doing over there?" There was no calming her down. "He is a prisoner under our supervision the same rules apply to him in the hospital as they would as if he was on the property." The redneck Warden informed my mom. "Well if my lawyer says different how would that make you feel?" Mom spat. "Listen ma'am you don't have to get the courts involve we can handle this on our own." The petrified Warden new this was a close book lawsuit case that he would not win weather Rock made it or not. "Then let me see him for Christ sakes! I'm not gonna break him the fuck out he's going to probably be cuffed up from the toes up anyway." Mom stated rudely. "I'm sorry ma'am if I could I would." Click mom's pleas went unheard as she hung up that damn phone and began to pray.

—

"He's a strong one." The doctor said as he patched up the final hole in Rock's lower back. Altogether he had 14 holes in him all ranging from his elbow to his lower back and on his side. The doctor couldn't believe how Rock pulled through this, but all he knows is that a strong will to survive can bring anyone back to life. In all his years of practice and medical he seen all types of tragedies. Very few make it out alive but the ones who do become a great success in life for the most part. "Let him rest he needs all the sleep he can get. We'll check up on him when he decides to wakes up.

Chapter13

"I don't know shit"

It's been almost a month in recovery which hasn't been too pleasurable. The injuries were definitely life-threatening but gladly I'm pulling through it all. I still was not 100% and may not be for a while to be honest. I somehow managed to cheat death twice. I felt born again. My mind and conscience felt at peace with itself. The doctor ordered me to be on bed rest for the next couple months and to stay away from all contact events, such as sports, weights etc. etc. yeah right! I had to get myself back into shape, I was well rested long enough. I haven't made it to the county jail not more than two weeks after the incident and I can count on two hands on how many times authorities from the prisons kept trying to question me about something that I knew nothing about. I asked to call my family and guess what they say? "You have to wait to you get back into the jail." How ironic. I was informed that mom had already been informed, but I had to assure her that I was okay for myself. Knowing those two they were causing all hell. I was moved right back into my cell with Slash but there was another unfamiliar face in the room. He was short and chubby, he too was light-skinned. He wore a regular with a chinstrap that looked a bit too thick. He had dark eyes with thick eyebrows. I noticed all his things were on my cabinet. I wondered if Slash told him about what happen or was he just waiting for me to get back. Slash helped me with the medical bag I had in my hand, had all types of toys. You know gauzes and antibacterial ointment. "Damn Rock I thought you was never coming back." Slash said looking at me from head to toe. "Where's my stuff?" I asked Slash. Now I didn't have much but I still wanted to know where my belongings were. "There exactly where you left them." Slash stated. I looked at chubs and looked at his things on my cabinet. The look on my face wasn't one that showed cheery go jolly. He moved his shit on the side on the floor.

"Yo this is "Bigs" he from Pennsauken." Slash introduced us. "Sup" I gave them a head nod. "I heard what happened man I hope you are right." Bigs said. Go figure Slash could never keep his jaws tight. "I'm good." I reply sitting on the desk. I had to talk but I wasn't sure where to begin. I just gathered my thoughts. "Listen I'm still a bit fucked up and I was told that I had to relax." I said. "I'll be out of your way man." Bigs said. I just looked at him. He was on point. "I don't need any extra bullshit in my way. I'm not saying that you will be in my way but what I'm saying is I have to get myself back into shape. A few muscles and nerves may have been damaged, so I'm going to try my hardest to get them back to normal." I spoke. "Ayo Rock, I found out who both of them niggaz are that got you. They running around as if they kings, trying to extort all the new guys who come in with the same shit they did to you." Slash was doing his homework. I nodded in approval I like that he was keeping his word. "What else do you know?" I asked. "They selling numbers and who else they be with." Slash went on. "That's Wassup." I praised Slash for his careful observation while I was gone. I gave him dap. I felt the pain in my banck and how much it forced me to wince. "My bad my nigga." Slash notice my pain. I reached in a bag and took a few pain relievers. "I'm handle that but not at the moment if anyone ask about me, I'm in my room fucked up." That's it nothing more or less" I looked at both of them. "That goes for you to big man." Referring to Bigs. "What is your name anyway?" I asked Bigs. "Lewis" he replied. "You Spanish?" I asked him. "Yeah mixed with black." Lewis informed me. How old are you?" I asked him 1 million questions. "23" he replied. "Did you check his work?" I asked Slash. "You already know I did that." "Guns and drugs." Slash informed me. I noticed Bigs was searching for his papers, "You good Lewis don't worry about that." If you going to stay here with us you either going to be with us all the way or you can pack up and leave now." I said to Bigs. Has face had no emotion .I kind of liked that. "I'm already here and this is going to be for a while it's whatever." Biggs stated. "Is that your word you given me? The room got silent. "Because you know its worthless if you don't stand behind it?" I stated. "My word." Lewis replied and gave me a pound. I noticed marks on the edge of the toilet that looked to be carvings. The last time I was in here Slash was using that spot to sharpen up that toothbrush to show me what he could make out of nothing and turn it into something. "Where is it?" I asked. The meds were beginning to kick in. I was numb all over but was fully conscious that I was still a wounded body. "Where's? What?" Slash aske. He was lost as to what I was asking for. I pointed to the mark on the floor. Slash smiled. "Damn you notice everything don't you?" Slash joked. "Apparently not, look at me?" I joked back causing everyone in the cell to laugh a bit breaking the awkwardness. I only got one in here the other is stashed away in the dayroom." Slash said. He flipped his mattress and began to dig in it deep inside until he finally located what he was looking for. He had his hand so far up in that mattress it made me laugh. It even hurt to laugh. I hated this pain. He pulled out a fucking whack that was almost as long as my forearm. "What the fuck is that?" I asked him. "It's a work in progress Rock. It was made of wood." Slash said. I took it from his hand and enjoyed the power a useless item can possess if used properly. It looked like a plunger stick to me but I couldn't understand where and how he got this. "You know they going to come up in here and search the cell right?" I said. "They already did twice." Bigs corrected me. "Okay but just in case let's finish it up and move it just in case." I stated. "All right I'll finish it tonight and pass it off."

With my court date approaching rapidly, mentally and physically I was fucked up. I couldn't let it show though. The same week I get situated into the prison I'm called out for a visit. Just in time, I needed a change in my bid even if it was for a few minutes or hours. You would think that. once your relatives came up to see you they wouldn't be treated as criminals, being that they aren't criminals. A thick glass separating us from actually being able to touch and hug one another, was worse than not having a visit at all. Mom look so beautiful with her hair pinned up in a bun. She was showing off her ears, showing off her earrings. She looked very radiant, just seeing her put a huge smile on my face which was like a chain reaction Linda also smiled trying not to show any pain hidden behind her eyes. It was clear to see but no one wanted to show how much you actually hurt.

"How are you baby?" Mom asked me. "I'm okay mom, I'm hanging in there." I replied with a sly smile. My pain was too visible. It was a touchy matter. "I tried to see you in the hospital but they just wouldn't let me on the floor where you were being held on." Mom stated. "I know mom I tried to call you because they told me that they notified you about what had happened." I stated. Linda just watched with her hands over her mouth listening. I wasn't sure what she was doing but I watched her closely. "Did they catch the guy who hurt you?" Mom asked. She was hoping I was gona say yes. I shook my head. "How in the world didn't they!" Mom raise her voice in complete anger. I put my index finger all my lips so she could hush. She obeyed and looked at me with this concerning look. "You know who did it." She mouth it off to me in a whisper. It was hard to hear her but I read her lips. I didn't say yes or no. My devilish grin was all she got. Linda observed me. She ran her fingers under her neck. Again I didn't say word. Now, Linda was the one grinning. It scared me to see that the innocent face she once possess no longer existed. She was the one given me a sinister grin now. Instead I could see the coldness in her eyes.

"Are you okay?" I asked Linda switching topics and putting her on the spot. "I'm not okay Manny but I'm being strong for you and mom." Linda admitted. "Good I need you to be strong, and how is school?" I asked. "It's going, I'm working now too." Linda informed me. "That's good where are you working at?" I asked. "In the school as an ambassador." Linda said. "Okay Balling!" I joked. Linda smiled was soft. I really miss them. I couldn't do shit about it either. "We got you a lawyer to try and help in the case, he's an old friend of mine. He's almost charging me nothing to help you." Mom said gracefully. "Oh yea?" I asked in complete shock. I wasn't expecting no lawyer in fact. I thought a lawyer would be a waste of time. I couldn't tell them that, they were trying and for all I know it could actually help if they really believed it. "He'll be coming to see you soon. Be patient Manny and be truthful about everything." Mom emphasized the word everything. In my mind I thought she was crazy but then again Linda told her everything I know that much. There were no secrets in my household amongst the three of us. "Manny?" Linda call my name. "/Quein fue?/" /who was it/ she asked she stared dead in my eyes. I wanted to tell her but to speak so flagrantly in this room wasn't a smart move. It would be straight telling if anyone with bad intentions would overhear the name. Instead I decided to write it on the glass with my finger. She would have to use our imagination because I wasn't going to do it again....c....u....r.....t... .i....s....." I spelled out the name. Linda's mouth opened soon as I finished off the letters. She couldn't believe it. Mom's nosey ass wanted to know what I was writing Linda. She whispered in her ear. Mom's jaw dropped. "That boy don't learn." Was all mom said? I smiled he would learn the hard way. "I'm working on something out here Manny don't be mad at me but it's something I can't stop myself from doing. I just want you to know I'm on your side no matter what." Linda spoke looking at me. I had no clue what she was saying but I'm sure she would get her point across to me. My quizzical look went on answered. "Be good and don't do nothing stupid Linda." I said to her. Her cold stare hit me hard. This wasn't Linda anymore she was still this pretty sexy female, but she had this look that gave me the chills. "You listening to me?" She shook her head. "No." That was the first time Linda has ever went against my word. This point on I may have lost my baby girl. Mom just sat there not saying a word.

Just letting me see for myself that Linda was going through all of this differently. "Your truck Manuel?" Mom broke me out of my trance with Linda. "What about it?" I asked. The impound called and they told me to go pick it up with $575. What do you want me to do?" Mom asked. "Sell it." Was the first thing that came in my head and the first thing I blurted out? "How much?" Mom asked is banged up in the back." I said. "Sell it for $2000 or whatever you can give for it to help the two of you out at home." I said. "That car is trouble so whoever is driving the truck could be mistaken to be related to me, I don't want anything else to happen to you because of me." I explained.

"I'm sorry Manny." Linda couldn't hold in the tears. I knew it would come and it did. Mom follow suit. I bit my bottom lip to hold in my sorrow but my eyes gave away my pain again. If anyone can say that they have been through a similar trip like this and say it was easy to deal with. You must not have any one on the outside who really truly cared for you or love you at all. I'm aware it would get better but for now it still hurt so badly. "Stop." I said. "It's not that bad." I tried to sound convincing. "I love you Manny but I can't do this right now." Linda stated getting up and leaving. Mom stood and inhale deeply. Her hands went up on the glass. I put mind on the glass not seeing the point in his but gave a good sense of satisfaction. "I don't know who she is anymore Manuel she comes in at all hours at night and hardly speaks." Mom began to vent. Linda has changed and mom just confirmed it. "You know mom she trying to deal with this to the best of her ability, just give her time and space." I suggested. "I hope you're right. Did you get the money?" Mom asked. "Yes I did thank you very much." I replied.

"Guess who asked me out?" I couldn't believe what I just heard come out of mom's mouth, but I was happy. "Pete." Mom said very happily. "Who?" I asked not catching the name. "Your boss Pete." Mom was like a kid on Christmas. "Yeah right mom." I was speechless. "For real I didn't tell him anything because I wanted to hear what you thought about all of this first." My mind was on froze as I listened to what mom was saying to me. "I thought he was married?" I asked. "No he separated there not compatible anymore." Mom reassured me. "Are you sure?" I asked. "That's what he's telling me Manuel, I believe him and why would he lie about something so serious?" Mom asked. "I don't know mom just make sure before you jump off the cliff." I responded. "So is this a yes?" Mom held her hands on her chest. "You are grown and if you feel as though you truly like him then go for it, whatever makes you happy mom." Her smile was priceless in my eyes, there was no way I could take that moment from her. "Just keep an eye on Linda and you watch yourself please." I said before the guard spoke. "Rap it up, five minutes left!" The CO barked. "Make sure you call us and let us know everything that is going on in there. I'll do my part out here as good as I can." Mom said in one breath. Just like that it was all over with an I love you, and a blow of kisses were exchanged.

So much happening and I wasn't sure what to think. Mom and Pete? Where the fuck did that come from? The way I see it is, if mom saw something in Pete other than his money then there might be hope now. If Pete is running game then he just may made my shit list.

The rest of the day went by quietly and smoothly for the most part which wasn't the norm but I knew that in due time this tsunami would crash it's way through all of this again shortly. As I made my way back to the cell, the guys were in their playing chess as always the pain didn't seem to go away fast enough. "A yo Rock there is a note for you on the cabinet." Slash stated. "Another fucking note? These niggas is worse than females in this bitch. They remind me of grade school when a girl is feeling you and vice versa. We would send each other a love note and shit." The guys were laughing their asses off now. It was a nore but it wasn't from no nigga. It was from Kiki. I heard what happened and I'm sorry you going through all this. You don't deserve it but service is tomorrow, please go so I can see you Rock." The one and only Kiki. This girl was feeling me, and I wanted to see that thick ass too.

"That same nigga again?" Slash asked. "Nah Shorty from the other day." I informed them. "Damn nigga how you get all this attention and you wasn't even here for a while." Bigs asked. "I want some love too." Bigs joked. I smiled at his remarks. "You gota be cool man. It'll all come to you but be careful what you asked for because it's a pain in the ass." I replied to his remarks. "I got winners." "Al man, you don't want none of this." Bigs joke about my skills. It was my turn to play a good game of chess.

"Oh my god girl, how have you been?" Jacqueline asked Linda. Hugging one another as if they were the bestes of friends. They were both got off the speed line meeting up at the gallery in downtown Philadelphia. The people were moving by the hundreds left and right. "I'm okay I couldn't wait to see you girl since the last time." Linda played smoothly. "So what's going on with you?" Linda asked her taking her hand. Lets grab a bite to eat I'm hungry." Linda request. "Sounds good." Jacqueline agreed. "Well I wrote the guy I was telling you about, but he hasn't wrote me back. I really want to see him." Jacqueline spoke about Rock. "Well he's probably not interested because of his current situation or he just need some time to gather all his thoughts." Linda suggested. "Yeah you're probably right, but in my heart this man captured me and I'm actually in love with him. I think he loves me too." Jacqueline admitted her feelings about Rock. Linda wanted to slap this bitch, she must be an idiot my brother loves her? The only woman my brother loves is mom and me, especially not a broad like this Linda thought. Was she right? "Let's eat here?" Linda saw a chicken spot. The line was long but who cared they had nothing to do and their bellies were one step away from starving. "How are you and your boyfriend James doing?" Jacqueline asked Linda. We are hanging in there, you know going through the motions." Linda said. "Is he still beating you?" Jacqueline asked Linda. "Not lately but he has choked me last week because he said the house was dirty." Linda look down as she spoke. Linda was lying out her eyes, you had to know your enemy by any means right? There was no way Joel could ever muster the audacity to put his hands on Linda let alone choke her. After, what Jacqueline said to Linda a couple weeks ago Linda had no choice but to play victim as well. Jacqueline put her hands on her mouth. "Oh my God girl, you gota try and get some help because this will only get worse. If you don't stop that crazy ass nigga now who knows what could happen next." Jacqueline said speaking softly to Linda. They ordered their food and found a spot all the way in the corner. "Jasmine?" Jacqueline called over to Linda "yes." Linda answered. "What kind of drink do you want? Let me get a Sprite." Linda replied. Linda sat back and played out her scheme on how it would all go down smoothly, only if no one intervened. This wasn't going to be an easy task but it would be completed one way or the other. "Here you go." Jacqueline handed Linda her Sprite. "This place is packed girl." Jacqueline stated. "I know I can't believe all these people here spending money. Shit, I need to open a business." Linda replied. "So where you want to go first?" Linda asked "It don't matter I want to buy outfit for my son and some sneakers. Ima buy me something if feel like it not to sure yet." Jacqueline was always on top of her mother game. She had no choice. "So where is the baby now? With your baby dads?" Linda asked.

"Hell no that nigga come and see his son once a month if that." Jacqueline said with an attitude. "Damn that shit is crazy." Linda replied. "That nigga had the nerve come by the job with his little girlfriend name Star and try and start some shit, all because I wasn't down with the threesome with his dirty as bitch!" Jacqueline went in. "With who?" Linda probed. "This girl he with, her name is Star. She got a few stars in the back of her ear. Don't get me wrong, she is cute but hell no. It was not happening not in this lifetime. Maybe if he was a decent father I might have done it but he fucked that up." Jacqueline admitted that she would defintely do it. This was Linda's angle. If Linda's memory served her correct, the bitch Jacqueline was referring to was the one she boxed out that night. "Let me get this straight your baby dad want you and his new girlfriend "Dusty Betty" to have a threesome with one another?" Linda joked. Jacqueline was balling out laughing. "Yeah girl and he crazy I think this nigga done lost it completely." Jacqueline admitted. "This chicken is good aint it?" Linda stated changing the subject for second. "It definitely is." Jacqueline replied. "Wow." I'm shocked" Linda said in between bites. Jacqueline noticed this light-skinned nigga eyeing her down from the other side.

"Look at this thirsty mother fucker. I can't even eat without someone down my throat." Jacqueline said. Linda followed her stare and homie was still stalking his prey with his hazel eyes. "He is cute, go for it." Jacqueline just stared at Linda. "Jasmine! You got to be kidding me I have enough drama in my life with the men. To bring in a stray dog would only bring in more fleas." Linda burst out in laughter. "I got you." Linda got up fixing her tight fitted black jeans and walked over to Mr. Hazel. Jacqueline couldn't help but to stare at Linda's ass, it was phat and dipping in that Jacqueline wouldn't mind. She like girls that's why her baby dads wanted that threesome. She had given him that gift years ago when they first met and now he expected on command. Jacqueline watched as Linda flirted with him. The guy wrote down his number and that's all it took. Like taking candy from a baby. Linda took it. She had all eyes on Jacqueline as she was walking back to her table. "Here you go ma." Linda handed her the piece of napkin. "Maurice." A.k.a. "Hazel" what a coincidence. "Jasmine you are too much let's get out of here please." Jacqueline was embarrassed. Hysterically laughing they both exited the chicken spot.

After hours of yapping and spending money Linda decided to dig a bit deeper into Jacqueline's personal life. "I was thinking about how you and I have a sleep over at your spot?" We can invite a few girls and just have an all-girls night." Linda needed to find out where she stayed. She wanted to see who else she could run into and be able to chew some more information out of. Jacqueline's facial expression show some uncertainty. "It'll be fun we can talk about men and sex. We can even play with some toys." Linda joked was all serious. Jacqueline's smile was plastered on Linda's last comment. "Okay but when? I'll get someone to watch my son." Jacqueline agreed. Too easy Linda thought. "What should I bring to drink?" Linda asked. Anything light, dark liquor gets me a bit too angry." Jacqueline admitted. I don't have any friends so you have to invite yours if you want." Linda said. "You got me Jasmine." Jacqueline hugged Linda as she spoke her caring words. "How about next weekend so I'll make sure I'm off of work, that'll give us enough time to clear our schedules." Jacqueline suggested. "Sounds like fun and a plan ma." Linda showed her pearly whites excitedly. "I know you might think I'm bugging but you should try to work things out with your baby dads." Linda was heading towards another route with this one. It caught Jacqueline by surprise. "Work what? With who?" Jacqueline replied. "You heard me girl." Linda said walking towards the escalator leading upstairs. Jasmine I don't think you understand me when I say this but this man is on some other shit. If I give him access to me and my pussy, he'll be hooked all over again and think he can control my every move. This means no friends, no friends, and no life." Jacqueline spoke not liking this idea at all.

There was a concert going on the floor up ahead at the gallery the music and the singing could be her very loudly and clearly. The crowd of people were all over, this mall it was huge. I mean blocks after blocks there was no ending to it. Linda got closer to hear Jacqueline words clearly. "It must've not been that bad if you had a baby with him." Linda tossed up. Jacqueline stood quiet. Linda had planted the seed and now it was time to water the seed and watch it grow. Date was set now it was go time.

—

"I talked to my son the other day and he said he didn't have a problem with us seeing one another under one circumstance?" Mom said to Pete. "Oh yeah and what is this?" Pete asked in his loud usual voice. Mom and Pete were at Ponderosa waiting to be seated. Pete had offered to take mom to eat, and mom didn't object to it. "That you proved to me that you and your wife are separated." Mom held her ground waiting for peace reaction. "That's it?" Pete said. "No!" Mom interjected. If you going to play games go somewhere else, not this mom Pete." Mom stated. Pete knew this had to be serious and he planned to. "I'll agree to those terms." Pete put his hands out to lock in the deal, mom took his hand and Pete kissed it. "I'll have to thank him for this gift he's given me." Pete said. Mom blushed

"Your table is ready please follow me." The tall waiter instructed. In case you never heard of Ponderosa. It's an all you can eat buffet with all types of food ranging from white rice to fried chicken to mashed potatoes and everything else you can think of. Dessert was the best. They all types of pastries and ice creams. "So how is he doing?" Pete asked switching lanes. He is strong that's all I can say he'll need us by his side and I plan on being there for the long haul." Mom admitted. "I know, I like your son from the very first day that he walked into my shop asking for a job. His face showed a deep determination to find employment. If I would've said no but there was no way I would let that kid slipped through my fingers. Yes we all made mistakes but I know that Manuel was reacting in self-defense because I've seen killers and your son didn't strike me as that type. He is sweet and loving." Mom informed Pete. The conversation was lightened as they began to eat.

"Not bad for a first date Pete stated mom smiled "thank you she spoke softly to Pete.

—

What went from one lousy push up turn into 15. The pain in Rocks body was sharp but he knew he had to pull through it all. He didn't go to any meals, stood in the cell getting his body and mind right was all that Rock had in his mind on. It was game time and he would come out roaring. "Getting stronger." Bigs said noticing. "It was a few days ago you could barely do a push-up. I'm 100% I still can't do a push-up." Biggs joke. The men all laughed. Commissary was all Rock was eaten.

"You ready for court tomorrow?" Slash asked. "Not really." Rock admitted. "Just remember you don't want no deal and you want to proceed with the hearing." Slash informed Rock. Rock payed close attention "deal?" What you talking about?" Rock asked completely lost. "The DA is going to try and give you a deal so you don't take it to trial, now by taking this deal you are admitted to the crime and taking a so-called plea-bargain in return for your guilty plea. You under no circumstances want the PD or lawyer to talk you into taking a deal." Slash said in one breath. What if is a good deal?" Rock was to uneducated. He asked the most ridiculous question. "Why? Would you admit to something that you could get away with if the evidence doesn't convict you?" You want to go home or do you want to stay here with us?" Slashed asked a dead serious question. "You are here for murder Rock if I was in your shoes. I would most definitely try and go home by any means." Slash said being experienced in the law department. This was good because knowing Rock he would do something he had no business doing. "Okay I'm getting it, so no deal and trial all the way?" Rock put the puzzle together. "You got it bro and don't worry, I'm no lawyer but I beat a homi before. Don't get your hopes up because this doesn't mean you can beat yours, but it's a process. I'll help you as much as I can and siphon through the law books with you. "Slash had Rocks attention to the max. He was going to take his advice and try his best not to let the DA and his lawyer dictate what he should do. Your freedom couldn't be taken lightly. No one would fight for his freedom the way you would fight for yours.

The cold steel pressed up on your skin, was a feeling that one could never get used to. Shackled from head to toe, It felt so wrong to treat a human being like an animal. We were all lined up with cuffs on our wrist, on our ankles.They made sure to secure our feet from moving too quickly. The chain that connected our two ankles was about 10 inches so you can only take a baby step as you walked, anything faster or longer than that would only shoot paint straight through your Achilles heel, but for the most part tripping and falling. Let's not forget there was another big chain around your fucking waste. This one kept your hands close to your waistline so you couldn't even think about striking anyone.

"Everyone head into the pod." The big belly CO Bark. Just as if we were programmed with software, one by one in a line formation everyone moved inside the pod. The loud thud from the door isolated everyone. It was 6 AM and our bellies could be heard from one another.

"When was going to eat?" I thought out loud to myself. The room was big enough for half of us to sit down. Everyone else just stood up waiting impatiently. The stale air got worse by the minutes as the chatter grew. The room got much noisier. It went from stale to straight smelly. You have at least 50 grown men in a 15 x 10 room with one toilet and one sink that don't do shit. Mind you about half or even a third didn't brush their teeth because the smell of breath was being thrown around as if no one cared. My breath could be smelled and I brush my teeth. So just imagine the others who didn't.

"So what you hear for?" One asked the other. "Aggravated assault." Answered the other white guy. "Yup you're going to jail." The younger light skin prisoner joked. Laughter grew as well. It was amazing how all of us were in here about to see a judge to either be sentence or just go to a prelim as I was. Somehow, someway everyone had smiles on their faces. The ones who didn't have any type of facial expression, didn't because they were asleep or at least trying to catch a few z's before the bus transported us all to the courthouse. For what seemed like about an hour and a half, the Sheriffs walked in with their black and gold on. There uniform screamed power and authority. "There they go." Shouted one alerting everyone else that wasn't paying any attention to anything.

"About fucking time you pieces of shit." Yelled another. I watched as the pigs just smiled and chuckled at us because we were pissed that they were late. My hands were numb and I had to pist. I made my way over to the can, there had to be at least five guys hovering the toilet as if they were staring in a wishing well. "Excuse me fellas." I said hoping they would fucking move. I was still in pain from my healing wounds and all this extra bullshit wasn't helping the situation any. "Damn nigga you gota piss now? One of the "thorough" bread mother fucker decided to pop off early in the morning. "I did say excuse me didn't I?" I had no choice but to combat with the same tone. It seemed like no matter who or what everyone wanted to spark up a flare without knowing shit about anyone. I made it my business to take a mental photo of this ignorant disrespectful piece of shit. "Well if you asked or not you ain't going to make this small as room smell like piss, knowing this room small as fuck." This tall mother fucker wearing a kufi was a little too hostile for no apparent reason. He couldn't be serious. I too step towards him but one of his brothers got directly in my way.

"No need to take it there brother." The shorter and stockier one of the crew said in his deep modest tone. "It's your man, I gota use the bathroom that's all I need to do. If I piss on myself the smell will be all over the bus then what?" I tried another angle. With a swift head nod the toilet was open to my disposal. I release my bladder and just like that we were thrown into a van heading to the court house. Crammed like sardines we all sat shoulder to shoulder. There was no moving without the other one bumping into the other so if you had a problem with that then you were in for a rude awakening. The trip wasn't a long one but the anxiety began to build amongst everyone. The loud chatter ceased down into deep thoughts amongst our own thoughts. Many of the cases were very serious. My main concern was me, me and me at the moment. How would all this pan out for me? Will I make it out of here or what? Or would I sit in this place for very long time? Was there a way to escape all of this in one piece? Or better yet was there a way to not get any time at all? So many questions filled my head. " Ayo G?" A voice called over to me as we were exiting the van to enter another fucking holding pod that appeared to be underground. "Wassup?" I replied staring at his hands, than his eyes "I'm here for a robbery right? You'd think they gonna slam me?" The man I was listening to had two visible teeth that look as if they wanted to jump out of his mouth and fing the others.

His grays on his face needed to be trimmed down. His top lip was hardly noticeable. "I'm not gonna sit here and bull shit OG, but I don't know a mother fucking thing about law or anything else that is about to go down up in here." I answer truthfully to his question. The guy in front of me must've heard what I was telling the man. So I guess he decided to play jailhouse PD.

"What you hear for?" The middle age white guy asked him. "Robbery" toothless answered. "Okay you gota be a bit more specific than that okay." The jailhouse PD told him. I use that term very loosely. "Armed robbery" toothless corrected himself. Now we getting somewhere. You don't have to make me a believer you gota convince the jury because they the ones was going to slam you." The jailhouse PD stated clearly. Everyone stared at him as the PD try to help him. "You think they gonna hit me harder." Toothless answered desperately wanted to confirm his confirmation bias. "Everyone in the pod shut up and listen up for your name." Yelled another sheriff.My name was damn near last. The conversation between the two men continue.

"Let me ask you this. How many times have you been locked up?" The PD asked him scooting closer to hear his response. "About 22 or 21 times." Toothless answered my eyes popped out of my head. I just couldn't believe what I just heard. "Okay." The PD responded. "Now how many of those times have you been convicted of felonies?" Asked the PD. This old head had to check in his memory bank to find the answer to that question. "Seven".... No wait "six" toothless was a little confused. "Let's say seven just to be safe." Now how many years have you done altogether in your life?" The PD was really probing for his clues to get his assumption of all his case. "23 years." My jaw dropped now, fuck my eyes they done been fell out. 23 years I thought to myself. He has my whole life behind bars and some how was this even possible. I've only been here a few months and I know I'll never step foot in here again if I get the chance to be release. "Okay old head now out of all those convicted of felonies, how many of them were armed robberies?" Asked the PD. "Five of them." Toothless replied. The PD shook his head in disbelief, I hate to be the one to tell you this but I think you are done! You are definitely going to jail. The PD concluded his free consultation. By now half of us were dying of laughter, not because of the time old was about to get. He's been in and out of this prison for a great majority of his life and for some reason thinks that this time will end up less. Knowing damn well he knows better than that.

"If you want to eat come up and grab a bag lunch!" Yelled another sheriff with a trash bag full of bags with food in it. One by one we each grabbed a paper bag of food. It wasn't the most tasteful but it would most definitely serve its purpose.

You had your experienced criminals who already knew that their cases would be dropped from the rip, due to lack of evidence. They were planning what they were going to do once they got up out of here today. Then you had your ones who knew they weren't going anywhere no time soon. They talked about how they would be going to a certain state jail and of course reminiscing about the time they did at the state jail before. Lastly, you had your first timers who could be notice from a mile away without even searching for them. Fortunately, I was a lucky contestant to fit into that category. "Mr. Johnson and Mr. Ortiz." The names were being called in no particular order just names that corresponded to someone who committed an act of criminal mischief. This was there moment to shine and to be heard by the "State of New Jersey."..... "Mr. Ricardo and Mr. Rivera." I froze for a second. Here we go I thought to myself, the other Spanish man was already up ahead of me. I followed him as we exited the pod. I noticed more empty pods on the side of ours, but one pod stood out because there were females in that pod. I search for Kiki but I didn't notice anyone that resembled her. A few of them notice me and began to shout out through the window. I really couldn't make out what they were shouting. I did notice someone say good luck by reading their lips because their lips were full as fuck.

"Straight ahead." the blue eyed sheriff instructed us. "Now a left." he ordered again. "Have a seat."

It was a wooden bench that was bolted into the concrete floor so that no one could move it let alone break it. It too had a chain with a single cuff on it that was used no other than to secure us even more from being a threat to anyone who could come in contact with us. "Your lawyers will be here in a second." The sheriff with the silver name plate that read Sgt. Kowalski, John. That was a hell of a name to have I thought. "Yo pa who is your lawyer?" Mr. Rivera asked me. To be honest I had no fucking clue, no name, no description and no nada just a message from mom that I had a lawyer. "I don't know man." I replied to his question. Which was the dead ass truth, I didn't know. I was about to find out.

This mother fucker walked in with another man in a suit. One wore a navy blue with a white button up shirt with a light blue tie and the other wore a khaki color suit with a black button shirt with a brown tie. They look and played their part visual wise. They was fresh. I just only hope that their litigation style looked and played as good as they look. "Mr. Ricardo." The man with a khaki suit called out looking at both of us. "Right here." I anwered. "I'm Mr. Stoski." he shook my hand firmly. "I'm a friend of your mother Ms. Catherine and she told me that you had got yourself in a tight jam. She asked if I would or could represent you for as long as I could in this case. I decided to help the both of you out off the strength of your mom ok?" My lawyer had dark black hair, his eyes were also dark, dark eyebrows, neatly cleaned up and no facial hair. He wasn't as tall as I was but he wasn't as short as the other lawyer next to him. The other lawyer was also a paid lawyer for Mr. Rivera. It was a bit uncomfortable that there was no privacy no matter how low they decided to talk. I could hear them clearly as I'm sure they could hear us just as clear. "So let me look at your file for second." My lawyer Mr. Stoski scanned my file "Wow!" He said not stopping his eyes from scanning. "So you managed to catch a murder one and a weapon possession charge?" Mr. Stoski asked me looking at me dead into my eyes. "You want the truth or do you rather work with what they're saying?" I asked him. Even if the truth is far from what they're are proving, they have evidence and a witness who both are willing to testify." Stoski replied. I felt hopeless as those words came out of his mouth. "I'm sure this was a mutual conflict that wasn't one-sided, so our defense will have to be self-defense no matter how we look at this." Stoski said. "It was." I tried to agree with his educated guess. My palms were sweaty and as we spoke. Normally the prelim would be waived, but we are not going to do that. I want to see what tehy are working with. This will work in our favor." So how much time are we looking at?" I couldn't hold it in any longer. I wanted to know my legs were shaking so rapidly that it caused the fucking bench to rattle. My lawyer noticed it. "Nervous?" He asked. "What?"... Am I." I answered. "We are going to work through this." Stoski assured me. He was avoiding my initial question. It couldn't be good was all I thought. "How much time?" I reiterated. I'm not sure yet but you are definitely going to serve some time if they have a strong case built up against you, that's all I can say for now. We should be up soon is there anything I can do for you? As far as relating a message to your mom or whoever?" Stoski asked. "No.... Well yes tell mom that I said thank you and thank you to." I replied don't thank me just yet it just begun. "Stoski said. "Even if it doesn't go as planned thank you anyway because you didn't have to do this." I was grateful for his presence today. The Spanish guy next to me was in sobs. He was looking at two life sentences off the gate that was his initial offer. I didn't want to hear that but I didn't doubt that it could very well be me. So I was grateful for the little help that I was getting. The two men next to me had concluded their meeting with their attorneys and were escorted right out of the courtroom. There was no one in the room.

"So you want to tell me what really happened, because your affidavit is clean and cut but there might be a few loopholes hidden. I'm going to file a motion to obtain your discovery, but I need you to tell me exactly what happened that night detail for detail so I can help you better. No shortcuts every single detail" Stoski explained to me.

Linda was up early there was no way she was going to miss this day for the world, she had to know and support what her brother was going through. "Mom!" Linda yelled over to her mom's room. Mom slow steps could be heard. "Yes baby?" "Did you call the lawyer?" Linda asked. "I called but no answer but I did leave a message." Mom confirmed to her beautiful daughter. "All look at you getting all prettified for your brother's big day." Mom complimented her. It just so happened that Linda was wearing the outfit that Manny had helped her pick out the day in the mall, when he bought mom those expensive shades. "You look gorgeous." Mom complimented Linda again. "Why aren't you ready yet mom?" and "thank you." I'll be quick Linda can you put the coffee pot on when you go downstairs please." It's already on mom." Linda was on her a game this morning. "Nice." mom replied leaving to go get dressed. Linda modeled in the mirror talking to herself. "If anything happened to my brother everyone is going to pay a small price until I feel as though it's enough." Linda had that sinister grin on her face as she modeled in front of the mirror while applying some eyeliner. The phone rang hysterically....." Hello" Linda answered. It was Felicia hey Linda are you going to the hearing this morning?" Felicia asked the million-dollar question as if she wasn't "of course why wouldn't I?" Linda answered. "I don't know just asking." Felicia replied. "You want to ride with me because I'm almost ready." Felicia offered "hold on." Linda bolted to mom's room. You want to ride with Felicia she's almost ready." Linda asked mom. She didn't say a word, she just put her thumbs up and Linda turn around and left. "Just come on by when you're ready girl." Linda switched up her attitude. "See you shortly." Felicia ended. "I don't know what to do with her." Linda spoke again to herself, what did Felicia ever do to Linda? Everyone's ready sipping on a hot mug of coffee waiting for little Ms Felicia to arrive. "This girl is going to be late" mom said with an attitude. "The cab would have been here already." Mom was losing her patients. She lit a cigarette and sat back down. "Come on mom with the cigarettes." Linda whined. "It's not me it's my anxiety I can't miss Mannys first hearing imagine how that boy will feel." "Beep, beep!" The sound of the blaring horn could be heard all the way inside clear as day. "There she go, put that out smoky" Linda made light of the situation hurrying towards the white Lexus mom took her cigarettes wherever she went.

—

They all jumped out of the Lexus which was parked up the street. The breeze was picking up it was a matter of time until the snow would began to fall. Entering the big establishment that contained so much authority felt odd,. Linda had never entered this building before, neither has Felicia.

"Put all metal objects in a plastic container and all bags, pocketbooks and jackets coats on the conveyor belt." The security guard asked in a deep voice. After passing the metal detector and clearing it swiftly everyone except Felicia. She had change in her pocket that she didn't notice. "Thank you ladies." The security guard permitted them to continue about their business. "Fourth floor" Felicia said. Heading straight towards the elevator. Linda looked at her. "I hope we made it." Mom said. Felicia and Linda simultaneously looked at their watches. "We should" Linda assure mom. "Bing!" The doors of the elevator opened and it was so spacious inside, there had to be at least 8 people inside and the floor still could be very much visible. "Fourth floor please." Mom said hoping the lady with the pinstripe suit would push the button. She didn't need to because it was already lit. She pushed it anyway. Linda grabbed mom's hand. They were frightened from Manuel, no one was ready to deal with any of this. A few people got off ont he second floor and others got on "nine please" the white male asked filling the elevator with his strong cologne. Mom step closer to get a better smell. Linda laughed and pulled her hand back as if she was a child. Fourth floor the elevator slowed down as it finally came to a halt. A good portion of everyone in the elevator got off. 4B, Felicia was repeating. Thats what she was told when she called earlier this morning confirming all her doubts. She was going to see Rock by any means. Exiting the door slowly and quickly Linda was behind mom so mom initially was first entering the dead silent courtroom Linda noticed a familiar face in the front corner as she backed up almost instantly. "Go in, I'll be right back." She directed Felicia to proceed. Linda had her hand on her chest as if her heart was about to explode from her body. How could I be so stupid and not think she wouldn't show her face. This is the most important day of her brother's life, What was she to do now? Linda thought. "Fuck no!" She was beating herself up. She was pacing back and forth in the hallway where the elevators were. After about four minutes of pacing she decided to abandon entire building because this could turn into a real problem if she were to be figured out. Mom and Felicia found seats in the middle row that was almost clear. There were only about four people occupying the pews. The judge had not exited his chambers yet, so they were clear to speak amongst themselves as everyone prayed for their love ones, who were about to be judged for his or her actions in a few moments. Mom noticed Mr. Stoski and he noticed her. He winked at mom. Felicia noticed the wink. "Oh my God he's cute." Felicia stated. Mom gave her the stank eye. "You got your man honey." Mom joked. "I know but did he just wink at you?" Felicia asked in disbelief. "He sure did." Mom boasted. That's the lawyer I got for my baby." Mom brag some more. "Oh really?" Felicia was super excited now, knowing that Rock didn't have to go at this bare ass. Somebody has to look out for my baby." Mom made that clear. "And where the hell is Jalinda?" Mom asked. The female in the far right front row kept looking back to mom and Felicia as if she recognized the two from somewhere but would change her stare every few seconds. Ms. Cathy you know that girl in front of us?" Felicia asked. Mom her eyes moved over to who Felicia was talking about but it wasn't until she was able to get a full view of the woman's face that it rang a bell. Mom change her visions. "No she's probably looking at the people next to us are behind us." Mom tried to take the attention off this woman." Would everyone rise." the bailiff announced in his early manly caffeinated voice. Everyone rose mom looked around for Linda and it was pointless because she was nowhere to be found. The black gown appeared in the courtroom. His present screamed attention and authority.

"You may be seated." All white male with very few strands of hair left on his head announced. "Is everyone ready?" He asked the DA. "Yes we are." The skinny female DA reply back at the Honorable Judge. "Let's proceed."…. "Well your honor to begin we would like to introduce case number CL265563 state of New Jersey versus Manuel Ricardo.

I was brought out of the room and escorted towards the table where my lawyer was standing tall. His face wore a look of determination plastered on it. I noticed all the faces in the pews and the first two I noticed was mom and Felicia. My stomach settled at the site of those two standing in front of me. I didn't even get the chance to notice the other female in the far right. I had so much running through my mind it was unbelievable. I stood about 1 foot taller than my lawyer. He whispered into my ear. Don't laugh but why are you so tall?" Stoski joked trying to get me to ease up. I held in my reply "who is representing Mr. Ricardo?" The judge asked. "Michael Stoski criminal and civil law attorney." Mr. Stoski replied swiftly. "Your Honor Mr. Ricardo is being charged with murder one and possession of a legal instrument used in a crime." The little feisty bitch spoke with authority, getting out her point of interest. "And how do you plea?" The judge asked. "Not guilty you're Honor." Mr. Stoski answered for me. "You may be seated." He gave us permission to sit down and listen, but the DA took it upon herself to continue standing. "Mr. Stoski and his client have chosen to proceed with the hearing that is scheduled for today, I contested to this and opinionated to waive the hearing until a later date so matters could be resolved, in which the state of New Jersey would consider their cooperation to our needs." The DA was a blonde blue-eyed sexy white girl, her legs were exposed up to her knees. Her muscles look more defined and to be honest I wanted her to take me prisoner all on her own. Her diamond earring shined brighter than the florescent lighting in the courtroom. Her voice was soft but it had an edge and power behind it. The judge listen to what was being said by the district attorney.

"Mr. Stoski." The judge looked over to my lawyer. The spotlight was on him now, please don't freeze up on me let's do this I thought looking up at the DA. Her pink lips wouldn't dare to go unnoticed, I was in love with this woman who was trying desperately to lock me up and throw away the key forever. "That is absolutely correct your honor my client and myself will likely proceed with the hearing as Ms. Miller has informed you that is in fact scheduled for this lovely morning." Bull's-eye I thought this man was insane. The judge wore a smirk his face. I look back and looked at Felicia she was as gorgeous as the first time I met her at the hospital. I diverted my attention to mom but the slap on my thigh by Mr. Stoski indicated for me to pay a fuck intention. I did just that. "Very well." The DA began to prove what she knew from what the officers, the phone calls and what so-called witnesses informed her.

"Mr. Ricardo is being accused of murder one, possession of instrument of a crime used in this murder.

On 7/30 at approximately 12 o'clock midnight to 12:30 AM Mr. Ricardo had gotten himself in a physical altercation with the deceased. For reasons that are unclear, the fight began as a fistfight as it rapidly escalated into Mr. Ricardo plunging a butterfly knife into the side of the deceases jugular vein in his neck, in which has caused the deceased to lose a vast amount of blood causing the deceased to die on the scene. The paramedics were called but were not able to resuscitate the deceased." I hated how she kept on using that deceased word. "Our witnesses who have not shown up today after making many failed attempts to get in contact with them. It was too late when the authorities and medics arrived on the scene to resuscitate a lifeless body. Mr. Ricardo was present at the scene with blood on his persons and an object later recognizes as the butterfly knife by the corner department after the autopsy was completed. It was brought to our knowledge that the size of the puncture wounds match identically to the knife that was located a few feet from the accused. When questioned about these accusation Mr. Ricardo failed on numerous attempts to provide and cooperate with authorities. The accused is being held at the Camden County jail till this day." The DA didn't sugar coat anything she hated me as soon as I walked in the courtroom. "That's all for now you're Honor." Ms. Miller concluded for now sitting down in her chair crossing those sexy legs. My tongue was dry as fuck. I couldn't find room to swallow. I was beginning to actually believe that I could very well be a killer, if I would go by what she just put together.

"Mr. Stoski." The judge diverted his attention on him. This was where he had to counter her accusation, to see if he could get all this thrown out or convince a judge that they had no official grounds to proceed with the case. "Your Honor thank you." Mr. Stoski began. The stenographer was typing away. "Ms. Miller did you personally see my client do any of what you're accusing him of?" Stoski asked. "No" she answered. "Thank you. You have informed the court here today that you in fact have witnesses, are they here today?" Stoski asked. I like where he was going with this. "Yes and no." Miller answered. "So no?" Stoski asked "I don't know." Miller answered. "You don't know?" "How about the arresting officers are they here today?" Stoski asked trying to throw some curveballs. "No they are not, they are in the field." Miller answered. "Another no." Stoski stated moving on after a series of questions. I was sure that the judge would dismiss this case. "Anything else Mr. Stoski?" The judge asked. "Yes Your Honor. I asked that the state of New Jersey dismiss this case on lack of evidence, lack of witnesses that apparently aren't not here today." "That's all." Stoski had this in the bag. That was all I was thinking. "Ms. Miller." The judge looked at the DA for a comeback. "Your honor I disagree, if you dismiss this case you'll be releasing a murderer back on the streets. The witnesses are there and the evidence is clear as day, so with that I say we hold Mr. Ricardo so we can properly put the case in better order and believe in our investigators and uphold our end of the law." Mrs. Miller was a bitch for real, she had a strong argument and it could work in her favor. Our next hearing will be held on July 18 Mr. Ricardo will be held in the county until further matters. Clank! Clank! The gavel spoke and just like that the matter was closed. I wasn't going anywhere but even with all that said I had some what type of hope in my lawyer. Plus I had to do my own homework in the prison in the library. By now all I wanted to do was head back to my cell and eat a honey bun. "Is not over we are off to a great start." Mr. Stoski informed me. "Like I said thank you." My personal escorts walked me straight out of the courtroom with no time to speak to anyone. It was fucked up, no hi, not even a hug or nothing. I was so close to them but yet I felt so distant from them.

Chapter 14

"Game on"

"Oh my God girl what took you so long to get here?" Jacqueline said opening door to her second-floor apartment over in Westfield. Linda just had gotten out of the cab she called from her house about an hour ago, and she now arrived at Jacqueline's house in two hours. "You know how these cabs are around here. They come and pick you up when they feel like it instead of arriving at the time you really need them to arrive." I'm here though." Linda said cheerfully. Come on and excuse the mess. I didn't get a chance to clean up yet. The girls are already up stairs eating munchies and doing each other's nails. I like your PJs baby." Jacqueline complemented Linda. Thank you they are my favorite. Linda had on some Scooby Doo PJs that looked a bit too big for her small body. The smell of cake was lingering amongst the air, it caught Linda's attention immediately.

"Tell me that isn't a brownie being baked." Linda had a good nose to smell out things. "Yes it is girl and I got us some ice cream too." Jacqueline escorted Linda towards the kitchen. "I don't see no mess, you must of clean before we got here because this place is far from messy." Linda spoke about her observation. "So what did you buy? I see the bag." Jacqueline change the subject. I bought a fifth of Henny and a fifth of Vodka. I hope you have some juice or soda." Linda asked. Opening the fridge. Linda watched as Jacqueline ass filled up her PJs. Her's had a bunch of marijuana leaves all over it. "Which one do you prefer? She pulled out a 2 Liter of Coke and a big gallon of Florida orange juice? It doesn't matter. I'm drinking Henny I know that much." Linda said opening the Henny. Me too Jacqueline decided to drink Henny as well. Linda began to play bartender. "So how many people are upstairs?" Linda asked after making the 2nd cup. Four of us altogether." Jacqueline informed. "Oh look." Digging in the freezer Jacqueline pulled out a tub of cookies and cream ice cream. "For our brownies."

Jacqueline said. "So who's upstairs?" Linda asked a bit anxious to know who was up there and wondered if any of them knew Linda and vice versa. "My friend Mary and Denise." Neither of their name sounded familiar. Linda assume she was in the clear. After all the drinks were all put together Jacqueline grab the bag of mixed nuts and lead the way upstairs.

The girls were listening to some old school Stevie B and like Jacqueline informed Linda they were doing their manicures and pedicures on one another.

"Oh yeaaahhh! Finally the drinks have arrived." The Burnett said. Getting her nails painted. "I'm so sorry girls but the cabby was an idiot." They all laughed. "We already know how that is." Other girls spoke. Taste it and let me know if is too strong or not strong enough." Linda said with a big smile handing the drinks to both of the other girls. "Thank you." They said in unison. You are welcome." This is Jasmine" Jacqueline introduced Linda to her friends, and Jasmine these are my best friends the one with green eyes and blonde highlights her name is Mary and that's Denise with the jet black hair with them dark mysterious eyes." They all shook hands smiling and greeting one another. "A toast." She waisted no time. Jacqueline spoke eagerly taking a sip from her glass. "Clank! Clank! Clank!" Friends are all we need." Friends" they all shouted together taken sips out of their glasses. They all made a sour patch face. "Is it strong?" Linda also scrunched up her face. "No!" Once again they all said. They all laughed. "Perfect" Mary said taking another sip. So girls now that we are all here what do you want to do?" Jacqueline was heading towards a closet and grabbed a paper bag with two string handles. "You want to watch a movie she threw on the bed or you want to get straight to the fun stuff. She tipped the bag upside down and all its contents came out dropping onto the bed. Linda eyes grew big. "Oh my God!" Jacqueline this is supposed to be a sleepover." Linda said in complete shock. She couldn't believe what her eyes were witnessing. There were dildos, little bullets, tongue vibrators, sex balls, lubrication etc. etc. "You are a freaky little one." Mary said joking sipping her drink. The look on her face shows she was ready to slam it all up in her virgina. They all laughed. "Once we get done with all this fun you will be sleeping over more often." Jacqueline joked. The movie was called "hit me hard" it was rated triple X so we already knew it was a porno. "I said it would be fun plus it wasn't my idea." Jacqueline told Linda. "So it's you Jasmine, you are the horn dog." Denise joked. "I suggested a sleepover not a toy orgy." Linda defended her case. "Well I added a twist, you don't want to play?" Jacqueline held up to 10 inch dildo that had to be at least two or 3 inches in diameter. They all blush. "Exactly we are all freaks." Jacqueline blurted out. Tonight will be a memorable night Linda thought, but she had other things on her agenda and it would be a task worth completing.

—

"Come on!" Leak pushed Rocks to his max on the Smith machine. "Eerrgg-hhhh!" Rock let out a growl as he pushed the 380 on the press for his eighth repetition tenth set. He was getting closer to his mark. "That's what the fuck I'm talking about Rock!" Go hard or go home ain't no room for no soft ass niggaz!" Leak was all hyped it was just a couple of weeks ago Rock was almost offed and now he was stronger than ever.

The two of them concluded there work out and headed to a spot that wasn't occupied they went straight to business. "So when you try to make your move?" Leak was a thoroughbred hood nigga for real, no questions asked. "Soon." Rock replied. Still with a bad taste in his mouth over these two mother fuckas. Well good because I talked to a few people and I'm going to fill in the empty slot." Leak informed me of this new information. I dapped him up. "Early!" About fucking time, you sliding back over. I thought you change your mind about coming through." I said checking out who what was moving around us. Ever since the incident. I've been on extra paranoia which was a good thing because I was on mega alert with everyone's movement. Not saying I wasn't before but now I could spot a fly coming towards me from the other side of the room. "Slash gathered all the info we needed?" Leak asked "he sure did." I replied. "That's what's up we gonna need all that because I'm a bang his man's the fuck out until he is breathless." I can't stand that pussy." Leak built up some serious animosity toward them Niggaz. I'm content with just leak willing to ride out with me, I really didn't trust no other man in this facility.

"Lock it in gentlemen!" The Sgt. yelled at everyone who was out in the gym. "Ima get with you tonight when I come through." Leak headed to his cell and I did the same. I noticed this big black guy who resembled Jamal's brother from the club. I got closer his face seemed to not fit my mental description anymore of his brothers. I was highly mistaken. "Can I help you?" The big brother asked in his deep voice. "No just you resemble someone that I know." I didn't want to rip with this big ass nigga. "I get that a lot." The big man said with a grin and proceeded his away.

I thought about how much Kiki wanted to talk to me when she saw me at the service. You can say that there was no service. All we did was talk to one another the whole time. Her uniform hugged her sexy ass body. I wanted to rip her open so bad. The problem was that the distance between us was quite a distance and when it was time to go, the ladies left separately which was fucked up because with that being done. There was no way for me to come in contact with her. She informed me that Banga and Jigz never did what they said they were going to do. I somehow already felt that would happen knowing how fast these two live their lives. To worry about someone who isn't even in the picture could be forgotten in an instant. I kind of felt bad for the hood rat, but I had my own shit worry about. Bigs was asleep as I walked up in the cell. I slammed the shit out the door. He jumped up. "Get up nigga, you going to sleep all day, every day?" Slash was in his own zone, writing down some lyrics. I'm tired nigga we stood up until 3 AM." I laughed. "My bad I forgot." Joking, Slash caught what I was doing and shook his head while still writing. I was scheduled to go to the library with Slash later and I couldn't wait. "What time is our passes to the library?" I interrupted Slash and his thoughts, he held up his index finger not breaking his train of thought. "1 o'clock?" I asked. He nodded in agreement with me. I washed up quickly and lay back on my rack. I had already replied to all the letters that came my way with all respectable and truthful responses. I wanted my women to be on board with me in this troubling time but on a friendship level. After seeing Felicia the day at my hearing brought back some deep emotions I couldn't wait to see her again.

—

By now all of the girls were feeling tipsy with the bottles in Jacqueline's room. The fifth was by Linda. There was no more soda and no one wanted to go anywhere so Jacqueline, Mary and Denise were all sipping it straight on the rocks.

"So look y'all." Jacqueline was slurring a little. Let me tell you what happened a couple weeks ago." This is what Linda was waiting for some personal information. Linda took a straight shot, and blew it out so the burning sensation could be tamed. Mary reached into her handbag and pulled out a white tube like cylinder. It appeared to be a joint. The lighter confirmed that

"I know you not gonna lite that in here." Jacqueline contested. "Come on, it too cold to go outside Jacqueline." Mary pouted until Jacqueline gave in. "No more after this one." Listen, I need your advice." Jacqueline was asking the ladies. "Okay sorry what happened?" Denise filled in. Now Linda was on the top right corner of Jacqueline's bed sitting up, Jacqueline was on the left corner also sitting. Denise and Mary were both on chairs at the side of the bed one on Linda side and the other with Jacqueline. All the toys were still on the bed waiting to be experimented with. Jacqueline sipped off her glass. The smell of marijuana was circulating and it smelled so familiar to Linda. "What is that?" Linda asked Mary who was passing the joint over to Denise. The words that her brother told her in the truck that night, echoed as if he was in the room with her. "It's some Cush I got it for my brother." Mary stated. "And what else is in it?" Linda challenged. Mary looked at Linda then at Jacqueline. "Nothing else just some high grade bud." "Why?" Mary asked. I just want to make sure that it's just weed that's all." The joint made it to Linda, she took a couple drags and passed it off.

"I went to Rocks hearing." She had everyone's attention now. Linda was curious to find out what she could possibly say but knew it would lead to some more valuable information in just a few seconds. Mary sipped and pulled on the joint "you did go?" Mary asked in shock, but most of all excitedly. "So tell us how did it go?" Denise asked. Linda waited for a response. "He is so fine girl." Jacqueline said. They had him all shackled up from head to toe." Jacqueline looked at Linda. Linda shook her head in disbelief showing some type of emotion but didn't say anything. "He is such a criminal." Mary said jabbing Jacqueline with her comment. "He isn't a criminal!" Jacqueline defended her man. Linda watched her attentively, she was hurt with the accusations. It was bad enough that the courts were accusing Rock of being a murderer, now Jacqueline's friends had their mind already set on a guilty verdict as well. I'm glad they weren't on the jury panel to determine his verdict Linda thought. The case didn't even begin and a guilty plea was already instated by the public. Jacqueline got quiet for a second. "What's wrong?" Linda asked sensing the change in attitude. "He didn't even recognize me." Jacqueline said in a mumble, Mary went right towards her besty and hugged her. "He did, I'm sure he did." Mary said in her feminine soft voice trying her best to console her friend. I sat in the front row hoping and praying that he would be all right." Jacqueline's voice was cracking Linda waited for tears to fall, but no tears came. Was she putting up a façade to see what Linda would say or do? Does she know who Linda really was? Did she in fact notice Linda at the hearing and just played as if she didn't know anything? Linda's mind began to spin a thousand miles per hour. The alcohol and the marijuana had her very paranoid. She needed to gain confirmation on all of her suspicion before they get out of hand. How could she go about doing that without setting off the alarm and jeopardizing her cover? The last thing she needed was to raise suspicion on herself, even with little evidence that she could possibly have against her and being already exposed. "Did he look at you?" Denise asked. "No." Jacqueline replied "how come?" Denise asked a stupid question. "I don't know." All I know was that he look back and smile at the people sitting on a bench behind me but I didn't see no type of actual communication." Jacqueline explained. "So how do you know he was smiling at them and not anyone else on the side of the room?" Mary took the words right out of Linda's mouth. "I can't be 100% positive but the look this girl had on her face made my stomach turn. I wanted to go up to her so bad, and ask her if she knew Rock. There was so much being said about him that it caused me to freeze." Jacqueline spoke with her eyes closed, Replaying the events in her mind reliving the moment. "What did they say?" Linda asked. Jacqueline opened her eyes and looked at Linda. "They called him a murderer, a cold-blooded killer who didn't deserve to be let back out in society until the outcome of this case." Jacqueline spoke in pain. She grabbed a glass of alcohol, and pretty much chugged half the glass. Mary pulled the cup away or at least tried too but Jacqueline shook her head finishing it all in one gulp. Jacqueline was hurt and didn't want to be held back from drinking her sorrow away. "Do you think what they are saying about him is true?" Denise asked. "I don't know, I wasn't there. All I know is that they were presenting the case. It made everyone listening to actually think that he did commit a terrible criminal act point blank." Jacqueline informed her friends in her own summary of the events that took place that day. "What else did they say?" Linda asked. Well he had a lawyer or APD. I don't know the difference between the two because they all look the same to me." Jacqueline was also very ignorant when it came to the law and the court System. "APD is an attorney appointed by the courts. It just means that a PD in most cases is known to sell you out in most cases not really caring about the outcome. I may be wrong and a lawyer is or can be an appointed lawyer or just a lawyer, that you and your family can hire to represent you and he will actually try his best to help you win the case. He has a name and a law firm to uphold in order to keep his clients to keep coming to him for his help." Denise was ranting on about the whole lawyer incidents well basically just stating her opinion between the two. It helped a lot because none of the ladies knew anything about neither. "So what did his lawyer do to help?" Linda asked. "Well he asked a lot of questions trying to make the DA sound as if he didn't know anything about Rock. He questioned all of his alleged accusations just to see if thet were fully accurate. It sounded as if he was putting up a good argument, but it didn't work out because the judge and the DA didn't fall for what Rock's lawyers was trying to prove." Jacqueline spoke. "Were there any witnesses?" Linda asked. The DA said they had witnesses that were willing to testify but no one was there. My baby dad said that he was going to testify along with his little girlfriend but I don't know, because no one showed up." Jacqueline went on to explain dropping jewels. "So they're going to testify at the trial?" Denise asked. I think so he would rather see Rock in jail than to deal with him in the street like a real man." Jacqueline spoke negative about her baby dads. "Is there any way you can try to get him, to not show up so that they could potentially drop the case?" Denise asked curiously. Linda listened attentively while looking at the toys on the bed. I wish there was a way for me to get him to not show up but it seems as if he already has his mind made up already. He hates Rock and it's all because of me." Jacqueline said putting her head down. "Is not your fault you didn't force your baby dads to hurt Rock, nor did you force Rock to fuck you. Everyone that's in this situation is grown and knew what and who would lead to what." Mary said sipping on her drink. "Yet it's not your fault." Linda spoke also trying to console the now depressed Jacqueline.

"This is supposed to be a night for us to have fun and for us to enjoy." Denise got up and picked up the sex balls. "I want to know how the hell you use these." Denise joked.She changed the mood inside the room. We all were pretty much intoxicated. Linda picked up the DVD and threw it in the player. After a few seconds a woman getting fuck by two men vigorously popped up on the TV screen.

"That's what I'm talking about." Mary said pouring a row of shots for everyone. Linda noticed Jacqueline's mood. She was down and depressed. Her hands began touching herself not caring who was watching her. Her hand slid down her pants and found her love button. She massaged it slowly getting comfy on her bed.

"Oh my God are you....?" Mary notice what Jacqueline was doing. Jacqueline smile confirming all of Mary's questions. Denise opened the balls and took them out of the package. One by one, all the ladies found a spot on the bed. The moaning and the screaming from the porno caused all four of them to get moist down bottom. Linda picked up the small bullet. She made her way getting closer to Jacqueline. What came out her mouth made completely no sense at all. "You know what just popped in my head?" Jacqueline asked still touching herself. "What's that?" Linda asked. "There was an older woman there at the hearing that look familiar, but I can't figure out exactly where I saw her or even if I really did." Jacqueline's mind was still on Rock. The humming of the bullet got everyone's attention. "Let's clear your mind a little bit. "Linda said with a big smile on her face enjoying the vibration in her hand. Mary was all over Jacqueline's breast once, Linda said the magic words. The older lady was mom and Linda had to eliminate that thought. Mary kissed Jacqueline and slid her hand up under her shirt fondling her breasts. Linda slid off Jacqueline's PJs and exposing her bare legs and her vagina. With no hesitation the bullet had Jacqueline moaning loudly. Jacqueline let go of all her pent-up emotions and enjoyed all of the attention. Denise also found a spot to play with but it wasn't on Jacqueline it was on Linda. She touched Linda softly. This caught Linda off-guard. She flinched but Denise's soft spoken words relaxed her. It's okay Jasmine it's only me and the three of us." Denise kissed Linda's lower back, lifting her shirt to see her skin. She licked around her waistline. She too remove Linda's PJs but unlike Jacqueline. Linda had a sexy booty shorts that were baby blue hugging her ass. Denise didn't take them off yet. She wanted to feel Linda up first. With the bullet causing a rainstorm in between Jacqueline's legs with Mary sucking and biting on her sexy round breast.

The orgasms, after orgasms were for certain. Jacqueline tugged on Mary's PJs trying to get her naked. Mary got the hint and decided to stripped down to her birthday suit. Her pink nipples were extremely erected. Her breast were no smaller than an A- cup. Her pussy wasn't completely shaven but it was neatly groomed with a landing strip that was not thicker than a stick of gum. Jacqueline slid her finger inside of Mary, the sound of her fingers swishing in and out of her pink pussy, also had her moaning in ecstasy. Linda licked Jacqueline's clit while she played with the 3 inch bullet that was still causing uncontrollable orgasms inside of Jacqueline. No more thoughts of Rock at this moment Linda thought. Denise let herself under Linda's waistline, since Linda was on all four playing with Jacqueline and began to eat Linda out with the dildo in her hand. "Oh yes?" Linda shouted out of pure excitement. She had been eaten out by Joel on many occasions but for some reason Denise made her feel pleased more. Maybe it was because they were doing so much and their levels of sexual attraction have increased so much, due to all the touching of one another. Linda thought.

"Finger fuck me baby yes! I love it Jacqueline yes!" Mary was about to cum. "You like it baby?" Jacqueline looked in Mary's eyes, cum from me if you like it she said sliding three fingers inside of her. Linda felt some pressure down low but didn't oppose to any of it. Whatever Denise was doing she would let her do because it was feeling so good Linda was thinking. "Jasmine fuck me to baby, make me come some more." Jacqueline was letting it all out. They were all on each other forgetting about the video that was playing. A camera in this room at this very moment would've been priceless.

"Oh my God! Linda maneuvered her waist to invite the dildo that was being driven into her wet walls by Denise. "Damn!" She took a nice deep breath. Denise slid the dildo right inside of Linda slowly. Everyone was getting action except for Denise. Her love box was just as wet as all the others there was no denying it. Mary came while kissing Linda. "You like that Jasmine?" Mary asked watching and rubbing all over Linda. "Oh..... Yes! It feels so good." Linda bit her bottom lip also enjoying it all. "Don't stop." Yelled Mary. "Right there, right there!" Mary was about to cum again. Her tiny thick body shook all over as she released her juices. She moved over to where Denise was lying and ripped off her PJs, she grabbed the sex balls she so desperately wanted to know how they worked. Lubing them up, one by one disappearing inside of Denise's love box. Each ball had a tiny metal ball in it so the vibrating sent a wave of excitement through her body. All the balls forced her to stop was she was doing. "What the fuck!"..... All! All my God have mercy....!!!Denise yelled from under Linda. She grabbed Linda's tities and began to purr like a kitten. "I want to try them." Jacqueline cried out in between her burst of pleasure. It was a pure orgy going on in their room amongst the four of them. What was supposed to be a sleepover turn into a rated X fuck fest in a matter of seconds. It didn't end there the shin-dig went on until about midnight. After eating all the goodies and junk food all four of them ended up passing out on top of one another.

—

It's been a couple of days Slash and I did our research on my case in the law library. To be frank if it was up to me entirely. I would've gave up the very second I picked up one of those law books. The wording in those books gave me a migraine. Slash understood the wording a bit more accurately than I did so his help was very much needed and appreciated.

"Here." Leak passed me some gloves that he managed to swindle out of the kitchen from a worker. I put them on. "Just in case." Leak spoke putting his gloves on as well. Bigs and Slash were both sent to go to the yard. We decided that they didn't need to know anything that we were plotting on, even though they knew something was going to happen in the near future after I got hit up. "I am nervous as shit." I said to Leak being completely honest. "That's all right I am too." I wondered if he was lying to me because he didn't look as if he was anywhere near nervous. "Just try and relax, take deep breaths this is going to be quick. If you don't want to do this you don't have to Rock." Leak tried to make me feel better. I looked at him. "I have to do this, if I don't it will never stop." Leak nodded in agreement to my statement. "I'm not gonna stop this fight I'm going to end all these future fights." I went on silent after those words left my lips. We were in the cell. I was sitting on the toilet, I had the wooden wack in my hand. I was examining it wondering how perfectly crafted it was. It had a nice point at the end of it. Just by looking at it anyone could tell that they could inflict some serious pain on the human body. I touched the tip and just let my imagination run. Leak had the plastic one that was about

7 inches long and just as sharp. He decided he wanted this one because he had to take care of Curtis's boy who was a lot muscular than Curtis.

"These niggas are done, that's all I'm going to say." Leak was ready. I wondered if our plan would work and if it didn't how much time would we be forced to do. We went over our plan about 100 times until we both were sure that we had a down pack. It was only about 15 minutes left of yard. "One more final-round from the CO." Leak informed me. I was shaken my left leg uncontrollably. I was about to shed blood and it would not be my blood on this particular day. The blood of a menace who thought he was untouchable. The word in the county jail was that, me getting poked up changed my whole demeanor to a soft ass nigga. I didn't mind the rumors because I knew that they were not true. They did change me into something but that's something was far from soft. I was facing a lot of time and let's get this straight, there was a good chance this case would drag me down into the dumps way after it was resolved. I was becoming a SAVAGE my anger was beginning to seep out my tear ducts. I was no longer Rock I was "ROCK!" I was going to make sure my name would travel all the way to state prisons. Or even further. My wrath is going to be felt.

"It's go time." Leak said. The doors would open in a matter of seconds. This was our Q to wait for the rush of people to come and we would split up. I was going right and leak will head left. With only one thing on our mind and that was to meet up at our targets at the same time. Which was only few feet from the entrance where Curtis and his man's would split up? They would head to their individual cells, but before they would split they would talk for a few minutes about who knows what. Since they were not living in the same cell. This was there routine. This is what our sources have informed us. The crowds of people began pouring as they did every day on the hour on the second. The thing with all and most prison/jail was that they were all set up to run themselves, every day like clockwork. There was hardly a day when the system was off schedule and when it was it was because there was a state emergency or a shakedown.3......2.......1 game on. I kept close to the wall on the perimeter avoiding any and every individual in my site. There was no room for not even a 10th of a second of distraction. It would sabotage the whole plan and that wasn't going to be part of the script.

“Wassup Rock.” Homeboy in front of me put his hand out, I would apologize to him later because for now I blew right by him. “It’s like that?” I kept my hands in my pants as every other person did in this jail. It wouldn’t be looked at as something out of the norm. I had to be about 75 feet away from our midpoint. I grab my waistline which was only to be occupy with Mr. Woody and I’m not talking about my wood but the wack, it was still in place. It was hard for me to see Leak but I was sure that he was on point. I noticed many individual but today two individuals’ days were numbered. I tried not to look so obvious but my determination caused me to look all my prey like a lion who has seen his meal as clear as day, that was soon to be captured. Curtis back was towards me he was engaged in a deep discussion with his right hand man. The man who had a deadly vice grip on me. I glanced at his face but he too was wrapped up exchanging words with Curtis. He looked my way but a quick side step over hid my face, with the guys that were coming in towards me bought me some more time to get closer. 20 feet away now I sped up my pace. I noticed Leak directly on the opposite end where I was standing. The mass of bodies help camouflage the attack. 15 feet from them my heart was beating rapidly. The closer I got the sweatier my palms got. I gripped Mr. Woody, that was patiently waiting on my hip to taste some human pussy. My fingers wrapped around it, just like I practiced numerous times in a cell. 10 feet, they had their heads down as if they were staring at something in each other’s hands. This was going too smoothly. I cared less about the COs or any other matter that was being conducted in this very moment. We had about five minutes before the crowds would begin to disperse completely making us oddballs. 5 feet, I could see Leak clear as day. The sinister grin on his face look so devilish it made me walk faster. Curtis boy decided to look up an alert Curtis, but his words could only be made out as “Oh.” The sharp pain was already fucking his flesh. I poked Curtis right below his kidney with the same force I used almost 10 years ago when I swung that stick at him. It went in so flush with no problem. The smell of his perspiration flared my nostrils. He must’ve been working out. I saw Leak’s arm dance in and out so rapidly I cloned his every move doing the same increasing the number of pokes. I counted 15 pokes give or take one or two. Curtis and his boy were hugging one another as if they were lovers. “Move!!” Leak growled. I removed the wack and walked the way Leak came from and Leak took the route I came from. We were done, we had to conclude our lap which would put us exactly where we started. If Biggs and Slash were on point they should be exactly where they were instructed to be. My feet were moving faster than they were supposed to be moving. So I tried my best to slow down my heart rate. A rookie move to run would only alarm everyone that I did something. I saw Slash he was heading towards me. Gloves were off and wrapped around the wack, handoff. It had to be discarded immediately. It didn't matter where but it had to be far away from Leak and myself. As long as it wasn't on our person it would be damn near impossible to pin this bullshit on us. The alarm was blaring loudly it was a lockdown. I was already in my cell on my bed. Leak wasn't in yet. I wondered where the hell could he be and why wasn't he in here yet. Bigs came in with a look of uncertainty on his face. I knew something was wrong.

"Where is Leak!?" I asked in a pist off tone. He stood quiet. "Yo!" I barked he flinched. My reflexes where to go in his mouth hard. "I'm as you again where is he?" Just as I balled up my fist ready to splash his face again. Slash was in "Ayo chill what you doing?" His eyes met mine but my stairs showed no time to explain, he threw his palms up. "whatever" minding my business." Slash Said. Leak rushed inside the cell. My mood calmed down, but not completely. I felt better that Leak was in but Bigs and Slash were supposed to be the last ones end, not the other way around. "Relax" we'll handle him later too much going on right now set up the chess boards and start playing. Leak was still focus on the mission. I had gotten sidetracked by Bigs. The boards were supposed to have been up two minutes ago. If everyone did as they were told and instructed earlier. The sound of the COs barking into their walkie-talkies ordering the medical staff to bring all their equipment. Echoed threw threw the tier. It was useless there were two lifeless body spewing out a tremendous amount of blood all over the floor. I couldn't keep my eyes off Bigs. He sensed the animosity towards him. I cut my sights on Leak. He played the game with Slash and shook his head in complete disappointment. I knew he was mad because his jaw joint was popping out as if he was chewing gum. COs made their rounds looking into every cell on the unit. They had to be at least 50 guards on the unit and none knew how all of this took place so quickly. When you sit on your ass all day in a facility like this you get accustomed to being lazy and very unaware of your surroundings. You are the authority who is in command to watch over all of us. Slip ups like these lead to fatalities on every occasion in any institution. Our stories were rehearsed just as much as the routine was. The security will question all suspect first thing in the a.m. Just my luck I'll was their number one suspect because their mind was set on retaliation on my behalf.

The next morning and I was already being cuffed taken down to security.

"Stand up, turn your lights on and head all the way to the back and get on your knees now!" Security Sgt. barked from outside of the room. "For what?!" I shot back. "Mr. Ricardo we will not ask you again." The other white prick barked. I did as they asked me to do for all I cared they didn't have shit on me. So what the hell let's go for the ride. No brushing my teeth or anything of that nature, straight Viking status. After getting on my knees, there orders were far from over.

"You good man, just play dumb". Leak said from under the blankets I could hear him as clear as day. I smiled following their orders "you think this is funny!?" The Serge was even more pist. Turn around and face the fucking wall!" Mind you there are four walls. "Which one?" I asked. "The back wall asshole!" Oh boy he was really mad. I turned to face the wall as he shouted. I didn't even get to rotate all the way when the keys were jingling and the door was open immediately. I close my eyes just in case a blow to the face was on his way. Lucky for me nothing came but the cold steel around my wrist.

They dragged me to the security office, there they sat me down at a table and left me alone. I assumed it was a tactic they would use on many occasions. To try and get you to drive yourself crazy in your own thoughts about the matter. I was half-asleep almost falling over when Humpty Dumpty and his partner came barging in with a file in his hands. They sat right across from me. I had my head down in my own world. Mr. Humpty Dumpty slammed his file on the table very hard making a loud banging noise. I acted as if I didn't hear shit.

"Wake up bad ass!" His partner said looking like Sherlock Holmes. "What do you want?" I asked them. "You know what we want from you." Sherlock said." You are already here for a murder Mr. Rock!" I found it hilarious how they directed me by my alias. I kept my mouth shut. I gave them the raised eyebrow waiting for their next move. "Look all you have to do is tell us why you stabbed those two guys yesterday and maybe we can work out something." Humpty Dumpty tried to negotiate. "Stabbed two guys?" I don't know what you're talking about." I replied. "You know exactly what we are talking about, a few months ago you got stabbed up during line movement. So you had to get back at them didn't you?" Sherlock asked. These two men were so pathetic with their little show that they were trying to put up. It was so cheesy and so unprofessional. I don't know who stabbed me and more importantly why would I hurt someone in this place? I'm not a bad person." I stated with confidence that they would back the fuck off. "Well guess what you're about to be charge with another murder if you don't get the talking soon. I was over with this shit. I went into shutdown mode. We found the whack you used to kill them two men. As soon as the results come back you won't be so quiet. I am going to make sure of that. You going to wish you have spoken to us when you had the chance!" Dumpy was furious he was spitting every time he spoke a syllable. "So who did you get the weapon from?" Sherlock asked. Adjusting his glasses. This had to be a military reject, his lip had a cold sore on it I put all my money that it was a herpies. When we look at the tape it will tell us everything buddy so make this easier on yourself." Sherlock was my friend...Not! He didn't get any words from me either. After about 30 minutes of doing the rain and dance they were tired of not getting anywhere.

"Your fucked boy we know you did it and also know you been nothing but a problem since you arrived in his prison." They grip me up causing an excruciating amount pain on my wrist. "Assholes!" I said. Before I was finally allowed back to my cell. They had nothing I thought to myself.

"What they say?" Leak asked off the top as soon as I entered the cell. "A whole bunch of nothing." I replied. "They said they found the wack that I used to kill both of those niggas." I repeated "There is no way that's even possible." Leak said. "I know but since we know that they don't know shit, if they somehow mysteriously obtained some valuable information, we will automatically know who it came from." I walked closer to Bigs bed and pulled his blanket off his face, he was up. "You heard me right?" I barked at him but in a low tone with much authority. "I'm not gonna say shit. I'm sorry I panicked yesterday but I ain't no rat." Bigs tried to convince us about his loyalty. I didn't trust that nigga for shit and to be honest he might have to go to. I wouldn't tell anyone about this though. Leak and Slash were listening and watching me very attentively. "You too Slash!" I was a little pist I must admit. "You already know nigga I ain't talking. "He confirmed. "Don't sweat it. We gonna waited it out Rock fall back and try relax. I'm a get at you in a bit." Leak threw his covers over his head and fell out. Neither of us got up to go to breakfast. Slash was the only one which was good because he could make sure no one tried to creep up on us.

—

Mom and Pete were heading to Cherry Hill Mall these two were all over each other. Holding hands as they walked through the parking lot.

"When are you going to see your son again?" Pete asked I found it amusing how he would always talk about me. Until this day he still sends me funds every now and then when he has a chance. He even went as far as sending me a letter thanking me for allowing him to talk my mom. He didn't say that but you get the drift. "I was thinking maybe next week around the weekend, I miss him." Mom said going through the door he had open for her. We'll let me know and I will be more than happy to take you up there so you don't have to take the bus or cab baby." Pete was sharp. He had managed to enter mom's heart something I would never have foreseen. I wondered if I would have never gotten locked up if mom would've went out to seek some male love and attention? It's a coincidence on how I'm out the picture and all of a sudden mom is shackled up with Pete. Anyway good for them.

"Oh so this is the woman you got up and left me for huh?" It was Pete's ex-wife, this bitch was at the Cherry Hill Mall with about five bags in her hand spending all of Pete's money. Pete's face got cherry red, don't even do this right now Maggie." Pete pled. "No! I gave you nine years of my life and you leave me for another woman just like that." Maggie was causing a hell of a scene in front of Macy's. "Listen this is between you two I'll be over there baby." Mom had to call Pete baby. She didn't give a fuck about his ex-wife all she knew was that Pete was hers. For now she was confident in herself to leave and let them handle there shit. Maggie would try to drag mom into her childish games but mom knew better than to feed in. Now

Maggie was the same height as mom but she was pale white and her eyes were green with dirty blonde hair. She maintained herself well but her face wore massive wrinkles around her eyes and she had visible grays that could be sprouting as they spoke. Now, mom had a few grays too but the beauty parlor always got rid of them for her every month. Maggie's body was also thick but her breasts sagged almost to her belly button. Not sure if it was because they were huge or just because she wore no bra. Mom sat on a bench and watched all the passerby's being nosey. She would look every now and then to the raging Maggie. She was getting annoyed on how long Pete was taken to dismiss his psychopathic ex-wife. She got up to help out but he ended it right on time.

"I'm so sorry baby I didn't mean for this to happen tonight." Pete was copping a plea. Mom listen and walk side-by-side with Pete. So what did she say? And don't you even think of lying to me." Mom was straight forward. "She wants me to get back with her. She says that she misses me so much, she feels so lonely without me laying by her side." Pete admitted to mom. "And what did you tell her?" Mom asked Pete "I told her that what we had died years ago and that it was to broken to fix any of it now. I told her that I am in love with you and that I can't see myself going back to the bull shit and nonstop drama." Pete went on to say. Mom had a strong warm feeling inside of her. She couldn't believe what she just heard this man just admitted to her and his ex-wife that he had fell in love with another woman and that woman was my mother. The night went on and ended in deep lovemaking. My mom was content with this man and I wouldn't impede on her emotions.

—

The bus dropped Linda off a block away from Pennsauken Mart. Mom and Linda haven't seen one another in a day or two, but today was the end of Linda's semester and she had passed all her classes with honors. She was upholding her part of the deal we had made to each other. I didn't get the chance to speak to her lately but mom told me her progress. Days were going by faster than usual and Linda had some shopping to do. She wore the shirt we had gotten made the last time we were at the mart together, with some tight fitted blue jeans and some blue and white chucks. She was styling as always and she was alone. She headed towards the entrance way but the tall lamppost where Rock parked his truck brought back flashbacks of the painful night. She envisioned the whole scenario not even blinking just stopped and stared at nothing. Her heart pounded as her mind pictured all the hideous images all over again.

"Excuse me sweetie." A soft spoken voice spoke waking Linda up from her daze. "I'm sorry." Linda sidesteps. It was cold and Linda's vest wasn't doing his job because her nipples were extra hard. "I got you bro... I'm here for you." She said to herself. "They will pay for what they think they got away with." Linda was self-talking again. The Mart never change no matter what day of the week it was. Everyone ripping and running enjoying the sales. Linda had to come in here and grab something that she couldn't leave without. She made her way passing many different stores. The loud music echoed all throughout the place and it would switch to reggaeton. She passed other stores and it would go back to hip-hop. She decided to grab a funnel cake first then head to the store that was waiting for her presence. It was warm but the draft from the cold breeze would sneak up on her as she walked.

Her and the girls have really gotten much closer. All thanks to what took place that night at Jacqueline's house. Jacqueline had let her in on all her personal intimate possessions. Streets now had a face in Linda's mind that she would never forget. She knew his occupation, she knew his hideouts and she knew where exactly to find him if and when the time came. Who would've known that a little sexual encounter would be so satisfying and so helpful in so many ways? It was so easy. Linda didn't even have to pry any of it from her. Just being a bit curious and asking why's and a few where's led to almost the impossible. What she didn't prepare for was what she was looking at from a distance. His face made her stomach turn. His smile rose anger inside of her. She had to be around 70 feet from him. What am I going to do? She asked herself. She was frozen in her steps. She didn't even make it to get the funnel cake. Who is he with? She asked herself observing him attentively. Zipping up her jacket so that her brother's face wouldn't be exposed just in case he glanced her way. Linda leaned up against the wall and pondered her next move. Here it is her brother's righteous enemy, in Pennsauken Mart again in the flesh with a big smile on his face as if he had no care in the world. She had to do something but what was she to do Linda. She decided to freelance the situation. She couldn't let him get away, nope not that easily. She forced herself to put 1 foot in front of the other. As the distance between the two decreased her nerves cause her to hesitate. What will I do if he notices me? Linda asked herself. She needed to come up with a backup plan just in case. She was all alone with a mass of people walking back and forth. He had on a bomber jacket, his diamond stud earrings sparkled from the lights above. His shape up looked as if it was sharp enough to cut the razor that did it. Baggy blue jeans with high top construction where on his feet. The boy was fly Linda admired him. She caught herself, this was the enemy by no means will I look at him any other way. Stopping at the funnel cake spot, the lady took the order "a few minutes." The older lady said. By now he was about 5 feet away from Linda, Linda try her best not to make eye contact as she walked back and forth slowly keeping her mind off this nigga . Well she at least she tried but she could feel his eyes on her. Who wouldn't be eyeing Linda's fine ass. She was fly as always. But that ass was a showstopper with them jeans. She looked up and guess who was eyeing her down? He walked over to cure his curiosity. Now Linda's heart began to bang harder than ever. She reached in her pocket and held on to her mace. If this nigga trips, Ima empty this whole can in his face. Linda thought, she was like a deer in the headlights.

"Large funnel cake ready!" The lady yelled allowing Linda to break her trance and retrieve her cake. She grabbed it and left already paid.

"Holdup girl." The nigga who she didn't want to exchange words with just tried to catch her attention. Linda hated when a mother fucker called her anything but her name. She kept walking. "Excuse me pretty girl." He said speeding up to her. He grabbed her arm ever so lightly to get Linda's attention. "Get the fuck off of me nigga!" Linda barked. "Oh shit!" Damn gorgeous I don't mean no harm. I just wana rap to you for a second is that cool?" He spoke in a soft but assertive tone. "You got a second." Linda said. Taken a bite of the funnel cake. He watched her as she chewed. The way her fingers grab pieces of the cake had him in a trance not to mention the way her pretty lips moved as she chewed on the cake. "Times up." Linda said turning and walking away. "Nah man holdup." He tried again. "You set a second and you didn't say anything." Linda spat with an attitude. "Are you always so mean?" He asked. "Only when my time is being wasted." Linda had to be sharp. There was no telling how this was going to end or even go. "My bad.... Alright let me get a piece of that cake." He asked Linda. Linda's eyes got serious. This nigga must've lost his mind out of all the things he could as say he chose to ask for a piece of my funnel cake. "My what?" Linda asked with a smirk on her face. He moved in closer. Linda didn't move he smells so good, so masculine. Linda thought. "You heard me mini let me get a piece. The way you chewing on that making my mouth water, that shit gota be good." He said with a smile exposing his perfect whites. I see why he has these bitches going crazy over him, he cute. He not all that tall but he smelled good and he has a helluva voice. Deep and smooth. "Buy your own." Linda joked. He had managed to keep her more than a few seconds now. He was winning this match. "Nah how about I buy you a fresh hot one and you give me the rest of that one." Damn he was smooth Linda thought. "Order it and pay for it first. Linda pulled his car. It didn't take too much for him to call that bluff, he sure enough pull out a hefty knot a payed for a fresh funnel cake. "And give it to her." He told the lady pointing to Linda. "Okay no problem." She replied Linda took another bite before given it to him. "Sit down for a second." He spoke pulling out a seat in an open area, Linda looked at the table up ahead and remember that her and her brother would always choose to sit at this particular one.

"So I only have a second huh?" He asked. "Don't push your luck." Linda reminded him who was in charge. "All right my bad." He stuck his hand out to give her a handshake. "My name is Streets." Nice to meet you what is your name?" It was most definitely him. This nigga is Jacqueline's baby dad and he is exactly who she thought he was. He doesn't recognize me or he is a hell of an actor. Linda thought. This wasn't going to end well, as long as he didn't see Linda shirt or remember her face everything would be okay. Linda was playing with fire and it was sizzling. The longer she would stay there and exchange more words with this man the deeper the pit got. Linda grabbed his hand to avoid suspicion. "My name is Janet, nice to meet you too." Linda was flirting with the enemy. "Janet?" Streets repeated. That's a cute name. So where are you from Janet?" Streets emphasized the name as he asked a question. Linda didn't know what to say she was running out of ideas. Too many lies were becoming harder and harder to remember. "That's none of your business. I don't know you to be telling you all that." Linda said. "Wow." Okay I can respect that, so are you going to let me get to know you sometime?"

Street asked. Hell no Linda said her mind. "Maybe" she said out loud. "I can't predict the future." Linda spoke eating her fresh funnel cake. "Well I can." Streets joked. "Oh really?" Linda asked with a smile on her face. "So tell me what the future is?" Linda challenged. Streets rubbed his goatee and ponder for a quick second. "You and I will go out next week and enjoy each other's company." Streets tried his best. In the back of his mind this woman look very familiar. Streets has been so rampant all over town and was with so many different types a woman he could be highly mistaken. So he chose not to assume, rather ask questions to be safe. "I think your fortune teller is wrong." Linda said. He is definitely a sexy Latino but all the stories that Linda has heard about this worthless piece of shit wouldn't allow her to see him in any other light, rather than the light she has already knows him to be seen in along with witnessing all his real intentions.

"You look like you are in deep thought Janet." Street stated. "I don't want to scare you away or anything but I feel like we have met before." Street said staring at Linda searching for a facial expression. Linda swallowed her food that was in her mouth almost choking. "So you mean to tell me that we fucked already?" Linda got straight to the point because just in case she was going to get up out of there immediately. Now it was Streets turn to almost choke but he actually almost did. Coughing and laughing. "I didn't mean it like that girl, I'm just saying that maybe you and I have crossed paths sometime before. I could be wrong but if my memory serves me right I could be right." The funnel cakes spot was getting louder and louder by the second. The empty few seats were now filled with bodies and also standing customers waiting for their cakes. "I can't think of a time that you and I may have hung out. I think you might have me mistaken with one of your hood rates or something because I don't chill with people." Linda shortened trying her best to conceal her identity and erase any images of her from his mind. All he had to do was see the faces on her shirt and immediately has memory would serve him correct no questions asked. "You trying to get out of here it's getting pretty loud." Streets asked Linda knowing better than to go anywhere with this man. "Yeah, gota get going I got a few things to do." Linda tried to avoid him, but it was pointless he had fell for her beauty and swag. "I'm saying can we chill until you ready to go?" Streets wanted to have Linda like now. Nah it's cool I already gave you more than a second Streets." And plus I wouldn't want your wifey to get her panties in a bunch if she'd catch you trying to holler." Linda got up ready to leave. "What wife I'm a free agent, I'm not in a contract with no female at this time." So your Intel is wrong Janet." Streets challenged hoping to win Linda over. This nigga is a liar for real. Last time I checked he and his bum bitch name Star were an item. This just proved to her that these trifling as dudes were all no good. "Well I catch you another time I got a go." Linda was cutting the conversation short. "All right here take this." Streets handed her a piece of paper with his pager number on it. "Hit me up whenever you got time for me, and no matter what I'm doing I'll drop everything to holler back." Linda blushed. She could never get use to the attention all these men would give her. She knew that they all just wanted to taste her love box but it wasn't gonna happen that easily. She was going to use what she had to her advantage. "I got you, stay fly." She flirted walking away. There is no way that this man is that dumb to not remember my face Linda thought to herself. Even if he did remember and he was wheeling her in he was just as smart as I never thought he was. Heading to her store she went and picked up and exact replica of what she came to buy and found the closest exit and went home.

—

After about a week the security squad kept on harassing Rock about the incident. They weren't getting anywhere and they wouldn't as long as everyone who played a part in the incident kept their mouths shut. "Damn! Rock why you hit them niggaz up like that?" This big Spanish guy asked in the gym fishing for information. Leak was on the squat rack. He put the weights up just in case the question got answered the wrong way. "What?" I don't know what the hell you talking about big man." Rock delivered to the question in an off-the-wall answer. It seemed as though no one in this facility or even in his world knew how to mind their own fucking business. How and why could so many people be so fucking nosy? Everybody knows you had something to do with that. "What comes around goes around right?" The big Spanish papi boy said. "He had it coming his way somebody had to slow that nigga the fuck down aint nobody mad at you." Big boy went on to say.

"Ayo my man you heard what the fuck he said he don't know what the fuck you talking about, so why you still pressing the issue don't no one know what you saying?" Leak had the menacing look on his face that show not to be fucked with. "I wasn't talking to you." No later did the last syllable slip his mouth Leak had two pieced the shit out of him. He didn't drop but the sound that his face made upon contact with Leaks mittens sounded as if something was broken. "I'm not gonna say it again get the fuck away from us with this bullshit or else!" Leak moved in closer just in case big boy has something crazy to say, but by the taste he had in his mouth he knew better than to come out his face again. I grabbed Leak and pulled him away so that all the attention that was on our end could dissipate.

"Damn! Nigga you all right?" I asked leak. "Fuck no I'm not all right we got to fight these cases and on top of that we gota put up with all these nosy females up in here. If they're so nosy why they won't be man enough to approach us directly and asked if we did what every one is saying we did instead of beating around the fucking bush. That's some broad shit for real! Leak was mad. "That goes for whoever!" Leak was now calling out everyone who has something to say or assume. I felt what he was saying and where he was coming from with all this because it was true. You wouldn't get a direct question you'll get a he said, she say shit with no proof just a bunch of mother fuck trying to get you to admit something that they think you had something to do with. It was getting annoying and I'm sure with this small incident mother fuckers would get the picture.

"I feel you my nigga" come on let's get this paper "I had to hype him up to get a set in with me on shoulder shrug. Slash was inching his way over to us. The b- ballgame picked back up and everyone else fell back into what they were doing. Big papi boy could be seen talking to his people who weren't going to do a damn thing, not because they were soft but because he was wrong. One thing I know about my Spanish bloodline. If you go talking crazy to someone just because you think you deep and big and bad and get punched your mouth for being disrespectful. You brought that mess upon yourself being nosy. So don't expect to drag the rest of them in your unnecessary beef. Now if you don't do shit to cause the situation then now is yard out with no, if, ands or buts about it... "Let's get it!" It was my turn to get my set in. "Yo yall good?" Slash came with his gangsta walk. "Man we good Wassup?" Leak asked. "Nah I saw you punch main man in the mouth and wanted to know what was up because my people want to ride out if shit get crazy."

Slash informed. I was listening. "That's good to know but we go for now." Rock said. We had about five minutes left. The rec I got side track talking to leak about these two bitches Felicia and Jacqueline.

"Ayo pa!" A Spanish voice yelled over to where I was at I didn't pay it no mind. "Rock!" Was yelled. My senses flared up instantly. It was big boy's homie. "/que fue?/"/what's up/I asked. He waved me over to him. I went to walk but Leak grab my elbow. "Want me to go wit?" I was enthused by how tightly Leak and I were becoming, for real I would've never thought this to be the way it turned out to be. "No I got it." I assured him walking away. I felt his eyes on my back. I headed straight over to the thick squad they were deep but I didn't care. My heart began to pick up.

"/que paso ayi?/"/what happened there?/ The 5'9" tattoo wearing papi asked. He had two teardrops on his left eye and one on his right. I noticed a scar above his lip a much bigger scar on his eyebrow. This man look as if he meant business when he spoke. He asked. "Ask your homeboy." I said. "Already did but I want to hear your side to see if the two size matchup no need for hostility." I looked at him his eyes they were cold, emotionless. "We have a way with dealing with our own people, you are Spanish right?" He asked I nodded. "/si/"/ yes/I answered. So then you should know how we operate." Mr. Teardrops said. "Not necessarily but I'll tell you what happened and maybe you can explain to me how you operate." I wanted to know everything about everyone and how they thought and interacting with their own. After the small explanation of what happened the big boy eyes got big as I told the truth. Teardrops look back at him. He didn't seem too happy about the story I was telling him. "Is that what really happened?" Mr. Teardrops asked his big friend waiting for a response. Big boy put his head down and nodded. "Listen Rock let me be the first to apologize for my brother stupidity and nosiness. He was wrong as he got what he deserved but now I'm asking you if you have another problem with any of these men behind me and I mean any problem with any of the man behind me he repeated twice to please come and tell me what the problem is, they represent me and I'll fix it up." He pulled out his hand to call it a truth. I thought about what he said carefully I grabbed his hand and we tighten grips. "Machete" he told me his name. "/tabien/"/ok/.I replied and walked away back to where leak was standing with his arms folded. "You good?" Leak asked. "Yeah" "Rec is over everyone back to your cells!" A voice yelled over the PA system. "I'll tell you about it later." It was almost time for lunch and I was hungry I couldn't wait to stuff my face with whatever the lucky meal was today. Little by little the reputation and respect one would accumulate in a place like this was based on how you conducted yourself. I don't mean you have to be ruthless because that will only get you killed if you don't check yourself. I mean as far as handling your situations and not backing down from shit out of cowardness, but backing down as a man using your head instead of your mouth or unneeded physical altercations. Yes, you gonna have your times when you have no choice but to face disrespect which is evitable and sometimes this may be thrown at you but other than using violence there are other ways to handle situations. Man fuck that shit they talking about. If a nigga got a loose mouth tightened the shit up and if he still don't learn kill that mother fucker! Because for some odd reason, a nigga don't respect that humble shit. They quick to run all over a nigga who ain't in no mood. So what happens when the humble ass nigga is pushed to his breaking point? The so called loudmouth gangsters are in complete shock when he lets loose and then they have the audacity to label the humble guy who never wanted any problems from the beginning as the bad guy any troublemaker. So to get right into the mix give them what they understand the most. Which is blood and tears! But nah if all can be avoided than do right. It ain't working for me! Like they say different strokes for different folks. "Ayo Rock." Bigs said as soon as we entered the cell. "Wassup little big guy." I joked. I was in a good mood and no one was going to ruin it for me. "When I went to medical this Shorty name Kiki told me to tell you to go to church this week and that she got in contact with Jigz and Banga. They coming up to see her supposedly." Bigs had his slanted eyes closed while trying to tell me exactly what was said. "What else?" I asked "ummmmmm oh and she misses your sexy ass." We all laugh because it felt weird hearing that come from Bigs mouth instead of Kiki's. "All right good looking." I said. "So why did you go to medical? Slash was curious of his little story. He pulled up his shirt to show us his band aid. "Did blood work." Bigs answered. "Blood work? What you infected nigga?" Slash asked very concerned not with Bigs but if it was contagious. "No but is good to get it done just to be 100% sure." Bigs said with much seriousness and sincerity. "Yeah I got check too, why wouldn't you it's free and you know we've been fucking all types of females out there like there was no tomorrow." I agreed with Bigs. "Fucking right I remember a couple years ago I got locked up on some bull shit. I was fucking this shorty who was badder than a mother fucker." Leak was speaking. "Man this girl was a full-blown freak we did everything with one another from 69, tea bagging all the way up to 77." Leak joked. "What the fuck is 77?" Slash asked cracking up we were all laughing. "Not right now" Leak said in between breaths. I just so happen to get locked up with this broad and I ended up biting the possession charge but let me tell you how I woke up in that morning in the holding tank and my dick fell as though it was spewing out lava. I yelled like a fucking bitch because of how bad that shit was burning. I didn't dare to piss again. When the CO came up to the tank door asking me "what the fuck you hollering about?" I told him that when I use the bathroom my pee whole burn so bad that something had to be wrong. The way his facial expression turned up I knew he knew exactly what I was talking about. He laughed and told his coworker and he too had to be continuously cracking jokes about these dirty bitches. I must have been fucking and whatnot. I was fucking mad but I couldn't do shit neither could they. They told me "go see the medical department when I got into the jail." Leak was telling us one of his lived experiences. "What did they do when you was finally was in here?" Rock asked to be curious. "What did they do? I had to fill out a sick call slip which I had to pay for but when they finally call me down to get a checkup there was this fine ass Spanish short thick curly haired Latina that looks so badder than a motha. She smelled even better I was so embarrassed that I acted as if it wasn't me who had the penis problem so I went another week almost setting my dick on fire again. I wanted to cut it off that's how bad it hurt when I use the bathroom." Everyone in the cell was holding their bellies because this shit was hilarious. Leak had no choice but to force a laugh with this. "You are all fucked up I'm tryna to share something with y'all and all you doing is laughing at me." Leak was all smiles. For what seemed like three minutes. It fell as though there was no tension in the cell and for these couple of seconds, I didn't feel locked up. All the laughter that we were channeling on to one another felt so genuine and was so real. To be able to feel like this in this predicament we found ourselves in was great. "So what else happened?" Bigs asked in between last. I signed another sick call form and waited with my penis in my hands to get called down again." He shook his head, not wanting to tell us the rest. I threw my pillow at him. "Spit it out what did they say?" Already knew where this was going. He tossed my pillow back at me. "It was the sexy doctor again I remember her like it was yesterday. "Miss Martinez." She asked me. "What is wrong?" And it took me a few seconds before I spilled the beans. "My private area hurts really badly when I use the bathroom." I said so embarrassed. Our burst of laughter could be heard all over the tier. My eyes were all watered up from all the laughing. "You don't have to feel embarrassed it happens to a lot of people this is what happens when you decide to experiment with unprotected sex. You end up catching these curable diseases. "You are lucky it wasn't as bad as AIDS or HIV. What would you have done if you wasn't so lucky?" Miss Martinez asked leak that day. "I don't know what I would do." Leak replied. "You guys have no idea how stupid and dirty I felt in the presence of this woman, if in the back of my mind I could of thought that maybe one day this woman would give me. The time a day my dreams were shot down almost immediately once I had to tell her what was happening to my penis." Leak was a smiling anymore but we were still dying in laughter. "You know what hell she told me?" Leak had us hooked on the fishing line. "What?" We all said together. That she knew that, the first time I came into the office. She could tell that I was the one who had issue that was written on a sick call form, not just by the wording and how I spoke. How I stood with my legs crossed and I look as if I had to use the bathroom. She told me that she wasn't gonna stop me because she wanted to see how long I would take in all this pain until I would finally break. Because the pain would only get worse as time went by. I didn't know where to hide my face." Once again we all burst out into laughter. So how did she get rid of it?" Slash asked. She gave me some antibiotics pills that I had to take for a week straight." Leak informed us. "And that's why I get checked up every now and then." Bigs stated proving his point through leaks story. "You don't get no pussy so you good nigga." Slash joked as the day came and went.

—

Had to be around 10:30 PM and all the lights in the house were off, mom had gotten dropped off by Pete he was supposed to stay the night but change his mind. He didn't want mom to get tired of his presence so he decided to make her miss him for a bit. You know keeping things interesting and spicy. "Are you coming with me tomorrow?" Mom asked Pete leaning on the driver side door. "If you want me to I will go with you honey." Pete said to mom. He always knew what exactly to say and when to say. "Of course I do baby why I wouldn't?" Mom challenge. "Why don't you stay the night with me so you don't have to drive back down this way?" Mom pled. Because I have to feed my dogs and plus I want to make you miss me when I'm not there." Pete stated. I have an idea how about after we pick up the truck we go and visit Manuel?"

Mom said hoping that Pete would agree. "Anything for you, I couldn't deny you from going and seeing your son baby." Pete worked his magic as always. "Now go and get some rest and call me as soon as you get up in the morning." Pete said. He perked up his lips so that mom would lay a big wet one on him. "Good night baby." Mom said. As she walked towards the unlit house Pete stayed in the car and watched as mom made her way into the house. She turned and looked at her boo one more time before she disappeared in through the doorway. Mom slipped off her shoes and stood at the entrance of the house and listen. The house was dark but it felt odd. She didn't hear anything and figured that no one was home.

In the kitchen she flicked on the lights and heard rummaging in her backyard. Her heart began to speed up a bit. She was afraid. Where was Manuel was when she needed him. He would always check on all the noises in a house that fell out of place. Mom grabbed the biggest knife from the kitchen and tiptoed towards the back door. Once again the noise grew a bit louder. Who in God's name is making all that damn noise? She asked herself turning the doorknob she took a deep breath and forced herself to find out what was causing all that noise. She opened the door very swiftly and swung the blade in her hand hoping to cut someone but all she managed to do was cut the screen mesh on the screen door. The noise continue. Mom looked over to the trash and saw a mess that appeared to freeze up in her stair. It was two raccoons vandalizing the garbage, Linda must have forgotten to cover the trash can when she threw out the trash last night. Scared the hell out of me. Mom said to herself.

"Pop.... Pop, pop, pop, pop! Forgetting about the raccoons that was enough to send her back inside and remind herself that being outside was not worth a stray bullet. The front door slammed. "Mom!" Linda voice shouted from a far. "Yes baby!" Mom answered. "Are you okay?" Mom asked. "Yes oh my God mom I saw the flashes from the gun that was shooting all the way from up the block." Linda was scared. Mom hugged her. I'm glad you are okay, now why are you in outside anyway?" You know how this gets around this time at night." Mom scolded Linda. "I know mom, I'm sorry I had to meet up with Joel and take care of a few things." Linda tried to ease mom worries. I'm going to see your brother tomorrow if you want you can come with us." Mom informed "us?" Linda asked. "Pete and I." Yes I would love to go just remind me. Linda informed mom. "Linda?" Mom wanted to talk with her. "Yes?" Linda politely replied "are you okay baby?" Mom asked Linda. Linda stared at mom and took a deep breath and shook her head. "No mom I'm a wreck." Linda admitted. Mom was excited that her baby girl was willing to open up. "Have a seat for a second." Mom went back into the kitchen, she came back with cocoa as she always had ready for Linda but lately is been going to waste because Linda hasn't been around nor has she been herself lately. "Mom I can't control was going to happen in the next few days or even months." The statement caught mom by surprise she had no idea what to think of those words that her daughter had just spoken. "Baby what do you mean you can control was going to happen? Of course you can, if it's one thing I know is that you yourself have the power to control all of your actions that pertain to your living being." Mom spoke trying to find the rule of Linda's dilemma. "You don't understand there are things that I have to do that are out of my reach because I will succeed in accomplishing what is needed to be done." Mom still wasn't following along as if Linda was speaking in riddles. Linda you are scaring me please tell me what are you talking about and what are you about to do?" Mom was worried now more than ever. Linda wasn't Linda anymore. Somewhere deep down inside of her body Linda was hidden or even trapped inside. "I'm going to fix the pass and adjust the future." Linda face was a nasty one she sipped the hot cocoa and got up and left the seat. She headed upstairs with no more words, being spoken. The words ricocheted around mom's head. She grabbed a cigarette and puffed on it slowly trying to decipher the conversation she just had with Linda. She knew that this had everything to do a Manual and no one could tell her anything different, but what was he trying to say? The past was already set in stone in the future could very well be altered but to what extent. Mom had to talk to someone. No one would be able to help her understand this but one person and Pete was definitely out of the equation. Picking up the pen and paper she began to put down all her worries and concerns down to the only person who could possibly help her see things in a much clearer light.

—

"You have a collect call from "Rock" from the Camden County jail system to receive this call please press...." The recording from the phone system recited its already programmed recording. Rock couldn't take it anymore he had to hear a woman's voice but not just any woman one who would show some affection and be very supportive. The phone call was accepted. "Hello?"

Felicia sounded very excited as she answered the phone call. "What's up ma you have a few minutes?" Rock asked her. "Of course I have a few minutes for you I have all the time in the world for you." Felicia informed Rock. "Why would you think otherwise?" Felicia went from feeling excited to feeling sad. "How have you been doing?" Rock asked. "Missing you like crazy, why haven't you been responding to my letters lately?" Felicia asked. Rock inhaled. "You don't want me anymore do you?" Felicia asked and answered her own question. "Mommy look!" Rock heard a child's his voice could be heard in the background. "Way to go baby, can you give mommy a few minutes, I'm talking to Rock." Felicia said to her princess. "I want to talk to him." Eliza whined. "Okay I'll let you know when okay?" Felicia spoke to her daughter "okay" Rock was listening and missing them both. "Hello." Felicia said. "I never said that I didn't want you anymore." Rock continue the conversation. "Well it feels like it and I want to go see you but I wasn't allowed in." "What was that about?" Felicia asked. I didn't put you on the list yet, but I'll be sure to do it by the end of this week." Rock assured her. "I need you to come up because I have a few things that I need you to help me with." Rock said. "This call is being monitored and recorded." The recording interrupted. "Okay I'll come up next week then for sure, but in the meantime talk to me right to me. I miss you so much Rock why did you leave me?" I thought you wanted to be with me. I can't stop thinking of you, your body, your smile, your smell is all beginning to fade little by little." Felicia spoke from the heart. "I know I think of you too and don't worry I'll see you soon one day." Rock tried to console her worries. "Have you heard anything?" Felicia asked. "No not since the hearing but my lawyer should be coming up to see me soon." Rock explained. "Have you seen or spoken to my sister?" Rock asked. "No I haven't, I've been so busy all I do is work and be a mommy to my princess." Felicia informed him. "I know keep up the good work. I'm sure she enjoys every minute of you." Rock referred to Eliza. "Yeah she is getting so big and so smart." "She remembers you." Felicia said. "I remember her too." You have 60 seconds." The recording stated. "Hello?" Eliza small voice chimed over the receiver. "Hey princess are you behaving for mommy?" Rock asked. "Yes I am my mommy misses you when are you coming over." The words hit Rock like daggers. Someday Eliza I promise. The phone went silent. Rock held the receiver and just stood in deep thought this was the only piece of mind he could find at any given moment in these walls. He wanted to shout until his voice would give out. He held his composure and return back to his cell.

CHAPTER 15
"What's good?"

hen the time finally came to go and pick up the truck after waiting for Rock to send us the notarized paperwork. It was a hassle to obtain ownership of it. No one had authority to remove the vehicle from the police impound. Pete was up early and on his way to take mom to the truck.

"Are you hungry?" Pete asked mom. "A little mom lit up a cigarette and so did Pete. Instead of these two mother fuckers trying to help each other stop or even slow down. It was as if they were in a race to see who could smoke more than the other. I already told mom to contain herself and to tell fucking Pete to not aid her habit. "Where you want to eat it?" Pete asked mom. "It doesn't matter babe you pick the place." Mom replied. With no restaurant close by or diner Pete opted to hit the nearest Burger King or McDonald's. "So you still want to go and see Rock later?" Pete asked. "Let's see how this goes first and if you still feel like it then yes we can stop by for a few." Mom informed Pete. "Did you have your discussion with Linda?" Pete asked. Ever since mom had explained to Pete of all the changes mom noticed in her baby girl, Pete became a bit worried himself. So he definitely encourage mom to try and find out what was going on in Linda's head. "Yes I had a few words with her and to be honest I'm lost I don't think I can help her Pete." The words we had were very brief but the worst part was that they weren't loud and abusive but they surely were scary." Mom said looking at the side of Pete's face as he focused on the road ahead. He put on his turn signal and pulled into the Burger King. The line of cars was longer than usual but he pulled up behind the last vehicle. A rusted green Honda with a missing taillight. "Scary?" How come scary babe?" Pete looking over at mom. "She was talking about something that she needed to do to change the future and a lot of other shit." Mom put her handle her for head. "Future?" Pete repeated with a chuckle "It's not funny Pete the look in her eyes was so evil that I had nothing else to say. She changed ever since that night." Mom scolded Pete, his face had no choice but to get serious. "No one could understand that Linda had taken a human life. For some this is a way of living and can deal with the memories or even toss them out, than move on with their life as if nothing ever occurred without any worries. Now, no one was smart enough to actually see that in this case my beautiful sister wasn't one of these individuals who could live with that image in her mind. I'm not saying she isn't strong enough to delete such images. I'm saying that Linda could be being possessed by the human soul that she had taken that night. How was all this going to pan out? Would it cause her to commit the unthinkable? The voices, the memories and all that she's been putting together inside her own mind. Suicide could be the answer just to end all this madness that was taking place inside of Linda's head. Many could say that they understood,but in reality they all just wanted to act as if nothing was wrong with her. How could they try and make someone accept, when they weren't the one who took a life. Easier said than done agreed?

"I'm sorry baby how about a psychiatrist maybe she's going through something mentally disturbing. she may need professional help with." Pete advised. "I thought of that but there was no way Linda was going to sit down with a complete stranger and confined in that person or explained to them what she is feeling and why." Mom spoke to truth it was hard enough for us to open up towards one another let alone a complete stranger. We only confided in one another, the only way that I could see what Linda was feeling would be on a one-on-one visit. Now getting her to show up by herself was another challenge. Pete pulled off once the food was in there hands and headed to their first destination while chomping down on his egg and cheese sandwich. They both sat in silence eating and watching everyone scramble in their early commute.

—

"Get up nigga" Rock poked Slash. "Come on my nigga I'm tired as hell." Slash replied. One of the most convenient things in jail was that, one you are a grown ass man and by that you are grown which meant you could sleep all fucking day and not expect anyone to tell you to do anything different. This was a dream for the "man" who had nothing going on for themselves nor did he want anything going on for himself. "Man you got all day to sleep nigga they about to call for library soon." Rock tried to get him up. It wasn't working, Leak was up already ready. Big's fat ass was knocked the fuck out too. He was always lying in that bed, for all I cared he was better off in that rack. I didn't want that man out mingling with anyone, it wasn't hard to pick his brain. "We working out later?" Rock asked leak. "You already know we are." Leak replied. A few minutes later they called for library passes. Leak and Rock walk side-by-side wide awake, while others had eye crust being taken out their eyes as they exited their cells. Many still wore that I'm still half asleep look on their face. Vulnerable and unaware of how quick things could go from 0 to 1000. Rock learned his lesson that almost cost him his life. Machete was coming up on them with his crew about five deep and saluted the man and kept it moving with his entourage.

"That nigga run those niggas hard." Leak gossiped. I didn't say shit. "Look how he got all of them niggas behind him. He got to be some type of big baller." Leak suggested still talking shit. "Probably" I said. "Either that or they know what he does out in the streets, a cold killer I bet." Leak spoke some more. "What does Machete mean Rock?" Leak asked. "It's a large knife that is used on the island to chop niggas limbs off in one swift motion. The farmers use it for many other reasons like cutting grass or even cutting down branches from trees and shit." I explained "damn! That nigga look like he did chop the few limbs off . He better leave my limbs alone." Leak joked. We laughed all the way to the library. "When you next court date?" I asked Leak. "Man I got about six months till trial you know I'm fighting mine all the way. They going to pick 12 and spent all that money on me fuck that!" Leak was robust all eyes were on us as we didn't care.

Eventually we shut the fuck up and got focus on the books. I was always getting frustrated but had to remind myself getting all worked up wasn't the answer when reading these books. I noticed some old head who was reading to the far end of the library concentrating on his case and I decided to ask him for some assistance. I was hesitant at first but my freedom was a lot more important than my pride at the moment.

"Excuse me OG." I called over to him in a low whisper. He put up his pointer finger at me as to give him a second. This mother fucker gave me the finger after

I done said excuse me. I was about to spin around and leave. "What can I do for you young'n." Old head was speaking to me. "If you busy it can wait no worries." I tried to sound not too desperate. "I have nothing but time youngin." Old head informed me. "It's your case huh?" He read my mind. I naturally put my head down embarrassed as always when it had to deal with my case. "Let me see your paperwork." Old head extended his hand. I handed him the paperwork. He scanned it quickly and shook his head, this isn't looking too good young man." Old head said in his raspy voice I can only imagine how many cigarettes this guy smoked in his years. "Let's have a seat over here." Old head walked with a limp he was about 5'4" and may be about 145 pounds soaking wet. The grays he had all over his face and head covered him well. The top of his head was leathery and shining with no strands of hair lingering at all. Gone completely. As I sat down across from him. I noticed leak out my peripherals looking my away. He smiled. Old head wore so many scars on his face that I'm sure if I counted them I would miss a few. He caught me staring deeply at his face. He smiled. "I've been to hell and back youngin." I snapped out of my days. "I apologized." It was automatic, it was rude to stare. "For what?" You didn't do this to me I did this to myself." Old head said to me in all seriousness.

"Manuel Ricardo?" I am Jeremy Brown." They call me OJ. I shook his hand and he only had four of his five fingers, the pinky was gone. How could someone have gone through so much and still be alive. I thought to myself. "Do you have a lawyer?" OJ asked. "Yes I do." I replied. He looked at me "a real lawyer not these public pretender's." OG joked. I laughed. OJ had most of his teeth and had a good personality. "Yes his name is Michael Stoski. I replied. "Any good?" OG asked. "Not sure yet." I answered honestly, if you have a lawyer why are you down here doing his job?" OJ was right asking me this question. I didn't know what to say so I went on my first answer that popped in my head. "Just in case the money begins to dwindle and he decides I'm not worth the chump change." I hoped that this wouldn't occur, but just because he owed mom a favored didn't mean he didn't want to get paid. Regardless of the fact he was an attorney who wanted to build his capital, and my life doesn't mean anything to him if you wanted to get technical about it.

"That's a good answer." OJ stated. "From what I see here they have a hard case built up against you but this isn't something that has all truth to it right?" He read the affidavit. He was absolutely right. It had a lot of bends in it. "What did your lawyer say his angle would be as your defense?" OG asked. "He said self defense." I replied. That would be the most logical defense." OG said. "It says here that the knife was found a few feet from your person." Is that true?" OG asked. "Yes it is." I replied. "So they are waiting for the autopsy report to confirm that this weapon was used in the murder?" OG asked. "Yes they are. It also says your next hearing is around the corner which is good because you'll be able to see all the evidence that they have against you." OG stated. "If your lawyer is on his job he'll make sure that your rights are protected." OG spoke not looking up at me. "Do you know your rights youngin?" OG asked. "You mean the right to remain silent?" I answered dumbfounded. OJ laughed. "That's one of them." He rose up out of his seat and located a book and searched through the pages until he located what he was looking for. "I want you to read these and become very familiar with them because if you don't have any knowledge of your own personal rights from our Constitution then you might as well admit defeat "checkmate" youngin. By you learning this you'll be one step ahead of all those crackers. When they try to play you stupid you be one step ahead of the game. Now and days yall don't know or care about anything that carries any real meaning besides, who is bigger and badder." OG was schooling me. I wanted to know more on my case but for some reason I saw that he wasn't going to get completely involved unless I showed interest.

"Break it up now!" The sound of blows being exchanged could be heard but the voice of the librarian is what alarmed everyone. One of Machete's boys were beating the shit out of another male. He appeared to be a black male. It seems very unfair, the other four men blocked so that no one else would get involved. But it was a one-on-one as a matter fact. Machete was at a table reading a book watching his soldiers following the hit that was instructed. I looked at Machete and he caught my stare, he winked at me and went back to his book. It took seconds before the two Co's came running in with batons in her hands. The four men standing in line formation stepped aside as if they knew exactly what was about to come.

"Break it up now!" The fist and blows kept on going with blood on both faces. I'm not going to say it again." By now all of the men were sitting at Machetes table as if they knew nothing just watching attentively. The two officers began to beat the men with the batons. Two more COs rushed in.

"Everyone out of the library now!" One of the two barked at everyone. No one argued I took the book and we all exited the library as instructed. Leak was up ahead. I fell back and kept talking to OJ. "When can I catch you again Mr. J I asked."It's OJ" he corrected "and I'm in the library every day I work down there so you will always see me if you look for me. Next time I see you, you should be a bit more knowledgeable with your rights, right?" OJ asked. "You bet." He went his way and I went my way. I caught up Leak

"Yo they whipped that niggas ass." Leak said excitedly. It was pure amusement whenever you would see action in this place. After waiting for the med lady to fianally come, I was high all over again "you need to leave that shit alone." Leak scolded me. "Man you have no idea how much this she helps me." I spoke slowly to Leak. "I see, it get you feeling all nice and shit." "You can take them but this is every day Rock three times a day, you can be off your game like that." Leak was right but the truth was this was my getaway drug. "You told me that you wasn't into drugs out there right?" Leak asked. "Right." I answered. "So now you are becoming more and more dependent on them in here Rock how that sound?" Leak said he hated when I would be all doped up. I gave him a dose one time and he wasn't into it at all. He slept all day so he didn't have to feel the effect throughout the day anymore. I joked with him about that, he told me that he would never take that again. Slash and Bigs on the other hand went to the psych and got prescribed some of their own cocktails. "Ima stop Leak, just not right now." I said.

I ran into Mandy and asked her to help me handle a few things, She was definitely unsure but my charm had her hypnotized. I wasn't sure how or when all this would take place. I only hope that she would play her part whenever she had the opportunity. Having her as a major player on my team would be crucial. I sensed a lot of benefit to come out of this relationship between us whether it was intimate or not.

—

"Ma'am I'm sorry but you have to pay me $675 to get the truck out of here." The owner at the impound shop was out of his mind. "When I called the girl who answered the phone told me it was only a few dollars less than $400 and now you are telling me that my balance is now almost $700 what the hell do you take me as!?" Mom was furious. "Where is your fucking boss, I want to speak to him?" Mom Barked with her hand on her hips. "Ma'am you're speaking with him." Jack was the name written on his shirt. Mom shook her head in complete disbelief. "You guys are the crooks here not the men being put in jail!" Mom had a point they didn't care. Their job was to get the money for the space the vehicle was occupying and either take it or leave it either way this price would go up if mom left it in the space any longer.

"Babe how much do you have?" Pete asked trying to defuse the situation "about $400" mom answered annoyed. "You are $275 short." The disrespectful clerk chimed in. "Listen you piece shit I'm not talking to you. Please mind your fucking business while talk to my lady!" Pete barked out of nowhere. I've only heard of and seen Pete lose his cool one time, but today he lost it completely. Even mom looked at him confused. "Don't worry I got the rest, we are going to get the truck out. Don't let that piss you off or ruin our day baby" Pete was humble now and very smooth. "Look at me" Pete held mom's chin. Her deep blue eyes met his muahz he kissed her and mom close her eyes. Pete erased all mom's fury with that passionate simple kiss. "You are too beautiful to let this scum bag take you off your square." Pete informed mom. Mom dug in her purse and pulled out $400 using what Pete gave her for the truck's release.

"You drive my car and I'll drive the truck just in case we get pulled over." The smashed up bumper and busted left tail light will most definitely raise suspicion so Pete figured he'll take the plunge if anything went wrong. Baby just stay behind me the whole time okay?" Pete instructed mom. "I got you, thank you." Mom yelled out the window over to Pete. "No problem." Pete jumped in the truck and lead the way all the way home to mom's back alley. As mom looked at the back of the truck she put together the story Linda had told her about that night. She pictured the car smashing the back of the truck and Manuel jumping out in a tantrum. She held back her tears.

"Babe I will sell it and I'll give you back what you put in for it today okay." Mom told Pete. "I'm not worried about that, just make sure you do what Rock asked you to do and get rid of it. I'll tell a few people that I know that I have a truck for sale, so we can get rid of it quicker. Rock needs the money more than I do." Pete was an honest man. "Plus we can come to an agreement later." Pete said kissing mom again and again. "Oh yea?"

Mom teased. "Oh yeah." Pete kissed her neck mom squealed with laughter, she was ticklish. "Well I'm going to open the shop. You call me if you want to go to the jail." I will thank you again." Mom said to Pete he handed her the keys and set the alarm on the truck. Once Pete left mom stared at the truck for a few minutes then finally headed inside. Linda was already up cooking some breakfast for herself. She didn't know the truck was out back.

"Oh my God you did?" Now she did.She hurried to the back door to see the dusty truck parked out back. "Can I have it?" Linda pled. Mom looked at her and saw how happy it may her daughter to see her busted brother's truck out back. "That was my first intention baby but after talking to your brother. He told me to sell it and use the money to get you another car of your own." Mom broke her baby's heart. "By why would you spend money on another vehicle when Rocks truck is outback mom?" Linda wasn't going to give up this fight so easily. "Is not me baby, It's your brother he doesn't want you to be seen in that truck. The news made it very clear to everyone that this is the truck Rock was in when he "killed" that man. Those other people who don't know exactly who you are might be able to distinguish you by the truck." Mom spoke so it would all sink in. "One plus one equals two right?" Mom asked after a few seconds. Linda saw the reasoning behind her brother's word. Linda could care less who saw her in that truck. She was not giving a shit of what could occur. The truck was the only piece of tangible material she had left. besides the deep memories of her and her brother. She had to have his truck by any means. "How was she going to get it from mom?" "So how much is he selling it for?" Linda asked biting into her omelet and bacon sandwich. Mom took a deep breath he said $1500-$2000."That's what Manny ask for." Mom said. "Who you selling it too?" Linda was curious. "I don't know yet but Pete is going to tell his friends and I'll spread the word and wait." Mom said. So far no one was in mind to purchase the vehicle. "Well I'll tell a few of my friends too." Linda cleaned up the mess. "Okay you do that." Mom replied. I got the kitchen you going to be here for dinner or am I going to eat alone again?" Mom asked Linda. Probably not but put a plate aside if I do come in early mom." Linda had to go to work. "Always baby." Linda gave mom a peck on the cheek. "How you getting to work?" Mom asked "Joel should be here soon." Linda said. "I love you baby." Mom spoke washing dishes. "I love you too mom, tell Manny I said I'll be there sometime next week." Linda said walking away grabbing her backpack.

—

Jacqueline's house phone was ringing like it never rung before. She hadn't answered it because she was off and wanted to relax for the most part until Eliza would wake up at least. From the looks of it this wasn't going to happen. She wanted to curse whoever was blown up her phone. One would think that if no one would answer on the first two attempts, than maybe nobody was there. So maybe one should call back later right? No this call had to be urgent and it had to be answered from what Jacqueline noticed.

"Hello!" Jacqueline answered with an attitude. "I'm sorry for blowing up your phone but I need to speak with you its really important." The female voice on the other end was saying, sounding far from a hood chick. "Who the hell was this?" Jacqueline asked not liking this one bit. "It's a friend of Rock, He gave me your number so I could talk to you in private. That's why the call was so urgent. I wasn't going to stop until you answered. I'm just following what I was asked to do." The voice over the phone instructed. "How could you have got my number from Rock if he is locked up? If you have nothing else to do you need to get a life because I don't have time for games." Jacqueline was getting a little upset. "Look I'm not playing games with anyone. When and where would be a good place to meet? I can explain all this to you. And No! We can't do it over the phone." The female voice spoke with authority. She wasn't playing games, what did this woman want from Jacqueline? Could she be trusted?

"Well I'm off of work today, so today will be the best day for me and I swear you better not be on no sneaky shady shit!" Jacqueline was a bit paranoid. "Okay I'm off too, where? The female asked. Meet me at the 7/11 on Federal." Jacqueline said. "Okay which 7/11?" The woman asked. By 36th Jacqueline said. "Time?" The woman asked. "3 o'clock" Jacqueline spoke into the receiver. The call was ended.

Jacqueline didn't know what to think. She knew Rock which that alone ease her mind a bit, but what could she possibly want? Jacqueline's mind went bananas and why in the hell would Rock give her my number? He didn't even consult with me first? Was he in trouble? He hasn't been answering my mail nor has he called. For someone to be away Rock was sure making an impact in everyone's lives. It made perfect sense on how one's actions can truly affect everyone in your circle. No one really paid much attention but it's most definitely true. There was no way to erase the emotional attachment one builds for anyone. Over time yes it can subsided but it wouldn't ever vanish permanently. Especially if the attachment was sincere. It's possible for it to fade to a certain degree though.

That entire morning and afternoon Jacqueline couldn't stop thinking about the phone call. It would be a relief when she got to the bottom of this. 3 o'clock couldn't have come any faster.

"Can you watch him for a second?" Jacqueline asked her friend who was staying over for a while. "Sure where you going?" Her friend asked. "To the 7/11." Jacqueline answered. "You want anything?" Jacqueline asked bundling up her coat. "Mommy I want ice cream." He told her mother. "Ice scream?" Jacqueline repeated. "Yes mommy the red one. "He described the ice cream which was more like a Popsicle. "Okay baby mommy will buy you an ice cream." "Yay! Mommy is the best, mommy is the best!" he jumped out of excitement. "Mommy will be right back." Ay Jacqueline grab me a slushy." Jacqueline's friend Charmaine asked. "All right." The walk was a straight shot downhill.

The niggas on the corners all tried to kick game but Jacqueline being Jacqueline kept her head up and that ass moving. She swore her shit didn't stink. It was a little earlier than 3 o'clock as a matter of fact it was 10 minutes earlier. She wasted time in the store as she looked out the big glass windows to see if any familiar face would show up but nothing. There was a light-skinned woman walking up and Jacqueline swore it was her, she came up in the store and nothing no eye contact or anything. "Can I help you find something?" The India man behind the counter spoke to Jacqueline with a curious look on his face. "No I'm waiting for friend thank you." Jacqueline said placing some candy on the counter. "I'm not done." Jacqueline advised him so he wouldn't ring her up. She felt awkward and uncomfortable all in one bunch. She wasn't gonna wait anymore. She poured herself a medium cup of French vanilla cappuccino and grabbed the Popsicle her son wanted. "Let me get a black and mild." She asked the man sitting behind the counter. His eyes kept on scanning the store. You would be surprised how many robberies occurred in this area alone. It was known to get held up on a regular. Now Jacqueline was mad that this bitch was playing games. As soon as she stepped out of the store a silver Volvo pulled up scanning the area. They locked eyes and Jacqueline threw up her hands. The white girl hopped out.

"I'm so sorry. Are you Jacqueline?" She asked with her seductive eyes that were masked with eyeliner. White girl was pretty as shit, a bit thick but she was a cutie Jacqueline thought. "Damn girl I thought you wasn't coming. Wassup who are you?" Jacqueline got straight to the point. "Get in." Mandy instructed Jacqueline. "It's cold we can sit in the car." Mandy assured Jacqueline. "I can't I got ice cream and I got to get it to my son." Jacqueline admitted. "Oh okay so let's take it to him we can talk on the way." Jacqueline finally got in the car.

"I'm sorry I took so long but traffic is pretty bad today." Mandy kept apologizing the look on Jacqueline's face showed no emotion. "Who are you I asked and what do you want for me?" Jacqueline was rude. "Turn right up here and go straight up." Jacqueline gave Mandy instructions to get to the house. Her car was clean and smelled almost new. White girl has some money in the bank. Jacqueline thought to herself. "Listen I don't mean to be rude but I don't want shit from you. I'm doing this favor for Rock. He told me that you are his rider and that you would be more than helpful to help him." Mandy came out straight forward with her own attitude. Mandy wasn't having it anymore. "Why hasn't Rock notified me? And why doesn't he answer my letters?" Jacqueline asked Mandy as if she was supposed to know the answer to her concerning questions. Mandy didn't have the answers why would she. "You can pull over right here I'll be in and out." Jacqueline said rushing out the car.

"Why am I doing this? What am I getting myself into? Mandy look at her rearview mirror and spoke to herself atarring at her own reflection. "Damn Rock you better be happy." She said to herself. Jacqueline jump back into the car.

"I'm sorry my son is a handful." Jacqueline came into the car with a whole new attitude. "I'm sure he is." Mandy replied. "I can't wait to have my own baby." Mandy admitted. "Oh yes you can." Jacqueline joked. "We'll look the only way I came to know Manuel a.k.a. Rock I work in the jail so when he came in he was hurt pretty bad and on top of that he's been going through a lot up in there." Mandy let the cat out the bag slowly. "A lot?" What do you mean?" Jacqueline was worried now. "Girl that man is a problem in that jail, he's only been there for a while and he's already getting into so much shit with the cops and with the other prisoners etc. etc." Mandy informed. "Oh my God that can't be Rock he's not a troublemaker." Jacqueline protected Rocks reputation. "I know he is not a troublemaker but if you fuck with him, he just lets go of his humbleness and becomes this evil person that most guys are intimidated by him now. A few months ago someone stabbed him almost killing him." Mandy informed Jacqueline. "No!" She held her mouth in complete shock not wanting to believe any of it. "He's okay but a few months ago two men turned up dead and all the staff swore up and down that it was Rock who had something to do with it." Mandy look at Jacqueline sexy face seriously. "Did he?" Jacqueline asked. "Nobody knows for sure if he did it." Mandy admitted. "Do you think he did it?" Jacqueline asked Mandy. Mandy nodded her head and confirming her suspicion. "So why are you helping him?" Jacqueline asked Mandy. "I don't know.... I mean I know when I talk to Rock which is only a few seconds a week. He's not that bad person everyone portrays him to be. He is smart and caring." Mandy spoke highly a Rock. Jacqueline smiled. "Yes he is, I know definitely he is a charmer I went to his court hearing and he didn't even notice me. It hurts me to know I can't see him or touch him. I miss him so much I want him to know this. I'm sure he might still have a girl but I don't care. I want my friend back. Tell him that I'll never leave his side and that I'll do whatever he wants me to do for him." Jacqueline's eyes teared up but she didn't allow any tears to fall as she spilled her heart out to this stranger. "This brings me up to this now. He wants you to help me buy him and a ball of some powder and a half ounce of weed. If he can't afford both just grab one or two." Mandy spoke dropping the bomb right on her "What!?" Jacqueline couldn't believe what she was hearing. I know that man must have lost his mind." Jacqueline was pist. "I'm just a messenger if you don't want to do it, don't worry about it. I'll get someone to buy off someone else." Mandy proved her loyalty. Jacqueline stared at her. "Are you serious, you going to do this with or without my help won't you?" Jacqueline asked mad. "You want him to yourself right? That's what you're trying to do?" Jacqueline eyes got red. "No he needs my help and I told him I would. I know what it is to have no one in your corner and I see you are here but he feels alone in their. If I can help him this one time, I'll do it because he deserves that much." Mandy was definitely on board. I couldn't believe she was willing to go the extra mile for me. She didn't know me from a hole in the wall but I was more than greatful to have met her. I didn't care how many other guys she helped in my situation but I knew that I wouldn't let her lose the job for me. "So you going to bring it inside for him after I get it for you?" Jacqueline was putting the pieces of the puzzle together. "Yup" Mandy replied. "So Rock is an addict now huh? Jacqueline asked annoyed. "No he's not an addict. They have him on psych meds that's all. I'm guessing he wants to make some money so that he isn't a burden on anyone on the outside." Mandy summarized. Let me call someone you can come in, or you can wait out here." Jacqueline informed Mandy. "No I'll wait out here." Mandy said. Jacqueline rushed in the house and made a phone call. She refused to call her baby dads for anything. She reached out to a few other people that played in a game. She located the soft, the bud would be later.

"Charmaine, I need a half of all of some loud can you get it for a good price?" Jacqueline was on a mission. "Of course I can get it, l I didn't know you blew?" Charmaine said picking up the phone now. I don't is for a friend. "I got you girl." Charmaine was ugly as hell but her breasts were huge. $110" Charmaine repeated over the receiver. Looking at Jacqueline putting up her two thumbs. The order was placed a ball was $90 and that brought the total to $200. Back in the car Jacqueline informed Mandy of everything.

"I got it but I am $40 short." Jacqueline let Mandy know. She began to dig in her glove box Mandy pulled out $50 bill and gave it to Jacqueline. "I'll be back in an hour I have to take care of something else." Mandy informed Jacqueline. "All right" Jacqueline jumped out. She pulled away Rocks words echoed in Mandy's ear. "Condoms or balloons will work just fine." Mandy decided to go with the latex condom because balloons didn't sound too convincing. She went back to the 7/11 and bought a pack of Trojan condoms and had to burn some time until her hour was up.

—

Linda was on break at work with about two hours to go before her shift was over. She thought a lot about Streets and how nice he was. She was undecided if she would call him or not. Her Curiosity got the best of her. She punched the number into the payphone and waited till she heard the tone. If Joel only knew what she was up to? She hung up and waited for the call back. It took forever but the pay phone finally rang, she was nervous as hell.

"Hello" Linda answered in her sexy his voice. "I didn't think you would ever call mami." Streets was putting on his game. "I wasn't but I guess my curiosity got the best of me." Linda spoke very sweet. "Oh yea?" Streets replied. "What are you doing?" Street asked Linda. "Nothing chilling." What are you doing?" Linda asked. "Making money." The same as every other day." Streets boasted . "So you are busy huh?" Linda asked. "No not at all Janet. I'm never too busy to see you why Wassup?" What you doing later?" Streets wasted no time. "nada at the moment why what you got in mind?" Linda play with him. "Is all up to you whatever you want to do we can do, except for sex." Linda make sure to set her boundaries off the rip. "Come on mami I didn't even bring that shit up you did." Streets use her words against her. "I know but I know how y'all niggas be all in a rush to get in a woman's pants." Linda worked her magic. She had to get him where she wanted him and right now he wasn't anywhere close to her mark. "I got you I'm a gentleman keyword gentle." Streets joked. "See there you go being a bad boy because trust me you getting nowhere Streets." Linda warned. "I'm joking Janet so we on for tonight or what?" He asked "Just make sure to call back faster next time or I won't pick up." Linda was feisty. "Oh my bad, you got it though." Street gave in. Linda had to get back to work. "All right talk to you later." Linda hung up quickly with her stomach in knots. She couldn't believe that she was playing with the enemy like this.

She was attracted by Street swag though. She wondered how do Joel would be if he had a little bit of street swag in him. She was wrong, she was thinking a little too much. Joel was a man who worked and took care of all of his responsibilities another way. There was no way she could play both sides, the adrenaline was building up as she thought about it alone. Was she wrong for what she was imagining deep down inside of her head? It was only thoughts wasn't it? She had to stop she had to get back to work and focus.

—

The horn was ripping through the sky that was beginning to darken little by little. With the four ways on she was parallel parked in the middle of the street in silver Volvo. It stood out like a sore thumb. The dope boys were coming out toward the Volvo. They were looking to see if she wanted to cop some drugs. She did but not like that. Jacqueline came down her still steps.

"Leave her alone, she ain't no fiend!" Jacqueline fended off the many hungry dope boys. "All right baby my bad." The one young bucks said. Let's go around the block." Jacqueline instructed Mandy. Mandy's heart began to beat faster as the smell marijuana hit her nostrils. She wanted to back down at this point but there was already too much money involved to quit now. "How much was the coke?" Mandy asked sounding like an undercover. Jacqueline was nervous now, "It was 90 and the bud was 110. Jacqueline pulled out a small clear plastic bag that contained the coke. It was a small ball that looked a lot smaller than an ice cube. The bud on the other hand was light green and smelled strong. How the hell am I going to get all this inside of the prison without the Guard smelling this shit?" Its bad enough my car smell like this it now." Mandy was panicking now. "What did Rock tell you to do with it?" Jacqueline asked he told me to break it down the bud into almost dust and pack it into a balloon or a condom and to shove it in my pussy." Mandy said with a smile on her face. Jacqueline laughed. "Okay there you go it should be that simple." No one is going to smell inside of your pussy girl." Jacqueline tried to sound convincing. "Plus inside the condom should help conceal the smell too." Mandy parked up on the other end of the block. She looked at the product and her hand. "All right I guess I have no choice now." Mandy said. "No you have a choice, you don't have to do this girl." Jacqueline said. "Yes I do and I'm going to do it." Mandy forced herself to be strong. she would do her best to pull through for Rock sake. "I'm a let you go I'll call you and let you know what's going on okay." Mandy pulled up to Jacqueline's corner and dropped her off.

"Tell Rock to put me on the list and to call me that I'll be waiting for him." Jacqueline said before she shut the door. "Fucking Rock had all these woman going crazy over him. I didn't even get to go on a date with him" Mandy spoke to herself. On her commute home she looked in search for cops breaking her neck at ever head light that approached her, there was no telling what will happen if she got pulled over.Tomorrow she would make it a must to clean and wash the car after she packed all the stuff up. Paranoid as can be she finally made it to her small town apartment. She took a deep breath and put all the contents in her brown bag where the condoms were put in. She stared at the white ball and wondered what this do to people? It would have them going crazy in these street but also in jail.

Finally, in her kitchen she didn't even bother to change clothes she searched for a sifter so she could break down the coke, she looked for a silver spoon. She was a certified nurse she had all the gloves she needed in her first aid kit. Putting a pair of latex glove on she opened the clear sandwich bag slowly to not spill the rock like substance anywhere but on the kitchen counter. It was rocky so she placed it in the sifter and began to grind it back and forth. She noticed the rock was getting smaller and smaller with every stroke. The pile underneath the sifter was getting bigger. She smiled as Rock's instructions were clear and accurate. The coke was broken down into practically dust. She grabbed a condom which raised suspicion. The condom box red Trojan extra lubricant. There was no way she could put this dry powdery inside this condom that was lubed up with spermicide and whatnot.

"I bought the wrong one!" She yelled out loud. "What the fuck now!?" She was beating herself up. She sat back and looked at all the mess she was making on her kitchen counter. Not with food or drinks but would drugs, drug that could get her in deep trouble and make her lose her career. She looked at her hand "gloves" she said. "I got it." She went back to the first aid kit and pulled out some more gloves. She found some scissors, That would be used to cut off the fingers. Once satisfied she used a piece of paper to scoop up the powder and emptied it in the biggest finger from the glove. It took up almost about inch of the glove she packed it down until she thought it was compressed enough. Tying a knot at the end twice she snipped off the excess latex that was unnecessary. Had to be bigger than a marble now. She put it aside and did the same with the bud. The same sifter was used not even washing it out. Mandy didn't see any harm and in what she was doing. She was totally unconscious of her actions. What she was doing? She did the same thing. The Weed was a lot fluffier, she made four balls all compressed down tightly. Finally she pull all the balls in one condom putting a tight knot on it as well. She looked at it thinking of how she was gonna shove all this inside of her pussy. After putting it all together she cleaned up her mess and threw away all the extra paraphernalia.

S decided to stripped down or her clothing until she was bare ass, she decided to tie a piece of thread at the top of the knotted condom so she could have something to pull on it easily. She grabbed the condom and slid it up her pussy slowly. The ripples of each ball may her juices flow. It slid out and she did it again she was getting herself ready for the big day. She continued sliding the condom in and out. This was arousing her to a higher degree. She ended up masturbating to Rock and finger popped herself all the way into the shower satisfied herself for more pleasure. She practiced pulling the string until she felt confident that it would work in her favor with her first exhibition coming up. She stashed the goods after wiping them down and waited for her shift to begin.

—

Linda's was just getting her night started. She went home and got freshened up and ate the full meal, that mom had put aside for her. She decided to call Joel. He picked up on the first ring.

"Wassup baby?" Joel answered. "Boy how you know it was me what if it was a man or somebody else?" Linda joked with her man. "Baby you the only one that calls here at this time." Joel made Linda feel special every time. "Awwww you to sweet baby I'm so tired. Ima call it a night. Am I gonna see you tomorrow?" Linda asked trying to rush Joel off the phone. "Of course babe, just call me tomorrow, get your beauty sleep my sexy princess. "Joel fell right into what Linda was doing. "All right baby." Linda wanted to sell it even more. Blowing good night kisses. The call was ended immediately. Linda turned off the ringers on all the phones in the house, even mom's. Mom was out as always Linda was looking sexy as fuck, she never looked anything but sexy.

Tonight, she wore black spandex with a fitted polo sweater that hugged her body nicely. She wore her coffee snow boots. The weatherman was calling for a chance of snow and this was a perfect day to Rock them. Her hair was still in micro minis but she had managed to get them redone a little bit thicker. She wore them all over the place. Her smelled was intoxicating. Fresh!" She stared in the mirror. "It's like taking candy from a baby." She grabbed her jacket and a few things and out the door she went.

She walked on a mission, passing the club Elegante and picked up a pay phone dialing Street's pager and hung up after punching the pay phone number. Not even two second pass after hanging up and it was already ringing. "Quick learner." Linda thought. "Hello." Linda answered. "Where you at sexy?" Street asked. At the 7/11 on Federal." Linda responded. "Which one?" Linda asked. The one down from the millennium." Linda answered. "I'll be there five minutes." Streets wasn't wasting no time to get to Linda in Linda's guts.

New pussy will make any nigga do things that they say they would never do. I've seen it all. Trust and believe, I fell victim to it a few times. There's nothing better than a challenge to get in any woman's drawls that you'll never touched before. What's fucked up is that once you get that shot it's nothing anymore to you then a piece of ass. Once the chase is over is no longer a thrill, now if this woman's fucking game is on point a nigga would keep her in the stash until the woman finally got tired of it, feeling like just a fuck. Then there is love, for those who have been privileged to enjoy. Good luck with that one! Streets only took four minutes as he pulled up in his Lincoln. The front bumper wasn't smashed in and his lights were sparkling as if they were installed brand-new. His smile was worth 1 million bucks. He hopped out and went straight to the other side.

"Shall we?" He joked. Linda had no choice but to smile at his cheesy self. "Damn! Janet you look gorgeous tonight." Streets looked at Linda from head to toe savoring her body in his own mind. Linda caught him drooling. She held up her manicure pointed finger. "Don't start your shit because I will stay right here." Linda didn't get in until Streets straightened out. "You got it Janet it's all about you tonight." Linda was happy with his attitude switch up, but knew that this horny mother fucker would be a handful tonight. "Where to?" Streets asked lighting and L. "Boy if you don't put that shit out." Linda barked. "Put it out you know I haven't eaten anything all day and this is the only thing to cure my appetite. You gota be crazy if you going to make me put this out." I followed all you little rules but this one I will not comply with." Streets puffed and inhaled deeply. He pulled off before Linda could even think about jumping out a moving car. Let's go to the theater in Cherry Hill." Linda said. "What do you want to see at the theater?" Streets asked blowing smoke. The car was hotboxed. "Gladiator with Russle Crowe." Linda informed Streets "okay we can do that I've been meaning to see that movie." Streets informed Linda he passed Linda the L. She hesitated but eventually took it also smoked with Streets. "So Wassup with you Janet how come you single?" Streets probed. "Because I don't have patience with men all yall want is the pussy." Linda said in between puffs. She handed the L back over to Streets. "Wow that's a lot of people you put in one big category." Streets defend himself. "Well I ain't like the rest of these hoe ass niggaz. I'm not trying to get committed I just want to have fun and live a little. I have kids and I can't deal with the headache myself." Streets was keeping it 100 will Linda for once, Linda was listening to his bullshit. She admire how truthful he was trying to be. He was different he said. I'm sure this is what a lot of woman didn't like about him. The fact that he didn't want a commitment . "So in other words you're a dog that goes around poking everything in its path huh?" Linda asked. Streets laugh. "No I have limitations and standards I only tend to be drawn to thoroughbred woman. I'm not all that into pretty go lucky prissy females. I'm from the street so I want a woman that I am dealing with to have the capability to hold her ground down. As well as hold me down when the going gets rough." Streets laid it all out on the table. "So why you trying to mess with me?" Linda asked with an attitude. High as hell both of them wore chinky eyes on there faces. The theater was about five minutes away. The L was gone but the clouded Lincoln held the smoke inside. Street was about to light a cigarette. "Oh man! Don't light that for real that shit stinks. I can't walk up in their smelling like an ashtray, we are almost there." Linda begged in one breath. She really couldn't stand the smell of cigarettes. "All right Janet you got it. Ill smoke it when we get there." Streets made an exception he liked Linda just like every other nigga did. So he respected showing her that she mattered. Pulling up into a parking lot Streets parked up and hopped out rushing to open Linda's door so she could step out. "You don't have to do all that." Linda said to Streets. "We grow as bad as you are you shouldn't have to touch any doors." Streets was determined to get that pussy. Linda blushed. She stood a few feet away from him as he took a few puffs from his Newport and ended up throwing the rest out. The lights illuminated the parking lot with reds and blues from the theater. "Streets extended his hand out Linda grabbed it feeling warm and safe feeling inside. The place had people all over the front smoking, getting high and whatnot. Linda scanned the area not wanting to be noticed by anyone that could potentially blow her cover again. Streets was bigger than her, she used his broad shoulders to shield her face from the other people.

Once inside there were even more people mingling around she had no clue this place would have so many people today. "I'm use the bathroom I'll meet you in the arcades." Linda informed Streets. "Gladiator right?" Streets reiterated. "Yes" Linda went on her way as Streets went to purchase the tickets. Linda didn't really need to go but wanted to check up on her look. The bathroom was sparkling there was a crowd of white college girls in the far corner. It looked as if they were snorting something but Linda couldn't really tell. They were passing around a small bottle that was definitely a flask. They laughed and gulped it all down. Satisfy where her look Linda decided to step back out of the bathroom and fianlly head to the arcades.

What could come out of all this? Linda asked yourself walking to find Streets who was in the arcade playing one of the games. She stared at him from behind and wonder how his dick game was. "Was she taking it that far?" Linda was falling for this nigga herself. Why not? She was up close on Streets.

"Wassup baby girl who you here with?" A short stocky spanish guy was trying to holler. Streets radar went up immediately. Linda sucked her teeth. "A friend" Linda replied. Streets turned around "yeah a friend so back up playboy." Devastated, homeboy threw up his palms "My bad, no problem." He went back to doing what he was doing. "So mean." She said to Streets. "Not at all you would've seen mean if you was my lady but since you said friend, you only get friend protection." Streets was a character he joked. They both laughed.

"We got 10 minutes you want to play a few games or you want to find some seats before he gets packed in their?" Streets asked. "Let's get our seats." They racked up on all types of candy it was a bit overpriced but Streets didn't care he was balling. The total on candy alone came up to almost $30 soda and popcorn was on his way too. "Janet grab the candy ma." Streets instructed. He did have a temper that he like to show that he was in charge. Linda noticed all of his body language. "We out." Streets lead the way to theater number six that was showing the movie they had agreed to watch. "You can pick the seats." Streets told Linda. There options were limited being that it was practically already packed. "Top corner." Linda pointed finally seating.

They began to have small talk while eating chocolate and gummies.

"So how you feeling?" Linda asked. "I'm good, high as hell."... I'm not gonna lie. I need another cigarette though." Street said. "Yuck." Linda contested to that one. "Why you don't like cigarettes but you smoke some that ganja?" "I have a relative that is close to dying all because of cigarettes, ever since seeing her almost losing her life I told myself I would never pick up a cigarette in my life." Linda shared a piece of her life with Streets. "Who is this person?" Streets asked. "My aunt." Linda lied. "Damn that sucks." I still need a cigarette." Street didn't care about dying. It wasn't him dying anyway. He joked. "You are too much." Linda said.

The movie was about to begin it got real dark and "Please remain quiet." was spread across the screen. "Fuck you bitch is this quite enough for you!" A voice from out front yelled joking. Linda shook her head in disgust. "Rude." Linda spoke. "Aren't they" Street agreed? The movie lasted almost 2 hours and it was a movie that was worth every cent. The candy was all gone and so was the popcorn it was time to call it a night.

The lights came on blinding everyone who stood in the theater Streets and Linda waited for the jam-packed room to disperse. "That was a good pick." Streets commended Linda for the choice of movie. He stared at her eyes that were no longer red. They were white as the clouds on a cloudy day. Linda stared at him and made a mental know of his face, every scar every blemish everything she made sure to never forget his face. "Are you ready?" I'm tired." Linda was cutting the night short "me too I gota work still." Street said "work?" I gota work, you gota run around." Linda joked. "It still work Janet just a little more dangerous." Streets tried to uphold his lined of work. Linda laughed. Street stared at Linda's ass. Her curves were to die for. He couldn't wait to bus all in that ass. Linda already knew his eyes were locked on her body this is why she wore this outfit. She put a bit more authority in her step which made her ass shake even more. "Damn!" Streets couldn't hold it anymore. Linda turned around. "What?" She smiled.

"You!" is what happened" Street was on it. "Stop it." Linda put her finger up until Streets came in close. "I'll bite that finger." Street said leaning in for a kiss but Linda turned her face and gave him the cheek. "You're too sweet." Linda spoke. Streets enjoyed the games eventually he was going to dick Linda down by choice or by force. Street was the type who always got what he wanted no matter what it was. He would ask for it, he would stick you up for it. He would just kill them and take it no matter what the case was he always got what he wanted. They held hands and marched towards the car. "Have you ever been to jail?" Linda came out of nowhere with this question. "Jail?" Streets repeated he didn't like those words. "Why would you asked me something like that Janet?" Streets was curious and annoyed now. This woman was trouble Streets was thinking to himself. "I mean in your line of work I know a lot of people who go to jail doing what you do. That's all I'm saying" Linda stated. Streets was in deep thought. "I'm not them, I know how to do my shit. The people who end up in jail are the ones who get real comfortable and think that they are untouchable. In the streets everyone can be touch whether it's by the cops or even by your enemy, you can't ever think that you are above everyone else." Streets schooled Linda. I don't trust anyone and the very few I let in my circle I watched closely because everyone isn't as loyal the way they say they are. My right hand man was killed a while back ago." Till this day I know I will never find a nigga like him to have my back the way we had each other's back." Linda got quiet and in deep thought he was talking about Kay the man she killed to protect her brother. "Oh my God, that's what I'm talking about aren't you afraid of one day losing your life over something so petty?" Linda asked. "To be straight up, I don't care if I die tomorrow. As long as I die with my head up high and die knowing that I didn't go down like a bitch. I'm willing to live with that." Streets played the all mighty gangsta role Linda, she fell for it. She was naïve to the life so anything that Streets would say she would most likely believe. I'm sorry to hear that about your man but if you don't mind me asking how he died." Linda was walking on eggshells.

"All happen because of my stupid baby moms I told her to stop talking with this lame ass nigga." That nigga was Manny Linda was getting the missing pieces she needed. "I had gave her the option to stop talking to this nigga because I didn't want my son around no other man thinking that he was daddy." Street went back to the scene recounting the beginning to the end. "I didn't know who this nigga was nor did anyone else in the hood low him. This mother Fucker was low key." Streets talked about Rock. He was right the only people who know Rock were the people who went to school with him. So if you wasn't in school you would never cross paths with him. All this worked out to his advantage. "All I knew was what kind of truck this bitch ass nigga drove." Linda's blood was getting hot. She didn't like to hear her brother's name being slandered the way it was right now. She held herself back because blowing up wasn't what she needed. "How did you know what car he drove?" Linda cut in. I was waiting for my baby moms at her job one day to talk to her and I saw her jump out of this fresh Expo was some shiny as rims. Then on top of that I was waiting for her at her house when she showed up late and I saw the truck again. That shit had me pist." Streets informed sparking up another L. "Drop me off at the 7/11." Linda cut in. "All right" Streets replied pulling the L strongly. "What else?" Linda asked. "I tried to get her to set this nigga up for me because I was going to kill him on site, but she liked him so much that she protected him from me." Streets admitted. Linda looked at Jacqueline from a different perspective now she now understood why Jacqueline admired Manny so much. She really did care for him." Why didn't you just let her fuck this nigga and move on? And just tell her to keep your son away from him?" Linda tried to find a late solution. "You still love her don't you?" Linda asked. "I'm not gonna lie Janet this woman will always have my heart no matter how many woman I've done been with none can compare to Jacqueline." Streets was in love with his baby moms not because of the baby boy but on a more intimate level. "So why she don't want to be which you anymore?" Linda asked. Streets took get deep breath passing the L to Linda. "Nah I'm good Streets I gota get up early." Linda refused the L. "I hurt her very bad and even hit her a few times, but she is those types that love to get hit and love to hit back. So don't look at me like a woman abuser because that's not me at all." Streets tried to defend his character. "That's what it sounds like." Linda said. "You see this is why I don't talk about my past relationships." Streets was about to close up. "Okay I won't judge you, tell me what else happen with you and that lame ass nigga." Linda couldn't believe she just referred to her brother as a lame ass nigga which he was far from." Well since I couldn't find this nigga I stopped looking and eventually he fell on my lap. I was with my main Kay and my home girl Star on this particular night. We all decided to go to the mart and guess what I saw when I showed up there?" Streets let the question dangled in the air. The 7/11 was approaching. "What?" Linda asked. I saw the truck that belong to this mother Fucker!" Streets got excited as he told his part of the story. He put out the L as he pulled into an available parking spot. "Saw his truck?" Linda asked "hell yeah it I saw his whip." Now all of us was smoking weed, wet and we were drinking so we were all fucked up in my car. Parked away from the truck because I didn't want to be seen. We stood out there sipping getting all fucked up for almost 2 hours if you had to pist you better have did it in a cup because no one was leaving the car." Street went on to explain. He is a pussy Linda thought. He made sure no one left because he didn't want to go one-on-one with Manny Linda thought. Finally, this tall as nigga came out with this short ass nigga or woman I still don't remember who he or she was. Star said it was a tomboy because she was digging all up in Star's face after she stabbed my man in the neck with a blade." Street still had no clue who this chick was, but Star would recognized Linda if she would see her again. Linda had to stay away from Star in the meantime. "So what happened to the tall man?" Linda inquired. What you mean we beat the shit out of that nigga. He stabbed me twice but Star and myself managed to get up out of their. They took that nigga to jail for the murder of my man and I got a hit out on this girl he was with that night or man." Street said with hatred in his blood. "But the nigga didn't kill your man what if they let him out?" Linda asked. "You're right about that Janet but Star and myself are going to testify against him in trial so either way he going to pay for my man's death." Streets admitted to taking the stand to put away the man who didn't even kill his right hand man over a woman. "Yes somebody going to pay right?" Linda agree with Streets, trying not be too suspicious. "That's right." Streets confirm how pathetic he was in Linda's eyes. "Well look I hope we can chill again but I got a go and get some rest. I have fun and be careful Streets." Linda warned. "I had a good time ma, I'll see you another day." Street spoke to Linda. Linda leaned in and kissed his cheek softly but tenderly. Street smiled. "Night" off she went disappearing in the darkness heading home.

Back in the cell the guys all were all talking about what was on their agenda for tomorrow. "I know I had to meet back with OJ" Rock said. "Who the fuck is OJ" Slash asked. That's the old head who got up that morning to help me fight this fucking cases since your lazy didn't want to get up." Rock was ready reading the book that OJ gave him to study and talking shit at the same time. "Damn Rock I be tired as hell in the morning. "Slash reply. "Yeah because you be up all god damn night, what do you expect?" Rock said. "I'm hungry what's up with that pot?" Bigs said. "You always hungry mother fucker." Leak said. He checked the potato chip bag to check if the meal was done. "A few more minutes the rice and noodles aren't done completely." Leak advise everyone. "Put some more hot water on that shit." Slash said. He did just that, they ran the hot water some more. We all had commissary lately so we all pitched in two items so we could all eat a nice healthy Chi chi every night which is exactly what we did. Rock learned what all the ramen noodles and dicing up all the sausages and smashing the cheese nips or cheese toast for the cheese, makes it all together and add water then presto we had a Chichi. It was a helluva a concoction a mixture of a little bit of everything. For dessert we had two honey buns with peanut butter and jelly on them. We would cut it in half and a piece for everyone. The juice was tang which was simple just add water. "Wish we had some iced tea." Rock said. "I know but it ain't happening bro." Bigs said.

"Give me your bowls." Leak ask ready to divide up the meal. It smelled good as always we were all ingesting over 1500 Cal in one sitting, but then again who gave a fuck. The meals could always get better but they always got worse so we made it do with what we had.

"CO, CO!" Give me out of here!" There was always something going on behind these walls. A voice yelled loudly as if he was dying. My nosy ass rushed to the door. "CO, CO!" A voice yelled again a couple other prisoners also yelled to get to CO's attention "where you at?" The officer yelled. "58 cell!" the prisoner yelled" another CO rushed to his aid. "You are a bitch I told you not to fuck with me bitch ass nigga!" His cellmate yelled at his celly pleading for help. "Put your hand behind you head and kneel down!" CO barked at the man doing all that hollering. You two get up on your bunks and don't move!" The CO order to the other two cellmates. "I ain't doing shit!" The aggressor yelled he jumped back on his victim. "Help me! What the fuck!" The victim was bitching the guards rushed inside the cell with backup and pride Mr. Aggressor right off his prey. It didn't stop there, they began to beat him the fuck up. Stop resisting! Stop resisting! The CO's yelled as an excuse to continue to beat the man. The small white guy had his face all marked up with all types of markings. He had gotten beaten up badly. "I'm not fucking resisting bitch!" The other man could be heard trying to submit to the guards. Once they finallydecided to stop beating on him. They subdued him for after about five minutes his face was a lot worse than the other guys. He was much bigger than the other white guy but the CO's did a helluva job rearranging his face. His t-shirt had blood all over it his eyes was swollen shut. The man looked as if he was in pain. "Damn, they fucked him up bad!" It wasn't a pretty sight to look at no one deserve to get beat like that but then again sometimes bullies need to be taught a lesson. Someone yelled out the cell. "That's police brutality!" Fuck you before we brutally beat the shit out of you too." The block went crazy at the sound of that comment.

"Here Rock, fuck them niggas." Leak got me off the gate. Bigs said a prayer even though I would eat way before he finished. The guys already knew my belief. "Amen."

Rock's mind went back and wondered about his family, this sucked to be alone. Prison wasn't the place to be, but at this point this was Rock's life. A life that couldn't determine if he would leave or if in fact he would remain here for a good portion of his life. The hours passed and the tossing and turning wouldn't let Rock sleep. The pills had not fully kicked in, so his mind would not stop cycling all that he had encountered in the past years of his life. Your mind is your worst enemy, once you lose balance of it. It has the ability to destroy you from within. Rock jumped up and decided to write to Jacqueline. To get his mind off the bullshit.

Mira hermosa!

First and foremost I want to start this letter by hoping that you and your son are in the best of health. To inform you, I have received your letter and my apologies are being sent to you. I just hope that you can find space in your heart to forgive me for all the troubles I may have brought your way. I need you to know that my intentions were never to cause you any pain whether physical or mental. I am very aware of how you feel about us and that you are very much willing to be by my side through all of this. I am very grateful to have met you and I'll never reject anything that you and I have built. I only asked you. That I'm not sure how long I will be behind these walls and in no way am I asking you to stop living your life just to accommodate my feelings. You are a beautiful woman who is free to do what she wants. I'm no one to impede on your freedom. I understand that you want to show me your loyalty if you choose to keep your word.Than, I'll have no choice but to accept all that you have to offer to me.

Rock has so much on his mind that had to be let out. He couldn't hold it in anymore. "Can't sleep huh?" Bigs asked. "No." Rock replied. "Me either." Biggs said. "You want to play a game of chess?" Big asked maybe once I finish this letter." Rock replied going back to what he was doing

... I do miss you and I miss my family a lot! I wanted you to know that me being incarcerated isn't your fault. You can't beat yourself up for something that I've been accused of. You have no control of my actions nor do you have any control over the next man's intentions. Who would've known that things would end up this far? I for one would've never have thought that I would end up in jail for a murder. Let's just hope that my lawyer can work his magic and pull some strings to get the ball moving on my court. I can't stress what I can control. You have made an impact on my life, this is why I took so long to reply to you. My emotions were all out of place. I did see you in the court room as well I can only imagine that you may have thought that I didn't notice you this was not the case. I still am in contact with one of my female friends till this day. I told her that I can't keep this relationship between her and I. It's too much for me to handle in here, as you met me in a small relationship. I'm sure you accept me for me not by who I was fucking, I hope? All I need in my circle is loyal friends who will be by my side when I need them the most. Not a wife or a girlfriend because I cannot give you what your body wants and craves for. Please understand all that I'm saying ,don't stop being the person I met at the store. I will try my best to keep in contact with you. I have received the money order you sent me and I will call you soon, before I forget some lady will be getting in contact with you about some help that I need from both of you. If you can please help her to help me. If it's too much to ask just disregard what I'm asking of you. I once again I didn't mean to put you in a tight predicament, but I need you. Send me your info so I can put you on my visitation list. I would love to see that beautiful smile of yours. I want to make sure my memory serves me right! (Smile) once again thank you for everything!

Love always,

Rock bottom

Rock could hear light snoring Bigs fell asleep there was no waking him up, I knew I wouldn't. I let him sleep, I picked up the law book and wondered about all of our rights and how they're being broken while I sat up in this place. It's been said that a prisoner has its own set of rights how true this may be on that. I wasn't 100% sure of this, I had to look into this as time went by. The sight of the mouse running from cell to cell me my stomach turn. These tiny little animals were having a field day and everyone's trash bins. These are the things you don't notice when you're asleep but know that once every one is settled you can see and hear the squeaking from them all too well. I rose my feet just in case one decided to sneak up on me. Rabies was something I definitely didn't want or need right now. It gave me the chills. I stared out the window and the street lights always stayed on illuminating the streets, cars driving by coming and going to the clubs to and from the after hours. So much crime being committed out of their but I'm in here for nothing. If only there was a way out of here, would I take the chance? Would it be worth going on the run for the rest of my life? I smiled at my reflection in the thick glass. What would be my way out? I look back down at the thick book in my hand.

Chapter 16

"What the...."

The tapping on Manny's window only prove that the forecast was more than accurate. The atmosphere that the rain creates, for some makes my body lazier than the usual. Till this day I never figured out why that is. It felt as though you are weighed down by ton of bricks, and not wanting to move. There is a sense of peace and relaxation that takes over your body. Let's not forget the warm feeling of being wrapped up in one's blanket, being saturated in your own body heat. It's such a wonderful and pleasing feeling in my opinion.

Her vision blurred not wanting to intentionally force her eyes open. She peeks and what she sees disappoints her, five after 5 AM as usual. She has to be up at 5:15 which gives her about 45 minutes to wash up and be on her commute to work to punch in by 6:30 AM. She's not even close to wanting to get up out of her queen-size bed. She pries herself loose from this imaginary hold her bed possesses, walking like a zombie. With her eyes not fully open yet she almost runs into the bathroom door. That woke her up. The bathroom is white all over with baby blue lines in the tile seems. Crispy white towels with baby blue butterflies on each corner hung neatly for pure decoration. The knobs on her sink were crispy white with silver trimming holding them in place. The floor would have you thinking you were walking on fluffy white clouds, not an ounce of color just straight white rugs comforting your feet. Anyone would notice that she put some good time and effort to get this bathroom exactly the way she wanted it. Not a speck of mildew anywhere, her cosmetics were still boxed up in the corner shelf on the wall. The smell of fresh aromas filled the air, the bathroom looked as if it's been laid out yesterday. I was once told that when you are dealing with a woman that you are unsure of, check out her bathroom and you'll determine your decision based solely on that. A woman's bathroom is sacred that is where they perfect all of their beautiful attributes.

So if there bathroom looks like shit and it's disgusting you might want to reevaluate this woman before you do the unthinkable. Beautiful qualities are not just looks there is more to a woman that this. A woman dropped this jewel on me and I'll never forget it. After washing up her appendages and her goddess. Mandy was now's racing to finish up so she could jump in her vehicle and speed to work as she did every day. Her mind, was on eating a quick breakfast two yogurts and some crackers. She had her bag in her hands while running down towards her vehicle. The rain was down pouring. It was going to be an ugly night. "What the hell!" Mandy yelled from inside the vehicle. Her keys were already in the ignition. "How could I be so stupid?" Mandy insults her herself. Removing the keys she sprinted back to her apartment. Her round voluptuous breasts bounced all over the place. Her Nikes stomped the pavement trying to avoid the drops of rain, which was impossible. Back in her apartment she went straight to the kitchen and dug inside a bowl of rice. What she came up with was, what this whole day was about. "This better work" Mandy said to herself. She wash off the rice starch and drop her scrubs. Her booty shorts also slid down her plump ass. She was bear ass now, she inserted the packages in her already moist vagina with ease. She enjoyed the feeling again. "No time for that." she told herself. Making sure that the string hung out a bit, pulling up her drawls. She stormed out the door again.

She thought what would be the best possible way to pass the drugs to Rock. Rock got medication three times a day but it wasn't a guarantee that she would be assigned to his housing unit. She also knew that she couldn't recommend the block, because the last nurse that did that ended up on desk duty for a month. It rose to much suspicion once a nurse would request a block to work on. You don't want anyone to think that you are fraternizing with the prisoner. To many rats and a whole lot of jealousy. The nurse's gossip amongst one another about prisoners they thought were handsome and a few other thoughts, but it stayed at that. To risk your career for a fling, would be Ludacris. One would be amazed by all the stories you would hear, about the state prisons and even in the county jails. Bitches didn't give a fuck. It's one thing when you're out in society and you have a one night stand with a random nigga or bitch in the street, but when you're that desperate to feed into a niggas lines in a prison. I think you deserve to get what you get for risking your career for someone who obviously can't get it right for themselves. I dont give a shit how or why he ended up in here. Doesn't mean you should join a mother fucker. I'm speaking about myself for the most part. The ride to the county jail was a short one. The anxiety of what was going to occur made matters a bit more intense. The rain not wanting to seize, only guaranteed that Mandy would be drenched by the time she walked into the facility. She bought herself a few extra minutes in the car. Her palms were sweating.

"I hope this works, I hope this works". Mandy repeated over and over to herself psyching herself up. She flung open her door and grabbed everything that she needed to enter the facility. ID wrapped around her neck and her lunch bag along with the smaller backpack that carried. A few feminine products along with a book or two. She approached the door and to her surprise, the LT. and Sgt. Miller were posted at the entrance looking out at the downpour. Mandy being Mandy was paranoid as can be. She didn't know where to plant her eyes. What should of been a normal day with a bunch of "hi's, and how are you gentlemen's doing?" She freezes up. Why was it that we would throw ourselves under the bus when we would be under pressure? All she had to do was play it off as if nothing was out of the norm. Talk about being suspicious.

"Ms. Dusive" the LT. called out to her. She slid by him. "Hey guys.... Good morning." Mandy tried her best to sound as if nothing is up. "Ugly day huh?" Sgt. Miller chimed in. Not noticing that her key ring was on one of her fingers. She placed all the bags on the conveyor belt to prepare her every day routine of getting searched and wanded. "Yes it is terrible and the cold isn't helping either." She manages to get out with her hair drenched. She slides through the metal detector "Beep! Beep!" Her heart wants to explode from her chest. "Remove all objects." the C.O behind the small counter states. She has no pockets or no jewelry but she goes back through. The LT stares at her as if she's carrying a contraband on her person, she passes through again "beep! Beep!" "What the hell!" Mandy is getting frustrated and scared at the same time. The CO notices the key on her finger on her right hand but doesn't say anything. "Remove all objects please!" The jackass behind the counter is playing with Mandy now. No one else sees the joke but him. Her mind is so clouded that she is far from conscious of what she is overlooking. The LT notices the keys.

"Ms. Dusive!" The LT called over to her. Mandy's face is red and so terrified. "What!" She answers so humbly. "Your key he holds up his right hand and points to it with his left. "OH!" Mandy takes a deep breath of relief. Now she went from frightened to a total embarrassment. She buried her wet face into her chest. "It's okay, it's the rain" Sgt. Miller jokes. She smiles and grabs all her belongings. The C.O behind the counter is laughing hysterically. Mandy mugs him with pure hatred. She's in, she is buzzed inside the metal doors. She waits inside the port for the other door to open. Looking up ahead the cameras are dead in her face. She shakes her head at what just occurred. She began to beat herself up about how stupid she was for not seeing or feeling the keys on her finger. "Clank!" The door was unlocked. Walking down the corridor she was going head-to-head with three more officers who were ending their shift. "Ms. Dusive good morning." the CO in the middle spoke out to her. "Morning gentlemen." Mandy replied and kept her head down and her steps moving forward. She hated herself for putting herself through this emotional roller-coaster.

—

"Ayo get up Slash." Rock shoved Slash again.... "For what nigga?" Slash was still half asleep. "Your breakfast!" Rock said. Bigs and Leak been up. Man that nigga ain't getting up." Bigs says, Leak laughed at Rocks attempts. "Come on nigga, do me this favor." Rock says. Just get it and head back, you don't even have a sit down." Rock tried to convince Slash. "Damn niggggaaaaa! Only because is for you." Slash gave in. He jumped on Slash. "My nigggggaaaa." Rock joked. Yea Rock may be a bit more mature than your average 19 year old, but he was still a kid at heart. "All right.... get off me." Slash pled. "Y'all niggas is crazy." Leak said with a smile.

"It's almost time they about to pop the doors". Bigs said. Oatmeal and toast with fruit was on the menu for today. "Ayo this mother fucker Braze owes me four dollars today, he better have my money." That comment caught me off guard. I'm with Leak all day and I have a notice him doing any hustling on the side but then again that's how it was supposed to be done right? "Oh yea he owes you?" I asked Leak. "For what?" I was nosy and I could be because I had to know all that went down with mine, just like he always knew what went down with me at all times. It's how we made sure there weren't any surprises amongst one another. "We placed a bet on a definition of a word?" Leak informed me. I couldn't believe what I just heard. "A word?" I asked. Leak laughed. "Yeah we was at the library when you when you was with OJ and he swore up and down that glaucoma was a coma" Leak was laughing while he told me about the bet. I immediately had a smile on my face. That was easy money. I already knew that Leak was an educated man. He may have not graduated from school and shit, but the state prisons has helped him to polish up his knowledge tremendously . By the way he speaks you can tell that he has some type of education with him. Bigs stared at Leak while picking his nose with a tissue. Slash was out again with his body leaned up against the wall. He was listening to us though. "Oh yea, so what he say when you told him he was wrong?" I asked him. "He offered the bet, being that in his mind he actually thought that his definition was accurate." Leak explained. "So I said. "bet that!" I said shaking his hand. "If your right I'll pay you five dollars but if I'm wrong you only pay me four dollars. This is made the bet a even more irresistible. I went on to tell him that glaucoma is a disease of the eyes and that shit sent him on fire. He didn't stop until he found the dictionary which took almost an hour to look up the damn word." Leak was explaining all this to us laughing. I couldn't believe I missed all this. That goes to show you how much I was invested in my case. "You wrong nigga he kept saying to me as he looked so desperately lost in the Bible the words." Leak joked we all were laughing now. "After me spelling it out for him, he finally found it. His hopes and pay day all came crashing down tragically." More laughter amongst us. "You got that stupid mother fucker." Slash says still with his eyes closed. "He got himself" Leak said seriously. "All I know is that this nigga better have my money today. We went to the store yesterday so they are no excuses. Don't write a check your ass can't cash." Leak checked his face in the raggedy mirror.

"Chow time! Chow time! The P.A system screamed" All the doors open and everyone who was hungry went to eat. I dumped Slash's tray right onto mine. Slash was MIA in the blink of an eye. Leak sat across from me. "/Toma/" I offered to him. Not touching anything, he slid his tray over so that I could give him rations off the extra food I got off Slash. It was just something we all have made a habit of doing. We treated each other equally with everything that we had. It's not mandated but it has rubbed off amongst us. "Hit me" leak said....."that's good of my nigga" Leak was looking around but he wasn't spotting what he was looking for. "This nigga going to make me fuck him up".... "Chill yo he got you I'm sure of it." I tried to calm this hot tempered ass nigga down. Leak was a stick of dynamite with the fuse already halfway live ready to blow. I called him a Livewire because he was jailing for real. We all wanted to change and not live a violent lifestyle, but for those who may not know. Time and places change and dictate a lot of our actions. Especially if your mentality isn't at 100. Many will beg to differ but in here it's eat or be eaten. Even more when you are doing a trip like this. "He better, fuck that!" I change the subject because I couldn't allow Leak to focus on that for too long.

"So when they coming up?" I asked referring to his baby moms and kids. Supposedly this week. I can't wait see my baby girl and my little man." His face glowed replacing Brazes initial thoughts. "That's what's up I see you are excited." The convo was flowing, we ate and spoke rapidly. We only had a few minutes to eat so we did both. We scarfed down our trays while politicking with one another. "What's up with Kiki? You still didn't ask her about any friends over on the female unit did you? Tell her to holler at your boy?" Leak was worse than I was, at least that's what I thought. Tomorrow I'll see them at church." "You horny bastard." I joked while laughing. "You going out?" Leak asked. "Yup as soon as I get my meds." I answered. "Come on nigga you don't need that bull shit anymore." Leak said getting up from the seat. I got up following suit. "You're right probably I don't but I want them for now though." Truth was I didn't need them. My mind was driving me crazy. All I thought and felt was the blood and the shank in my hands whenever the meds wore off. I didn't like that feeling inside my head. The drugs got my mind off all of that.

I fell back in my rack but no sooner did I slam my eyelids, the door popped and my name blared through the PA system. "Visit!" I automatically thought it was for Leak but it wasn't. "That's you "G" Leak said to me. I hopped up freshened up, not wasting any time. "Go to the multipurpose room." The CO in charge yelled from the bubble. "Multipurpose room?" I asked myself who the fuck could this be?

My hopes went up at the site of Michael Stoski. He had on a fresh suit and tie. It was dark and crisp, his hair was neatly cut and his shoes looked as if they were just polished. His cologne smacked the shit out of me. This man had some serious class. The way he was dressed looked as if he did live an expensive lifestyle. He was reading as I walked in the room. His head was buried in my file I assumed. "You supposed to have that memorized already." I joked as soon as I was about 5 feet away from him. The echo in the room could be heard even though I wasn't screaming. "Imagine that." Stoski rebuttled. A low blow I thought to myself. "You know how many cases I have? Memorizing any of them is rare." Stoski admitted. He smiled and rose up to his feet and shook my hand. His grip was firm but not firm enough. "So how we looking?" I asked holding his hand. My size alone was much bigger than his soul. My hands over powered his. I let go of his hand right after I asked the question. "Too early to tell at this moment but I just wanted to come and tell you what they are offering you if you decide not to go to trial." Stoski said with all seriousness. My ears didn't want to register what they were hearing. This can't be right. I thought to myself ."So what are you telling me?" I asked in disbelief. He noticed a change in my attitude and in my voice. His attempts to make my spirit come back alive would not be accomplished. "I'm not saying anything Manuel. I'm just letting you know what I came across and what I put together in our defense." Now he said what I wanted to hear. "That's what I'm talking about man!" I was back to being happy with the dream I was being sold. I thought to myself. He put his finger up. "I need you to be on the same page. We already discussed what we are going to do and if it doesn't work out as planned we will appeal this until it's heard and handled correctly." Stoski stated with that look in his eyes that showed he was not playing any games with the DA. I hope he wasn't blowing smoke like most lawyers tended to do. Lawyers are just as grimy as PD's and some just didn't give a fuck about you, your case or even themselves. They came a crooked as you typical criminals. Only difference, was that they had a degreee to do it. They'll sell you out faster than the work moving on a dope block. "I been doing my homework in here to try and see what I can help myself with." I wanted to see what he was going to say about this. "Oh shit! You hitting the law books now!?" Stoski asked shocked but joking at the same time. Why wouldn't I hit those books? There in the library and their free and let's not forget to mention, it's my freedom we talking about." No one will fight for your freedom like you will. What if you find a case number that you're PD or lawyer may have overlooked? That could be your get out of jail free card right? It's a slap in the face to your consul. They are supposed to do all this extra work to find cases as such right? Wrong! it's all a money game with them rich wealthy mother fucker's. It goes the same way when you was out on the block grinding or working a nine to five. You was putting together all that bread chasing every dollar that was presenting itself. You would hustle day in and day out right? Why not put that much energy into yourself? Because we are lazy? No! We are not! We may act lazy, even complain about going the extra mile for oneself. When something captivates our attention we make sure we go that extra mile though. Why not find that same drive and hit those book, and fight for what one truly believes in for once. For those who may like to use the excuse that we are not capable to learn or become knowledgeable in certain topics, This was just a cop out to give up on yourself. We are only as dumb as we choose to be. These lawyers and doctors didn't wake up knowing the law and medicines did they? Didn't think so they picked up a book, read and read until it started to click and makes sense in their own heads over and over again. So what makes us any different than any of them? There not any different!

"Leave that work up to me Manuel. I'm glad to hear you are trying to help but those books are very complicated." He advised. "I have a friend." I tried to tell him of OJ but he cut me off. "Who knows the law?" he tried to finish. "No he's helping me read and comprehend a few fundamental things." I tried to back up what I was saying, he was helping. "Even if he's not a bar graduate, it doesn't mean he don't know any of this." I stated in defense mode now. "Obviously he can't get it right either if he still coming to jail and hasn't gotten himself out of his own situation. How is he going to help you, help me get you out?" Stoski was being a jerk I now noticed. A part of me wanted to curse him out but another part of me made me see what he was trying to explain to me. It made a lot of sense for the most part, but I couldn't give up on my own personal mission. "All right check this out I may not have the best guidance in here. Besides mom I never had it anyway, so whatever I can benefit from in here I'm going to try my best. I mean I am going to do my best to better myself in here." Stoski was taken back from my words. "That sounds like it was well put together. I will not object to this. You go right ahead and learn statues and maybe you can work for me when you get out." Condescending was all I thought. "Funny." I joked, he laughed. "So what's the deal?" I asked. I could care less what it was. I just wanted to take the attention off Old J and what I was doing to help the matter. "The deal?" Stoski said loudly staring at me. "I thought you didn't want to know what that was." He asked sarcastically. "You don't want to know this trust me when I tell you it's off the charts Manuel." Stoski said in all seriousness and being truthful. I didn't want to know what the DA had to say, but my desperation and curiosity always seems to get the upper hand. "I talked to your mom." Stoski changing the subject or at least tried. I laughed shaking my head "the deal boss" I gave him the authority position. He referred to his notes and slid the file to my side of the table. I looked down and saw a big 35 to 70 written in red pen circled. My body went numb my vision got blurred my heart raced my palms began to sweat. I was about to faint. Stoski noticed the switch in my demeanor. "Easy!" We are not even considering this so relax. I told you, you didn't want to see." Stoski was so fucking right. I didn't want to see that shit, no man in my situation wanted to see that shit. "That can't be right." I said in a desperate tone looking for some type of closure. I watched Stoski's face and his eyebrows shot up. "I'm afraid this is about right for an offer, now of course we can counter it with an offer of our own but the number isn't going to change that much at all Manuel." This is a murderer one they are charging you with remember that." Stoski reminded me as if I forgot. "Thanks for reminding me I thought it was a DUI." I tried to joke but no one was really joking right now this was serious as fuck. No time for games. "You want to counter just to see what they'll say?" Stoski asked me for my input more like permission to plea bargain. "I took a deep breath filling up my lungs to the max and held it "tell them since I never got in any type of trouble to give me a 5 to 10 just to see what they'll say." I was tripping, I know but we wouldn't know unless we tried. "You can't be serious? Are you?" Stoski asked rubbing his four head. I smiled "fuck it." "Now what happens if we go to trial?" I asked "trial?" He repeated after me. "Yeah" I said wanting to know all that I could before this man decided to get up and leave. "Well first things first your counter deal is a no go and is kind of making me look like I don't know my shit, but if it'll make you happy I'll do the counter offer. Trial on the other hand seems a bit more promising being that I'll have your back and it's up to the jury to decide your fate. This doesn't mean we will beat the case even though that's what we are trying for. Like I said we need to prepare for all possible aspect. This is how you win this mentally because there is always that chance that we may lose "if" the DA has a strong case in their favor." Stoski spoke very confident in his words. "What am I looking at if I lose trial?" I asked. "If we lose." Stoski corrected. "Together remember" Stoski corrected. "We could be looking at life with the possibility of parole." Stoski let right out. Staring at me dead center in my eyes. My eyes grew wide. "No! No! That's not an option" I said frightened. "The deal sounds good right about now." I blurted out trying to take away that last comment Stoski said. "I bet it does now" let me tell you this, once you deny the offer they will not put it back on the table. The offer is long gone, so please think about everything that we are talking about in this room. Also don't let all these jailhouse lawyers contaminate your head Manuel. Remember you are the one who is going to have to serve all this time at the end of the day. So listen to yourself and make sure all of the decisions you make. You will be able to live with them because those jailhouse lawyers are not going to do the time for you worst case scenario." Stoski preached straight fire. My nerves were going ecstatic. "I'm not saying that were going to lose this case but you have to prepare your mind for the worst possible outcome." I listen to what he had to say very attentively it was all making sense the way he was putting it together. This was my case and every plausible outcome was only going to directly affect me whether I would beat the case or lose it. I didn't have anything else to say. What was exchanged amongst the two of us within this hour was more than a mouthful to ingest. "Are you okay?" Stoski asked knowing the answer to his question. "This is as real as it's going to get Manuel, I know you didn't want to hear any of this but you have to look at it in another perspective. Now that you know the worst outcome. Everything that comes from here on out will be surprises that could possibly benefit us." I must've heard him wrong but none of that made any sense to me. "So how's mom?" I didn't want to hear about law anymore, I asked him. "Ms. Catherine?" Stoski repeated excitedly. "Oh man, she's missing her boy like crazy. She is handling it a lot better now than she was at first." Stoski informed. I had a slight smile on my face.

"Gentlemen" a voice from behind me was heard, Stoski's eyes followed the person who was making his way over towards the far end of the room to another table. "Morning" Stoski said to him. I had to admit the tapping of his thousand dollars shoes annoyed the fuck out of me. Is there anything that you want me to tell her?" Stoski asked me. Now he was Mr. lawyer/messenger I thought. "No not a message but be sure to tell her what we talked about and that I'm hanging on strong. I love them." Rock stated. He wrote on his big yellow pad. Another set of footsteps could be heard from behind but the steps weren't thousand dollars shoes. They were a lot softer and slower they were more like three dollars Skippy's. I turned around and the face shocked me. It was "Braze" small jailo. "Sup nigga?" I say very rudely on purpose. "Tell Leak I got him." Braze said "he better." I said amongst Stoski and myself. "That's another thing." Stoski said. "It almost slipped my mind." "What's that?" Rock answered. "What's all this bullshit I've been hearing about you being a problem in the jail?" Stoski asked in a low professional tone. My smirk gave it all away. "Problem?" I acted dumbfounded. "You said it, it's bullshit." he gave me the arched eyebrow. His look was very suspicious of my answer to his question. "I need you to try your best, to not be such problematic individual in here Manuel. The DA will use all of this extra ammunition in their defense and anymore negative knowledge of your character is what we don't need to be brought up against you right?" Stoski asked trying to get me to coincide with him, but that wasn't happening. "This is my first rodeo and if we are one then you have to either do this time with me or you have to let me do it because it isn't a walk through the park in here. I'm surrounded by nothing but blood thirsty animals and you're asking me to be a vulnerable kitty cat huh?" Rock was speaking low but his tone was scary as fuck. Stoski swallowed hard as he tried to visualize the scene Rock painted for him. "It won't really make a difference anyway as long as you don't catch any more charges while in this county jail system." Stoski admitted. I wasn't as gullible as I perceived to be, even with all that in mind I still knew what had to be done. My jail house lawyer would help me as much as he could. A lot was said to me in the past hour and a half but the only thing that stuck out like a sore thumb was how the DA offered me some crazy ass numbers. You would think these numbers were the amount of yards in between a pass on a football field. "Insane."

The halls were pretty scarce only a few bodies up and about. I missed med line but I may my way towards one of many bubbles and inquired about them. "Go straight up to medical." The CO granted me authority to roam a bit. I took my time walking up the steps until I reached the floor. These woman couldnt be up so early. I step foot on the block and those horny little dick chaser began to holler "he's back bitches." one yelled. Obviously one that knew of me from the last time I stepped on the block. "Kiki! Your baby boy is here to see you!" I heard and smiled on my way to the bench. I was ordered to go straight to medical but hey what the fuck I didn't hear that part right? I sat on the bench and enjoyed all the comments even though not all of them were good but I didn't give a fuck. "Rock!" It was Kiki voice yelling out. "Sup ma!?" I yelled back. "How you holding up baby?" Kiki pushed it. Knowing that I wasn't her baby but hey who cared. She wanted it to be known. "I'm all right ma. I just came from seeing my lawyer" I yelled over. "I bet he ain't no help?" A voice yelled from my left side. I was almost about to agree with her but I couldn't doubt my "partner" in all of this. "He's working his magic." I defended him. "I know that's right." Kiki said. "What he tell you Rock anything good?" Kiki asked. "Not really but is too early to tell ma." I tried to hold onto my words. "It'll get better I been praying for you baby don't worry god is good and he gonna look out for you!" This bitch gota be crazy with all this holy moly shit. I thought. I wasn't going to stomp on her parade though. "Wassup with you Kiki?" I asked. Last time we spoke she had gotten in contact with Banga and Jigz and I can't remember what happened between them. "They took my kids. It's fucked up!" Kiki yelled out loud and clear. "Stay strong girl." Another prisoner yelled towards her. "You'll get them back. Jesus loves us." That same girl yell. "I know" Kiki yelled. "You coming to the service?" Kiki asked. "You already know ma." I had to see her, that was as close as I was going to get to the hood. "I can't wait to see your smile." I talked to Banga a Jigz." Kiki yelled. "What's up with them?" I asked. "You know them crazy ass niggas is out there causing chaos. It's what they enjoyed doing. I mean they supposed to come up but I haven't been waiting because I've been hearing that for some time now. It gets old babe." Kiki had no more hope. This was going to be her last time up in here because it hurts knowing that everything you have out there is getting taken away slowly from you. "Sorry to hear that ma, make sure you keep all this in mind when you head back out there to them niggas." I yelled over to her. "That's right tell her Rock!" She gonna listen one way or the other!" Two different voices must have been trying to tell her what I was telling her as well. "She better fucking listen!" I barked loudly trying to get Kiki to feel my words. Kiki was quiet, she had to be soaking it in. "Ay Rock my cousin is down there. He told me you down there putting in work for real!" A soft voice said when the commotion ceased a bit. "Nah ma, not me." I defended all accusations. "Oh yea it's you, bad ass" her words put a smile to my face. "Look at that smile!" Yelled the one across from me who had a direct view on my face. "You better stop Rock you can't get out acting like that." Kiki took advantage to scold me now. "Girl I'm like you I have no one but my mom and my sister. I can act up if I want. Especially! If it's my life being tampered with" Rock yelled not admitting anything just stating the obvious. "I know that's right!" Yelled one. All these voices and no faces to distinguish them. I wanted to see them all. "Don't worry baby when I get out I'll be there I promise." Kiki said. "Don't make promises you can't keep ma." I said. "You'll see" Kiki defended.

"Manuel Ricardo" Ms. Peg came out to get me. The CO said that he told you to come straight in didn't he?" Peg asked leading the way with her wide hips. Not that I can recall. I lied straight threw my teeth. "Uuuhhmmm" Ms. Peg didn't believe me at all. "Your meds." she picked up a cup and dumped them in my hand. "Water" she pointed towards the fountain. Down they went immediately. "You can go" Ms. Peg said. "Thank you" I replied. "How's your injuries?" She asked as I began to walk away. "I'm good thank you for asking."

I headed out the door not stop for anything. I ignored all the calls and whistles heading straight to the bubble. "I thought I told you to head straight to medical." The CO was fishing and guess what there weren't any fish over here. I extended my hand to get my pass without saying a word. He must've got the message, I wasn't biting his bate. "You go boy. Fucked that no pussy getting ass fag." Girly yell from behind me as I left. I laughed, This woman could be just as bad as out unit. They didn't give a fuck.He handed me my pass and off I went. By the time I made it to my cell the meds were kicking in, not sure why they hit me so hard but they did today. "Damn!" I thought to myself.

"How was the visit?" Bigs asked. He was the only one in the cell. The cell was spotless. We would all took turns cleaning this small as cell. Slash had to break him in because he was a messy one. It took some time but he was getting it now. "It was okay" I answered finding a comfortable spot on my rack. "Okay?" Bigs said. "What's wrong with mom and them?" Bigs Probed trying to find out why I was so down." "She didn't come, it was my lawyer." I replied. "Oh" Bigs already knew to end it there. The guys went to yard to find Braze." Bigs informed. It was freezing outside the summer was long gone by now. Snow was bound to fall within the next week or two and there was no stopping it. I was warm right were I was at. I smiled underneath the covers with the thought of Braze not being out there. These two were out there freezing looking for someone that wasn't going to be out there. I ended up dosing off.

They had Mandy up on another floor handing out meds. She was upset because she wanted to pass to shit off to Rock already. She had to use the bathroom but held in every drop of urine. She wasn't in the mood to remove the stuff condom it was too much. The only way she would remove it was to hand it off to Rock no exceptions. The only thing she was worried about was how she was going to get it to him now. She didn't want to go through all this again. They had Alisha on Rock's block and she wasn't gonna be moved unless she left but this wasn't going to happen. Mandy handed out the meds on the block she was assigned to.The CO watching her was glued onto her every move. They made sure that she wasn't being harassed or bothered by any of the prisoners. She waited patiently as he reached Mr. Gonzales who was an older male that was no taller than 4'9. "/que linda tu te ves mi angelita, quisera dalte besos por todo tu cuerpo/" Mr. Gonzales fantasize about giving her kisses all over her body. Mandy had no clue what he was saying but she understood. "/besitos/" which meant /kisses/. She dump the meds in his palms and he tried to touch her finger. "Mr. Gonzales take the meds now!" The CO barked into the PA system. With no further incident he gulped down all of the meds and opened his mouth to show they were heading down his throat. She moved along to finish off her rounds on the unit.

Within an hour to lunch break Mandy couldn't come up with any ideas. She figure she would have to try again another day, but keeping all this work on her was something that she didn't want to do.

****

Back in the cell half asleep I could hear the ruckus but didn't pay it any mind. "There he go!" Slash said loudly. I know you never ever mess with the man sleep, but being that all I did was talk while Slash was asleep I couldn't expect anything less from him to do it to me. Remember when a man slept you let him sleep. Why you may be asking? Because behind these walls is our only means of escaping the reality. Let him or her dream. That's as close as to home a person that is incarcerated will feel. So don't ever fuck with someone sleeping. Many people get hurt over shit like this. You could only imagine and experiece how dreams felt so real. So just imagine who or what the individual was dreaming about. There you come waking him or her up just to ask for a cigarette or a shot of coffee, to meet your instant gratification. Good luck with that one!

"How was that visit?" Slash wasn't going to quit until I talked to him. "He asleep" Bigs said. Yeah I see that but I don't believe that." Slash spoke. Leak plopped down on his bed not saying a word. I could only bet he was pissed that old boy wasn't out there in that yard. "The visit was shit." I mumbled under the covers with my face dug into my pillow. "What?" Slash said. I rose up "it was a shitty visit." Laying my head back down on the pillow. "Why was it shitty?" Leak asked. I was up and I know he wouldn't stop until we got to the bottom why I wasn't having a good morning. "Who came? Your mom? Or one of your chicken heads? Leak joked. "Neither" I replied staring up at the top bunk from the bottom. "So who was it?" Slash asked getting impatient. "My lawyer." I said. "Oh boy." Slash said not wanted to interrogate me anymore. The room got quiet for a second. "Rock?" Leak wanted to know. "Wassup?" I replied down and out. "How bad was it? If you don't want to talk about it is all good. I'm not forcing you but maybe I can help a bit." Leak said. "How the fuck you going to help?" I stated frustrated. "You know the DA? You going to fuck that bitch and talk her into giving me a better offer?" It was quiet, I exploded. "Huh?" No one said shit. They knew I was going through it I would never burst out intentionally at the guys I've been privileged to live with. "Let it all out bro" Slash said. "My bad no." Rock apologized. "It's all good Manuel, we know it's not easy." Bigs said. "The offer is 35 to 70 years and if I take it to trial, life with the possibility of parole." Leak was shocked as if that was some crazy shit to even offer a man like that. "You didn't take a right?" Leak asked. "Fuck no! That's 30 fucking years locked in a cage!" Rock said to the guys. "I wouldn't take it neither." Slash agreed. "They better convict me fuck that." Slash went on. "So did you get the chance to tell him a counter offer?" Leak asked. I laughed at the words that were just spoken. "You fucking right, I told him a 5 to 10." I laugh my ass off because I had no other emotions left that would help me in this crisis. The guys noticed and understood this was far from funny but it was one of the best ways to deal with all this pain. To cry and laugh and crying was done and over with. They didn't laugh with me thought they knew I was in pain. I tried to stay strong but what the laughter told me. I was hiding my feelings and couldn't stop laughing, it was uncontrollable. "Fuck these mother fuckers! They want to put me away for life! Ima make everyone's life in this place to living hell. They say I'm a fucking killer? Guess what I'm kill till someone kills my fucking ass. Fuck the Sgt! Fuck the prisoners! Fuck me! They want to play let's see who is more bold!" I was yelling at the top of my lungs out the door so everyone could feel my fury. I was far from angry my laughter transformed into rage in seconds. The guys in a cell let me go, no one tried to stop me. "Open this fucking door!" I kicked it making a loud bang that almost shook the whole block. The first nigga to get in my face is dead! Body count is going to soar. I'm a so called killer!" Leak gave me a tight ass hug. "It's all good bro you don't have to hurt anyone anymore." Leak was trying. "Yes the fuck I do" I spoke into his shoulder my tears fell on him. My snot was all on his shoulder. "No you don't we are going to get through this." Leak tried his best to console me. "Ima never get out of here, they don't want me out there!" I cried it was true it finally hit me. I was balling out I couldn't hold it all inside anymore. Is not easy being tough and strong? That shit takes a lot out of you. To be weak is so easy and it surrounds you in places like this. For after about 10 minutes of letting go I compose myself.

"You going?" Leak asked if I was going to lunch. I shook my head. "Nah my nigga, I'll eat a honey bun or something." I answered. "Fuck that meal right now!" Leak joked. "I laughed. My bad my nigga." They all left as I gathered my thoughts. They were bouncing around my head. I stared in the mirror and told myself to never show weakness like that again. It had to be done today because it was so much being held inside with mom, Linda, Felicia, Linda and Jacqueline everyone at home I let down. Especially myself.

—

Sitting inside the car eating a sandwich with a juice. Her mind thought of ways to succeed with here plans. She wanted to complete them today. She wasn't going to get back into her vehicle with that package inside her vagina. She bit into her turkey ham and cheese sandwich. She chewed as she scanned the parking lot and noticed all the females who came up to see their love ones. Showing them there support. Her eyes grew large as she came up with a plan that would either work or not. Either way she had no choice but to attempt it. What she knew about Alisha was that she had a son who goes to daycare by Pennsauken. What she was about to do was far from ethical but she had no choice at the moment. Is not like she was hurting anyone. She had about 10 minutes before her break was up so she had to move fast.

Jumping out the car without the sandwich and drink she ran to the payphone inside the lobby area. She grabbed a phonebook looking for a certain number and dialed out

"Camden County prison." The male's voice answered about 20 feet away from Mandy. She was ballsy for this one. Was it worth getting caught up? "Hi I'm calling from the family daycare in Pennsauken. I wanted to know if I could speak with Ms. Alisha Figueroa?" Mandy couldn't believe the extent that she was taken to do this. "Give me a second ma'am." the CO could be heard from the receiver as well as crossing the lobby. He put Mandy on hold. The CO called over to medical no answer. Over the walkie-talkie, no anwer. Alisha had to be on her break. "It appears Ms. Figueroa is on her break, is everything okay?" The CO spoke into the receiver. "Can I take a message for her?" The CO asked. Not knowing what to do Mandy did the unthinkable. "Yes please tell her to come and pick up her son immediately because I have to close down the daycare. I have a family emergency and that her son is fine but I have to head to the hospital." Mandy spoke into the receiver as low as she could. She was stretching her voice a little trying to avoid bringing any more suspicion her way. "Okay ma'am, I'll relayed the message to her as soon as she comes back from break." The CO took the bait. Now we wait and see what Alisha does. Hopefully she doesn't call back and just leaves to go pick up her son. That would buy her enough time in covering for Alisha on the next med line. It was something that had to happen since pill line would be within the next half hour. Mandy stood in the lobby until she had about one minute left until she had to get back to work. She noticed Alisha's car parked up. Hanging up she headed through the detectors again. She did what she did every day working her shift. The phone rang. Mandy's heart raced. "Okay thank you." Ms. Peg spoke into the receiver. That had to be the call. Mandy prepared for meds as usual for the units she had to cover. It only took her about 15 minutes to get all the meds cupped up and placed on the portable table with wheels. As she was heading out the door that's when her name was yelled out from Ms. Peg the supervisor. "Mandy." She parked the car and headed toward Ms. Peg. "Yes?" Mandy answered. I'm sorry to do this to you but I need you to prep all of the meds for the units Alisha was covering. I'm sorry baby." Ms. Peg apologized to Mandy. "What happened to Alisha?" Mandy asked concerned knowing damn well she already knew what was up. "She's okay, she had to go pick up her son from daycare." "Is her son okay?" Mandy asked worried. "I'm sure he is because she didn't say anything of that nature." Ms. Peg said. "All right I'll take care of it. I'll hand them all out too no worries." Mandy said "no darling you don't have to do that." Ms. Peg stopped her. "That's too much." Mandy was fast with how she handled her job. "Too much I got this babe." Mandy went to work. She had managed to do what she had planned out but now it was time to put the last piece of the puzzle in the right spot. This was where it could all go down-hill quickly if she slipped up. Her career her reputation will all be ruined in the blink of an eye. Not to forget to mention the charges she would accumulate over all of this.

—

Back in the cell Leak and Rock were having a push up competition. "You can't fuck with me youngin." Leak joked talking heavy. "You ain't got the mileage to keep up with me Rock." Leak was on his fifth set of 50 clips. Rock inhaled and waited for Leak to get up from doing his set while running his mouth at the same time. Once he was finished Rock was on his heels on his fifth set. Slash and Bigs just watched and ran their mouths. "He struggling, he struggling." Slash joked. "Nah you crazy he got this!" Bigs defended. "48....49... ughhhh! 50!" Rock got up with his chest poked out from all of the blood being sent to it. His breathing was hard. "It's on you old timer." Slash hyped up. "Holdup" Leak said "hold up!?" Rock repeated that sounds like defeat" Rock cheered. Leak got down to force his body to back up his mouth. There was no way he was going to let himself lose this battle to Rock. Maybe if he didn't talk all that shit but since leak wrote the check now he had no choice but to cash it out...45...46...47... As big counted out loud. Rock got low. "come on man, I got you let's get it." Rock hyped him up "48....49..... Leak couldn't. His arms began to shake. "One more!" Rock yelled. "One fucking more!" Rock wasn't going to let Leak not complete his set even if he had to help him."50!" Leak finished.

"Attention on the block medication, medication!" The CO yelled through the speaker. I ignored it as I always did. They came when it came. I dropped and gave 50 more almost collapsing towards the end. The perspiration was dripping off both our faces. "Damn! Leak him still holding strong Wassup?" Bigs had to voice his opinion but what was that for? "I know you didn't." Leak was halfway on the floor when he stopped. "Your fat ass can't even do 10 straight and you been here nine months already whats up with that!?" Leak didn't like his side remarks especially when he in his mind didn't give up. Leak got to 30, Rock was on his ass. I'm here let's go take a breather and back at it... 40 then he stopped again.

"Mr. Ricardo medication." a familiar voice spoke into the door. It was Mandy. "What's up pretty girl? How you been?" Rock asked. "I'm okay, you ready for you meds?" Mandy asked him. "You already know." as he approached the door. "Tell me if the guard is looking at me?" Mandy asked at first. Rock didn't understand he looked over her shoulder. "Yeah he is." Tell me when he's not all right and pay attention Manuel." Mandy said getting Rocks meds. A second or two passed by Mandy had her back towards Rock. She watched threw her peripherals. She use the cart to block herself from the waist down she tugged on her string dropping something on the floor as an excuse to finagle the package out from inside. She bent down to retrieve what she dropped getting back up, and went back to what she was doing. The small package was in her hand now. She was nervous as fuck. Her hands were shaking uncontrollably. The beats per second could be felt in her fingers. She regretted every second of this. "Now he's not looking." Rock said in one swift motion with the guard on her right she held the package with her left and meds in the right. She dumped the meds and Rocks hands and tilted her body ever so slightly to cover the guard in case he decided to look. Mandy handed it off any quick motion. She took a breath of relief. "Ms. Dusive to the bubble!" A CO call for her. "hide it now" Rock didn't know what to do with the shit. "What is it?" Leak asked. He showed Leak. "Work" Rock said. "Oh shit" Leak got on the door to watch. They called her they probably saw her yo!" Leak said "Booth it" Leak said. "What?" Rock didn't understand. "If they come up in here and find that we are all fucked Rock, you got to hide it." Leak stated "Give it to me. I got it." Slash took it and put the sheet up.

"Where those guys giving you a hard time?" The CO asked wanting a reason to come at Rock. "Oh no." Mandy was so happy and surprised with what she was just hearing. She was at ease with herself and how everything had worked out for everyone, but I do have to give Mr. Ricardo his last pill." Mandy stated. "You sure because I saw you hand him his pills." The CO said there was no way he saw all that. "Wow! You must have great vision how many pills did I give him?" Mandy put her hands on her hips and smiled. Alright I saw you dump the cup but there was no way I saw the actual amount of pills." The CO confessed. "Just one because I dropped one but I picked it up." Mandy tested the waters. All right, Be careful with that bunch they're all being watched closely." The CO gave up some detailed information. Mandy headed back to the door. They were all doing push-ups now.

"Mr. Ricardo here take this." Mandy said. "More what you tryna overdose me?" Rock joked. "Here boy and make sure all of you watch yourself because he just told me that there watching you and you're welcome. Oh and I need $180 off of that if you want it to keep coming. See you when I see you." Mandy said adding her tax on the situation. "Thank you baby girl." Rock said to her back. She slid over to the cell at the end to finish handing off the rest of the medication. That was close. Mandy thought to herself the rest was all up to him and his small crew. "What the fuck!"

Slash said. "How did you know she was going to do that?" Slash asked with the package hidden. "I didn't." Rock said. "What the fuck you mean you didn't?" Leak asked. "Well I had put the bug in her ear but I didn't think she would actually follow through you know?" Rock said. "Well shorty came through" Bigs said. "What is it?" Asked Bigs. I'm not sure it could be some crack or coke." Rock said. I thought you didn't know anything about that shit?" Asked Leak. I don't but that's what your here for to school me and help me right?" Rock asked. "I got you my G but we gota find out what it is first." Leak said. "And right now it's a no go." Slash joked we all laughed. "You crazy as shit nigga." Rock said looking at Slash. Man you have no idea how many things I had to move in this joint to get by. That shit ain't nothing." Slash said. "But I'm on right?" Slash asked. "We all in but I want to establish what it is first." Tonight Bigs and Slash will go to yard. Leak and I will stay in and figure out what we gonna do, and how we going to do this alright?" Rock was playing his position he didn't know shit but being a boss came natural to him. Plus the work was his no matter what. "Hello it's in my ass." Slash said being a smartass. I know that and you going to make sure to get it out before the last rec." Rock said giving him the only look. This wasn't something to fuck with. He didn't like the face he made when Rock explain what was going to be done instead of asking how it should be done. Rock was far from greedy but he wasn't about to let anyone fuck this up for him. Not leak, not Bigs and definitely not Slash. "No one is to know about any of this, understand?" Rock made it a point to make things clear. "How you gonna sell it if no one knows?" Bigs had to be the smartass. They will find out when the time is ready." Leak chimed in. He took the words right out of my mouth. "We can't sell shit, until we see if we can trust certain people. I'm not trying to sell to everyone.Only a selected few that's all." Rock said. Leak nodded as he agree with what Rock was saying. This is what Banga and Jigz saw in Rock all this time. No matter how much Rock denied it he still ended up doing what he didn't want to do. "In the meantime Rock had no clue how to bag this shit up. This is why Leak and myself are going to contemplate on all that later." Rock said. "I'm sure there is work already in his building and I'm not trying to take nobody show. There's enough for everyone to eat." Anyway I don't even know if there will be another package after this one." There was no need to try to start something that was not going to be steady or long term. No one could say how far this would go so there was no need to try and be greedy and take over the jail. Rock thought to himself "I need you to give me your word that no matter what happens we stay true to each other here in this cell." Rock needed confirmation. Leak got up and dapped Rock up "you already know I got you" Leak said "you got my word too Rock" Slash also dapped Rock up. "I got you too my nigga." Bigs said. "Word." "We will always be taken care of that's my word. No one will go to bed hungry or need anything but I must say this if you have your gambling issues on the side don't think that this is your meal ticket because we going to make money not lose money." Rock looked at Leak, who put his head down. Rock realized a while ago that Leak did have a gambling problem and guess what? If he wanted to gamble it would be his problem not ours. Even though I'm sure Leak already knew that. "That goes for me too." I am no different." Rock treated them and himself all equally including himself.

Later that day they all shot to the library. Rock met with OJ. "How is it going young man?" OJ shook Rock's hand. "Maintaining" Rock replied. "That's a great start, how's the love ones?" OJ inquired. "They are all doing fine I can honestly say. Dealing with all of this a little better than I had expected." Rock said sadly. "Yeah they will as time goes by which is a good thing, it doesn't mean they're losing love for you young buck. It just means they know they gota wait and can only do so much. Being down on their end isn't helping the cause either. You have to make the best of it as well." OJ always kept a real when it came to me. I have my respect for him to the fullest. It was hard to find people who didn't bullshit the other just for the pure benefit of their own. "So what did you learn?" OJ asked. "I read a little here and there but what I learned this morning was a lot more relevant" Rock said. "And what's that?" OJ asked. "I saw my lawyer and he had not so great news for me." Rock sounded like a broken record. Then again that's how this jail shit went. It was the same shit every day nothing hardly ever changed, but the number of days left for you to be released. Even with that it was hard to ingest especially if your days didn't have an end date.

"Is it always bad news with these guys? Don't lose hope or discourage yourself, with what that man had to say to you. He's just delivering a message." OJ knew because I didn't even begin to tell him what Stoski had told me. "So how much was the offer?" OJ asked. "You don't even want to know." Rock said. "You're right I don't but is good to know." OJ replied "35 to 70" was all I said. OJ shook his head. "They already have you hung without even giving you a chance." OJ said. "That's what it's looking like." Rock said "It don't have to look like it though. Usually a high number like that will fall lower. It always seems to fall once they see you are not taken the bait. So if you go to trial, life without parole huh?" OJ asked. "With parole" I corrected his last statement. "Oh with parole that's a new one." OJ joked. "Anyway, we'll look into that in a bit. Name a few rights that you and I as citizens of old America the beautiful actually don't have but say that we do have?" I laughed with OJ. I named a few. I didn't know all of them but we kicked it back and forth on each one discussing, how and why they affected us in good and in a bad ways. I wasn't aware of all of the information that OJ was spitting, but then again how was I to know them? If the government tried their best to keep us from knowing them. It was mainly our fault for allowing all this to happen. I noticed Leak and Slash wrapped up in deep conversation. I could only wonder what they discussing with one another. No one could be trusted and I made sure of it sad to say. Too many personalities to have around I had to double check everything. OJ looked up some cases that were similar to mine but not completely identical. He located the section that dealt with numerous homicides by deadly weapons. He instructed me to read through each case until I found a case very similar to my own. Many weren't anywhere close but how things occurred in these cases could be used to decipher how the DA would try to use it against me in my case. This was only helping me become more knowledgeable on what's wrong in my case. If noone objects in these situations thea could tear us up. My lawyer better be on point. I read for about an hour and found nothing yet. My head began to hurt deciphering all the terminology.

"Look at this one?" OJ slid the hardcover criminal law book over to my side. The case involved a shooting of two dead bodies at a cookout with numerous witnesses but the shooter fled the scene. The suspect or the accused somehow got placed at the scene as the shooter when in fact the actual shooter that fled was the brother of the accused. You have 50% of the witnesses accusing the shooter that left the scene who no one knew his identity and the other 50% are accusing the man who was close by when it all occurred. The case ended in a hung jury which brought grounds to throwing out the case. "I don't understand OJ" Rock said after analyzing the case. "The man who was accused ended up going home because the jury couldn't decide if he was guilty or not." OJ explained. "So why did it happen like that?" I asked not knowing anything. I was completely lost. Only half of the witnesses knew the shooter and the other have pointed at the other man. It made the other witnesses look as if they didn't know anything at all and vice versa. Now a witness is supposed to help either side and in this case the witnesses jeopardized both sides by not having or sticking to one side. This forced the jury to be undecided on what to believe." OJ went on to explain. He made me understand it. It was all making sense now. My mind began to wonder on ways I could make this happen in my case. OJ noticed me thinking.

"That is right you gota think out of the box young man. Like I said I'll be right here to help you as much as I can but you have to make things happen on your end." I listen to OJ "You have to control your pieces so you can win your battles. There are loop holes all over. It's up to you to utilize each one when you see it fit." I love how this old man thought. It was all useful information. "Five minutes" the librarian yelled. "I'm a take this one with me." I told OJ "No! You'll take the first one I gave you and this one and remember you only get out of this what you put in it. It's your freedom not mine I have already lost my battle, but they can't stop me from helping guide others to win there's." OJ was right so was the lawyer. "So what you come up with?" Slash asked walking on the opposite side of where Leak was walking on my left side. "Came up, with enough to open my eyes a lot more then they have been. They were damn near shut completely . "Slash didn't comprehend what I said. "I like that one." Leak understood. "So how about y'all? I see you two deep in conversation at the end table?" I looked at Leak for the answer. "You already know I was telling Slash how we need gloves and wax bags depending on what we had." Leak admitted. "Where we gona find that?" I asked. "Gloves are easy. My man works as a block janitor he can get them. The wax bags could be found in the kitchen. They put the bread in them sometimes. Spoons and the salt and pepper plackets for bag lunches. Since it was cold it shouldn't be a problem to keep the candy safe from the heat." Leak was planning all the moves getting everything ready. "That's Wassup." He also told him that we would all end up splitting up one day. so they wanted to school me on as much shit as possible. That day would be inevitable Rock" I didn't like those words. What you mean? We all got some time to do." I contested. "Yeah but I'm up for trial soon. Leak should be transferring soon, Bigs is probably the only one that is going to be there by your side within the next year or two." Slash was right. "You're going home but we not sure when." Leak made me feel better saying that, even if it wasn't going to happen. "I gota shit my niggas." Slash cut everyone off. "Damn! You can't hold it?" Leak said. "Not really." Slash said. Bigs fell asleep as always.

"Cell search! Cell search!" The guard on the block yelled. "Now you definitely got a hold it." He joked. "Fuck you!" Slash joked back. It was too good to be true. How the fuck the day Mandy comes by and drops off that package smelling like fresh pussy. She comes and gives us the heads up that the guys and myself were being watched, but to make matters more interesting now the shakedown team is on the block how fucking ironic. I was beginging to analyze things deeper I noticed. I could only wonder what the other guys thoughts were. Im sure they had to be as well. This shit is crazy Leak jumped on the door to see what was going on. "They searching cell to cell my nigga. Trash anything that could possibly put us in the hole." Leak said looking back. The cell was already clean." Bigs reminded. It's clean right why? Because you cleaned it?" Leak got hyped. He opened the cabinet and tossed the open razor on the cabinet, he reached in my cabinet and pulled out rigged batteries. He reached in his cabin and pulled out a 3 inch whack. It's clean right?" Leak growled. I laughed. Slash bent over joking. "I got some shit too" He tried to take the heat off Bigs. "Fuck you Rock, flush it" Slash said. I followed what he say "whoooshhhhh! "Whoooshhhhh!" That's what you heard coming out our cell and just about every other cell and the block. All the contraband needed to be flushed but didn't get the chance to be flushed was thrown on the block buy the pigs. The tire look as though a tornado ran threw it. You saw all type of trash that wasn't supposed to be in our cell. Chemicals were being splashed all over the place as they hit the floor. If you had extra blankets, covers, pillows batteries, etc.etc Anything that was altered or an item that was excessive would be thrown out and you better believe if it was the right pric. You was receiving a misconduct and probably going to the hole. No if or butts about it. Thanks to Leak all our contraband has just been flushed down the toilet, with the wack just barely making it through the drain. I laughed my ass off talking shit. "If you bend over and that ship pops out my nigga." Rock joked. "That's fucked up Rock!" "Don't worry I'll tell them it's mine." Rock said after Slash's his remark. "And how do you explain how he got your shit up in his ass." Bigs joked. "Okay let's leave the jokes out of my ass. I'm doing you a favor and this is what I get huh?" Slash didn't find our jokes amusing at all. There by our cell." Bigs informed " It's all good let them come in we are clean and we are recovering addicts." Leak joked. "Yeah I bet." We all shared a laugh and joked around some more until they finally barged in our cell.

"Any contraband gentleman?" The Marine looking ass prick asked in his drill sergeant voice. His colleague was on his heels. Three step out and one stay in." Only contraband in herer is the one you plant here." Leak pressed his luck. "We'll see about that smartass." The prick shot back. Leak, Bigs and I all stepped out. Slash went first and get his strip search out the way. We listen as they gave a few demands and routines to follow. After a few moments Slash was done. Safe and sound I said to myself. I could only imagine how Slash was feeling going through all that. It was my turn I was clean but for some reason I was fucking nervous. I was almost all the way to the back wall. The only object that kept me from touching the wall was the bunk at the end. "Turnaround" super high top fade ordered. I was standing tall. "Manuel Ricardo, I hear so much about I could write a fucking biography on your stupid ass." I smiled. "You can't always listen to what you hear about others." I shot bac. being a smartass. "Oh my resources are very reliable with all their Intel Mr. Rock!" This piece of shit was serious. "Drop them." He order for me to drop my pants underwear and all. "Shirt off!" I was completely naked in front of this man who looked at dick and balls his whole career working in the prison system. "Ay Slotiz! He called in his colleague. "Sup" his colleague answered. "This is my big old bad guy huh?" High top couldn't be serious. "That's what they say." replies his collegue. "Look at that small thing." They both laugh hysterically. "Ask you wife how big it gets when is happy." The laughter stopped immediately as I let those words ripped from my lips. High top went from white to pink but I mean almost reddish pink. He was so humiliated, it was my turn to laugh my ass all with my little man's out and all.

"Fuck you mother fucker." he was pissed. "It don't feel too good to be made fun of right?" Rock was in his bag. "Run your hand through your hair.... Let me see the back of your ears...... open mouth..... Tongue up....... lifted penis..... Balls up.... It was ridiculous of how much a nigga had to go to up in here on a regular basis,...... hands out..... Elbows..... Turnaround...... left leg up, wiggle toes...... right leg up, wiggle toes..... Bend over and cough.... get dressed smartass. I was out the door. Leak than Bigs. By the time these white mother fuckers ransacked our cell it was a .2 on a richter scale. The beds were all over the floor, this was my first time getting flipped. I didn't know how to take this shit. I felt so violated and disrespected.

"Ayo Slotiz!Why the fuck you trash our cell for?!" I Barked "Bitch I'm talking to you!"..... "Suck it up! "Slotiz barked back being a complete ass hole but not engaging in my shit. "That's the same thing I tell wife soon as I get done coming, you aint shit I hope you die tomorrow!" I was bugging. I didn't care. I was yelling all types of obscenities out the door. "Rock fall back." Leak said. Trying to get me to relax. "Is not that serious will get the room back together. That's how they roll remember this is their house and we just guest here." Slash said. "Look at my sheets on the ground, pillow by the toilet. These mother fuck is are out of line, this is what they call a cell search?" No one said anything. "I'm asking please tell me so I know?" Leak found this funny. "You have so much to learn, yes that is a cell search and if you keep on screaming out that door guess what else they going to do?" Leak spoke smooth and deep as he picked up his belongings. "What?" I asked very ignorantly. "Going straight to the mother fucking twist." Leak said. "Twist?" What the fuck is that?" Rock asked. That's where you gonna go if you keep on testing these people's patients." "How long do you think you will last if no one schools you? Knowing this is your first time up in here?" Leak asked. "Not long at all" Slash opinionated. "Now that is the correct answer." at the moment I was still wondering what the fuck was the twist. How many niggaz in here do you think will help you stay out of the hole like we try to do every day?" Leak asked. "None" Bigs answered. "Correct" Leak looked over at Bigs who was having a hard time setting up his bed with all that weight moving around. "All right I get it, what is the fucking twist?" Rock asked frustrated. Looking at Leak and Slash. "The twist is the bucket." Slash didn't help "I'm still lost, explain." Rock asked. "It's where you go if you are a problematic individual in here, it's known as the hole Rock . It's cold and damp and smell fucking filthy" Leak let that sink in before he went into more detail. "It's lonely, you sleep on a slab of cement, a foot off the ground. They feed you food loaf, one shower every three days. One hour rec in a cage. No games, no weights, no phone calls, and you barely get your mail on time. I didn't want to go where Leak was describing, not today not tomorrow not ever. Sounded a whole lot worse than the place that I was in now. "Oh I almost forgot no commissary and your visits are only 15 minutes." Leak said still cleaning up. "So go right ahead and act up all you want. I learned the hard way with no one helping me or showing me the ropes once it was too late. I can only help you with so much but at the end of the day you're going to choose to learn the way you want from what I see it's going to be the hard way." Leak words impacted all of us. Especially myself the most. "What's food loaf?" Was all I ask ed. The cell burst out in laughter once we cleaned up the cell?

It looked as if nothing ever happened. No one got caught with contraband and no one went to the twist. I cooled down. "You see? Back to normal and I gota get on the shitter." Slash advised us throwing up the sheet. "Don't flush that shit. Leak barked. "Damn Leak I'm not Rock." Slash joked. "Ha,ha real funny" Rock didn't like that joke not one bit. I never understood how anyone could ever get comfortable with listening to another man piss while pushing out his turds. It was just so inhumane. That shit was punishment enough. The sounds of turds dropping was disgusting. "Here it comes" Slash felt the need to direct us on every turd that touched or even pierce to surface. What made it all worse was how everyone was so quiet wanting to hear if it was being tampered with. We were all anxious to open the package. "I'm done" Slash said cleaning up. "Who's going to get it?" Slash had to be kidding, right? I looked at Leak and he shook his head. I looked at Bigs and he had his face buried in the pillow. I'm fucking with yall I got it, yall niggas is bugging. I can't make you dig in my shit literally." Slash laughed. He gagged as he fished through his shit which made me gag. I couldn't take it anymore. Man let me know when you done playing in your shit" I now buried my face in my own pillow. That shit had the cell up in flames. Now I understood the concept of the courtesy flushing. The smell of shit was way to potent to let it linger around. There were three other lungs in the cell that needed oxygen to breathe. The sound of the sink echoed. Leak was in his own world. I kind of wish I knew what he was thinking. To bad, it was impossible to do such tricks as humans. It's best that it couldn't be accomplished anyway. It's all we have that noone could control. Just imagine what it would feel like to have the ablility to hear what the others are thinking. Slash pull down the sheet and flushed the toilet. The package was in the sink all washed up. "Y'all do what yall need to do my job is done." Slash step back and jumped on his bed. I dashed to the sink and examine the package for particles. Particles a what? SHIT!. "Its clean man I took care of it." Slash was mad. I took my time looking at the package. "Gota be sure Slash." Rock said. I grabbed a roll toilet tissue and wrapped a nice chunk around my hand to use it to dry off the tied up condom. You could see the grooves in the sealed condom that gave the impression of the smaller balls inside of the condom. Get your head out the gutter people. I picked it up, I counted four individual balls inside one condom. "It looked loaded Rock." Leak informed me. Your girl pulled through. Whatever you do keep her happy and don't ever piss her off because she can lift you and just like that and drop you my nigga." Leak was right I had a piece of the outside world in my hand or better yet in our cell. You could feel the anxiousness in the room. Everyone was eager to figure out what the fuck was in the condom. I was about to bust it open

"Don't do that yet!" Leak let out not waiting for me to do something stupid. "Why not?" Rock asked. We gota find out what's in here Leak." I bargained. "You already know what's in there Rock." Leak was smart. I knew but I didn't. If that made any sense. "Now if you break that shit opened you'll be setting yourself up for failure. You should know why?" Leak asked. "No but I bet you going to tell me" Rock answered sarcastically. "You bet your ass I'm a tell you." Once you open that is going to be all hell to close back into that individual package first of all, second once you open that the smell of the Coke or weed is going to saturate the room with its potency. No one on this block has any type of work here. So when the guards go around to do their rounds the smell will be so obvious that another cell search will be the next thing smoking. And three, you my friend better get used to throwing up for the next few mornings because you don't know exactly what you're opening unless you do open it?" Leak challenged. The ball was in Rocks court now. Leak was so fucking right with every possible solution that came up out of his mouth. I was not risking it not evening a bit. "Nah man I know its work but I gave her three options it could be anything you're right. I think we should wait." Leak smile. Smart man.

"Well we fucked "because I'm not putting that shit up my ass again." Slash felt some type of way. We had him thinking we was going to open it up but I actually wanted too, but the situation wouldn't allow it at the moment. We need to work on getting gloves and the things we need that is our main priority by tonight. Slash talk to your people and asked them to get gloves or plastic trash bag over as soon as possible. If they ask, its for food seasoning or whatever. You already know the deal. Try to get a lighter my nigga. I'll ask the guys I know outside. "I thought we was staying in?" Rock asked. Yea we was but we can't waste time with this now, time is money and bullshitting can get us jammed up. We gota make moves Rock. You can stay in with Bigs since he don't like coming out anyway. Leak informed. "Nah fuck that I'm going outside too." Leak gave me that here we go again look. I can give this to Bigs to hold down and he can stay in with it. Right Bigs?" I asked the man. He shrugged his shoulders eating not giving a fuck. He did what we wanted him to do. That man don't even want to hold it. He didn't even answer you." Leak spoke. He was right. Fuck it I'll stay just make sure you get the shit we need to make all this all come together." Rock said. "We got you my nigga." No sooner did the doors pop and it was rec time. "Plus I gota find Braze." Leak said heading out the door. "Oh yea he was with his lawyer this morning too. I saw him he said he got you my bad." Rock informed Leak all late. "Damn! Rock my mind wasn't in a good place when I was going outside right now, I'm so glad you told me that. Next time do me a favor and let me know earlier. This shit been bugging me all day." Leak said. "I got you my fault. I should've known better." I said. "Aint bout nothing, check you in a bit." Leak was ghost along with Slash and the rest of the block. I fell back on my rack and fell in deep thought. "What you going to do with all that shit?" Bigs asked the dumbest question ever. "I'm a get so high and over does." I joked with Bigs. "Nah don't do that Rock you have a family that loves you too much." Bigs thought I was serious. "I'm playing Bigs, Ima sell it and try to get some more and sell it again." I said not really thinking. "But for what Rock?" Bigs asked again. "So I don't have to depend on anyone for anything for as long as I'm in here Bigs. There is a good chance that I will be behind these bars for a very long time. That type of money being spent on someone in jail is alot. I don't want to be a burden on my family." Rock spoke with his heart but Bigs wasn't done. "By you doing all of this do you think that your love ones will stop sending you money?" I didn't know where Bigs was going with all of this but it was getting annoying. "I'm not sure but if all goes according to plan I can tell them not to send me any money because I'm okay without the cash. I haven't thought that far yet and why are you asking me all these irrelevant questions?" Rock asked with some attitude. "I don't want you to get in more trouble than you already find yourself Rock. I hope it all goes in your favor but you have to weigh your pros and your cons too. You can't just expect everything to go your way all the time. That's all I'm saying." Bigs said. His last words he made perfect sense which was true on how I always expected everything to go the way I wanted to go knowing damn well it wouldn't be like that every time. He was only trying to help like Slash and Leak but on another level. "What do you think I should do Biggs?" Rock wanted to know what this nigga would do. "I don't know man I don't know much of this lifestyle and believe me after this I don't care too much for I'm sure you'll figure it out just don't let yourself be so easily influenced like me." Bigs admitted. I took into a deep consideration what Bigs said. I understood now what he meant he didn't want to come out and say it but in so many little words he put it all on himself to really get the message across.

What felt like eternity rec was finally over and the guys were on their way back in. I must've dozed off because I didn't even hear when they called it. The sound of all the slamming of the doors is what woke me up out of my nap.

Slash and Leak came in all hyped and swollen from working out. "Man we was getting that money" Leak talked to Bigs. "I bet, ya mother fuckers is crazy how much bigger yall want to get." Bigs asked. "Well we gota handle some business too you know. If we don't do it who going to handle it Big man?" Leak asked. We all know you ain't. All you do is sleep and eat." Leak joked. Slash didn't help the situation not one bit. "Yea fat boy, you need to get up that big ass of yours and work out too. Slash clowned Bigs. "Man being big, the honeys love it. So let me be." Bigs shot back not caring what they had to say. "What's the plan my niggas?" Rock asked changing the subject. "Well my man said they will send the trash bag over tonight." Slash informed Rock not skipping a beat. "That's what's up." Rock replied. "That's all we need right?" Rock stated. Technically yea that should do but is good to have everything, just in case we do need wax bags. What if that's some dope, especially if it's that good shit?" Leak suggested. I had no clue about the dope shit and trust and believe I damn sure didn't want to get sick off that shit. It was wise to get the equipment needed to put all that shit together. "We have to wait for the gloves tomorrow morning when my man's a supposed to clean the showers." Leak informed me. "Wassup, so if anything we can put all this together tomorrow right?" Rock asked. The important thing is this we just got searched and they found nothing. So we have a good amount of time to put all this together before our next shakedown because once we start moving best believe all eyes are on us. Your little girlfriend warned us but now they gonna swarm us like bees on honey!" Leak projected.

Chapter 17

"Getting it"

After standing Jacqueline up for the past few weeks. Linda finally decided to call her up and link up with her. They agreed to meet up at the terminal. It was snowing and its cold, bundled up from head to toe on this beautiful chilly day. Mom was nowhere in sight. She didn't even bother coming home last night. Pete and mom have been wrapped around each other like two teenagers. Linda is in the kitchen preparing a quick sandwich to hold her down when the phone rings. She looked at the caller ID and didn't recognize the number so she didn't even bother to answer it. Two bites into her sandwich she heads towards the door. Once again the phone rang, she almost didn't even bother to check who it was but she wondered if it was Joel.

"Shit, I'm about to hear it." Linda picked up. "You have a collect call from Rock you will not be charged for this call, to accept press one." recorder spoke in its monotone recording. "Hello" Linda answered. Rock couldn't believe what he just heard. "I know this isn't Linda he growled excitedly." "Hey Manny!" Linda plopped down on the couch. She knew this would be a while and Jacqueline would have to wait a minute. "Linda?" Rock said over the phone. "Yes?" Linda tried to put on her innocent voice. "Don't even try it girl." Rock already knew what she was trying to do. "Why haven't you been around when I call?" Rock lowered his tone a bit. Not wanting to piss Linda off knowing that she would hang up on him. "You always call when I'm not around." Linda lied. "Girl don't sit there and lie to me." Rock spoke knowing she was lying. "So now we lie to each other? I feel like I lost my other half." Rock spoke truthfully feeling like Linda wasn't on his boat anymore. He needed her the most but felt that she was long gone. "You didn't lose me Manny. I'm just tying up some loose ends out here before your court date you know? It's around the corner and I'm going to try my best to show up." Linda informed Rock. "And if you don't its okay Linda, but how come you don't come up with mom when she invites you to my visit?" Rock was in his feelings. Now that he finally had the chance to have Linda's undivided attention he couldn't let it go. "That's because mom is always busy where her baby boy Pete and doesn't ever have time for me anymoretoo. So to be honest I feel like I lost both of you." Linda was right but if she could recall, mom only looks for comfort and support in Pete because Linda is hardly around. When she is around Linda is a closed book now and days. "From what I know Linda ever since all this happened you haven't been the same. I hate to side with mom but even I feel and noticed the change in you Linda." Linda tapped her heal quickly while listening to her brother. Feeling the change Linda made ever since all this transpired. It wasn't a behavior she wanted to display intentionally, her circumstances required her to make a few modifications in her behavior. "I'm sorry Manny and you're right I had changed up a bit but I need you to know it's because of you I'm acting the way I am." Linda sent Rock clues. "Because of me?" Rock almost exploded. I don't need you to change. I need you in my corner Linda, like we've always been for one another. I'm alone in here, with you and mom everything else I can deal with. Knowing your losing love for me is tearing me up inside." Rock informed. "It's all gonna get better soon I promise just give me some time and you'll see your rider going to come through." Linda advised. "Wassup with the truck? Did they sell it yet? Mom said no one has come by. We made a few phone calls but nothing yet." Rock asked about his long lost treasure. "Nobody wants that truck Manny I don't know why you don't just let me keep it and do what I want with it." Linda said. "Because it's hot baby girl and you deserve something that's not tainted." Rock's words made Linda feel warm inside, she missed her brothers voice. She missed his presence in all actuality. She felt so bad for abandoning him the way she was, but she knew now that she had to put her priorities first. "I miss you Manny." Linda blurted out. Rock got quiet. "I know you do ma and I miss the hell out of yall too. Do me a favor tell mom to sell the truck for $1000. I want here to keep the money as a gift from me to the two of you. I don't need any money for now. I call or I asked for it when I need it ok. I can't be a burden on you anymore." Rock said not going in depth with what he meant. "You know you're no burden, so don't even try it." Linda informed Rock. "I know." Just tell her what I said. "Rock said over the receiver. "As for you, I'll be expecting you to come up and see me soon right?" Rock didn't give much of an option. "Yes Manny." Linda smiled over the reciever. He alway was the same she thought to herself. "Promise?" Rock said "I promise Manny." Linda satisfied Rock's request. "It's cold as shit outside so bundle up if you going out Linda don't be getting all sick because you trying to look cute." Rock joked. "I will Manny."

"You have 60 seconds left." Just like that the call was coming to an end. "I love you Manny be careful in there and I'll see you soon." Linda tried to race the clock. "I love you too ma and you be safe." She held the receiver in her hand, replaying the whole conversation over and over. She smiled and grabbed the pencil on the stand and wrote a note.

I spoke with Manny and he said he loves and misses us, he asked about the truck and I told him is still out back. He told me to tell you to sell it for $1,000 and to keep the money I'll tell you what else he said later. I love you mom love Linda. The small note was placed on the phone so whenever mom would come in she would notice it immediately on the receiver.

The cold pierced Linda's face as she headed towards the nearest bus stop with one of her scarfs Manny had brought for her. There were two men at the stop and one woman who had on capris.

"This bitch is crazy" Linda said under her breath in between shivers. One male must have heard Linda and laughed. What felt like forever was only two minutes. The big New Jersey Transit bus came moving slowly until it came to a halt.

It was jam-packed. It's where the heat was and the homeless would ride the bus all day keeping warm until they finally got kicked off. The ride to the terminal was a complete disaster. It was too crowded and the smell got worse as the days went by. Linda wished someone would open a window so that some fresh air could kill the foul odor that lingered all around her nostrils. Many standing bumped into every person that came on board and exited the bus. Linda refused to sit down especially after putting on fresh blue jeans. She'll be damn if she would get a stain on them. After a few minutes of torture she got off the bus. Instead of waiting in the lobby area Linda decided to shoot to the sub shop.

"Ay look what the cold dragged in." Pete had this big smile on his face. "Hey! How are you doing?" Linda got warm. The shop was dead. Jamal was sitting at the table up front checking out Linda from his view. "I know that voice." Mom came from the back. "Is everything okay?" Mom asked Linda. "Yes everything is, where have you been young lady?" Linda joked with mom. "Well baby with this man." Mom patted Pete on his ass. "Oh man." Linda was disgusted. "How's your brother?" Jamal grabbed Linda's attention licking his lips. This nigga must be crazy if he even think Ima ever give him the time a day. Linda stared at Jamal in deep thought. "As a matter fact mom." Linda turned towards her mother. I just spoke with him. He is doing good. Missing us for the most part, but I did leave you a note at the house with a few things Manny and I spoke about." Linda said not going into the detail. "Is that what brought you all the way up here?" Pete asked. "Oh no I'm going out with a friend. I'm supposed to meet her at the terminal." Linda informed. "So he's good?" Jamal asked getting Linda's attention again. "Yes he is." Linda replied. "Are you going to be home for dinner later?" Mom asked. "I plan to, if Joel doesn't take me out again." Linda had to throw that up in the air. "That man got you spoiled baby." Mom said smiling. "Look who's talking." Linda stared at Pete and Mom with her hand on her hip. Jamal admired that plump ass, but turned away not being so obvious. "Well I got a go I'll see you later on tonight."

Linda parted from the shop crossing the street. She headed straight to the lobby in search for her so called friend. No site of her anywhere. She decided to pick an empty corner and leaned up against the wall watching the entrance way. . It made Linda cringe and reminded her how grateful she was for the little things she had. The site of a few homeless laid out on the floor near the back wall was a scene that no one could enjoy seeing

"Hey girl!" Jacqueline popped out from the side that Linda wasn't watching. "Damn girl you got me." Linda put her hand on her chest. "What or who were you thinking about?" Jacqueline asked. Linda smiled. "That man got my girl Jasmine sprung huh?" Jacqueline joked. Linda smiled with her beautiful smile. "Is you ready?" Linda asked. "Let's do it, where to today?" Jacqueline asked. Not knowing exactly where their destination would be. That wasn't even discussed. "How about the Moorestown Mall?" Linda asked. "Wow, it's been a while since I been to that mall." Jacqueline said. "No?" Linda asked. "Let's go." Jacqueline grabbed Linda's arm and they waited for the bus that was headed their way. "So what you got planned for tonight?" Jacqueline asked Linda. "I don't know yet. Why?" Linda asked. "Because I got an itch that need to be scratch and I want you to scratch it." Jacqueline whispered in Linda's year. Linda's mouth dropped as the words tickled her ear. "Are you serious?" Linda asked not believing what she just heard come out Jacqueline's mouth. The look on Jacqueline's face wasn't showing any signs of joking. She was dead serious. "That was a one time thing." Linda tried to refuse the offer. "I know it was and it was the last time I did anything to myself and I think you are so fucking sexy I would rather enjoy a moment with you then with my baby dads or just some random nigga in the street." Jacqueline whined. The bus showed up. Linda's mind was appalled she didn't know what to do. "Let's sit here. Jacqueline pick the seat at the window and turned towards Linda to continue her quest for seduction. Linda was embarrassed at the proposition "Why you don't call your other girlfriends to have this so called itch to be scratched?" Linda whispered so that no other ears to hear. "Because you understand me more and are sexier than they are naked." Jacqueline held nothing back. Linda had this wet feeling building up with all the sexual comments being thrown at her. No need to ask Jacqueline how she was feeling because her hand was in between her thighs enjoying every second of this. Plus her bottom lip was in between her teeth as she tried her best to persuade Linda into a night of passion and intimacy. "I'll let you know Jacqueline but I am making no promises okay?" Linda was going to consider it but how? If Joel was supposed to come over and claim his girl as they did every other day. Whether it was at his house or at mom's house. Linda wouldn't dare to tell Joel of the sexual experience she had the night with the girls. Even though he had expected it when she asked him if it would be okay to have a sleepover with her friends. He wasn't gona infringe on her fun with the girls, but he also didn't want to hear or know what happened that night. "So what you plan on buying at the mall?" Jacqueline change the conversation. "I want some new boots and a jacket." Linda added. "Oh okay." Jacqueline said. The ride to the mall was going to take a few.

—

"Ayo, got that?" Asked an older white man with grays all over. He wore tattoos all over his forearms. The gym was smelly and sweaty due to all of the guys working out heavy. We all did this trying to eliminate some stress and any other unwanted feelings that were pinned up inside. "Rock good, I'm not." Leak answered. Rock was down on the shoulder press hitting his set and listening to the exchange of words. "Gota wait, and of what?" Rock was buffed up. He was about 98% from fully recovering from his past injuries to the naked eye. Everyone was saying he was at his peak but Rock and Leak knew that he still had a few weeks left to reach his peak. "Soft." Old head spoke softly trying to be inconspicuous. "You got that money on board or is this going to be something I'm a have to wait for?" Rock wasted no time with getting to the point. "I have items in my cell but if you want something in particular I'll have to order it for you." The older man was feining. Rock had already been spreading his work with in his guys. He had it broken down almost to a science. We all had a job to do and it's been working smoothly. "How much do you want?" Rock asked old head while spotting Leak. "Come on three more." Rock push Leak. "About 100." the old man said. "What the fuck is about?" Rock hated the slick shit. He now understood why mother fuck always ended up on the front page and on the news. These niggaz always tried to play games with their words and send the next man to get what another man needed or wanted. "I..... I need a whole one." he said now. "Man get the fuck out my face now you stuttering and shit. Come back later either with all the money or better yet send me a money order and once I get it you have your shit." Rock had a serious attitude now. "That mother fucker must be high already." Rock was transforming into a vicious animal. He was no longer Manny. He didn't want to be like this but it's the only thing people understood. "What he wanted?" Leak asked. "He didn't even know! Fuck him! I need the money first fucking with him." Rock snarled. "He pays though." Leak tried to get the man when he needed. "I know but how much more money you think his people is going to keep blowing." Rock said. He had a good point, yes the old man paid the first few times, but how much more juicing was he's going to get out his family? "Leak agreed. "You are right." Leak was in charge of the muscle and pretty much Rock's right hand man. Slash was in charge of the shit we had out on credit with the help of Leak. Big's job was to write all the shit down so that no one could figure out what was recorded with Rocks help. Rock made it a must that some way somehow everyone who was involved had to use the other no matter what. This would eliminate the sneaky shit amongst one another.

Mandy had gotten her cut plus an extra hundred so that she could keep the product coming in like clockwork. The method she used was the same as the first time. We had competition on the other floor but that wasn't interfering. Stash spots were used by two people which were Rock and Leak. No one else had no clue where the stash spots were. The bud was as green as it came and the powder was extra soft. Everyone loved it. The food in our cell was for whoever wanted to eat. All the cabinets were overstuffed with chips, soups, candy bars, cookies and juice. Everything you could buy on the commissary we had it. Cosmetics was all top of the line products. Rock enjoyed the feeling of having a portion of the jail under his wing, but he couldn't do it all on his own. There is a saying that goes. "The more money you make the more problem one accumulates." This couldn't have any more truth behind it. You had your addicts, that are only addicted to using drugs. Right? Wrong! You have so many different types of addicts. Rock now just added another addiction on his platter which was? Money! A quick dollar could become engorged in his or her addiction like this one. The cell has so much food stored in it that their only option other than to eat it all was to?

"Ayo Rock you want to open up a store?" Slash asked. The conversation was brought up one night. "A store?" Rock asked a bit confused. "Why would I want to open a store for? We got all this food and cosmetic for us. Why would I want to sell it?" Rock didn't see the proposition that Slash was requesting. "You don't sell it Rock.... Well you do but you don't." Leak tried to put in his two cents. "Which is it you sell it or you don't?" Rock asked not understanding. "Ayo Bigs you want to start emptying the toilet?" Rock also asked. "Not really but I got it." Bigs was a softy which all three of the guys knew, but he was no saint either. "I'm still lost on the store concept Slash." Rock admitted. "It sounds like you want to sell all that we hustling for?" Rock didn't like what he was put together not really understanding it all. "You're not getting it, passed me five soup Slash. This is the only way he going to get it watch." Leak said catching the five chicken flavored Ramen noodles shoes. "You running a store right?" Leak went on to do some role playing. While Bigs was taken out all the water in the toilet. "I need two soups." Leak held up two soups in his hand. "You the store man give me these two soups and tell me that you want three soups back. You are charging one soup for the interest and lending me two soups, you following me?" Leak demonstrated. The smile on Rock's face wasn't fully reaching ear to ear yet, but his smirk was getting bigger. "Now if you give me three soups, how many do you asked for back?" Leak asked Rock. "I want four soups back." Rock said. "No you can do that but that's not how it's done, you want five back." Leak smile. "So you're not selling anything my G you're flipping what you already have for nothing. People are always hungry and never order enough food to last them through the next store week." Leak had Rock by the ears. "What if they want one soup?" Rock asked then you tell them that you want two back, no if and or buts." Slash said. "And this goes for everything not just soups, with everything from soap to socks. It don't matter what you have you can flip it. So what you don't have in here that's on the commissary list get it so you have everything that the jail needs." Now Rock's face was Kool-Aid type smiling. He liked the idea. "All right I'm with it." Rock agreed to the store proposition, but if that wasn't enough. The tickets that were in the process of being ran were being put together as we spoke. "Skill that." Rock tossed a bag of some high grade bud to Slash. "Damn I thought you said we couldn't blow or do any of our shit?" Slash reiterated what Rock had once said when they first started this business venture. "I remember that to." Leak also added kerosene on the fire. "All right fuck you give me the bag back. I tried to be nice and treat my niggas because I know ya be wanting to blaze and this is what I get for trying to show my niggas some love." Rock shot back. To be honest he's the one that has been dying to feel another type of high besides the high he was getting with the pills within the past months. The time was flying by and the feel for the streets or home as we call it has done left his mind little by little. The system was taken Rock away and molding him, into the creation that Rock always despised. "Nah chill Rock they just fucking with you." Bigs wanted to smoke too. Everyone laughed. "Yea man we just fucking with you." Slash said with two joins already skilled in his fingers. Now lighting it would be the task. "You got a light?" Leak asked. "Hell no." Rock replied with the look of pure embarrassment on his face. He had all the answers to all the questions but he still was lacking the "how to jail mentality." He still didn't have the how to make anything out of nothing type mentality. "So how are we going to spark these joints?" Bigs asked also lacking the knowledge. "Damn! You killing me I can't keep teaching you're all my secrets." Slash said. "Go head nigga, he need to learn that too, obviously he know of it but just don't know how to yet. " Leak was right. After selling Machete a lot of bud he wondered how the hell these guys were smoking all that shit. Because lighters wouldn't last forever and were almost impossible to get in, but possible if you pulled the right strings. Rock slipped up and asked Machete for a lighter one day. "/No tengo/ /don't have/, you have to improvise with what you have in your cell hermano." Machete said. "Plus you the man making the moves I was going to ask you for one myself." Machete joked. Machete and his crew all always copped green from his own people on the other floor but after the last shipment they got it had him very disappointed. They were being fed garbage lately which forced Machete and all of his crew to spend the money with Rock. "Listen I like how you move Rock. I'm not sure why it is that I've learned to care for you as one of my own but I do. I wanted to put you in a position where you can have men move for you with just a snap of a finger. I've used your style and your character to lecture my men, well the younger ones at least because they are the most stubborn ones. They still have a lot of maturing to do." Machete spoke highly of Rock in the gym a few weeks ago. Rock already sensed where all this was heading.

There was no need to even be disrespectful to such a well-respected man who took great care of his men. "I don't understand what you are asking of me Machete?" Rock asked. "I need more men of your stature to inspire and motivate the others, to carry themselves in a structured manner. "/Como tu/" /like you/ "/piedra/" /Rock/ Machete spoke softly. "All you have to do is consider it, that's all I'm asking from you "si tu no lo siente "/if you not feeling it/. It's all love anyways. Stick to who you are and I'll make sure you will be respected as a man, when dealing with my people." Now if you choose to go another route in this lifestyle Rock I can't help you /mi hermano/ / my brother/" Machete spoke how he was feeling. "I appreciate you and your offer and I'm not declining but I'm not seeing yes either, I have a lot on my plate right now, I'll let you know if and when I'm ready to handle so much responsibility." Rock's answer was more than intelligent enough. "That's what I'm talking about. I'll see you around. If you need anything from me just let me know." Machete replied. "Look Rock." Slash called over to Rock. He jumped up to his feet and headed towards the light switch. "You see this?" Slash unscrewed the cover to the light switch on the wall with a nail clipper. This took only a minute but it worked. Rock studied Slash every movement. The smell of the food being warmed up in the sink with the hot water scorching tickled the guy's nostrils. "Are you crazy nigga? You trying to get electrocuted or what?" Rock stepped back. "Or what?" Slash joked. "Chill my nigga watch and learn. "Slash felt in power now. He had a pencil and broke it, he extracted the lead as carefully as he could. He made sure he had three nice long pieces. "You see these?" Slash asked Holding up the lead. "Yea." Rock answered. "First you grab one and wrap the middle with toilet tissue, the other two pieces. You shove one where the red wire is like this." Slash jimmied the lead in until it was wedged in on the side of the switch where the red wire was screwed on the side of the light switch. "You don't want to break it."Slash said once it was in place. "Take the other one and do the same on the other side." Once they're both in place grab the last piece of lead, with the tissue tied in the middle so it hangs on tightly on the tissue. Then you put the last piece in between the other two wedge pieces carefully." Slash played with lead pieces, Rock sat back and watched in amazement as the little lesson was taking longer than expected. "This shit isn't working Leak." Rock was impatient. "It'll work keep watching." Leak instructed. At this site of the heat brewing in the middle but no actual flame may Rock's doubt go away? "You gota be careful Rock because if you hit both of them pieces too much at the same time you can blow the power out, then the whole block is going to be on lockdown until they find out where the shortages is coming from. "How much work we got in here?" Rock was getting paranoid. "Chill only the two joints and one bag of bud." Leak answer swiftly. "Don't be scared now." Leak joked. "Fuck you!" Rock eyes closed at the sight of the spark and the smell from the flame ignited finally. "Pass me the joint and get the towel ready." Bigs was soaking the towel in the water that was running already. "Shit hot as fuck!" Bigs was bitching. Laughter filled the cell. Puff and pass the cloud of smoke disappeared in the toilet bowl. Their heads had to be covered with a damp towel the moisture help tremendously. In a matter of seconds both joints were gone. Ashes was all that was made of them. Bigs was the last one with his head in the toilet. "Man I don't feel it." Slash was the first one to deny the feeling. "What you want to blow some more?" Rock asked feeling it already. His eyes were slammed. You'll be surprised that he could even see. Leak had his head leaning on the wall relaxing. "Man I feel this shit I don't know what you talking about." Leak was talking smoothly. "Ayo Bigs why you still got your head in the toilet?" Rock was laughing his lungs out. "Yo that mother fucker fell asleep in the toilet!" Slash was also in tears busting into laughter holding his stomach. Rock looked at Slash to see if he could notice any visible side effects that displayed to be intoxicated. The big old cheesy smile he had was enough but the sound of his dry as mouth smacking in a search for some saliva or whatever other liquids to hydrate his cotton mouth also gave him the impression that he was. "You wasn't high though?" Rock asked. "Man fuck that I'm fffuucckkeedd uuuppp!!!! Sup with that food though?" Slash asked. Leak finally opened his eyes and tried to gain focus of everything. "Ayo?" Where the CO?" Rock and Slashes' ears shot up at the sound of CO being brought up.

"Oooohhhh Weeeeiiiii" someone yelled out onto the block. "Must be nice!" Yelled another. The smell must have escaped enough to alert the other guys on the block. "He coming?" Leak was tripping. "Why the fuck is Big's head still in the fucking toilet?" Leak asked staring at Bigs motionless body with the towel over his head. They knew he was alive because his belly moved in and out with every breath that he took. "Nah the guard is in the bubble aint nobody nigga." Slash said staring out onto the block. "Bigs." He moved, but didn't get up.

"Ayo Bigs." Rock kicked the fuck out of him. "Yo." Bigs replied. "Get the fuck up man." "Oh shit." I'm up." Bigs tried to play it off. "Okay you up, now get up." Slash joked laughing hysterically. He got his ass up embarrassed. "Yo that shit got me all fucked up, what is that?" Big asked. Laying up on his bed. "What else would it be?" Leak answered. "Damn it's good." Bigs said. "I know it's been some time since I've blown any bud, but I ain't never been stuck on stupid like that." Bigs was tripping he went from laying on his bed to digging in the locker he didn't know what to do with himself. "Why is my mouth so fucking dry though?" Slash asked. "My shit dries as fuck too." Leak agreed "Maybe this will help." Bigs pulled out a big ass bag of breakfast orange juice mix. Slash and leak both jumped up. "I'll make it." They both wanted parts. "Man pass me the pot of food before your get all that juice all over it." Rock was focused on the food. "Yo... The keys." Slash said peeking out the door. It was the CO. "Oh shit him coming." Slash was paranoid as fuck. Rock got up to look because all of these nigga were bidding off each other. He grabbed the bag of food and headed towards the door. The CO was making his rounds like always. In their eyes it look more like he was coming to get them but in all actuality the CO did not want anything from them. "Shit he is coming. Leak jump up on his bed and just waited. Slash kept preparing the juice quiet as a church mouse. Jalinda crossed Rock's mind but he dismissed the thought. Right now wasn't the time to get caught slipping. It's bad enough the weed had total control of all four of them. While the sound of the keys kept getting closer the quieter they all got. Knowing that Rock is on top you would think his attitude would be a bit cockier. But it seems as though that the small pep talks were getting or have already gotten to him. "He's coming, he's coming." Slash whispered. Waiting for the bullshit to erupt but the keys jingled right on by. He just kept on moving about his shift making his rounds. "You scared asses that mother Fucker ain't sweating us." Leak was bold now.

"Nigga get the fuck out of here you had nothing to say when he was coming, all the sudden you got a voice." Rock was bidding now. "Man I was just watching you three bitch up." Leak joked back. "Yeah I know." Rock began to break down the food. "Let me get them bowls." Rock said. The meal was ready. Their bows were big enough to feed two grown men a piece. Talk about an appetite. Now the juice on the other hand was made in a small trash bag. Don't worry it's a new bag and is clean. It had to be made very carefully because the bags were great for cooking but they were shitty when it came to make juice. Someway somehow the juice would find a whole and marry it allowing the juice to leak out slowly. It was a typical night in a jail cell for us. If your funds weren't were you wanted them to be you would possibly go hungry every night. You could be lucky and have some thorough ass cellies that wouldn't let you go hungry. That wasn't the case in most cells. You'll be lucky to get a soup or two from someone if they had it. After that you would be all on your own. Just think about it. How would you look if you would be doing your bid plus the next man's bid? It's hard for you to fill your belly, let alone another man's belly that is it nowhere near attached to your own. Sorry but in here it's every man for themselves so if you don't have anyone to ride with you. Than guess what you better get your hustle on. I can actually say that out of the four of us. Bigs is the only ones that would be financially okay if the work would've never made it. Slash gets bread once in a while and Leak rather not ask his baby moms for money because she got them kids to cater to. I respect him for that for the most part. He's the type that will go without, than to ask the next man for anything. So just for that if I got it, guess what? He got it to. We are up now, it's our turn to go to bed with our bellies full every night.

"Ayo this is salty as hell." Bigs was bitching. "My bad it is a bit salty." Rock agreed. "You can't cook you suck at all this jail shit nigga." Leak said. "Fuck that! This shit is on point. Put water in it." Slash was up in his corner near the door sitting like a kid on timeout. Stuffing his face talking shit. We laughed at Slash, he was a bid all in himself. The juice was sweet as hell you could drink half a cup and fill it up with water to make a whole new cup. "I was thinking about. Where could we find another spot to stash all this grub as it gets bigger?" Leak asked. "What do you mean? Was wrong with where we haven't now?" Rock got defensive. Leak may have been paranoid but he knew exactly what he was saying. "Right now nothing but as the store grows and the items begin to triple there will be close to no room at all in this cell." Leak said now getting to the actual point. "So we eat it faster." Rock blurted out with a mouthful of chi chi. Everyone almost choked with what they had in their mouths. "Eat it all?" You are bugging Rock, even if we all tried to eat all the food that's in one cabinet out of the four we wouldn't even get a third of the way." Slash said. "I like that idea." Bigs said. Also with his chubby cheeks loaded. Leak looked over "I bet you fat ass does like that idea." Leak joked. Bigs put up his stubby thick middle finger. Leak just smiled. "But seriously Rock is just something to think about." Leak informed Rock. "All right but for now it stays here where we all know and can keep our eyes on it. Deal?" Rock said. "It's your call. "Slash agreed. "Say no more." Leak agreed. "I'm all in." Bigs also agreed. All right who got the dishes? "Slash added. "You set yourself up for that one, you do my nigga." Leak said. "All right I'll get it, fuck it." Slash didn't protest. "Nah Slash I got em." Rock volunteered. "What?" Somebody put in a sick call. This man gota be sick, first the joints now the dishes. What's next foot massages." Bigs joke. The cell was all laughter. "You got that fat boy. I lined myself up for that one." Rock took it all in. The night ended well and the fellas were getting to know each other more. Rock wasn't the only one who was raised by a foster family. Slash and Bigs were products of that as well. Leak grew up in them streets literally. They made him a ruthless man but also a devoted father. I earn some more respect for the guys as they earned more respect from myself. The high began to take a toll on the guy. The conversations grew lighter and lighter.

—

"Manuel Ricardo!" Report to the visiting area immediately!" The CO barked early in the morning. Rock was so tired and drained from the previous night that sleep felt as though it was the only thing to do at the moment. My eyes were cemented shut, well that's what they felt like at least. The door clicked again and again. It loudly alerted Rock to get the fuck up. "Ayo it's for you!" Bigs informed him still half asleep. "I know man, I'm fucking beat." He replied just as groggy. Bigs was up already. I wasn't even sure of the time but it had to be around noon. The light coming in through the window was shining brightly. The bed had Rock in a cobra grip not allowing him to pry loose from the warmth that the bed contained. "Click, click!" Manuel Ricardo you have a visit!" The CO sounded very irritated by my presence not being on command like all the others who were accustomed in doing so at the snap of the finger. "I'll go for you if you don't want your visit." Bigs said. "All right I'm up, I'm up!" Rock answered. "I wish someone would come see my ass you see how fast I'll be out that door." Bigs didn't understand the lack of initiative from Rock's behalf. This man should feel special knowing that he has love ones out there making time for him. "If we only knew how ungrateful a man could be in this world. How could we be so unappreciative and inconsiderate to make his or her family wait as if their presence wasn't cherished enough." These are the thoughts that ran through Bigs head. He just sat back and stared at Rock voicing his thoughts. It took him about 15 minutes to get ready and out the door. "I'll see you later don't sleep too much because I'm coming back to go straight to bed myself." Rock said grabbing a handful of candy and putting it in his pocket. "Man get out of here." Bigs said getting back to his reading. The day would be a great day. It always was especially when a visit came by to get anyone out their cell. The last visit was for leak. That day wasn't a bad one from what I can remember. Rock forced his body to make his way to the visitor's room. He saw a few faces roaming the hall. Many were either heading to medical or going to a designated group program as scheduled.

"Sup Rock you good?" Asked the youngin who would always grab some soft. You would be surprised on how lucrative jail can really be if you have a commodity that people would love to buy or need. "Yea but I'll talk to you later because I'm headed to the dance floor." Rock said slowing down his debt. "All right dude just a 30 piece of anything." Jessie stated.

Jessie was around Rocks age but he lived over by Cherry Hill. He got jammed up with some possession charges on him which would be considered a misdemeanor. He'll be sliding up outa here soon. He gets no fronts because everyone knows that he is temporary in this facility. "I got you just put the bread together." Rock said walking away.

The visiting room was dead, there was barely any visits going on down there but two other guys. Rock wondered who made time for him on this special day. His anxiety began to drive him a bit crazy. The chewing of his fingernails was a habit he was developing in here. It was a nasty one but it's how he dealt with it, when he wasn't all drugged up from his CVS remedies prescribed by Doggie Houser. Imagine that one. The sight of Felicia's beautiful flawless face appeared out of the blue.

—

The most interesting thing that occur when Jacqueline and Linda were at the Moorestown Mall. They were heading over to the food court, Jacqueline notice her baby dad with his girlfriend Star.

"Oh my God there he is." Jacqueline grabbed Linda's arm redirecting her walking towards a totally different path. "Who? Linda asked. She scanned the area quickly while walking in the direction Jacqueline was pulling her into. "My babydad Jasmine I don't want him to see me. I don't feel like dealing with his bullshit right now." Jacqueline said going into a clothing store. Once inside the "Gap" they hid behind a clothing rack. "There you see them?" Jacqueline moved Linda into the direction where she could spot them. "I don't see them and I don't want to see them." Linda lied. She did want to see who Streets was with but she damn sure didn't want Streets to see her with Jacqueline. That would start the only drama. Drama that Linda knew better than to get caught up in not now and not yet. She finally spotted Streets with his arm wrapped around this female. "Is that her?" Linda asked. "Yeah that's the bitch." Jacqueline ideed both of them. They laughed and walked around to the food court. "That is her." Linda didn't mean to blurt out. "What you say Jasmine?" Jacqueline didn't quite catch what Linda was saying but asked anyway. "That bitch ain't got shit on you Jacqueline." Linda switched it up quick. "I know right." Jacqueline agreed with Linda's opinion. Linda's memory didn't steer her wrong. The beaten she put on that bitch was a beaten to remember. She swore that night she was going to give Linda some work, not a chance. "Come on girl let's look around fuck them two dirt balls." Jacqueline was hurt and any blind man could see that. Linda just got the confirmation she needed. In Linda's mind her Star's image was faint. Now it was engraved permanently. "It's okay Jacqueline let her go through all that shit he put you through." Linda noticed Jacqueline change her attitude. It wasn't easy to see someone you love for so long be all hell bent with the next chick. No matter how bad the relationship was. All that time invested in one another along with the thoughts of it being thrown all away one day would torment anyone. The memories and feelings never seem to wash away quick enough. "I'm good Jasmine and you are absolutely right." "But what I want to know is how the fuck this man always knows where I'm at or was this pure coincidence?" Jacqueline asked. "Maybe it is coincidental." Linda suggested. "Because I picked this place so yeah it has to be.

—

"I thought you forgot about me." Rock said with a small smirk on his face. The windows no cleaner than before, it's like no one cared enough to do their job correctly down here. The smell was as if there was dried up semen on the floor and walls, it was so disgusting. The visits were great to have let's not be mistaking about that one. It's the extra shit one must put up with while in a visit. Especially if the guard that's on duty gave two shits about who was doing what. You would think that you was in a rated X film with all the horrible graphics you witnessed behind the glass. But then again desperate measures require desperate acts huh? One was left to imagine and partake.

"Now why would that even cross your mind baby?" Felicia's smile sent chills down Rock's spine. She was beautiful. She had on her work uniform. Her breasts were up and perky. Her hair was down straight onto one side leaving her whole left side of her neck and ears exposed. Her neck had all my attention yelling bite me. "It's been a minute since I last saw that pretty face." Rock spoke sweet to her. She blushed. "I'm sorry baby. It's just that I don't want to bother you or be an inconvenience to you. Im not sure how you feel about any of this." Felicia said. "Why and how would that be possible ma? You have to understand maybe the writing can be a little stressful but I'll get to it eventually. I don't write as much because I don't want to sound stupid." Rock down played himself. He looked deep into Felicia's beautiful eyes. He followed them because they broke contact staring past him. Someone was walking up towards him. The individual wasn't coming up at Rock but to receive his own visit as well. "You don't have to worry about sounding stupid babe. You are far from stupid. I love your letters. I need them to help me get over my obstacles in my life on the outside. I need you to remember that no matter how difficult life may get. Having an inspiring letter from you, knowing how bad your situation is gives me so much power. I can see and read that you are not giving up on yours obstacles and that alone can drive me to pull through on my end baby." Felicia came to speak to Rock on a much needed eye opener. Many had no clue what it was to go through a situation as this one, but what make this impactful is all on how one handles it all. "Wow ma I didn't know a few words on my behalf could be so meaningful to anyone. Let alone help you get through your problems out there in your life?" Rock was speechless. "Well they do babe, the phone calls are great too but if you rather not speak to me at least write to me. Ima send you a few pennies for the phone or for whatever you may need while you're in here." Felicia was doing her part but Rock was too stubborn to show his appreciation in return. How could any man expect to keep any real woman out there if he does not give her what she's asking for? Which had nothing to do with sex. Many found it very difficult to believe that a woman couldn't control herself more than a man would ever try to. If a woman is holding you down working, plus raising a child all on her own, the only thing that she asked you is for emotional support in your letter and what was being said over the phone. Having all these small but very meaningful actions can be the leading cause for her to stay by this trying time and possibly stay devoted to you. While still taking care of all of her other priorities in life on her own. So when a man becomes blinded by his own thoughts and assumptions and begins to second guess the loyalty of his lady. He will act out due to his own insecurities which will lead him to ask numerous amounts of questions that are very hurtful let alone disrespectful on a regular basis. If a man can not deliver 1 ounce of emotional relief to his already stressed out woman. What the fuck you think is gona happen? She will go in search to find some emotional support in a 'friend" all because your insecurities couldn't read in between the lines. This is all your lady really wanted from you in the first place to east the pain she is holding. How could one not muster a few moments to deliver this to her wholeheartedly . Now she has found this someone. Who has offered a lending ear, so she could vent too. When all this shit could of been avoided if we would just shut the fuck up and listen. Oops, I almost forgot she gave up the pussy because this nobody took time out his so called busy life to listen and provide feedback. The same shit she was asking of you to do. Now you are way beyond pist and want to kill her and every nigga she came in contact with. So in all actuality who was in the wrong? For every action there is a reaction and that shit goes hand in hand on how we dish that shit.

"I don't mean to ignore your letters is that I'm still trying to get in the swing of things in here." Rock admitted. "I know baby but I want you to know that I'm right here for you for as long as you want me to be." Felicia put her hand on the glass. She informed Rock. "Thank you I'm glad to have you in my corner. I'm here for you too, you are not alone." Rock said with a smile. Felicia's eyes watered but she didn't drop any tears. "Good, keep them in your eyes." Smile for me baby girl." Rock joked. Felicia let out a light laugh. "So how's work?" Rock asked Felicia. "Very stressful but somebody has to do it." Felicia informed. "I wanted to ask you if it would be a problem for me to bring Eliza up here with me the next time I came." Felicia asked. "No problem at all ma, you know I enjoying seeing that little girl." Rock assured her. "I need her information." Rock replied. "Good because she has a crush on you I think." Felicia was bugging. "A what?" Rock asked. He was shocked at what Felicia just told her. Felicia was laughing hard nodding through the glass. "Yeah baby there isn't a day that goes by that she doesn't mention you. I asked her why does she like you so much you know what she said." Felicia asked. "Why?" Rock asked. "Because you love him mommy." Felicia said. "It was so sweet it made me wonder and think of you so much more." Felicia spoke staring into Rock's eyes. "So do you love me?" Rock asked. "You know I do Rock. I feel so empty without you by my side. I can't find it in me to move on knowing that you are still holding a special place in my heart. Maybe one day I'll have enough strength to work you out but for now you are still mine." Felicia wasn't playing. Rock noticed Felicia staring at her wristwatch. "You gota go?" Rock asked. "I don't want to." Felicia didn't answer the question but she did at the same time. "I had to get back to work, I'm already late." Felicia admitted. "Well you can't do us no good if you get fired ma." Go and come with the princess another day." Rock was being considerate. "I will remember what we talked about." Felicia said raising up fixing her pants. Her ass was loose in them scrubs. As she fixed them her booty jumped up and down. Rock stared at Felicia She noticed. She did it again Rock looked up at Felicia and she was blowing kisses. She knew how to make a nigga feel appreciated. The visit was terminated after almost an hour. Rock slowly headed back to his cell.

"Damn nigga why they jump on Bigs like that?" Asked a black medium build tier runner who was heading up the stairs. Rock stopped him in his tracks. "What the fuck you talking about?" Rock asked with a menacing look in his eyes. "Your celli. The fat boy they just rushed him to medical and took two niggaz to the hole. I guess they caught themselves trying to steal some shit off him but ended up with nothing." The tier runner chirped like a bird. "What's your name?" Rock asked. "Greg" he replied. I don't got shit to do with that though I'm just letting you know because I know that was your cell." Greg was a bit paranoid now. "Nah you good but when you get a chance slide by my cell later tonight." Rock said. "Yeah I got you." Greg confirmed. Rocks heart began to beat faster as his steps grew with more speed. "These mother fuckers are really pushing me." Rock said out loud to himself. He noticed that there were moving bodies in his cell without even going to the bubble he went straight to cell full speed. It was Slash and Leak cleaning up the mess that was all over the cell.

"Yo what the fuck happened in here?" Rock barked. "Oh shit!" Slash was caught off guard. "Niggas try to hit us, that's what happened." Leak said in a low growl. His eyes read pure hatred. "Who?" Rock asked. "Mr. Ricardo to the bubble." CO yelled to the PA system. "What the fuck!" Rock barked. He noticed a few faces on the gate watching his moves. "When you come back from any pass you report back to the bubble before you head to your cell!" Rock threw his pass through the small slot in the glass. "Open my cell!" He barked walking away. He didn't have the time to engage with the fucking prick. He slammed the shit out of the cell door. "When?" asked Rock. "While we were at yard." Slash answered picking up crumbs of all kinds of food on the ground. "Did they take anything?" Rock unconsciously asked. He must of forgot the work wasn't even kept in the cell. "No there isn't anything to take plus I heard they went to the hole." Leak said. "Who went to the hole?" Asked Rock. "Two niggas from Philly supposedly." Slash informed. "From Philly?" Rock asked. "Yeah but I'm not sure if that's on point we will have to find out more once they let us out." Slash said. "What about Bigs?" Rock asked. Leak dug in the trash and pulled out two t-shirts that were redder than cherry water ices. "They gonna get it." Leak didn't like Bigs all that much, but by all the blood they caused Bigs to spill on those T-shirts. Would make anyone mad enough to cause the same harm to whoever caused Bigs to lose that much blood. Bigs was far from a problematic individual in fact he was damn near harmless in our eyes. "That's all Bigs blood?" Rock asked with his eyes almost leaving his eye sockets. "Hate to tell you this, yes it is." Leak answered. "Oh yea. They are definitely going to get it. How long will they be in the hole for?" Rock asked pacing from the sink to the back wall. "I'll say about 60 to 90 days. "Slash answered. Why the fuck would they do something like that to him? He ain't got shit to do with anything?" Rock was getting madder as the seconds went by. I can't tell you why they did that to Bigs Rock, but to be straight up with you I think whoever would of stayed in today would of went through what Bigs went through. From the look of this cell those two mother fuckers were after one thing and one thing only." Leak was putting all this together inside of his own head alone. "There wasn't shit in here though." Rock protested. "All four of us knew that. Remember no one else knows this. To them all our work was inside of the cell. So to me, once they heard your name being called all crazy over the loudspeaker. It gave them two bitch ass niggas an idea. You would be at a visit then this would be a great opportunity to hit the honeycomb. Since you was headed to the dance floor." Leak was speaking as though he may have been the one to orchestrate all of this. Rock was thinking irrationally. "Could it be because Leak knew exactly where the stash was at? So for him to even try some slimy shit like this would only be a dummy mission but then again it could have been a decoy. Rock's thoughts were fucking with him. "Did you check on the stash?" Rock asked Leak. "I'm already on that. Everything is exactly where it is supposed to be." Leak assured him. "So why did they beat the shit out of Bigs?" Rock asked not understanding. "He wouldn't tell them what they wanted to hear possibly." Slash opinionated. "I'd have to agree with Slash on that note. First I didn't get it neither as to why they would have to take it that far into beaten the shit out of Bigs. If they came in and didn't find anything what would I do? I looked around and I put myself in their Skippy's. I also have some experience in home invasions as well. But we will keep that between the three of us." Leak spoke. "Once you searched a house looking for something that you know is in the house somewhere stashed away and couldn't seem to find it things always tended to get really frustrating and disappointing all at the same time. So your last result was to find out where the items were hidden and the only way to find that out is to get the homeowner to tell you where all that good stuff is located." Leak took a deep breath Rock looked at Slash who was nodding in agreement with everything leak was saying. "So you are telling me that since they couldn't find what they came in here to find. They asked Bigs where the work was, Bigs wanted to prove his loyalty to us. He told them that he didn't know where the work was at? So instead of believing him they took it upon themselves to beat it out of him one way or another?" Rock may have not been a street nigga but he was learning at an heirs pace. Rock's assumption was all good and dandy but the reality was "what if Bigs would've known where the stash was at would he have still taken that beaten? This is what you needed to consider. Yes, Bigs took a brutal beaten for the house but if you wouldn't of kept everyone out of the loop the way your mind had instructed you to do. Bigs would've probably still be in the cell with us at this very moment but the work would've been lost. Bigs couldn't swim to save his own life. We can't say that he proved his loyalty because he didn't know where the work was... At all. The only two that knew that was you and I. It was a good thing that Bigs didn't know. There is a good chance they would have took it all Rock." Leak was right on the money. "He's right Rock." Slash agreed with the hypothesis that was being made. ""So what do we do now if all this is true? Is all of Bigs belongings still here?" Rock asked. "Nothing we can do, we wait for Bigs to come back. If they do allow him to stay, if he doesn't Bitch up. We gona gather as much info as we can from..." Tap, tap, tap" all three of the guys inside the cell got quiet freezing everyone up. "Who the fuck is that?" Leak asked. "It's Greg." He peaked his big nappy head into the small Plexiglas window. "Ayo what's good." Rock jumped up over towards the door. "I just got word from the CO that your boy is good but they got him under investigation for a few days." Greg had pull being that he was a tier runner. He could go places where none of us could at any given time. "Did you find out who the two jackasses where?" Rock asked leaning on the door. "I don't know them, but I know that in about 30 to 45 days they'll be back out. Maybe not back on this block but on another unit. Supposedly they from Philly, they here on attempts. They not going anywhere anytime soon." Greg was very useful.

"Ayo Slash pass me honeybun." Rock slid it under the door. "That's for you, find out all you can and trust me I got you." Rock paid the man for his info. He bent over and snatched that shit up fast, tucking it away even faster it was unbelievable. "I don't care if Bigs would've told. I'm going to make sure all these these mother fuckers that want to try some shit like this, will think twice before they even consider taking a leap." Rock was way beyond mad. "You already know Rock!" Slash commented. "From now on we have to be on point with everyone, not just the people who were buying from us. I want to see and interact with everyone in this jail. I want to feel and see and how everyone looks. I want to know what they are thinking because deception is a mother fucker.

—

Back on the Block Street is sitting in his car was Star watching the runners on the block. Thoughts of Linda and her sexy body came into his mind. Star was feeling all over him. She was kissing him from behind the tints in his car. Her hands roamed as she unziped his jeans and puts him in her mouth. The thoughts of Linda and Streets getting it on added some extra excitment. He used these thoughts to intensify his arousal. The clouded interior of the vehicle had him in ecstasy. The slurping of Star's mouth and hands going up and down his shaft is such a beautiful feeling. Any and most men love enjoyments as such. He pulls on the L that is held with his left hand, with his right hand is all under Star's sweatpants feeling her all up. By now he's clearly lost focus on what was going on around him and what was being conducted on the block. Stars moaning like a bitch in heap puts the icing on the cake. Linda's ass bent over throwing it back is what Streets is wanting to due to her. Sooner or later she'll give that pussy up. Then out of nowhere it finally hit him right in the face. That's where he knows Linda from. Could it be? He was thinking. It had to be. Linda's face wasn't completely unidentifiable but the glimpse of the side of her jawline and her body was all very well identified. It is her.

"You okay baby?" Star asked. His erection was getting flaccid with these thoughts of Linda being the girl who was with Rock that night. "I'm good, don't stop." Taken another puff of the almost unlit L. He brought it back to life. The slurping continued as Streets tried to refocus on climaxing. Janet is going to die, I'm not sure when but I'll make sure she'll pay for what she did to Kay. As he envisioned raping and killing Linda his erection came back to attention. "That's it baby." Star went harder. Streets grabbed her by the hair and faced fucked her throat not stopping until he came all in her mouth. Star swallowed every drop of his semen until she was sure that no more would come out savoring every bit of it.

"You have me worried there baby I thought I wasn't doing it right." Star said fixing her hair in the sun visor mirror. "/Toma"/here/ Streets handed her the L "Na ma you know what you doing. I just got sidetracked for a second but you brought me back." Street confessed to Star. "What's on your mind?" Star asked inhaling the THC from the L. "Nothing really." Streets lied. He was plotting on Linda now. He's finally put a place on her face. It was time to put her face in the dirt. How could she think that I'm so stupid and I wouldn't figure this out. Linda was in trouble her plan was soon to backfire on her now. Getting emotionally involved was about to cause her life. With her out the picture Street could sleep better. He was going to prove his loyalty to his right hand man that lost his life to this stupid bitch. When and how, was Streets going to make his move? He had to do this shit right because getting caught up with a body on his hip wasn't part of the plan.

"I know that's not ..."Clip!?" Street focused on the man with the navy blue coat walking up towards the block. "I can't tell but it looks like his walk." Star opinionated. "It is him." Streets watched as he busted it up with the fellas on the corner. None of his men noticed that it was Clip on the other side of the building. These niggas better handled that or I'm going to have to handle them." Street said reaching under his seat grabbing his big boy. He popped the cylinder open and all shells were occupying every available space in the cylinder. The chromed glisten as the sun pierced right through the front windshield. He wrapped his hand around her rubber grip so that he could get a secure grip on the 357 snub nose in his hand. "What you going to do?" Star asked worrying now. "What I've been dying to do to this nigga after he stole all that work from the stash a while back ago." Streets informed. He always said more than he had to when he came to Star. He really trusted his girl and through all that they been through she has never gave him any reason to not trust her. "Look!" Star yelled. "They're going to get him." She said excitedly. Streets reached over to pull the lever on the door to make sure the situation was going to be handled the way he wanted it to be handled. Star grabbed his hand. "No! let them." Star didn't feel right letting Streets leave her side with that big ass hammer on him. "I got this." Street said opening the door. "What the fuck you pay them for?" So you don't have a get your hands dirty Babe right?" Star was absolutely right and the last comment kept him where he was at. "You know what?". He sat back. "You're right let me see what these niggas going to do." Street put the big boy on his lap and watch the whole scene unfold. The ass whopping was about to begin. "When did he take that work from?" Star asked. "This is almost 6 months ago." Street asked. "Damn baby six months ago." Star reiterated. "Yeah he's been ducking and dodging ever since." Streets explained."Oh shit." One of his workers two piece him. His runner was standing over top of him barking some shit at him which couldn't be made out but what was being said. It really didn't matter what was being said, what was important was what was being done. That was what matter right now. Another guy ran Clip's pockets. All his pockets were emptied out the beaten began some more. The stomping and the kicking was brutal.

"Baby they're going to kill him!" Star felt bad for Clips "That's what he gets for stealing from me and my men, let them kill him." Streets was about 50 feet away from everything. His blood boiled as if he was there participating in the brutal beating. The beating was getting worse. Clip's sneakers were stripped from his body. He was balled up in a fetal position trying to cover his head from getting busted in even more. It didn't work, it exposed his ribs. "Make them stop Streets." Star pled. "Not yet." Streets had a big smile on his face watching all this unravel. "No baby he is bleeding a lot." Star thought not even being able to see all the blood on the floor but she was right. Clips was losing vast amounts of blood. Streets tapped his horn twice the men looked over at Street's direction. Streets hit his high beans twice and the beating ceased. "Oh my God thank you. That nigga gets the message he won't steal from you again." Star was still protecting Clips.

"Bitch! Are you fucking that nigga?" Streets grabbed his gun and put it in Star's face. This mother fucker was super bipolar as fuck. "What!?" No I ain't fucking him and get that gun out my face before it goes off." Star had balls but her mouth needed to get checked every now and then. "So why you protecting that bitch ass nigga?" Street asked. "Ain't nobody protecting him, go kill him! Don't write me when you asses all jammed up!" Street was gone, he was biting his bottom lip in anger. This bitch was testing his gangsta. "I will watch." As soon as he opened the door the site of his men running in different directions made him stop dead in his tracks. Two squad cars rushed up into the towers right where Clips was still picking himself off the ground. "Oh shit." Street was back in his car. "You see you don't listen to me right?

Fuck what I say, huh?" Star was talking shit now. Let's get out of here before they start questioning us." Star went on quiet mode the whole time they were crossing the bridge.

—

"Baby what is wrong where is your oxygen tank?" Pete asked mom with mom still smoking like a Navajo Indian she was only making her situation worse. Linda wasn't home. She ended up linking up with Joel before she would head over to Jacqueline's house to scratch her itch. "In... the... Closet." mom tried to speak as she gasped for air. She searching for the next breath almost frozen. Pete and mom just got done making some good loving. They both always tended to enjoy a cigarette between the two after the fact. Pete rushed and grabbed the tank and mask not trying to trip over the hoses. Mom wasn't even three puffs into her cigarette that her breathing began to get shallower and shallower. Instead of reaching for the oxygen tank she decided to take another drag of her cigarette. Mom wasn't making absolutely no fucking sense right now. "We going to the hospital." Pete said scared out his mind. Mom had the mask in her right hand with a cigarette in her left hand. "Give me that shit woman!" Pete snatched the cigarette out mom's hand. "Would you stop?" Mom protested. "Stop!".... "Stop!" Are you seeing what's happening?" Pete was furious. He put out the cigarette. "I'm okay babe." Mom tried to justify. "Yeah maybe you are at the moment but what if I wasn't here?" Pete scolded. Mom stayed mute. "Get dressed we are going to the hospital." Pete ordered he wasn't even asking. Mom was moving slowly. The air that was being administered into her lungs wasn't sufficient. Pete helped get her dressed faster. He didn't like the way she was moving. She was moving slower than normal and there was no way he would allow her to fatigue herself more than she had to.

At the hospital the doctor immediately admitted her into the next available bed in admissions. Once the nurses reviewed her file and noticed the words "immediate admission." In bold letters under the doctors comments. There was no hesitation. Pete stood by mom side as he always said he would. "You're going to have to..... You know what? We are going to have to quit smoking Catherine I can't afford to lose you. Your son will fucking kill me." Pete was right he loved mom. Therefore to let anything happen to mom would kill him inside. He promised to be there for her to Rock. "I'm... Okay" mom said in between breaths. "I know baby but we are going to try our hardest to ensure that you will always be okay." Pete's words struck mom's heart. "We'll be taking her down for x-rays and running a few test on her. You are more than welcome to join us or you can wait here for her." The nurse said in her professional soft tone. Mom held Pete's hand. "I'll go with her." Pete answered. "Okay right this way." Pete never did enjoy the smell of hospitals, he once told me that the air smelled like death. I laugh but in a way it had some truth behind his words. They say the average person dies every 3.2 seconds in the country. Now if you think about it those odds can be stacked up against you.

—

Joel hugged his girl after he had come over for some love. "Babe what you doing tomorrow night?" Joel asked. "Nothing yet, why babe?" Linda asked. I wanted to do something new for us tomorrow if you are free." Joel missed his girl even though Linda love him so much. With all that she was trying to accomplish, plus keep her relationship intact wasn't an easy task she admitted. "Oh yeah baby and why something special huh? Linda asked curious. "I think you deserve something special and it's been some time since we actually spent a romantic night out with one another. "Joel admitted to Linda. "Yeah you're right baby and I think that's a good idea, set it up." Linda got up and began to get dressed. "Where you going?" Joel asked. "Home." Linda said. "Why don't you stay here tonight?" Joel asked with a confused look on his face. "Because you young man have to go to work early in the morning and I have to go to work as well." Linda said. "Okay I'll get up early and take you home." Joel suggested. "That's why baby, I don't want you to wake up extra early. Its bad enough I'm losing sleep at night tossing and turning. I don't want to get up early?" Linda was making up excuses. So she could go meet up with Jacqueline. "I'll take you home right now then." Joel suggested. "No that's okay pass me the phone." Linda asked Joel. "Dialing the Gonzales Service. She asked for the next available cab. "Five minutes." Okay thank you" Linda repeated. "You have to get your rest as much as I do. It doesn't make any sense you driving all the way to my house just to drive me back killing more time. I'll be okay I know you hate when I take the cab service but I got my..." Linda whipped our butterfly showing him how she makes it float. "Watch out kill girl don't hurt nobody." Joel joked but being serious as fuck. "The look in her eyes along with a grin on her face made Joel question her intentions. He decided not to. Linda jumped on the bed fully dressed and snuggled up with her man. "Are you sure you're okay Linda?" Joel questioned. "Yeah baby I just can't wait till I get my car." Linda said. "Yeah and when you do I'll be here to help you out." Joel replied. "Speaking of car I have a car that I want to buy can you help me get it?" Linda asked. "Of course baby where it is and how much does it cost?" Joel asked. "Well I got the money but I need to put it under your name." Linda asked. "Okay so where is it?" Joel asked. "In my backyard." Linda answered. "You mean your brother's truck?" Joel asked shocked already knowing the deal. "That's the car." Linda warmly snug under her man's arm. "But what about your mom?" Joel asked already knowing what Linda's mom had said. "I'll handle her but can you do that for me baby?" Linda pouted. "Of course, but I don't need your mom hate me." Joel enjoyed the fact that Linda's mom loved him and didn't need her to begin to dislike him. A few quiet moments pass by when the blaring of the horn startled the two of them. "Baby." Joel shook Linda. "The cab is here." Joel informed. "Love you" Linda said giving her man a reassuring kiss goodbye. "Love you too and be careful." Joel didn't even get up off the bed he was already worn out.

Getting dropped off a few blocks away from her man's house. Linda couldn't believe she was led into leaving her man, to sexually satisfy another woman's needs. In a way she felt guilty. At the same time she was helping Jacqueline from cheating on her brother. She was thinking irrationally to a much higher degree. She didn't feel all that bad though, even though Rock and Linda both had sexual relations with Jacqueline. Linda was the only one bouncing all around trying to please everyone but herself. "Ding, ding!" The doorbell rang. All the lights were off Linda cursed herself out if this bitch wouldn't answer the door. " Ding,ding!" The cab driver already sped off and the next payphone was almost a block away. The clicking of the door brought a relief to Linda knowing that Jacqueline was there. "I thought you wasn't coming." Jacqueline slid over to allow Linda to answer. "I wasn't." Linda said. "So why did you?" Jacqueline asked. "I don't know." The hall was dark. "Give me your hand." Jacqueline reached for Linda's hand as she led her all the way up to her room. "Where is the baby?" Linda asked. "Sleeping." Jacqueline answered. "I want to shower." Linda stated not having the chance to shower at Joel's. How would that have looked if she had decided to jump in the shower after having sex with him? "Come on" Jacqueline whispered. Following Jacqueline's panty wearing ass. Her tank top showed no trace of a bra being worn. Linda was turned on a bit. Her bouncy ass was stared at her from behind all the way till they got to the bathroom.

Jacqueline turned on the water until it was hot and steamy. The steam in the bathroom got thicker, Jacqueline decided to steal a kiss from Linda.

"Jasmine are you ready." Jacqueline asked backing away to get a good look of Linda's face. Linda took off her shirt with the help of Jacqueline. The cool air cause her nipples to get hard immediately. Jacqueline stared which made Linda feel a bit uncomfortable. "What?" Linda asked "Nothing" Jacqueline answered. I'm just admiring your pretty body. Jacqueline took off her shirt exposing her already naked breast. Jacqueline's breast were nice despite having a son who was breast fed. Linda's breast had nowhere near a stretch mark nor did they even sag not one bit, unlike Jacqueline's which sagged ever so slightly. The still weren't a bad sight to look at. Jacqueline unbuttoned Linda's jeans and helped her slip off of them. Her beautiful body was fully exposed. Her soft smooth thighs look so tasteful. Removing her own booty shorts they embraced for a second, touching one another softly enjoying the moment. Jacqueline's hands moved closer towards Linda's love box. Linda stopped her dead in her tracks and turned to jump in the water. The water was perfect. Just how Linda enjoyed it hot, Linda smiled. "Come on." She pulled on Jacqueline's hand. The two played with the water kissing and caressing each other's bodies, biting on each other's nipples and exploring ever inch of there body. Linda bit her bottom lip enjoying how rough Jacqueline was but gentle at the same time . Her touch couldn't compare to any others touch, Linda let her hands roam all over Linda's body. She enjoyed this a little too much to be a straight female. I guess after the second episode she fell into the bisexual category huh? They both washed up thoroughly helping one another. No words were spoken to each other. They simply allowed their hands and body movements do all of the talking. They nearly spent almost 45 minutes in the water until the water began to come out a little colder. Thats when they finally decided to jump out of the tub. Not even bothering to put on any clothing, their anticipation couldn't wait till they got to the room.

Jacqueline took advantage that Linda was sitting on the toilet seat dropped down to her knees and stuffed her face in between Linda's thighs.

"Oh my God girl right here?" Linda was caught off guard but as soon as Jacqueline tongue pierced against Linda swollen lips, her words fell on deaf ears. "Oooohhhh!" Linda let out a soft moan. Jacqueline took that as she was hitting the right spot. Not stopping or slowing down Linda had her legs up in the air now, leaning back on the toilet seat. She used it to hold her balance, her thighs began to tremble as Jacqueline ate her love box like a pro. She had to admit Joel couldn't compete with Jacqueline by a longshot. Linda's free hand buried Jacqueline's face into her love box. She was moaning and leaking all her juices all in her mouth. Jacqueline was enjoying all of it. Linda's juices were sweet and tasteful to her. "Let's go to the bedroom." Linda suggested "Oh yeah?" Jacqueline wanted to please her already. She didn't object to the request at all. They walked expeditiously towards the bedroom, where it was all ready for excitement. Linda was behind Jacqueline. Once she was close to the bed Linda pushed Jacqueline onto the bed. "Damn so rough." Jacqueline says smiling adjusting herself on the bed. It was Linda's turn to work her magic on Jacqueline. "Wait." Jacqueline reach under her bed pulling out the box of toys the girls had that night at the sleepover. Linda reached in the box and grabbed the dildo. Jacqueline laid back and pulled Linda up to her. She kiss Linda on her neck and bit her. "No hickies." She got serious using her pointer finger. "Okay sorry, I got you." Jacqueline kissed Linda's warm body. She caressed hers as Linda laid on top of her. Linda kissed and licked her breast tasting a bit of breast milk. Her face scrunched up. The tarp taste caught her by surprise but she kept mining towards her mark. She hit Jacqueline's waistline. Jacqueline let out a light moan. Linda wasn't good or even use to this. Linda knew what she liked to be done to herself. She used what she like to be done to her on Jacqueline, She nibbled inside on Jacqueline's inner thighs. This drove Jacqueline wild. "Whoa baby, I like that Jasmine." She let out. Linda looked at Jacqueline's pretty pussy, her lips were tucked away neatly and her click peaked out getting erected slowly. Linda flicked her tongue on her click causing Jacqueline to flinch. "Got it." Linda says softly. "Yes you do." Jacqueline replied. It wasn't hard for Linda to stimulate Jacqueline. Her back was arched and the dildo wasn't even inside of her yet. Jacqueline ran her hands over her breast. Her hands ended on the back of Linda's head. The closer she got to climax and the harder she forced Linda's head on her clit. It was as though Jacqueline wanted Linda to literally put her whole head inside of her. "Right there baby! Right there don't stop!" Linda licked and sucked on Jacqueline's pussy lips while massaging her clit with her wet fingers. "Yes! Yes!" I'm Cumming!!" Jacqueline came hard, her legs trembled as she reached her climax. Linda spit on the toy lubercating it while she was massaging Jacqueline clitoris. She was going for her second. "Ooooo mmmyyyyy gooooddddd Jazmmin....!" She didn't even get Jasmine's full name out when Linda rammed the dildo on high vibration up inside Jacqueline. "FUCK YEAAAA!!!! FUCK YEA! FUCK ME HARD JAZMINEE! Oooohhhh! She scream so loud that Linda doubted that her son was still sleeping through all of this. "You're the best, you're the best! Linda was wet as hell. She played with her pussy as she was smashing the dildo in and out of her love box. Linda wasn't doing it out of pleasure now, her face wore that malicious stare she had been wearing a lot lately. She was trying to hurt Jacqueline but it wasn't working. This is exactly how Rock used to fuck his woman when they wanted it like this. This was only making Jacqueline believe that Rock was pounding in her tiny love box. The juices leaked all over the bed. The sheets looked as if she had pissed the bed. "No more please, no more." I want you now baby!" Jacqueline wanted to give Linda the same pleasure she had just received from Linda. Linda slowed down. The beads of sweat were running down Linda's four head. It was a site that was worth capturing with a few pictures. Jacqueline jumped on Linda. She grabbed the sex balls and lubed those up good. Linda was spread eagle on Jacqueline bed. She was all in. Linda played with herself. "Damn you sexy!" Jacqueline said licking her lips. Just relax and enjoy all of this okay." Jacqueline said. Linda's head tilted back as her finger popped herself. Jacqueline also grab the bullet and turned it on. The humming was low but powerful Linda could hear it. It sounded like a hummingbird in her imagination.

She almost hit the ceiling when the vibrator touched her love button. "Whooaa!"Relax." Jacqueline instructed. "Just lay back and enjoy the feeling, let it take you wherever it wants too." Jacqueline instructed. Linda took a deep breath. Her heart rate was racing trying to catch up to the vibrations of the sex toy. It was a game of tag and Linda was it. "Oooohhhh! Yea!" The chase has begun and my money was that Linda wasn't going to catch up. "Yes!" Jacqueline had Linda's left leg on her shoulder and the other on the opposite shoulder. Linda couldn't go anywhere. She slid the small vibrator in and out of Linda's walls slowly. This sent chills all over Linda's body. Jacqueline kissed and licked around Linda's thighs. Her goal was to get Linda so wet and horny enough to slide the sex balls all up in her ass. All while fucking her pussy so hard.... Little did she know Linda wasn't ready for all that yet? Linda rocked and pinched her nipples. She tried hard to hold in her cries of fulfillment.

"Oh shit! Oh shit! Linda cried. "What is it baby?" Jacqueline asked. Linda's pretty shaved pussy was smooth. It was something to enjoy looking at, let alone to taste it. Jacqueline put down Linda's legs and began to suck on her fully erect clit that was screaming for attention. She tried to swallow it whole, instead she woke up the moans that Linda couldn't hold it in anymore. "That's it Jasmine, let me hear you." Jacqueline gave her the green light. "OH YESSS! I love this shit don't stop baby please don't stop! "AAAYY!" Linda began to moan as the vibrator began to swish as it went in and out of her wet pussy. Jacqueline was ready to shove the first sex ball in Linda's ass. "Relax baby please".... "I am" Linda replied taking deep breaths. As soon as Linda went to take her first deep breath Jacqueline began to eat her ass out too. "What the fuck!" That's nasty! Linda said but became quiet because Jacqueline didn't stop. Jacqueline took it as she enjoyed it very much. She wasn't complaining at all. Licking ass and pussy fucking was what the girls wanted and this is what they did tonight. The first ball went in but had to be removed immediately "OH NO, NO! Sorry but we not going in there baby girl." Linda wasn't comfortable with that yet. The night ended on that note but not on any type of anger or animosity both fell asleep drained and fully satisfied. Two beautifuly naked women laid side by side all over one another. The toys were all over the bed. What a night, what good could come out of all of this?

—

Mom and Pete were both in the hospital room. Mom was asleep and Pete was nodding in and out of his sleep. It was close to 3 AM and the tests results had not been concluded yet. What they both were waiting for, was what everyone was scared to know. They had to inject mom with some steroids to get her stable and breathing normally again. Her lungs couldn't keep up with how much air was being needed for her body to function properly. Pete prayed to his higher power. I wonder if he actually thought if anyone was listening? That didn't matter I guess. Who am I to deter someone's belief in any way? I remember like it was yesterday when they recounted this to me in the visiting room. After about another hour and a half. The doctor came in with a blank look on his face. He shook Pete's hand.

"Is she awake?" The doctor asked, "No I'm sorry, she isn't." Pete apologize like it was his fault. "No need to apologize. If she is asleep she can't smoke right?" Not sure if he was being a dick or what. The doctor was sending a clear message though. "When she wakes up you can call me or you can tell her yourself." Said the elder doctor with the grays in his head. "Tell her what doctor? Is she going to be okay?" Pete had this sad and depressed look on his face. The doctor inhaled deeply. "Ima be straight up with you. You are her husband right?" The doctor asked. "Yes I am." Pete assured him. "Okay it's like this. Ms. Catherine had stage 1 cancer almost a year ago if I'm not mistaken. This is what her file says. Today, I just so happen to look at her situation and it has gotten a lot worse. He let it all now. If your wife doesn't quit smoking those cigarette soon.The doctor stared right in Pete's eyes. I'm sorry to be the one to tell you this but I don't see her making it to see the next year this time." The doctor stared at Pete waiting for Pete's reaction. Pete felt his heart break. "Do you smoke?" The doctor asked Pete. "Yes I do." Pete answered honestly. "Well if you love this woman I would request that the two of you quit together. So that neither of you will lose each other in the long run. I'm just giving you a professional opinion." The doctor knew exactly what he was suggestion. The question was did Pete understand completely what he was saying? Pete rubbed his head profusely not wanting to believe what his ears just heard. "I'm not saying that she will die tomorrow because that's not the case but you two need to come up with a very serious decision, and a fast one." The doctor explained. "Like I said is up to you to relate this message to your wife or I'll do my best to tell her when she gets up." The doctor was going to have to because Pete couldn't find it in his heart to tell his wife the bad news. "I'll call you when she is awake doctor. Thank you so much." Pete said. "No problem I'll see you soon." Pete grabbed mom's hand. "Baby we gota stop smoking. I can't lose you to a fucking cigarette." Pete's voice was cracking. "I won't lose you baby." Mom was up. Pete was shell-shocked. "Did you hear?" Pete asked. "Yes I did baby and I don't want to die yet, not without holding my son again." Mom was already making plans. "Good. This is very serious babe. Why didn't you tell me that this was more serious than you have explained to me?" Pete asked. "I didn't think we would actually get this far. I'm so sorry baby." Mom apologized. "It's okay I'm here for you baby but you have to want it to work or it won't." Pete assured mom.

Chapter 18

"Don't touch!"

Linda managed to talk Joel into putting Rock's truck under his name. Mom made him swear that Linda was not to be inside of the truck no matter what! Joel was hesitant because he knew that the truck was going to end up in her hands. I took it mom was just covering her ass, so when the news broke out no one could come at mom for allowing any of this to occur. Linda had a friend who went to the same school as she did. Her friend's father owned a body shop. She had spoken to him in advance about holding down the truck, until she was ready to get it out of the shop. Being that this "classmate" had a bit of attraction towards Linda. He talked to his father into helping him help Linda. Linda was specifically told to not drive or be seen in Rock's truck. These were orders that she was blatantly disobeying without any concern for her well-being. Linda was dancing with fire and she had no knowledge that Street was doing his homework on Linda and confirming his suspicion. He played it off as if everything was cool when they would hooked up. Nothing would change he would play clueless and just make sure that he kept his eyes on her just in case. He felt no imminent threat. He enjoyed this and was going to continue having Linda around as much as he could.

Streets and Linda was supposed to meet up for a Christmas show. A show that was being held at the Staples Center a few days before Christmas. They continued to meet up at the designated spot at the 7/11 on Federal St. Linda was cold, the flurries kissed her face ever so lightly.

"Where the hell is he?" Linda asked herself shivering. She decided to enter the store and wait the temperature always dropped towards the evening. "Hey little lady." The dot head said. He was noticing Linda more. She would always came in waiting for Streets. "Hello how are you?" Linda made small talk. "I'm okay and ju" The clerk asked. "I'm fine waiting for my friend." Linda admitted. She decided to grab a hot cocoa. It was nothing like moms but it would do.

Ever since mom's last episode. Linda tried her best to accommodate mom with all that needed to be done. Espercially when it came to taking care of our home. Joel asked Linda if she would consider moving in with him in his new apartment, over by Creamer Hill. Linda rejected the offer. Not because she didn't want to be in a defined relationship or because she didn't love Joel. Linda's plate already had, close to no more room to occupy another type of entrée on it. She had even portions and moving in with Joel would throw off all the rations on her plate. This couldn't be done at the moment. Joel didn't understand why Linda didn't want to make the move. After a brief and sincere explanation Linda gave him, he clearly understood. Instead of being judgmental or even jealous that everyone else occupied Linda's time. He offered a lending hand with everything that Linda needed from him. Linda grew more attached to Joel. "Are you ready for Christmas?" Asked the clerk. Linda was over by the cocoa machine pouring herself a medium size cup. "Not really." Linda answered. "Oh no?" The clerk asked surprised. "It's in a couple of days isn't it?" The clerk asked. Linda walked up. "Yes it is and it's not the same this year. There is a missing part to all of this." Linda spoke sadly referring to the absence of Rock. "I'm very very sorry to hear such things." The clerk said trying to brighten her up. "You know what my little friend? This cup is on me." The clerk brought a smile to Linda's face. It wasn't the $1.50 that brought her joy but on how thoughtful this man was to her. "Awe thank you." Linda was very grateful of this gesture. "Merry Christmas." The clerk said. "You two." was Linda's reply. The loud horn caused Linda to look past the entering customers and noticed Streets pulling up. "There he goes, be careful with that man and drive safely." The clerk advised. "We will and have a good night." Linda exited the store with her cup of hot cocoa. Streets observed Linda as she walked up to his car. Her hips swayed from side to side. He still couldn't wait to shove his dick all up inside of her either by choice or by force. Either was this was going to happen, there was no stopping him. The aroma of the loud hit Linda right in her face as soon as she opened the door.

"Damn party started without me." Linda joked. Sitting in the passenger seat. "Nah baby girl never that." Streets pulled off, his car slid as he accelerated his car. "Whoa" Linda grabbed onto Street's right arm with her left. "Scared?" Streets looked at her. "Don't be I got you Janet." Streets passed the L over to Linda. "These roads need to be salted." Linda said while hitting the

L. "Yeah you would think they would but being a poor city this is how we get treated." Street spoke. Watch when we cross out of the city lines and just see the difference in the roads. White people take care the own real well." Street had a point, as soon as they hit the outskirts of Camden. The blacktop couldn't be missed with how clean and clear the snow was quickly removed off of it and maintained. It was a shame. You can't expect the unexpected, when it has always been accepted this way. "So when are you going to finally let me know where you live at? So I don't have to keep picking you up at the store?" Streets was high and he wanted to get some answers from Linda. He didn't want her to become suspicious of his questions. His mind wanted to know who exactly Linda was, and what was she up to? "My peoples don't like it when I bring people over. It's best for me to try and keep my business to myself. I'm saving up some money to get my own place soon, I'm hoping." Linda lied. "That's Wassup ma." Streets like what he was hearing. If he could help her find a place. Then he could use her house to kill her once he had all the information that he needed to cure all his curiosities. "Anywhere in particular?" Streets asked. "I don't know yet, but anywhere really. As long as I'm in my own place, then maybe one day I'll let you come over and pick me up from there." Linda tried to sound convincing. "Yeah that'll be nice. You'll be freezing out here waiting for me to come through." Streets explained watching the road attentively. "I'm good is not a problem. I'm sorry I know it don't look right with you picking me up at the store, but like I said soon you won't have to." Linda reiterated. "So you don't have any other family out here?" Streets asked. Linda wasn't liking all the questioning. She knew that she had to be quick with her responses. "Out here in Camden no, but I do have an aunt and uncle that live in New York. They moved away when I was younger, they got tired of all the bullshit out here." Linda lied some more. "Yeah it can get real tiresome with all the shit that goes on out here." Streets agreed. "I've been out here for years and I must admit I love my city but it does get to be too much sometimes." Street said. "Well look at what you do, you're constantly involved in all this madness right?" Linda asked. "Damn that's what you see when you are with me?" Streets was offended. "Not like that." Linda slapped his thigh. "I mean you see it a lot more because of your occupation." Linda tried to clean up her last words. Streets listened. "I like how you switched it up, but yeah you're right. I am more involved with the bullshit and at times it's rough, but it's a business that I'm running. I have kids to feed and bills to pay just like every other mother fucker out here you know?" Streets asked looking at Linda. He couldn't find the connection in her eyes but he knew he had to tread lightly. So have you ever been in any type of trouble?" Streets was bombarding her with questions. "I mean I've gotten in some trouble with my parents for not listening, but as far as anything serious. Never. I always tried to stay away from all that bad stuff." Linda was definitely player her position to the tee. "So you mean you never got suspended from school or never gotten into fights?" Streets was probing. "Fight?" Why would I want to ruin these pretty nails?" Linda displayed her beautiful manicured hands joking. Streets had no choice but to laugh. He pulled into a parking spot at the Staples Center. They made great timing. Linda wasn't feeling all this interrogation and knew that she was running at a time. Streets lift up the arm rest that served as a barrier in between the two of them. The low reggaeton played as Streets got closer to Linda. She couldn't keep playing him any longer she assumed that he would only keep getting closer to her as time would go by. Linda wasn't feeling this but how long could she keep duçking this nigga kisses? Linda already made it a point that she was far from a fast chick. How much more could she hold this up? Streets hand touched the side of Linda's face. "You know you are very pretty?" Streets asked, but more or so stating it. Linda cringed inside, she forced a smile outside though. She blushed. "Thank you.You're not too bad looking yourself?" Linda stated. I know you don't want to rush anything but I've been dying to taste those beautiful juicy lips of yours." Streets was leaning in. Linda wanted to slap all fire out of Streets face, but instead she kissed him. She held herself with the thought of him being a sloppy kiss her but the moistness down her pants served her otherwise. She was actually lip locking was Streets. This was Jacqueline's baby dad. Her mind floated as her hands felt on Street's chest. They eventually made their way to the back of his neck. Streets didn't cross any more lines that he knew wouldn't be accepted. He let his tongue work do all the magic. Linda was enjoying this a little too much when she realized what the fuck she was doing.

"Oh my God!" What am I doing?" Linda shot embarrassed from her actions. "I'm so sorry Janet it's all my fault I didn't mean too." Streets tried to take the blame for what just occurred. The snow had picked up and covered the front windshield with a light visible layer. "No it's not your fault Streets it's that I like you but I can't right now I..." he put his finger on Linda's lips. "Sshhhhhh you don't have to explain anything this is what you want and feel Janet." Streets was moving just as he wanted because he removed his finger and was planning another welcoming kiss on Linda. With a few moans and scratches on his neck. Streets slipped his hand under Linda's shirt cuffing her right breast that felt so soft and firm. Her nipples were harder than a Jolly rancher he pinched it and Linda moaned and bit his bottom lip. "Ugh! Streets complained, but was loving the roughness. She pulled away and pushed his hand from under her shirt. Both of their lips were swollen. The blood was surely flowing up and down on both sides. "Let's go, I'm not ready for this." Linda opened the door. Streets was on her. "Hold up ma. /perdona me." /forgive me/ Streets asked for her forgiveness. Linda had this horny nigga right where she wanted him. Streets put his arm around her and they both walked in the show.

—

Listen Rock, I had a meeting with my boys and they are waiting for me to give them the word. In the next day or two they are going to let them two mother fuckers out the hole and I'm not going to let this issue slide." Slash wanted to prove his loyalty on a daily basis. "What you think?" Rock asked Bigs who was back in our cell within weeks of the incident. "Look they didn't get anything from us, yea I got beat up but they didn't kill me. So I say we just let it go." Bigs was always on some peace and love type shit. I respected that to a certain extent. "Man fuck that shit! We going to fuck them up and you're going to get your fucking hands dirty too Bigs." Leak wasn't trying to hear any of this soft shit right now. "I've been telling him to calm down lately. With all the shit he's been saying ever since them tried to hit our spot. "I'm not fucking anybody up I want to get the fuck out of here to my family." Bigs was bitching up. "I wasn't asking Bigs." Leak said. "If you want to leave from the cell remember your word you gave us. As a matter fact we all gave our word to have each other's back didn't we!?" Leak barked. "Yea.... But" Bigs answered. "But nothing!" We are going to make these two mother fuckers wish they were locked up in another county jail. You can put you money on that! So you either a part of the solution or become a part of the problem up in this mother fucker!" Leak was beyond mad his veins on his neck and arms were all getting thicker and thicker with every emphasis of his words. "Ayo Leak we got this." Rock said. "If he don't want to participate he can be a lookout or whatever.

The man ain't no killer and no fighter." Rock said. Leak was pacing. He had Bigs and Slash both watching him closely. Leak could be very unpredictable at times. He was gun powder looking for a spark by any means. That wasn't a good combination. "All I'm saying is that I am beginning to lose trust in this nigga!" Leak pointed his finger at Bigs. "And if he going to be up in here with us with all this dirt that is being done. He needs to get on board and prove his loyalty or get the fuck out. I don't mean on your own 2 feet either. He got too much dirt on all of us to leave as if nothing is going on. Fuck that I read this story before and it don't end well." Leak was wrong but absolutely right at the same time. I examined Bigs. His facial frustration was very noticeable. He was type scared. I looked at Slash and his face showed determination. Leak's face wore pure evil and you could tell that this had to be resolved and it would.

With business still going on, the cash flowed in at an alarming rate. We had a few guys who couldn't pay on time with the credit but eventually they pay once the interest kept rising. I was not holding back with any of these niggaz.

"Listen Ima be a week late because the money didn't get through yet." Old head papi admitted to Slash for the last two weeks. "Look that's all we expect from you is to tell us what's going on don't leave any of us in the dark. Ima talk to my man and most likely he going to tell me to tell you that he understands but the meter will rise a little. Slash already knew what our model was. We had a formula and it was working like a charm. "Make money off the money already owed." The tickets were pure gold. It seemed like no matter how many times people lost. They always thought they could cover the spread on the next one. Those points was something not to fuck with if you didn't know your shit. I never enjoyed but could care less how much money they lost. It was clear that our tickets couldn't be fucked with. It got so bad that we labeled them. "Got Cha!" Because it was becoming a war with the tickets and the gamblers. We had out days when we would get cracked. "Shorty" cracked us in the head twice. He was the only one that really knew his sports. We couldn't argue with him. Shorty was from South Camden and he had 12 brothers and sisters he was the oldest but was the shortest at 5'2". He had to weigh almost 140 pounds soaking wet. He was cut the fuck up and just because he was short he took no shit from anyone. I loved that about him.

"Ayo Rock was up? What you got for me?" Shorty made his way over to our cell. "Man nothing if you going to keep trying to clean me out. You one ticket from getting band." I joked with him. "Who on?" Rock asked inquiring about the CO on duty. "Asshole." I already know who that was. "That mother fucker always on duty. He had no life a real." Rock slandered the CO's character. "Man, than they wonder why their wives be cheating on them. They are never home to take care that pussy." Shorty joked. "They not ready right now." Rock said amongst the laughter going on inside the cell. "I'll come see you as soon as they come fresh off the press bro." Rock informed. "All right, I'm out." Shorty disappeared just as fast as he showed up. "That little mother fucker is funny as shit." Slash said. "I know, I fuck with him." Slash said. "He down for a minute." Slash said. "Yeah?" Leak asked in shock. Yea over some broad." Slash informed. "Damn I don't know how they do that shit. I mean, I love my women but to lose my life over a chick? Nah not me fuck that." Leak spoke. Only two I'd go out for, would be my mom and my sister. I could care less about my baby moms or any other bitch that aint close to me like those two. I know it sounds fucked up but I learned that these two are the closest to my heart. So that's what I truly believe." Rock opinionated. "I agree." Bigs said. We all looked at Bigs. "Fuck with my mom and sister, I'm on that ass too." Bigs Agreed. It felt weird hearing that from Bigs but for some reason we all felt he was dead serious. "For one to fend for others may not be a priority but to fend for your own. Your whole mindset would go into another dimension and make you act out in ways you would never imagine. Now if the people weren't as close. One wouldn't even consider a thought as such. You know what I am saying." Leak said. We all nodded our heads understanding what he was saying. To kill another person wasn't on anyone's to do list. To be straight up I was due for a fight just to keep my tools sharp. For someone to catch a body would only happen if it was a life and death situation.

"A yo what's the count on everything in the cell?" Rock asked Bigs. He pulled out his sheet that had all the money coming in and all the money that was out. He went over it. "In the house we are over $250 in food. That's not adding what's owed, which is roughly $150 in food. That's only food from the store. The work that is out is over $600 which is broken down and 50's and 30's. Keep in mind we are at about a stack altogether." Leak whispered. "Wow I didn't even think it was that much out there." Leak was shocked at those numbers. "How much in work Leak?" Rock asked. Shit, close to 700 with both the soft and bud." Leak shot at me. "We going to move some of this shit." Rock finally saw what they were trying to tell him a while ago. "Now you thinking Rock." Leak said with a smile. "Smart move." It's the only way to keep rising without actually drawing a lot attention." Leak said. "Yeah but who and where?" That's in your hands. I don't want to be responsible for anything that happens with all that crap." Slash suggested. "I have to agree with Slash on that one." Leak agreed. "What you think big boy?" Rock looked at Bigs with his wife beater hugging his body. I think you should keep it close, so you can keep our eye on it. Sorry I don't know anyone up in here to vouch for." Bigs opinionated. Rock like how the three men were thinking. It was a sticky situation to get involved in so they knew better than to drag themselves into a mess that couldn't be cleaned up if he got out of hand. "Ima talk to a few people on the block and see what they're talking about." Rock stated. The day went by as it always did, there was always some type of controversy going on in this place. Avoiding it was the most challenging part. There was work to be sold and money to be made. The kids and families could always be seen outside on any given day. The hand signs could be seen as families and loved ones spoke to one another. The sacrifices some of us constantly overlook unintentionally. Our loved ones truly cared. Here it is we are warm and cozy in our cells staring out a thick glass window out to the street. Down below you could see the women, children and families all bundled up. They wore there scarfs, skullies, coats, gloves and snow boots. All this was for who? For the ones sitting up in jail cell. The love was real and in most cases unconditional. For what though? It was done to put a smile on our faces. The people who hurt them the most in most cases. The did it so that we knew, that there were people who cared about us. Even when we thought the world has forgotten about us. I sometimes wondered, if we would do all that our family did for us? Would we if it was the other way around? It's easy to want when it is a time in need isn't it? But to give when one isn't in that hazy situation, these are the real and loyal test. This separates the real from the selfish individuals. This is what I use to keep me grounded when my mind begins to get clouded.

"Yo look at the snowman it looks so small from here." Slash said wiping the window. Leak was the first one to shoot over towards the window beside Slash. I couldn't see over there two big heads, they were all up in the way. So

I just waited patiently until I could finally see. I'm was sure they were thinking of their kids and how they were missing out on quality time with them. Can't cry over spilled milk though right?

"I can't see with these big ass melons in my way." I joked. I know your pen shaped head isn't talking with those small ass ears." Slash shot back at me. ""Ooooo" Bigs tried to hype up the situation laying on his bed eaten a Snickers."Oh so you want to instigate? Sounded like a fucking cow given birth.... Fat ass!"...."ooooo" Rock came at Bigs. Leak was Balling. "Your black ass got some nerve with your hot ass breath fogging up the window more than it already is." Rock was coming at everyone now. Leak stepped away. I took the window and looked out, but the reflection from the window behind me alerted me of what was about to happen and it was too late. Bigs, Slash and Leak all jump on me. Bigs was sitting on my back while Leak and Slash beat me up hitting all my exposed body parts. "Mother fuckers." I snarled at them. They weren't soft blows either. "I'm a get y'all, you know you're not going to keep me down here forever." Bigs fat ass was heavy. I couldn't even get a good deep breath in. I swung as much as I could, this was effortless thought they had me. I was pinned down and I was getting a beaten by my celly's out of pure love. I must admit I wasn't used to playing much. The last time I played like this had to be almost 8 years ago. I was in school and this was a past time that we used to do. "So you gangsta huh?" Leak was punching me but not for real. Slash had my shoulders and arms. I was useless and with Bigs fat ass on me. I became almost powerless. I admitted defeat. "All right you got me I can't do shit." Rock admitted "Oh hell no!" Leak wasn't trying to hear it. We not fucking quitters up in here, that's what we do now? Huh Rock we quit?" He kept on with the blows on my thighs. They were numb. I couldn't feel them but I was getting mad at what he was saying. Those words and those punches were a hell of a combination that made me dig deep for some strength. "Yeah you a quitter all that tough Tony shit and now you're tapping out." Slash was also feeding into what Leak was doing. I was done playing now. Bigs let all his fat ass weight dropped on my lower chest which gave me an advantage, he was relaxing. He was my way up, staying down on this concrete floor was not an option. I concentrated and controlled my breathing. I waited for my chance. I counted Leaks blows which was 4 to 6. Then he would talk a bunch of shit. "Sup nigga you gave up let me hear you say you give up and I will let you up." Leak said. He exactly as I expected right on Q. Slash would hit me twice and back away. I was for certain that Slash was enjoying this. Exploding in one rush I managed to knock Bigs fat ass off balance. Thanks to him it wasn't hard at all. "Oh shit!" Bigs barked almost hitting the bed. I did a quick burpee and sprang to my feet and just began to throw haymakers at Leak. He was the biggest out of all of us. I controlled my breathing and blocked almost all of his punches that he threw at me. None of my blows were thrown with fury. I knew we were all just joking around. I jumped over to Slash and he just balled up near the door trying to block all my punches. His obliques were wide open. I went to town on them. I noticed Bigs trying to get up and a swift kick to the back of his knees put him right back down. Leak was cracking up, he had his hands up.

"I'm good youngin you got too much energy for me. Yea you got that!" Leak joked. My heart was pumping rapidly. I could feel it through my shirt. It felt good to play around and let go of some of that seriousness. Where we found ourselves there wasn't much time for horseplay. "Come on! Now you want to quit right?" I was hyped as fuck now. "Nah, it ain't going down like that y'all better step up or Ima get at yall on my own." Rock was enjoying every second of this now. "Slash, get up tough guy." Rock barked. Slash darted to him tackle him. "Yeah! That's what the fuck I'm talking about." Rock was still talking shit. Slash had him pinned to the ground. Rock found some wiggle room and grabbed Slash's left arm and pulled it over to Rock's left and managed to somehow flip him over. "Bang." The sound of Slash's elbow hit the side of the bedpost. "Fuck!" Slash yelled not giving up for one second. Slash was pretty strong. They both tussled for a few more seconds until Slash put Rock in an arm bar. "Ughhhh!" Rock grunted as the pain shot right up his arm. They both were on the floor but Slash had Rock. "Tap out!" Leak suggested. "Fuck you!" They both were sweating. Rock could box his ass off, but proven at the moment he wasn't much of a wrestler. "Ughhhh!" Rock grunted louder. "You better tap out!" A voice from the door yelled. Leak looked over and noticed a CO peaking in. Normally if this was on the block and they would see this type of horseplay, the bucket would be our next move. "Tap out!" Slash tried to compromise. Tapping out was giving up and giving up was something that Rock couldn't do. He would rather let Slash break his arm then to admit defeat. It wasn't part of Rock's repertoire nor would he even start to show any signs of it. Rock tried to control his breathing. The guard was still watching at the door. This was just as good as watching to pitbulls go at it for money and if you're from Puerto Rico a cockfight match. It was a live match in a small fucking cell. It was our cell there was nothing anyone could say to any of us, as long as no one was killing the other. "Ayo Rock just tap." Bigs fat ass said curled up in his bed watching and feeling the pain. "Yeah just tap Rock." Slash said. Rock felt him loosen up this was where he made his mistake. He had the chance to break it or to squeeze it tighter. He was too busy trying to show off his control. Rock flipped his whole body in the direction Slash was holding him which only gave him the same two choices break it or let it go he did exactly what he had planned out in his mind. Rock reverse the hold and put Slash in a headlock. "Oh shit!" The CO at the door yelled. "Never tap out!" Rock barked. "Tap!" he was smacking my forearm gasping for air. I let him go. "Damn my nigga that was a nice reversal." Slash said as the sweat dripped off his four head. "Come on Leak, I'm not done." Rock wasn't done "Chill Manual." Leak said looking in the mirror. "Yall jump on me remember? One on one every one of you till I can't go no more." Rock challenge. Leak didn't budge. "Rock fall back please my nigga." Leak spoke seriously. Rock fell back he knew that he wasn't your average bear so he decided to leave it at that. Sometimes moods could be felt without many words being spoken. Especially if it was real. It's amazing how our body's intuition has the capability to detect these things instantly. Leak felt how real it had gotten between Slash and myself. Knowingly he probably didn't know how to keep a situation in a joking manner and possibly break my arm or neck by accident. "Good because I don't feel like dying tonight anyway." Rock joke. It was time to go eat.....

—

It's been some time now that mom and Pete have been keeping their word on keeping their lips off a burning cigarette. It wasn't an easy task but no one ever said it would be. "Baby I'm going to put together a meal for us to eat, is there anything in particular you want?" Mom asked heading towards the front of the shop to whip something up. "Anything is just fine babe but no hot peppers please." Pete informed mom. He stayed in his office punching in numbers into his calculator. Pete had no one to help him with any of his accounts. He learned through so many mistakes, and has taken so many losses dealing with the IRS. It wasn't easy filling out your own taxes. Till this day he can honestly say that he finally mastered it. Pete would've been better off paying to attend a seminar to cut his losses but at the end of the day he finally perfected his own craft. His profits were all positive at this point in his career. Pete had money and he damn sure didn't display any sign of his success. Anyone in their right mind could see past all of that. "Jamal how many orders you have to prep?" Mom asked. Just two why? Want to help?" Jamal asked joking. He and mom ended up getting to know one another more as mom would come by more often with Pete. "Sure I'll help you. Did you eat?" Mom asked. "Not since earlier why you hungry?" Jamal asked "a little" mom said. "What do you need Hun?" Mom asked. "Fries and six mozzarella sticks." Jamal instructed. Mom did as Jamal asked of her. "And dropped them all in two separate baskets in the deep fryer. Thank you Ms. Cathy." Jamal said. Mom grabbed chicken breast and put them on the side of the grill. It was almost 6 o'clock on the nose. It was a good day. The sound of the doorbell rang as two men came inside the shop entered being rude and robust. Mom didn't utter a word and really didn't pay them any mind. That was normal for a few people to come in under the influence with some noise with them. Than you had your certain few people who were always just loud for no reason. "Can I take your orders?" Jamal asked the two males. The fries and sticks were crispy enough to send the other customers who have been waiting impatiently on their way. "Yeah I'm a get a cheese steak with a small fry." Jamal repeated the order. "Let me get the same shit" The other man said. Early that's my shit right there, let's hope they make it just as good as the other spot by Federal". The tall skinny black man with lanky arms and legs said to his boy. Mom didn't realize who this kid was probably because she wasn't paying him any attention. She was focused on cutting up some fresh lettuce for her man's sandwich. The fries were packed up and so were the mozzarella sticks. "Thank you have a nice night." Jamal said to the customer. "I'm going to smoke a cigarette." The one guy said to his lanky friend. The tall one took off his coat getting comfortable at the table. Mom glanced over as she heard the words to smoke a cigarette. "I need one of those." Mom said in a low tone. "No you don't woman." Jamal interjected knowing the deal with these two. The guy in the waiting area had on a short sleeve shirt exposing all of his artwork all over his arms. He worn many tattoos on his arms. His necklace was glistening from the light from the ceiling. Mom looked at the man and stared for second but went back to doing what she was doing paying no mind to the "gangsta" in the shop. "Ayo my man can you put extra cheese on one of those subs?" Bam went up to the counter. "If that's what you want, that's what you'll get it." Jamal's job was to accommodate whatever the customer wanted. Staring at mom for a long moment. Mom looked at him. She knew his face from somewhere but couldn't pin it at the moment. "You have a son ma'am don't you?" Bam was fishing. "Yes I do and you asked because?" Mom had an attitude not knowing who this was. "And a daughter too right?" Bam was getting his confirmation. The stakes were all sizzling on the grill. Jamal didn't think anything wrong of the questions that were being asked. "That's asking a little too much now, do I know you?" Mom asked disturbed that she couldn't pin who this kid was. He had to be around Rock's age but a bit older. "His name is Manuel and his sister is Jalinda right?" Those words made mom's hairs in the back of her neck stand up. Her heart began to race as her breathing picked up at the same time. "Yeah you are his mom that stays on 28th and federal over by Creamer Elementary school." Bam knew exactly who Ms. Cathy was now. "What is it that you want?" Mom asked. "From you nothing lady but as for your son I want his life.... Better yet I want his sou.l I'm going to put his face on my arm permanently as a trophy." Those words almost killed mom. "What!?" You better leave my son alone." Just as she said those words Bam's face found a spot in mom's memory bank. She remembered the day she made Rock fight Bam and Curtis for stealing his goods every time he would go to the store. "I can't touch him now Ms. Cathy, but let me tell you this. When he comes out you better find a spot to bury him because he is mine and make sure you tell him what I'm telling you." Bam wasn't loud or aggressive but his words cut deep like a sword cutting flesh. "I know you are not still mad that he beat you and your brother up when y'all was younger?" Mom search for a reason. Instead she got what she wasn't expecting. "No that shit is old news. I know you remember Curtis my brother, yes u do." Bam answered his own question "Well your son killed my brother while in the jail, so therefore he is going to die as a revenge for Curtis's sake." Bam was putting on his coat as he lifted his arm to put his jacket on. The steel on his hip went far from unnoticed. "You better not touch him because I will deal with you on my own!" Mom was raising her voice now. Bam smiled. If you bring me back my brother I will spare his life. Until then your son is better off in jail. You were already warned of what is going to happen to him." Bam's boy came in "Wassup the food done?" "Nah ain't no food playa, you might as well bounce." Jamal stepped up angry at all the harsh words and threats that he had just heard. "What the fuck you mean no and bounce?" The other light skin gangsta said. "You her what I said." "Fuck that bitch! I'm hungry give me my shit now." He barked over at Jamal. Mom wrapped up the food. "What the fuck is going on up here." Pete came from the back with his hand by his side. "I want my food." Light bright barked again. "Here" Mom put it on the counter and stormed to the back. A crusty 20 dollar bill was thrown on the counter by Bam. He winked at Jamal. "Keep the change you need it." Bam walked off leaving his man's to pick up the food in the bag. As soon as they left Pete put his 45 mm back on safety. "What the fuck was that about?" Pete asked Jamal. He pointed his head over to mom's direction "talk to her boss man I don't know." Jamal said. "Close it up early." Pete headed to the back. The site of mom sitting in Pete's favorite chair hooked up to her breathing machine could have killed Pete. She wiped her eyes and filled her lungs with fresh oxygen.

"Baby do you mind telling me what happen out there?" Pete was far from angry but he was very confused about what had just taken place not quite understanding what he walked into. He put his hammer back in the safe which was accompanied by two more. A 22 revolver and a 380. Pete had his share of guns and no one knew about them till today.

"We all locked up boss man" Jamal came in from the back inform Pete that his instructions were met and followed to the tee. "Thank you give us a minute Jamal." Pete said. Jamal spun away. Mom held up a finger needing some time until she was breathing normal again. She couldn't believe the threat she had just received from Bam. "Could all that he was saying be true? Or were they all lies? These are the questions that ran through mom's head. She already knew her son had a temper but for him to be a murderer, this couldn't be anywhere near the truth. Manuel was a sweet boy who never started or instigated any fights. He protected us as much as he could. Why was everyone considering her son a full blown murderer? It wasn't just what Bam had to say. It was all the other comments that have been circulating throughout the city about her son that has gotten her to the brink of tipping over.

"That kid..... That was just here..." Mom spoke in between breath. "Take it easy baby." Pete loved mom. She was gorgeous to him despite her condition. Mom was a shell shocker with that thick body. He and Manuel had gotten into a couple fights over the years." Mom said. "Okay." Pete said as if that was nothing out of the ordinary amongst the youth growing up. "Yeah

I know but he has a friend that grew up with him. Everyone considered that they were brothers. The whole block knew these two bad asses. Bam and Curtis they would torment all the other kids together by taking their snacks, money, baseball, toys and whatever they wanted. Those two made sure they did it baby." Mom inhaled swallowing. "So they pick on Manuel didn't they?" Pete jump to conclusion and landed right on the clues. "Yes but Manuel grabbed a pole or a stick, I can't recall exactly what he used. He beat them so bad causing them to lose so much blood that they never bothered him again after that. This was years ago I'm talking about." Mom emphasized. "So what's the problem with that kid and you?" Pete asked still not getting the full picture yet. "Once he noticed who I was. He decided to use me to send a message to Manuel. Telling me that once Manuel got out that he was going to kill him as soon as he came across Manuel." Mom began to breathe faster again. "But why the hell does he want to hurt Manuel?" Pete question. "He told me my son killed his brother in jail." Mom couldn't believe what she was saying. "Manuel did what?" Pete was lost. "So you're saying that Manuel your son, that is locked away for a murder." Pete use his fingers to quote the word murder just killed another man while being incarcerated? This man he killed is suppose to be Bam's brother Curtis?" Pete asked now putting it all together. "That's what he said to me. This is why I got so bent out of shape and lost it. My son isn't a murderer." Mom defended Manuel until the end. If he was, she was still was going to side with him no matter if he was wrong or right. "Babe I've been in the county jail once too many times and it's rough in there but I can't see Manuel going on a killing spree." Pete tried to rationalize what he just heard. "Me neither." Mom agreed with Pete. "Come on let's get out of here." Pete instructed. "But the shop." Mom contested. "Don't worry about the shop, the shop is fine. I'll reopen it in the a.m. bright and early that's all." Pete assured mom. Pete didn't want to take a chance and gamble with Bam and his boy. He was young and the mentality of a young mother fucker with revenge on his mind was nothing to sleep on. Pete was old school and he was hip on game. Bam didn't give a shit about anyone and the possibility of Bam taken out his anger on Rock's mom were very high. So to avoid any mishap it was a wise decision to close up and leave for the rest of the day. It was best to be safe than sorry in moments like these. A shootout coming from Bam wasn't a very bright idea to engage with. Pete thought, even though he had a license to carry and kill on sight. If the threat presented itself that was a different story. Pete wasn't trying to go through this at his shop. Building a bad reputation due to an involvement in a shooting was a situation that Pete didn't want. Being the owner he had to consider all of the following factors. Pete was wise. He allowed Jamal take the rest of the day off. "I'll see you in the a.m. its slow today." was all Pete said. "Is everything okay?" Jamal asked. "Of course." "See you in the A.M than." Jamal accepted. "All right call me if anything." Jamal exited out the back door Pete watched as he left to make sure he made it to his car in one piece. Going back to his safe he pulled out the 45 mm and buried it in his waistband. "You ready?" Pete asked mom "yes."

—

The smell of sweat and stale air lingered. The guys were working out as a normal past time. Many would wonder how we ended up so big. There was nothing else to do. Amazing what a few push-ups and dips off the bed could do. Bigs and Leak were engaged in a war in chess. Leak had just came back from a visit and he couldn't wipe the smirk off his face.

"Damn! My nigga she got a spot for you at the crib?" Rock asked in disbelief. Leak had come back almost an hour ago. The last time he spoke to his baby moms it was okay, but over time the comments and statements got harsher and harsher. There was no understanding as to what was going on there. "Yeah that's what she said." Leak said. "I think she want you to put her back in the passenger seat." Rock opinionated. "I know, that ain't happening Rock." I don't know what the fuck she up to but I guess Ima find out." Leak said. "Or she might want you to put another bun in that oven Mr. Baby daddy." Rock joked. "Is on you Slash." Rock said. Slash was working out and busting Bigs ass in chess. His breathing was getting heavier as the sets got harder. "You might be right because she's always said she wanted to have another baby. That crazy bitch." Leak joked. "You just as crazy." Slash countered while doing his dips and laughing. "You sure is." Rock agreed getting down to do his set. The day was already coming to an end. Every day after the last meal it was an indication that the day was already gone. Time behind these wall seem to fly by as you got dug in. You just had to make sure that your mind stood busy. "Damn I know but she so fine and wetter that Niagara. I wouldn't mind getting her pregnant again if that's what she really wants." Leak's baby mom lived in Centerville and was living on government assistance. She was living a comfortable life if she was exactly how Leak described her to us a few months ago. She wasn't your average party animal chick. She did go out on occasions. Her time and energy was focused on her children for the most part as Leak vouched. "Yeah why not but are you going to be there and stay for the long haul?" Rock was poking at open wounds now trying to get Leak to see things as they really were. Instead of seeing it as a double dutch game when you hop in and out whenever you want. Rock was keeping shit real. We as men tended to do this to woman some did it on purpose and others did it uncontiously. Either way it was fucked up to fuck with a woman head as so. Now if she was that type to play that game too, because we all know that woman tended to play this dumb ass game too. One would reap what they sow.

"I hope to be a great father but coming in and out of jail is what's fucking meet up with my family." Leak admitted. "I see that, so then you know what you have to do to stay out don't you?" Rock questioned. Right as he did the mail slid right under the door. There was three pieces of mail one for each of us except for Leak. "You don't get mail today because you got something a lot better than mail." Rock joked. "Yeah checkmate." Bigs said while grabbing his piece of mail. "Yeah right." Leak looked at the board. "Damn! Shorty gotcha head all fucked up. I know you just didn't get checkmated by Bigs at that." Rock joked opening his letter coming at Slash. "It's my sister." Rock said. "It's my mom." Bigs stated. "I think this is my cousin." Slash informed. "He got me he got that" Slash admitted defeat.

Manny!!!

I'm a keep this short and to the point you may not fully understand but I need you to think. Things are best left alone as many would say, but we all know that this here is no fun. Now, who isn't to say that karma is a process just waiting for things to occur on their own? Or can karma be sped up so that it happens faster? A smile brings laughter and of course many more smiles will be attracted, but can a smile bring or bear hatred all in one? To inquire about things like this is to experiment and finish our very own quest in life. To live, to be alive and to be alive is to stand up for what is right. I hope you don't get the wrong impression as you read this letter, but I'm on a quest that is needed to keep many with smiles. Our last conversation wasn't the last nor will it be. I'll see you soon, stay strong and positive for me and mom. I am my brother's keeper for now and forever. Smile because it's a smile that will be worth showing for many more years to come. Embrace and cheerish all that is formulated. To formulate can be the key to escavate. I love you with all my heart

Tu Linda!

Silence in the cell was heavy, no one spoke a word just allowing the other to soak in and digest what was written in their own worlds. A letter was gold when it was written to you but let me be the one to be the bearing of the great news. These letters had the power to make your day but destroy your world all in one reading. The thoughts inside of Rocks head were driving him insane. No one could understand what was going on. Nor did one want to accept what the possibilities could be,

"What is this woman talking about?" Rock broke the silence thinking out loud. "Who?" Leak asked. "My fucking sister she sounds as if she is really losing it." Rock stated. Rock passed the letter to Leak. Yes mail is definitely personal and for yourself to read. After some time with the person you live with and once the bond is built. It'll get to a point where you and your celly are constantly talking about each other's lives. You pretty much learn and know everything about your celly. So reading each other's mail under their consent isn't too bad. Only if you allowed it and are comfortable enough to allow another person to share some of your life with you. The feedback may be needed in some instances. "What is she saying?" Leak asked the same question back to Rock. "I don't know but knowing my sister this isn't good." Rock opinionated. "Why wouldn't it be good? Everything that comes to us in jail doesn't all have to be bad news." Leak said. "I know but you don't know Linda. She is sweet but she is a fucking problem and by what she just wrote in that letter I don't get anything good from it. That's some subliminal shit she sending. I know that much and feel that shit." Rock explained not too happy at what he was putting together. You're bugging and she isn't saying anything out of the ordinary." Leak damn sure didn't know Linda which is why he was saying what he was saying. I took the letter back and put it away. I would have to write her later because I know she's gonna end up doing something stupid. He felt that shit deep in his stomach. Rock's irrational thoughts wouldn't let him sleep at all that night. One's mind was the worst possible enemy anyone could have. There was no fighting it once you lost control of it.

"You fucking that dumb bitch Star right!? So go and get some pussy from that trifling as bitch!" Jacqueline was going in on her baby dads. She just went on break and it just so happened Streets was waiting for her up the block from her job. She was heading over to the McDonald's mining her business. He crept up on her. The people who worked around the area stopped and looked as Jacqueline and Streets went at it back and forth. "I love you Jacqueline I'm not in love with any other female I be fucking. You have my heart." Jacqueline kept her step up laughing which only forced Street to keep up with her. "I'm sick of your lies and all of your broken promises. I've been dealing and putting up with your shit for too long and all of the sudden you realize you had something good in your hands. It's too late! Stay with all your dirty chicken heads and be a father to you son! Forget about me because I no longer exist in your life!" That last comment sent Street up the wall. "You know what you did this to us bitch! You couldn't keep your dirty ass legs closed for one second!" Streets flip the script on her. That caught Jacqueline's attention and everyone else who was walking to grab a bite to eat "I couldn't keep my legs closed? Ha! Let's be serious nigga. You cheated on me numerous times. You beat me numerous times, you didn't care about your son or me when we had nowhere to go. You are the selfish one, you want me to keep..."SLAP!" Streets lit the side of Jacqueline's face with his right hand. Her nose was red due to the cold and now her eyes filled the water. She wanted to cry but instead she held them back. "Go ahead hit me again! You're a fucking coward that's what you always been! You know one ain't enough, come on slap me you bitch ass nigga!" Streets backed up as she came closer. Jacqueline's fury and tone could be seen through her eyes and her stair cut deep into his eyes. Jacqueline was possessed but the devil himself her eyes showed pure evil. She wasn't afraid anymore. She wasn't going to cry anymore. She was fed up with all the verbal and physical abuse. No woman had to endure any of this no matter how smart of a mouth she had. This is what women did. They bitched and complain about everything us men did. It doesn't mean you beat them up every time she gets out of line or does it? Or maybe once or twice is good enough right? Fuck noooo! We real men walk away from a spicy situation like this. I know there are a few of you reading this who like to abuse woman on the low but now that I have your attention allow me to say this. You too are a COWARD and should take a good look in the mirror. Ask yourself why are you so weak to allow a woman to bring you to the point that you have to strike her to get a point across or to prove to her your lack of masculinity. Streets didn't like to walk away he enjoyed to have power over women. Maybe it was because he had already built that bad habit and couldn't find an antidote to get a cure for it. He tried to hug her. "Get the fuck off me!" Jacqueline screamed loudly. "I'm sorry mami." Streets now felt bad he just put his hands on his baby moms again. In front of many who just stared not doing a fucking thing. Especially in this fucking cold weather. "Leave me alone! I hate you!" Jacqueline stormed off into the restaurant. She headed straight to the bathroom and cried and cried so much her eyes began to hurt. "Why did she love him? Why did she bear his seed? Jacqueline felt helpless and felt as though this would never stop for as long as she was alive.

"Hey are you okay in there?" A customer asked on the other side of the bathroom stall door. Jacqueline saw her shoes they were flats. "Yes I'm okay just going through some personal stuff that's all. Thank you for your concern though." Jacqueline got herself together. The voice and shoes disappeared from the bathroom. She went to wash her hands and looked up in the mirror and saw the bottom of her left eye beginning to swell, it wore a greenish tint. From previous experiences she knew that it was a matter of hours before it changed to a darker color from the veins being swollen or even ruptured underneath her beautiful soft delicate skin. "I hate him I swear! I do! If you ever get back with him you deserve what you get!" Jacqueline was scolded herself in the mirror. After a few minutes she got herself together and headed out the door. She swallowed her pride, holding her head up as she walked to order something to eat. She knew she was a bad bitch but to keep on living this nightmare over and over could destroy the prettiest of the prettiest in a heartbeat.

Later that night, Linda had Jacqueline on her mind. She felt uneasy about something so she decided to call her. Joel and her had plans. Joel was on his way to pick her up. Mom of course was with Pete doing who knows what.

"Hello?" Jacqueline answered on the first ring. "Hey!" Linda said happy to hear Jacqueline's voice. "Hi baby girl." Jacqueline's voice wasn't as it was when they spoke to one another it felt unusual. "Are you okay?" Linda asked. "I'm all right I guess." Jacqueline was still replaying the episode in her mind. "Well, I called because I was worried about you but if you're okay then I guess I'll let you go." Linda wasn't going to sit there and beg her to tell her what was wrong with her. Instead, she would dismiss the conversation. "I'm not okay Jasmine I want to die already." Jacqueline barked into the receiver losing it again. She cried pouring out all her emotions. She was glad that Linda had called but what she really wanted was for Linda to come over and console her the way she knew she could. To help her get rid of all her stress and frustration once and for all. "What happened?" Linda asked. She sat on her bed dressed. She was ready to go out with her man looking her part in high heels and all. She looked in the mirror as she laid on the bed speaking into the receiver. "It Streets?" Jacqueline dropped hints of information. "What about him?" Linda's blood begin to boil at the sound of Jacqueline's words. "We had a very bad argument today." Jacqueline spoon fed Linda the story. "What you mean an argument? How and why?" Linda asked getting angry from within. On my break today." Jacqueline said. "You had lunch with him and it turned into an argument?" Linda was getting very upset. Why was she getting so angry with what she was putting together? "No." We didn't have lunch together why would I even want to see that nigga?" Jacqueline asked irritated in tears. "Well you said you seen him on your lunch break so what else could that mean?" Linda spoke back into the receiver. "I was going to lunch and he showed up out of nowhere. I didn't invite him to go anywhere with me." Jacqueline defended herself against the accusations. Linda looked at the clock behind her on the nightstand it was 10 till 9 PM. "So tell me what did he said." Linda tried to speed up the conversation. "He followed me all the way to the McDonald's trying to convince me." Jacqueline paused to take a breath. "Convince you to do what?" Linda got a bit nervous at the words that Jacqueline was using at the moment. She was getting very tired of this mother fucker Streets and also she was fed up with all the lies that she was accumulating. They were beginning to consume her. "He wanted me to bring the baby over to his apartment and hang out for the night." Jacqueline said not finishing. "What's wrong with that?" Linda asked "What the fuck do you mean was wrong with that?" Jacqueline snapped. Linda look at the receiver. This girl is losing it Linda she thought. "Yeah was wrong with that?"

Linda reiterated. "He just didn't want to spend time with me and his son Jasmine he wanted to stick his dirty dick in my pussy! That's the same line he used to use when I was pregnant with his son." "He think I'm stupid. I pulled his card and he didn't like the fact that I don't want the dick no more. So he wasn't trying to hear that." She told Jasmine." Jacqueline was going in on what really went down earlier. "So why are you so mad? That's good that you told him about yourself." Linda wasn't getting the full scope of the picture and she obviously didn't fully understand who Streets was as a person. "I know but it's what he did once I say what I said." Linda had her blade her hand and was playing with it as she listened to Jacqueline's distraught voice. "What did he do please don't tell me that he tried to rape you in the McDonald's bathroom or something?" Linda was clutching the blade her left hand. "No but he did slap the fuck out of me in front of so many people walking by us. It was so embarrassing Jasmine. I couldn't believe he actually would ever do that in front of so many people." Jacqueline was balling her eyes out now. Her son was asleep. She just wanted to take her son and leave the city or even the state. "I'm so tired of him Jasmine. I'm never going to be happy as long as I stay here." Linda listened attentively her vessels in her eyes swelled with blood as her animosity and fury began to escalate rapidly. She knew she had to get rid of Streets but how and when? She knew he wasn't an easy target. "I'm so sorry to hear that Jacqueline why don't you put a restraining order on him?" Linda asked already knowing the answer to that question. "I know I thought about that but I still don't think that's going to resolve anything Jasmine." Jacqueline admitted. She was absolutely right. "Beep-beep!" The blaring horn was loud enough to hear from the back room. "I'll see you tomorrow, I got to go girl." Linda spoke into the receiver. "What!? Where are you going!?" Jacqueline barked. "Out." Linda answered getting straight to the point. Jacqueline didn't like the answer. "Out? I need you right now and you're blowing me off because you got a go out?!" Jacqueline was bugging now. "I have a man Jacqueline and I do have to spend time with him don't you think!?" Linda informed. "Yeah whatever!" Jacqueline was being very selfish. "I'll see you tomorrow." Linda said eager to hang up the phone. "Whatever." As soon as Linda heard those words she hung up immediately. Now she was even more pist over something that she had nothing to do with. She grabbed her jacket and threw it on grabbing her tiny pocketbook, she headed down the steps. The phone rang and rang and it kept on ringing even as she finally shut the door and set the alarm to the house.

As she carefully made her way down the few steps Joel hopped out and made his way to her grabbing her hand so that she wouldn't slip in the snow or black ice on the ground.

"Hey beautiful." Joel said leaving his car in the middle of the street. Linda smelled the marijuana in the air. Linda wanted to blow an L before she left but that wasn't going to happen. "You smell so good baby I'm going to try my best to keep myself from jumping all over you tonight." Joel joked. He opened the door for his wifey. "You look real sharp yourself who did you get all dressed up for?" Linda complemented her man. "For the woman who deserves to see her man dressed up. I had to ,to represent such an elegant queen." Joel worked his cheesy lines. Linda loved his charm. "Can I get a kiss baby?" Linda asked. "My pleasure." Joel planted a small juicy kiss on his woman in the blistering cold. He held her as the headlights crept up behind them. Sitting in her seat on the passenger side Linda fixed her lipstick in the sun visor mirror. Joel sped around and jumped in the car and drove. "You ready?" Joel asked. "Yes" Linda said excitedly. She stared at Joel thinking of all that she had been doing ever since her brother had got locked up. Joel didn't deserve any of this. He was too sweet for anyone to treat him the way Linda was treating him. Even though he was oblivious as to all the dirt Linda was doing but Linda's conscience was beginning to take a toll on her slowly. She knew that in due time all this would either be over or it would only get worse as time went by. "Wassup baby?" Joel asked looking over at his beautiful queen. "Nothing." Linda smiled brightly putting her innocent mask on. "I'm just admiring how handsome you are that's all." Linda felt the need to show Joel how much she actually cared for him. "I'm all yours baby." Joel smiled back. "You better be." Linda said with attitude but in a joking manner. "You are babe I just hope you're all mine." Joel didn't even bother to look at her way. Linda swallowed hard. That staement hit her hard, cutting deep into her heart. She was wrong. "You are baby don't ever think otherwise." Linda tried to sound convincing lying. She wasn't right but she promised herself not to play Joel for no one anymore. "I'm a hold you to that." Joel said stopping at the red light." He looked over. "You are sexy as hell." Joel burst out. "I want you tonight." he leaned in for a kiss. "You already have me baby." Linda assured him "uuuuummmmm" Joel moaned and moved the car as the light turned green. "So where are we going baby?" Linda asked. "Where are we going?" Joel repeated as if he was thinking of the place in that very moment. "Well we are going to the Sheraton over by Mount Holly." Joel said. "The Sheraton?" Linda wasn't sure what the Sheraton was."Yes to Sheraton. Have you ever been there?" Joel asked her. "No I haven't what is it?" Linda asked. It's an upscale club. No sneakers, blues jeans or any of that extra baggy ghetto gear babe." Joel informed. "So it's for white people?" Linda asked sounding ignorant. "For white people babe? Really?" Joel joked. Linda put her hand over her mouth laughing. "Yeah." she said in between laughs. "No is not for white people it's for people with class my love. It doesn't matter what your nationality is. You are allowed to enter but like I said if you look like you belong on the corner trapping, you won't be allowed in. It's not that type of place." I wanted to show how elegant I see my lady, my woman and my queen, not my bitch or my chick." Joel had Linda's love box wet. He was doing a number on her and he didn't even touch her yet. "Awwww babe you are my man and my gentleman, not my nigga or my boo but my hubby too." Linda caused Joel to smile. "So what going on in this place?" Linda asked. "Well every night it is a different theme but tonight if I'm not mistaken its salsa night. So you better get ready to dance your ass off." Joel couldn't wait to go up in there. He never been there either but his mom and his boss at work always talked about this place. They would say how much fun it is and how elegant it feels. So Joel had no choice but to take advantage of the time and take Linda to this place. He wanted to really see it for himself on how the so called "Sheraton" really was.

Finally arriving the parking lot was flooded with cars. "Oh my God baby is this the place?" Linda asked staring at this big building in front of them with the words "Sheraton" in red lights at the top of the building. "Yes it is." Joel circled the lot scouting for a parking spot which was almost impossible. He noticed a car pulling out in the back of the lot "Babe Ima drop you off in the front and tried to make that parking back there." Joel was a gentleman for real. "No you're not I will walk with you." Linda was his rider and he didn't argue. "All right let's go then."

Hand in hand the two exited towards the building Linda had on a burgundy mini dress that was a one piece. It hugged her hips and body like a glove. Her black heels made her dress stand out even more. The braids were gone on this night. She wore a straightened out Bob her hair was soft and had bounce as she walked. Her white gold diamond studs reflected off the lighted chandeliers from up above. Her neck was naked which only gave her the only sex appeal. Her cleavage was exposed slightly. It was just enough to catch any man's attention that came her way. Her black jacket put it all together. The burgundy pocketbook didn't go unnoticed in her left hand. After giving the lady at the reservation booth their names,she escorted them to the tables which was near the wall. The bar was on a higher platform. The chandelier is what grab Linda's attention. This place was enormous the people were dressed to impress, just like Joel had explained to Linda in the car. The men all had on suits with button ups under their blazers. Those who were already hot from dancing song after song had their jackets off. Their button up sleeves were rolled up. The sound of the Spanish salsa was blaring over the loud-speakers. The hostess introduced herself

"Hi I am Yolanda. If you need anything you can come and get me. If you cant find me just go up to anyone wearing a white polo,m they will help you with anything that you need." Yolanda had a gorgeous face and her body was so fucking thick. You had to know what to do with that because she was built like an ox. It was about Linda today though. "Thank you we will." Joel kept his eyes on Linda. "This place is so nice baby is so different." Linda was mesmerized. "I told you we had to go somewhere nice. I could of just taking you anywhere but you deserve a different scene. Where did you think I was going to take you?" Joel asked. Linda she shrugged. "I don't know I wasn't expecting this." Linda admitted. "Well this won't be the first or the last time. "Let's dance" Joel got up. Jerry Rivera "Cara de Nino "came on. The night had just begun and guess what? It was far from over. Everyone wore smiles on their faces. This was a magical moment.

Streets pulled up into a Home Depot parking lot. After what had transpired with his baby mom he was beyond furious he wanted to kill her. He wasn't going to stop there, he also had already made up his mind to get rid of Linda. In his mind he knew that Linda was that woman that night. Plus the angel dust he was inhaling all by himself in his car wasn't helping him not one bit. He was stuck and listening to music and pulling hard on the L. "She is!" he kept saying to himself looking in the rearview mirror. He wasn't thinking consciously but no one could stop him now. They were both dead Linda and Jacqueline were in deep shit. If this man didn't sober up fast. They were going to set him up. The more he kept on thinking about them. The crazier his thought process was becoming. The more he confirmed what he was going to do to them. His mind was planning out his every move. Home Depot wasn't going to close no time soon and Streets already knew exactly what he needed to buy. After finishing the dust he decided to go shopping. He left his gun under the driver seat and put on his fitted cap. Lighting a new port he walked right up towards the entrance. The heat in the building caused his high to reach its peak. Streets was no rookie and smoked on a regular but he was far from thinking rationally. The store was a couple hours from closing which gave him ample time to do what he needed to do. He had tunnel vision and be sure that he wasn't going to let anyone get in his way. No man, no god or Satan himself would stop this man. Who's not to say that Satan was driving this car on this trip? Strolling with his cart he picked up a variety of items. You would think that Streets was going to do some serious work on house or yard work, but in this case no one was going to build or bury anything in this weather.

After almost two hours and a half the PA system blared.

"Attention all Home Depot shoppers. We thank you for your support. Home Depot will be closing in the next 30 minutes. So if all Home Depot shoppers could please bring all your checkout items to the front for final purchase that would be greatly appreciated. Thank you enjoy the rest your night." Streets was so high he didn't pay the warning any mine. He didn't make his way up to the front of the store. He wasn't done looking for what he was looking for. He headed towards the grills which were to far end of the outing section. To him time wasn't moving as fast as he thought. Him being so out of it he didn't realize it. "Sir we are about to close can I help you find something?" The small lady with a brush cut asked. She was standing about 15 feet away for Streets. Streets face scared her on contact. She walked away probably to get some help because she wasn't going to engage in any verbal combat with the sinister look he possessed. "Attention Home Depot shoppers! We will be closing in three minutes once again please bring all checkout items to the nearest register for final checkouts please and thank you once again." The voice over the speaker spoke once again this time a man came up to Streets. "Sir can I help you with something we are closing." The man said walking up to Streets. He smell of the abominable fluid coming off him was strong. The man wasn't familiar with the smell but knew that he smelled something out of the norm.

"I need kerosene do you carry that shit here? Streets was moving slowly. He was leaning on his shopping cart. "Yes we do how many do you need?" The white guy with the long straight hair asked." Two cans or whatever they come in." Street said not even looking at him. "What you need them for?" The man wearing the name tag with the named Jacob on it asked being nosey as fuck. "Streets looked at him as if it really fucking mattered what he needed it for? "Okay dumb question. I'll go grab it for you while you go over to the register right there and pay for the rest of these items you have in your cart." Jacob suggested. "No! I'll go with you and I'll pay once I have all my items how about that?" Streets countered his office. "Sounds good come on. Jacob led the way not arguing with him. After finally getting his two tin gallons of kerosene the man rang him up. "The total is $168.39 Jacob said to Streets. Jacob knew that Streets was up to no good but it wasn't his business and he probably was just assuming shit anyway. Even though the two rolls of duct tape, one hammer, 2 gallons of kerosene, a few feet of chains, locks and a bunch of other useful items could mean a lot of things.

"Have fun." Jacob said to Streets as he walked away into the cold night. The parking lot was lonely only a few vehicles that belong to their employees.

"These bitches are dead I'm tired of them both they are going to die and I'm going to enjoy every moment of this." Streets was talking to himself repeating the words over and over again sounding possessed. "Ima fuck them and kill them! Streets was filling his head up with all types of pollutants. He jumped on the highway. He was driving recklessly, he made it home to where Star was waiting for him at his place. He left all the toys he bought in the trunk of his car and passed out in his bed with all his clothing still on.

—

"Come on baby you tired?" Linda teased Joel who couldn't keep with Linda's nonstop dancing. Is been a while since Linda had this much fun with anyone. She was enjoying every bit of it "I'm tired baby I can't believe you have so much energy in you." Joel commented. Go dance with one of the guys on the floor and I'll watch from over here. I might learn some new moves. "You are tired now imagine when I have you all to myself later. What you going to do then?" Linda teased Joel. "Oh baby that's a different ballgame. I gota save some energy for that because that fine ass is mine." Joel bit his bottom lip. "I can't wait." Linda spun off to dance some more and jumped on the next available man that she seen. She was turned on how Joel let her go and dance with random men. He wasn't an overly jealous type because she gave him quite a show to watch. She dance to Eddie Santiago with the Spanish man who had his hands all over her but being respectful at the same time. "Is that your man staring at us?" The Spanish man asked enjoying his dance with Linda. Linda could move, even though she wasn't Spanish. Rock had raised her in his culture and as far as the language. He taught her the basics moves with a few songs and dance moves. Mom helped a lot with the food being that she had her fair share of Spanish men in her time. "No, that's my husband." Linda answered with a bright smile on her face. "Are you two fighting or arguing?" The Spanish accent man asked. "No Linda smiled again. "Why would you assume that?" Linda asked. "Because if you my woman there is no way I would let any man touch you the way I am touching you." This nigga was tripping. "You're not caressing me, you're holding me because we are dancing he knows this. He's not insecure he knows what he has and knows that I'm all his and that I'm not going anywhere baby." Linda flirted. "Oh yeah?" Mr. Sauvé said. "Yeah and guess what?" Linda wanted to get Mr. Sauvé thinking. "What's that?" He asked staring at Linda's pretty flawless face. "When I'm done dancing with you. I'm going to suck my husband's dick so bad. He's gonna bust in my mouth so hard, that I'm going to come all over myself by him being pleased by my head game." Mr. Sauvé's jaw dropped and Linda spun away from his grip. She winked and sashayed her hips as she got closer to Joel. "You ready baby?" Linda asked. "Only if you are." Joel asked. "Yes finally leaving the club the night got even colder. Then wait here while I get the car." Joel said. "I said no, I'll walk with you no matter what." Linda demanded. "All right let's go." They spend walked over to the car. Linda did what she set out to do with Joel keeping him hot while they rode towards his apartment. Linda has been here but hasn't had the chance to stay and enjoy the whole night with Joel. Tonight would be all about his needs just as he put her needs first every day and night. Linda wasted no time pulling over her tight dress over her head. She exposed her bra and thong, that she had disappearing within that juicy ass. She walked away making Joel chase her. She kept her heels on to make the foreplay become more appealing for her man. Joel was practically drooling. He wanted to eat her up and give her a serious rub down with his tongue. Linda pulled out the chair in the room. "Sit down please." Linda instructed Joel. Not putting up a fight he followed her demands. Linda's bra and thong was silk it fit and cupped her sexy breast perfectly. Linda gave Joel a lap dance without any music, just her humming a melody and grinding on her man. This alone was causing his dick to fill with blood. She kissed him on his neck as she made her way towards his back and caressed his neck and shoulders. She unbuttoning his shirt Joel touch Linda she quickly slapped his hands. "Don't touch!" Linda said not letting him satisfy his desires in caressing her beautiful body. She would make him want her so bad that he would be forced to jump on her. She bent over exposing the thong string in between her crack and grabbed the back of her heels. Joel bit his lip. "Damn baby come here I want to taste you." Joel begged. "Not yet my love." She took off his shirt slowly. Joel's back touch the coldness of the seat but Linda's tongue took his mind somewhere else. She would kiss his lips, he would try to kiss her back she would pull away. She unbuttoned his belt. His erection was trying to rip threw his slacks all on his own. Linda bit on his pants wear she could see his imprinted erection. Joel couldn't hold it anymore. Linda unclipped her bra and took it off all while dancing in a winding motion her breast stood exactly where they were, no sagging just perky and soft. Her nipples were erected. Joel's mouth watered he could tasted her already. Linda was a sexy piece of work. She put her breast all in Joel's face, he licked one but didn't have time to get to the other one. He tried to grab Linda but slapped his hands away again. "Patients baby please." Linda seductively spoke. She continued her dance routine. She got closer again her scent was intoxication it drove him insane. She could feel his manhood in between her thighs which cause her to become wetter as she grinded on Joel's lap. She was pleasing herself on his lap. She too fought the urge to stay away. It was hard but she had to. She was making Joel wait and she did to. She turned around and allowed him to suck and bite on her breast. "Bite me baby." Linda instructed him. She purred as he bit and sucked on her nipples hard. "Oooohhhh! Yes baby like that." Linda was enjoying herself. He stared at her pretty feet. She slipped out of the thong. The show was far from over Linda put one leg on the arm of the chair and rubbed her click with her fingers. Joel was taking back by the show. He couldn't believe this was happening. Linda threw that same leg up on Joel's shoulder so that her love box was only inches away from his face. Joel licked her clit but couldn't do any more without using his hands. Linda wanted to taste her man and that she did. Dropping to her knees on his soft carpet in his room she pulled out his manhood and lick the tip. Joel wanted to keep tasting her and touching on her so bad. He had to put his own two hands behind his head so that he wouldn't. He was losing. It was too much to hold back. Linda was going to make him climax this was her mission. Linda focused on the tip of his manhood sucking on it as if it was a tootsie pop. She would look up every now and then and noticed how his eyes would roll back. She wiggled him out of his slacks and underwear. Joel lifted one of his legs and put it on Linda's shoulder. Linda was going to make it happen. Sucking harder using her mouth juices to keep things moving in a rythm. Joel couldn't hold it anymore. "Baby I'm coming!" Joel warned Linda she didn't stop her nor did she slow down. She still stayed locked on the fat tip of his manhood sucking so she could feel his heartbeats per second increasing. ". Baby... Oh shit here I..... cummmmmmmm!!!" Joel pushed a mega load in Linda's mouth. It almost came up out of her nose, But it didn't. Linda slurped and swallowed all of him not dropping a drop. She made sure that he wasn't coming anymore and just like that. "Popped!" him right out. "Patience baby I got you my love." Linda assured him "Yea you do?" Joel asked. "Yes" Linda confirmed. "All right let me get you now." Joel picked her right up and laid her down on his bed. He touched her with two fingers and the swishing noise of his fingers touching her drenched pussy walls made Joel hard again instantaneously. "Wow! You like that? Joel asked. "You make me like that baby." Linda assured Joel. Joel went to work as he always did. He claimed what was his every time. Making his lady come again until they both passed out exhausted. "I love you." Linda said I love you more" Joel replied.

CHAPTER 19
"You bitch!"

Dear Madre,

Before I begin this letter my only wish is that you and my beautiful sister find yourselves in the best of health. I know the two of you can be very religious at times so I can also only hope that the two of you are in the highest of spirits. Before, I forget tell Pete I send him my regards.

I know that this has been a long journey that has been put in our path. I've learned to try make the best of a bad situation. Even if it means to go about things in a manner that I may have not been accustomed to. Mom I want you and Linda to do your best in all of this. I need you to tell yourselves that no matter how hard things may get everything will be just fine. I understand the distance from each other can hurt more than imagined. I know you two love me unconditionally and I do love you guys just as much. I know that you may have already been informed as to when my trial date is. I can't believe how fast it's approaching. My lawyer is doing his best to assure me that I will not get a life sentence. (That shit sounds crazy just saying them words) I'm sweating just thinking about it. As I was saying he gonna do his best to get the DA, to work just as hard to prove that I am guilty. I'm doing my homework in the law library with this man named "OJ." He's has been helping me on a regular bases with my case. He raised a great argument, if I'm not found guilty of the murder itself that I will be able to go home scoot free right? Sorry mom this isn't the case, that won't happen. If they dropped the murder charge that clears me of that, but then the DA can either asked me to give up the person who did commit the crime. We know that isn't going to happen. Instead, I'll just practice my right to remain silent.

Enough of that mom. How are you holding up? I hope you and Pete are sticking to y'all "non-smoking oath. You can't keep getting rushed to the hospital mom. You may not have someone there when you really need them.

Please stay strong keep fighting temptation. I know you have it in you to help live a longer life with us. Pete will help you. You can help him quit too.

As for me I'm doing better than you can imagine inside behind these cold walls. I live with three men who aren't bad men. We all take care of one another and we protect each other as well. They all help me keep my sanity when they see or sense that I'm going to lose it. Tell Linda to be good and to please stay out of the jungle. There are plenty of known and unknown animals that can be ruthless out there. She will know what I'm talking about. "I hope." I'm going to cut this letter short. I love you both and hope to see you when you get the opportunity. From the inside all the way to your side.

Your son,

Manuel Ricardo (one and only)

She was in her baby blue gown as mom sipped on her coffee reading Rock's letter. Pete had dropped her off early in the morning after spending the day and night with her. "I'm so proud of you my son." Mom said softly kissing the letter. She had no cigarettes but the urges were so strong they were driving her insane. She wore a patch, in her opinion didn't work not one bit. She knew that going to the corner store and getting a pack of cigarettes was out the question. So instead she took a deep breath and exhale slowly. She decided to cook something to eat. Considering she didn't have much of an appetite. She had to do anything to keep her mind distracted. Those powerful urges to pick up a stick had her on the edge.

—

"Baby where are you going?" Joel asked feeling Linda get up off the bed. "I'm going home I have to check up on mom. I haven't seen her since the incident." Linda said. Can you just call her babe? I'll drop you off later." Joel suggested. "I'll call but I'm going over as soon as I hang up." Linda had on her panties and bra as she walked over to pick up the phone. Joel admired her ass, it bounced up and down as she walked. He wanted some more of that girl. "Hello?" Linda spoke into the receiver. Linda smiled. "I at Joel's apartment." Linda informed. "How are you feeling?" Linda asked. Waiting for a reply. "You what?" Linda's attitude change almost immediately. Joel watched as his wifey's mood changed. He could only wonder what was being said on the other end of the receiver. "You better not even." Linda barked. "I'm on my way." Linda hurried up. "What's wrong?" Joel asked. "Nothing!" Linda was taken it out on Joel now. Joel didn't say shit. He wasn't in the mood. Linda sensed it

"I'm sorry babe but it's mom. She's telling me that she wants a cigarette, this woman don't seem to learn." Linda put on her clothes. Joel follow suit. "She'll learn babe, I just hope it won't be at the last minute. "What you got planned for today besides going home?" Joel asked. "Not sure yet why?" I'd like to spend the day with you later." Joel suggested. "We'll see." Linda looked in the mirror. "You ready?" "Let's go." Joel instructed.

—

Back in the Camden County jail Rock had a pass. He had to attend a violence group which he despised. Rock didn't see himself as a violent person, let him tell it. Everyone would beg to differ. He would go three times a week, or whenever it was scheduled which. It's funny how you would be mandated to participate in all these programs and other groups. The civilians who were in charge of running these groups, would never show up. Group would be canceled because they didn't feel like showing up. Rock hated this shit. This was supposed to help us. This is what they would say to us. On the brighter side of going to these groups. We would always encounter a few transactions along the way. Whenever they did decide to have it. So you could say it was worth going or was it?

"Oh shit, when did you sign you up for this shit?" Rock asked the Spanish man who lived two cells down from his. "Men this is my first day. How is this shit?" Jonathan asked. "Corny as hell." Rock replied giving his honest opinions. The session had not begun. The room was filling up slowly. "Ayo I need you." Rock said moving closer to Jonathan. "For what?" Jonathan didn't like this not one bit. He knew who Rock was but not personally. By all the rumors and the day to day gossip he overheard while making his way around the jail. He didn't want to be associated with Rock. Well not in that light. "Want to make some money?" Rock had to approach this on an angle. Everyone in jail wanted to make an easy quick dollar if it was possible. "Always." Jonathan replied interested. "All right you ain't gota do much but hold down a few things for me. I'll pay you weekly. Rock searched Johnathan eyes for any red flags. If things ends up missing than that's your ass." Rock explained in all seriousness getting to the point. The counselor finally decided to join the group. "Good morning gentlemen." The obese man waltzed in. "Is everyone here?" Mr. Klinger asked. "You're the one with the attendance sheet, you figure it out." The man in the far left corner shot with a lot of attitude. "You see, now that's what we are trying to work on right there." Klinger joke but was dead serious. He counted, pointing at everyone until he was satisfied with the number of guys in the small room. He radioed in the count over his walkie-talkie and a quick. "Copy" confirmed his last remark. "So who wants to go first?" Klinger asked trying to get some momentum started. The classes were for an hour and believe me that hour dragged every time. I will be the first to admit it was rare that I ever actually payed any attention on what was being said. My mind would take me to Felicia and I would just wonder what she was up too. At times it'll stop by at Jalinda's. I would put some gas in my truck then head over to mom and Linda. I was never mentally in those classes, I was free. My imagination always gave me a sense of freedom. The bullshit that was being conducted in this room was more than a Violent Prevention session. You had mother fuckers talking about their favorite pick on the tickets. You had Rock selling shit. Mr. Potato head was up front talking about how to control your anger. "Blah blah blah." Little did we know. The information he was telling us was in fact pretty valuable. It would only work if applied directly to one's own situation and use correctly. How would any of the guys know this if our attention was focused on something totally different? When we should've been focused on what we needed to be focused on which was ourselves.

The session came and went. Rock stood behind so that Jonathan and him could finish the discussion there were having that was interrupted earlier.

"So what is it that you want me to hold down?" Jonathan asked. "/Yo no voy guardar drogas mi hermano./"/I'm not going to hold drugs bro/ "/lo siento/" /I'm sorry/ Jonathan said already paranoid of the proposition. No one wanted to hold down any drugs in his place, but everyone wanted to get paid. What was he thinking? There was no way Rock was even considering him holding any of that? "I know that. I like you but I don't like you that much." Rock informed Jonathan. I need you to hold down two bags of food that's all. You don't have to worry about anything else. Just make sure it's all there, and we are good." Rock said walking slowly. "That's all you want me to do?" Jonathan asked. "That's it unless you want to work?" Rock asked. "No I'm not with all that. That's why my ass is in here now." Jonathan joked. "I know why you hear, this is why I choose you." Rock did his research on homeboy. "I mean as far as tickets? You know anything about sports?" Rock asked him "do I? I love that shit." Jonathan like that idea. Alright then I'll talk to you at our next group. Ima send the food over later alright?" Rock needed to hear confirmation. "Yeah but how much you paying me a week?" Jonathan asked. "Five dollars a week" Rock just threw out a number just to see how Jonathan would react.

"Take it in gentlemen!" The voice was talking to Rock and Jonathan. They were the only two lolly gagging to their cells. "All right sounds good." Jonathan dapped up Rock. "Got one." Rock said as he entered his cell leaving Johnathan. Leak and Slash were playing a game of chess and talking mad shit to one another. "They both looked over at him. "Got who?" Asked the nosier of the two. In this case it happened to be Leak this morning. "Damn you nosy." Rock joked. "Fuck you." Leak joked back falling for it. "You know homeboy that lived two cells over?" Rock questioned Slash pointed over to the left. "That side?" "Nope" This side." Rock use his hand pointing in the opposite direction. "What about him?" Leak asked looking down at his pieces. He's going to hold for us. Well some of the food not all of it." Rock corrected himself with a grin on his face. "That's a good move, about time." Leak joked. "What you think if I put him to move some tickets too?" Rock asked. "Whoa whoa!" Leak was shocked. Are you serious?" Leak asked not liking the proposition not one bit. "Easy. It was a suggestion don't stroll me again now." Rock joked. "I'm saying you don't even know this nigga to be giving him shit like that." Slash opinionated. Bigs rolled over. "Yeah if you do that, you gota watch him and the rest of the mother fuckers inside his cell. Plus all the niggaz he hang with too. Shit in my eyes is only going to lead to more bull shit Rock." Bigs was saying staring at the wall. Leak gave him the head nod as to say he was on point. Rock listened carefully at what was being said to him by his intermediate circle. "Bigs I didn't even look at it like that go point." Rock admitted. "I'm still going to pass him the food though. I said I would, so that's a done deal for now." Rock informed the others. "Yeah that ain't a problem, how much you paying him?" Slash asked. "Five dollars a week." Rock replied. "Not bad he can live off that, shit its free money for doing shit." Leak stated. "I thought that was reasonable." Rock stated looking in the mirror. After tweaking a few things and crunching a few numbers. Rock bagged up almost $150 the commissary with a little bit of everything except cosmetics. The cosmetics weren't going anywhere. Rock had a thing for his cosmetics. His locker and box consisted of nothing but that. Tube after tubes of toothpaste with all types of generic brands to top brands. It was like that with everything else that was sold in the hygiene category on the commissary. There was no way he would let those items go he may sure he and his crew were on top of their hygiene game. Plus cosmetics always seem to be more expensive.

—

"Hey Joel!" Mom rushed over to give Joel a big hug. It's been a while since I've seen you baby. How you been?" Mom asked excited to see Linda's man. "Busy Ms. Cathy. Working and school you know that takes up a lot of my time." Joel admitted informing mom. "How is Miss Thang treating you?" Mom looked over to Linda. Linda scurried off towards the kitchen. "Baby you're thirsty?" Linda asked as she walked away. "Coffee if there is some already made, if not don't worry about it." Joel replied. "Now you know I always got coffee on boy." Mom said. Linda and I are doing just fine. We see each other when we can. It's a little hard because she works and goes to school but we make it work when we can." Joel informed. "Did you have a good time last night?" mom asked. "Mom that's none of your business." Linda blurted out thinking with her mind in the gutter. "Babe relax she only asking because you still have your dress on from last night." Joel tried to correct Linda's unnecessary attitude. Linda felt stupid. She handed her man one of the mugs of coffee and handing mom the other. "Oh I'm sorry mom." Linda apologized for jumping the gun." "Girl don't even worry about it. I already know that man got you going crazy." Mom joked laughing. Linda blushed. "Ima go change you two are too much." Linda bolted up the steps. The room had laughter all in it. "How are things with you and Pete?" Joel asked taking the spotlight off him and his girl for a few seconds. "He's good he's at the shop taking care of his business." Mom informed. "So I take it yall happy together." Joel didn't like the answer mom gave. She avoided it completely and Joel wasn't going to let her off the hook that easily. Mom smiled. "Yeah he is a great man I'm so happy he is a part of my life for now." Mom ended. "That's good to hear Ms. Cathy, and your son?" Joel asked. "He just wrote me, he is holding on stronger than I had imagined." Mom admitted. "That's great to hear too." Joel sipped his coffee. He looked at his watch. He had to run a couple errands in a few himself.

That's why he wanted Linda to stay with him. He needed her to pick out a few things that she'd like at his place. It was too masculine for him. He wanted Linda to feel welcome in his apartment as if it was hers two. "In a rush?" Mom asked. "Oh no rush just have to go and take care of a few things soon that's all." Joel said. "Is Linda going with you?" Mom asked. "I don't think so. She wants to stay with you for a while to make sure you don't relapse." Joel slipped up telling the truth on Linda. Mom scrunched up her face as if she smell something foul. "Little heifer." Mom held her mouth were her hand. "Oops you didn't hear that." Mom tried to cover up the last comment. "I made some breakfast you want some?" Mom offered. "Yeah why not I'm already here." Joel follow mom towards the kitchen. He stopped at the dining hall taken his seat. "How has Linda been taken this?" Joel asked mom. "I mean with me she is somewhat normal but I know it's affecting her a bit still." Joel informed mom. "I mean when I'm not around." Joel was talking close to a whisper. "She is okay, I agree she has her moments. I have to understand that they were very tight. It's not easy for someone that close to you to be ripped away overnight." Mom put the plate on the table. It had fresh bacon and an omelet with all types of onions and peppers in it. "More coffee?" Mom asked. "Please" Joel replied. The two of them engaged in small talk, but the creaking of the steps only meant one thing.

"What are you two talking about?" Linda asked wearing her PJs. "I guess she's not going." Mom stated the obvious. "Yeah I see that, but I gota be going soon. I have to take advantage of this day since it's my only day off this week."

Joel placed his empty plate into the sink and gave mom a kiss on the cheek. Remember it's in your best interests to leave that crap alone. I enjoy having you around." Joel shot a subliminal message at mom. Hopefully she felt that one. "Tell her babe, since she don't care what I have to say or what Manny has to say from the inside." Linda also added some jazz to the shot. "Why you leaving already?" Linda switched subject. "I asked you to stay with me so we can handle a few errands together." Joel spoke staring at Linda as if she was a bit lost. "I know but mom." Linda tried to use mom. "But mom nothing girl don't be using me as an excuse." Mom interjected blowing up her spot. "I'm here because of you. I can't keep my eyes off you for a few seconds without you already looking for them cigarettes to suck on.Shit." Linda countered. "Well Ima leave the two of you so yall can handle your lil disagreements." Joel gave Linda a peck on the lips. She smelled so good. Joel thought to himself. See you another time. "Ima call you later babe." Linda walked her man to the door. "Don't be picking up no hookers out there on your way home." Linda had some insecurities that would only reflect in her own behavior. Do you think she noticed them? I highly doubted it. "You're my only hooker." Joel joked just kidding babe. "I better be." Linda perked her lips. "MUAHZ!"

"Why didn't you just stay with that man on his only day off. You don't work either. Don't you like him Linda?" Mom was curious. "Of course, I love him. I was with him all night mom. I have to take care of a few things that's why." Linda had a smart mouth at times. "Love? Alright, that's right baby. Make him miss you huh?" Mom had one hand on her hip as she spoke with a big grin on her face. "Oh my God. Mom stop please, it's so embarrassing mom." Linda covered her bashful face and sat on the chair. "Don't be embarrassed. Pete got me wide open too baby. "Uuuhhmmm." That man something else." Mom joked. "ill! I don't want to know this mom, you are so crazy." Linda whined the two enjoyed their morning, but Linda's time was pressed. Punching in the number to Streets phone which by the way he didn't answer. "Pick up the phone." Linda dialed out again still no answer.

"You probably out there on the go with some hood rat." Linda was talking to herself. You would think that after all the time that she was spending with the Streets. She would have some hatred against him right? The way she was acting, your average person would think that she was becoming emotionally involved with this man. "Hello?" Street finally answered. "Damn! What you with the next bitch already?" Linda spat acting out her emotion. "Wow!" This is how you greet me over the phone?" Streets was still lying in bed with Star laid out right next to him. "Wassup?" Street asked. "Nothing I wanted to see you today that's all. I figured that I call you early so you wouldn't make plans and not fit me in your busy schedule. I had to be everybody to the punch." Linda said. "Okay that was smart. Well call me at seven or eight and I'll come grip you up." Street spoke into the receiver. "Who's that?" Star asked still half asleep. Linda could hear the voice faintly. Streets slapped her bare ass. "Don't to worry about it." Linda heard him say over the phone to Star. "Later." Linda said before hanging. This nigga was all laid up with the next bitch. I need to find out who and where this chick be at." Linda thought to herself. Her mind was racing. Something's would be better off just left alone. Why was it that we always wanted to kick the hornets' nest knowing the outcome could be drastic.

—

The door popped, we all stared at it waiting to see what the pigs had to say. "Randy Robison visit!" The guard yelled over the speaker. "Oh shit Mr. I don't get no love." Leak mocked Slash for what he said the other day. "I don't, shit." Slash said jumping up to brush his hair and his teeth at the same time. "Well your day is here take your dusty ass out there and enjoy that shit." Rock joked. "Shit I don't get no love." Bigs said. Leak and Rock both simultaneously spoke. "What!?" Maybe if I say I get no love too I might get a visit too." Bigs joked laughing at his statement.

"You wanted to see me?" Greg popped his face in the door. He had the best job running around the tier cleaning and passing shit to whoever and whenever he wanted too. "Yea mamao." Rock answered.

I need you to pass some shit to Jonathan he is two cells down." Rock instructed Greg. "What is it?" Greg asked. Leak got up and picked up two bags. "This." "What the fuck. I gota get this door popped for that one." Greg said. "Make it happen and I got you with the honey bun with a bag of chips." Rock had to pay every man that he needed to make a move for him,. "Na you good I got you." Greg denied the offer for payment. "Man fuck that Ima lookout, make it happen." Rock snapped. He disliked when mother fuckers didn't want to take his money. He felt disrespected, plus he damn sure didn't want it to be thrown in his face later. "Nigga you still here." Leak joked. "Alright, all right I'm out." Slash darted out the cell. That nigga still ugly as fuck." Leak could be very comical at times. He had Bigs and Rock balling out with laughter.

"Set it up." Rock declared war on the chessboard. "Who want it?" Chest was a serious game so if you played you should always take it serious every time you played. Your opponent will destroy you the minute he notices you slipping up. "Ayo we running low too by the way." Leak spoke softly. The topic grab Bigg's attention he turned his big ass over to face the guys. Rock notice but didn't say anything. "How much?" Rock asked in a low tone as well. "About 10 of each." Leak put all his pieces where they belonged on the chessboard Rock on the other hand was in deep thought. Usually Mandy would already have dropped off the work. He looked over at the calendar. "She still had a day left." Biggs read his mind. "That's what I don't want to get rid of your big ass." Rock liked how on point Biggs was at times. He might not be the most ruthless out of the crew but he had what we may have been lacking in each of us which was patients and memory. Having all his pieces set up.

"Was the money sent already? Rock asked not looking up at Bigs "$500 just like you said." Big was in charge of that shit. Rock didn't feel like gambling with his money like that. It's fucked up, how a lack of trust was floating in the air at times. It was always a good move to be wise and aware. You always had to know who and what surrounded you know matter where you found yourself. Wouldn't you agree? "Give her a day or two, can't rush her you already know she got her own shit to take care of. A few days without some work will only let us cool down a bit anyway." Rock spoke making the first move with his fourth pawn for two spaces. The cell went silence for a few as the two battled for their victory.

It was nothing to get accustomed to live in the jailhouse lifestyle. If you had things going and had a couple people in your corner these small trips weren't as bad as they were made out to be. This is crazy because this how many people that were institutionalized thought. Do not get me wrong. For those of you who are doing or may have done a significant amount of time. Yall could agree that this had the power to make anyone age quicker. Your stress levels would rise at times , but once you mentally set yourself up and accepted what you have done. You'd be able to live a life at ease. Yes, the thought of not having a woman by your side would drive any man insane. Besides that, a strong mind could help you conquer everything as long as you put your all into it.

—

Mandy on the other hand was going through her own episodes. "Why the fuck isn't this bitch answering the phone!" Mandy was pacing back and forth in her jeans, with her navy blue sweater that hugged her body snugly. She decided to let it go and just wait for Jacqueline to call her back. Who knows when that would be? Not knowing this was going to happen it only made her mad at herself for not being better prepared. "I should've called her yesterday and handled all of this last night." Mandy was really beaten herself up. Was it that important to keep Rock happy and content inside? Even if her job and her freedom could be placed in jeopardy? She didn't give a fuck. She had another cash flow coming in from Rock, she didn't mind this not one bit. The money was coming faster than her checks at times. She tried to relax on her loveseat.

The loud ringing of the phone startled her. It was definitely the call she was waiting for. "Hello!?" Manny answered. "Damn bitch! What the hell? I've been trying to call you all morning." Mandy had already gotten to know Jacqueline. So much that they had built a nice bond with oneanother. "Well Sorry but I do have a thing called "A life" as well, but I couldn't expect you to understand that one." Jacqueline shot back. "You already know what I need from you." Mandy spoken to the receiver. She was more relax knowing that it was Jacqueline's voice she was speaking to. "Yes baby the same as always." Mandy kept it simple. She knew better than to put a bigger cargo on herself. She was already accustomed to carry a big enough load. It's got to the point where all the feelings she use to have for Rock, all went out the window. She liked Rock but getting too involved with him could only lead to disaster. Mandy didn't have seniority or pull like that yet, to pull stunts like that in the jail. So for the better she made sure to contained herself and put her lust in the backseat. The money was grabbing her attention more than Rock was. That was a wise move because if it was up to Rocks horny ass. That pussy would be first on his list. That man did love all his woman. "Call me right back then." Mandy ended the call and waited patiently in her cozy love seat dozing off.

—

30 minutes didn't go by, that the phone's annoying ring snapped Mandy right out of her nap. She answered it immediately. It wasn't the call she was waiting for. "Hey mom." Mandy tried to sound inviting. Her eyes weren't fully open yet or should I say that hearing her mother's voice only put her in a state of relaxation again. "No I had off just trying to tie up a few things that I need to do." Mandy informed her mother. If her mother would find out what she was up to she would probably disown her own creation. Her mom wouldn't understand. How her innocent daughter's mind, has evolved into what she was thinking lately. "Yes I will stop by when I get the chance today. I want to see my old room anyway." Mandy was reminiscing how quick time has passed her by. "I love you and I'll see you later." Mandy knew that the chances of stopping by her mom's house were slim. She had to pacify her mom so that her mother wouldn't just pop up while Mandy

was prepping up the work. She had to feed her all that false information for now. It was a must to keep her as far away as possible from Mandy's home for the next couple of days.

Jacqueline finally called close to 1 p.m.Mandy's day was half way gone already. "We gonna have to do this earlier next time Jacqueline, my whole day is gone." Mandy was annoyed. "I know I don't have to do this but I want to do it. So wassup?" Mandy didn't allow Jacqueline to say much. He got the snowfall but no green growing?" Mandy reiterated. "Damn! Fuck it double up on the snow then." Mandy didn't know what she was doing. Rock was going to be so happy once he found out that he was only getting more of the raw. Everyone's profits were about to skyrocket with just a simple double up. "Yes I'm sure, how long?" Mandy waited for a response. She slid on her on unlaced Tim's. Mandy was finally coming in contact with Jacqueline. She knew after this it was smooth sailing. This was the worst part. Getting a hold of one another. when things had to be done was something everyone dreaded. "All right I'll be there 15 minutes." Mandy peeled off a couple of bills and took the rest with her. She was coming up. How long was all this going to last? Would Jacqueline forced Mandy to find another line because Jacqueline wasn't eating like Mandy was? Or would Rock finally be halted in his tracks causing him to stop and lose all that he worked for? Everything was moving so fast and going so well. There was no way any of this would last. Things like this never did.

—

"You have till 3 p.m. ma'am." The pink faced correctional officer said. After passing through the detectors upon more detectors. Jacqueline was dressed in a fly ass outfit. She was looking as if she was one of the baldest bitches in the small city of Camden. She had on her fitted with a deep burgundy color with the matching jacket. She showed off her belly button. She happened to have a small visible piercing exposing complimenting her beautiful soft skin. Her hair was in a ponytail it hung on her left shoulder. Her eyebrows were on point. her walk, her body and character was all neck turning. Her presence screamed attention. The G string was holding nothing but her pussy lips because that small plump ass stormed as she walked. It demanded everyone's attention with her small frame. This was Jacqueline and she was waiting to see no one else but Rock. She knew she was a sexy bad bitch. Her eye was a lot better but you could still noticed a tint of discoloration. Jacqueline was never the heavy makeup wearing type. Why would she ruined that picture perfect face? She had her flaws but who didn't? What made one beautful was on how they embraced there imperfections.

"You can sit at the far end, or in the middle miss." The CO's jaw was dragging. "Thank you." Jacqueline replied not even turning around to face the CO. She gave him her back. It was funny because you could always see your haters from up close. They all tend to give you that "know she ain't" look as if you're doing something wrong. If a mother fucker look good thatn let them be The visitors mainly consisted of women supporting their man, as they should. If that's the life they wish to live with their significant other so be it. A few had there family and by family I meant intermediate family. The ones who made time to come and support there loved ones was rare but they still did exist.

Lastly, you had your broads that only came up to shut you the fuck up. Because your nagging and bitching about how come they don't come up to see your ass got annoying as fuck. As if they ain't got a life to live of their own. So to put it plain and simple, they'll show their face and answer your little 15 to 20 minute phone calls to keep you happy. Many did this to keep you thinking that you are still running the show. When in all actuality they balls deep with the next nigga. Are we that naïve? Hate to burst your bubble but you could be one of those niggaz. As much as you tried. You couldn't keep a hot ass from getting dicked down playboy. If she wanted some dick you best believe she gonna go get that shit from whoever she fucking felt like. So how about we just accept the fact that a bitch is only as loyal as you are to her my friend. Ima break it down a little more, you can't call after last count which is around 9 right? That's the time when everything starts to pop off. As far as clubs, parties, strip clubs, dating and fucking etc. etc. you following me? Good now you have your phones on the tier that are on after 8 AM and that's assuming you can get one that early. Either your was bitch was laid up in bed with the next man with cum all over her ass, pussy and throat unless she kicked the nigga out that same night. So when you do decide to call her like clock work. The next man knows who you are nine times out a ten. He gonna play his part to the tee. Why? Because all he wants is that shot on command. All she has to do is win her Oscar, for actress of the day and there you are my friend you are pacified. Stupid mother fuckers. The mental torment of this shit was beyond with in reason. Cut those tainted relationship unless you enjoy the mental break down. As for Rock I hated to say it. Jacqueline was playing him like a saxophone on a hot jazz night or was he playing her?

Rock walked in with his tall glowing cinnamon complexion, his toned up body didnt go unnoticed. Jacqueline looks right on cue. She searching his eyes for any emotion that she would be able to go off of. Rock checks out every who is out on the dance floor with him. He gives a few head nods in acknowledgment than his attention is back focused on Jacqueline. He moves in closer towards the glass to get a full view. Well at least he tries to get a full view. Jacqueline was so small he could only see her from the belly button up. He flags her with his hand telling her to back up. She smiled so vibrantly. She did exactly what he asked of her. She put her hands on her hips and striked a pose. The look Rock gives her ment he wanted to devour her given the opportunity. He bit his bottom lip. Rock twirled his finger. She spun her ass around and shook it like a tsunami. Jacqueline winked at the CO who was checking her out. The other crazy mother fuckers in the visiting room with their visits couldn't help but look. A couple of the females begin to talk shit to their man for looking but none of that shit fazeds Jacqueline. She had one thing on her mind and that was to please Rock for this small amount of time that she was permitted with him. Jacqueline was done with her show and knew that it was very much approved. "Hey baby boy." Jacqueline said smiling vibrantly. "Wassup ma?" Those words hit her hard. Those words instantly brought back a wave of memories. When they would talk to each other in his soft manly swag. That same swag that captured her from the first time they met. "How are you?" Jacqueline asked. "I'm good. I'm really good now that I see you in front of me." Rock didn't want to say anything out of the ordinary that could ruined this joyful moment. He thought rationally starting small talk. "I didn't think you would ever come up." Rock said. "Why wouldn't I come? I can't stay away from you forever. I think of you almost every moment that I'm up and moving. I been going through so much. Babe... I miss you so much." Jacqueline looked down at her fingernails as she spoke what she was feeling. "/Mira me/"/ look at me/Rock spoke softly instructing her. She was hesitant but eventually gazed deep into Rock's eyes. Rocks visage turned sinister in seconds. "What?" Jacqueline asked. Forgetting her visible wounds. "Why?" Rock asked. Jacqueline wasn't too sure what he was inquiring "Why what?" She asked confused. Rocks corner of his lip curled up. "Why did he hit you? Rock asked. Not loud but with enough tone for her to feel his question. Jacqueline shook her head not wanting to get into this conversation. "I didn't come here to talk about that. I came to see how you are doing Rock." Jacqueline whined knowing this was a match she was not going to come close to winning. I didn't asked you that ma. "/porque te pego?/"/why did he hit you?/ Rock asked her again. "Because I didn't want to be with him." Jacqueline didn't want to go into the exact reason but she figured this was as close enought to the truth. Being that they were only about a foot away from the other visitors she didn't wan everyone in her business. An unnecessary embarrassment wasn't something that she wanted right now. For the record this visit wasn't going as planned in Jacqueline's eyes. She kind of wish she would've waited till her damn face was 100% to come up. "Are you fucking serious?" Rocks tone grew louder. He banged his fist on the small ledge. Wishing he could get out on that nigga Streets. "I'm okay baby ain't no need to get all worked up over nothing." Jacqueline tried to console Rock. "Why is it that your baby dads can't seem to let you go? I'm beginning to think that you are playing with this nigga mind. Why is he so hell bent over you?" Rock fucked up opening his mouth and speaking out of emotion. Jacqueline's jaw dropped. "What!?" Are you fucking kidding me. You know that since day one I've been going through with this with him. You're right he is my baby dad. There is a chance he will never let me go but for you to say some off the wall type shit like that. It's so wrong and so disrespectful! I thought you knew me better than that." Jacqueline's left hand was shaking. She was getting just as hyped as Rock was now but she had all the right. Rock was dead wrong and he realized it checking himself.

"I'm sorry ma that came out all wrong. I meant to say, is it that hard for you to stay away from him?" Rock corrected his angle. "I can't, remember he knows where I work at. I really don't have no control over him Rock. It's just too much to worry about. I'm seriously thinking of getting all my stuff and relocating far away. It's getting out of hand with this nigga. I thought he got the picture by now but apparently not." Jacqueline was going through it. "I'm sorry once again. Ima make a few phone calls and see what I can do for you." Rock was on another type of time. Who did he think he was? A Cartel boss. "No Rock. I'm okay I don't need you to get into anymore bullshit over nothing." Jacqueline said. "You are something don't ever say that you are nothing. Maybe to him you're nothing but to me you hold a special part in my heart. Remember that." Rock assured Jacqueline. Her eyes retained a lot of water but she wasn't going to cry. This was her baby and she would be strong for him. The same way he was always strong for her. "How's the baby?" Rock switched up the convo. Jacqueline's face lit up like fireworks in the dark blue sky on Independence Day. He is my inspiration, my world. He is my everything Rock. "I see that ma. Your facial expression said it all." Jacqueline you are so beautiful... Take care of yourself. If you have to find yourself a real man, who will love and protect you as I once did go for it." It took almost everything that Rock had inside to say something like that to Jacqueline. Jacqueline's eyes now dropped a lonely tear. "You don't want me anymore?" She asked. "I didn't say that baby, all I'm saying is that if you find yourself a man that is thorough and really likes you. Go for it. Maybe your baby dads will see that you want nothing to do with him for real. If he sees that you are alone. He isn't going to stop trying to get in between those sexy thighs of yours." Rock was manning up. He was giving up his spot so the next man could actually provide, and do what he couldn't. Jacqueline was understanding what Rock was saying. "Now this don't mean to get all dicked down than forget all about me." Rock was bringing back the humor in the conversation. Jacqueline smiled. "How would that ever be possible, no man out there will ever treat me the way you did ever." Jacqueline emphasized "Ever" I'm sure there is one out there." Rock challenge. "What if he is a she? Does that still count as the same thing?" Jacqueline blurted out being completely honest as she had always been with Rock. "A what?" Rock was taking back a little with that one. Jacqueline laughed as if she was being tickled. "Why you going to wait for me to fall up in here to come out the closet with that one? That's not right I want to have some fun too." Rock couldn't believe what he just heard. "Don't worry when you get out I'll have something special for you." Jacqueline teased."Oh yea?" Rock asked. "Yes I do." Jacqueline teased some more. "And what may that be?" Rock was getting an all aroused by this conversation now. Jacqueline unzipped her jacket halfway exposing only a bra. Rock's eyes grew larger than normal. Jacqueline stopped not wanting bring any attention over to them. "Better yet how about you explain all those nasty thoughts, In the next letter you write to me. With some pictures of you looking as you do today or even sexier." Rock was planting the seed. He needed some excitement from his lady friends "pictures?" Jacqueline replied licking her lips. Jacqueline always knew how to make Rock feel appreciated. She leaned in and popped out her breast. She was exposing it, she squeezed it and pinched her nipple. Rocks dick grew solid immediately. "He was enjoying Jacqueline today. She was going out her way risking the visit and all. She plopped it back where it belonged in the purple velour jacket. Rock couldn't wait to get back to the cell, everyone had to go. "Pictures that?" Jacqueline teased. "All of that." Rock wished he could have taken a nose dive into Jacqueline's love box. He was almost for sure that it was moist and getting worse by the second. She knew what she was doing right? It's what a rider chick does for her man in a times like this. "I got you babe." Jacqueline assured Rock. So did you hear anything on the status on your case yet?" Jacqueline change the subject taking a glance over to the backside noticing the pig staring over in her direction. "Yes and no. I'm gonna be here for some time if these witnesses do come and testify." Rock informed Jacqueline. "I'm a try to talk to him so he doesn't because that some bitch ass shit." Jacqueline suggested. "you better not say shit to that bitch ass nigga!" Rocks barked. I know you want to help but knowing his type he use that against you to try and get you back and still renig on his word." Rock replied to her suggestion. He was right "what can I do to help?" Jacqueline asked. Just keep doing what you doing with the white girl because that's helping me so much you have no fucking clue." Rock he knew better than to talk to reckless especially while the CO behind him was steady listen into his every word. Waiting for one of these idiots to slip up and say something out of the norm. "Oh yea. Speaking of that you should have gave me the heads up a bit sooner Rock that shit almost got ugly." Jacqueline had her sexy mean mug face displayed. Rock smiled "I know my bad but yall getting along just right now." Jaclyn smiled. "Yea once she gave me the 411 on everything I couldn't resist not helping my baby everything is for you too." Jacqueline was confirming the next shipment without Rock even having to ask about it. "You got five minutes." The CO on Rock's side informed. "Time flies when you have any good time ain't that what they say." Rock said. "Well at least that's what they say Rock clearly didn't want to end the date. "Baby I'm a try my best to come when I can. Make sure your bitches don't show up on the same time I come because I'll fuck around and be up in there with yo ass." Jacqueline was joking she wasn't gonna do anything to end up in jail she better not Rock was savoring and enjoying his last few moments we Jacqueline. "Which side you on?" Jacqueline asked. "By fifth why?" Rock asked. Got the window when you go back so I can see which window is yours." Jacqueline was a trooper for real. You know how cold it is out there and she was willing to stand out there and freeze just so she could identify Rocks window. "I will be safe out there baby and do me a favor?" Rock suggested. "Wassup baby?" Jacqueline's smile was priceless look into getting your license to carry when you get a chance is only a few dollars." Rock was on some other shit for real. "I thought about that and I am glad you read my mind. You just gave me the extra push I needed to do it." Jacqueline was even more excited than before.

“Muahz! Muahz!” Jacqueline blue Rock kisses that wouldn’t be felt physically but Rock felt both of them and blowing one of his own back at her. “”The window” Jacqueline reminded him as she was getting up pulling her velour pants up so that her ass crack would be concealed. She walked away so Rock could enjoy all of her and he sure did. The walk back to Rock cell was a bit stressful but he couldn’t let all that was going on out there fuck up his mind and emotions in here. There was no room for any of that he had no choice but to start jailing again. He remembered Jacqueline specifically told Rock about the window so he picked up his step heading towards his cell. He felt bad leaving her out there just staring. All the guys were inside talking about whatever it was that they were debating about it was always something new every day. Rock headed straight to the window.

“Yoooooo! You good my nigga?” Slash asked. Wondering why Rock knocked over everything that was on Leaks footlocker by accident. “Yeah I’m straight.” Rock focused his eyes out the window. “Oh shit! He getting window love.” Bigs said. So far no one in the cell got window love yet. No particular reason but no one’s family really had the patience and time to sit out there getting a crook in there neck staring up at the high as windows. “What’s her name bro?” Bigs nosey ass asked. “Jacqueline.” Rock said smiling. Leak noticed his cheeks go up. “Man this is the one he feeling. Look at his face.” Leak challenge. “Chill I’m tryna find her.” Rock was a little child looking for his toy in the toy box. “Yea he definitely sprung over Ms. Jacqueline.” Slash emphasized. Rock’s eyes scanned the people outside which weren’t many, but enough to get your eyes exhausted. “Burgundy pants” Rock said. Leak got up to helped Rock look. “That girl went home you know how cold it is out there to be just standing out there?” Slash was sounding like a hater but in a way he could be absolutely right about her going home. “Nah, she told me to look out the window.” Rock defended his Shorty. “She wouldn’t do me like that. I hope not” Rock had doubt. “I’m not saying she would but it is cold.” Slash was right there was no sign of Jacqueline. “You prolly right she aint coming.” Rock plopped down on his bed.

“So how was it?” Bigs asked referring to the visit. “Man she a rider for real, you don’t know what she did down there. I wasn’t even expecting none of that shit. Rock had everyone’s attention. “What did she do?” Slash’s horny ass asked. “She got nasty?” Leak backed away from the window waiting for the answer to his question. “No she didn’t get nasty, what the fuck are you thinking?” Rock got serious. Bigs fat ass didn't want no parts of this, all hell was about to break loose. Bigs stared out the window. The snow captured his eyes as he just stared at the freedom that he couldn't touch. "Yo my bad got a little hyped, by the way you said it. "Slash didn't want to come off as no slimy ass nigga who gets off on the next man's woman. "Na you good she did show me her sexy breast though. Oh my god it was better than the smut we got in his mother fucker. The way she touched yourself had me ready to jack off right in the visitor room. Now I see why niggaz be letting off rounds down there. That's as good as it fucking gets unless you fucking up in here." Rock recounted the episode.

"Burgundy pants?" Bigs asked "I see them." Rock shot up. "Where!?" He asked. "Walking over." Bigs had his eyes locked on someone. "I don't see shit Bigs." Rock was getting frustrated. "Okay don't pay attention to anything out there okay." Bigs was instructing. Just focus on what I'm telling you to look at." Bigs spoke. It didn't help that Rock's vision was far from perfect too. "You see the dumpster over by the light pole." Bigs asked keeping his eye on Jacqueline's body. He wasn't even sure if who he was looking at was even her. "Okay I see the dumbster now what?" Rock was getting desperate. "Count three light poles to the right." Bigs was mapping out Jacqueline's coordinates to the tee. "Alright, I see two people one with a white coat and one with the blue one." Rock advised Bigs. "All right now you see the mailbox that's almost at the end of the corner?" Big asked Rock. "Yeah I see it." Rock was getting excited. He was getting closer to Jacqueline and his emotions could be felt. "Now look to the left of the mailbox." "That should be her, because no one else out there has Burgundy pants." Bigs informed Rock. "That's her!" Rock was excited. She had on her coat with the hood on looking up.

"How do I get her attention?" Rock asked not knowing shit about this one. "This is the fun part." Leak said "Slash get the light." He was already at the light switch. "On it." "Pass me a cup Rock." Leak said. When I say flick it you already know." Leak said. The Cups banged on the window with full force. "Tap! Tap! Tap! Tap!" Jacqueline looked around. Leak did not stop until he thought she was looking up at their direction. "Flick it" Jacqueline turn her vision elsewhere. "Holdup"..... Tap, Tap, Tap! Leak's veins could be seen growing in his arm and his four head. He was really trying to put a hole in that window, banging it hard on that thick ass window. Jacqueline looked up again sensing that it had to be for her. All that noise that was being made caused her to look up again grabbing her attention. But where? "Flick it." The lights in a cell danced like a club scene on and off. Leak would wave his hands trying to get Jacqueline's full attention. After almost 10 minutes. Leak finally managed to get Jacqueline's attention. "Rock it's on you." Leak instructed. Jacqueline threw up her small arms. R – O – C – K Jacqueline spelled out. "That's her. She spelled your name Rock. The two engage in small talk for a brief moment. With the help of the guys the conversation went well. Rock realized that Jacqueline had done this one too many times. And to be honest he didn't even care because now she was riding for him.The temperatures dropping drastically caused the conversation to be terminated

—

Linda's outfit was slighly different. This time the tights were out the window. Linda had no fucking clue what she was getting herself into. The rug was about to be pulled right out from under her. She couldn't just let bygones be bygones, was this worth all the damages. No one in their right mind had the power to stop Linda. Her mind was set on attempting the worst. She looked at herself in the mirror. Her all black sweats that were pretty loose, even with that apple bottom could still be very visible. She had on her money green tights under her sweats. Her heart rate was steady, as she finished up the braids in her hair. She rocked those braids good, looking sexier than ever. Today she wore no earrings, no type of jewelry was on her body at all. Streets was way ahead of her game. He was ready to do the unthinkable. Linda was ready to pull this fucking stunt and there was no turning her back now. The worst part of all this. Linda had no clue that fucking Streets knew who the fuck Linda was. Linda strongly believed that she had the upper had in all of this, but this was far from the case.

—

Streets dipped his Newport into the small valve that contained the awful smelling liquid. "Baby what time you coming over?" Star asked. She stared at Streets pulling on a cigarette to get as much as the embalming fluid to saturate the entire cigarette as much as he could. "Around 10:30 to 11 o'clock. Make sure you answer the door and don't go anywhere." Streets was getting ready and putting together his alibi. He was a lot more experience in this department than many. This man literally went out of his way to purchase equipment to murder and dispose of Linda's body. He was on a mission, only difference was. Streets was dead serious. He waited patiently for the phone call that would only mean one thing and one thing only. It was causing his heart rates to race every time the phone rang. The sherm stick was engulfed in flames. The cherry turned bright red with every pull he took. It was go time. "So what you going to do tonight?" Star asked. She knew when her man smoked that shit it only meant that something was about to happen., and it wasn't something pretty. She learned this from all the previous experiences with him. Streets didn't say a word. It only took a minute for his hallucinations to kick in and become the pilot of his body. I ran into so many so called men. Who all had to do what Streets was doing before getting ready to commit acts of war. It took me some time to understand why this was done. As time went by, I put the equation together all by myself. Killing wasn't something many could do or could live with after they committed these types of acts. So therefore, to help give them the strength to push through there subconscious. One either was a cold blooded killer or one just needed to be heavily intoxication to play. Then you had your stone cold killers who do it off the muscle with no worries. Just for the adrenaline rush murder after murder. Those who didn't care about a mother fucking thing. They got high after the act has been done or might not even get high at all. The killing alone could be the only high that they wanted to experience. These aren't the ones you have to worry about it's the cowards like Streets one must try their best avoid.

"I'm going to..... handle.... something right quick so chill." Streets was talking real slow. He passed the saturated smoking cigarette over to Star. She took two pulls and passed it right back. "You better be careful." I'm not going to be doing this jail shit I'm warning you." Star knew damn well she was riding no matter what. If Streets would let her she would be right by his side helping him with this murder. Streets had something twisted planned out for this night. Streets wasn't paying Star no mind, she knew better than that. She's lucky Streets hasn't tied her ass up yet and threw her in his trunk. If you knew your cars anyone would know that a Lincoln town car was known to fit at least three. If you were bold you could squeeze in a fourth. Streets and Kay done filled that trunk up with countless bodies over the years. This is why he was so eager to get revenge on that bitch that killed his man's. Even though this was only an assumption that he was making. He was not hundred percent sure if it was Linda but at this point he didn't give a fuck. She was enough to fit his vague description of the broad that night. Linda was soon to be another statistic once her lifeless body would be found. The odds were stacked against her. "Ring, ring!" The phone was sitting right in front of the two stuck wet heads. "Ring, ring!" They just stared at the phone. "Babe." Star said. "I got it." Streets replied moving slowly to answer the phone "yooooo." Streets answered. "Damn wassup you forgot about me?" Linda spoke into the receiver. "No, I didn't forget." Street sounded like a robot going dead. "are you okay?" Linda asked. "I'm on my way give me 15 to 20." Streets hung up. "He stared at Star. "Come on, I'm dropping you off then I'll be back tonight." Streets stated still not moving. Angel dust was known as one of the worst drug to ingested. You would be surprised how many people enjoyed the near death experience every time you're high on that shit.

—

Linda waiting for about five minutes in the living room by herself. Mom was upstairs probably asleep already. "Let me call my baby." Linda said to herself. No answer. "This nigga out playing me?" Linda mumbled to herself. Again still no answer. Why this mother fucker not answering! Linda was tight. "Fuck him." She got up putting on her coat over her sweater and storms out the door. The snow was still falling. The news cast declared a snowstorm in effect, but we all know how that goes. When have you ever seen a news company ever be on point? The KYW news crew was no different, but they were accurate like a mother fucker for once.

Linda's all suede black Tim's stomped the snow. She tucked her head low and walked up towards the same spot where she met Streets. The hustlers were out holding down what was rightfully considered their turf. Every corner all the way to the 7/11 had different set of crews drinking and dealing. This was home and it wouldn't change no time soon for any of us.

The kids played throwing snowballs at one another chasing and freezing their little bodies off. Their adrenaline was the only thing working to keep them warm. A snowball almost hit Linda but she didn't pay it no mind not one bit. As she got closer to the 7/11 her lower back began to perspire a bit. Her adrenaline was on overload as well. Her breathing began to get heavier. Could she pull through with this? Was she having doubts?

What she would normally do when arriving at the store. She did the complete opposite. Instead of waiting inside with Mr. Hobbiebee sipping on hot chocolate and having smalltalk. She didn't do the normal routine. Why? The hood on her coat didn't allow any live feed to identify who she was. The dark clothing she decided to wear was also on her side. She posted up on the side of the building. I may have of under estimated Linda. She was trying to avoid being recorded on a surveillance system that the 7/11. Why wouldn't she? She thought she was covering up her breadcrumbs. She was going about it the wrong way. These tapes could be the way to get her murderer behind bars. Instead she was only helping him out by keeping her face nowhere to be identified with him. Too much thought into something could be just as detrimental as to not thinking about it at all. Wouldn't you agree? When you tended to plan things out to a tee. There was always that one misplaced segment that catches everyone off guard. That alone had the power to paralyzes the majority, that alone could results in a catastrophic event. There was a car parked in the far distance she noticed. The exhaust only signified that the vehicle was on. The cloud it blew out the exhaust didn't want to mix with the freezing air. No one really noticed the vehicle. It was irrelevant. "Here he comes" Linda mumbled to herself. She waiting for the Lincoln to park in the available spot. Linda walked briskly towards the vehicle and jumped right inside. "Damn! It's cold what the heck took you so long?" Linda asked. She leaned over for a kiss. Streets dug his tongue straight down Linda's mouth not being in the mood to play her little games at the moment. They swapped spit for a minute. Linda tastes something nasty in Streets mouth but didn't alarm him of it. Instead she popped in a stick a big red in her mouth.

"The snowww maaann, look at them rooaads." Streets was still slurring his speech. "I know, it's so bad right?" Linda asked. "Who you telling. I don't even want to drive in this for real." Streets informed. "You don't have to. Let go to your place if you want." Linda suggested. "My place or a telly?" Streets asked. Linda liked that idea but refused it. "What you got your wifey at your spot?" Linda countered. "Wifey? Haha." Streets was laughing. I told you I don't do those." Streets informed. "Aright then I want to lay in your bed." Linda reached over touching Street between his thighs. Streets bit his bottom lip. He couldn't wait to rip Linda's ass wide open. He never had any plans on going to a fucking telly. All the things he needed for his little charade were at his place. It was just a stunt to throw her off just in case she was suspecting something. "Let's get out of here." Linda suggested still not uncovering her head. Streets ended up removing her hood as they pulled off. "Why you hiding?" Streets asked her. He put his hands on her thigh as they drove towards his crib. Linda's heart was pounding.

She stared out the window. "I'm not hiding from nobody." Her cornrows were fresh as always when she snatched her own hair back. "I'm feeling the cornrows." Streets complemented. "Thank you I'm glad you notice them." Linda played her part. "So what you got to drink at your spot?" Linda asked. "Shiiitt. What don't I have?" Streets was cocky as always. "Well let me see. I got some Henny. I have some absolute and a half a case of old English, and some vodka I think. Is there anything in particular you want to sip on?" Streets was driving steadily through the slippery roads. "Damn this shit picking up or is it my eyes playing with me?" Linda asked. "No it's not your eyes, this shit is fallen." It was perfect to catch a body. Linda only weighed about a buck and some change. He would do her dirty and dispose her body where ever he thought would be the most convenient.

Kay and Streets were so thrown off that they done dumped bodies in the Cooper River one night. For those of you who may not know of the Cooper River. It's a public River where everyone goes to swim, fish and do whatever they do at that River. These two didn't even care if those bodies were found. That body was found the very next day. That's how stupid and bold these two were at times. "No I guess that sounds good. How about movies do you have any?" Linda asked. Streets looked at Linda. "Of course, but I rather make our own." Streets suggest-ed. "Uumm I don't know about all that. I can't trust you with the tape of all of this. You probably copy that shit than sell it to every person in the city and get rich." Linda joked. "I'll give you half" Streets joked back "Half you going to have to come better than that baby." Linda replied. "All right I'll give you 75% and I get 25% plus that pussy when I wanted." Streets counter offered. "Damn whenever you want though?" Linda wasn't feeling this conversation but the situation was evolving all on his own. "What if I'm in Maryland than what?" Linda joked. "Well you going to jump on a plane and bring that ass to me then jump back on that plane and head back to Maryland when I'm done." Streets joked. He dug into the ashtray after finding what he was looking for. "Lite that." Streets told Linda. "What is it?" Linda asked. "Its chronic." Streets admitted. Linda smelled it not 100% sure if. He was telling the truth. Rocks words echo to ear once again. "If you didn't see it rolled up don't smoke it." Those were his words. Linda was very hesitant and Streets was getting annoyed "I said light that shit for me!" He snapped. "What the fuck you smelling it for?" He was bugging out that wet. "All right I got you relax." Linda's hands trembled as she held the L with her lips and use her hands to light it up. "Was that hard? What you thought I'm poising you Janet?" Streets snapped a question her way. Linda inhaled the chronic. The smell was something that she recognized but then again even if it wasn't she was fucked anyway. "I don't know I hope not." Linda's voice showed fear. He had her exactly where he wanted her. Linda had an option . She could hop out of the car as soon as it came to a stop and get somewhere safe or follow through with the plan as planned. This wasn't going to end well for her. Streets killed the half of clip and the rest of the ride was a bit awkward. Linda had a small taste of what Jacqueline was going through. There was no escaping the madness of Streets. Especially when a child was involved with this lunatic.

He finally pulled up to his apartment. Streets was no longer that gentleman when they first met each other. The opening of the doors, the holding of the hands. The arm locking was all a play to get what he wanted. It all played off. It was soon to come and no one was going to intervene in his mission. Linda opened her door and stepped out pulling her hood over her head. So that the snow wouldn't creep down her back Streets was already far ahead.

"You coming?" His attitude was shit now. Linda look back. She was wondering if she should run and not stop until she was clear from what she had gotten herself into. She was scared for her own life now. This shit was getting real and fast. As soon as she would enter his house, she wasn't sure what was bound to take place nor did she want to contemplate any of it. "Yeah I'm right behind you." Linda had to play the hand that was dealt. She had no choice but to play it out now.

Linda's heart pounded as she walked up the steps to enter the apartment. She noticed that Streets sneakers were at the door. She did what she saw and kicked off her own boots. The apartment had this distinctive smell. Linda wasn't sure what the smell was but it sort of resembled what she tasted and smelled when she first kissed Streets upon entering his whip. She tried not to pay any mine to it. She closed the door and walked slowly. "Where you go?" Linda yelled. I'm upstairs take a seat in the living room. You want to smoke?" Streets was yelling from upstairs. Linda put her coat near the door. She made her way towards the living room as instructed by Streets. She had to admit his place was warm and inviting to an extent. His sofas look damn near new. The large TV that was in front of the sofa had to cost a few thousand. The wall to wall persian carpet felt so soft under Linda's feet. "What you doing?" Linda yelled getting impatient. "I'm coming." Streets replied finally shooting down the stairs. "Roll it up." Streets tossed Linda a small baggie with a Dutch. "I can't roll like that." Linda admitted.

"Well keep learning, you gota learn one day." Streets said. "If I fuck it up." "Blah blah" Streets interrupted. "You won't Janet." Just try your best." Streets said. Linda was confused she didn't know how to take his attitude. He was bipolar as fuck. A minute ago in the car he went off, now he was acting as if everything was great. Like the car incident never even occurred. Streets went to the back of the house where Linda was nowhere in sight. He lit up another sherm stick and suck on it till the empty filter was almost burning. He was far gone as he walked in. The aroma clearly hung on to his clothing for dear life. "A yooooo, what you want to drink?" Streets asked moving super slow. He searched through his cabinets in search of the alcohol. Linda was still slobbering all over the dutch leaf tryna to place them as they went. You would think she was putting together a puzzle. "It don't matter." Linda replied. Streets put together a Henny and Coke for her and off the bat he swigged the bottle downing almost half of it in one gulp. The burning in his throat caused him to gasp for air a bit. What was suppose to be a friendly movie with the two of them. Turned into a kiss and feel up session between the two. Linda was high as hell and the Henny and Coke was serving her right. She straddled Streets with her breasts all up in his face. He bit hard on her erected nipples. "hiissss" Linda let out a comfortable moan. He was being rough as hell. Linda was enjoying this a little too much. She was losing focus on what she had come to do. Streets hand dug under her sweats and tights and managed to palm her soft ass. They were grinding and kissing. Linda's pussy was wet as fuck. "Fuck this." Streets picked her up as if she was a ragdoll. She was light as a feather. The wiggles had him feeling like Incredible Hulk. The movie on the tv screen just stood there playing. No one was watching as the two went upstairs to his bedroom. The bed was waiting patiently for both of them. Linda was nibbling on Streets ear biting him as hard, so he could see how it felt to be bitten exaggeratedly. "Streets let out a light growl as they both dropped onto the bed. Streets took his shirt off exposing a portrait of Jacqueline on his left pec right on his heart. Linda snapped out of her sexual intoxication. Streets felt her all up but Linda managed to turn him on his back pulling off his pants. Expecting him in his boxer, his manhood pulled right up at attention. Streets was lying comfortably on his pillow. He put his hand behind his head way under his pillow. The cold steel confirmed what he was searching for and it was still there. Linda bit his thigh and made her way down to where she was looking for. She pulled off his boxers, she grabbed his manhood with her small hand began to strok his ego. Streets was enjoying every minute of this. Linda couldn't believe what she was about to do. She licked her lips and she rubbed his thick long dick. She made his veins become engorged with blood. She finally lick the tip then eventually put him completely into her mouth. The saliva found room around her lips to seep down as it reached her small manicured hands. It was slipping and Linda was soaked herself. "Uuuhhmmm that's right baby suck my dick." Streets words caught her by surprise but it didn't slow her down one bit. She rubbed his thigh feeling all the way up to his stomach and chest. "You like this dick? Streets was psyching himself up as she sucked on the head of Streets dick. She made his toes curled. "Damn! You dirty bitch, you got some skills." Now he was just getting carried away. His hands had a tight grip on the wooden handle. His face was on the back of Linda's hair. He followed her every stroke. It was pretty hard for him to stay focused with the buffing of the helmet Linda was performing. Linda reached down to her ankle to retrieve what she was carrying with her the whole time. "You stupid bitch, how dare you!?" Streets moaned. Linda almost paused but her rhythm picked up as she sucked him even more vigorously. It was almost impossible for Linda to see Streets hand so she was oblivious to what was about to happen. The rowdier he got with his mouth the more vigorous Linda got with her hand and mouth. She had her blade in her right hand and with the left one she held and stroked streets dick firmly. "How long was you going to keep this up Jalinda?" Streets cocked back the hammer and gripped up the back of Linda's head forcing his dick down her throat as he was about to explode down her throat. Linda clutch the blade and in one swift motion almost decapitated streets dick missing it by millimeters. She sliced his testicle. "Aaaaahhhh you bitch!" Streets growled letting her head go he swung missing her completely hitting himself dead on his left thigh. The blood he was losing saturated the bed completely. Linda knew better than to try and jump on him. She jumped off instead. "That's for Jacqueline you worthless piece of shit!" And this is for my brother!" Streets managed to roll off the bed with his left hand clutching his balls or just one ball. The bleeding slowed down. "I'm a kill you bitch!! You not getting out of here alive!" He charged at her pissed as hell. Linda was small. She got low and made her butterfly float slicing his thigh next ughhhh!! Linda had two up on him at the moment. Linda sidestepped and tripped over a pair of sneakers. Streets jumped right on her. She was fucked now. She stuck the blade in his shoulder but that was useless. Streets adrenaline was pumping something serious now. The blows were all over Linda. He punched her so hard in her face that all she could do was scream. "Shut up you dumb stupid bitch you're dead! This is for "Kay." He punched on her. The cracking in her face could be heard. Linda's cries fell on deaf ears. Linda couldn't move. Streets got up and retrieved the construction hammer he was going to hit her with from the very beginning. Linda was conscience. But she wasn't she wasn't no match for Streets. Even with all the damage that was done to him already. Her vision was blurred. A few more blows made contact with her face. and Linda was not moving now. At this point all those blows to the face could be deadly. Streets didn't want to kill her so quickly. This wasn't the purpose. "Aaaaahhhhhh!" A sharp blow on Linda's left knee with the round part of the hammer sent a charge of pain through her entire body. "Don't feel too good right!?" Streets Barked. That hurt? The hammer was dropped again but this time right on her ankle. She tried to grab her ankle to ease the pain but the hammer was faster than her already paralyzed body. He managed to blast every joint with the hammer before finally noticing that Linda was no longer a threat. Linda wasn't ever going to win this one as she had it planned. Where was Manny when she needed him the most? He dropped the hammer about a foot away from Linda's body close to the end of the bed. "Somebody help me!" Linda was pleading for help. "Streets, no please!" Linda was pleading for his mercy crying hysterically. "Now you want to play nice bitch! Look what you did to me!" The butterfly was on the floor, nowhere near close for her to grab. Linda was helpless. Streets tied up a sheet around his waist line like a toga focusing tight pressure on private area. The sheet went from baby blue to a dark maroon color instantly. He was losing a lot of blood. He could pretty much die a slow death if he didn't get it to slow down. He straddled her again "Why did you have to get into it?" Why didn't you just let us kill your brother? Why did you have to be so nosy? Jalinda "You thought I wasn't going to put it all together? How long did you think it would take me to find out you were not Janet?" Streets tightened his grip around Linda's neck "...t...op! I ca...t bre...athhhh." Linda was losing oxygen fast. She was no longer going to be a part of this planet we called earth it was for the best of her. "You are dead and Jacqueline is next!" "Thump!" Streets eyes grew larger than ever as a stream of blood paced down the side of his face. The grip on Linda's neck was almost completely lose. Streets body was stiff. Linda didn't understand. She grasped for air. Trying to push Streets body from on top of her. She couldn't move her body was in pain and she was weak. Her vision became clearer as the levels of her oxygen began to flow through her body once again. The figure in front of her was still unclear. It just stared at her confused, the way his hand was clenching the construction hammer caused her to still be frightened. The look in his eyes only showed he too wanted to kill Linda himself. Linda gasped for more air. Was this man going to kill her too could this possibly be after being saved momentarily? Was she was going to die no matter what?

CHAPTER 20

"Light it"

The tears ran down his face. His heart was broken and ached in so much pain. He couldn't understand why did she have to take it this far. "Joel help me baby please! I'm begging you please don't leave me here. I'm sorry I need you more than ever, please don't not leave me here." Streets was slumped over with his legs still over Linda's body. Joel finally snapped out of his trance. What ever was going on his mind caused him to really want to hurt Linda. The hammer dropped down to the floor. He to dropped to his knees and held his girl in his arms. The tears came down. He cried as to not believing what has just happened. He was hurt and he didn't want to live a life like this one. Was she worth his time? Could he do better? Would he allow her to get away with this one?

"How did you know?" Linda whined in excruciating pain. Joel carried her body over to the bed. "I didn't know shit, what the fuck were you thinking!?" Joel was flaming with anger inside of him. This was a totally different Joel. "I wasn't thinking, this is the man who was going to testify against my brother." Linda admitted. Joel looked over at the puddle of blood. His stomach turned there was blood everywhere. "Oh my God." He was breathless. "I just killed him. No we have to help him." Joel was starting to panic. "Babe its okay I have a plan." Linda tried to erase all the paranoia that was building up in Joel. "A fucking plan!? From the looks of it your plan wasn't working! From the looks of it this man had a plan of his own and it was killing you! What the fuck you think this is!? A fucking game!?" Joel began to look around the house. "Babe don't be so loud. Turned the stereo on please." Linda plead to him speaking in so much pain. It was clearly not the time to listen to music what was wrong with this woman. She must've lost it completely. "Stereo you got to be shitting me." Joel walked over to Linda. "The music will muffle our voices from the neighbor's babe. Ouch." Linda had to go to the hospital. Joel understood her logic now. He headed towards the stereo and did as he was told. He did not play it excessively loud but loud enough to do what she said it would do. No one wanted to alarm the neighbors. "You have a lot of explaining to do if you and I make it the fuck out of here." Joel said searching the place. He came back with a big can of kerosene in his hand. "What was this man into?" Linda's eyes grew big. I don't know but I think that was going to be used on me. What else is back there? She asked. "Rope, duct tape, and a bunch of other tools that could be used to torture someone or build a house." Joel began to put it all together. He was far from stupid. The hammer that he had picked up was brand new, not a dent or scratch on it. What were the odds of a man owning a hammer and it not have not a single scuff on it? The man lying on the ground was definitely far from a construction worker. The only construction that he was going to perform was on Linda's beautiful reconstructed face. "We got to get the fuck out of here." Joel suggested. "Yes you are right"....uggghhh!" Linda complained. "And you have to go to the hospital." Joel didn't know what to do. He did what he thought was best. "Pour it all over him first then the rest around the house." Linda was still running the show. Joel did exactly as he was told. A small box behind the mattress caught Joel's attention. "Oh shit!" Was all he could say? Rushing back over towards Linda. "There's an open safe back there." Joel was like a small kid. Half of him wanted to snatch everything out but the other half wasn't sure what to do. "What's in it?" Linda asked. "Money and drugs." Joel stated okay take the money and leave the drugs in it, then shut it." Linda ordered. Not thinking twice the money was put into a pillow case. "/Toma/" Joel tossed a pillow case over to Linda. "Come on babe we gota get out of here. The longer we stay the worse all this is going to get." Linda suggested. She was right getting caught inside of Streets house was not a good idea. It didn't matter if Linda was all fucked up they would still be hauled away to a jail. They would try there best to charge Linda up. The apartment smelled like nothing but kerosene and there was a pillow case filled with money. There was a lifeless body that wasn't able to say a word. Joel analyzed all of what Linda just said and began to move swiftly with the other gallon of kerosene. "I can't believe this." Linda observed how Joel was handling the situation. She had turned Joel completely out. She wasn't able to move to help her man. She was fucked up for real. At the door ready to leave Joel had to helped Linda all the way down to the car. The car was parked two apartment buildings down from Street's apartment. "Go light it babe." Joel didn't say a word he had his girl out of the place safe in his car. Now he had to go back. He hoped that all the flames would destroy every fingerprint, partial print, every follicle and burn all the blood that did not belong to Streets that was spilled in the apartment. Linda and Joel could not be linked to any of this if this bullshit was gona work in there favor.

Joel headed straight to the kitchen stove. It made a loud ticking trying to ignite. The flames were bright orange with shades of blue. It didn't take much to light up the apartment. The car engine was already idling. Linda tried to hold in all her pain. Joel wasn't back yet. "Where is he, why is he taking so long?" Linda took a glance to her side view mirror to see if she could see him coming, but nothing. She was worried. She notice a figure coming from up ahead. She saw that Joel finally came from the front of the vehicle. "Where did you go?" Linda was now panicking. I had to go around because I heard something. When I was going to come out the front I heard the noise so the back was my only way out." Joel put the car and drive and the wheels spun until they grabbed traction.

He looked into the rearview mirror and noticed a car behind them. Joel's eyes were glued to the rearview now. He kept driving as cool as he could. He made a left going up three blocks than making a right. The car was still following them this couldn't be happening. Someone was fucking following theem. Someone saw them commit or exiting the house that was already engulfed in flames? Panicking Joel didn't say a word to do Linda. He did not want her to panic too. What was he going to do? Was he going to speed away and try to elude from the vehicle behind them? He positioned his car on the right side of the lane ready to make his next move.

He was going to go for it. He had to get away from this car as much as possible. The car behind him made a left, it was never following him. It just happened to be they were going the same way until he reached a certain block. The sound of Joel of exhaling was deep was a breath that was really needed. His heart was literally coming out his ass.

"You okay baby Linda sensed something was wrong. "Yes baby everything is good." Joel grabbed the bag and pulled out a rubber banded stack of bills. He couldn't believe what he was holding in his hand but most of all he couldn't believe what just happened. It looked like they just did a home invasion that resulted in a homicide. "Hospital." Joel said trying to erase the images of

Streets wide dead eyes open. That image kept resurfacing in his mind as he stared at nothing while driving. "West Jersey is to close us." Linda clearly was delusional. "How about Temple." Joel was planning far ahead. A hospital close by wasn't a smart idea. "That's too far babe I can't hold in the pain anymore. The potholes and turns are killing me. I can't feel my legs." Linda was in tears. "I know baby but at least you're alive, it's our best option." Joel looked over to Jalinda and her face was so swollen bad. She looked as if a hive of whasp had attacked her face. That's how swollen it was. She didn't look like Linda anymore. It would take months for her to heal. Joel wanted to get the questions so bad, but he knew that this wasn't a good time to interrogate Linda. "When you get to the hospital you're going to tell them that a bunch of crack heads tried to rape you, that's all. Your homeless too ok?" Joel noticed she had too much blood on her to say all that blood wasn't hers. He was thinking. "Do you have clothes under what you're wearing now?" Joel asked. "Yes but the blood soaked through them, I can feel it." Linda knew what Joel was thinking. It was almost 10:30pm and the next clothing store was a few miles away. "Try to take your clothes off babe." Joel was watching the road. After crossing the Ben Franklin Bridge he was looking for the nearest gas station.

Finally locating oneJoel pulled in. He parked on the edge to the closest available parking spot. He rushed in and rushed right out with some towels and a gallon of water. He rubbed Linda down erasing a good portion of Streets blood. Well at least the spots he thought where his on her. It was impossible to get rid of every drop. Whoever she would come in contact with would say she had been involved in something life threatening. They would judge her almost immediately. Joel took off his pants, that left him in his basketball shorts. He slipped Linda in his big ass jeans and in his big ass shirt. "It was freezing outside baby what are you doing?" Linda asked. It was brick, Linda was right but Joel was sweating. He didn't care about any of that. He was scared to death and trying to be smart at the same time. "I'm okay let's get you to the hospital." He said happy with Linda's presentation. 10 minutes away from Temple Linda felt every shot of pain that was caused due to the movement of the vehicle.

Joel didn't enter with her right away there was no way that he would. He left her in there care for now. He would enter after a few hours have past. He didn't want anyone to think that he was the cause of this brutal beatings. He decided to stay away until he felt as though enough time has passed by.

—

Back to the house that was engulfed in flames. It took almost 20 minutes for the authorities to arrive at the scene. Neighbors were bundled with coats and blankets watching the show from a distance. All in awe, their hands covered their open mouths in disbelief. The thing with kerosene was that it's a more hazardous chemical than gasoline was. It has a chemical agent in it that causes it to combust alot more. Gasoline works well in starting a fire but not like kerosene and Streets knew exactly what he was doing. Kerosene burns but instead of simmering down a bit it gets hotter and more uncontrollable as it is engulfed. The fire engine came with backup. It was definitely needed because the fire did not want to go out. That was a good sign on Linda and Joel's behalf. It took about three hours of water to finally disperse of all the flames. Once the fire was out the firefighters could finally step foot inside and begin their search. The police questioned all the nearby neighbors. It was pointless since none of the neighbors never had the opportunity to meet Streets. The life that Streets was accustom to live plus being very secretive with all that he did wouldn't help the cause. His neighbors rarely saw him due to the late hours he would come in and out of his home. Even when they did see them, they couldn't due to his tints on his car. So the law had to work double time on this case but we all knew that they were doing their job. The real question was how well they were doing it? Time would tell.

—

Rock was tossing and turning in his rack, something wasn't right. He could feel it in the pit of his stomach. Bigs was up writing a letter to someone ."You good?" Bigs notice Rocks discomfort. "Yo man, my mind is spinning something serious right now. Something isn't right?" Rock admitted to Bigs. Slash and Leak were both sound asleep. "Na don't think like that. Everything is okay. It's your mind fucking with you ,don't let it get to you." Bigs said in between writing sentences. "I hope so because if she ain't right Ima lose it Bigs. Shit is going to get crazy. Damn I need to call home." Rocks intuition was hitting him hard. There was no way that Rock would fall asleep. He couldn't sleep at all like this.

He stood up all night until it was time to go eat breakfast. He was sitting on the desk as everyone in his cell got up one by one on their own.

“Yo, you up early, you was up all night?” Leak asked rubbing his eyes. “Man I gota get on that Jack.” Rock replied. “The phone?” “You been up all night thinking about that mother fucking phone?” Leak asked not believing what he was hearing. “Not right now Leak.” Rock wasn’t in no mood for his sarcasm.

“You have a collect call from Manny.” The voice recording said. Rock wasn’t going to stop until mom answered the phone. “Hello?” Mom answered. “Ma are you okay?” Rock asked still not feeling any better, he wouldn’t until he heard confirmation that they all were doing just fine. “Yes baby, I’m okay. Why are you okay?” Mom asked flipping the question on him. “Yeah I’m good I just couldn’t sleep all night. I felt that something wasn’t right.” Rock admitted. I think your sister is in her room. “Mom got up to check if Linda was asleep or if there was any sign that she was there and left this morning. Mom was still half asleep. “She’s not in her room, She’s probably went to work or school.” Mom tried to ease Rock’s worries. Its 8 o’clock in morning mom. She don’t leave to school until 9 o’clock. Rock said knowing his sister schedule. “That’s right she’s probably with Joel you know how she is.” Mom wasn’t helping Rocks worries now. “Let me call Joel and see if she’s over there with him.” Mom did a three way quickly. “No answer.” Mom find her. I’ll call in a few hours please. Something isn’t right.” Rock was 100% sure that something was wrong. “Boy, she is okay don’t worry yourself to death. Call back later I’ll get in contact with her.” Mom stated. Rock ended the call not accepting what mom had told him. Hanging up but he wasn’t done.

“Ayo man I got an 8:30 phone call.” A voice from across the room informed. Rock picked up the phone and dialed out. The phone rang and rang with no answer. I don’t know what it is about these walls but they had this power over you it was out of the norm. Once they instilled something in you, you weren’t happy to you figure out what is going on. You wouldn’t stop until you find out what was disturbing you. Everyone around you can tell you that everything is okay till they were blue in the face. That wasn’t enough. You wouldn’t stop until you spoke to the person you wanted to talk to and attain that closure for yourself. A letter ,a phone call is what you needed and wanted at that moment. To know that everything was okay. Rock heard from mom so he knew mom wasnt the cause of his uneasiness. Rock needed to hear from Linda, he needed to hear from Linda that she was ok. “This shit it is crazy, why nobody picking up now.” Rock mumbled to himself. He slammed the phone down infuriated.

"Medication!" Yelled the CO. "Medication!" Rock went to retrieve his meds, maybe the meds would get him to zone out and stop being so anxious. They had to calm him down a bit because he was losing his mind. Even after mom specifically informed him that everything was okay. He noticed Mandy with her tray of meds. Rock had this devilish look on his face. Mandy figured the news was out already. "Did she tell you?" Mandy asked in a low tone. "Tell me what?"... Who?" Rock asked. "Jacqueline." Mandy replied trying to buy some time before given Rock his meds. "Her baby dad is dead." Rock's hair all over his body flared up like a cat when it's about to attack. "Dead?" Rock repeated. "Yeah he was burnt to death at his apartment. Well at least she think it was him. The autopsies still need to be done so there is no definite identity yet but she thinks it is him for sure. I thought you knew." Mandy said softly. "When was this?" Rock asked. "She call me this morning crying hysterically." Mandy said. "If she called you this morning and we just got let out from meds, how would I have known now? I know thanks now thanks to you." Rock was rude to Mandy for no reason. She was not to blame for anything. He spun off to get back on the phone. He had tunnel vision. The only thing on his mind was Linda. "I told her to leave it alone. This fucking girl don't fucking listen!" Rock was speaking to himself loud enough for everyone to hear him though. All the phones were occupied. Go figure, Rock looked at the phone he was on and charge straight to it. He was about to get himself in some more dumb shit.

"Yo my man!" He says staring at the guy on the phone who looked as if he was speaking to no one. Rock's assumption was right. He handed the phone right over. Mother fuckers like this are the ones who take up phone slots for no fucking reason. You got to make a phone call? Good make it but if you don't and want to give the impression that you are balling with no money to blow. Your on the phone talking to no one but the fucking operator you are in the fucking way. Rock didn't even say shit. He snatched the phone right out of his hand and dialed out. The more times he called the more times no one anwered. His nerves were rattled, he finally got the message and gave up for now. He Stormed back to his cell and slammed the door behind him. "Wassup nigga, you all right?" Leak asked. "No I'm not fucking all right. I told her to let it go. Now nobody know where the fuck she's at." Rock barked leaving everyone lost for words, no one wanted to say anything for second. It was best to not even try at the moment with this hotheaded mother fucker right now.

"I just seen the fucking nurse right? and she just fucking told me that the nigga." Rock was interrupted by the popping of the door "Manuel Ricardo multipurpose room now!" The voice over the PA barked leaving Rocks sentence in midair. "The nigga what?" Slash nosey ass wanted to know what was going on Rock's head. Rock just stared at him and stormed out the cell heading straight to the multipurpose room.

Unaware of who or what wanted him. His heart began to beat rapidly as he rushed over to see what was up. The two gentlemen that were waiting for him were standing with their arms folded. His heart stopped instantly this couldn't be happening. He knew better than to freeze up, his steps grew so much heavier. He walked as if he had cinderblocks on the bottom of his feet.

"Well, well look who we have here." Detective Hasnoff was the first one to speak sarcastically. "Wassup? How can I help you too?" Rock swallowed hard regaining his mindset. This wasn't the time to show fucked up emotions. Especially after what the fuck was told to him this morning. "Oh shit help? So you're willing to help us this time huh?" Detective Defenchi asked. This two had the game fucked up. "First off let's start with a good morning. How's your morning going?" Hasnoff asked taking a seat following his partner. They both were suited up in their hundred dollars suits. "I'm in fucking jail how else would I be in this rat infested place?" Rock got just as sarcastic as them. "Not so good I take it then. You don't like your new friends?" Hasnoff answered his own question. "You been a problematic prisoner behind these walls Mr. Ricardo. We been hearing but to everyone else on the outside you are this little angel. Something isn't adding up at all. You may fool everyone else but we met hundreds of guys like you." Hasnoff was a prick. It was hard to conceal that shit. Not sure how people gotten like that over time or was that the way a family would raise a child? It didn't matter at the moment because this prick wanted everyone to know how much of a prick he could be. "If you know so much about me and my character why the fuck are you here and why am I not out of here yet?" Rock wasn't gonna stay quiet this time going around. He was already in jail and expressing his innermost thoughts. Who the fuck cared what they thought? They couldn't do shit else to him. "Either you just don't know or you have a lot of pull on the outside." Defenchi stated. He slid 2 photos over to me on the table that was separating us. I almost threw up everything I ate for breakfast at the sight of those pictures.

"This is the man that was supposed to testify on your behalf to keep your ass in jail for the rest of your life." Definchi's voice was rising. "Can you tell me who this man is?" Defenchi asked. I could only see his eyeballs which were white as cotton. The man was complete charcoal. All that was needed was some barbecue sauce and you could feed a small village with this mother fucker, that's how well done this man looked. If Mandy was right I knew exactly who it was but if she was wrong this shish kebab could be anybody. "Who is he?" Hasnoff yelled. "How the fuck should I know?" I'm in fucking prisoned idiot." Rock snapback. Was he stupid enough to give up a name? Probably not but Red and Stimpy here were not going to give up that easily either. "All we want to know is how and who did you have go and do this to this man?" You give us that and we'll drop some of your charges and then maybe you'll be able to go home on your appeal." Hasnoff proposed. "You gota be shitten me. You want me to give you a name so then "maybe" you'll drop the charges." You two have to be the dumbest detectives in the unit. Leave me the fuck alone and go find another innocent man to pin another murder on. Apparently I'm already in jail for a homicide you two dumb asses can't figure out." Rock knew more than he was portraying but cooperating with the pigs wasn't gonna happen. "Listen! You maniac were going to find out who did this and guess what?" Rock just stared at them. "You not going to go to jail you know why?" Defenchi asked. His veins were swollen on his forehead. "Why is that?" Rock wanted to hear this. Not because he cared what they had to say but because Rock wanted to see if he could make his vein his forehead explode. Rock smile at his own thoughts. "I am getting whoever did this to say you told them to do it and then you'll be looking at two life sentences. Those will hold you imprisoned for literally the rest of your little useless life. You peice of shit. That means no pussy, no clubs, no family and no nothing ever! I am going to make sure of it!" Defenchi blew a head gasket. "If thats the reason why I wont be getting no pussy than whats your reason since your free you little faggot." Rock wasn't shutting up for this one. "Get the fuck out my face you piece of shit!" Defenchi was mad as hell dismissing Rock. "Have a good day gentlemen. I hope you find who you looking for and stop wasting time coming at me for some more nonsense. It was just more ammunition for me and my lawyer's bitches." Rock was enjoying every moment of this. "Don't drop the soap you little bitch!" Hasnoff also got way out of character. Rock needed to locate Linda before they did. How was he going to manage to pull this one off? Rock couldn't believe what his mind was fabricating. It couldn't be possible, that Linda had managed to kill Streets. This is what his gut was warning him about but was it true?

"What the fuck was that about?" Leak asked. Looking at Rock. "Nigga that was the detectives." Rock said. "What? They still harrassing you over this case?" Leak asked surprised. "Hell no! Another homicide that they can't seem to solve. They trying to get me to say something on that one." Rock informed everyone in the cell. Bigs just shook his head not believing what he was hearing. "Damn Rock what are you actually into out there?" Leak was starting to see Rock as another person. "What you mean by that?" Rock asked confused. "I'm saying the detectives are questioning you for another body. They just don't bother people if you're not into that shit." Leak challenge. "Yeah nigga I understand that but the murder was last night." Rock snapped. "How the fuck they questioning you? If you're in here with us? What you fucking Houdini?" Slash asked." Who you telling if I was I would leave and never come back, not catch a body than come back!" Rock defended himself.

"Yo that nigga was torched in his house." The images stayed in Rocks head clear as day. "Who was torched?" Slash asked. "I don't know his government name, but they call him Streets?" Rock said "Streets?" Slash repeated. "That name sound familiar as shit." Slash informed. "Where he be at?" Slash asked. "I can't answer that, I don't know that nigga like that." Rock said. All I know is that he was supposed to testify against me." Rock informed. "That's a good thing Rock. Why you all hung up about it then?" Leak was ruthless. "Because they trying to pin all that shit on me now." Rock was sick to his stomach. He couldn't take this anymore. "They can't do that shit man, they just trying to scare you that's all. The only way that's possible is if they have a person actually tell them that you told them to do that shit? Did you tell anyone to put a hit out on this charcoal rat ass nigga?" Leak asked. Trying to prove a point. "Fuck no!" Rock spoke truthfully. "Are you sure?" He asked again. He didn't answer Rock just gave him that look. "All right I'm just asking so your good then don't sweat shit." Focus on this case. You have a chance now to get your sentence reduce. If this nigga Streets was going to show face in court this was your angle now." Leak was making a lot of fucking sense now. He was right if Linda or whoever had a vendetta against Streets and got away with this. Than one of my credible witnesses were out of the equation. I signed up for the library immediately. I wasn't scheduled to see OJ until that following day, but I had to tell him some of my good news. Leak was in my head. "So who you got moving out there for you Rock?" Leak asked in all seriousness. "Moving?" I must admit I never did understand half the shit these niggas talked about. I would use context clues with these niggaz but even with that it was far from any help most of the time.

—

Joel still hasn't shown face at the hospital nor would he anytime soon. He was at a local diner still wearing his basketball shorts and a wife beater. He was headed to the local k-mart after he got his mind together. He didn't know who to even call or even what to do. His best bet was to call Ms. Cathy and he did just that. Walking over to the far back he dispensed two coins into the pay-phone and punched in the number to Ms. Cathy's house she answered almost immediately. "Hello?" Mom answered. "Ms. Cathy." Joel spoke into the receiver. Initially mom thought that Linda was with Joel but his phone cause mom's heartbeat to pick up instantly. She headed to her breathing tank and prepared it just in case. She knew this wasn't going to be a good call. "I need you to sit down and relax." Joel spoke calmly into the receiver. "Oh my God where is she?" Mom asked taking a deep breath from the mask. She is okay but she is hurt." Joel was cutting mom's flesh with a sharp blade as he mustered himself to bring out the words from his mouth straight into her ears. "Where are you?" Mom's eyes were dropping streams of tears down her cheeks. "I'm at a diner. I don't want to get into the details at the moment with all these ears around me but Linda is okay. Like I said she is hurt, can you meet me?" Joel asked not saying much. "Why aren't you with Linda? Did you hurt her?" Now it was mom's turn to take the air out of Joel's lungs. "No I would never. I need you to come and meet me." Joel repeated firmly not liking the accusations. How could he couldn't blame her. "Where are you?" Mom asked. "In Philly at the IHOP confused, are you coming?" Joel needed some help and this was the only person he could trust and rely on at the moment. "Yes! I'll be right there." Mom assured him. The IHOP closest to Temple hospital." Joel said before hanging up. He knew that it would take some time till they arrived so he decided to go purchase some clothing as he intended to.

—

Mom couldn't tell Pete any details but he didn't need any once heard mom's voice and Linda's name in the same sentence. Pete left Jamal running the shop without telling him anything. "I'll be back can you hold it down on your own?" Pete asked. "Would it be the first time?" Jamal replied. He could handle the spot any given day all by himself . That was a no brainer. No words were exchanged during the drive to Philly.

Finally arriving at the diner, mom was so anxious to see Joel. He was sitting in his car. Joel was in a daze in his car with the heat up fully dressed in his new clothing. Pete yanked open the door pulling Joel out the car in one swift motion. He was a big man but Pete was a strong man. Mom just watched as if she wanted this to happen.

"What did you do to her?" Pete growled at Joel. He punched him in the stomach. Joel didn't say shit, not because he didn't want to because he couldn't breathe. Another blow to his oblique's dropped Joel. "I... didn't do anything!" Joel gasped for air as he tried to tell the truth." Where is she then?" Pete growled. "That's enough babe." Mom pulled Pete off Joel. Everyone looked at the scene from inside probably calling the cops who knows? "Let me fucking explain what happened please. Than you can make up your mind and continue to beat me up for nothing or I can tell you what's going on?!" Joel snapped with his eyes red as fuck. After the whole story was recounting mom was in tears and Pete was feeling like shit. "That girl is brave." Pete said. Mom looked at him. "Brave? More like stupid!" Mom corrected. "Thank you hun, I'm so sorry for all of this. Everything is going to be all right I promise." Mom was making a promise. She damn sure knew she couldn't keep. "What name is she checked in at the hospital? "Angelina Metz" Joel made this name up for her to check in. Everything had to be fake that's one thing that just had to be done, no bread crumbs.

It was already close to noon. "Let's go what are we waiting for?" Mom said eager to go and visit her daughter. "This is what Linda was up to since day one." Mom said speaking out loud reflecting on her daughters strange actions. "So you knew of this?" Pete asked. "No I didn't know but her attitude wasn't the same. She was very secretive lately and acting strange. All three were in Pete's car riding to the hospital. "How did you know? Mom stared at Joel from the front seat looking back at him. I didn't know like you said. She wasn't the same and I wanted to know what she was up to." Joel admitted. "So you never left that day on your day off?" Mom asked. "No I parked down the street and waited for her to leave and I followed her." Joel was a hero and mom would be in his debt for ever. Too bad she couldn't take back those breathtaking blows Pete unleashed on him. Better yet Joel should be lucky that's all he got.

"How can I help you?" The nurse at the desk asked mom . "Umm yes I'm here to visit my friend she came in earlier this morning." Mom was nervous. She didn't want to raise any suspicion. "Name ma'am?" The young beautiful black nurse asked. "Angelina Metz." Mom said waiting for the nurse to say something. "Oh here she is. She is headed for surgery on the third floor. Would you like to wait or would you prefer heading up? You can have a talk with one of the doctors or nurses that may be able to answer any of your questions?" The nurse was very helpful. "Yes I would like to go up and wait." They all jumped in the elevator. She's been in too many hospitals and no matter how religious or fancy they try to present them. They all smelled like death. "Bing!" The elevator dropped her off at the third floor which was where her baby was heading to undergo surgery. She rushed to the front desk once again on that floor.

"Angelina Metz." was all mom said. "She's about to go into surgery would you like to see her before she's taken away?" The nurse with finger waves asked looking as if she was in her mid-30s. "Please can I?" Mom asked. "Of course right this way ma'am." The fine nurse led the way. Shorty was holding seriously. The air in this place was icy. It made no sense why these hospitals where alwasy this cold. They both stopped at room b12. "I will be back in about 15 minutes to take her." The nurse said. Linda was asleep must be some serious pain medication. Mom held her mouth as she walked slowly towards her baby girl. Linda's face was fucked up bad. Her eyes were swollen shut, her lips were fat and her cheeks were a dark black. It look as if every vessel and her face was imploded. Even her ear has some type of cut on it. "Oh my God." mom whispered. "I'm so sorry baby." Mom allowed her tears to fall immediately, not withholding any of them back. The site she was seeing wasn't one that any mother wanted to see their child in. I don't care how much you hated or want to disown your own, This was enough pain to forgive and apologize to your child. If not then you wouldn't even have shown up to see your child in the first place at the hospital. Mom put her hands on Linda's bruised hand.

"Why couldn't you just let it go?" Mom whispered. Her head was down. Mom said a prayer. "I couldn't do..... It." Linda answered mom's question. "You up?" Mom asked still crying. "Yes, bar...ly . The drugs are strong...... how do I look?" Linda asked tryna make light of the situation. "Beautiful baby, beautiful." mom couldn't tell her the truth. Linda forced a smile. "You lie...." Mom laughed. "Where... Is... Joel?" Linda asked wincing in pain.

"Baby he is with Pete he is okay." Mom advise Linda. "Tell him I love him." Linda said in between breaths of pain. "I will Angelina." Mom said. "I like that name why didn't you give me that name." Linda was too much after all that was going on she still managed to keep the warm loving personality. She was being Linda again. "Save your energy baby they're going to take you away for surgery." Mom informed. I'll be out in the waiting room area until they are done fixing you." Mom wasn't going anywhere how could she? "Okay I love you." Linda managed to say. "I love Manny too." She finished. "I know you do baby trust me I know you do."

In the waiting room. Mom had managed to inquire everything that was going to happen to Linda physically. Linda had to get a left knee replacement and put back together because it was shattered. Her left ankle was also broken. She had a fractured jaw which also needed some wire work. A bunch of stitches inside of her mouth. A few more stiches on her right eyebrow. The damages were minor but mom was grateful that her baby was still alive kicking and ticking. The doctors approximated about three hours until Linda was all said and done. Recovery was unknown depending on how the surgery went.

How is she? Joel asked rushing towards mom. Joel and Pete headed out so that Pete could smoke. They waited down the block from the hospital? Mom broke down in Joel's arms. "Is she okay?" Joel didn't like this at all. Mom nodded her head. "Thank you so much Joel. Mom said in between sobs you saved my baby girl." Mom was bawling like a baby wanting it's bottle. Joel hugged mom tightly. "You are welcome Ms. Cathy." Joel drop a tear as well. "How is she?" Joel asked again wanted to know. "She says she loves you baby.... I love you too Joel." Mom didn't answer his question she confessed how much she truly love him for his bravery. "I love all of you too." Joel confirmed. "She is fine they just took her into surgery now hun." Mom said in between sobs. She made her way over to Pete. "You okay babe?" Pete asked concern. "Yes I am now. This is going to be a rough recovery but she'll make it. She is very strong "mom said. "Yes she will babe." Pete assured mom's last comment.

Joel was spaced out while mom and Pete held one another. What was he going to do now? The images of Streets dead body didn't go away, nor did they even attempt to dissipate.

"Are you okay?" Pete asked learning of all the details again. Joel shook his head. He wasn't okay. "You are going to be okay. I know it doesn't feel as though you will be, but you have to be 100 times stronger than you was a few hours ago. He got what he deserved Joel if not him then it would have been Linda. You did what you had to do." Pete spoke softly soothing Joel from his guilt. "So if I did the right thing? Why doesn't it feel like I did the right thing? And if that is true that I did do the right thing, that means I can go to the police and explain to them what happened right?" Joel was more than confuse. He was paranoid to the max. "Baby Linda was at the scene and that man was supposed to testify against Linda's brother." Mom said lightly. "Pete is right you going to have to be stronger now for all of us." "Because now we are all in jeopardy because we all know what happened. So in order for this to stay as it is. We can't say a word about this to anyone ever." Mom was right and she was going to go through all this with Linda and now she was going to have to deal with Joel as well. "We will all get through this, come here." Mom put her arm around Joel. Joel had to be watched closely the ball rolling down the hill was too big to be stopped now. A minor slip up on his behalf could land everyone in jail. "But I will tell them it was all my fault." Joel said biting his fingernails. "You can't it will automatically involve Linda. Then they would ask why did you take Linda to the hospital in a totally different city. Why did you use a false name to get surgery done on her beat up body?" Pete was stating the facts now too. "You can tell them what you want Joel but what you need to remember is that a body was torched and was hit with a construction hammer. That's where the trial will start all the way till this very spot where we are discussing this. If you're smart and you love your freedom ,let it go and have your guard up for anything. Tomorrow morning the paper will disclose all of what we need to know about what the police may know and if any suspects are being sought." Pete had one hand on Joel's shoulder as he gave him a detailed quick analysis of what and how he should play his hand. "You're right.... I can't they won't believe me they won't help us... Yes you are right." Joel was talking but dazed out into the street ahead. He was still in shock. He had to lighten the fuck up that's all that needed to happen. But could he? Would he keep his mouth shut? Would this many eventually put everyone is jail? A weak link this could destroy anything.

—

That evening Rock had one of the few jacks on lock. Greg was on it. He would pretty much do just about anything that Rock needed. All Rock had to do was say the word because he paid to play. The phone just rang and rang. On the four attempts Jacqueline finally answered sounding horse like a mother fucker. "Why the fuck you not answering the fucking phone? Rock snapped off the gate. "Oh my God!" You too!?" Jacqueline yelled back still dropping hundreds of tears. "What you mean, mean too!?" Rock snapped not liking Jacqueline's attitude. Rock didn't give a fuck if Streets have been murdered. Why should he give a fuck? "My baby dad is dead and all everybody cares is about themselves." Jacqueline was crying bad. Rock bit his tongue once he remembered that the calls were being monitored so he decided to save all that riffraff shit for a visit or even a letter but even with that Rock had to be extra cautious. "He's what?" Rock asked. Putting in on his best act. "He's dead Rock." Jacqueline reiterated as if he didn't hear the initial question. "How did this happen?" Rock asked starting his recorded conversation. He had to play likea prisoner not knowing what the fuck was going on out in the world. "Sometime last night. His bitch Star called me early in the morning going on about how he was supposed to meet up with her at 11 o'clock so she stayed up waiting for him to show up and the night came and went and no sign of Dante. So she decided to go by his house, in her mom's car that she stole and the fucking...." Jacqueline stopped as she tried to regain her composure."rode was blocked off by the police and ambulance. She walked down to where Dante's apartment was, she noticed that it was his house up in flames!" "He's dead!" What the fuck!" Jacqueline was hurt it was sad on her behalf. Deep down inside Rock knew that Jacqueline never did erase Streets completely from her heart.Being the father of her child was something that couldn't be undone no matter how bad you wish it. All those hateful words that came out her mouth were out of spite. Rock now understood of how tight of a bond a man and woman create when a man and woman bear a child together. "I'm sorry to hear that." Rock swallowed as he didn't give a rat's ass about that lame. "Everybody saying you have something to do with it but you are in fucking jail how the fuck!?" Jacqueline was saying all the right things because the detectives would definitely be hearing this recording and examining all my calls tomorrow so they could fabricate another case on my ass. It wasn't happening. So far Rock knew Streets was no longer a threat to mom or Linda's lives anymore. This allowed him to gather peace. Another important piece of information was how Star was still out there. Was she willing to testify against him in court? She was still a valuable asset to the district attorney. One thing hadn't been confirmed yet. The whereabouts of where Linda was, was still unknown. Did she make it or was she laid up in the ditch holding on to dear life herself? So many endless thoughts smothered Rock's mine. Everything that was being said was great but it was all irrelevant if his pride and joy was suffering. It wasn't her position to be suffering for anyone nor anything. He wanted to ask about his sister but Jacqueline never brought her up as if they ever spoke. It didn't come to a surprise to Rock due to the type of person Linda was. So he decided to leave it alone. "Listen Rock I'm sorry but I got to go. I'll be up there sometime next week." Jacqueline was terminating the call which was fine with Rock. "Take it easy baby girl and keep that head up." Those were his last words. He clenched his jaw as he hung up the phone not knowing who else to call. He decided to call Felicia. There was a small chance that Felicia would know something. Rock took a deep breath as he watched his surroundings. The few prisoners that were up had him on point. He now didn't trust anyone more than he already didn't. If anything he had to watch his back even more. No answer from Felicia, Rock glance back at the time it was useless Felicia was at work faithfully every day getting that money at this time. She was due for a visit but Rock hardly ever press the issue. If they arrived great and if they didn't it was all good too. The rest of the day was still a worrisome day. Leak handled whatever these niggaz wanted. "Ima fallback I will not control myself I am one second away from Tipping." Rock was far from beyond stressed out he didn't know what to do. He was gonna take it out on who ever.

Still no word from anyone, the Courier Post was slid under Rock's door as requested from Greg. Rock didn't think he was ever in the mood to pick up the carrier post and read about who or what was going on in the city. That wasn't the life he had endured so he didn't give a fuck. Rock got up as soon as he heard the noise. It was the paper just as promised. The paper on the front page was a torched building. It appeared to be two buildings. Ihe image was heart racing. "Damn!" Rock said under his breath not wanting to alarm the guys. They were all still in deep sleep. Rock sat on his bed and began to read. The headline was in big bold letters. The headline didn't make much sense until Rock began to read:

"On December 1st local authorities were notified of some screaming at the above address. Dispatchers took more than enough time to show up at the scene due to hectic traffic. When law enforcement finally showed up it appeared to be too late. The flames engulfed the small apartment building, stretching over to the next building that was only a few yards away. A corpse was discovered at the scene inside of the torch building. An autopsy is being immediately performed to identify the corpse.

Police gave this account: at approximately 10:30 PM the New Jersey police department have been notified numerous times of what seem to be a domestic disturbance. The Camden Police Department took this account as your ordinary domestic case and would send a squad unit to check out the call. Authorities arrived almost at 11 o'clock due to the heavy traffic in the area and the high rate of calls that were considered to be more drastic and more severe. They were handled as priority. Upon arriving on the scene the dispatches had also informed squad car number 43 that a fire had broken out at the same address as the domestic dispute. This was when the call became a priority. The bright orange and yellow flames confirmed exactly what was being reported on the radio. The squad car immediately radioed the fire department alarming them of the enormous fire at the residence house. The uniformed officer was supposed to check out three minutes earlier. It had taken all local fire companies to work collectivly for almost 2 1/2 to 3 hours to disburse all of the flames. After flames had been maitained and the fire chief gave the crews the green light to conduct a thorough sweep of the already charcoaled house.They searched for the so called domestic disputed bodies that may have still been inside. After firefighters only recover one male body the rest of the building was secured. The flames made its way over to the neighbors so that home too had to be secured as well. No one else was injured just two cats who couldn't escape the tragedy. An autopsy was schedualed immediately. The how and why has yet to be determined? The ruling of a potential arsonists was already ruled out. Despite the tin cans of kerosene that have been left at the scene. That could only indicate that the suspects knew that the raging flames would discard all of the physical evidence if any have been left behind, eliminating any foul play if considered. A wooden handled construction hammer was also found by the deceased body, which also led for the immediate autopsy. It appears that a homicide may be the cause of the deceased followed by a quick fire to finish off the hideous act. Investigators are carefully analyzing as to who the the deceased body was affiliated with prior to the days of this and even are going as far as months before.

The corner of Rock's lip curled up as he read this part twice.

The investigators are looking for the other potential witnesses in the case. To keep the individual under protective custody in the case that is being handled.

The autopsy revealed that the victim was stabbed and struck upside his head with the construction hammer that took his life but not before one of his testicles being severed off before the scorching of the apartment. Whoever did this was someone close and had to be a coldhearted individual. Dante Imposa's life was pronounced dead at the scene leaving his 29-year-old body lifeless. He left his almost 2-year-old son and the mother of his child alone. We are asking the city of Camden New Jersey to please step forward in helping us solve and find this individual or individuals responsible for such a heinous act in this incident. Prosecution is a must and will be done with everyone's help thank you.

Rock almost dropped a tear as he read on how innocent and good Streets was painted as.

"Yeah right that's bullshit" Rock said loud enough to wake up Slash. "What is it bro?" Wait to you read this." Rock tossed up the paper he was ready to locate his sister. He felt responsible for this so-called hideous act. So far his mind was at ease for the time being. No evidence of a woman's body was mentioned anywhere in that paper. So he had a small bit of closure until further notice was available. He busted open a honey bun and put together a nice cup of instant Maxwell's coffee with cream and sugar. The articles words bounced around in his head as they describe how Streets was killed. He got what he deserved. This was all that Rock was thinking. It didn't matter how it happened, but that it did have to happen one day in the near future with or without Linda's help. Rock couldn't wait to head to the library and speak to his jail house attorney OJ. Rock would have to take this shit to his grave. Whatever Linda was doing she had better thought out all her actions because now there was nothing that Rock could do to protect her no matter how much he wanted too. "Damn! This is the nigga that has the spot over by the Northgate Apartments. No wonder I knew that name." Slash admitted. "That nigga was grimy as fuck. What the fuck these crackers talking about he was innocent? They don't know shit about none of us, stupid mother fucker's." Slash was going in. "Yo they took off one of his nuts?" Slash laughed confirming how heartless he was. "That shit is bugged out." Rock opinionated. "This is good news bro. Your witness is gone, if you can get the other one off too. Then you might not be looking at much time to do at all." Slash was already pointing fingers without actually pointing. Rock listened but didn't cosign shit. "Some people aren't meant to be sitting in jail you know?" Slash said handing me the paper. So that's what them pigs were harassing you about yesterday huh?" Slash asked. "Yes that's exactly what they were talking about. It's funny how they was quick to throw that man's death and pin that body on me. They didn't have the balls to put it in the paper if it mattered that much though." Rock was irritated. He waited patiently until it was time to get on the phone which only made time go by that much slower. He eventually passed out not even being bothered to be awakened by the guys. They knew not to bother him with the extra nonsense. There was too much going on, to be bothered with the dumb shit. Rock was being hammered emotionally. It was a matter of time before he exploded on someone. No matter how hard he may have tried not to it was going to happen regardless. Things were going in his favor even if they seem that they weren't.

—

A full week went by with no word from the family. Rock went as far as telling Felicia to call and deliver a message to mom. No one returned her calls nor did they even bother answering when she called. "How could they be so rude and not answer the phone?" Rock asked the guys. "Is not that they are rude. They are probably just a little busy handling who knows what." Bigs said. "Busy?" Doing what?" Rock answered without thinking before blurting out them words. Man they are all bugging and we got no work because Jacqueline going crazy over her baby dads. So much for hating someone and now we all gota suffer for a bit until she gets her shit together." Rock said being selfish. "Wassup with Nurse Joy?" Slash gave Mandy that alias because she would always get joyous when she would see or come around Rock. So much for not given up the pussy. "She riding but it's up to Jacqueline. She ain't dealing with nobody else on that tip." Rock informed the guys. Shit we up, we still got the tickets popping off crazy and main man down the tear still holding mad shit and the store is up. To be honest we are not hurting foreal." Leak took it all in stride. He was absolutely right. "I know but I'm trying to blow some of that good good."

Rock joked simulating the joint putting it to his lips. "You got pills you don't need no bud nigga." Slash reminded Rock as if he wasn't already aware what he had tucked away. "Yeah but that bud is where it's at. Fucked them pills." Rock had grew accustomed to smoking whenever he felt the urge to smoke. He didn't have anybody telling him no, too cool out or even to up the price. It was his shit and if he wanted to smoke it all fuck it. He could and no one could say a fucking word about it to him. "I'm saying we can grab something off them niggaz upstairs." Slash suggested Rock looked at him. It was only a suggestion, don't get all stupid on me now." Slash surrendered. "I know and I almost forgot about them because upstairs. They owe us some money anyway don't they?" Rock searched his rolodex in his brain. "Bigs how much?" Rock couldn't remember so he went to the next best person who knew the numbers to the tee. Bigs search until he located a piece of paper in a book. He studied his made up codes for a second. "Well you got Junito who owes you $230 and you got them North Camden boys who... all together owe $175. Rock was listening until Greg showed up. Rock jumped on the door as soon as he saw Greg swing by. He scanned the tier not seeing him as if he disappeared. Rock let out a loud whistle.

"Damn nigga that shit Loud as fuck." Leak held his ears. "There isn't no-where for that noise to go but inside our ears." Bigs was bitch in. Slash laughed as the comments were being shot. "A warning would've been nice." Bigs said. "Wassup yo?" Greg stopped what he was doing, he came right over to the gate. "Can you do your thing right now?" Rock decided to get straight to the point, fucked the delivering a messages. He was Jonesing. ""Depend why wassup?" Greg was always out for the challenge. "I need you to send a kite upstairs." Rock said. "To?" Greg asked. "Junito" Rock answered immediately. "Junito, Junito? Greg repeated the names making Junito name sound all fucked up. "Oh that's the short stocky poppy boy always doing push-ups?" Greg needed confirmation. "Exactly." Can you get up there?" Rock asked. Probably not until second shift but get the kite ready just in case I can right quick." Greg said. "Let me know I got you." Rock said. "I know you always do." Greg disappeared moving throughout the tier. You could only imagine all the running around this man did for everyone. A bunch of errands for the guys who had some change to spare.

—

"So the doctor is releasing you today. He wants you to do a follow-up at the therapy center about a half a mile east of here and to take all your pain meds as needed." The blonde with the bad acne all over her face explain to Linda. She was surrounded by all these doctors and little mamas couldn't get some medical attention to tame that acne breakout. Linda's mind always had a way of expressing itself. "Thank God I was getting tired of being stuck in here with no air, no nothing." Linda wanted out already. She wouldn't be walking on her own, not just yet. That would be some time until she would be ready. "Thank you for everything." Linda added feeling stupid after her last comment. "You're welcome I hope you get better, you too pretty to be sitting up in the hospital." Acne face shot a cheap shot back at Linda, It was only fair. "I know, I hope so too." Linda agreed with Ms. Acne. Mom hugged Linda. "Let's go home baby I'm tired of living here with you too." Mom joked. Mom hasn't left Linda side, not even for a split second. Pete would bring her clothes every day and mom would wash up in the hospital and even eat the hospital food with her daughter. It said when a mother loves she loves her all, when a child suffers a mother suffers all. It had to be some truth to it is because mom and Linda were inseparable. Mom had learned so much about Linda in these past few weeks that it only made her want to protect her that much more. "Yes I miss my bed too, I know you miss your bed and Pete's bed." Linda joked. Her smile was picture perfect as it always been, even with the rubber bands on her back molars cause her mouth was to remain close. The healing process was far from complete. "Ima call Joel so he can come and pick you up." Linda suggested. "I bet you can't wait to see that man." Linda blushed. "uuuhhmmm" she could taste him now. Once the release papers were signed and dated Linda's body was plopped in the wheelchair and hauled away to the nearest exit. Where her baby Joel was parked waiting with a dozen red roses and some chocolates. Linda loved her Sweets and Joel knew this. Her eyes watered as the thought of what Joel had done and how he was still by her side despite the madness.

"How are you feeling baby?" Joel asked handing her the flowers and chocolates when she was sitting comfortably in the passenger seat. "" I'm feeling well, how have you been babe? I missed you so much." Linda was opening the chocolates not wasting any time. "You hungry?" Joel asked. "Not really just dying to have something sweet." Linda replied. "Linda didn't get too far when she remembered she couldn't open her mouth to put chocolate in her mouth the look on her face was priceless. He could tell. She wanted to cry but she didn't."Mom how are you holding up?" Joel looked at mom's blue eyes through the rearview mirror. "Exhausted, hungry and mentally drained." Mom answered. "Did you read the paper?" Joel asked Linda. Linda was looking down at the chocolate. "Yes I did. You think it's over?" Linda asked not wanting to look up. "I think it's over if you want it to be over. If you have any more bright ideas I think it will be wise for you to inform me or your mother of your little side adventures. "Joel wasn't being rude or being mean but he really wanted Linda to confide in him more now than she did before. Was she going to be straight up with Joel now? Time would tell. "Linda are you listening to him?" Mom asked from the backseat. Mom smiled staring at Joel from the rearview mirror. Linda knew this conversation was bound to happen. She didn't expect that it would be so soon. Linda nodded her head and everyone in the car knew exactly what happened that night. This is where it had to stay if they wanted to remain free. "So did you have sex with him?" Joel asked out of nowhere. Linda snapped her neck and glared at Joel. She couldn't believe what he was asking her. Mom's eyes almost popped out of her face. "Were not going to talk about this now Joel." Linda snapped. "I'm sorry babe but we are. Your mom knows all about us. This is no different." "No! Joel I didn't and don't you ever think any less of me again." Linda was mad at the assumption but how could she be so mad when she had sex with Jacqueline and two other females. Did that make it okay because they were females? "I'm sorry Linda but it was killing me inside. I needed to know the truth." Joel admitted mom was silent in the backseat, while listening to all of the scandalous news. "I wouldn't do you like that, if I would I would leave you first. I wouldn't want you to do it to me." Linda informed trying to make light of everything. "All right we can talk about something else." Joel suggested. "You want to go and visit your brother?" Linda's frown turned upside down. She was excited at the thought of seeing her brother and knowing what the hell he was gonna say about all of this. "He's going to be furious." Mom said already knowing her son. "Why you say that?" Linda asked. "Because I haven't been home for the past week. Our last conversation he was a mad because he couldn't get in contact with you." Mom forgot to inform her about that one. "Ouch ma." Linda whined. "That's nothing compared to what your brother is going to say to you. If he could get his hands on you I think you would want to stay in the hospital." Mom joked. Everyone knew that Rock wouldn't dare put his hands on a woman, but verbally he could unleash a wave of pain with words. That would make you want him to put your hands on him instead. Linda knew this and second guessed the visit. "We can go tomorrow how about it?" Linda asked. "Whatever you want babe." Joel would grant Linda's every wish if you could with in good reason. The long ride home felt never ending.

A snowstorm was approaching from the north as the news crews mentioned on the radio. Joel and mom help Linda walk up the steps entering their home. The dope boys made there way over to Ms. Cathy's house as they notice Linda and mom entering the house. "Ayo! The one called out wearing a Scully with his bomber on. Joel looked back and noticed that they were hollering at them. He came back down. "Can I help you?" Joel was not starting anything just curious as to what they wanted. "You Linda's man and shit right?" Homie with the fitted asked. They both were fresh to death in winter gear getting that money. "Yes I am, what's it to you?" Joel was pushing a fine line. "Damn G, no need for all that. All we came over to tell you is that the detectives been coming around here knocking on this door a lot lately." Those words struck Joel like a ton of cinderblocks. He didn't think this was going to happen but it was happening. He swallowed hard. "How long ago?" Joel was curious." This morning and two days ago. They not gonna stop until somebody answers the door and gives them a few answers to whatever it is that they want to know." Main man with the Scully informed. "Alright thank you for the info. I'll make sure to pass the info along to Ms. Cathy." The conversation was terminated. Joel legs were wobbling as he darted back into the house. It's been more than a week since all of this had transpired. You would think that those pigs would let it go or just sweep it under the rug as they did with every other unsolved killing in the city. This case had their nose wide open. They wanted to get to the bottom of it one way or the other. So if knocking and showing up to a specific house on an everyday basis had to be done, this is what they would do. "What did they want?" Linda asked laid out on the comfy couch. "Nothing they just wanted to tell us that the detectives have been showing up at his house for the past week or so looking for someone to talk to about something." Joel said sitting down. "Mom can I get some coffee please." Joel was getting nervous again. How would they cover this one up or did they even have to? Maybe they were blowing all this out of proportion? Mom was quiet and reappeared with the coffee mug in her hand. She handed one to Joel and handed the other one to Linda. It was her hot chocolate. "Mom what do we tell them if they come back." Linda asked nervously. She blew the top of her mug trying to cool it down before taking a sip. She didn't want to burn herself. "Nothing." Mom said. "What do you mean nothing we gonna have to say something." Joel had a bad taste in his mouth and it wasn't the coffee. "I won't let them come back to me I'm a go to them instead." Mom was losing it or did she have an idea? Mom knew that if she allowed the detectives to show up at the house unannounced it wouldn't be a wise choice. Joel and Linda were to intimidated and wouldn't know how to conduct themselves. You couldn't say or mention cops to either one of them right now without them getting paranoid and jittery. They didn't know how to handle the police let alone handle being questioned. They would get so paranoid when mom and Pete would talk to them about what happened. Mom and Pete could notice the shakiness and they were far from trained professionals. So you could just imagine if the detectives got a hold of one of them alone. It would be like feeding crackers to a parrot. They would tell you everything for another bite of that cracker right? Mom picked up the phone and dialed a number. "Who are you calling?" Linda asked. "A friend." Mom replied. "Hey how's it going?" Moms smiled was so radiant as she spoke into the receiver. "I have a small issue I was wondering if you could meet me at the County Police Department in the early a.m. tomorrow. It will be in and out I promise. I just need your presence there for my sake if is not too much of a burden on you." Mom was crossing her fingers. "Oh thank you I'll see you at AM have a good one." Mom ended the call. "Mom was that Pete?" Linda as wondering who had mom all giggly like that. "No that wasn't Pete it was a friend I said." Mom left it at that. "knock,knock,knock".. "What a fucking coincidence timing couldn't be any worse, don't you answer the door." Mom scolded Joel as he made his way to peak. He stepped back "It's a female." Joel stepped away not wanted to do anything or say anything else. "Female?" Mom stared at the door. "Oh!" She opened the door and it was Felicia.

"You are some hard people to find." Mom stepped aside so she could step in. Felicia kicked off her work sneakers at the site of Linda all banged up laying on the couch. It made her wish she didn't blurt out the nonsense that she did at the spur of the moment.

"What the hell happened to yoooouuuu?" Felicia was by Linda's side and two big steps. "Who me girl. I fell." Linda lied. Felicia gave her a sly look. "You know your brother has been going crazy trying to get in contact with you two." Felicia looked at mom and Linda. "I bet" Linda said. "That was a nasty fall Linda. You need to be more careful girl." Felicia was too gullible or she was a good actor as well. "I went to see him the other day. He is getting so big. I hate going up there because I can't touch him or nothing. They be acting crazy up in there with all that extra security." Felicia said "I know, we might go up tomorrow sometime not sure exactly when but it's in our plans." Linda said. "It's in your plans. Linda I got something to do in the morning." Mom reminded Linda. "Who you going with?" Felicia asked wanted to know more details. "My baby." Linda answered looking at Joel. Felicia looked over to Joel. "Oh my God he looks so much like Rock, let me find out." Felicia joked. Joel smiled he hated that shit. "No he is all mine, yours is in the county jail." Linda made a joke. A joke that wasn't very humorous at that. Felicia put her hand down at the thought of Linda's words. "Come on girl I'm joking. He'll be out one day chill." Linda tried to make light of what she just said. "We'll look ma. I gota get to work, I just came by because your brother told me to stop by rather than to keep calling since no one seem to answer the phone. This was my second time coming. I'm glad I caught you though." Felicia said putting on her sneakers. "Listen if Manny calls tell him that you saw us and that we are okay. Don't tell him that we might show up at the jail because it is a surprise." Linda instructed Felicia. "A surprise?" He's definitely going to be a surprise when he sees your ass all fucked up in all those bandages and cast girl." Felicia was more than on the money with that one. Rock was gonna have a heart attack once he would see his pride and joy in that light. "But yeah I got you. I won't say anything just make sure you go up and visit him because he's really going through it. Felicia turned the knob on the door and headed out. "I'll stop by later on tonight if you want." Felicia disappeared in the cold bright blue sky.

I'm going upstairs if you need anything let me know Linda. Joel you are more than welcome to stay as long as you want." Mom went upstairs leaving the two love birds alone. Mom had to think.

—

If you have no witness to testify against you then you are most likely declared to have a dismissal because those are the only things that is keeping you here. Two people are claiming that they saw you kill that man and now one of those two people are dead. Now that is a major coincidence or you have some major pull out there." OJ was talking very softly to Rock. OJ read the paper.

They never have gotten the chance to meet up that following day because OJ had other matters to attend to but today he was all Rocks. "Tell me the truth did you know this was going to happen?" OJ wanted to know the truth behind all of this. He stared deep into Rocks eyes searching for lies. "No I didn't OJ I was just as shocked as you are right now. I don't know of anyone who would even consider doing anything like this to anyone." Rock told the truth. He didn't know that Linda did this for sure so he kept it as it was. "Your sister would she have the capability to execute something to this magnitude?" OJ. had his suspicions. Rock couldn't confide in him. It was a smart thing to do. Too many victims became victims of their own, by misinforming other prisoners of a little too much personal information. Let's just hope OJ wouldn't be the type to turn in the next man so he could have a get out of jail free card in his wallet. "Hell no that girl is scared shitless to do anything, thinking that is all going to come back on me." Rock defended his sister, that's all he knew how to do. "Well you must have an angel looking out after you because somebody wants you home and not to be sitting up in here wasting your life." OJ's words may Rock think, when he had the chance to escape all of this. All he had to do was take his mother's hand and follow her where she was staying forever. He would have been with her until eternity, but went against it all. He smiled as OJ's words disappeared from his thoughts. It could be possible, if mom was watching from up above her method wouldn't be to kill. In order to get me out of this hell hole or would it? At least that's what he thought. No that still wouldn't be right. "All I can say that this could be very beneficial on your behalf as long as everyone keeps their mouth shut, and lets the judicial system take his course in all of this. It's a process but it's a process that if it's done correctly can pan out for everyone and yes it has is kinks that need to be addressed but that's Congress job. We are very small in all of this." OJ was a wise old man. Rock appreciated all that he had to offer him. He somehow wish that he could help him as much as OJ was helping Rock. Rock wasn't qualified in that department what he did do was throw him a joint every now and then. That would ease OJ's mind from all of the demons that were possessing him from within. He would never ask nor did he have to. OJ was old school and the majority of them didn't give a shit about much, being that they lived it all and rolled with the punches. Rock just hoped one day he makes it up there in those years. Many would say by the way he's going, he might not even see 30. He was moving to fast many would say. To be honest who the fuck cared what they thought?

—

"Can I speak with Detective Defenchi or Detective Hasnoff." the soft voice spoke into the receiver with a lit L in her hand as she waited patiently. She put a few items in a duffel bag wondering what she was going to tell them. "Hello?" Star responded. "I heard you were looking for me?" Star asked. What was she doing at the moment? "I know his trial is in less than a month." Star snapback. "All you worried about is getting a fucking conviction, don't fucking sit here and try and make it seem that you are worried for my well being because you don't give a fuck!" Star was snapping as she inhaled big pulls from the lit L in between her lips. She was absolutely right the detectives could care less if you lived or died, Their main priority was to get a conviction as Star just mentioned. She could turn up missing or even dead. All they would was place the ad in the paper looking for people to help solve and complete their work, so that they didn't had to do a fucking thing. "I'm not going into protective custody so just leave me the fuck alone. If I show up for the case I do and if I don't it's the same shit to me so fuck you!" Star hung up on the Detective's. Star had her mind already made up and her plans was to go and stay with her cousins over in "Badlands" until all of the shit blew over. Rock would be set free if neither of the two witnesses showed face right? How ironic that would turn out to be. The DA had another scheme up their sleeves. Since the murder of Streets, they had to move on to Plan B. Which was brewing as we spoke. The DA, let alone our government were the most crooked. They needed to be watched heavier than the so called criminals. This shit was about to take a turn for the worst. No matter how many loose ends that needed to be tied up. There was no stopping them no matter who didn't show, no matter who didn't wanted to testify, no matter the lack of evidence. If they wanted to have you. They would hold you there until you did everything you had to do to get yourself out of there. For those of you who could care less and kept rolling with the punches accepting defeat. You were the ones who would be sitting up in there the longest. Sometimes rolling with the punches we forget to punch back and that my friend could end up in defeat.

Chapter 21

"Conspiracy"

Mom was up early as she went to go check up on Linda. She peeked in and saw the two hugged up sound asleep. Joel was just completely laid up with Linda. Mom smiled at the site of the two. She crept back into the hall shutting the door quietly. Mom was stronger than most, not sure if it was because she dealt with children who were always neglected. She would go the extra mile for the kids when no one would have. Even if you had to deal with issues like the principal or even with the local police department. Mom always showed us that even if they weren't blood. Loyalty had to be Learned and earned amongst the people and family. She knew what the consequences were if all this would blow up in her face. The Camden County Police Department would have a field day. If they found out what was being done. Mom was playing Russian and roulette with this stunt she was about to pull. This matter was the cylinder that held one sole bullet ready to kiss to hammer if any of them would slip up. She contemplated bringing Pete along for the ride but decided to leave him at the shop where he was suppose to be running his business. Pete would be a big distraction on mom's part anyway. Let's not forget to mention another innocent person that would get caught up in the eye of the storm. I'll leave him out of this. I'll fill him in later she thought to herself. The fresh coffee was brewing as mom put together a small breakfast for herself. The time was tight she would eat the bagel while she walked towards the nearest bus stop.

The dope boys were posted getting that paper like clockwork at the abando. "Morning." mom said not skipping a beat. "Wassup Ms. Cathy." One of them said as if he had no breath holding in the smoke. Mom smiled as she remembered the first time she ever tried that shit.

It was cold and the bus needed to hurry up. Mom thought finishing up her breakfast. "Hey there young lady." The older man greeted sitting at the bus stop. He was smoking like a chimney. "Good morning to you too." Her nostrils flared as the smell of the second hand clouds of smoke were inhaled. Her palms began to sweat under her gloves. Her eyes widened every time the men would bring the cigarette up to his lips. He saw mom starring. She didn't give a fuck what brand it was. The craven was eating her up slowly. Mom has been doing exceptionally well these past few weeks, even after all that what was happening. She managed to push away the thoughts of lighting a lung buster. It hasn't even crossed her mind. "Do you have an extra cigarette?" Mom asked not able to control herself. The man reached into his jacket and pulled out a box. I need to quit this shit. My fucking fingers feel like they're about to fall off." The raspy man voice admitted. He extended the pack, his words were sharp but the sound of the loud engine could be heard from up ahead. "There she comes." The old man said. "You know what, thank you but I'm good." Mom made up her mind quickly realizing on the great progress she was making in the past few weeks. "Why give up now." Mom said out loud. The man quickly close the box. His hand was probably freezing just holding it up in the air waiting diligently for mom to grab what she had asked for. She now changed her mind. "Give up? Yes you will!" The old man joked helping mom win over her urges. "Stay strong young lady I wish I was as strong as you." The man let mom board the bus first. Mom did great even though she almost gave in for a blast of nicotine. Mom wore a smile the whole way to the county police headquarters. It was 7:56 AM.

"I hope he shows up" Mom whispered to herself as she got off the New Jersey transit bus. She had to only walk about 30 feet until she would finally reach the main entrance. She decided to wait patiently hoping to encounter her longtime friend. Everyone was bundled up heading to work walking briskly on by. Dress shoes and high heels is all you could hear and see hitting the pavement as they made their way to work. No one knews how these two became so well acquainted. As as time went by we would all find out sure enought. I noticed how the two shined so vibrantly at the sound of each other's names and presence around the other. It drove Rock crazy until he finally asked the question that he was dreading to know the answer to.

Mom was bundled up from head to toe, her long hair was up and styled in a fashionable messy bun with her hoops displaying her small cute ears. She had to apply her light lipstick that matched her well kept nails. She enjoyed her jewelry and decided to keep a few rings on, her marriage finger stood open and would until Pete finally decided to put one on her finger or whoever the lucky man would be. Mom was cold but from the looks of her outfit she looked warm and snug.

"Good morning isn't it?" The man's cold voice said staring mom from behind. Mom did a 180 and stared into his dark eyes. Mom's smile was beautifully lit. In amazement and excitement. Michael Stoski also returned the smile with his pearly whites. The two had deep history, that could never be erased. Stoski fucked up years ago. Mom and Stoski met at a club almost 2 decades ago they had instantly fallen for one another. Mom was is thick but it was a nice thick. She would never lose that beauty that she carried with her. She was thick in all the right places and had been like this for her entire life. The two were young and pretty much didn't know what it was to be in a "committed" keyword committed relationship. Well, mom gave him her all. She was brought up wanting something more and long lasting. Now Michael on the other hand, had a bit of a womanizing addiction. He never disowned mom but neither did he disown any of the other woman he enjoyed fucking around with. Stoski wasn't a bad man. The things he did made him a not so good partner. After mom allowed all of this to continually go on for months, ending being a full year dealing with his womanizing behavior. It was hard for her. All mom wanted was for him to love and accept her as time went by. He didn't, the more time Michael spent in school the more distant he was becoming. Mom never gave him the ultimatum to choose between his schooling and her because mom was the one who pushed him through every semester. Whenever Stoski wanted to quit, she never left his side. Eventually that's when mom admitted defeat. She no longer wanted to be third place in his life. If school was going to be first and foremost mom was more than okay with that. All these extra affairs apparently came in second, then came mom. "I don't think so." Those were her words. She finally filled me in with a glimpse of her past. She decided to just be there for Michael as a friend nothing more or less. Stoski was so wrapped up in his life that he never realized that he was pushing mom away unintentionally. It was too late. He was a year away from passing the bar exam when he tried to capture mom's heart again. He was hurt but not more than mom was hurt. He understood all that he had done to cause emotional pain and he still till this day feels as though he is in debt to mom. He has hopes that maybe this flame would ignite again one day. No one knew if that would ever resurface.

"You're so handsome as always." Mom flirted a bit given him a quick hug. "Not as gorgeous as you Catherine." Mom blushed at the sound of her name rolling off Michael's tongue. "I'm sorry to bother you but I'm having an issue with these detectives coming to my house looking for me for no apparent reason. They are already fabricating the case on Manuel. I'm getting tired of it, this is why I wanted you to spare me a few minutes of your valuable time." Mom appreciated his time and got straight to the point not wanting to waist any more of his time. She knew this was why Michael went to school and study so hard. He earned his living protecting the people from the law itself. "You are in no way, shape or form bugging me. I'd actually rather you bug me more often than not at all." Michael was still a charmer. "I think I can most definitely help you with them assholes." Stoski assured mom. "Under one condition." Michael asked. "And that is?" Mom asked. "We grab a cup of coffee before we part ways." Mom inhaled making a hissing sound not really knowing if that was a good idea. Pete was working around the corner a few blocks up. "If not we could rain check?" Michael sinced the refusal and looked for a common ground. "Yes, we can do that." Mom figured getting it out the way now would be better than dealing with it in the future. "One quick cup." Mom challenge putting up her pointer finger looking cute as ever. Michael playfully snapped at it like a hungry snake. "Stop." Mom said with a frozen big smile plastered on her face. "Let's go and see what these pricks are harassing you for now." Michael led the way. "Remember you cannot talk. I'll do all the talking from here on out for you, your son and your daughter." As long as you let me do this we should be all right." Now in Manuel's case it's going to be a bit more difficult but I tell him the same thing?" Stoski made it clear, they made their way to the basement floor taken the steps. "So I hear your seeing someone." Michael said taken the stairs slowly. "I am" and you?" Mom asked wanting to know. "Yes and no." Michael admitted. "Some things never change." Mom jabbed him twice. "Oh boy I knew this was coming." Michael said softly in the corridors with one flight left to go. "It's like all they want is my money. They are all the same Catherine." "Excuse me." Mom stopped at the top of the steps and looked at him questioning his last statement. "No I don't mean it like that, they are nowhere compared to you. That's what I'm saying. In fact I been trying so hard to find one that can come close to you but to no avail it's useless, pointless and meaningless. I can't find happiness after you put that hex on me." Michael joked. Mom burst out laughing. She admired Michael's personality. He never changed with mom. He was always this adorable man. Who made some errors in his youth that would be hard to forgive. "I'm sorry to hear that, maybe if you stop searching she will come to you." Mom said. I don't think she will come twice after I let her go the first time." Michael said opening the door. Mom didn't reply to his comment. Her smile spoke for itself leaving Michael's thoughts of what would of been her reply of his own. "Have a seat on the bench. I have to ask a few questions." Stoski informed mom. She did exactly what she was told. This was Michael's realm no need to intervene what he knew best.

"Can I help you sir?" The woman at the desk asked. She was wearing a T-shirt with a vest covering her shirt. Her shiny badge dangling from her neck displayed the words detective spelled on it. "Yes actually you can. I'm here with my client. There has been a few visits by your detectives on numerous occasions to her place of residence. I'm here with her to see what all this is about." Stoski wanted to know what was going on at mom's house. Why would they persistently keep on visiting her if her son was already incarcerated? Something wasn't right. They knew something or assume something and Michael was getting to the root of it all today. "Your name?" The DT asked. "Michael Stoski attorney in law." "Okay Mr. Stoski what is your client's name?" The lady at the desk asked. "Catherine" Stoski didn't finish her name when she already knew who Michael was talking about. "Give me a second Mr. Stoski." The detective disappeared. In seconds two other detectives appeared. It was no other than detectives Ren and Stimpy. Those were the two pricks causing all this ruckus. Yes, I know they're doing their job which is to be in everyone else's lives but their own but damn.

"Mr. Stoski." Hasnoff extended his hand. Michael didn't take it. Hasnoff face scrunched up. "Well, no need for the rudeness. You can come to the back with us if you wish. Bring her to while you're at it." Defenchi requested turning his back to Michael leading the way. Michael signaled over to mom so she would come over. Don't say a word please. No matter how much you want to bark something back at them. Can you do this for me? I don't know how serious this is. I want to play this by ear." Michael instructed mom. She zipped her lips and threw away the key. "Don't lose that key because I want to talk to you later." Michael put a small mom's face. It felt real good to have someone in your corner, to defend you when you had no one else. You can take a seat if you wish." Hasnoff said already sitting down. "Would you two care for a beverage or some coffee?" Defenchi she asked. "No my client and myself wish to get out of here as soon as possible we have many things to do today. Please and thank you." Stoski was always that type of man. He always got to the point. No wonder he loved his career so much. "Well in case you haven't read the paper about one of our material witnesses turning up dead. We find it to be very coincidental if we may say." Hasnoff was a true prick. He stated with a smirk. "And what does any of this have to do with my client detective?" Michael asked. Staring coldly in the eyes of Hasnoff. "We are not saying that she is involved but we are entitled to ask a few questions as to her whereabouts are we not?" Hasnoff was beginning to growl slowly. Mom was feeling uneasy. "I believe that's what I'm here for don't you think? To protect her rights since your department is known to get a little reckless and disrespectful with the questioning. I'm sure you're aware that her son is locked up for a homicide that he didn't commit aren't you?" Stoski wanted to run the show. "Well according to our only witness now he did." Defenchi chimed in. "We'll see how all that holds in court." Michael shot back. "All we want to know is where Catherine was the night of the murder?" Defenchi asked. "You don't have to answer that question Catherine." Michael instructed. "I was home with my daughter and her boyfriend." Michael gave mom a seriously cold stare as to say what the fuck I told you before we came in this room. "Home, you heard her." I hope you're not harassing my client that's already in the Camden County custody?" Michael tried to diverge the attention somewhere else. "We tried and that boy is a tough cookie to crack." Defenchi informed. "Let me tell you something, if you don't have a case on my client. I'm going to ask you this one time and one time only to let her live her life in peace. She is already dealing with so much with the fabrication of her only son being tried for murder. Now you want to throw the rest of her small family into the mix of another murder that has nothing to do with them? Are you that useless and empathetic that you can't get a conviction honestly? Why don't you find a new career in construction or something because you two suck at this shit?" Stoski was going in on the two pricks. Their ears were red as the sly comments were being shot back to back in their faces. "Whoa whoa listen up Mr. Stoski you're protecting a murderer for all we know, so I wouldn't be so quick to shoot down on our careers. We put the bad guys in prison you make money keeping them out!" Hasnoff shot back. Michael didn't like this at all. Gentlemen we are done here if you have any question pertaining to any of my clients. You go through me and only me or we skip the bull shit and I start filing harassments civil suit charges on the both of you. You can throw your plastic badges on the line so I can add them to my collection." Mr. Stoski was pissed. He tossed his card on the table and got up and left with mom following suit. "See you in court." Hasnoff had to get the last word in.

"Something isn't right here." Defenchi said to his partner in the room. All by themselves re-evaluating what just went down. "Yes I agree, all we wanted to do was ask a few simple questions does it seem interestingly odd that she went as far as hiring an attorney without even knowing what we wanted from her to begin with?" Defenchi was rubbing his chin pondering deeply to what he was hearing. He was right did mom just raised more suspicion on herself and Linda or did she think productively in advance to avoid entrapping herself in a mess that she couldn't get herself out of? "I don't know about you but I want to hear what her daughter has to say." Defenchi opinionated. "Yes I do too but didn't you hear what the lawyers said?" Hasnoff asked sarcastically. Defenchi let out a laugh that's what he thought of Mr. Stoski's warning.

—

Heading towards Michael's car the temperature had to have dropped a few more degrees. Michael tried to shield mom from the blistering cold but it was of no use because the wind could not be tamed no matter how much you tried. They made it, fianlly settling in the Bens.

"I know the seats are cold I'm working on it." Michael took the words right from mom's mouth. The leather has no perks besides looking good. You should try sitting on them in the scorching summer." Michael joked. "I'm okay I think the cold gave me an idea of how that wouldn't work too well." Mom joked back. She slipped her cold hands in between her thighs searching for warmth. "I need you to be straight up with me Catherine." Michael asked as the car was idling. The cars air was getting warmer as the engine gave off some more heat. "Wassup?" Mom asked already knowing where this conversation was going. Please don't tell me that you know who had anything to do with that murder that took place over a week ago? Before you answer this I want you to know that I am on your side in all of this, but I need you to know they think you have some idea in who is responsible to what happened." I can't protect you if you lie to me." Michael took a moment of silence. Mom didn't know what to do or say. Michael already knew too much, would this put him into deep as well? Could he help as much as he wanted to? Was it worth dragging Michael deeper in all of this? Mom took a deep breath and exhaled slowly. "I'm sorry Michael but I have no clue as to why they are harassing us so much." Mom looked at Michael's eyes for a few seconds but eventually bypassed his eyes looking out the window. I know he didn't like that reply but he didn't even bother to search any deeper. If mom wouldn't open up now maybe she would do it later. Let's just hope it wasn't too late.

"How about some Dunkin' Donuts?" Michael didn't feel like working if mom wasn't going to make his job any easier. "Sounds great." Mom said accepting the offer. So who is this lucky man that has managed to sweep you off your pretty little toes?" Michael didn't waste no time as usual. Mom's smile solidified what Michael was saying. "Well he must be a hell of a man?" Michael admitted. "He is. He's not a doctor or a judge but he is a true man. He is divorced, well in the process of finalizing all of the legal documents." Mom didn't say too much. "Oh yea? You managed to rip him from under his wife's claws?" Michael joked. Mom pushed his shoulder. "No silly they were already separated when we began to talk to each other." Mom defended the accusations against herself. "So how did the two of you meet?" Michael asked wanting to know who this man was exactly. "Through Manuel." Mom admitted. "Your son hooked you up. Well tell him to match make me a girlfriend." Michael joked "I really got to get him out now." Michael was the comedian at times. Mom was tearing up on how much he was making her laugh. She did miss Michael and often did wonder how he was. She could just never really work up the courage and belittle herself to give in to him again. "He gave Manuel a job when he needed it the most at the sub shop that he owns. He took him in and showed him how to make an honest dollar even if it was making sandwiches. He enjoyed his little gig at the shop. He would help me out knowing that I didn't need a dime for anything but he still would help out so much." Mom's voice was cracking. She missed her boy so much. Everything that mom would do was for Manuel and Linda and no one else mattered. "Its okay, Ima do my best. I promise Catherine." Michael was putting two and two together he remember going into Pete's shop one day and did notice a male that resembled Manuel. He decided to let it go. He didn't want to believe that mom was referring to Pete. Those two were the complete opposite when it came to him and Pete. You could since a little jealousy in the air of the Bens. Did he lose mom completely to Pete? Or would mom go back to her long last love?

"Mr. Hasnoff I have a fax from the corners office." The sexy slender secretary wearing a casual woman suit said coming over with a piece of paper held in her manicured left hand. Defenchi looked at his partner and shrugged his shoulders not knowing what this was about. "Thank you Trish." Hasnoff examine the paper. His face turned sour in seconds. "You got to be fucking kidding me this can be fucking happening!" Hasnoff was pist. "Whoa?" What is that?" Defenchi asked. What are the odds of this little shit actually being not guilty?" Hasnoff tossed over the paper on the desk. Defenchi grabbed it anxiously wanting to know what this disturbing content was. "Oh shit?" So he is innocent?" Defenchi asked. Shocked with what the paper had written on it. Defenchi had confirmation that the blood on the butterfly knife found on the scene was in fact Rock's knife due to his fingerprints being all over the handle on it. The man pronounced dead on the scene had no blood matching on Rock's knife. "But the fucking wounds matched up perfectly with the weapon we found on the scene." Defenchi was confused. "We may have jump to conclusion on this one." Hasnoff admitted "now what?" Defenchi asked. Hasnoff shook his head "we are missing someone here. If he didn't kill him then who the fuck did and from what we are observing he has us thinking that he committed the murder. I know if it was me, and I didn't kill anyone but knew who did. In an instant I would give up that person up. There is no way I'm about to stay in a cage for the rest of my life." Hasnoff was dead serious about what he was saying. Go figure he would give up the person, never doubted it. "That's you and I this is a man from the street who is following street code that's the difference." Defenchi rationalized. Living by a street code isn't something you do sometimes. It's a way of life 24/7 or you just don't do it at all. I'm almost 100% positive all my real thorough bred brothers and sistahs out there know this. A lot has changed but if you are in that life you should know already. These pigs will tell on their mother so they wouldn't have to set foot in any jail. Thats their code. "He is going to beat us in trial and this little shit knows it." Hasnoff projected what the future will contribute. "Oh no he isn't. If he doesn't give was what we want then he'll have to bite the next best thing." Hasnoff had a hard on for Rock. He wouldn't rest until the key were thrown away or lost for a few years. "And what's that?" Defenchi wore a quizzical look on his face asking. "Conspiracy to." Hasnoff had an evil grin on his face unleashing the beast from within. This shit was fucked up for real. There motto was by any means. "Shall we?" Hasnoff asked. "Yeah let's go visit that so called tough guy." Defenchi suggested smiling at the thought of his partner's vindictive attitude. There was no slowing him down. Everything was moving so fast, what is there a man to do when all is against you? Even when you aren't the one to blame? Adapt and accept? Is one way but what if it's too strong that you become codependent on the effects of the adaptation process no matter what that may be?

—

"The he go right there." Slash warned as he kept his eyes on one of the guys they've been waiting for. "We going to get him he thinks shit is sweet." Leak said. "Damn I thought yall was going to let it go?" Bigs was tired of the scheming and plotting. "It's only right they gonna get what they deserve Bigs they could've killed you in there. They didn't because the Co broke it up. Did you ever think of that?" Rock spoke softly trying to put some sense in their heads. Bigs blood was boiling he was getting tired of all of this shit the guys were up to. There was five minutes left for Chow, they waited patiently for the opportunity to present itself. You will be surprised what peer pressure can do to a man if he isn't aware of his own weaknesses. The plan was already set in motion on the next block out, the mission was going to be executed regardless of the fact. Well that's what Rock, Leak and Slash were up to.....

Chow time! Chow time!" The doors were cracked Bigs was always the first to exit the cell. He stood behind the guys. Was he a bit worried or just scared? To get him to speed up was useless instead he eventually got lost within the masses of the people. Leak and Rock made it a habit to walk side by side. Whenever you saw one the other wasn't too far off. "Look at em right there, you see them?" Rock was extremely tall, towering over everyone else wasn't hard at all to see further ahead. "Yeah I see those pieces a shit." Leak said through clenched teeth noticing those niggas who beat the shit out of Bigs. The plan was simple and couldn't wait to be executed. Slash was with his squad as always. He was within eye shot distance from where we were. His crew loved the fact on how much Slash was eating. Slash would break bread with all of them out of his own cut. I could care less extra security around the board Rock thought. There were aiming towards the end of the week to handle the Philly cats. Two on two was what Leak and Rock had discussed. Jumping on one at a time would only show weakness and that's exactly what wouldn't be displayed today.

Already sitting down, everyone who was somebody saluted each other. Showing the respect everyone demanded towards one another. "Damn Rock I want to put that nigga down like now." Leak was too anxious he couldn't wait. "Chill my nigga no point in getting sent to the bucket because we couldn't be patient for a few days." Rock said. He looked down to take a spoonful of his meal. He looked up and notice Bigs fat ass walking straight across the dining hall. His mouth was full of food. The look in his eyes was one I never seen. Leak's initial reaction was to look behind himself. He noticed Bigs too."What the fuck is he doing?" Leak says softly not to alarm anyone. His back pocket weigh his pants down you could tell. Rock notice and couldn't understand though. "He's going over there." Rock said again. "Shit!" he got up to but it was too late. Being that there was a trash can right next to the marks who moved on Bigs it looked as if he was heading towards the trash can. The marks didn't notice a thing. This was not the case today. Bigs has something up his sleeve and the dining hall was about to be in complete uproar in a matter of seconds. Just as Rock has suspected Bigs did have something in his back pocket. They were unsure of what it could been exactly. The sight of the sock gave away all uncertainties, it was a lock in a sock. By the time the Philly's boy informed his homey that someone was approaching on him the "CRACK!" from the lock catching his head as he tried to turn around. "CRACK" it was as quick and as fast as the whip cracking Jesus Christ. They both endured so much pain in his time. The chow hall rose up to see were all the commotion was coming from. Slash and his boys were sitting at the table across them and didn't give the other man from Philly any chance to help his boy. "No you don't play boy now 3 of Slash's boys put foot to ass on the other mother fuckers given him a taste of what they did the Bigs. The sock that Biggs had in his hand was no longer white it was doused in red thick blood. The CO was on Bigs but he didn't move fast enought. He didn't stop cracking that man until the sock and Lock was snatched from his hand. It took three CO's to calm Bigs down. "Stop let it go!" CRACK! I said let it go "CRACK!" I said stop!!! Bigs was too possessed. There was no getting in it there were too many guards trying to defuse the situation. I held Leak back. "It's over, he handled it. We can't do shit fallback!" It took all of Rock's might to hold him back. There intentions were to join the brawl but that wouldn't do them no good. All three of them in the hole was a smart move, was it? Someone had to think quickly and Rock was the thinker this time. For once.

EVERYONE BACK TO YOUR CELL NOW!!!....I SAID NOW"!" the PA was wailing with orders. "Fuck you! One prisoner yell. "You lock in!" Another yelled. No one was about to start a riot but from the looks of it. The baby blue shirts flooded the chow hall. Bigs was cuffed immediately so was one of the guys who jumped the other man. The other two got away swiftly. Two out of four these odds were acceptable. Instead of four out of four. The blood was leaking from both men heavy. The one Bigs got out on had to be rushed on an emergency unit over to the hospital quickly. The other one will go to the infirmary in the jail, he wasn't as bad as the lock and sock victim.

"Why didn't this mother fucker wait for us?" Leak was pissed. Slash wasn't back yet." Where the fuck is Slash?" Leak was mad for no reason. Rock looked at him then looked out the cell searching for Slash. "I say get in your cell now you piece of shit!" The CO was yelling at Slash as he took his sweet old time walking towards the cell. Rock smiled. "You always got to be the last one for everything don't you?" "Fuck you!" Slash was also being very insubordinate right now. Yelling back at the CO who was demanding him to lock in now.

"Ayo! Bigs is crazy as hell. Please tell me that you knew he was going to pop off like that?" Slash was all the way up hyped pacing back and forth in the small ass cell. "Fuck no, we didn't authorize this shit." Rock said. We just as surprised as you." Rock informed. "Did you see all that fucking blood?" Leak asked calming down a bit. It was pointless to get all wound up, knowing we were the cause of all this whether we knew it or not. If we hadn't been nagging Bigs and making him feel belittled. He wouldn't of over reacted the way he did this morning. "He snapped." Rock said. "Yes he did." Leak agreed. "What was that with your peoples?" Leak asked Slash. "Man they been dying to get at main man. They saw the opportunity and ran with it. That was destiny at his best." Slash was joking about the situation. This is what it was all about, blood, guts and glory huh? You would think otherwise but not here.

"We mind as well pack up Bigs shit because he might sit for a while for that stunt. Wouldn't be surprised if they bring up charges on him?" Leak said wondering out loud. Sooner or later you will get got especially if you did some grimy shit like that. That ass whopping was already dated on your ass. Unless you got juice like that, to be honest no one would even care. If you got caught slipping that's on you, blood loss is only payable by blood spilled. "I wanted them pussies!" Leak shouted out as if he had a bad case of Tourette syndrome. "I knew I couldn't wait for that shit to have jumped off later." Slash Agreed. "Ayo Slash?" Rock called over to him interrupting there conversation flow. "Wassup? Why your man's disliked homeboy anyway if I may ask?" This was bugging the fuck out of Rock. He didn't mind but for every action there is a definite reaction wouldn't you agree? "Well I ain't supposed to be talking about it but since yall my niggas I can tell you. I'll say about four months ago they had some words in the shower which was left alone but it really wasn't. t just been brewing up as the minutes passed by. So when those to clowns decided to run up in here that shit just put the icing on the cake that was the bottom line. Even though that shower incident had nothing to do with me. I'm riding all day with them and they know that. So when that shit took place they felt disrespected too. So that's what led them to take advantage of the opportunity today fucking homeboy up. It was going to happen sooner or later. It was a coincidence it all his very morning." Slash informed us on the details. "Those dudes was going to get it regardless." Slash opinionated. "All Bigs had to do was wait." Leak shook his head in disappointment.

"Manuel Ricardo report to the bubble now!"Manuel Ricardo report to the bubble fully dressed!" The CO yelled over the speaker. "Damn you stay on the hot seat." Leak joked. "Be easy." Slash suggested. "Be easy? What the fuck these mother fuckers want with me now?" Rock was pissed. Everything that goes on in this punk ass jail seems to lead back to my ass!" Rock was getting annoyed with all this extra shit.W all know it wasn't like that but it dame sure felt like that to him. "Just go see what they want you know what to do." Leak suggested. Rock left his cell in no hurry lolly gagging the whole way, not running for anyone. He felt as if he was on everyone's hotlist "Someone dies. Rock was present. Someone kills. Rock orchestrated it. Rock's cell is ransacked blame it on Rock. Someone almost killed someone let's see what Rock had to do with it." Rock mumbled under his breath. He stepped up to the bubble. "You are a very important man." The big belly CO says sarcastically. "What do you want?" Rock return with so much attitude. I don't want shit from you boy, but I know people who do want you though. Go to the multipurpose room smart ass to see how much attitude you got you come back from you little visit." The CO was antagonizing the whole situation.

Rock snatched his pass and strolled on over to the multipurpose room. So far the only people who waited for him when he was called to the so-called multipurpose room was his lawyer and Bevis and Butthead head. These were the two detectives only came to be a pain in my ass. It wasn't a smart thing to engage with them verbally and especially not physically. If you had any brains at all you could use them to your advantage. When it came to these two clowns one had to be a few steps ahead of them. Since they always thought they were five steps ahead of their suspects. Ha! Imagine that. Rock's stomach tighten when his retinas focused on the image that was in front of him. Shaking his head in disbelief his body wanted to turn around and not even feed into the Dick heads that he couldn't stand.

"Mr. Ricardo a.k.a. Mr. Rock." Hasnoff voice echoed all throughout the room loud enough for everyone to hear. "Fuck it!" Rock said under his breath. They could see the look on Rock's face. Rock didn't want to see them he'd rather strangle one them, if lucky both of them. "What's wrong? You're not happy to see us?" Defenchi had a few words of sarcasm in him to let out before the news would be finally dropped. "What is it with you two? You must not have any lives let alone get no pussy, if all you want to do is deal with men in prison all day." Rock shot back. "Wow that was cold, coming from a man who is surrounded by dick and balls 24/7." Hasnoff shot back. "What the fuck you coming down here for? I don't have to be out here without my lawyer you do know this right?" Rock snap getting their undivided attention now. The CO stood up as if ready to jump on Rock at any given moment. Rock look back at the CO. "All right, all right enough with the bickering" Defenchi suggested. Hasnoff followed his partner's request. These two had to be the most unprofessional pricks in any unit. "How you doing Mr. Ricardo?" Defenchi tried to straighten out the situation by starting over again. "Fuck you what the fuck do you want?" Rock wasn't taken the bait. He was done with the extra shit. You teach a mother fucker a little law and he grows some balls quick. "All right look straight to the point. That's what you want right?" Defenchi asked. Hasnoff noticed Rock with his observant eyes watching Rock's body language under the microscope. Rock gave him a once over nod. "We have some great news to tell you, what would you think if we told you that you didn't kill "Kay"?" Defenchi let it marinate. Rocks palms began to get warmer than the normal. His heart beat must've increased by two beats per second. He was about to scream his lungs out. "I would say I told you that. I'm innocent." Rock said. This could not be good at all Rock thought silently. These two jackasses had something up their sleeves. "We have reason to believe that you may have been telling us the truth. You may be innocent after all. You see the blood on your knife didn't quite match the blood of the man that was pronounced dead at the scene." Defenchi was doing all the talking. Rock didn't know how to take any of this. His lawyer needed to be present right now but he wasn't. Rock was gonna fuck this who case up. "So what you're telling me is that you two men fucked up this case by putting me Manuel Ricardo behind bars? For alomost a full year now right?" Rock asked not trying to give them any type of information that they were looking for.

Defenchi bit his lip haten the words express from Rock's mouth. "You're not here because you are innocent Mr. Ricardo let's get that straight. It's possible that we may have jumped the gun in all of this but you are still a valuable asset to the DA. If you didn't killed Kay we are all confident that you Mr. Know it all, knows exactly who is the person responsible for the murder of Kay." Defenchi corrected. It was funny how they wouldn't even call Kay by his birth name. They addressed him as if they knew him. Could the dead man get some type of respect from anyone? They had a solid point. Here Rock is thinking that he was going to get away scott free because of the mistake dumb and dumber made but this was far from the case. Rock may be capable to be acquitted of charges. Even if he did dumb and dumber were here to make sure this error wouldn't make it to trial because if it did, the case would be an acquittal for sure. So maybe these two did have a millimeter of some type of brains left in there big heads that rested on their shoulders. Rock already knew where this was going. "You can help us help yourself and get yourself out of this stinking hell hole, or you can stay as you are and get even more comfortable behind these cold brick walls." Defenchi was an asshole. Rock saw what he was trying to do and it wasn't going to work. "We are willing to take away all these charges and give you a pass right out of this place within the next few days if you give us the name of the person who was with you the night on the murder." Defenchi asked. Hasnoff never broke his stare. I was there by myself why would you think that there was someone else there with me?" Rock had a few questions of his own. "Well come to look at it from another view your passenger door from your truck was left open. We picked up a few unidentified prints on the truck as well but that's all inconclusive at the moment. If you didn't kill him. Whoever was with you had the same exact knife that you had. The corner's examination told us that the cuts fit together perfectly like two puzzle pieces made just for one another." Defenchi was gaining on Rock. Was Linda in any trouble? Why the fuck hasn't anyone come and notified Rock of anything? Where was Stoski with his help? No family, no lawyer nobody what the fuck? Rocks mind was traveling at a velocity beyond light speed. He couldn't believe how this was about to blow up in his face. These assholes couldn't have all this information. Rock thought. "The door was open because that mother fucker tried to come into the passenger side." Rock was digging himself in deeper than he realized it. "I don't believe that Manuel. Someone helped you and now you are protecting that person why?" Defenchi was expected Rock to finish his words. "Y'all bugging I killed him because he was fucking me up. As you already notice when you're man came and picked me up. I stabbed him, than I cleaned off the knife" Rock had to shut the fuck up fast. "So you are confessing to it then?" Hasnoff spoke up. "Yes that's what it sounds like."

"What the fuck is going on in here? I specifically told the two of you what I would do if I found out that you two were harassing my client!" Stoski came in the clutch out of nowhere hooting and hollering from behind. Rock smiled he was relieved. Rock was on the verge of putting his foot deep in his own ass. "We are done here anyway your client just confessed to us." Hasnoff had a big smirk on his face before he even attempted to stand up. "Yea good luck, we will see how that shit holds up in court." Stoski shot back. "Listen my secretary obtained some vital information on this case which I'm sure can be extremely beneficial to the both of us. So instead of using it as leverage over my clients head. Why don't we lay out our cards and get this settled right here right now." Stoski was attempting the impossible could it work? Was I on the verge of being set free?

"I like how you talking. What about your client." Hasnoff pointed at Rock with his big head. "He doesn't seem to want to cooperate with us. That is what we are trying to do here in the first place." Hasnoff lied. "Yeah okay." Rock mumbled. "Give us a second would you." Rock and Stoski got up and walked all the way to the other side of the room in low whispers. "didn't I tell you not to talk to these guys Manuel?" How the hell in sweet Jesus name am I able to protect you? If you are willing to walk out your cell, walked all the way down here just to accommodate these men. Who are trying to put your life away behind bars for the rest of your life?" Can you give me a reasonable, better yet logical explanation for this?" Stoski was mad. I failed to following his simple instructions. Rock shook his head, ashamed in his own actions "I just wanted to know what they knew about with everything, as you can see they saying that I wasn't the one who killed the man." Rock smiled as if he was saying something of importance. I mean yes it was terrific news but the detectives intentions were all malice. Rock was too uneducated to compete with them in their own game. "So what? You think you're scot free huh?" Stoski's words wiped off Rocks smirked instantly. "They are not letting you go. I need you to see this. The only way you are getting out of here is by striking a deal which I know you are not going to do. Are you?" Stoski put his hands on Rock shoulder. He wanted to get a direct look into his eyes. "Hell no." Rock retorted. "Alright then so remember they are going to use this new information to their advantage to get you to talk. The only way you can be set free is by bail now and a not guilty verdict by the jury. So their little hopes and dreams that they are trying to sell you it's all a ploy and I'm going to show you right now. Don't say anything." Stoski instructor once again. Rock took in all that was said by Stoski and put it in his memory bank for future use.

"All done with your powwow?" Hasnoff never quit. "So I've been informed that the blood on my client's knife isn't a match to the victims." Rock sat back and listen as Hasnoff words played out just as Stoski warned. The law was a real piece of work. You had to trust in them as they were obligated to take an oath to protect and serve right ?..... Fucking wrong! Yes they do take an oath to uphold the constitution but we all know in this game they are only protecting their asses so they don't look stupid. To accomplish this everyone in their way, will get ran over and guess what will happen? ... Yup, you got they would end up road kill. "What is it that you need from my client detective?" Stoski asked not really giving in or giving a fuck. He wanted to prove a point to Rock and it was being proven for the most part. "We don't want him to do anything, all we want is the name of the person who was at the scene when Kay was murdered. He doesn't have to testify, make any statements. All we need is a lead...." The auditorium was quiet. "We can take care of the rest on our own." Hasnoff wasn't loud or being rude anymore. In fact he managed to put on a friendly act for an audience. "If my client gives you a name or a lead as you guys call it, he then will be free to pick up his belongings and go back home with his family today right? Is this what our terms are sounding like?" Stoski wanted to keep playing his little game with these two brainiacs. Definchi's face was all scrunched up as Stoski finished his last comment "Must be some sour grapes huh?" Stoski stated noticing his visage. "We'll have to run it across to DA first just to make sure it's approved from up above." Defenchi replied knowing damn well the DA wouldn't pass up on one fish to get another fish especially when they had a nice case built up against the first fish. What if the detectives did their job hard enough that the State of New Jersey could have both suspects in jail? "So make a call and will be right here waiting." Stoski pushed harder. "All right we all know that isn't going to happen like that, so I'll stop it right there. What we can guarantee you that your client's charges will be dropped to conspiracy charges. He will see the time of the light in the near future if he is cooperative." Hasnoff tried to sound convincing. "Bullshit!" Stoski burst out not playing anymore. "If we go to trial the charges will be dropped either way to conspiracy no matter what. Whether he decides to cooperate or not, so don't try that shit. He's not given up no name so we can do this two ways because I'm getting tired of your fucking games now. You can drop the charges now and find your own lead or you can go back to your bitch and tell her or him that my client isn't helping anybody but himself get out of jail with his innocence only. Not with your help nor the judge's help and definitely not the DAs help!" Stoski took the wind right out of both of their lungs with that one. The room was silent for a minute everyone was thinking about their next move. It was predictable to an extent. If Star testifies Rock was assed out but if she didn't he would have a chance for mistrial but they had to play it safe. "This is what we'll do. Your client will be charged for conspiracy within the next few days or even hours how about that?" Hasnoff was admitted defeat. "But the case will still be investigated until we find the individual responsible in the murder. Your client still has to show face in court." Defenchi stated being a fucking prick. I don't care what they promised you I need to make this shit fucking clear they don't give a shit about you or you dying mother. So save yourself the embarrassment of being labeled a rat and do your time with your head up. If not stay the fuck out the way and out the game. Sounds somewhat fair. They asked walking away knowing damn well that shit wasn't working The meeting was over it was just Stoski and Rock in the room now.

"I told you, I'm not here to steer you wrong Rock but you can get yourself in a lot of extra trouble by opening your mouth a little more than you supposed to. Especially in this ugly predicament you are in." Stoski informed. Rock felt good to know someone had a positive interest in him. "Have you heard from your mom? "He asked changing the subject. "Actually I haven't and I've been fucking worried sick." Rock admitted. "She is okay, but those two knuckleheads had been harassing and knocking on your mom's door looking for answers to the questions about their key witness being killed." Rock's face looked sick. Here they were Stoski and Rock sitting in a room. Stoski just got done schooling Rock on how the Dt's play mind games and now Stoski was also trying to get into Rocks mind, since mom didn't give him any ammo. "Why would they be harassing your mother?" Stoski asked searching into Rocks eyes for the truth. "You asking me? I have the slightest clue I'm in jail. I told you I haven't heard anything from them. This is the first good news I've heard about them. Well at least somewhat good news from you about them." Rock admitted. "Did you put your sister up to do something?" Stoski asked. "Damn Michael I haven't had any communication with either one of them. Why you asking me something like this?" Rock wasn't too happy with the accusations. It's a fucked of feeling when you think you know something, but you don't for sure. When people also think they know you had something to do with anything could drive anyone up the wall. "All right, all right I apologize I just thought that you may have heard from her at least." Stoski tried to clean up a spill, more like low key accusations.

"So how is it going to pan out in court?" Rock switched up to talk about the case now. "Good I think you still might not get out of this unscathed, but it will be better than a life sentence. Wouldn't you agree?" Stoski asked. Rock was a bit down at the news. There was no way any of this would go away. Stoski was absolutely right. "Yeah I guess you're right?" Rock said. "So how much time now?" Rock asked. He had to prepare himself for what he was about to get into for the long haul. "Well you got a year in basically in now right? So maybe we are talking 15 years at the least, if I can pull some strings." Stoski said looking in his notes. Rock rubbed the back of his head feeling up his fade. "So if this is what I can get you you'll have 14 more left." Stoski said. Now if this witness shows up appointing fingers at you is not a good look for us." Stoski explained. "I know this though, they are here because they are 100% positive that there only credible witness isn't looking so promising after all." Stoski informed. "So if they do process you again for conspiracy, that's a good thing don't be alarmed. If they start questioning again dont answer anything unless its about sports. Can you do that for me?" Stoski asked. "I got you just work your magic with the DA. I know you're trying but I want to slide up out of here." Those were the last words for either one of them. The lucky number 14 was all that was on Rocks mind now.

—

"Linda you have to try to put some light pressure on that leg." Mom pleaded with Linda. She hasn't a move from her bed ever since she got home from the hospital. "It hurts when I walk on it mom." Linda whined. "I know it does baby but the doctor said not to baby it to much. That's what the boot is for and your crutches."

Mom would be as persistent as she could when it came to getting her daughter back up and walking. She felt bad because she was pushing Linda to do something that was causing her an excruciating amount of pain, but if she didn't do it no one would. "Mom?" Linda called over to mom. "Yes?" Mom answered. I'm starving can you make me something or should I just call over to the Chinese spot and order?" Linda knew this would change the subject. Linda was supposed to see Rock and from what her level of pain was it wasn't on the agenda today. "What do you want?" Mom didn't approve of her tactics switching subjects at all, but then again Linda must have not eaten anything all morning. "What time did Joel leave?" Mom asked. "I don't know I was asleep when he must've left. I woke up and he wasn't by my side. Did he say he had to work?" Linda's asked. "I want a cheesesteak mom that way we can split it between the two of us with some onion rings. What you think?" Linda asked mom. "Sounds good baby." Mom replied.

"So I went down to the City Hall to have a word with the detectives that have been harassing and coming to the house with my friend." Mom said. "Your friend? Was he the one that dropped you off to?" Linda didn't hesitate to ask. Mom smiled confirmed the truth. "Who is this man?" Linda asked. "He's your brother's attorney." Mom admitted. "Oh really." Linda smiled while dialing out to the Chinese store to place her order. We shouldn't have to worry about them anymore. If they do decide to pop up again I was told by Michael that we are not to say or answer none of their questions about anything. If they catch you alone you are to call Michael or simply say that you rather have your lawyer present to answer any of there questions. I have a small feeling that they want to talk to you especially. Just an FYI Linda. This is why I need you to recover quickly." Mom said. "What kind of drink do you want mom?" Linda asked. "I want a home iced tea with two lemons in it." Mom answered. "Homemade lemonade for me." Linda spoke into the receiver. "Did you hear what I said?" Mom asked Linda as she hung up the phone. "Yes mom I heard you, do you think they know?" Linda asked. Mom looked at Linda not knowing how to answer that question. She hoped not, for her daughter sake, She wasn't a hundred percent sure yet. "I can't answer that hun. We all have to be very mindful of what we talked about to anyone." Mom said a bit paranoid but speaking all facts. She sat by Linda on her bed staring at the blank TV screen. "You think we should move?" Linda asked mom. "No baby we are not going anywhere if you just listen we will be just fine. Plus, where will we move to? This house is almost mine 100%?" Mom asked. "The Bahamas or Hawaii." Linda said joking about the situation. Deep down inside Linda was this frightened little girl who was scared of herself. Containing herself was an issue she would have to adjust immediately. If not who knows what else her little mind would come up with. "Call Joel when you can and relate the message that I just related to you please. He is the other one I'm worried about Linda." Mom admitted to her daughter. Joel is going through the motions himself the most. Linda has somehow learn how to push the death to the back of her mind. If she didn't she was putting up a good front. "Ima go pick up the food right quick give me a few minutes." Mom left grabbing the other cordless.. "Don't forget the fortune cookies mom!!!" Linda mumbled as loud as she could hoping she would hear her

With the wind's coldness wanting to slice mom's face. She tucked her head down and walked briskly over to the store. She stepped in and just like any giving day it was crowded with most from around the way.

"Excuse me." Mom made her way over to the window. "Excuse me we was here first." The nappy headed Spanish girl said with a serious attitude not knowing what was coming to her mouth. "I see that but I'm here to pick up an order is that okay with you?" Mom spat back with an attitude herself. "Ayo you better calm the fuck down, you don't know.... the small heifer came out her face. "One of the males gripped her up. "Yo shut the fuck up you know who mother this is? Unless, you want to keep that pretty face I suggest you shut the fuck up before her daughter fuck your whole world up." One of the dope boys interjected trying to calm little miss thang down. "Her daughter? That bitch aint doing shit." The dope boy laughed all right when she put your stupid as in the body bag, you won't be talking that tough shit." The pre hyped chick didn't like those words at all. She pipe down. Mom couldn't believe what the Street was talking right in front of her face. How did they know? Or where they just talking shit? Mom decided to play along. "What's your name honey?" Mom asked starring at the motor mouth. "Sharmaine." mom grabbed her bag. "You in trouble now I don't want to hear your mouth later when they start digging down your throat." The boy chimed in. "Sharmaine" mom said to herself. These kids have got to be so disrespectful nowadays it was unbelievable. The sound of the phone ringing mom caught moms attention. Linda must've answered it.

"Who?" Linda couldn't believe what she was talking to. "Well it's been some time since you called over here." Linda was on the phone with Jacqueline. She had to keep her voice normal she had almost gave herself away once she heard the name Jacqueline. Why was she calling now? How the hell did she get this number? Ima kill Manny. "I'm not sure when I'm going up to see Rock why?" Linda asked confused as fuck. This was getting complicated. How would she finessed this one without exposing her cards? She wasn't sure if she should already come clean since a major part of the plan has been executed already. "You want to come over?" Linda repeated over the receiver. Mom walked in Linda's room, with paper plates and the bag of food. Linda put a finger on her lips so mom wouldn't say word. "Well I'm heading out to Philly so today wouldn't be a good day. If you want I can call you and let you know when we can meet up is that okay?" Linda wasn't sure this was going to work. "All right I'll call you then." Linda hung up the phone. "Who was that?" Mom asked with a lost look plastered on her face. "What are the odds of this happening?" Linda buried her face in her pillow. "What Jalinda?" Mom asked.

"That was Jacqueline" Linda said. Mom shrugged her shoulders as if what was the big deal. "Mom that was Manny side chick remember?" Linda reminded mom. Mom thought for a second "Oh yeah it's been a while since she called over here what does she want?" Mom asked. She wanted to go and see Manny together. Manny must've told her to call and check up on me. Since I haven't showed up or wrote to him lately." Mom hypothesized. "Okay so go with her." Mom wasn't following the picture. "Mom she is Street's baby mom. First of all and remember when we met her at the value plus a while back ago?" Linda threw a few pieces to see if mom was putting all this together. Moms jaw dropped. She thinks you are Jasmine but you Jalinda." Mom struck oil. Her face was priceless. She laughed digging in the bag leave me out of this one." Mom said filling up the plate's with food. "Mom what do I do?" Linda was laughing to. Mom was focused on what she was doing she did not want to get involved. "I don't know but I'm sure you'll figure it out just like you've been." Mom said biting down on her onion rings. "How are they?" Linda asked diving into her sandwich piece by piece. "Crispy just how I like them." Mom said. "If she comes over and sees that I'm Jasmine she gonna know something was up. She going to want to know why I lied." Linda could not shake off the thought of getting jammed up in this lie. "You see what happens when you lie." Mom said in between bites. "I know but I did it all for a good reason. It's not like I lied just to lie. I had to gather some information. She was very useful in all of this little did she know. "So why don't you just be honest and tell her the truth? I'm not saying tell her about what happened but tell her that you..." Mom stopped mid-sentence. "I don't know Linda this is an ugly situation." Mom admitted. "I'll figure it out."

Meanwhile Felicia had just gotten home from work. The mail on the floor was all bills but there was one that stood out from all the others it was a letter from Rock. She smiled no one was home. It was a long day her daughter and her roommate must've went out somewhere probably to go eat. She kicked off her shoes and headed straight to the bathroom turning on the water and let it run. She picked up the unopened envelope and decided to read it. Her anxiousness got the best of her. She couldn't wait to see what rock had to say...

Hey ma,

Hope by the time you get this few lines you find yourself in the best of health. Tell Eliza I said hi and that I hope one day I can see her pretty little face. Well as I said in my previous letter my mind seems to drive me in so many directions, but my final destination seems to end with you on my mind. What did you do to me? Do you think of me as much as I think of you? It's been a stressful couple of weeks since the last time you have come up to see me. I haven't heard anything from my family I hope all is well. I sit here and wonder staring at the cinderblocks on the walls. Will this ride be as lonely as I didn't intend it to be? Am I gonna die here alone? My trial date is approaching fast and my destiny feels as if his been set in stone already. How could I get myself out of this? I remember you telling me that you want to be here in my life Felicia. I'm going to be totally honest with you I don't know if this is going to be possible. I mean I'm grateful to have met you don't get me wrong for a second, but we are humans you have needs that I can't satisfy nor fulfill as much as I wish I could. It's not possible this might not be a few years we are talking about. This could very much be forever, how would you think if I would accept your offer to stand by me and devote yourself to me? I'd feel so selfish. A man who is behind the razor wire. A man that when you need a tight hug can't give it to you or when you desperately need someone to talk to at night because you can't sleep. I won't be there. I will be in the way instead of being there for you. I'm not telling you what to do nor would I ever impose on how you choose to live your life. I need you to know that being a true friend will work better for the both of us. You can still be my number one baby girl as far as holding each other down as friends. That may sound silly or it may come across the wrong way. Don't feel like that because I want you by my side but I don't want you to stop your life because there's a chance that I may have already stopped mine. This isn't set in stone but the more friends I have the better I'll feel internally. I find it stressful wondering a little too much, wanting to know what or who you're doing even if you're not doing anything at all. These walls say bad things to me. My mind is my worst enemy. Please think about what I'm saying and please don't take my words out of context because I don't mean any harm by them. I hope to see that pretty face of yours in the near future. With nothing but love and respect do I choose my words wisely. Write back

Rock!

Felicia couldn't believe it. "This nigga trying to get rid of me on the low?" Felicia said to herself. "Why is he letting his mind push me away?" Felicia couldn't understand where Rock was coming from. It's hard for man to stay sane in a relationship while incarcerated. It was too much unnecessary bull shit. Who she fucking with? Why she aint write? Why she not picking up the phone? There are so many unanswered questions that have already been addressed by your partner, but a missed call or a week's reply in a letter can cause any man to break his head wondering the worst. Felicia jumped in the bath. She would address this letter later when she had a chance. She wasn't too happy with what she just read. She fell for Rock hard and this is who she wanted.

"I can't go anymore." Slash was burned out they were all working out in the cell since the jail had been issued on a lockdown. The block was all shouts and uproar. It was a pain in the ass when you had to be locked down for 22 hours a day. When these lockdowns were put into effect you would be lockdown all day, for days. Those little two hours that you did have to go to the gym or dayroom when it was given. You actually learn how to appreciate them seriously. "Two more!" Come on Leak said hitting the dips off the sink. "One...... two... Slash Collapse on the floor. "Get up its on Rock." Rock got down and began his 50 clip. "So they might drop your charges and give you a lesser charge huh?" Leak was excited about the news that Rock had told them earlier. "It's... a..... Possibility." Rock said in between push-ups trying to keep his flow going nice and steady. "That's a lot better than doing a life sentence. I know it sucks to be in here, but 15 years will go by so fast you won't even believe how fast they are flying by once you're dug in." Leak was talking from experience. "48.... 49.... 50." Slash counted making sure Rock pushed out every last push-up as he always did. "Come on Leak I know you mean well, but 15 years isn't going to go by that fast. Its 15 fucking years." Rock said breathing heavily doing a set of squats right after. "I don't mean it's going to fly that fast but I'm telling you once you your home jail you will have a set schedule and get into the swing of things. Just as long as you keep yourself busy throughout the day you'll see how fast it goes." Leak said while pushing down on the floor down. You're right he wishes he could do that." Slash said. "Stop how long you been in a cell with this?" Slash asked. "Almost a year." Rock calculated. Leak was up on his feet. "Already!" He repeated. "You see what I'm saying? You just got here not too long ago, and a year has passed by already." Leak was doing his dips now. Rock tried to see it how he sold it but it was still a year and many more to go. It wasn't working. "Upstate is nothing like this shit hole, this is all lockdown and maximum security all around us. Upstate is more freedom. You can roam the yard three times a day if you want. You can sign up for school or vocational training programs. You can smoke all you want, you can fuck bitches if your game is tight." Leak went on and on. Rock didn't want to go upstate. He didn't want to think about that yet. Even though he should be because his day was approaching whether he wanted to go or not. He didn't dare to tell the guys about upstate, but he was afraid of heading upstate. This is where all your real killers stayed. They were all set in their ways not having any time for any bull shit. He has heard so many stories. Rock was not in a rush to experience any of those stories he heard. Now leak was painting a picture that sounded a bit too perfect. "It can't be that great up state Leak." Rock contested. "You won't want to leave once you get all dug up in your home jail. I promise watch." Leak admitted. "It's a lot better than being here Rock. I'm not gonna gas you up, its still locked up." "Leak is right. There is so much more to do up there, you aren't lockdown like this. I mean every now and then you have to get shaken down but the jail is so big you have to wait until they hit every part of the jail, but it's only for a day or two. Other than that you are back to your normal schedule. You have contact visits with your family and fuck your hoes if your balls are big enough. It's a different atmosphere." Slash spoke up informing Rock of all the fine qualities of jail/prison. "You two kill me with the shit... How can you learn to love all this so much?" Rock asked not understanding it. I want to be home, not in a cell smelling the next man shit." Rock said missing the point. "Were not telling you to learn how to love this shit Rock where you are telling you to learn how to adjust and accept what you're going to have to accept regardless. For one, no matter how much you wish or desire to be home you won't make it happen. You are only setting yourself up to be angry every day. We all want to be home with our family friends or kids, but we can't because there is no way out. Unless you have balls to kill yourself or have a helicopter come pick you up which I totally doubt. So whats the next best thing?" Leak asked wanting to know what Rock was thinking. "Make the best of it." Rock said not so happy. I know that's what Leak wanted to hear. "Now you getting it. Yes, this sucks but like I said it's a whole another world upstate. You have your fights, killings as you do in every fucking Jail. You not going to go up there on that type of time. I mean yea if a nigga try you, you gonna have to put in work but for the most part you'll be all right. Now give me my money stop stalling." Leak finished. "Get him!" Slash joked. "Stalling?" Never that." Rock dropped to pay his dues. "Ayo!" Greg was up on the door. "Damn what is this Gold's gym up in here?" Greg joked seeing the sweat on all three of them. "Smell like it, why was up?" Slash asked. Jacob over on the other block, he hit on the no-hitter" check it out I'll be back in a few." Greg disappeared. "Who?" Rock asked. "Jacob" Slash repeated. "Who the fuck is Jacob?" Rock asked. "That's the white boy they call him "Stix". Oh okay I know who you talking about." Rock checked in the note-book he found his name. "You have to wait because I don't know the final scores yet. If he did it's a nice hit on his part." How much if he did hit?" Leak asked "$20 Rock said. "Damn" Slash said. "Yeah I know fuck it." I'll check tomorrow morning." Rock said. "You should get Greg to get the scores before he locks in." He suggested. "No I want to see the scores with my own eyes." Rock new Greg couldn't be trusted too much entirely. He was a criminal just like the rest of us. That was a good call his behalf.

CHAPTER 22

"Baby boy"

It wasn't even breakfast time yet but the guard was waking me up early in the morning. It's been several days since I see my lawyer. "Manuel Ricardo your needed down in control." The guard opened the cell door and grabbed my attention. My eyes felt as though they been glued shut. I couldn't open them as much as I tried. "Did you hear me?" The guard asked. "Yeah I heard." Not really given a fuck. He left the cell door open and disappeared. I tried to pry my eyes open.

"What the fuck don't tell me this shit." Rock mumbled under his breath not wanting to wake the others in the cell. "What the fuck they want?" Leak asked with his face covered. "Your guess is as good as mine." Rock replied. "Yo!" Rock said. "Wassup" Leak replied. "I think I got the pinkeye yo." Rock said prying his eyes open. "Oh shit." Leak buried himself deeper in his covers. "How you know?" Leak asked. "I got all the shit in my eye and I can hardly open them on their own." Rock admitted. "Yup that's definitely the symptoms." Leak laughed. "Fuck you." Rock said as he flushed his eyes so he could finally see clearly. His eyes were bloodshot. He would have to sign up for sick call as soon as possible. He cleaned up everything that he came in contact with hoping not to spread it. That feeling of not being able to open your eyes when they're supposed to wasn't a popular feeling. It's said that your eyes are the most sensitive part of your body wouldn't you agree? I've learned that the main cause for when one gets the so called pinkeye, was mainly because you have someway somehow allowed some type of bacteria to enter your eye. Which only than gives your body the green light to flush it all out pushing a shit load of sticky yellow discharge from your eye. It can be so bad, that your eyes get sealed shut. It's a disgusting feeling and it's very contagious if it isn't treated properly. The odds that Leak or Slash would contract that shit were slim but also likely if I didn't disinfect the cell.

Rock made his way over to the bubble trying hard to not to wipe his eyes with his bare hands. The tissue in his left hand absorbed the water his eye was leaking.

“I see you got that shit out of your eyes.” The CO said handing him a pass. “If you want I’ll send you to medical right after you’re done.” The CO wasn’t the regular he was the shift relief officer. “I don’t need that shit floating around I got kids at home.” The CO saw the damage in Rock’s eyes. He was a father so he already knew the deal. “I was going to sign a sick call but if you can make that move for me I appreciate it.” Rock needed his help so for the moment he put his pride aside. Rock gave the guard his back and made his way down to control. The feeling to scratch his eyes was something he wanted to do to soothe that itchy irritation that was hounding him. Rock knew better than to allow temptation to get the best of him. “Control?” Rock said to himself was he going to court?

“Mr. Ricardo have a seat.” The husky Sheriff instructed. He was almost completely bald. He had about a hundred follicles left before officially being labeled bald. I never could understand why men tended to do this. If a man has less than 50% of his hair why not get rid of the rest voluntarily. Instead of hanging on to it for dear life. It’s gone to let it go baldy! I was talking shit now, I’m sure Id’ prolly be the same way once I started to lose some strands. “Can I ask what this is for?” Rock asked innocently wanting to know what the fuck was going on.

“It looks to be a new conspiracy charge to homicide.” the Sheriff informed. “Sound familiar?” He said nonchalantly. “Somewhat.” Rock replied “Somewhat?” The Sheriff repeated sarcastically. “You have to know something about it, this is why I’m here.” The sheriff said. Setting up the ink and a new charge card ready to be filled in with my identity. “So what’s going to happen to the murder charge?” Rock was a bit confused. He wasn’t sure if the new conspiracy charge would erase the homicide charge or if it would stay. “I can’t answer that Mr. Ricardo. I’m not a lawyer or a judge. My job is to get you printed and run it through the books on file. Rock tried to remember the conversation the lawyer had with him. It would all depend on trial. “You’re a little too young to be sitting up in here for killing people, don’t you think?” The sheriff asked. Being nosy as fuck. “It’s a long story” Rock wasn’t about to tell this man anything that he had no business knowing. “Left index finger.” The Sheriff doused it with black ink, until he saw it was perfect. He ran through Rocks 10 fingers in about five minutes. “That’s it you can head back up to your cell, but before you leave let me tell you something.” the Sheriff said. Rock took a couple steps back making eye contact with the sheriff for the last time. "I'm an old man Mr. Ricardo, I done took prints from so many people of all types of race, colors and sizes. Women and men, most of them you can see it in her eyes. They will not discontinue to commit crimes or even try to slow down. The reason I'm telling you this is because when I look into your eyes. I see a lost child who is in the place that he doesn't belong in and that has an eye infection as well." The sheriff joked. Rock smiled. "Seriously this could be the end of your life or could be a new beginning. It doesn't mean for you to get lost in these walls and become something you are not. Yes we all have our tempers but you young man. If you want to make it out of here in one piece you need to control yours." The sheriff words were hitting Rock hard. Mind you the two have never met a day in life until this very moment. It was weird how this older man has spoken as if they know each other for some time now. "Take it easy." Rock left with his mind still boggled at the thought of all the words spoken from the pig. He was right. Who was Rock? He wasn't the man he was portraying to be in these past days. He was weak. I'm not talking physically but mentally. He would allow others to blow his fuse. Rock headed back to the bubble on his unit. The relief CO was gone.

"CO?" Rock called into the bubble. "Drop your past and take it in." The pink nose pricked ordered. "Can you give me a pass so I can go to medical it's urgent." Rock was out of luck. Good guards were rare and Rock was about to witness this for himself. "Urgent? I don't see anything wrong with you!" The guard in the bubble spoke behind thick glass. "I have the pink eye I just want to get it checked out before gets worse." Rock kept his cool. The CO got closer to take a better look. "You sure do, you better sign a sick call than." CO did what they did best which was not give a shit. "Take it in. "Your a piece of shit you know that." Rock walked away his ears were hot and his blood was even hotter. He hated them, he hated himself. How could so much hatred be felt by someone. The guys were all still asleep Rock fell back and tried his best to calm his heart rate down.

—

"Excuse me do you have change for a $10 bill? The machine doesn't want to accept the money." The sexy femanine voice asked the man posted up on the side of the speed line wall. He was waiting for his train to arrive. "Yes I do." The man dug into his pocket and pulled out some bills. He eyed girly up and down following her curves. Shorty had a body, there was no taken that from her. "So where you heading." The man asked. He had to be at least 26. He had on a jacket over a button up. That was exposed from the top, fitted jeans with some fresh crispy forces. "I'm not sure yet but far away from here." She answered. "And you, where you going?" She asked him walking towards the machine to get a pass. The man followed her, it wasn't a long walk. "You going to miss your ride." Lil girly advised him. "I'm not worried about that, there will be another one behind it." He joked. "What is your name?" He asked little mamas. "Star." "What is yours?" Star asked. "I'm Devon." He answered extending his hand. Star looked at it for a second. She smiled and took it. "Nice to meet you." Devon said. "Likewise." Star made a new friend. "I'm going to Philly." Star admitted. "What part because that's where I'm heading?" Devon asked. "North" Star answered. "Do you mind if I ride with you? That's exactly where I'm headed, no need to go alone." Devon wanted to taste Star, she was fly as always. With trial a week or two from now Star was already heading out of town. "What you going to do out in Philly?" Star asked being a little too nosy. "Business." Devon answered. No need to feed her too much info. Devon just met Star for all he cared she didn't need to know shit. All he wanted was to get in them drawls. "That's us right there." Devon said looking towards the train. "I got that for you shorty." Devon offered to help with her duffel bag. "Awe you're so sweet." Star said. The train wasn't as packed as usual. Devon picked a seat towards the rear of the cart. "What kind of business you in to?" Star asked. Devon inhale thinking that there's a good chance I might not ever see this bitch again. Ima smash fuck it. "I'm a pharmaceutical representative." Devon said with a grin. Star smiled but trying to hold it in at the same time. "You can smile it looks good on you." Devon worked his game. "I know but my ex used to say the same thing." Star was reminiscing about Streets. "Oh yeah so I take it he sold drugs to?" Devon asked. "He used to." Star answered. "So what? He locked up or something?" Devon asked. "No he's dead." Star said with her head down. "He was murdered a while ago." Star informed Devon. "Damn Shorty I'm sorry to hear that, he got robbed or something?" Devon wanted to know how and why her ex got killed. This girl could be bad news or she might be an accomplice to murder. Thats why she was very secretive at first, not wanted to say pretty much of anything. To make things more suspicious she had a duffel bag. What was inside the bag? Money? Drugs? Whatever it was Devon wanted to know. "He was lit on fire, inside his house." Star said. "What the fuck? So why are you getting up and leaving?" Devon asked. "It's a long story." Star said. "When we get off you want to blow one with me? I got it?" Star asked looking for a listening ear. She had so much shit pinned inside and it was killing her deep down inside. Her family all turned her back on her. Why because they warned her about being with Streets. Star was so hard headed and madly in love with Streets. She would rather put up with his shit then to steer away and listen to her family's caring words. Star was warned about the beatings and the major influence Streets had on her lifestyle. You would be amazed on how much pain a woman will endure for just a few minutes of attention. What's more pathetic is the man who takes advantage of the woman in a situation like this. She would become so afraid of him, that whatever he would asked of her to do. Would be done to the tee. Rock hated men that would display these characteristic. He called them cowards. "Yea we can blow one I got a spot we can head to if you want?" Devon asked. Already seeing his plan coming to fruition. "Yea we can do that." Star accepted the offer. "Well we got some time you can tell me why you leaving town?" Devon wasn't going to stop until he knew what Star was running from. "The man who killed my ex's friend is going to trial in a couple weeks and they want me to testify against him. I wanted to testify.... but " You wanted to do what?" Devon cut her off. "I can't fuck with you, your rat Shorty." Devon was taken aback by what had just come out Star's mouth. He was already getting the impression that she couldn't be trusted. There is a saying that has been around for centuries. "Your first impression is your only impression." Star just fucked up. "I'm not a rat!" Star barked causing a few passages to look back at them. "What the fuck you looking at?" Star snapped. "Alright Shorty my bad chill." Devon didn't know what he was getting himself into. "I said they want me to testify but I'm all the way out of here for that reason." Star tried to clean up what she said. The ride went smooth with light conversation.

—

It was a little past noon and Rock had already put his sick call slip in. Now all he had to do was wait until the medical department finally gave a fuck and called him down. "So what did they say about the other charges Rock?" Slash asked. Breaking the silence in the cell. It would get really boring at times in the cell. It didn't matter if you had your boys in the cell with you. When a man would get lost in his imagination. That was as close to freedom one could experience. It could be something as simple as you going to the store in the cold, or just heading out front to get a feel for the weather before you got dressed to start your day off. Small things like this a man usually learns how to value the most when its stripped away. When he or she is out in society we would take all the small these precious moments for granite, but once you were put away. We would wish to get one second of it. By then it was too late like always. "Man Slash, I don't know what the fuck is going to happen. All I know is that trial will be the last say so in all of this." Rock said snapping back from home. "That's the only thing that can happen now. Either you win or you lose. There is no in between with the courts." Rock said.

"Let's just hope that when you pick you jurors, you will have some ethnicity on your side. For some reason in most homicides. A brother always ends up with a lot of white people on his side. Sike! That shit is a conspiracy I tell you." Leak was in his conspiracy bag. Rock noticed Slash rubbing his eye. "Damn don't tell me I got you." Rock shook his head with a dead serious smile on his face. "No I'm good my shit be itchy that's all. "Slash Replied. "So you going tomorrow?" Rock asked. Ima take the deal because they're not offering a lot, and to keep it 100. I want to get all this stressful shit out the way and just do my bid." Slash had his hearing tomorrow. He was already dug in, it wouldn't make a big difference. Well at least that was his opinion. It's all the extra psychological shit that played a major part in driving a nigga insane in this hellhole.

Jail was easy for the most part. It was only considered difficult and hard when you're too busy trying to live both lives. It's damn near impossible to live both lives, unless you have a team that will ride with you and a team that adheres to what you say than maybe it's possible. For your regular Joe Shmoe, you'll drive yourself and your loved ones insane trying to tell them what to do. Demanding shit all because you say so. Please tell me how that will work in your favor. People have lives to live, trust and believe dropping everything that they are doing just to accommodate your needs. You better has some serious paper. That shit don't happen for too long though. If you have a little time to do that maybe, key word I said maybe it's possible. It seems like everyone had their minds made up as to what they were going to do as far as plea-bargaining's etc, etc. Leak told us from the gate you always go to trial fuck them. Make the state spend that paper, no freebies over here. Slash just admitted to a plea deal and Rock wanted to go to trial but wanted to take his mind off all this bullshit. He wanted to get it out the way but that wouldn't be a good idea. "Clank, clank the door was being hit once again. "That's for you Rock it's always for you." Slash joked. "Manuel Ricardo visit!" The guard yell. If being in jail was always like this, with the drugs and the visits coming and going along with mail and phone calls. It was easy to believe why a majority of people took the deals. It was a walk in the park with all that love coming and going for those who had it. "Damn!" Rock said as if it was bad. It was crazy how often their cell door was being constantly hit.

"What nigga you don't want to go? Shit I'll go for you since you sound busy or upset." He joked. "Is not that asshole, it's my fucking eyes. I don't want them to see me like this." Rock was dabbing his eye with Raw wet coffee. It was instant but his mom had done that to his sister years ago. "Boy if you don't cut it the fuck out. There is a thick glass between the two of you anyway. We the ones that should be worried." Leak was bugging. So was Rock. Rock dashed out the door heading straight towards the bubble. "You got to be the president as many fucking visits you get around here, you might as well be out in the fucking street." The same prick that denied him medical attention said. Rock took his pass without uttering a fucking syllable to the prick. His stomach flip flopped. Who the hell could this be? It's probably Felicia. Rock thought. The walk seem endless towards the visiting room.

—

"This isn't your house is it?" Star asked. "Damn Shorty you ask a lot of questions. No it isn't but it's like my house. The only difference is I don't pay any bills here." Devon joked. "You got some smoke?" Star asked not wanted to be rude or disrespectful, she was company. No one was inside the house. They were somewhere on eighth and Butler about five houses from the corner. The corner had over a dozen men on the corner. You could only imagine all the selling of everything you could think of. The spot that they were in was a dingy ass house. The pile of clothing were in the corner. It smelled as if nothing was washed in weeks. The house didn't or feel welcoming at all. You had 40 bottles of Old English and empty liquor bottles all on the table in the living room and floor. Incents were burning but that shit didn't help the house one bit.

"Of course that's why we hear." Star placed her bag in between her legs not wanting to let it out her site. She was keeping it close, it was her valuables? Devon looked and scanned her every move. "Just asking, no need to get smart." Star playfully joked lighting the L she had rolled up. Devon disappeared over to the kitchen. He was putting together a concoction of his own in the kitchen. He broke up the bud until it was almost dust. It was that sticky so that was almost impossible. He reached in his jean pocket and pulled out two clear sandwich baggies. One had off white color substance in it and the other had a sandy color substance it. He used it to spiced up the L he was rolling in the vanilla Dutch that he bought. He gave one to Star so she could roll up her shit. He was lacing the L and it wasn't him that was going to smoke this L. It was Star who was going to smoke that shit. "I can't stand rats." Devon said to himself. "Devon!" Star yelled. Devon wasn't from down south to be calling girls Shorty. He was put on a front so that Star would not know him at all. With the L finally rolled up tightly, he went back over to the living room where Star was sitting comfortably with her legs crossed looking sext as fuck. She was puffin on the already lit L reaching her high. "He sparked his but never inhaled it he just put the lighter to the tip. Until it was cherry red and passed it to Star. I just got this its call white widow." Devon lied right through his teeth. He switched L's with the L Star rolled puffing on it with no care in the world. Star being the gullible person that she was took the L almost snatching his fingers off his hand. "White widow I been dying to smoke that shit give me."

—

Rock's eyes went from red to fire engine red as he noticed his sister all bruised up. Her left eye was alot more swollen than her right. Her once beautiful face was mangled so badly. It would all go back to normal as time went by, but for now at this very moment in this visiting room at the Camden County jail. Rock wanted to hurt someone so bad right now. Mom was standing next to her. Joel was on the other side. Good thing Rock did put Joel's information down on his visit list, because he would have been one sick mother fucker if he would have been denied admission into the jail. Mom had her face down, no one said a word. Just letting the visual sink in. Rock broke the silence.

"I know you didn't do this to her. Ima give you one chance to tell me the truth. Did you do this to my sister and don't fucking lie to me?" Rock was not loud but his voice was most definitely deep and forceful. The vibrations could be felt as if he was holding in all his anger from deep down inside for some time now. Mom still didn't look up. She answered for Joel by shaking her head. "No it wasn't him Manny." Linda finally spoke up. Do you think he'll be right here if he did this to me? Come on think?" Linda spat through the bottom of the vent. Mom help Linda sit down. Her face was in so much pain as she spoke. "What happened Linda what are you doing out there?" Rock asked. He wanted to know some answers. It was going to be more than difficult to have an open honest conversation with the guards on both sides. They both stood on the sides of the window eavesdropping on every pronoun, verb, and adjective being spoken from everyone who was out on the dance floor. "I told you I would watch over you Manny." Linda say like a little girl. She had always made it clear that this what she would always do. Who would've thought she was that serious about it though. "Look at yourself, you know how bad it hurts me to see you like this?" Rock spoke through his clenched teeth. Linda looked afraid. Mom held Linda's hand tightly as she too heard the words her son was speaking. Joel just sat there and waited. He new that his turn would come to talk and answer some questions, until then he wasn't in a rush at all. "Was that you?" Rock asked not trying to be obvious with his questions. "What?" Linda wanted Rock to be more specific. "/El cabron ese/, /that nigga/"? Rock asked using some Spanish since he noticed the guards weren't Latino. Thanks for that one Linda looked over to Joel and nodded her head. Joel now put his head down. Rock couldn't believe what his eyes and brain were registering. Rock shook his head. "No you are lying." Rock said refusing to believe any of it. Mom looked at his son. Shaking her head. Answering for Linda and Joel. "What the fuck is wrong with the two of you!?" Rock snapped not being able to contain himself. "Excuse me Mr. Ricardo there other visits being taken place keep it down final warning." The guard had Rock by the balls. He didn't respond. "Calm down Manny you going to get us kicked out." Linda said unhappy with her brother's temper. "You worried about getting kicked out now! Rock barked back. Look at yourself. You look one step away from death." Rock was losing his cool as much as he tried to keep it under control. "I did it for you. How do you think I feel? Knowing you're in there because of something you didn't do? What you think I'm supposed to eat all the shit up? You expect me to live my life all happy go lucky as if nothing ever happened?" It was Linda's turn to express how she was feeling. Rock just stared at her in complete shock. There was not one thing Rock could've done to get this girl to comply with anything he was saying. Linda had become a woman a while back ago. Now she evolved into an animal, that had tasted blood accidentally and now was evolving into a full blown predator. Linda stared at Rock hoping he would learn to understand who she was now. This isn't something that she dreamed to be. This was Linda doing what she felt that needed to be done. In order to bring the family back together. "You both need to calm down. This isn't why we came up here." Mom looked at Linda in her eyes. She was dead serious. Linda had to take it easy. "I'm talking to you, I know you're not to happy with the outcome of what's been going on, but we are all in the water together remember. I'm not saying I agree with any of this." Mom shook her head speaking. "But it's done so whatever comes after this, we are all ready for the end results." Mom spoke softly into the vent so that the only ears that could be heard where the ones that she wanted to hear. Her words were as clear as day. Was mom right? Some would agree, others would also think that she lost a few screws growing up herself. Just as the rest of us did. "I don't need you to be getting hurt like this Linda it's all I'm saying." Rock tamed his anger now. "I know you mean well but that wasn't a smart move right Joel?" Rock dragged Joel into the conversation. He shook his head. "You have no idea man. I don't know what I'll do without this lunatic." Joel joked cracking a smile on everyone's face. "Come on Linda please stop with the extra shit. You have me going nuts in here." Rock said rubbing his head. "Just you? I'm going nuts too." Mom joked as well. The visit had went from a scolding session into a memorable moment of laughter amongst the four. At this point it didn't matter who did what. What mattered was how the love caused people to act out in many different ways.

Star was nodding the fuck in and out. The combination of drugs inside that blunt had her high out her mind. One minute she would nod off, then up the next. "I'm so high." Star admitted to Devon. He wasn't even in the room. He was doing who knows what? He never even hit the blunt he had given to Star. Once her sweet juicy lips had taste the blunt, he already knew what would happen next. This wasn't his first time using this grimy low life method to get what he wanted from the woman he met over time. "Damn Shorty you look high as hell that was some good shit huh?" Devon already knew the answer. "Oh yes it is." Stars words would drag out. "Come here I want to touch you." Star said touching herself. "Bingo." Devon said. He walked right over to her allowing her to caress his soft skin. He gave in touching her hair and neck. He leaned in for a kiss, and it wasn't denied.

"Do you have... some more of that white widow?" Star asked. She actually thought it was actually white widow. This girl was beyond lost. "Yup a whole bag full Shorty." Devon could care less by now if she found out, the damage was already done. His hand slid down her shirt fondling her beautiful full breasts. Devon began to feel blood rushed down to his manhood. Star had her hand on his not stopping him but making sure he didn't go anywhere else too fast. Star hissed as Devon bit her bottom lip piercing it a bit. "Not so rough pa." Star enjoyed the rough but that bite wasn't passionate at all. She kissed his neck, he allowed his other hand to slip down her backside which was soft and warm. "Uh-uh" Stat said pushing his hand back up. He did it again. "Stop playing girl." He went towards the front now. "Slow down Devon, I just met you." Star said hoping he would slow down. Who knows if she probably gave up the pussy to him. If he would have just slowed down. Guess that's unknown because Devon had no intention whatsoever of slowing down at all. If anything that was his Q to get what he wanted ever since seeing Star at the speed line terminal. "Slap! Slow down Bitch you going to give me some of this pussy." Devon slapped all fire out of this girl. Star's eyes watered her high must of been slapped right out of her because she wasn't nodding out anymore. She fought back slapping him right back. "You don't ever put your hands on me!" Star shouted. This time it wasn't a slap Devon had balled up his fist given her a right jab knock her right on her ass. The fighting back was useless but Star was no quitter. She had learned to never back down from anyone no matter how small or big you think they were compared to you. If you felt threatened, you know what you had to do. That was defend yourself. "Aaaahhhh!"

Star ran towards Devon trying to gauge his eyes out with her nails. Bitch you must off lost your mind." He used her body weight and flip the shit out of her slamming her onto the ran down carpet floor. He pin her down. "I like this this shit. Im gonna fuck you up stupid bitch." Devon ripped her shirt off exposing her breast in a fitted bra. This just intensified his urges even more. How could a coward like him be aroused by such a hideous act? "Streets!" Star yelled as he violated Star. "Streets! Help me please!" Devon didn't bother to even cover her mouth. This was his spot that he used to do this to numerous of females. He thrust her fully penetrating her causing her to bleed out. That wasn't enough for his filthy satisfaction. He flipped her over and violated her from behind. The cries for help to Streets went unheard. Star finally gave up fighting back. She had been defeated. Fighting it wasn't her best bet. She rather get it over with. "This happens to rat ass bitches who think they are slick. Streets aint here to help you bitch he is dead remember." Devon was doing this to her because he thought it was the right thing to do because Star was going to testify. Star's cries turned into sobs. What felt like eternity lasted only three minutes of pure violating of this woman. Star laid there motionless not even attempting to move at all. How could something like this happen so quickly to someone looking for a place to stay with a friend? The world was a cold place. "Help yourself out you rat ass bitch!" Devon tossed a bag on the floor. It was a dope wax bag. "There goes your white widow." Star didn't move until she was sure that Devon was gone. Her clothes ripped off with her body fully exposed. She searched for her bag but it wasn't where she had left it.

"It was right here please don't tell me he took it?" Star was talking to herself panicking. "No, No! Please be here." Star forgot about her breasts being out, that she darted out the door in search for Devon. Her breasts were out in the open with no one insight that she knew. Her face was bloody and it was cold. "You mother Fucker!" Star yelled causing everyone to look at her half naked body. "He robbed me and raped me!" She yelled crying now. She did a once over again in the house. Her private areas were in so much pain. She had to go to the hospital immediately. "Is not here all she saw was a roach clip and a bag labeled. "The truth" she picked them up fixing herself and heading out the door with her jacket zipped up to her neck. She ran as fast as she could. She wished Streets was alive to help her.

It's always two sides to a coin when something happens regardless of what it is. It can be very beneficial to one, but it can be very detrimental to the other. In this case Star was receiving the detrimental side of Rocks beneficial side of the coin. Who was to blame? One should never be so open about anything. Regarding to one's personal life especially with someone you didn't know. It only takes seconds to lose your life if the next person is looking for a thrill in his own life. To find a balance is something only you can determine. Live, life and enjoy it how you wish but most importantly shut the fuck up, not everything is ment for everyone.

—

"You have five minutes Mr. Ricardo." The pink faced acne having CO interrupted the visit. "They kicking us out already?" Linda whined. "That's what it looks like." I love all three of you I'm here for you. I know I can't do much but if you come. I can listen and tell you what I think of whatever is transpiring out there." Rock said not wanting to end the visit. He was trying so hard to offer support from his side. Rock had gained a new vast amount of love towards Joel. After he put together all the bits and pieces of the broken up puzzle of what had actually happened the night Streets was put to rest. Rock was more than thankful for his true love towards his sister. Knowing that Joel was there to protect Linda. It allowed him not to fear too as much for her safety but definitely not removing all of his uncertainties. The thrilling ride was far from over. Star still had the upper hand in all of this.

" I'll be up here more often." I have a lot more things to tell you as far as your bitches and shit." Linda smiled. Mom shook her head in disapproval. "I can't wait to hear this one I can only imagine what you have to say? They should be coming up within the next few days or whatever. I don't schedule my days on visits. It's to stressful when no one shows. So if y'all decide to come up just come whenever you guys feel like coming I'm not going anywhere." Rock says standing up. He blew kisses to mom and Linda and gave a window pound. "Thank you and please look after them." Rock was exiting the visiting room. A part of him wanted to leave with them. It was impossible he hated the departing factor when it came to ending his visits. For some reason mom and Linda's visit hurt him the most.

"I hate it that he can't leave with us." Linda said limping her torn a frame out the jail with mom and Joel by her side. "What?" Girl if that guard wouldn't of calm him down that glass wouldn't have been enough to protect us from that boy." Mom said joking . "I know right, who am I kidding?" Linda knew better than that.

"Damn it feels weird leaving him back th ere." Linda said getting into the passenger seat of Joel's car. "I don't know about you two but I felt his temper through the glass I didn't even want to be there once you. "Joel stared at Linda. "Got him started." Joel finished. "You good baby he likes you now it's fucked up, how he came to like you but at least he does see you differently now." Linda said voicing her honest opinion. "Mom how come you were quite for the most part of the visit?" Linda asked. "Because that was a visit that had been in the waiting for almost a year. I come every so often. You are the one he wanted to see. I sat back up and just listened and made sure he didn't finish killing you." Mom joked. "So he wanted to kill me now mom?" Linda asked using the sun visor mirror to look back at mom to see her facial expression. They were heading home. "Who knows what would've happened?" Mom opinionated. "Babe stop at the rite aid so I can pick up my prescription please." Linda requested in her innocent voice. "I got your boss." Joel joked.

"I'm on my way." Jacqueline spoke to the receiver. Mandy was back on her shit bringing in that work. It's been a few weeks, Rock would be surprised to find out the work would be back on the block. "You know Rock's court date is in the next week or two right?" Mandy asked Jacqueline. "You know I need to get an outfit. Maybe this time he will acknowledge me." Jacqueline was still bitter from the last time she was ignored after preparing herself so early in the morning. She went as far as securing a sitter so she could see Rock for a minute or two. The amount of effort a woman puts into there looks. The hair, makeup, clothing and everything else they do just so they can be noticed for a fraction of a second or more by their man. This shit was was incredible. There was so much on Rock's mind. He was becoming a person that didn't acknowledge every person in sight. With his freedom dangling right over his head ready to be snatched away from his family permanently. Gazing at woman wasn't his main priority at the moment. Even though at times he did get caught up staring at women that work in the jail. That was normal, he knew he couldn't do much. The wrong assumption could be made in any woman's point of view, if they could actually know how a man thought. So a level of selfishness shouldn't be on the top of her list, knowing what this man was going through. It wasn't easy to find a balence with woman but it wasn't hard either.

"So I'm off until tomorrow you want to hit the mall up right quick?" Mandy asked. Not having anything to do at the moment. "Damn that would be nice but I have no sitter." Jacqueline never bothered to take her baby around people who didn't care for children. Her baby security always came first and foremost. "You have a car seat?" Mandy asked really pressing the issue. "Yeah I do but I don't want to be a bother you know?" Jacqueline admitted. "Come on Jacqueline hit me up when you're on your way it's no problem with me I want to buy something myself." Mandy tried to convince Jacqueline. It didn't take much because she had gotten dropped off at her place and phoned Mandy to come and scoop her up on many occasions. So coming to an agreement they both decided to head to the mall.

—

Rock had the bubble guts as the days came closer that came and went. "Everything is going to be alright." Leak noticed Rock's behavior. "You are going to get off, what you might have to bite is that conspiracy charge. So worst case scenario prepare yourself for that part, because if everything gets thrown out then that my friend will be the best feeling ever." Leak was a ruthless mother fucker and he had really come to like Rock. He may have influenced him on a couple of negative aspects in this place but it was all for his well being. "You know what Leak?" Rock had his serious look plastered on his face. Slash was on Big's old bed reading and listening to what was being said. It was hard not to. "Wassup." Leak replied I never in 1 million years would have thought that at the age of 19. I'd be sitting in the jail cell for no one. Ima be straight forward, this shit kills me every day I think about this shit. To be honest if I do have to spend my life in jail. It's not going to be a pretty picture but I know with time. I'll learn to accept this place for what it is. I have my health and I'm still laughing and crying. That is 1,000 times better than being buried 6 feet under and covered with dirt and green grass." Rock was preparing himself for the worst. This shit was renting a lot of space in his head. "I want you to do one thing for me, even if is the last thing I'll ever ask you to do." Leak got eye level with Rock. He didn't respond he did what he had always did. He listened but this time he had something to say too. "No matter what happens in the next couple of days whether good or bad don't you ever become complacent in this environment Rock? I know you don't mean what you say about this place but when any nigga becomes complacent in this place guess what?" Slash stopped reading because Leak was not joking he was dead ass. "He stops trying to get out, he stops putting in appeals, he gives up on himself, and he accepts what the man has given him which was a life sentence. Some find a man to become sexually involved with because he can't take it no more, he doesn't have control of his thinking anymore, he doesn't stand up for himself, he isn't a citizen anymore, he's a state number that will die behind the states walls for the rest of his life. Please Rock don't you ever say that you will accept this place because you my nigga still have a fighting chance to get your freedom back. Yes, I know you are hurt and scared. Most of us in this cell, let alone in his county jail are too. You know what? There are so many who will be satisfied coming back to jail on a regular basis. Then in time they will to become complacent in this place. Once that happens it is to late Rock." Leak spoke aggressively with his choice of words making Rock and Slash open their eyes a bit wider. Leak was loaded with wisdom. If he would stop with all his negative bullshit, he could very much help keep Rock sane up in this place. If wisdom was that easy to run across who knows? This world wouldn't be that corrupted as it is. Then again wisdom is just as useless as is the individual who chooses not to utilize. What's been said needs to be applied it to his or her daily living. Was sharing all these thoughts useless to a certain extent? Or did many individuals benefit from what they hear? It's very difficult to answer that question because some of us love the pain we endure when we fall on our faces. That alone can be a driving force to push you to keep falling many more times, that much harder than the previous time. Was Rock going to be one to enjoy the falling? He still had a major journey up ahead of him. That wasn't going to be a walk in the park so to speak.

"Now let me ask you this Slash?" Leak spun to look at Slash knowing he was listening very attentively. "Do you want to be complacent in his jail cell? Think about that very carefully before you answer because you and I have been coming back and forth in this place for some time now. For the record we are somewhat complacent." Leak opinionated while asking. "You're right about that Leak. I've been in and out of juvy homes and jails ever since I can think of.

I hate coming here but after I get release from here is like instead of looking forward and trying my best to stay out. I link back up with my boys and go just as hard as I was gone before I got snatched up the time before. I don't want to say I'm complacent but I'm saying that's what it feels like come to think of it. You get three hot meals, shower, TV, books and everything else you could ask for in here. Just to keep you happy. The only thing that's missing is for a bad ass nurse to come up and suck you off." Slash joked about the situation. Leak shook his head. "You are complacent, you see this Rock? This is how you want to end up?" Leak asked. "I'm not shitting on you Slash, but I'm using you as a prime example." Leak went on. "It's cool, it was the truth." Slash has been complacent in jail. He just now figured it out. Who knows maybe this conversation could help him steer away from coming back in the future. Whenever he finally decided to let the bullshit go." "So what about you Leak?" Rock asked not coming off as a smartass. "Me?" Leak smiled accepting the question by not getting offensive. "If I don't get my shit straight, Ima end up in this place for very long time. Shit, I'm looking at a possible 5 to 10 years if the witnesses shows up too." Leak was dancing around the bush. "I don't mean to stereotype you but if I had to take a guess. I see you enjoy all this bullshit that goes on around us. I mean don't get me wrong. I'm not saying you come back intentionally but the way you move and carry yourself in here. It's as though you don't care too much about anything." Rock may have jumped to conclusion but with his last comment. Leak thought of Rocks words. "I agree with what you're saying to a certain extent Rock. All I know is how to go! I'm not one of them niggas who sit back and talk about what they going to do when the time comes. They either switch up the plan or procrastinate putting together a bunch of excuses. Many talk about how and why they gonna do it this way instead of that way. I have a low tolerance for bullies. I can't stand liars, fake bitch ass niggas and those tough dudes who can't stand on their own 2 feet." Leak spoke calmly expressing his inner most feelings when it came to things that triggered him to explode. "If you do something to me. I don't care how small it is I'm going to get you back just as fast as I find out it was you. I'm not sure why I am the way I am. It's probably because of all the shit I put myself through. I have learned what I don't accept to be done to me, and how to take someone's bullshit." Leak had a low tolerance for certain things. Like when he wanted to get them boys that got out on Bigs immediately. It went a totally different way that no one expected. "So to be honest I can't say that I'm complacent because I done so much shit in the streets you would never imagine doing.

I'm not saying that I'm good at what I do, but the things that I did weren't for fun it was done because mother fuckers cross that thin line. Every now and then you have your moments when you slip up and react without thinking rationally. This will land your ass right back in jail." Leak defended his case. "So you're saying that as long as you protecting your own beliefs whether you land in here one or two times it's not considered being complacent? Because it was something that you had to do at that given moment?" Slash wasn't even into his book anymore. "No I don't think that's what he meant. I'll say that it doesn't matter what happens to you, it's how you go about taking care of your business. Whether you're going to stick up and stand up for you and your love ones or not. You have to be already mentally prepared to accept all possible consequences when the rain begins the poor." Rock gave his opinion on what Leak said. Neither of the two could understand how Leak thought. That's what is so unique about one's mind, it's yours for you to use it how you see a fit. "My reasons are my reasons and I can't expect either of you to understand why I see things the way I do. The two of you have a good idea on how to see shit for yourselves. What I can do is begin to correct a lot of things that need to be corrected in my own mind. If not this will be my new home as well." Leak admitted. Rock listened attentively.

"Chow time! Chow time! The CO yelled over the PA system. Greg was approaching at full speed. He wasn't a threat or at least that's the vibe the guys got from him. Slash went to find his people as he always did. "Ayo I need two of them." Greg said. "I got you at the table." Rock spoke loud enough for Leak to hear. "What your man say about the payment?" Leak asked referring to the payout that was paid a few days ago. "Man that mother fucker was happy as hell. All them soups. He said your tickets are the truth. The other ticket holders be slacken and pay up bull shit. Why you think they all come to you? You pay on the spot and they're always up to date." Greg was the man when it came to running around the blocks. Rock didn't care how he did it, all he cared was that he did it when he needed to be done. "You said two right?" Rock repeated at the table sitting with Leak. "Yup" Rock peeled off six and passed them all to Leak. He passed them to Greg. I put an extra one in their free play for you on us." Rock said. The way Rock always handled his shit was a lot different from every other person. Leak had done so much business with alot of other people, he too informed Rock that he appreciated him. He always included everyone in the circle when it came to handling business with us. He could have been selfish and no one could say shit but that wasn't him. Rock knew the value of having some true soldiers by your side when it was time to get things done. Why leave them out when things got bad? It wouldn't be smart to do that and Rock noticed it being the breadwinner. They needed some work and being that little Miss. Mandy was Rock's. He had no excuses for her but little did they know little Miss Mandy was on point. At some point in your life you have to trust someone. I don't care who it is. If you really have issues trusting someone that could just mean one thing, you can't be trusted yourself by anyone. Beg to differ? "You see that's what the fuck I'm talking about bro." Greg was far from a thorough bread from the bricks, but then again who was able to give someone that title. "I'm a have these filled out ASAP for tomorrow's game. Who you like?" Greg asked. He would always speak so fast and always be in a hurry to get nowhere.

Greg was in here for conning people out there dead relative's homes. When he first told Rock about this. Rock had no clue how he did such a crime. He was clever and he would swindle you into buying a home that belong to a dead body, without you ever knowing until it until it was too late. The person buying the home wouldn't get in trouble because they didn't know what was going on. Greg was so good at what he did that he managed to sell a house, that the police calculated to be worth over 456 grand. All the cash he made was gone. He was splurging on everything he could think of. Then again that's the whole point of making all that money right? To enjoy it because you damn you sure can't take it with you. If you did someone would probably dig you back up just to rob your ass for it. "That's cool just try to have them back to me in the morning. I'm not taking any tickets in the afternoon. First game was at 1 PM and I don't want to be writing picks down with the game on. "Let's go fellas." The CO was rushing us off the table. "Can we at least finish?" He shot back. The CO ignored Leak smartass remark. "Come on you know we all dirty, why even a draw?" Rock asked finishing up their meal. "Fuck them bitches, they expect us to swallow all our food without chewing it. It's bad enough it taste like shit already." He shot back in one of his fuck it moods that Rock already knew all too well.

"Oh yeah I almost forgot to tell you. You're boy might get shipped out to another jail." Greg dropped the information that Rock's been waiting to hear. "How you know?" Leak asked. Greg looked at Leak as they all rose up from the table. "Come on man it's my Intel ever not on point?" Greg asked. "I never said that but I still want to know how you know?" He asked again. "When I was handing out the new commissary forms two days after that shit occurred. I walked in on the serge and the one faggot looking CO, talking about how the nigga that Bigs hit with the lock was still in the ICU. He lost a lot of blood. They wanted to charge him up but they going to wait and see what was going to happen to old boy. That's when he said that the warden wants his ass out of here. It's either move him or move Bigs." Greg informed the two of us as we walked back to our cells. "Oh and guess what else?" Greg had all the latest gossip. "No time for guessing games. Wassup?" Rock replied trying to get all the information he could from the insider. Greg was the jails KYW news man for real. "Miss Peg got fired." Greg said not holding back. "She got what?" Leak asked. He could not believing what he just heard. "Damn you girl bro." Rock joked. She didn't get caught red handed. Her coworker dropped a dime on her saying that she was sucking dick. When she was supposedly doing checkups on a few guys in here." Greg whispered the latest news. "Get the fu...." Leak was tight. He always knew that Miss Peg has some sneakiness to her character. He hesitated too long in moving in on his prey. Miss. Peg had a body just like all the other woman that worked in the prison. She wanted to taste some real dick. "I wonder who told on her." Rock wondered. He wondered if Mandy was to blame. The only reason Mandy came to his mind. Was because eliminating players on her end, could give her the higher position. It would let her do things that she couldn't do being under the microscope all the time. Rock shook off the thought of Mandy being a rat just to satisfy her own needs. "Damn Bigs is out of here?" Leak repeated to Slash. "He's gone?" Slash was caught off guard. "We don't know for sure but it's a strong possibility." Leak informed Slash of the news. "Greg?" Slash signaled him out. "You already know." Rock said. "Well look we all have court dates coming up soon we can either get someone in here to take his spot. Or we can take our chances with the next nigga who comes out for quarantine." Slash was thinking ahead which was exactly what neither Rock nor Leak were doing right now. "I'm surprised we didn't get anyone when we packed up his shit the first time." Leak said. Already knowing that their days with just the three of them were dwindling down. "Who the fuck we going to move up in here? I don't feel like dealing with no nut." Rock said lifting his left eyebrow as he opinionated. "I don't either." Leak agreed. "Anyone in mind that can be trusted?" Rock asked. "My man wants.." Leak put up his finger up cutting off Slash request. "None of your boys and your crew sorry." Leak said being dead serious. "Why not?" Slash was offended. Because we all got to know each other from the first time. No one here knew each other from the bricks or did jobs or completed missions with each other anywhere. I think it'll be better if we all agree on someone we didn't know. Someone we can put on and not have to worry who he running with." Leak didn't go into details but he did have a strong point. "What about Greg?" Rock suggested. "Hell no that boy two steps away from being an informant." Slash said. Leak broke out laughing. "You too much Slash, why you say that about that man?" Leak was in tears, Rock also laughed at the remark but he did understand why the accusations. "That's facts or are you just assuming?" Rock asked wanting to know Greg status. "It's not facts but just see how that mother fucker be all up in the police face, he got to be doing something." Just as Rock figured it was all an assumption with no type of paperwork. "Yes, he may be up in their guards face talking about who knows what but as far as chirping. I haven't heard no shit like that from anyone else up in here." This is the first time now coming out your mouth." The room got quiet this wasn't something to play with talking about another man in that manner. This is how niggas got killed." Leak wasn't into all that rumor shit. He would rather you say that you don't like a man for your own personal reasons. Instead of saying that he was a potential rat. That wasn't enough to convince me that he was. "From what I see he plays his part and he gets his few dollars helping us run our shit don't he?" Leak was asking. "I never said that he don't move or handle his business." Slash tried to correct his accusations. "You didn't, but your words weren't carefully picked you was talking from emotions just now." Leak was checking Slash. Rock just listen and observed how things could get so tense in just a matter of seconds. Rock looked back and forth as the two exchange words. They weren't on a arguing level but more like tryna get the other to understand the other . Words could go a long way if you placed them in the right ears. Once you let them out there was no telling how far they would go, by the time they reaches the other side of the room the words will have changed up dramatically. It'll be almost impossible to believe what you're hearing, once its made it's way around. "Alright I don't like that fuck." Slash said annoyed at the fact on how stupid he made himself look. "Now were getting somewhere." Rock said. "Anyone else?" Rock asked. He accepted Slash wasn't feeling Greg's ghost at the moment. It's hard to accept anyone if you don't give them a chance to show you what they are about. "How about papi boy from upstairs?" Leak asked. Not being too specific. "Which one? There are so many up in this bitch." Slash asked joking. "What's his name? He got the waves on his head." Leak descried him vaguely. "That's not helping." Rock joked you know we all got good hair." Rock joked back. "Get the fuck out here." Slash shot back. "Think his name is John or Johnny not to sure." Leak said. "Oh you talking about quiet boy who always doing dips and pull ups?" Slash asked. "That's him." Leak said. "Who?" Rock was still lost. "He just said it young boy who is always doing pull-ups and dips." Leak repeated. Rock had this perplexed look on his face. "Damn nigga you gota tighten the fuck up as much as we be down there get in it.and you can't remember who he talking about." Leak didn't like that at all. How the fuck, was Rock so careless. These are guys who were around him almost every other day and he couldn't recall who this nigga was. "I can't remember everybody's face." Rock tried to justify his reckless actions. "I understand that but damn Rock you better try. "Oh okay he's the boy who copped three bags the one day? He sent you a money order with an extra $10 just on the lookout to right?" Leak let Rock think some. "Okay, okay I know exactly who you talking about but he be on the dip bar heavy." Rock said. "No shit we just said that like 1000 times?" Slash joked. Rock laugh. "We'll holler at him tomorrow and see what he wanted to. So that's our candidate agreed?" Rock asked. "No doubt" Leak said in agreement. "I'm cool with it." Slash replied...

The weather calling for a white Christmas which was something many have wished for, despite not having Rock home. He would still be able to see his from the window if it did in fact snow. Linda was moving a lot more on her own which a great sign. The detectives didn't bother them in the past few days. Mom did say that they wouldn't. We all know that everything good came to a halt sooner or later.

"Linda are you almost ready?" Mom asked. "Almost." Linda replied taking her time to prepare herself. Her face was almost 100% which made her force herself back into doing things that she lost motivation in doing. By all the time she was taken to get ready only prove that she was going back to normal. Mom and Linda were on their way to go shopping. They were going to buy a few items that they forgot to buy.

Joel spent the night three days before helping set up all the decorations and the tree. It all looked so beautiful. That was always Rock's job. The decorations look so pretty and would attract many eyes that would come in contact with them from the outside. The tree wore a big red star on the top of it. Linda put it up there. It took several attempts with her unbalanced handicap ass. Joel had to put her on his shoulders and hold her up high enough so she could put the star on the tree.

"Do you want me to bring the camera?" Linda yelled. "You mind as well Linda. We have to send the pictures to your brother." Mom answered. Rock's court date was in two days. He called yesterday. He sounded anxious and worried. Mom calm him down as much as she could. There was so much going on that things could not get any more complicated in Rock's household.

"Where is my lip gloss?" Linda yelled over to mom. "Your lip gloss? Girl it's freezing outside you don't need that stuff." Mom poked her head in Linda's room. The site of her limping around for her lip gloss caused mom to laugh. "If you don't give it up already." Mom joked. "Help me find it." Linda whined and winced in pain. Mom help her out. "I don't understand why you can't leave the house without that mess." Mom said looking under the bed. She got low and came up with it. "Here." mom handed Linda her cherry lip gloss. Linda's smile spread across the room. That's how happy she got. "The phone rang. "That's Joel" Linda hoped over to the phone, by the time she made her way over to the phone it rang three more times. "I would've passed it to you Limpy." Mom joked.

"Hello?" Linda put on her sweet loving voice for her man. Her eyebrows almost touched the ceiling. She wasn't as happy as she was supposed to be at the sound of Joel's voice. Mom faced follow Linda's visage. "Who is it?" Mom whispered Linda shrugged her shoulders. "I'm sorry can I ask you who you calling for?" Linda spoke into the receiver. "I think you have the wrong number." Linda said. Whoever it was must of had mistakenly dialed the wrong number because Linda wasn't trying to hear anything that was being said to her on the other end. "Yes, Rock is my brother." Linda informed. "And you say your name is Samantha?" Linda repeated. "My brothers in jail. I don't know if any of this that you're saying has any truth to it. You could be making this shit up." Linda challenged. "Give me the phone." Mom had her hand out waiting for Linda to pass her phone. Linda tighten her grip on the phone with her free hand. She held up a pointer finger making mom wait. Mom put her left hand on her hip. How could that even be possible if Manny has been locked up going on a year now?" Linda asked trying to put together the pieces. "He is in the Camden County jail." Linda informed the caller. "What the hell was that woman saying to Linda? Mom though getting annoyed. Just when you think things are done getting complex. Something always pops up from out of nowhere. "You want his address so you can write him?" Linda repeated it was Samantha. I'll have to get in contact with Manny first before I do any of that. To make sure everything is approved by him." Linda said. If you want you can call around New Year's and I'll have an answer for you." Linda said not given up any information on her brother's whereabouts. For all she knew, this chick could be a fling that was looking for some attention. Trying to wrap her brother up in more shit. Linda was astonished by what she was hearing on the other end of the receiver. "This shit is crazy." Linda said hanging up the phone. Mom was shaking her right leg wanting to know what the hell was going on. "You ready?" Linda asked. "I've been ready but we not going anywhere to you tell me who the hell was that on the phone. Why did they want Manuel's address for?" Mom blocked the doorway. "It's nothing." Linda said. "Bullshit!" Mom let out. Linda was caught off-guard by that one. Linda exhaled. "Well if all this information is true the way that girl was putting it." Linda paused for second. "You young lady are going to be a grandmother." Linda said ending it at that. Mom's eyes popped open bigger than the usual. Her hand cover her mouth as if she wanted to cry, scream and shout. "Manuel is a father?" Mom asked breathless. She gasped for air deeply and spun around headed to her room. Linda was behind her. "Are you okay?" Linda asked. Mom was going through one of her small episodes. They weren't as bad as they use to be since she has almost gave up smoking completely. "The air pumped in her lungs and mom took a deep breaths to fill her lungs. The phone rang again. Linda limped over to mom's nightstand. "I got it you relax." Linda said. "Hello?" Linda answered.

"Okay baby I'll be out give us a minute okay." Linda said. "Love you too." Linda hung up. "Joel is out front." Linda informed mom. "Okay." mom said still filling up her lungs with fresh oxygen. "Oh my God Ima to be a grandma." Mom said still breathing through the mask. "We don't know that yet mom that girl could be lying through her teeth." Linda wasn't convinced. Nope not today, nor tomorrow. She had to hear it from Manny's mouth herself. There was no sense in believing a woman, who neither mom nor Linda have ever heard of. Let alone didn't call earlier to inform us of such a thing that was occurring. "Samantha?" "She sound like a white girl." Linda said with a disgusted look on her face. "My grandbaby has colored eyes." Mom said. Mom didn't care if the news was true or not just by the fact that this woman has called. It was a clear indication that there had to be some type of convincing evidence that this new baby had to bear some resemblance to her son. For a woman to make a call like that. It did take alot of guts. "How old is the baby?" Mom asked excitedly. "He's only two months old." Mom smiled. "That only prove that the woman wasn't sure who the father was. She had to wait until the new born's face was a bit clearer to pin the baby on. Crazy how some woman just didn't give a shit. "It's Manuel's baby I know it is." Mom said. "You don't know that mom." Linda didn't want mom to get her hopes up too high. That would only hurt her if the baby turned out to be someone else's baby and not Rock's baby at all. "Come on mom I can't wait to tell Joel about this one." Linda said. "You want to bring that with." Linda as referring to the oxygen tank. "No baby I should be fine, bring my inhaler." Mom assured Linda's worries. "Grab my purse it's by the alarm clock baby." Mom told Linda. It was almost below zero outside with only a few cars on the road. Joel had taken longer than expected to arrive at mom's house due to the nasty weather. The snow wasn't fallen at all but it was very much still visible from the days before when it fell all night and day long. Mom paid the local fiens to hook up her sidewalk. He took care of all of the houses that would allow him to shovel out the snow. He would only charge a few dollars. Mom always give him $10. He would always make sure our house sidewalks and steps were clean and clear from the snow and any other debris.

Finally getting into Joel's car, a horn blaring from up the block took everybody by surprise and it didn't stop until Linda look back. "What the fuck?" Joel said. "That's Felicia." Linda said not moving from her position. Instead mom popped back out to see what she wanted. Felicia felt abandoned by the family. It wasn't done on purpose but mom told Linda that she refused to answer her calls not because mom didn't like her, because mom didn't want Felicia to lose a great portion of her life waiting for a man behind bars. Felicia was young and pretty. She did what she had to do with a beautiful daughter. To see her struggle, to keep a roof over head, clothes, and food on their backs all alone it was a task all its self. To also take on the responsibility of incarcerated man was daring moved. Let alone draining with all the letters and visits plus the expense or commissary and all the calls.

What mom was doing may have seemed cold hearted but it was something that had to be done. She was protectiong Falicia. If it worked in mom's favor Felicia was a free bird, let out its cage to soar in the big blue sky. If it didn't work then guess what? Felicia would stick around for the long haul.

"He has what?" Felicia burst out as mom stood in the middle of the road. Felicia was double parked in the middle of the street. "A baby by another woman?" Mom was hurt by what she was doing. When it came to mom, she wanted to protect everyone's interest at heart. "By who?" Felicia question very angrily. "I can't answer that Felicia. Manuel doesn't know so let's keep this between us for now. He's already going through too much." Mom said. Felicia face was sick. "Can I come by later so we can talk about this?" Felicia said. "Well how about you call tomorrow and you can come over because we are busy all day today." Mom said. "Tell Linda to call me." Felicia said. "I will let her know. You drive home safely baby okay?" Mom walked away heading back to Joel's car that was idling. "What did she want?" Linda asked. "What else? Your brother." Mom joked. The hot air coming through the vents warmed mom right up. "It's so cold out there." Mom said. "Yeah it is. Where to first?" Joel asked. "Well let's develop these photos or at least drop them off before we go anywhere. The right aid is right down the street." Linda instructed. Joel didn't ask any questions. He put the car and drive and spun his wheels until the tires found traction. "That girl is obsessed with Manny." Linda said. "You know your brother does something to all of these girls that drives them wild." Mom said. I wonder what that is." Linda looked over to Joel smiling. Joel smiled and kept his eyes on the slippery roads. Mom smile from the backseat. She knew the game all to well.

—

After running all the errands going from store to store everyone was famished. "How about we go to the Pete's shop and grab a bite to eat so that I can see my baby too." Mom said. Joel jumped on route 30 and headed toward the city. "Baby guess what?" Linda said. "Wassup babe?" Joel replied. "I'm going to be an aunt." Linda look back at mom. "But you was telling me not to get my hopes up, look at you now." Mom says smiling from ear to ear. "An aunt?" Joel asked. "How is that going to happen?" Joel asked not knowing anything about the baby. "Last time I checked you only have one brother that we know of and he is in jail. I can't see how that is going to happen." Joel said. "It's a story that none of us know yet, but the possibility is there." Linda said. "I'm going to see Manny right after his court date and tell him the good news. I wonder what he is going to say." "What if he denies ever seeing this woman?" Linda asked. "I can't see your brother denying a baby if he had sexual relations with this woman. He'll remember what he did and how he did it." Mom hope. "Baby Park outback." Linda instructed. Joel spun around until he reached the alleyway. "I don't know who this woman is but this must have been a long time ago because Rock's been in jail for almost a year now." Joel was doing his own calculations. "We will see what happens when the test results are brought up." Mom said.

"Look what the cold dragged in." Jamal joked. "Hey!" mom searched for Pete. "He's in the back." Jamal said. Linda sat right in front of Joel and grabbed the menu. "You hungry baby girl?" Jamal asked. "Am I?" Linda replied. "As soon as I'm done I'll hook you up with something." Jamal said "We appreciate that Jamal." Linda said with a smile on her face. The shop was beginning to gather up dust and stains again. The lack of Rock's presence was definitely being noticed. Rock make sure this place was kept tight and clean on a daily basis. "I don't owe you anymore money. I gave you what I'm mandated to pay!" Pete was bitching over the phone. Mom stepped in slowly looking gorgeous as always. She was all bundled up and Pete was pissed. He had to kick out thousands a month to his ex-wife. He didn't mind the money he was court ordered to pay as alimony, but when his ex would ask for more like the money she was getting for free wasn't enough. That's what got him going. Mom stood at the doorway waiting for Pete to turn his chair around. "I don't care woman my kids have what they need. Using them as an excuse isn't going to work. When they need anything I'll get it to them and put it personally in their hands. You just a fucking leach. This is why we were never happy! I hope you see the shit." Pete yelled. Mom was shocked at the words he was using. He finally spun around. "His eyes showed embarrassment. "I have to go my beautiful and lovely babygirl just walked in." Click." Pete hung up just like that on his ex.

"I'm sorry you had to hear the baby. Pete got up walking towards mom. Mom met him halfway with open arms and a big wet kiss. "What brings you over here?" Pete asked. I miss you and I'm with Linda and her boyfriend." Mom said. "How are they holding up?" Pete asked. "They are doing better than I expected." Mom admitted. "Oh yeah that's very good isn't it?" Pete asked. "Yes it is and how are you doing my big teddy bear?" Mom joked trying to wrap her arms around Pete's body, not a chance he was too big. "I'm okay glad to see your beautiful face." Pete complimented. "What did you do today?" Pete asked. "Joel took Linda and me out to buy some clothes. He spoiled her I thought that was cute. That boy is in love with that girl." Mom said. "I bet he is. I'm a love with the mother." "That makes two of us." Pete made mom blush. They got hungry so I decided to buy them a meal and where else to spend my money than at my man shop." Mom said. Pete laughed. "Come on baby you know, you don't have to pay for anything in here." Pete informed. "Oh yes I do I'm known different. Business is business I'll be damn if I'll become a Leach." Mom pushed it joking. "That's her you a nothing compared to her. Don't you put yourself in that category please." Pete may himself sound dumb with that comment. "That's why I'm paying. I don't want or need anything for free baby. We will pay for our meal. All I want is you and your love." Mom said patting Pete's zipper. Pete laughed. You have all of that already. "You sure?" Mom asked. "Absolutely, I want to see the lovebirds." Pete was referring to Linda and Joel.

The shop was always a fun spot to hang out, if you had a bond with the people who work there. Mom and Linda eventually told the guys about the good news and the possibility of a baby coming around. First, they thought it was Linda who was having a baby. Joel's face gave it away though. It was not there baby that was coming. Once the name were announced Jamal couldn't believe what he had heard. He didn't say anything but knew exactly who Samantha was. This could most definitely be true. He thought. She was the sexier of the two, not bad for a sexy ass white baby mama to be a man's first. Jamal kept his silence the way he should have. You had to let them details be ironed out by the key factors. No need for him to recap how that all went down. The news would get out when it was supposed to be and when the time was right he would do his part and help connect a few dots.

CHAPTER 23
"Verdict"

The courtroom was jam packed. Every pew was loaded with all types of people from, friends family, and lovers. Someone was about to sign their freedom away once the jury did what they have come here to do, or possibly gain it as well. It all depended on how the coin fell for them. Today, was the day that Rock has been anticipating for a while now. The judge was in his chamber doing who knows what. It's been rumored that the judge presiding Rock's case usually loaded his nostrils up with that old white girl. Too bad he didn't bring any with him. Imagine that one. Now and days that shit was more than believable if you'd asked me. It fucking crazy, the same mother fuckers that put you away for selling the shit, got high off the same shit you was selling. Someone please explain that fuck shit to me please. Sorry got a little side tracked.

Mom was sitting in the front with Pete. Her fingers were interlocked tightly with his, her palms were perspiring as their anxiety was taken over. Linda was sitting right by mom holding her other hand with Joel right beside her. Linda chose to wear the shirt that Rock had gotten her the day of he got incarcerated. She loved this shit. It was the last thing that had alot of sentimental value. Mom fought with her all morning. She was bickering that she wouldn't look presentable with that shirt on for today. Linda didn't want to hear that shit. "Mom, he's never going to see me in it if I don't ever wear it. That's why I got it so I could wear it one day with him." Linda wasn't taken it off. There was no one who could make her take it off now. Mom got the message loud and clear.

"You know what where what you want you are grown." Mom said to Linda. Mom on the other hand was dressed to impress. She wore her new knee high skirt with a burgundy blouse. She looked as if she was going to a faculty meeting. Pete also was fresh with his Steve Maddens shoes on. His button up was crisp with a matching striped tie. His placed his jacket on his knee. Joel dress casual. Felicia hadn't shown up yet, neither has Jacqueline. Last Linda heard they were both coming up to the hearing. If they did great if they didn't, go figure.

The Cherry wood bench stood tall and polished from all dust. The big United States military flag stood tall to the right behind the judge's chair. To his left the New Jersey state flag stood tall as well. "Mom, what is taking so long?" Linda whispered. "Whenever they ready that's when they will start be patient." Mom said. The jurors weren't even seated yet. If you knew anything about the courts then you knew that they love to take their sweet old time doing everything. Nothing was ever rushed. Oh wait I lied. Let your ass do something you not supposed to do and watch how fast they rush your ass to jail.

—

Meanwhile at the entrance of the City Hall. Felicia was passing her pocket book through the conveyor belt so it could be x-rayed. As she walked her fine ass through the metal detector it went off again. "Beep, beep, beep!" Empty everything in your pockets ma'am. The Hispanic looking security guard said. He sounded as if he was a recorded message. He continuously said this over and over again. Felicia stuffed her hands into a small jacket pocket and pulled out a pack of gum. "This can't be it?" She walked through with no other incident.

"Ma'am empty everything in your pockets and place your bag on the conveyor belt please." The security guard said to the small tan complexion woman behind Felicia. Out of curiosity Felicia looked back just to see who the guard was talking to. Thinking nothing of it she picked up her bag and walked over towards the elevator. Her heels hit the floor hard all the way towards elevator. Everyone was dressed up which only ment this was a place of highly well educated people handling straight business.

Waiting for the elevator to come down felt like eternity. The sound of the heels getting closer caused Felicia to be nosy again. She looked at the same woman who was behind her from head to toe. The woman notice so she stopped so Felicia could get a better look.

"I'm sorry, didn't mean to stare but I love those shoes." Felicia tried to make herself seem less disrespectful. "Oh thank, you I just bought them,.They are a little tight but I like them too." The dimples in her face emphasized her smile so much. "Bing!" The elevator doors opened on the main floor. Felicia was about 3 inches taller than the other woman but they both had some serious sex appeals on them. Inhaling deeply and exhaling just as strong. "Bad day?" The small woman asked looking at Felicia. "I hope not." Felicia replied in a sad tone. "After you." Felicia allowed everyone else who was waiting to get on the elevator to get on first. She did this so she be the first one out. She was thinking ahead. "Thank you." Everyone said almost in unison. Somehow Felicia ended up side by side with the small dimpled lady again.

"You know where courtroom 4B is?" The small woman asked. Felicia stared a bit. "4B? Yea it's on the fourth floor I'm assuming." Felicia wanted to ask this small bitch if she was going to see her man but she just kept her composure and didn't overreact. She could be here for anyone.

"So you have a court too?" Felicia was probing. "Yes I'm so afraid I don't know what I am going to do if they don't drop those charges." Everyone in elevator was tuned in to the conversation. Elevator stopped at the second floor. The door slid open.

"Whoa... I will catch the next one." The one male in an expensive executive suit said. Elevator was too packed for him. The elevator door slid back shut. "Who is it your brother or your sister?" Felicia was looking for some relief. Her heart was spedding up. "No this is not my brother or sister he someone very special to me. I wish I could trade places with him. He is such a nice person. He don't belong in jail." Every single word that little mama was speaking only confirm one thing. Felicia couldn't hold it anymore. She went off not wanting to hear anything else form the other woman. "Listen I don't know who you are, but if you are talking about Rock. I advise you to not show your face in that courtroom." Felicia came out of nowhere with that one. The chances of her being mistaking and jumping the conclusion were very high. She didn't hold back not one bit. "Excuse me?" Jacqueline spat. "You heard what I said." The elevator stopped on the 3rd floor and a lot of people got out. Probably not everyone had to get off on the 3rd floor but by the heat brewing inside in that elevator. Everyone was better off getting out of both those 2 crazy bitches way. "Rock and I have been seeing each other for a while and he's my man." "SLAP!" Jacqueline was already going through it with all her own personal problems. She sparked the confrontation off the right way. Fuck all that back and forth shit. Felicia just put the icing on the cake. "Bitch!" Jacqueline went to swing again but the Good Samaritan grabbed her hand. "Not the time or place miss." The man in his expensive suit said. "Fuck that bitch!" Felicia slapped the hell out of Jacqueline back. That's when all hell broke loose. Their hands and feet were being thrown all over in the elevator. The people who had nothing to do with any of this got caught up in the assault. "He's my man!" Felicia yelled trying to get to Jacqueline. "Fuck you bitch, he'll tell you he's all mine." They were both being pinned up against the wall. "Either the two of you calm the fuck down or I'll take you straight to the cops on the 10th floor." The man with the salt and pepper hair threatened. The girls did exactly what he asked of them. They calmed the fuck down immediately not wanting to miss the hearing.

"Bing!" Now from what I heard this is your stop. Go and support whoever yall going to see and figure it out." The two of them got off. "Those are two crazy bitches." The one male mumbled under his breath. "Bitch mind your business." Jacqueline said out loud enough for lady across the hall to hear. Felicia disappeared into the courtroom. She fixed her hair before she walked in. Jacqueline stood thinking about what just occurred.

"Ima fucked that bitch up, she better back off my man." Jacqueline said to herself. The lawyer speaking to his client in the far corner looked up. He heard what Jacqueline didn't want anyone to hear. Pulling out her small pocket sized mirror. She touced up her face to perfection. It was almost impossible she was a work of beauty. She inhaled deeply for a second staring at the swinging doors. Jacqueline prepared herself. She walked in with her head up high and her walk on straight sexy. She noticed Felicia up front so she sat on the opposite side of the room. "Humph." Jacqueline had the room's attention. Linda look back and turned her face away immediatly. She got whiplash, that's how fast she tried not to be noticed. Jacqueline didn't notice Linda yet. She had other things on her mind.

Woman were known to be thrown off a bit or maybe even a lot. Like many of us. If no one would've been in that elevator in that moment. You and I could only imagine how bad these two psychopaths would've been going at it. It would of been almost impossible to seperate them. The mayhem that would've been accumulated in that small confined area would of been catastrophic.

Felicia looked over and guess who had their stare locked on hers? Yup, Jacqueline. She was most definitely small but this girl has some scruff and we already know Felicia was a little nutty up top as well. Felicia mugged Jacqueline then broke her gaze from hers. Felicia was sitting next to Linda. Linda didn't want to look over at Jacqueline. This had to be the most awkward moment in history. Linda felt super uncomfortable "Felicia are you okay?" Mom leaned over and asked wondering what the hell was going on with this woman. She came in breathing heavy, breaking everyone concentration and prayers from those who did believed. "I just got into it with that girl over in the corner to my right, she says that her and your brother were fucking." Felicia through gas on the already lit flames that have been already sparked in the elevator with Jacqueline's first blow. Linda didn't know what to say or do at the moment. So she just shook her head not wanted to hear or believe what had just went down between these two obsessed bitches. "Is your brother fucking her?" Felicia asked. Linda darted a cold stare Felicia. "He's in jail and if he was I don't know who he fucking, that's his dick." Linda had to lie again and had an attitude. She whispered into Felicia's ear. "Well I know this, Ima whip that bitch's ass once all this is over." Felicia said. She was not joking one bit. Linda couldn't help either one of them because she too was about to be exposed. This day was destined to come. This shit was going to happen. How would all this transpire? Who would say what? Jacqueline and Linda are so called lovers. Linda is Rock's sister and the murderer of Kay and Streets. This whole ordeal was taken a turn for the worse. There was no turning back. "I have to use the bathroom." Felicia went to get up. "Can't you wait until this is over?" Linda grabbed Felicia's arm pinning her down. "Yes but I..." Felicia didn't finish her words.The 12 jurors filled the seats on the right side of the room.

"All arise." The bailiff with the pot belly yellowed. Everyone rose to their feet. The bald wrinkled face judge entered the room with his small golden frames down to the tip of his nose. "We now pronounce the Honorable Judge Kenneth D. Rose." The same bailiff yellowed. The judge did a quick once over scanning the loaded pews. One can only imagine how many people this man put away in his life time. It wasn't over yet. He was old but stable enough to bang that hated gavel still.

“Take your seats.” The judge spoke as if he was sick and tired of the bull shit. He must not hate it too much if he still on the scene. In my opinion once you hit a certain age you should be disqualified to be a so called honorable judge. As they loved to call these regular drug using men and woman. I will apolgize for the ones who took there oath seriously. Where ever you may be. Why allow a grumpy old grandpa or grandma to be the main factor in overlooking someone’s future? Because Judge Kenny looked pretty grumpy and my guess was you would too if it took a whole bottle Viagra to get your mojo going. Ha!

The DA was positioned on the right and no one was sitting at the opposite side. Where the fuck was Stoski? Rock was getting impatient. “Mom how come Manny’s lawyer isn’t here yet?” Linda asked the million dollar question. “He’ll be here Linda relax.” Mom tried to ease Linda’s doubts. “Are you ready to commence?” The judge asked rudely. “Yes we are.” The district attorney answered.

Stoski came barging into the entrance door. “Glad you can make it Mr. Stoski.” The judge said sarcastic like a mother fucker. The pleasures mine, I wouldn’t miss it for the world.” Stoski was cocky as always. He caught mom’s eyes and winked at her. Pete noticed and so did Linda. Linda bumped mom’s elbow with hers. Hoping mom got that one. This was mom’s friend? Linda thought to herself. Linda stared at Stoski. This man had him some swag on him. “My client?” Stoski asked the bailiff. “Coming right out.” The baliff informed.

—

Rock’s wrists had the indentations from the grooves of the cuffs.The leather strap around his waistline hugged him tightly. He wasn’t alone he was accompanied by a few other prisoners. A woman who was also down for a body also occupied the small room with him. She had murdered her father.He was touching her for so many years, it was a fucked up world. It wasn’t slowing down either. She had enough of it all and she finally exploded.

“Ayo why you put these cuffs on so tight?” Rock barked not even wanting to hear that they weren’t. “So you won’t escape.” The smart mouth Sheriff replied. “Escape from where and how the fuck am I going to do that? You got chains on my nuts for crying out loud." Everyone laughed but Rock wasn't laughing. "I can't feel my fingers, can you loosen them up a bit." Rock wasn't lying his hands were changing color. They were getting darker. "You'll be fine we not going far." The sheriff disregarded Rock's request. "That's why mother fuckers like you end up in the dumpster slumped over you piece of shit." The youngin next to Rock spat at the sheriff. He too was on trial for a homicide. He managed to kill his best friend because he stole an ounce of crack from him while he was out busting a trap. He didn't care either he was young and didn't give a shit. The lawyer asked. If he had a chance to do it different would he? The boy answered fuck yea! I should of made him suffer more before I killed him. Heartless and cold, he struck Rock as the type of person who has been living reckless since he first learned how to walk. "Shut the fuck up, you ain't doing shit but going to trial and eating that time you about to get!" The sheriff's partner look back in the youngin eyes and snarled. Now we all know that if we weren't cuffed up. These men wouldn't be treating us the way they did. "We'll see big man." Young boy had something up his sleeve.

"What's wrong" Stoski asked seeing the look on my face. "These fucking cuffs are cutting off my circulation. I can't feel my hands. The sheriff didn't think they were tight." The sheriff heard what I was saying. He rushed to loosen them up quickly. "He fucking told you they were tight. We all know you don't give a shit about them." Stoski whispered to him. Rock didn't say shit. He was already tight from not feeling his hands. "Sorry about that "Manuel." The suit Rock was wearing could of easily have been worn been a thousand other prisoners. Rock smelled it. It had an awkward smell to it. He was told that his family could bring him a suit but Rock went against it. He didn't want his family to fork out anymore unnecessary money for a suit that would only be worn for a few hours. It made absolutely no sense to toss away money like that. Even if it was rented. "I know it isn't the best but it's something that is better than what you wearing now." The sheriff tried to sound convincing. Rock once again didn't say shit. He was in his zone now wasn't the time to get all hyped over small senseless bullshit. If this suit could help even a little he was going to wear it,ven if it smelled like crap. Once the hammy down suit was put on with every button buttoned all the way to the top with a black tie he was ready to go. He couldn't control his future but what Rock could most definitely control was himself at this very moment. He didn't know who all was supposed to show up. What he did know was that he had no choice but to show up. His head would be held up high no matter who or what the outcome would be. This had to be done. One for himself and second for his family. "You're up Mr. Ricardo." The sheriff said snapping Rock out of his days.

Rock was on his way up a few small flights of steps he had no cuffs on now, but the ones on his feet which were just as bad as having them on his wrist. "Good luck man." The sheriff walked Rock out to the room where he saw bright lights and so many different faces. The first few faces he noticed was Jacqueline. He smiled at her being she was the first face he noticed turning his neck. A few more degrees he noticed the first row with Felicia, Joel, and Linda. Mom and Pete all sitting together. His eyes grew big at the site of all of them especially Felicia and Jacqueline in the same room.

"Hey Manny." Linda couldn't hold in her emotions. "Manuel we love you." Mom said. The whole time Jacqueline was watching mom and Linda. Her eyes couldn't believe what the fuck she was seeing. The white woman and Felicia brought back flashbacks when they were all in the same courtroom during the prelim months ago. Linda was Jasmine. Jacqueline's blood was boiling, so hot she couldn't believe how she had been lied to and why? Who could do such a thing? She felt played but most of all she felt stupid. Rock smiled but nothing was funny. He diverted his attention over to his lawyer. He was rummaging through his briefcase pulling out stacks of files and one of his law books. He was ready, he may have been a little late but he was ready.

"Proceed" the judge ordered as he noticed everyone was in position where they ought to be. "Of course your honor the state of New Jersey has brought up charges on "Manuel Ricardo Hernandez." Jacqueline was taken aback so was Felicia at the sound of Rocks full name. "And the charges are?" The judge asked the DA. "Homicide in the 1st degree, possession of an illegal instrument in a crime and conspiracy to commit homicide." The DA was sexy as hell. She was the true definition of a woman worth bringing home to mom. Her hair was blonde, pinned up in a nice bun that looked very conservative. Her eyebrows were done to perfection. She had to be about 5'4" weighing about 145 pounds. She didn't look like the type to starve to look her best, her nice toned up legs gave it all away. Her icy blue eyes could be seen from across the room. Too bad she was the enemy at the moment. She was still a hell of a view to endure while fighting for one's freedom. "Open an arguments." The judge allowed Ms. Hitchskins to open up her argument. She went to explain very carefully. She was walking slowly back and forth. She did her best trying to use all that she could to play a mental picture of the henious crime that occured that night. She made sure it was short and to the point not leaving out any important details from the act that was committed that day at the Pennsauken Mart parking lot. Linda swallowed deeply reliving that moment. The DA had the story down to the tee, there was a crucial element missing though..... Which was.... her! She was the peace that could make all this go away to set her brother free. She couldn't no matter how much she wanted too. It would only make Rock angrier. Now, there were other loose ends that would eventually be tied up around her neck as well. Her best and only action for her to commit? Was to shut the fuck up and allow the lawyer to work his magic. "Objection your honor." Prosecution doesn't know that." Mr. Stoski was paying close attention to her opening argument. "Sustained." The judge ruled in Stoski's favor. Ms. Hitchskins went on with her version of the story that she managed to put together and place on paper. From the rats and all the other shit she found looking under all the rocks and tunnels searching for clues. She finally came to an end, "That's all for now your honor." Ms. Hitchskins said moving swiftly across the marble floor. She was damn sexy. Stoski caught himself looking. He knew the DA and she was a feisty one that never gave him any play. "She's hot." He whispered in Rock's ear. "Are you serious?" Rock replied not believing what this man was thinking about. "Oh yeah." he smiled relax I got this." Stoski assured Rock. Rock remembered what Stoski said about having to serve some time even if they did drop the homicide it would've been a whole different story if the DA would have left matters alone. Than maybe Rock would've been able to go home scott-free.

"Mr. Stoski your opening statement." The judge looked at Stoski. He rose up calm and cool as he always carried himself. "Where did you find this lawyer?" Pete asked. He was watching how mom stared at him. The yellow pages." Mom lied right through her teeth. Pete didn't say anything. "Is he any good?" Pete asked. "We'll see." Mom said not breaking her stare whispering. Linda whispered in mom's ear. "He is cute." It's incredible how at a time like this everyone's mind were not where they needed to be. Who gave a fuck how cute the lawyer was? You got to be shitting me. "I know." Mom smiled. "Yes your honor." After Stoski made his opening statement the war began. "Yes, your honor Mr. Stoski went on to defend Rock to the end. He was going on how their so-called reliable witnesses weren't even showing up and how the other wasn't even in existence. He spoke directly to the Jurors disregarding everyone else. Why? Because no one else mattered. He was befriending the jurors. They were the on;y 12 people who matter the most in here. He had some great attributes in his defense. We all just hoped that they would be taken serious enough to raise some reasonable doubts.

"With this being said, my only request that this case against my client and myself be thrown out due to lack of..... Stoski paused in deep thought... Let's say everything." Mr. Stoski was borderline crazy. "That's all for now." Stoski ended. This was going to be a long and emotionally painful day. Linda peeked over to Jacqueline who was still eyeballing her from the far corner. Jacqueline shook her head. Linda put her head down. She had no choice but to patch things up with Jacqueline. How was she going to do it? This was the ultimate question?

"You know her don't you?" Felicia asked in disbelief. "Sort of." Linda answered still lying. "Please don't tell me you knew?" Felicia wanted answers right now but Linda wasn't even in the mood to even start answering anything at the moment. "This isn't about you nor her it's about my mother fucking brother. We can talk about this shit later." Linda growled through clenched teeth. Mom scolded both Linda and Felicia on how they were acting. She didn't know what they were talking about. It didn't matter because they shouldn't be talking about anything. Instead they should be paying attention to what was going on.

"Objection your honor this is not going to be thrown out we have a jury to determine if our evidence is substantial or not." Mrs. Hitchskins said with her head up high and full of confidence. "Sustained proceed." The judge announced.

"Well your honor I like to call in the responding officer on the scene who was in fact the first officer on the scene. "Off. Blanchard." Ms. Hitchskins called out proceeding. The uniformed officer approached the stand. "Put your right hand on the Bible." The bailiff instructed. Officer Blanchard did just that.

"Do you swear to state the whole true and nothing but the truth so help you god?" "I do." Officer Blanchard answered. "Thank you." The bailiff returned back to his position on the bottom left-hand corner of the courtroom, standing at attention. Good morning Officer." Ms. Hitchskins spoke. "Morning." he replied.

"Do you recognize that man sitting by Mr. Stoski?" Ms. Hitchskins stared at Mr. Stoski with her sexy blue eyes. "Yes I do." Off. Blanchard answered. "From where?" She asked. "He was present at a homicide scene. I was the arresting officer on the scene when I arrived." He informed. "Was he compliant when you arrested him?" She asked. "Some what he didn't give us too much trouble." The officer stated. "And who else was at the scene other than the man you identified at the scene?" Ms. Hitchskins asked. Guiding him to her other question. "No one other than a lifeless body about 2 feet away from where he was arrested on the scene." Mrs. Hitchskins bit her bottom lip. She had to be getting off on all this excitement on her behalf. It's fucked up this was one sided. "Upon the arrest of Mr. Ricardo, did you find any weapons on the scene?" She asked. "None on his person." The officer admitted. "Mr. Stoski's ears flared up really paying attention now. Somehow he wasn't supposed to say that part the way he did. The fact that he just admitted that the weapon was not on Rock's body could help a lot on the defense. "But there was a weapon on the scene right?" The DA asked again. "Objection! Your honor she's coaching the witness." Mr. Stoski was on it. "Sustained Ms. Hitchskins he answered the question the first time." Ms. Hitchskins inhaled but not letting up, where there any weapons located on the scene?" She rephrase her question. "Yes there was a small 8 1/2 inch chrome butterfly knife with the words Linda, mom and Rock engraved on it." The officer admitted. Ms. Hitchskins swayed her body back and forth. Her frame was something worth wondering what was under them sophisticated clothes. "How long till the corners arrived at the scene?" She asked the Officer. "About 15 minutes." Officer answered. "And was there anything you could've done to help revive the man, that was dying on the scene?" She asked. "No he had no pulse by the time I arrived." The Officer said. "I'm sorry you had to witness and experience such a detrimental thing." Ms. Hitchskins was a hell of an actor. "Thank you." The officer wasn't that bad himself. Wonder who would take home the Oscar today? "That's all for now you're honor." Ms. Hitchskins was talented. "Mr. Stoski, cross examination." The judge stated. "Yes your honor." Stoski rose up pacing back and forth quietly for a few seconds. Everyone in court was follow his moving steps. "Off. Blanchard, is it correct?" Stoski asked not looking at the cop. "Yes it is." He replied not understanding. "You did swear to say the whole true and nothing but the truth am I correct?" Stoski asked. "Objection Your Honor we all are aware of what he was asked to do." Mrs. Hitchskins was feisty. "Mr. Stoski, what are you doing?" The judge asked. "Getting to my point your honor may I?" Mom smiled at her ex. Pete noticed he was some type jealous. "Over rule proceed Mr. Stoski." The judge ordered in his favor. Ms. Hitchskins sat back down with a pout. "You did say that there was no weapon found in my client am I correct?" Stoski asked. "Yes I did." Officer answered wiping off the sweat on his four head. "If I'm not mistaken, at our last hearing you stated that he did have a weapon on him do you remember that?" It got real quiet Ms. Hitchskins had her beautiful manicure hands tied up now. "I..... I... can't recall." The cop stuttered. "You can't recall? You mean you're not taking the fact that you could possibly send an innocent man to jail for your irresponsible uncertainties?" Stoski was on him. "Objection! Your Honor" The DA didn't like where this was going. "Overruled Ms. Hitchskins." Proceed Mr. Stoski." The judge ordered. "Thank you Your Honor." Stoski enjoyed this part of his job the most. Cross-examining and picking apart the witnesses.This was how he won most of his cases. "I don't want to say he did or that he didn't." The officer was fucking up bad. "We don't want you to say anything but the truth Off. Blanchard." Stoski raised his voice. "So did Mr. Ricardo have a weapon on him or not?" Stoski asked again demanding an answer. "He didn't have a weapon on him at the time of the arrest." Off. Blanchard confessed turning bright red. He was sweating, the beads of sweat rolled down his four head. "Thank you, now you mean to tell me that no one else was at the scene when all of this took place?" Stoski asked. Blanchard didn't want to answer any more of Stoski's questions. He had no choice at the moment.

"When the homicide took place those were the only two bodies at the scene." Off. Blanchard admitted. "How did Mr. Ricardo's appearance look?" Stoski asked. "He was beat up pretty bad." Off. Blanchard said. "Beat up?" Stoski asked confused. "Yes, beat up bad. He had a lot of blood on his clothing. His eyes were almost shut with some cuts and bruises." The officer described. "So would it be safe to say that Mr. Ricardo was fighting a life or death battle? The description you just gave us sounds pretty bad." Stoski asked. "Objection! Your Honor the witness can't determine that on an observation alone." Ms. Hitchskins stood up. "Sustained." Stoski asked. That's not his line of work." The judge honored Ms. Hitchskins request. "So he did get beat up you said?" Stoski went around the question. "Yes." Off. Blanchard can you tell me what the other man's face look like as far as any marks on his face?" Stoski asked. "He had no marks on his face only the wound on his neck." Off. Blanchard informed everyone in the courtroom. "No further questions." Stoski walked away from the bench heading back to where Rock was seated. Rock was shaking his right leg uncontrollably.

"Nervous?" Stoski noticed. "Whaaatt?" You have no clue." Rock replied. "Trust me I have a clue." "Your next witness Ms. Hitchskins?" The judge ordered. "I would like to call upon Dr. Truitt's." Ms. Hitchskins look back waiting for her professional witness to come up to the stand to get sworn in to proceed with her case.

"Mr. Truitt's can you tell the ladies and gentlemen of the jury what is your profession?" Ms. Hitchskins asked shifting her weight on her left leg make it her body curves look that much more appealing for everyone especially me.

"I'm a doctor who specializes in deceased bodies. I examine them in and out to determine cause of death." Mr. Truitt was proud of his occupation. "And how long have you been doing this for Mr. Truitt's?" Ms. Hitchskins asked. "22 years and counting." Truitt's replied. He definitely looked the part he had to be at least 50 something. He too wore his glasses down to the tip of his nose. The wrinkles in his face couldn't be ignored not one bit. "So you're professional in this line of work?" Ms. Hitchskins asked. "You can say that." Truitt's agreed. "Can we get your hearts honest opinion on how this innocent man was killed?" Ms. Hitchskins held up a picture so that the jury could see Kay's lifeless body lying on the asphalt the night of his murder. Their faces looks scared at the sight of the photo. Some shield their eyes so that they didn't have to look any longer, others shook their head in disbelief. "That man die from a sharp punctured wound straight into the man's jugular vein on the right side of his neck." Truitts said. "From that observation can you determine the type of weapon use to commit the crime?" Ms. Hitchskins asked walking over to her table that had a number of Ziploc bags on them with numbers and labels on them. "I can't determine exactly what the weapon was or use. I can tell you the size and if the weapon. I can make a mold that will help me determine if the weapon was found, and was in fact the weapon used on the victim body." Mr. Truitt explained making sure all his words were chosen carefully and accurately but most of all understood. "Good." The weapon recovered at the scene had a set of prints on it didn't they?" Ms. Hitchskins asked. "Yes, when the fingerprints were ran through the system's database there weren't any match to them?" She asked. "No there was no identity to them." Mom's heart began to race. Was she understanding what was being said at the moment. I'm pretty sure she heard it clearly. "So if there was no identity to the prints, how did you and your agency come to determine that the prints belong to our defendant today?" Ms.

Hitchskins asked. "The prints had no identity because no one in the system matched." Mr. Truitt's went on to explain. "After a few hours a match came up on the computer matching those prints taken off the knife." Mr. Truitt's stated. "So what you're saying is once our defendant was processed his identity was entered into the computer system and after a few hours you were alerted that the system had found a match to the prints?" Ms. Hitchskins was putting the pieces together so the ladies and gentlemen of the jury could see the picture a bit more clearly. "Yes that is correct." Mr. Truitt's replied. "So If I may ask you, who did the prints belong to?" "The prints belong to Manuel Ricardo." Truitt said not skipping a beat. "Can you tell us if the weapon found did in fact match the puncture wound in our victim's neck?" Ms. Hitchskins was on a roll. Rock swallowed everything he had in his mouth which was nothing but dry saliva. Linda's palms were so sweaty mom had to wipe her hands every so often on her jacket. They were slandering her brother's character and she couldn't do anything about it. "The wound and the weapon matched perfectly." Truitts admitted to everyone. "Was this the weapon that matched the puncture wound?" Ms. Hitchskins held up another bag with Rock's butterfly knife open and stained with blood on it. "The two patterns matched yes." Truitts answered. Stoski was noticing something that has caught his attention again, something was missing. Was it enough to help him get his client off completely? The time was already close to 11 how much longer was all this going to take place until it was over? "No more questions your honor thank you Mr. Truitt's." Ms. Hitchskins darted her eyes at Stoski. "We'll take a brief recess and continue after lunch. "Bang!" the gavel was the only reply that was heard. "How we looking?" Rock asked wanting to hear some good news. "We are making progress. It's far from over Manuel." Stoski said. "Listen can you deliver a message for me?" Rock said. "Sure"

"Tell that woman in the far right corner with the deep dimples that I said she look so pretty that I wish I could hug and kiss her." Rock's words were whispered into Stoski's ear before the bailiff pulled him away.

—

Outside of the courtroom Mom, Pete, Linda, Joel and Felicia all stood stretching their legs. They all were talking about what was taken place. Jacqueline popped up from behind.

"Hey Jasmine." Jacqueline smiled showing off her sexy dimples unfazed by Felicia. Linda and Jacqueline locked eyes. Mom walked away not wanting any parts of what was about to go down she pulled Pete and Joel by their sleeves. They didn't even bother asking any questions until they were on the other side of the room. This was where many had congregated to wait for the trial to continue. The three of them were united for once and for all "Jasmine? Bitch you got the wrong person." Felicia spat. "Do I?" Jacqueline shifted her small frame on to her right to face Linda. "Give us a second Felicia." Linda said. "You got to be kidding me are you serious." Felicia temper was taken over. "You heard her give us a minute." Jacqueline snapped back very disrespectful. Felicia sucked her teeth clearly pist at how she was dismissed from the circle.

"What the hell is going on?" Jacqueline asked with her eyes blood shot red. They filled with water slowly. Linda shook her head. "Why are you here?" Do you know the nigga that's on trial too?" Jacqueline was shaken. "That nigga is my brother." Linda said. Jacqueline held her hand up to her mouth. "Are you serious when were you going to tell me?" Jacqueline asked. "Oh my God, That's the two of you on your shirt." Jacqueline was still going through it. Now it was on another level with Rock and Linda, plus Felicia. This shit wasn't getting better for her. First it was her baby dads murdered and now all of this. Jacqueline was on the brink of calling it quits with everyone. Her love for Rock was too strong but let's not forget it was just as strong with Linda as well on an intimate level. "It's a long story that I can't even explain right now." Linda said. "So you're Jalinda?" Linda nodded in agreement with Jacqueline accusations. "So who is that white bitch over there?" Jacqueline asked referring to Felicia. "That's Manny's girlfriend, if they still calling in that I'm not sure." Linda cleared it up quickly. "Girlfriend? Oh shit that's her?" Jacqueline looked at Felicia to get another look. "I remember he says something about having a girl back then. Fuck that he want me still." Jacqueline got back into defense mode. "I can't believe I'm talking to Rock sister." Jacqueline said softly. "Shut the hell up." Linda said through gritted teeth. "It wasn't supposed to go down like this." Linda said hoping to set things straight. This was almost impossible at the moment. "It what?" Jacqueline said shell-shocked. "How was it supposed to go down then? Please enlighten me?" Jacqueline was dominating this conversation. Linda put her head down. "I don't know but we can talk about us later please." Linda didn't want to be anymore embarrassed that she was already feeling. "Us there is no us are you serious that your man over there too?" Jacqueline's voice was rising a bit. "Don't even think about it Jacqueline I swear." Linda said staring coldly into Jacqueline's eyes. "You swear what Linda?" I lost him and almost everything else I had. The only people I have is you and your brother what am I supposed to do? Can you answer me that question?" Jacqueline was cracking slowly. "You won't lose us I promise but right now this isn't about you, Felicia or me. It's about my brother coming home." Linda regain the momentum of the conversation with her side. She had to use her brother, it was the only thing that would actually work in this heated argument. Felicia came walking over

"Are you too done?" She said with so much rudeness in her voice. "Ima tell you the same thing I told her, this ain't about any of us. It's about Manny. It's about if he is coming home with us or he is going to be stuck inside of a cell for a very long time. So if you two want to fight each other go right ahead. What Manny needs is friends not a wifey or a mistress he needs friends who are going to be there by his side no matter what. Yes he was fucking both of you at the same time. I didn't know but apparently yes, he must've been. There isn't anything we can say or do to change what he did or how he did it." Linda was heated. She had to defuse the bomb before it would count down on its own. Felicia hawked Jacqueline and Jacqueline didn't even break her stair. She was showing no fear in her presence. "I'm here for him." Felicia said putting her hand on her hip proving a point. "You're here for him? Jacqueline laughed. "Well I was here a few days ago visiting him, where were you? And we did signs through the window. Where you were?" Jacqueline also prove her point. Those words stung Felicia she couldn't come up as much as she wanted to but she wrote and did all that she could. "I...." Felicia was about to counter Jacqueline last argument. "I said not now." Linda rose her voice shutting her up. Mom approached the ladies. "Yall going to talk about this later because it's time." Mom said walking by the three girls shaking her head. Mom knew all this would implode one day and out of all days why today? "We'll look, you know each other now so deal with it for now. We are all going to sit together just to show Manny that everyone knows one another. Let's see what he has to say when he writes." Linda had her plan and this was it. To put the spotlight on Manny because Linda was still in a lot of pain and walking with a cane. That didn't make matters any better. "I'm not sitting by her." Felicia said like a little kid. "I'm a sitting in between the both of you alright." Linda ordered. They had no choice but to bite their tongue right now. How long would this little charade keep on going if no one would have showed face today? What's in the dark always comes to light sooner or later right?

"Anyway what the hell happened to you Jasmine I mean Linda?" Jacqueline asked with a quizzical look on her face. "I fell.... really fucking hard too." Linda lied again. Part of her wish she could just work up the courage to tell them both the truth. The truth of the matter was these two bitches couldn't be trusted with information like that. This was something Linda may have to take to her grave. "You fell? You walking like a truck ran over your tiny body." Jacqueline joked trying to ease her mind off jumping on Felicia for what she did earlier in the elevator. This was far from over there was no way these two obsessive females would be second in Rocks eyes. They both couldn't be first, or could they? Back in their seated positions Linda made Joel sit next to Pete. He sat away from crazy and crazier with Linda being the craziest. If he only knew what the hell was going on he probably leave Linda. This was exactly what Linda didn't want to happen. Besides being raised in a foster home with Mom and Manny, Joel was the second best thing that has ever happened to her and she knew this now.

The judge entered the courtroom leaving his chambers. The DA had not moved since the start and Mr. Stoski was nowhere in sight. With all the commotion no one even notice when he left or pass by. Even if he did. He didn't want to set any alarms off with Mom and Pete. He was respectful and cautious.

Rock was brought back out. His face was screwed up as if he had eaten a sour patch at the site of Linda sitting in between his two girls. He shook his head. It just so happened that Jacqueline and Felicia both blew kisses his way at the same time. This really caused Rock to stare at Linda. Something was up and Linda's face had a smirk on as if she was the culprit in all of this. Stoski came in late as always. Mom shook her head. "This man is crazy." Pete heard her. "He's what?" Pete asked. "Crazy" mom whispered. "You would think he'd be here earlier than the judge, but no he's now just waltzing in with no care in the world." Mom whispered some more. Stoski went straight to Jacqueline's ear and whispered. "He told me to tell you look sexy as ever and he wishes he could eat you all up." Stoski twisted up Rocks words all the way up. The message was close enough. Jacqueline smiled and blushed so much her panties got moist right on cue at the site a Rock's face. She bit her bottom lip. Felicia leaned forward not liking what she was thinking. She could only imagine what the lawyer had said to her as he came in.

"Are we ready to continue?" The Honorable Judge asked the district attorney and Mr. Stoski. Ms. Hitchskins was the first to respond. "Yes Your Honor, I'm ready but I can't answer for Mr. Stoski over there." That cheap shot wasn't even necessary from Ms. Hitchskins. It was a never ending battle when he came to the combat the district attorneys. "Mr. Stoski are you?" The judge asked. "Absolutely, let's proceed." Stoski winked at Ms. Hitchskins. Mom noticed that she had hidden feelings this man, but that's all that they were. Hidden feelings. "Did you tell her?" Rock asked. "Did I?" Stoski laughed. "And some." He said in a whisper. Rock smiled. "Something is wrong with you, you know that right?" Rock joked.

"Mr. Truitt's please approach the stand." The judge ordered. "Mr. Stoski the cross-examination." Stoski glanced at his legal pad. "Mr. Truitt's..... did I say that correctly?" Stoski asked. "Yes you did." Truitt's replied. "Before we went our little lunch break. You inform the ladies and gentlemen of the jury. That the knife found on the scene did in fact match the mold that you took from the wound on the victim's body correct?" Stoski asked and answering all at once. "I believe that is correct Mr. Stoski." Truitts answered. "So this so called knife killed our victim?" Stoski asked hopping that Truitt's would bite the bait. "That's incorrect Mr. Stoski." Truitt's wasn't dumb and Stoski could bank his salary that he wouldn't let himself get caught up in that net. "Ummmmmm." You could hear a pin drop the court room was dead silent. "So the blood on the knife in my hands belongs to our dead victim then?" Stoski asked staring at the jurors. There faces look so confused at what they were hearing. "The blood does not match to the man found dead at the scene." Truitts admitted. Ms. Hitchskins was shaking her head not wanting to hear any of what Stoski was saying. She had already anticipated all of this. She only prayed and hope that he wasn't on his game. She was out of luck because Stoski did bring in his a game. "Another question Mr. Truitt's?" Stoski said pacing back and forth. Rock was feeling good about what he was hearing, but wasn't enough? Linda had both of her hands full with Jacqueline's and Felicia's locked in with her hands. They were so quiet. Their attention was strictly focused on all of the intriguing facts between the DA and Mr. Stoski. "Yes?" Truitts responded. "Is there any

DNA on that knife blade that belongs to our victim?" The courtroom was so quiet you could hear the worms moving underground. Everyone waited for the answer which only took seconds but felt like minutes. "The DNA sample was of a male. It wasn't a positive match with the deceased." Truitt's admitted. "No further questions for now Your Honor." Stoski said. He was brewing something up and no one knew what it was. Our only hope was that it would work as planned. "You may step down Mr. Truitt's." The judge directed. "Your next witness Ms. Hitchskins." The judge asked. Ms. Hitchskins was running out of stops to go to. Her one and only credible witness wasn't showing up. She had till the end the trial to show up. The KYW news reporter was sitting ,writing away in her memo pad while her tape recorder was fitted snugly in between her thighs. She recorded every word being spoken in his room today. This would make the headlines if the case would be thrown out due to technicality. In the world's eyes, Rock was a stone cold killer. For him to be acquitted of all this, would cause a frenzy. If found guilty a retrial would be awarded and the state would do everything in their power to bring it back. "I like to call Detective Hasnoff to the stand." Mom's heart almost stopped as soon as those words left Ms. Hitchskins lips. "Oh man, Rock mumbled loud enough for Stoski to hear. Mom didn't want to run into these two and now it was an inevitable avoiding them now. Linda swallowed deeply as well. He made his way up in plainclothes with his badge around his neck. He was looking like a narc that has been out in the field all morning. He looked over in mom's direction and winked at mom. Her heart began to beat faster. What was she going to do after this was over? This was only about to get worse Linda thought squeezing both hands unconsciously. "Jalinda let go of my hand girl." Felicia said low enough for her to hear. "I'm sorry." Linda apologized. After swearing the Detective in. He locked eyes with Rock having him in his ball park now. This is where he would take him down as much as he could until he made his point clear as day.

"Good afternoon Detective." Ms. Hitchskins made small talk before getting started. "Good afternoon Ms. Hitchskins." Hasnoff replied. "Do you know this man sitting beside Mr. Stoski?" Ms. Hitchskins initiated the battle. "Yes I do." Hasnoff answered still looking at Rock. Rocks blood began to get hot. His leg began to shake at full speed. The clatter of the chains caused Stoski to tap Rock's leg forcing him to try and relax. "Can you tell us a little bit about him with the information you gathered up investigating this young man?" Ms. Hitchskins chose her words wisely. "Well for starters my first interaction with this young man was on the day he was arrested. He was a prime suspect in the alleged killing of another young man over a dispute, that may have gotten out of hand." Hasnoff paused. "Anything else?" Ms. Hitchskins wasn't satisfied. She wanted him to slander Rock's character even more. "Well since that incident. I've been called to investigate another murder that took place in the county jail which was also allegedly said to have to do with Mr. Ricardo." "Objection Your Honor that is irrelevant. He is on trial for this case not another so called alleged case in jail." Stoski jumped up pissed not even thinking that they took it that far.

"Your Honor permission to approach the bench." Ms. Hitchskins asked politely. "Granted." The judge said. Stoski and Ms. Hitchskins were both in front of the judge.

"Ms. Hitchskins what does this have to do with the case?" The judge asked. "A lot Your Honor this man is violent and is powerful. Just listen to the facts before you overrule anything." Ms. Hitchskins beat Stoski to the first punch. All that is irrelevant Your Honor. She is assassinating my clients character with events that are unclear." Stoski defended. Stoski your client isn't here for building parks or anything in that nature. So spare me the character guilt trip." The judge was hard. "Two minutes Ms. Hitchskins not a second over." "That's more than enough Your Honor, you won't regret this." Ms. Hitchskins got her way. Stoski was pist. He didn't allow this to be expressed in his demeanor towards Rock nor his family. He had a job to do and he was making sure he would fulfill it to the fullest. "Where were we?" Ms. Hitchskins knew exactly where she left off, who the fuck was she foolong. "Oh yes another incident that you have come across in regards to Mr. Ricardo?" Ms. Hitchskins reiterated. "Well besides the two I've just mentioned, no. His name was mentioned in the murder of Dante who was a key witness on this trial. We are still in the process of investigating this coincidence. It's leading us to believe that Mr. Ricardo has something to do with orchestrating these other murders that miraculously occurred. Now, if he didn't partake in them. He most definitely knows who did participate in them." Mr. Hasnoff was looking over at Jalinda and Felicia. His gut told him that the murderers were closer and possibly right under his nose. There was no proof yet, he had to stand his ground. Linda swallowed hard she was afraid. Joel on the other hand maintain his composure not allowing any of the detective words to phase him one bit.

"Objection! Your Honor this man is slandering my client's character with all those accusations he's proclaiming. "Sustained. Ms. Hitchskins gets to the point." The judge ordered. "Detective in your line of duty have you ever met any men like Mr. Ricardo?" Ms. Hitchskins asked. "Yes too many. There slick and smart. This is why we still have current investigations on them and anyone we have reason to believe who may be involved in any of this." Detective Hasnoff locked eyes on Felicia. "Why is he staring at me?" She whispered over to mom. "I have no clue girl just relax you don't have anything to worry about." Mom assured Felicia of what she already knew. "No more questions for now thank you." Ms. Hitchskins sashayed her round bottom back to her seat. "Mr. Stoski" Judge Kenny said given Stoski the green light.

"Detective this will be simple and to the point. A few yes and no's and you will be on your way." Sounds good? "First off have you ever made an arrest that was ever overturned?" Stoski asked standing still staring at the marble floor in front of him facing the jury. "Ummmmmm" Hasnoff was thinking. "It's a yes or no." Mr. Hasnoff. "Yes!" Hasnoff admitted. Could he have lied? Probably because Stoski was free styling. "Any more than three?" Stoski asked. "Yes" He answered. "Wow more than three over turned arrests. That means these were innocent people in jail." Stoski still wasn't looking up but shaking his head. "More than five?" Stoski pushed hoping the bait was tasteful enough to eat. "Yes" Hasnoff answered. "I might as well stop. I can only imagine how high it'll be till you say no." Stoski said sarcastically. "Do you believe my client is guilty of this homicide?" Stoski looked up at the jurors now. "We have reason to." "I said yes or no!" Stoski raised his voice. Rock was sitting on the edge of his seat. "I can't answer that question." Hasnoff said. "You can't answer my question huh?" Stoski repeated louder. He now was facing Ms. Hitchskins. How about we answer it together?" Stoski was going in on him. From my clients file, you just so happen to charge him with conspiracy to murder a few days ago is this correct?" Stoski asked. "Yes." Hasnoff was redder than a juicy tomato. "So homicide wasn't enough to convict him? You wanted my client to have a more horrible appearance with all these bogus charges huh?" Stoski was working. "No." Hasnoff wasn't thinking consciously. "You wasn't?" Stoski asked. "I mean yes." Hasnoff was confused making an ass of himself. "So yes these are bogus charges?" Stoski was working a number on him. "Which is a yes or no?" Rock had a smile on his face, so did mom. She adored Michael for all he has done and who he was as a person. "I can't answer that question."

Hasnoff blurted out. "You what? You just did twice this isn't three strikes and you're out." Too late for that one." Stoski was winning the race and Ms. Hitchskins couldn't bury her face any deeper and her palms. Stoski had things going the way he wanted, but he knew that a conspiracy charge would be the one to give him a headache. No further questions for now." Stoski announced.

"You see ladies and gentlemen of the jury my client was on the verge of getting this case thrown out. The district attorney didn't want to leave it at that so what happens?" Stoski looked into each of the eyes of the jurors searching for compassion. "They saw that the evidence wasn't evident enough to set my client free. He was brought back down to bookings and charged again with another crime on the same case. It wasn't bad enough that he had to endure all these traumatic injuries that he suffered that night alone. So with that being said why not charge him with another charge just in case you the jury see what we all see.

You're Honor if I may call upon my witness?" Stoski asked. The judge glanced at his watch. "Right after break." Just like that the gavel was smacked against its counterpart dismissing everyone's next words. You could hear everyone's breath exhaling. The room was filled with anxieties from both sides. They hauled Rock away again. He looked back for a split second but the bailiff shielded his view.

"Damn can I at least see them? You don't have to be all up in the way?" Rock wasn't too pleased with how he just blocked his only view of everyone. "Catherine?" Stoski knelt down right in front of her. Mom only wished this was 15 years ago when he would of knelt down and proposed. This wasn't the case not today. "Yes." Mom answered softly keeping her breath light and controlled. Pete held her hand. He caught Michael staring at it for a second. To be honest, I think we might continue this in the morning unless you want me to talk to the judge to get it moving today." Stoski asked staring at mom then over back at Linda. "No don't rush anything I don't want to irritate the judge any more than he is already feeling." Mom had some consideration. "Well I'll be out in the hall making a few calls but be careful with the detective. They will take advantage that they have you here to bombard you with questions." Stoski warned getting up to walk away. "Thank you" mom said to his back. "I think that man likes you." Pete joked. "Who Michael?" Mom asked blushing. "Yeah right he don't want no old lady." Mom joked back. Linda winked at mom not even saying anything out of the norm.

"What you think is going to happen?" Jalinda asked loud enough for Felicia to here. "I'll tell you was going to happen. Little old Manuel will be found guilty and he'll be sent away for a good portion of his young life." Detective Defenchi said with Hasnoff right behind him smiling. They waited for Stoski to leave the room so they could harass Mom and Linda. "Why don't you leave us the fuck alone you already cause enough damage in our family." Linda spat not holding her tone back. "Linda" mom said. "What?" It's okay she's can say what she wants. We do have freedom of speech." Mr. Hasnoff opinionated knowing exactly what he was trying to do. "You could help your brother Jalinda. Don't you want to help him?" Detective Hasnoff asked. "You guys won't help anyone, haven't you notice?" Linda smart mouth voiced. "Whoa we get a man off the street who kills people, or better yet takes the fall for someone who kills people off the streets. This is how we get treated? He could help us catch the man or woman responsible for the murder but he don't want to cooperate. Now he is forced to serve time for a conspiracy charge. Humph, but we are the bad guys." Defenchi finished off Hasnoff's statement. "No! You and your partner suck at being cops. You two end up with innocent people in jail for no reason just face it." Linda didn't practice anything that her mom had warned her of, nor did she listen to what Stoski just instructed them to do. Defenchi tapped Hasnoff on the shoulder alerting him that Stoski had just entered the courtroom. Mom noticed what was going on. She was mad on how Linda disregarded all of the instructions. "By the way I love that shirt, I think we may of hit the jackpot." Hasnoff walked away with his sidekick. Linda completely forgot about the t-shirt she was wearing. She looked down at it regretting wearing it today but it was too late. How could she just put herself out there like that? Please don't tell me you said anything to them jerks?" Stoski was over where mom and Linda were sitting in seconds. Mom looked at Stoski not saying anything, but then she looked at Jalinda. "Jalinda?" Stoski put his head down. "We can't be exchanging words with them as SOBs. Every little word you say. They will misinterpret it and misconstrue it. To make you sound as if you admitting or given them clues to whatever it is that want to know.Those guys are far from stupid this is what they do." Stoski didn't even know the words that had been exchanged between the two of them, but he knew their MO. "What did he say and tell me what you told him." Stoski wasn't enjoying this one bit. He was getting annoyed at how Linda wasn't complying with his simple request. "What was supposed to be a fast and easy pro bono assignment on his own terms was turning into a free nightmare. When his clients weren't listening. "She didn't say anything. All she said was the truth." Felicia decided she had to help Jalinda out for some odd reason. Stoski looked at mom. "Who is this?" "It's a friend of Manuel's." Mom answered. Felicia pouted at how belittled she was said to be, by mom. "A friend" Stoski repeated "Well look friend I was talking to Jalinda and Catherine do me a favor and mind your business friend. I have a job to do and believe me you are nowhere in my notes or in my thoughts of helping. So please butt out just for a moment." Mom smiled at how straight forward Michael was. He was absolutely right there wasn't any time to be wasted with then extra bullshit. So nipping that in the butt was mandated but unexpected. Felicia's eyebrows scrunched together. She was a mad at how this man just put her in her place. He was right it was none of her business. She had to stay out of it. She knew better than to argue. She dealt with patients in her line of duty at the hospital. She ate her words to avoid more embarrassment. After Linda had told Stoski of her exchange of a words. Stoski once again told them the same exact instructions as before. "If you allow these jerks to pin more cases on any of you because you self-incriminating yourself, I'm sorry but you are on your own. I'll do my best but you have to help me on your behalf not make it impossible for me to defend you." Stoski informed upset. He was hoping they understood why he was saying what he was saying in the manner that he was saying it. He had to be firm that's how he was, plus it was for their protection as well. "Let me go and find out if we're going to try and wrap this up." Stoski disappeared

"Jalinda come over here." Mom said Linda moved her fine ass over a few seats forcing Felicia and Jacqueline to scoot over. They tried desperately to keep distance in between them. The pews were already loaded with bodies, taking up seats forcing them to juggle their own spots. "If you don't keep your mouth shut you going to put yourself in hot water are you listening to me?" I don't care about what those detective say to you. All I know is that you need to not say a word to them." Mom wasn't in her normal happy self. She had to get her point across even if Linda wouldn't listen to anyone else. She made sure she'd listen to mom. Mom was far from loud. It was a whisper that was softer then a silent prayer damn near, and just as powerful. "I didn't say anything." Linda try to protect yourself from the accusations. "You said enough which was a lot more than you had to say." Mom kept going. "Don't get cocky because things can get real ugly in the blink of an eye Jalinda. So use your intelligence rather than your mouth on impulse." Mom was done. She wouldn't keep it up not in public at least. Linda leaned onto Joe. He just shrugged his shoulders not saying a word. He knew better, he did exactly what he was told. Felicia and Jacqueline were mumbling about something on their side of the pew. They were shoving each other.

"I don't care how long you known him I'm not going anywhere." Jacqueline snapped back. By now these two were causing some unwanted attention up in the front row. The bailiff crept out from behind them. "This is a courtroom ladies" was all he said calming the two down immediately. They bickered some more which might go on forever. Linda hobbled back over to sit in between the two. "Are you two serious?" Linda asked for getting about the whisper. "How about I tell Manny to cut both you bitches off. He don't need this drama." Linda said. "It's her." Felicia told like a four year old. "I don't care who it is you want to fight wait till we go outside then you can rip each other's faces off. If you don't want to fight, than let it go and deal with each other because neither one of you are going to be able to fuck him. Now what?" Linda was directing her scolding that mom gave her a few seconds ago and taking it out on Felicia and Jacqueline.

"We are going to finish this by the end of the evening." Stoski said. You can go and grab a bite to eat because that's exactly what the judge went to go do." Stoski said. "I'm hungry myself." Stoski informed. "We can head to the shop. Pete suggested. "All of us?" He assured everyone of a nice hot meal. "How about it?" Mom said excitedly. Stoski looked at both of them. "I love too but I'm already meeting someone." Stoski burst mom's hopes. "Well then, we'll meet you back here in?" Pete asked not knowing at what time to be exact. "In two hours." Stoski said. Getting up and leaving "you ready?" Pete asked. "Let's go" mom got up first.

—

Rock had no appetite all he could think of was on how trial was going. The bagged lunch the sheriff tossed his way just laid there. "I'm going to beat this shit." Rock told himself. He was really forcing himself to believe what he was saying. He took off his suit jacket as soon as he entered the holding tank. Pacing back and forth for what Rock counted 98 times, his stomach growled he looked at the bag wondering what its contents could be in it.

No surprise it was a straight bologna sandwich. Two of them to be exact, a warm milk and three cream filled cookies. "What did I expect a cheesesteak with fries?" Rock asked himself laughing. He wished it was a sub. A sub he would always prepare. The exact same way in the shop whenever he got hungry. "CO!?" Rock yelled out the gate. "That mother fucker is gone G" another prisoner hollered back at Rock.

"Hows your shit going?" The other voice hollered.He sounded like one of the guys who was with Rock on the way up here. "It's hard to tell." Rock replied truthfully. "What about you?" Rock asked. "Man I'm fucked. I'm waiting on the verdict now." Rock didn't understand how he was already almost finished. Yet he was still waiting to cross examine a witness and closing arguments yet. "Why so fast?" Rock wasntd to know what was up. "Man listen they got all this evidence on me. My fucking lawyer sold me out and I told him I was going to kill him whenever I got out. So that pretty much made everything worse on my behalf." The young bucks said mad as hell. "Damn!" Rock said to himself. It was odd to hear things of that nature when a came to one's own freedom. Did you not want to go home? Could it be you lost hope way before you even decided to show up for trial? There was a strong chance that this young man would never see the streets again. Especially seeing and hearing how much he didn't give a fuck. "Wassup with you?" He asked. Bringing Rock out of his thoughts. "I'm not even close yet. My head all fucked up but my lawyer doing his thing but DA is on her shit too." Rock admitted. "He didn't lose hope. In his heart but his words sounded as if he was being defeated. "Hang in there it's not over for you yet don't do anything stupid like I did." That comment got Rock by surprise. Here was this complete stranger in a similar situation as Rock. He had no regard for his own freedom but wasted no time to lecture Rock to keep hope alive in his fight for his. Why was this? How would this help the young buck in anyway? Preaching positive information onto a complete stranger but not following through in his own words for oneself. Rock wasn't about to get wrapped up in another meaningless conversation with the wall. This is what he was thinking of the young buck. He didn't care nor did he want to listen to anyone who wanted to help him. It was a fair assumption but it wasn't what

Rock needed. "I will my nigga. Ima fall back and get my thoughts together, I'll holler at you later." Rock ended his conversation. "I might not be here later if anything I'll see you back at the jail. They call me JT" "Alright JT, I'm Rock." "I know" JT replied.

—

"What are you two going to do when this baby comes into this picture? I sure as hell don't want to see neither of the two of you fighting around the baby or even trying to push away Rock's babymom." The whole shop got so quiet everybody's jaw dropped. Linda's head was shaken from side to side. "How in the hell would mom just dropped the bomb like that on everyone. Jamal was even confused for a second. Felicia and Jacqueline were sitting at two different tables. Jacqueline looked at Felicia with hate in her eyes. Who was mom talking about with a baby? Felicia presumed it was Jacqueline and Jacqueline thought it was Felicia was caring Rock's the baby. "You pregnant?" Felicia asked not holding her mouth. "No are you?" Jacqueline asked back. The two of them must've not heard what mom had just said clearly. They only heard what they wanted. "It's neither of you." Linda said sitting next to Joel sharing a sub and wings. "So who was it?" Jacqueline asked with a French fry in her hand. "It doesn't matter who she is at the moment. What matters is there is a baby in this picture. Mom said with a smile on her face. "How in the hell is there a baby in this picture Rock is in jail?" Felicia was asking a dumb question. "Look honey my son was out messing with a couple a woman." Mom said pointing to Felicia and Jacqueline. "Now what makes you think that you two were the only pretty girls on his list?" Mom opinionated. Felicia was disgusted at what she had just heard. "I lost my appetite." Felicia said. "Well good, it's almost time to be heading back. "Can we get a name at least?" Jacqueline said sipping her juice. "Her name is Samantha." Linda said. Jamal's eyes popped open not believing that Linda exposed her name to theses two maniacs. Why didn't he say anything he knew exactly who mom and Linda were talking about "Samantha" that sound like a white girl name?" Jacqueline said rudely. "What's wrong with that?" Felicia took offense to Jacqueline's remarks. "Girl please." Jacqueline said not even paying Felicia any mine. Would those two actually stick around? Long enough to wait for Rock. Even if he did have to do some serious time after all this?" Joel asked Linda "Doubt it baby. I don't care because I have you and Rock has mom and me by his side. That's all that matters in my eyes." Linda said. "Why would you stir them up like that babe?" Pete asked mom walking towards his car. "Because I got tired of the bickering back and forth about nothing. Now they have something to bicker about now." Mom was evil. "You are something else Catherine." Pete hardly ever called mom by her name "Catherine?" Mom repeated. "What? I can't call you Catherine?" Pete asked. "You can but you don't." Mom said wondering where this was going. "You don't have a problem when Michael calls you Catherine." Pete was mocking Stoski. "Mom giggled not saying anything. She didn't feel as though that comment needed a reply. "How did you meet this man again?" Pete asked. He pulled off heading back to the courthouse. "I told you the Yellow Pages." Mom said again. Pete chuckled "Yellow Pages?" It's funny because I checked the Yellow Pages and his name nor firm is in those pages." Pete wasn't smiling anymore. "Mom head snap in Pete's direction. "You serious aren't you?" Mom asked. "Yup." Pete answered. "So you didn't take my word on what I told you?" Mom didn't like the fact on how he was on some sneaky shit. "I wanted to but the way he stares at you wouldn't allow me to leave it at that." Pete was a man. He knew damn well when a man enjoyed what he was looking at a little too much.

"I know Michael for year's babe we went to school together back then." Mom confessed not wanting to ruin what she had with Pete. "Why didn't you tell me that the first time Cat?" Pete asked parking in a spot down from the courthouse. "I don't know babe, I didn't think it was important." Mom said. "It isn't but I can't tell you what Mr. Stoski is thinking. I have to believe in what you're telling me babe I can't do that unless you are completely honest with me." Pete said sincerely. He was right. If mom would have said this before he wouldn't be engaged in this conversation. "You're right babe I'm sorry. It won't happen again." Mom opened the door meeting Pete on the side walk given him a kiss on his lips. "Can I make it up to you?" Mom said in between kisses. Pete smiled already knowing what she meant by that.

—

"Mr. Stoski you may proceed with your witness." The Hon. Judge instructed. Rock was back in the chair. Ms. Hitchskins was relaxed in her seat at her table waiting for Stoski's next move. She could only wonder what was up his sleeve. "Yes Mr. Truitt's please if you may." Stoski look back for Mr. Truitt's who was already on his way up to the stand. I need a few questions for you to confirm, if you may?" Stoski said. "Sure no problem." Truitts agreed.

"I may have forgotten to ask you about a DNA sample but can you tell the ladies and gentlemen of the jury that the blood found on the knife on the scene belong to whom?" Stoski asked "Well after further analysis. The blood specimen came back to belong to Mr. Dante." Truitts said. "And are you 100% sure that the blood on that knife is his?" Stoski asked. "Yes is a perfect match Mr. Stoski." Truitt said. "No further question Mr. Truitt thank you. "The blood wasn't the blood of the man my client is being accused of killing." Stoski looked over to the jury. The blood belong to the so called reliable witness that ended up dead due to a fire. He burned in his own home. "If that doesn't strike you as out of the ordinary I don't know what will. I will let that marinate for a few minutes. Stoski walked away.

"Ms. Hitchskins your closing statements." The judge asked.

"Yes Your Honor, ladies and gentlemen of the jury my only concern from me to you is that all of you look at the evidence carefully because this man is responsible for the murder of the victim in this case.It's up to us to bring this man to justice. If we do consider letting him go we may not be able to stop any future crimes committed by this individual. Who is a threat to our society, where our children and family lay their heads." Ms. Hitchskins was putting all cards on the table. She could care less about any other person in that room. Her only concern was that she would get her conviction, so she could add another one to her trophy room. "But if we decide to bring justice who knows how many lives we will save. I put my faith in whatever decision you decide to come up. I know you'll make the right one."..... Thank you." Her heels clicked and clanked all the way back to her seat.

The judge jotted down some notes then took his glare up to Stoski. "You're closing statement Mr. Stoski." The court room was quiet. The sound of heart-beats was the only thing that you could hear and of course the typing from the stenographer not missing or skipping a beat.

"Ladies and gentlemen of the jury." Stoski walked over to Ms. Hitchskins table. "She couldn't have said it any better. She knows the truth and we all can clearly see the truth. My client isn't the person we are looking for. The culprit behind all of this will be found but for now what's important is my client's rights to trial. How much is enough?" Stoski asked. Taking his time choosing his words carefully. My client was a victim. He was protecting himself from the man who they had as a witness. Are they too blind to see this or is it that they are so adamant on convictions that they won't allow anything or anyone to get in there way to get it? I too trust in you all to make the right decision and grant this man his life back." Stoski walked back to his seat. "Thank you Your Honor." Stoski finished. This feeling was a terrible one. My fate was in other people hands. This felt so fake but it was so real.

"The jurors will be back after they deliberate on the verdict the judge informed. Stoski held Rock's shoulder. "This is what it all comes down to." Stoski said looking in Rock's eyes. "I'm shitten bricks." Rock said cracking a smile.

—

35 minutes later after deliberation........

"We the ladies and gentlemen of the jury...." A tall white bald man was holding an index card in his hand. "Find Manuel Ricardo....... the courtroom was as if it was an empty room. Not a voice, not a breath, not a soul could be felt. "Not guilty of first-degree homicide." The people let their breaths out of relief mom and everyone in the front pew held each other's hands. For once, no bickering, no talking just all listening carefully hoping and praying for the best. The old man said. "We the ladies and gentlemen of the jury find Manuel Ricardo.... not guilty in possessing an instrument used in a crime." This was it I was going home. I was estatic. I couldn't wait to go home. The elder man said. "One more, one more." mom whispered. "We the ladies and gentlemen of the jury find Manuel Ricardo..... guilty in conspiracy to commit homicide." Mom's head fell down Linda began to whimper. Rock also had his head down. In a split second my world came crashing down hard. My chest tightened up-.The commotion in the court was getting loud.

"Order!.... Clank! Clank! Order!" The gavel along with the judge calmed everyone down. It took almost a few minutes.

"We The State of New Jersey will impose a sentence no more than 40 years and no less than 20 years in a state correctional facility with the possibility of parole." The judge spoke not even thinking of repeating himself. "Clank!" The horror was over but just beginning at the same time. "Rock I love you." Yelled Jalinda causing him to turn around. "I love you all, don't go too far." Rock forced a painful smile that had no type of joy in it. "We will be right by your side!" Linda yelled to his back as they hauled him away. Tears filled up pails. It was too much pain in here. Everyone loved Rock and what they were feeling right now was heart ripping. Mom's streams ran down her face. She had lost her son to the system. The system that failed her. How would she live with herself as a parent. Why was she being punished like this and who knows for how long the pain and anguish was going to last?

—

Back in the cell, Rocks mail waited patiently for Rock on his bed. He couldn't breathe he was lost. He was hurt, broken, scared but most of all he was angry. He wasn't in the mood to say or talk to anyone and his face said it all. The guys sensed it. It was a no brainer. He laid on his bed, he had to get his mind right before engaging in any conversation with anyone. For those who knew. This was the time that was given to a man or woman so they could gather there thoughts. Anyone could catch the heat if you was at the wrong time and had a crazy mouth peice on you.

"Hey cutie"

I hope by the time you get this you are in the best of mood, if not I'm sorry. I have a brief letter and I hope it will bring your spirits up a little bit. I've been home for almost a while now and I couldn't stop thinking of you.

I cut off Banga and Jigz because they don't give a shit about me. I'm working on getting my kids back. I can't keep living this crazy lifestyle anymore. Listen cutie I want you to know that I know how hard it is to be alone. This is why I'm making a promise to myself and to you that I'll be by your side not as your girlfriend or wifey but as a loyal friend to you. Ima be by your side every step of the way. I hope you allow me to do this. I don't want anything from you. All I want is for you to stay strong and keep moving on. I say this because you still have a long life to live. No matter if you're inside on the outside. I'm going to keep this brief and to the point and wait for your acceptance letter, that is if you want. Good luck at trial. Can't wait to hear from you craziness.

PS.You ain't missing much cutie. Stay sharp and out of trouble

your friend Kiki.

Rock couldn't believe what he had in his hand, he was in complete shock that he was holding a letter written by Kiki he forced a smile on his face which felt pretty good despite everything that he just went through today. He had two more letters in his hands. One of them stood out like a sore thumb. It was a postcard in a bright green envelope and it read Sam on the corner....

"WHO THE FUCK!?....

Synopsis

Many have grown up in a stable home. Many have grown up in their lovely cities. Many have both parents in their lives to fall back on when things to for the worst.

Unfortunately, Manuel Ricardo didn't have these advantages in his life. He was fatherless but most of all he was motherless. A pill that size would be very difficult for anyone to swallow. The city of Camden N.J wants to swallow him whole, what is he to do?

No mother, no father just foster home after foster home one after another. Manuel is a magnet when it came to the woman who he came in contact with. He could use this to his advantage or it had the same power to destroy him. If he didn't find someone to quench his thirst for the lack of attention he would never be complacent. The feeling of not being accepted, with only major influences from the streets along with the peer pressure to run a money making block. With a decision to take on the responsibilities of a crew. He manages to dodge all of the horrible influences that faced him on a daily basis. He was finally taken into a temporary comfortable home with his foster sister and foster mom. He lands a small gig where he finally finds acceptance for who he is and is congratulated in what he offers the business. When all seems to be just going great just like anything else in life, it is halted immediately taking an unimaginable turn for the worst .

A night out with his foster sister that should of just consisted of heading to the local mart to buy a few items. It ended with his foster sister bailing her foster brother out of a violent scuffle. That only ended with his foster sister committing a horrible act just to protect her only foster brother.

To love is to endure all that comes with those emotion even at the cost of one's own life let alone ones freedom if not careful. Manuel took the fall for his foster sisters heroic deeds which lands him in an institution fighting for his freedom.

He no longer is that same person who didn't want any parts of the blood, drugs and murders but instead he is forced to become this animal that her tried so hard to not become.

Either one became a product of your environment but choice or by force.

With his foster sister free and not being able to accept what has occurred. She only ends up living a double life just to tie up a lot of loose ends before her bothers trial date.

www.ingramcontent.com/pod-product-compliance
Lightning Source LLC
Chambersburg PA
CBHW071727270326
41928CB00013B/2582

9780692180495